The Prentice Hall Anthology of
African American
Women's Literature

Valerie Lee, Editor
The Ohio State University

D0002587

PEARSON

Prentice
Hall

Upper Saddle River, New Jersey 07458

Library of Congress Cataloging-in-Publication Data

The Prentice Hall anthology of African American women's literature / Valerie Lee, editor.
   p. cm.
ISBN 0-13-048546-2
   1. American literature—African American authors. 2. African American women—Literary collections.
3. African Americans—Literary collections. 4. American literature—Women authors. I. Lee, Valerie

PS508.N3P743 2005
810.8'09287'08996073—dc22

2004057753

Publisher: Nancy Roberts
Editorial Assistant: Lee Peterson
Full Service Production Liaison: Joanne Hakim
Senior Marketing Manager: Marissa Feliberty
Assistant Manufacturing Manager: Mary Ann Gloriande
Cover Art Director: Jayne Conte
Cover Design: Bruce Kenselaar
Manager, Cover Visual Research & Permissions: Karen Sanatar
Cover Art: "My Mother's Friends" © Aminah Brenda Lynn Robinson/Licensed by VAGA, New York, NY.
   Courtesy Rocky and Suzy Saxbe and the Columbus Museum of Art, Ohio.
Director, Image Resource Center: Melinda Reo
Manager, Rights and Permissions: Zina Arabia
Manager, Visual Research: Beth Brenzel
Photo Researcher: Elaine Soares
Photo Coordinator: Cathy Mazzucca
Composition/Full-Service Project Management: GGS Book Services, Atlantic Highlands
Printer/Binder: Hamilton Printing Company

Credits and acknowledgments borrowed from other sources and reproduced, with permission, in this textbook
appear on appropriate page within text. Photo on p. ii courtesy of Art Resource, N.Y.

Pearson Education LTD., London
Pearson Education Singapore, Pte. Ltd
Pearson Education, Canada, Ltd
Pearson Education–Japan
Pearson Education Australia PTY, Limited

Pearson Education North Asia Ltd
Pearson Educación de Mexico, S.A. de C.V.
Pearson Education Malaysia, Pte. Ltd
Pearson Education, Upper Saddle River, New Jersey

10 9 8 7 6 5 4 3 2 1
ISBN 0-13-048546-2

CONTENTS

The Colonial and Antebellum Periods   1

"Slavery is terrible for men; but it is far more terrible for women."

Incidents in the Life of a Slave Girl

"She is mother, and her heart / Is Breaking in despair."

"The Slave Mother"

The Reconstruction Period   41

"But to be a woman of the Negro race in America, and to be able to grasp the deep significance of the possibilities of the crisis, is to have a heritage, it seems to me, unique in the ages."
Anna Julia Cooper, *A Voice From the South*

"Mrs. Willis was a good example of a class of women of color that came into existence at the close of the Civil War. She was not a *rara avis*, but one of many possibilities which the future will develop from among the colored women of New England."
Pauline E. Hopkins, *Contending Forces*

Expansion, Experimentation, and Excellence: 20th- and 21st-Century African American Women's Writings   86

The Harlem Renaissance   90

". . . Ah done growed ten feet higher from jus' listenin' tuh you . . ."

Zora Neale Hurston, *Their Eyes Were Watching God*

"She wished to find out about this hazardous business 'passing,' this breaking away from all that was familiar and friendly."

Nella Larsen, *Passing*

The 1940s–1959   180

"God help her when she grew up. God help the man who married her. God help her sisters not to follow in her footsteps."

Dorothy West, *The Living Is Easy*

"Sadie scraped life / With a fine-tooth comb."

Gwendolyn Brooks, *"Sadie and Maud"*

Literature from the New Millennium: The 1990s to the 21st Century   351

"Trifling! Trifling women! After all I did to raise them right."
Tina McElroy Ansa, *Ugly Ways*

"Every shut eye ain't sleep. Every good-bye ain't gone."
Itabari Njeri, *Every Good-Bye Ain't Gone*

Black Feminist Criticism and Womanist Theories   398

"For people of color have always theorized—but in forms quite different from the Western form of abstract logic."
Barbara Christian, *"The Race for Theory"*

"Black feminist criticism is a knotty issue . . ."
Deborah McDowell, *"New Directions for Black Feminist Criticism"*

CONTENTS BY GENRE

CONTENTS BY THEME
(a selected sampling)

PREFACE

"Because each had discovered years before that they were neither white nor male, and that all freedom and triumph was forbidden to them, they set about creating something else to be."

—SULA

There are many anthologies of American Literature, a growing number of anthologies of women's literature, and several noteworthy ones of African American Literature. *The Prentice Hall Anthology of African American Women's Literature* represents the first comprehensive anthology of its kind. This volume spans all the historical periods from 1746 when Lucy Terry Prince wrote the first work by an African American to the New Millennium texts of Pearl Cleage and Tayari Jones. The time periods run from Colonial and Antebellum, Reconstruction, the Harlem Renaissance, to the Black Aesthetic Movement, the Second Renaissance of the late 1970s to 1990s, ending with literature of the 21st century. In total, rather than the usual sprinkling of African American women writers found in anthologies, *The Prentice Hall Anthology of African American Women's Literature* parades more than seventy-five authors.

Equally comprehensive are the many genres that this volume covers. Expansive in its definitions, the volume contains autobiographies, spiritual narratives, letters, slave narratives, neo-slave narratives, detective fiction, genteel fiction, folk stories, science fiction, romances, historical fiction, melodramas, surrealistic dramas, dramatic monologues, lyrics, ballads, sonnets, choreopoems, prose poems, and all types of genre hybrids. In addition to breadth in terms of chronology and genre, the themes explore the full range of the human imagination. Informed and inflected by the distinctive voice of African American women, the writings comment upon art and the imagination, bodies and blackness, heritage and history, citizenship and nationhood, interracial relationships and conflicts, language and literacy, sexual harassment and violence, slavery and its aftermath, to name a few.

As a supplement to the primary materials, the anthology offers readers aids to increase understanding and appreciation of the works. Essays by Jacqueline Jones Royster, "An Era of Resistance: 19th-Century African American Women's Writings," and Valerie Lee, "Expansion, Experimentation, and Excellence: 20th- & 21st-Century African American Women's Writings," help to historicize and contextualize the readings. These essays, along with biographies of each author, provide a lens whereby readers can frame the texts. The map of where the authors were born is a distinctive addition to the field of African American literature and culture, as well as the timeline that focuses on African American women's literary history and culture. In sum, this is a student-friendly collection of some of the best literature in America's treasury of the arts.

To paraphrase the epigraph from *Sula*, "Because [African American women] had discovered years before that they were neither white nor male, and that all freedom and triumph was forbidden to them, they set about creating something else to be." That something else is a wordsmith, a teller of tales and poems befitting their status as sistah conjurers.

Acknowledgments

I wish to thank the reviewers: Susanna Ashton, Clemson University; Margaret S. Crowder, California State University San Marcos; Catherine Paul, Clemson University; Linda Wagner-Martin, University of North Carolina—Chapel Hill; Yvonne Wilebski, Clackamas Community College; and Robert Young, University of Alabama.

With much appreciation to my research associates:

- Elizabeth Simoneau, who helped at the beginning stages of the project, constructing a complicated Excel chart of all anthologized writings by African American women.
- Aaron Oforlea, who helped during the final stages of the project, even reading one author he dislikes.
- Wendy Wolters, for her diligence, patience, and ability to scotch-tape thousands of pages and think clearly and creatively at the same time.
- Tiffani Clyburn, who read all of the selections with care, eagerness, and understanding and laughed at all my academic jokes.
- Kim Kovarik, for drawing an excellent map of the authors' birthplaces and for helping me with *all* my projects during the last three years. You've been a blessing.

With utmost respect to:

- All the students that I taught in Women Writers of the Harlem Renaissance; African American Women's Writings and Oral Traditions; Women in Literature; Critical Race Feminisms, and Women Writing the Civil Rights Movement. I want to thank both of my departments, English and Women's Studies, for giving me the opportunities to teach what I want to teach.
- My fourteen-year-old reading group, Womanist Readers of Columbus, Ohio. As a group we have read over 100 novels by African American women writers. Thanks for being so opinionated.

With everyday thanks to:

- My mother, A.C., who every Sunday asked if I needed help with the anthology.
- To my sister, Patty, who wants her name in all of my books, whether she helps or not.

And as always, I want to thank my children, Adam, Andrew, Erica, and Jessica, for allowing me to read while at the kitchen table, basketball and tennis games, and family gatherings. A special thanks to my husband, James, for encouragement in the midnight hour.

Valerie Lee

WRITERS AND GEOGRAPHY: BIRTHPLACES

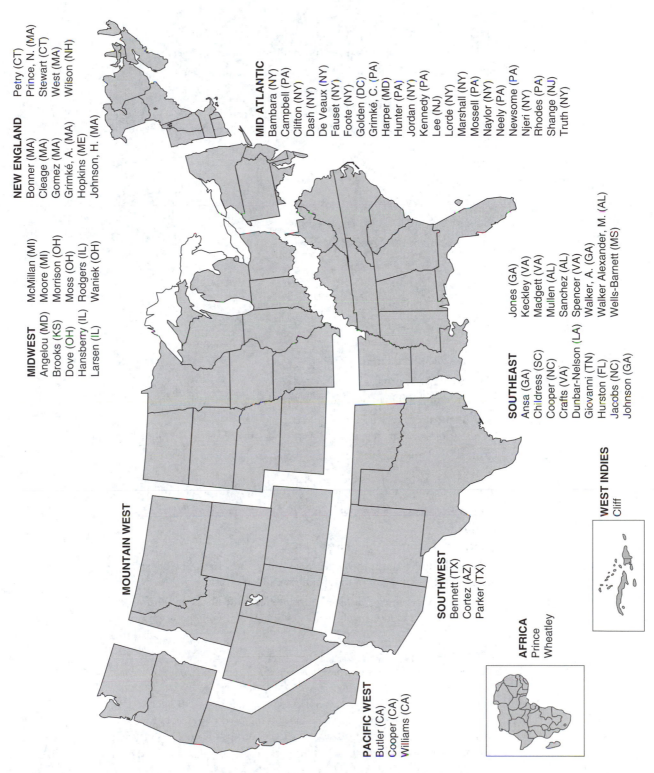

TIMELINE
African American Women's Literary and Cultural History

1730	Lucy Terry Prince born
1746	Lucy Terry Prince writes the first poem by an African American
1753	Phillis Wheatley born?
1767	Phillis Wheatley publishes first poem
1773	Phillis Wheatley publishes *Poems on Various Subjects, Religious and Moral*, becomes first African American and second woman in America to publish a book of poems
1775–1781	Revolutionary War
1783	Jarena Lee born
1784	Phillis Wheatley dies
1797	Sojourner Truth born Isabella Baumfree
1799	Nancy Gardner Prince born?
1803	Maria W. Stewart born
1813	Harriet Jacobs born
1820	Lucy Terry Prince dies
1823	Julia Foote born
1824	Elizabeth Keckley born?
1825	Frances Ellen Watkins Harper born
1828	Harriet Wilson born?
1830	Underground Railroad developed by Antislavery advocates
1831	Nat Turner leads rebellion in Virginia The Afric-American Female Intelligence Society of Boston is founded
1832	Maria Stewart is the first American woman to formally address a mixed or "promiscuous" audience
1835	Oberlin becomes the first college to open its doors to women and Blacks
1836	Jarena Lee independently publishes *The Life and Religious Experiences of Jarena Lee*
1837	Charlotte L. Forten Grimké born
1843	Isabella Baumfree takes the name "Sojourner Truth" to signify her spiritual conversion and mission to travel and reveal God's truth
1848	Convention in Seneca Falls, New York produces the Declaration of Sentiments and marks the official beginning of the Women's Rights Movement
1849	Jarena Lee dies?
1850	Nancy Gardner Prince publishes *Narrative of the Life and Travels of Mrs. Nancy Prince, Written By Herself* Fugitive Slave Act passed as part of the Compromise of 1850; required citizens to cooperate with slave hunters and imposed severe fines for concealing or helping escaped slaves, whether or not the area was officially free or slave (Smith Foster)

1851	Sojourner Truth gives speech at women's rights convention in Akron, Ohio, now known as "Ar'n't I a woman?"
1852	Harriet Beecher Stowe publishes *Uncle Tom's Cabin*
1853	Hannah Craft's *The Bondswoman's Narrative*, discovered by Henry Louis Gates in 2001, is believed to have been written between 1853 and 1861
1854	Frances Ellen Watkins Harper publishes *Poems on Miscellaneous Subjects*
1855	Gertrude Bustill Mossell born
1856	Nancy Gardner Prince dies Margaret Garner escapes from slavery in Kentucky
1858	Sojourner Truth bares her breast to an audience in Indiana questioning her gender and right to speak in public Anna Julia Cooper born
1859	John Brown and his men apprehended at Harper's Ferry Harriet Wilson publishes *Our Nig: Or, Sketches from the Life of a Free Black* Pauline E. Hopkins born
1861–1863	Civil War
1861	Harriet Jacobs publishes *Incidents in the Life of a Slave Girl*, the first slave narrative to be published by an African American woman
1862	Ida B. Wells-Barnett born
1863	Harriet Wilson dies Emancipation Proclamation created
1865	The Thirteenth Amendment abolishing slavery is passed
1868	Elizabeth Keckley publishes *Behind the Scenes: or Thirty Years a Slave and Four Years in the White House* Fourteenth Amendment is ratified, granting citizenship to all persons born or naturalized in the United States and granting the right to vote to all men over twenty-one
1870	Fifteenth Amendment gives Black men the right to vote
1875	Alice Moore Dunbar-Nelson born
1878	Sojourner Truth publishes *Narrative of Sojourner Truth*
1879	Maria W. Stewart dies Julia Foote publishes *A Brand Plucked From the Fire*
1880	Angelina Weld Grimké born
1882	Anne Spencer born Jessie Redmon Fauset born
1883	Sojourner Truth dies
1884	Ida B. Wells-Barnett is removed from a train after refusing to transfer to the smoking car; she later initiated a suit against the railroad Anna Julia Cooper and Mary Church Terrell graduate from Oberlin College
1885	Mary Effie Lee Newsome born
1886	Georgia Douglas Johnson born
1891	Zora Neale Hurston born Nella Larsen born
1892	Frances Ellen Watkins Harper publishes *Iola Leroy* Anna Julia Cooper publishes *A Voice From the South*

	Three young Black businessmen lynched in Memphis; Ida B. Wells-Barnett begins to write about lynching and incites a mass boycott and exodus of the Black population of Memphis Ida B. Wells-Barnett publishes *Southern Horrors: Lynch Law in All Its Phases*
1894	Julia Foote becomes the first woman in the A.M.E. Zion church to be ordained as a deacon Gertrude Bustill Mossell publishes "A Lofty Study" Alice Moore Dunbar-Nelson publishes *Violets and Other Tales*
1895	Lucy Terry Prince's "Bars Fight" published in *History of Western Massachusetts* Ida B. Wells publishes *A Red Record: Tabulated Statistics and Alleged Causes of Lynchings in the United States. 1892-1893-1894*
1896	National Association of Colored Women founded *Plessy v. Ferguson* legalizes racial segregation
1897	Harriet Jacobs dies
1899	Marita Bonner born
1900	Julia Foote dies Pauline E. Hopkins publishes *Contending Forces*
1902	Gwendolyn Bennett born
1907	Elizabeth Keckley dies Helene Johnson born Dorothy West born
1909	NAACP publishes *Crisis*
1911	Ann Petry born
1913	Ida B. Wells-Barnett founds the first Black female suffrage club, The Alpha Suffrage Club
1914–1918	World War I
1914	Charlotte L. Forten Grimké dies
1915	Margaret Walker Alexander born
1917	Gwendolyn Brooks born
1918	Georgia Douglas Johnson publishes *The Heart of a Woman*
1920	Angelina Weld Grimké publishes *Rachel*, the first play staged by an African American woman Alice Childress born Nineteenth Amendment ratified, granting women the right to vote
1921	Jessie Fauset represents the National Association of Colored Women at the Second Pan-African Congress The first three African American women receive a Ph.D. (Sadie T.M. Alexander, Eva B. Dykes, Georgiana R. Simpson)
1922	World's Woman's Christian Temperance Union posthumously awards Frances Ellen Watkins Harper a position on their Red Letter Calendar
1923	Anna Julia Cooper, age 65, is the fourth African American woman to earn her doctorate, completing her dissertation at the Sorbonne Gwendolyn Bennett publishes "Heritage" Naomi Long Madgett born Equal Rights Amendment first proposed Ma Rainey and Bessie Smith record their first records
1924	Jessie Redmon Fauset publishes *Plum Bun: A Novel Without a Moral*

1925	Marita Bonner publishes "On Being Young—a Woman—and Colored" Helene Johnson publishes "My Race"
1926	Dorothy West publishes "The Typewriter"
1927	Gwendolyn Bennett publishes "To a Dark Girl" Helene Johnson publishes "Sonnet to a Negro in Harlem" and "Magalu"
1928	Marita Bonner publishes *The Purple Flower* Maya Angelou born
1929	Nella Larsen publishes *Passing* Paule Marshall born
1930	Pauline E. Hopkins dies Lorraine Hansberry born
1931	Kristin Hunter born Toni Morrison born Adrienne Kennedy born
1934	Dorothy West founds the literary magazine *Challenge* Sonia Sanchez born Audre Lorde born
1935	Alice Moore Dunbar-Nelson dies Zora Neale Hurston publishes *Mules and Men*
1936	June Jordan born Lucille Clifton born
1936	Jayne Cortez born
1937	Zora Neale Hurston publishes *Their Eyes Were Watching God*
1939–1945	World War II
1939	Toni Cade Bambara born Maxine Clair born
1940	Hattie McDaniel wins Best Supporting Actress Academy Award for *Gone with the Wind*
1941	BarbaraNeely born
1942	Zora Neale Hurston publishes *Dust Tracks on a Road* Margaret Walker Alexander publishes *For My People*, wins the Yale Series of Younger Poets Award
1943	Nikki Giovanni born
1944	Alice Walker born Sherley Anne Williams born Pat Parker born
1945	Ann Petry publishes "Like a Winding Sheet" Gwendolyn Brooks publishes *A Street in Bronzeville* Carolyn Rodgers born
1946	Ann Petry publishes *The Street* Marilyn Nelson Waniek is born Michelle Cliff born
1947	Octavia Butler born
1948	Gertrude Bustill Mossell dies Dorothy West publishes *The Living is Easy* Ntozake Shange born Jewelle Gomez born Alexis De Veaux born

1949	Tina McElroy Ansa born
1950	Gwendolyn Brooks publishes *Annie Allen* and is the first African American woman to receive the Pulitzer Prize for poetry BeBe Moore Campbell is born Gloria Naylor born Marita Golden born Terry McMillan born
1952	Rita Dove born Julie Dash born
1953	*The Journals of Charlotte Forten Grimké* published Gwendolyn Brooks publishes *Maud Martha* Harryette Mullen born
1954	*Brown v. Board of Education of Topeka* overturns *Plessy v. Ferguson* and rules segregation in public schools unconstitutional Thylias Moss born Itabari Njeri born
1955	Emmett Till is murdered Rosa Parks initiates the Montgomery Bus Boycott
1956	Alice Childress publishes *Like One of the Family*
1957	Civil Rights Act of 1957 sets up a commission on civil rights Nine Black students integrate Central High School, Little Rock, Arkansas
1958	Angelina Weld Grimké dies
1959	*A Raisin in the Sun* by Lorraine Hansberry is first performed
1960	Zora Neale Hurston dies Paule Marshall receives a Guggenheim fellowship Civil Rights Act of 1960 makes it a federal offense to obstruct federal court orders by force or threat of violence, authorizes the appointment of federal referees to safeguard Black voting rights
1961–1975	Vietnam War
1961	Jessie Redmon Fauset dies Paule Marshall publishes *Soul Clap Hands and Sing* Freedom Rides begin from Washington D.C.
1962	Gwendolyn Brooks publishes *The Bean Eaters*
1963	March on Washington for passage of a civil rights bill A bomb blast in the Birmingham Sixteenth Street Baptist Church kills four little girls Equal Pay Act prohibits discrimination on the basis of sex and requires equal compensation for women and men who perform the same work
1964	Anna Julia Cooper dies Nella Larsen dies Civil Rights Act of 1964 prohibits discrimination on the basis of sex, color, race, religion, and national origin and establishes the Equal Employment Opportunity Commission
1965	Lorraine Hansberry dies Malcolm X assassinated
1966	Georgia Douglas Johnson dies Margaret Walker Alexander publishes *Jubilee* Black Panthers Party formed

1968   Gwendolyn Brooks publishes *In the Mecca*
        Kristin Hunter publishes *The Soul Brothers and Sister in Law*, for which she
        wins the Council on Interracial Children's Book Award
        Nikki Giovanni publishes *Black Feeling, Black Talk*
        Martin Luther King, Jr. assassinated
        Civil Rights Act of 1968 protects civil rights in housing, employment,
        and selection in federal and state juries

1969   Gwendolyn Brooks publishes *Riot*
        Sonia Sanchez publishes *Homecoming*
        Carolyn Rodgers publishes *Songs of a Blackbird*
        Maya Angelou publishes *I Know Why the Caged Bird Sings*
        Toni Morrison publishes *The Bluest Eye*
        Lucille Clifton publishes *Good Times*

1970   Mari Evans publishes *I Am a Black Woman*
        Sonia Sanchez publishes *We A Baddddd People*
        Nikki Giovanni publishes *Black Judgment*
        Angela Davis arrested after being linked to a shooting by the Black Panthers
        Tayari Jones born
        Essence magazine begins publication
        Anthology published: *The Black Woman*, by Toni Cade

1971   Marita Bonner dies
        Ann Petry publishes *Miss Muriel and Other Stories*
        June Jordan publishes *Some Changes*

1972   Toni Cade Bambara publishes *Gorilla My Love*
        Jayne Cortez founds Bola Press
        Jessica Care Moore born

1973   Toni Morrison publishes *Sula*
        Alice Walker publishes *In Love and Trouble* and *Revolutionary Petunias
        and Other Poems*
        Roe v. Wade legalizes abortion and protects women's right to privacy in
        matters generally related to procreation
        The National Black Feminist Organization was founded

1975   Anne Spencer dies
        Kristin Hunter wins the Christopher Award for *Guests in the Promised Land*
        Nikki Giovanni publishes *The Women and the Men*
        Carolyn Rodgers publishes *How I Got Ovah*
        Sherley Anne Williams publishes *The Peacock Poems*

1976   Adrienne Kennedy publishes *A Movie Star Has to Star in Black
        and White*
        Barbara Jordan keynotes the Democratic National Convention, the first
        African American to do so for a major party's national convention

1977   June Jordan publishes *Things That I Do in the Dark: Selected Poetry*
        Toni Morrison publishes *Song of Solomon*
        Ntozake Shange publishes *for colored girls who have considered suicide when the
        rainbow is enuf*

1978   Maya Angelou publishes *And Still I Rise*
        Ntozake Shange publishes *Nappy Edges*
        Marilyn Nelson Waniek publishes *For the Body*
        J. California Cooper named Black Playwright of the Year

1979   Mary Effie Lee Newsome dies

Octavia Butler publishes *Kindred*
Sturdy Black Bridges: Visions of Black Women in Literature, ed. by Roseann Bell, Bettye Parker and Beverly Guy-Sheftall
Anthology Published: *conditions: five—the black women's issue*, eds. Lorraine Bethel and Barbara Smith

1980   Lucille Clifton publishes *Two-Headed Woman*
Audre Lorde publishes *The Cancer Journals*

1981   Gwendolyn Bennett dies
Toni Morrison publishes *Tar Baby*
The National Black Women's Health Project is founded
Anthology published: *This Bridge Called My Back: Writings By Radical Women of Color*, eds. Cherríe Moraga and Gloria Anzaldua

1982   Henry Louis Gates, Jr. rediscovers Harriet Wilson's *Our Nig*
Alice Walker publishes *The Color Purple*
Ntozake Shange publishes *sassafras, cypress, and Indigo*
Sherley Anne Williams publishes *Some One Sweet Angel Chile*
Gloria Naylor publishes *The Women of Brewster Place*

1983   Paule Marshall publishes *Praisesong for the Widow*
Alice Walker publishes *In Search of Our Mothers' Gardens* and defines "womanism"
Gloria Naylor receives American Book Award for *The Women of Brewster Place*
Alice Walker receives American Book Award, and the first Pulitzer Prize for a novel written by an African American woman, for *The Color Purple* Anthology published: *Home Girls: A Black Feminist Anthology*, ed. Barbara Smith

1984   Paule Marshall receives the American Book Award
Michelle Cliff publishes *Abeng*
J. California Cooper publishes *A Piece of Mind*
Sage: A Scholarly Journal on Black Women begins publication

1985   June Jordan publishes *Living Room*
Sonia Sanchez receives American Book Award for *homegirls and handgrenades*

1986   Martin Luther King Day becomes national holiday
Rita Dove publishes *Thomas and Beulah*

1987   Rita Dove is the second African American woman to win the Pulitzer Prize for Poetry, for her collection *Thomas and Beulah*
J. California Cooper publishes *Some Soul to Keep*
Anthology Published: *Invented Lives*, ed. Mary Helen Washington

1988   Toni Morrison receives a Pulitzer Prize for fiction for the novel *Beloved*

1989   June Jordan publishes *Naming Our Destiny*
Tina McElroy Ansa publishes *Baby of the Family*
Marita Golden publishes *Long Distance Life*
Pat Parker dies

1990   Itabari Njeri publishes *Every Good-Bye Ain't Gone: Family Portraits and Personal Escapades* and wins an American Book Award

1991   Jewelle Gomez publishes *The Gilda Stories*
Civil Rights Act of 1991, an amendment to Title VII of the 1964
Civil Rights Act, defines sexual harassment and provides for compensatory and punitive damages for victims of sexual harassment
Anita Hill appears before the U.S. Senate Judiciary Committee during the confirmation hearings of Supreme Court Justice Clarence Thomas

1992   Los Angeles riots
            Paule Marshall receives the MacArthur Award
            Audre Lorde dies
            BeBe Moore Campbell publishes *Your Blues Ain't Like Mine*
            Gloria Naylor publishes *Bailey's Café*

1993   Maya Angelou delivers Inaugural poem, "On the Pulse of Morning," for
            President Clinton
            Toni Morrison receives Nobel Prize for Literature
            Thylias Moss publishes *Small Congregations: New and Selected Poems*
            Rita Dove is the first African American to hold the title of Poet Laureate of
            the United States, 1993–1995
            Julie Dash's film *Daughters of the Dust* premieres

1994   Alice Childress dies
            Rita Dove named Poet Laureate of the United States
            Gwendolyn Brooks receives the National Book Foundation's Medal for
            Distinguished Contribution to American Literature
            BeBe Moore Campbell publishes *Brothers and Sisters*
            Black women scholars nationwide gather at the Massachusetts Institute of
            Technology for a conference, "Black Women in the Academy: Defending
            Our Name"

1995   Million Man March in Washington D.C.
            Gwendolyn Brooks receives National Medal of the Arts from President Clinton
            Toni Morrison receives honorary doctorate from Howard University
            Helene Johnson dies
            Toni Cade Bambara dies
            Octavia Butler publishes *Bloodchild and Other Stories*

1996   Rosa Parks receives Presidential Medal of Freedom

1997   U.S. formally apologizes for Tuskegee syphilis experiments, from 1932–1972
            Million Woman March in Philadelphia
            Ann Petry dies
            Jessica Care Moore publishes *The Words Don't Fit in My Mouth*

1998   Dorothy West dies
            Margaret Walker Alexander dies
            Jewelle Gomez publishes *Don't Explain*
            Toni Morrison publishes *Paradise*

1999   Sherley Anne Williams dies

2000   Gwendolyn Brooks dies

2001   Bebe Moore Campbell publishes *What You Owe Me*

2002   June Jordan dies
            Tayari Jones publishes *Leaving Atlanta*
            Anthology published: *this bridge we call home*, eds. Gloria Anzaldua and
            Analouise Keating
            Ruth Simmons becomes President of Brown University, the first African
            American to be president of an Ivy League Institution
            Harryette Mullen publishes *Sleeping with the Dictionary*

2003   Toni Morrison publishes *Love*

2005   Tayari Jones publishes *The Untelling*
            Oprah Winfrey's Harpo Films presents a televised version of Zora Neale
            Hurston's *Their Eyes Were Watching God*

An Era of Resistance:
19th-Century African American Women's Writings

For African American women, the nineteenth century dawned as a world of danger and desire. For more than half of the century, the danger was ever present in the form of a society systemically dedicated to the peculiar institution of slavery as the "natural" condition of people of African descent. For the remainder of it, danger resided in the society's ideologically commitment to racist, sexist, and cultural domination. The desire, however, was also ever present. After the Revolutionary war and the founding of the United States as a land of freedom, African Americans, male and female, re-endowed their struggle for freedom, justice, equality, and empowerment with new passion. As the nineteenth century turned, the pursuit of these social and political realities constituted a core agenda that would carry African American women (and their male counterparts as well) with considerable momentum through the next century and beyond. Nowhere was this agenda more evident than in their passionate pursuits of education and their persistent uses of writing as creative and critical enactment of literary, intellectual, and also sociopolitical purposes.

A historical framing of African American women's literary accomplishment in the nineteenth century can be interestingly situated by one moment among a series of legal moments in American history. From March 16 to 23, 1790, the Congress of the United States engaged in a highly volatile debate on slavery in response to the most recent set of memorials from "the people called Quakers, and of the Pennsylvania Society for promoting the abolition of slavery," (Gales, 1500), with the latter as a biracial organization sending its petition for abolition via the writing hand of Benjamin Franklin, who served at that point as the society's president. Collectively, these petitions questioned slavery as an immoral and impractical institution, the Atlantic slave trade, and also the powers vested in the Congress of the newly formed United States to abolish slavery. The petitions were sent to a special committee for deliberation, and on March 16, the special committee made its report to the Committee of the Whole.

The results of both debates, in the special committee and in the Congressional Committee of the Whole, were deep wounds for the African American community, but strikingly so as the Committee of the Whole stripped even further the language of every opinion from the special committee, relieving itself from all but the narrowest interpretation of the new Constitution and the compromises struck between Southern and Northern politicians in order to actually form the Union. The special committee recommended and the Committee of the Whole made even clearer that Congress could and would do nothing about slavery until after 1808, as articulated by the signers of the Constitution; that they had

> . . . no authority to interfere in the emancipation of slaves or in the treatment of them within any of the States; it remaining with the several States alone to provide any regulations therein, which humanity and true policy may require. (Gales 1524)

They would only restrain and regulate the importation of slaves directly from Africa. In other words, the majority ruled not to disrupt the institution of slavery, regardless of the layers of arguments that were being brought to bear to do so. The nineteenth century was born, therefore, amid a legal context that set aside ethical and moral responsibility for the inhumanity and the incongruity of U.S. slavery and that simultaneously framed in the most negative of terms the conditions of life and liberty for African American people. Critical mandates for protest and resistance were inescapable for a people who were bent on freedom, justice, equality, and empowerment.

Acknowledging the oppressive historical context of the nineteenth century brings to bolder relief the highly compelling nature of the desire of African Americans for liberty and justice. Like their male counterparts, African American women writers were impassioned by the material conditions of their lives and by social and political imperatives that sharply defined the nineteenth century as an era of protest, resistance, and remarkable achievements against incredible odds. These women were socially conscious poets and fiction writers, as exemplified by the poetry of Charlotte Forten Grimké and Frances Ellen Watkins Harper, the novels of Harper and Pauline E. Hopkins, and the writings of numerous others. However, their nonfiction prose, and particularly their essay writing, offers a striking opportunity to understand the collective body of work, not just as creative and artistic expression, which certainly it is, but also as an indication of their active and passionate participation in the social and political discourses that surrounded them. During this period, then, the nonfiction publications of African American women can serve as a great cloak within which to wrap other expressions of creativity and intellectualism.

Starting in 1831 with Maria Stewart,[1] as the first known writer of political essays, we see a pattern forming. In broad stroke, Stewart articulated longstanding issues for African Americans: access to education, educational achievement, economic empowerment, legal equity, political participation, social justice, stereotypical images of African American people, the social constraints of women, and the possibilities of women. Her writings represent, however, a distinctive moment for nineteenth-century literate practices in that she symbolizes, both historically and metaphorically, the emergence for African American women of a *public* voice. Stewart made a new place, the first of its kind, for women as writers and speakers capable of reaching public audiences.

Stewart demonstrated an ability to negotiate complex triadic relationships between a *context* in which women should remain invisible; *the construction of a speaking/writing self* that could break through stereotypical boundaries that were so negatively drawn for African American women by both race and gender; and making **rhetorical choices** that were effective despite contending forces. Stewart crafted relationships between herself and others; made use of a wide array of persuasive strategies and argumentative techniques; connected her interests to the interests of others; and articulated pathways to positive action. Such practices constituted a resonant chord for generations of African American women writers who would follow Stewart as they too countered the continuities of their sociopolitical circumstances with staunch commitments to use language across various genres in the interest of social change. By the end of the century, there was evident a pattern, habits of mind and action, that functioned, in effect, as "ritual moves," as strategies for engagement that needed to be systematically deployed to counter persistent conditions.

Viewing the writing practices of nineteenth-century African American women from this perspective, we come to understand that they were drawing from available sociocultural resources to make choices that were proactive not just reactive, shaping themselves as writers complexly in balance and harmony amid an environment that was overtly hostile to them. By all measures, Stewart, as a case in point, could see from all around her that the African American cause, as mirrored by her own personal circumstances, was an urgent one. She envisioned a world in which the lives of African American people, and thereby African American women, should be better. She articulated a multitude of problems that contributed to debilitating conditions, but she also saw specific solutions to address them. Stewart was inspired to use writing to take a political stand, to fashion her own authority to speak, and to articulate mandates for community action.

In keeping with Hans-Georg Gadamer's view, Stewart experienced a fusion of horizons. She had a buildup of frustrations in her life at a point in time when the spirit of reform in her community was intense. This fusion created a space in which she as a linguistic being, a person capable of voice, was enabled to come to heremeneutic consciousness, i.e., to a more substantive sense of herself in the world and to a more critical sense of what is questionable in this world. She could ask with a clearer view of her own authority, Why is there no justice for African Americans? What are these wrongs about? How can we turn this world toward a better path? When will we see justice? With such questioning, Stewart could also raise for herself the most consistent questions in the struggle among African Americans for change: If not now, when? If not me, who? This pattern of inquiry, as it emerged so vibrantly from the fusion of danger and desire, would operate provocatively throughout the century and beyond. African American women writers played out across genres their views and responses, as demonstrated, for example, in Frances Watkins Harper's *Iola Leroy* (1892). They

---

[1]For a more extended version of this analysis of Maria Stewart, see my book *Traces of a Stream: Literacy and Social Change among African American Women* (Pittsburgh: U of Pittsburgh P, 2000).

brought literary flesh to the definition of social problems, and they laid out consequences for individuals, for groups, and for a nation in the face of refusals to act responsibly.

As we look from Stewart across the remainder of the nineteenth century and beyond to our own era, African American women, some of whom wrote essays or other nonfiction forms, some poetry, some fiction or drama, the evidence of both eloquence and artistic value are quite striking. These women exhibited a compelling desire to resist racist, sexist, and other oppressive agenda and simultaneously to proclaim, as demonstrated, for example, by Anna Julia Cooper's *A Voice from the South* (1892), not only their own possibilities, but also the extraordinary potential for all of us to make a better world—if we would only rise well to opportunity. They spoke variously of the desire to become all that they might be, as Harriet E. Wilson did in *Our Nig* (1859) with her character Frado who felt herself "capable of elevation." They yearned for the freedom to learn and to do whatever their talents and abilities permitted. As one example among the many who belonged to this pioneering group, Stewart, like those who would follow her, asserted an entitlement to speak, to pay attention to her own ideas and dreams, to assume authority for her own interests instead of simply serving the needs of others, to engage in political action, and to render those interests in writing. Despite the absence of societal support, these women claimed the privilege of space for their own intellectual needs, defiantly insisting on using their creative and intellectual abilities to express themselves in the interest of social change and human possibility.

In this era, African American women writers had an astute understanding of the burdens they carried as individuals and as members of two oppressed groups—African Americans and women—but they carried these burdens well. They left behind multiple legacies with regard to habits of mind and action amid contending social and political forces and in using their language resources and critical abilities across various expressive forms to transform their worlds. They garnered by various means the strength to engage with contentious problems. They created their own authority to speak and boldly raised pens and voices, showing to the world distinctive creative and critical powers and using those powers to remarkable effect. In doing so, they created a *public* presence and a trajectory of expressiveness that continues as we approach yet a third century of literary productivity.

As illustrated by the works in this volume, the legacies of African American women writers are noteworthy. We should be grateful for their courage, their tenacity, their inventiveness, their expertise, and their wisdom. We should feel honored to recognize and celebrate their talents, and we should feel obligated to make a rightful place for their literary work among others in literary history and cultural achievement. Beyond recognition for their literary prowess, however, there is the additional obligation to acknowledge that literary performances are resident on a larger cultural plain. For nineteenth century African American women writers that plain was definable by social and political imperatives that made it urgent for them to use literary talents and abilities to carry forth other causes—freedom, justice, equality, empowerment—words, as Maria Stewart asserted, that are the principles of our morality and the sure foundation on which we must continue to build. And build they did.

Jacqueline Jones Royster
Professor of English
The Ohio State University

Works Cited

Gadamer, Hans-Georg. *Philosophical Hermeneutics.* Trans. and ed. David E. Linge. Berkeley: U of California P, 1977.

Gales, Joseph Sr. *The Debates and Proceedings of the Congress of the United States.* Volume II. Washington: Gales and Seaton, 1834.

Royster, Jacqueline Jones. *Traces of a Stream: Literacy and Social Change among African American Women.* Pittsburgh: U of Pittsburgh P, 2000.

The Colonial and Antebellum Periods

Lucy Terry Prince (1730–1821)

Born in Africa and bought and baptized in 1735 by Ebenezer Wells of Rhode Island, Lucy Terry Prince remained in slavery until 1756 when she married Abijah Prince, a wealthy free black, twenty-five years her senior. Abijah bought his wife's freedom, and the couple settled in Massachusetts and later Vermont. They had six children. When one of their sons was denied admission to Williams College, Prince delivered a three-hour argument against the college's racial discrimination policy. Although she was unable to persuade the college to admit her son, her powers of persuasion were vindicated when she argued a property dispute before the Supreme Court.

Prince's "Bars Fight," the first known poem written by an African American, is a ballad describing a fight between Native Americans and white families in a part of Deerfield, Massachusetts, known as "The Bars" or meadows. The poem is considered an accurate, colloquial account of the 1746 event and was recited for many years before being formally published in 1895 in Josiah Gilbert Holland's *History of Western Massachusetts*.

Bars Fight

August 'twas the twenty fifth
Seventeen hundred forty-six
The Indians did in ambush lay
Some very valient men to slay
The names of whom I'll not leave out
Samuel Allen like a hero fout
And though he was so brave and bold
His face no more shall we behold.
Eleazer Hawks was killed outright
Before he had time to fight
Before he did the Indians see
Was shot and killed immediately.
Oliver Amsden he was slain
Which caused his friends much grief and pain.

Samuel Amsden they found dead
Not many rods off from his head.
Adonijah Gillet we do hear
Did lose his life which was so dear.
John Saddler fled across the water
And so excaped the dreadful slaughter.
Eunice Allen see the Indians comeing
And hoped to save herself by running
And had not her petticoats stopt her
The awful creatures had not cotched her
And tommyhawked her on the head
And left her on the ground for dead.
Young Samuel Allen, Oh! lack a-day
Was taken and carried to Canada.

Published in 1855 in *History of Western Massachusetts* by Josiah G. Holland.
Samuel Bowles & Co., Springfield, MA.

Phillis Wheatley (1753?–1784)

A child survivor of the Middle Passage, young Phillis Wheatley learned the language of her enslavers well enough to write poetry in it a few years later. Purchased in 1761 by the John and Susan Wheatley family of Boston and taught to read by their daughter, Mary, the young Phillis amazed white audiences who had thought that Africans were incapable of writing poetry. She studied a range of subjects: Latin, astronomy, history, geography, and the Bible. Her first published poem appeared in a Rhode Island newspaper in 1767. In 1770, she wrote an elegy on the death of the Reverend George Whitefield. Because of Whitefield's popularity as a Methodist evangelist, Wheatley's elegy brought her fame. In 1773 John Wheatley wrote an introduction to her first collection, *Poems on Various Subjects, Religious and Moral*. He did so to authenticate that Wheatley was indeed a product of West Africa and the author of the poems. This type of white authentication of black literary talent would become customary for many of the early writers. Freed upon her master's death in 1778, Wheatley, who was then around twenty-one years old, married a freedman, John Peters. They had three children, none of whom survived childhood.

Typical of her times, Wheatley's poems show the influence of such British writers as Alexander Pope and John Milton. To contemporary readers, her poems may seem a collection of writings that have little to do with the lives of enslaved Africans. Rather than emphasizing the trauma of the Middle Passage, she focuses on Christianizing experiences in the New World. Yet there are references throughout her poetry to remind us that she is of "Afric's sable race," an "Ethiop." Named for the *Phillis*, the slave ship that transported her, Wheatley became the first African American and second woman in America to publish a book of poems. Her writings to an Indian minister (Samson Occom), a black painter (Scipio Moorhead), and an American President (George Washington) attest to the beginnings of a multicultural tradition within American Literature.

On Being Brought from Africa to America

'Twas mercy brought me from my *Pagan* land,
Taught my benighted soul to understand
That there's a God, that there's a *Saviour* too:
Once I redemption neither sought nor knew.
Some view our sable race with scornful eye,
"Their colour is a diabolic die."
Remember, *Christians, Negros*, black as *Cain*,
May be refin'd, and join th' angelic train.

From *The Poems of Phillis Wheatley*, revised and enlarged edition, edited with an Introduction by Julian D. Mason, Jr. © 1989 by The University of North Carolina Press.

To S.M. a young *African* Painter, on seeing his Works

To show the lab'ring bosom's deep intent,
And thought in living characters to paint,
When first thy pencil did those beauties give,
And breathing figures learnt from thee to live,
How did those prospects give my soul delight,
A new creation rushing on my sight?
Still, wond'rous youth! each noble path pursue,
On deathless glories fix thine ardent view:
Still may the painter's and the poet's fire
To aid thy pencil, and thy verse conspire!
And may the charms of each seraphic theme
Conduct thy footsteps to immortal fame!
High to the blissful wonders of the skies
Elate thy soul, and raise thy wishful eyes.
Thrice happy, when exalted to survey
That splendid city, crown'd with endless day,

Whose twice fix gates on radiant hinges ring:
Celestial *Salem* blooms in endless spring.
Calm and serene thy moments glide along,
And may the muse inspire each future song!
Still, with the sweets of contemplation bless'd,
May peace with balmy wings your soul invest!
But when these shades of time are chas'd away,
And darkness ends in everlasting day,
On what seraphic pinions shall we move,
And view the landscapes in the realms above?
There shall thy tongue in heav'nly murmurs flow,
And there my muse with heav'nly transport glow:
No more to tell of *Damon's* tender sighs,
Or rising radiance of *Aurora's* eyes,
For nobler themes demand a nobler strain,
And purer language on th' ethereal plain.
Cease, gentle muse! the solemn gloom of night
Now seals the fair creation from my sight.

On Imagination (1773)

Thy various works, imperial queen, we see,
How bright their forms! how deck'd with pomp by thee!
Thy wond'rous acts in beauteous order stand,
And all attest how potent is thine hand.

From Helicon's refulgent heights attend,
Ye sacred choir, and my attempts befriend:
To tell her glories with a faithful tongue,
Ye blooming graces, triumph in my song.

Now here, now there, the roving Fancy flies,
Till some lov'd object strikes her wand'ring eyes,
Whose silken fetters all the senses bind,
And soft captivity involves the mind.

Imagination! who can sing thy force?
Or who describe the swiftness of thy course?
Soaring through air to find the bright abode,
Th' empyreal palace of the thund'ring God,
We on thy pinions can surpass the wind,
And leave the rolling universe behind;
From star to star the mental optics rove,
Measure the skies, and range the realms above.
There in one view we grasp the mighty whole,
Or with new worlds amaze th' unbounded soul.

Though Winter frowns to Fancy's raptur'd eyes
The fields may flourish, and gay scenes arise;
The frozen deeps may break their iron bands,
And bid their waters murmur o'er the sands.
Fair Flora may resume her fragrant reign,
And with her flow'ry riches deck the plain;
Sylvanus may diffuse his honours round,
And all the forest may with leaves be crown'd:
Show'rs may descend, and dews their gems disclose,
And nectar sparkle on the blooming rose.

Such is thy pow'r, nor are thine orders vain,
O thou the leader of the mental train:
In full perfection all thy works are wrought,
And thine the sceptre o'er the realms of thought.
Before thy throne the subject-passions bow,
Of subject-passions sov'reign ruler Thou;
At thy command joy rushes on the heart,
And through the glowing veins the spirits dart.

Fancy might now her silken pinions try
To rise from earth, and sweep th' expanse on high;
From Tithon's bed now might Aurora rise,
Her cheeks all glowing with celestial dies,
While a pure stream of light o'erflows the skies.
The monarch of the day I might behold,
And all the mountains tipt with radiant gold,
But I reluctant leave the pleasing views,
Which Fancy dresses to delight the Muse;
Winter austere forbids me to aspire,
And northern tempests damp the rising fire;
They chill the tides of Fancy's flowing sea,
Cease then, my song, cease the unequal lay.

Letter to Samson Occom (1774)

Reverend and Honoured Sir,

I have this Day received your obliging kind Epistle, and am greatly satisfied with your Reasons respecting the Negroes, and think highly reasonable what you offer in Vindication of their natural Rights: Those that invade them cannot be insensible that the divine Light is chasing away the thick Darkness which broods over the Land of Africa; and the Chaos which has reigned so long, is converting into beautiful Order, and reveals more and more clearly, the glorious Dispensation of civil and religious Liberty, which are so inseparably united, that there is little or no Enjoyment of one without the other: Otherwise, perhaps, the Israelites had been less solicitous for their Freedom from Egyptian Slavery; I do not say they would have been contented without it, by no Means, for in every human Breast, God has implanted a Principle, which we call Love of Freedom; it is impatient of Oppression, and pants for Deliverance; and by the Leave of our Modern Egyptians I will assert, that the same Principle lives in us. God grant Deliverance in his own way and Time, and get him honor upon all those whose Avarice impels them to countenance and help forward the Calamities of their Fellow Creatures. This I desire not for their Hurt, but to convince them of the strange Absurdity of their Conduct whose Words and Actions are so diametrically opposite. How well the Cry for Liberty, and the reverse Disposition for the Exercise of oppressive Power over others agree,—I humbly think it does not require the Penetration of a Philosopher to determine.

To His Excellency General Washington (1775)

Celestial choir! enthron'd in realms of light,
   Columbia's scenes of glorious toils I write.
While freedom's cause her anxious breast alarms,
She flashes dreadful in refulgent arms.
See mother earth her offspring's fate bemoan,
And nations gaze at scenes before unknown!
See the bright beams of heaven's revolving light
Involved in sorrows and veil of night!

The goddess comes, she moves divinely fair,
Olive and laurel bind her golden hair:
Wherever shines this native of the skies,
Unnumber'd charms and recent graces rise.

Muse! bow propitious while my pen relates
How pour her armies through a thousand gates,
As when Eolus heaven's fair face deforms,
Enwrapp'd in tempest and a night of storms;
Astonish'd ocean feels the wild uproar,
The refluent surges beat the sounding shore;
Or thick as leaves in Autumn's golden reign,
Such, and so many, moves the warrior's train.
In bright array they seek the work of war,
Enough thou know'st them in the fields of fight.
Thee, first in peace and honours,—we demand
The grace and glory of thy martial band.
Fam'd for thy valour, for thy virtues more,
Hear every tongue thy guardian aid implore!

One century scarce perform'd its destined round,
When Gallic powers Columbia's fury found;
And so may you, whoever dares disgrace
The land of freedom's heaven-defended race!
Fix'd are the eyes of nations on the scales,
For in their hopes Columbia's arm prevails.
Anon Britannia droops the pensive head,
While round increase the rising hills of dead.
Ah! cruel blindness to Columbia's state!
Lament thy thirst of boundless power too late.

Proceed, great chief, with virtue on thy side,
Thy ev'ry action let the goddess guide.
A crown, a mansion, and a throne that shine,
With gold unfading, WASHINGTON! be thine.

Jarena Lee (1783–1849?)

Jarena Lee was born in Cape May, New Jersey. Hired out at age seven as a servant girl, she converted to Christianity at twenty-one years old and joined the Bethel African Methodist Episcopal (AME) Church in Philadelphia. In 1811 she married Joseph Lee, who pastored a church near Philadelphia. Within five years, five of her family members died, including her husband, leaving Jarena Lee with two young children.

Although the AME church denied her requests to preach because she was a woman, Lee never gave up her desire to do so because she felt that the Holy Spirit had "called" her to preach. After previously having heard her preach an extemporaneous sermon, Richard Allen, upon becoming a bishop of the AME church, granted her request. Lee traveled hundreds of miles delivering sermons, most of the time alone. In 1833 she enlisted the aid of an editor to reshape her religious journal into a narrative and in 1836 spent $38 to have 1,000 copies of her manuscript printed. In 1844 when the AME church refused to support a new, expanded edition of her autobiography, Lee financed the printing herself, continuing her life up to her fiftieth birthday. Her autobiography captures the early writing traditions of black women who wrote within and against religious conventions.

The Life and Religious Experience of Jarena Lee, a Coloured Lady, Giving an Account of Her Call to Preach the Gospel. Revised and Corrected from the Original Manuscript, Written by Herself

My Call to Preach the Gospel

Between four and five years after my sanctification, on a certain time, an impressive silence fell upon me, and I stood as if some one was about to speak to me, yet I had no such thought in my heart. But to my utter surprise there seemed to sound a voice which I thought I distinctly heard, and most certainly understood, which said to me, "Go preach the Gospel!" I immediately replied aloud, "No one will believe me." Again I listened, and again the same voice seemed to say, "Preach the Gospel; I will put words in your mouth, and will turn your enemies to become your friends."

At first I supposed that Satan had spoken to me, for I had read that he could transform himself into an angel of

light, for the purpose of deception. Immediately I went into a secret place, and called upon the Lord to know if he had called me to preach, and whether I was deceived or not; when there appeared to my view the form and figure of a pulpit, with a Bible lying thereon, the back of which was presented to me as plainly as if it had been a literal fact.

In consequence of this, my mind became so exercised that during the night following, I took a text, and preached in my sleep. I thought there stood before me a great multitude, while I expounded to them the things of religion. So violent were my exertions, and so loud were my exclamations, that I awoke from the sound of my own voice, which also awoke the family of the house where I resided. Two days after, I went to see the preacher in charge of the African Society, who was the Rev. Richard Allen, the same before named in these pages, to tell him that I felt it my duty to preach the gospel. But as I drew near the street in which his house was, which was in the city of Philadelphia, my courage began to fail me; so terrible did the cross appear, it seemed that I should not be able to bear it. Previous to my setting out to go to see him, so agitated was my mind, that my appetite for my daily food failed me entirely. Several times on my way there, I turned back again; but as often I felt my strength again renewed, and I soon found that the nearer I approached to the house of the minister, the less was my fear. Accordingly, as soon as I came to the door, my fears subsided, the cross was removed, all things appeared pleasant—I was tranquil.

I now told him, that the Lord had revealed it to me, that I must preach the gospel. He replied by asking, in what

From *The Life and Religious Experience of Jarena Lee* (1836). Reprinted in 1839.

sphere I wished to move in? I said, among the Methodists. He then replied, that a Mrs. Cook, a Methodist lady, had also some time before requested the same privilege; who it was believed, had done much good in the way of exhortation, and holding prayer meetings; and who had been permitted to do so by the verbal license of the preacher in charge at the time. But as to women preaching, he said that our Discipline knew nothing at all about it—that it did not call for women preachers. This I was glad to hear, because it removed the fear of the cross—but no sooner did this feeling cross my mind, than I found that a love of souls had in a measure departed from me; that holy energy which burned within me, as a fire, began to be smothered. This I soon perceived.

O how careful ought we to be, lest through our by-laws of church government and discipline, we bring into disrepute even the word of life. For as unseemly as it may appear now-a-days for a woman to preach, it should be remembered that nothing is impossible with God. And why should it be thought impossible, heterodox, or improper, for a woman to preach? seeing the Saviour died for the woman as well as the man.

If a man may preach, because the Saviour died for him, why not the woman? seeing he died for her also. Is he not a whole Saviour, instead of a half one? as those who hold it wrong for a woman to preach, would seem to make it appear.

Did not Mary *first* preach the risen Saviour, and is not the doctrine of the resurrection the very climax of Christianity— hangs not all our hope on this, as argued by St. Paul? Then did not Mary, a woman, preach the gospel? for she preached the resurrection of the crucified Son of God.

But some will say, that Mary did not expound the Scripture, therefore, she did not preach, in the proper sense of the term. To this I reply, it may be that the term *preach*, in those primitive times, did not mean exactly what it is now *made* to mean; perhaps it was a great deal more simple then, than it is now;—if it were not, the unlearned fishermen could not have preached the gospel at all, as they had no learning.

To this it may be replied, by those who are determined not to believe that it is right for a woman to preach, that the disciples, though they were fishermen, and ignorant of letters too, were inspired so to do. To which I would reply, that though they were inspired, yet that inspiration did not save them from showing their ignorance of letters, and of man's wisdom; this the multitude soon found out, by listening to the remarks of the envious Jewish priests. If then, to preach the gospel, by the gift of heaven, comes by inspiration solely, is God straitened; must he take the man exclusively? May he not, did he not, and can he not inspire a female to preach the simple story of the birth, life, death, and resurrection of our Lord, and accompany it too, with power to the sinner's heart. As for me, I am fully persuaded that the Lord called me to labour according to what I have received, in his vineyard. If he has not, how could he consistently bear testimony in favour of my poor labours, in awakening and converting sinners?

In my wanderings up and down among men, preaching according to my ability, I have frequently found families who told me that they had not for several years been to a meeting, and yet, while listening to hear what God would say by his poor coloured female instrument, have believed with trembling— tears rolling down their cheeks, the signs of contrition and repentance towards God. I firmly believe that I have sown seed, in the name of the Lord, which shall appear with its increase at the great day of accounts, when Christ shall come to make up his jewels.

At a certain time, I was beset with the idea, that soon or late I should fall from grace, and lose my soul at last. I was frequently called to the throne of grace about this matter, but found no relief; the temptation pursued me still. Being more and more afflicted with it, till at a certain time when the spirit strongly impressed it on my mind to enter into my closet, and carry my case once more to the Lord; the Lord enabled me to draw nigh to him, and to his mercy seat, at this time, in an extraordinary manner; for while I wrestled with him for the victory over this disposition to doubt whether I should persevere, there appeared a form of fire, about the size of a man's hand, as I was on my knees; at the same moment, there appeared to the eye of faith a man robed in a white garment, from the shoulders down to the feet; from him a voice proceeded, saying: "Thou shalt never return from the cross." Since that time I have never doubted, but believe that god will keep me until the day of redemption. Now I could adopt the very language of St. Paul, and say that nothing could have separated my soul from the love of god, which is in Christ Jesus [Rom. 8:35–39]. From that time, 1807, until the present, 1833, I have not yet doubted the power and goodness of God to keep me from falling, through sanctification of the spirit and belief of the truth.

Sojourner Truth (1797–1883)

An early women's rights advocate, abolitionist, and evangelical speaker, Sojourner Truth is known for her oratorical skills. In May 1851, she spoke before a women's rights convention in Akron, Ohio. Frances Dana Gage, a feminist abolitionist, immortalized the speech, recording it as "Ain't I a Woman?" Contemporary scholars contend that Truth's speech was closer to the "Ar'n't I a Woman?" version that follows, rather than Gage's version of "black dialect." Although unable to read or write, Truth's speeches raise some questions that remain central to black feminist thought: Who gets to be included in the category "woman"? How do race and class inform gender? In 1858 some men in an audience in Indiana questioned her gender and right to speak in public. In a climatic and eloquent moment, Truth bared her breast to prove her sexual identity.

Truth was born Isabella Baumfree to a Dutch master in Ulster County, New York. She had at least five children during slavery and took one of them with her when she left her final master. In 1829 she successfully arranged the return of her son, Peter, from enslavement in Alabama. After working for Isaac and Maria Van Wagener, she took their last name. During the 1830s she lived in a religious commune and in 1843 changed her name to Sojourner Truth, signifying her spiritual conversion and mission to travel and reveal God's truth. Truth worked with several people to have her speeches and life events published. Olive Gilbert helped her write and publish the *Narrative of Sojourner Truth*. Gage rewrote a longer version of the "Ar'n't I a Woman?" speech that was added to the expanded version of Truth's narrative. The 1851 and 1878 versions of the speech are different in diction and tone, and there remains much debate as to what Truth actually said. In Truth's later years she was active in the Millerite movement, preaching the imminent return of Jesus. When Frederick Douglass became discouraged with anti-slavery work, Truth reportedly asked him, "Frederick, is God dead?" She spent her last years in Battle Creek, Michigan, as a woman preaching *truth* about earthly and heavenly kingdoms.

Ar'n't I a Woman? Speech to the Women's Rights Convention in Akron, Ohio, 1851

From The *Anti-Slavery Bugle*, June 21, 1851

One of the most unique and interesting speeches of the Convention was made by Sojourner Truth, an emancipated slave. It is impossible to transfer it to paper, or convey any adequate idea of the effect it produced upon the audience. Those only can appreciate it who saw her powerful form, her whole-souled, earnest gesture, and listened to her strong and truthful tones. She came forward to the platform and addressing the President said with great simplicity: "May I say a few words?" Receiving an affirmative answer, she proceeded:

I want to say a few words about this matter. I am a woman's rights. I have as much muscle as any man, and can do as much work as any man. I have plowed and reaped and husked and chopped and mowed, and can any man do more than that? I have heard much about the sexes being equal. I can carry as much as any man, and can eat as much too, if I can get it. I am as strong as any man that is now. As for intellect, all I can say is, if woman have a pint, and man a quart—why can't she have her little pint full? You need not be afraid to give us our rights for fear we will take too much,—for we can't take more than our pint'll hold. The poor men seem to be all in confusion, and don't know what to do. Why children, if you have woman's rights, give it to her and you will feel better. You will have your own rights, and they won't be so much trouble. I can't read, but I can hear. I have heard the bible and have learned that Eve caused man to sin. Well, if woman upset the world, do give her a chance to set it right side up again. The Lady has spoken about Jesus, how he never spurned woman from him, and she was right. When Lazarus died,

Published in *Anti-Slavery Bugle*, June 21, 1851; from *Narrative of Sojourner Truth 1878 with recollections of Frances Gage*. Gage version: Truth, Sojourner. *Narrative of Sojourner Truth*, with Olive Gilbert, 1850; revised by Frances W. Titus, 1875, 1884.

Mary and Martha came to him with faith and love and besought him to raise their brother. And Jesus wept and Lazarus came forth. And how came Jesus into the world? Through God who created him and a woman who bore him. Man, where is your part? But the women are coming up blessed be God and a few of the men are coming up with them. But man is in a tight place, the poor slave is on him, woman is coming on him, he is surely between a hawk and a buzzard.

When Woman Gets Her Rights Man Will Be Right

1867

My Friends, I am rejoiced that you are glad, but I don't know how you will feel when I get through. I come from another field—the country of the slave. They have got their rights—so much good luck. Now what is to be done about it? I feel that I have got as much responsibility as anybody else. I have as good rights as anybody. There is a great stir about colored men getting their rights, but not a word about the colored women; and if colored men get their rights, and not colored women get theirs, there will be a bad time about it. So I am for keeping the thing going while things are stirring; because if we wait till it is still, it will take a great while to get it going again. White women are a great deal smarter and know more than colored women, while colored women do not know scarcely anything. They go out washing, which is about as high as a colored woman gets, and their men go about idle, strutting up and down; and when the women come home, they ask for their money and take it all, and then scold because there is no food. I want you to consider on that, chil'n. I want women to have their rights. In the courts women have no right, no voice; nobody speaks for them. I wish woman to have her voice there among the pettifoggers. If it is not a fit place for women, it is unfit for men to be there. I am above eighty years old; it is about time for me to be going. But I suppose I am kept here because something remains for me to do; I suppose I am yet to help break the chain. I have done a great deal of work—as much as a man, but did not get so much pay. I used to work in the field and bind grain, keeping up with the cradler; but men never doing no more, got twice as much pay. So with the German women. They work in the field and do as much work, but do not get the pay. We do as much, we eat as much, we want as much. I suppose I am about the only colored woman that goes about to speak for the rights of the colored woman, I want to keep the thing stirring, now that the ice is broken. What we want is a little money. You men know that you get as much again as women when you write, or for what you do. When we get our rights, we shall not have to come to you for money, for then we shall have money enough of our own. It is a good consolation to know that when we have got this we shall not be coming to you any more. You have been having our right so long, that you think, like a slaveholder, that you own us. I know that it is hard for one who has held the reins for so long to give up; it cuts like a knife. It will feel all better when it closes up again. I have been in Washington about three years, seeing about those colored people. Now colored men have a right to vote; and what I want is to have colored women have the right to vote. There ought to be equal rights more than ever, since colored people have got their freedom.

I know that it is hard for men to give up entirely. They must run in the old track. I was amused how men speak up for one another. They cannot bear that a woman should say anything about the man, but they will stand here and take up the time in man's cause. But we are going, tremble or no tremble. Men are trying to help us. I know that all—the spirit they have got; and they cannot help us much until some of the spirit is taken out of them that belongs among the women. Men have got their rights, and women has not got their rights. That is the trouble. When woman gets her rights man will be right. How beautiful that will be. Then it will be peace on earth and good will to men. But it cannot be until it be right . . . It will come . . . Yes, it will come quickly. It must come. And now when the waters is troubled, and now is the time to step into the pool. There is a great deal now with the minds, and now is the time to start forth . . . The great fight was to keep the rights of the poor colored people. That made a great battle. And now I hope that this will be the last battle that will be in the world. Let us finish up so that there be no more fighting. I have faith in God and there is truth in humanity. Be strong women! Blush not! Tremble not! I want you to keep a good faith and good courage. And I am going round after I get my business settled and get more equality. People in the North, I am going round to lecture on human rights. I will shake every place I go to.

Major Speeches by Negroes in the U.S., 1797–1971, ed. Eric Foner (New York: Simon and Schuster, 1972).

Nancy Gardner Prince (1799c.–1856)

Few African American women of her era had the opportunities for international travel that Nancy Gardner Prince had. Born in Newburyport, Massachusetts, to free parents, she was interested in both evangelical and abolitionist work. Her maternal grandfather was a slave who fought at Bunker Hill. Both of her parents were born in Massachusetts. Her father died when she was three months old. Subsequently, her mother had a mental breakdown, leaving her to take care of six or seven siblings. In 1824 she married Nero Prince, who like her father was a seaman. Nero was also a servant in Russia's imperial court. Shortly after their marriage, the Princes went to Russia. After staying in Russia for nine years, she returned to America. In 1840 she traveled to Jamaica where she did what she could to help emancipated slaves. A participant in the 1854 National Women's Rights Convention, Prince was an advocate for the rights of black women. Her narrative focuses primarily on her travels to Europe, Russia, and Jamaica.

A Narrative of the Life and Travels of Mrs. Nancy Prince Written by Herself

Preface

By divine aid, I attempt a second edition of my narrative, with the additions suggested to me by my friends. My object is not a vain desire to appear before the public; but, by the sale, I hope to obtain the means to supply my necessities. There are many benevolent societies for the support of Widows, but I am desirous not to avail myself of them, so long as I can support myself by my own endeavors. Infirmities are coming upon me, which induce me to solicit the patronage of my friends and the public, in the sale of this work. Not wishing to throw myself on them, I take this method to help myself, as health and strength are gone.

Narrative

I was born in Newburyport, September the 15th, 1799. My mother was born in Gloucester, Massachusetts—the daughter of Tobias Wornton, or Backus, so called. He was stolen from Africa, when a lad, and was a slave of Captain Winthrop Sargent; but, although a slave, he fought for liberty. He was in the Revolutionary army, and at the battle of Bunker Hill. He often used to tell us, when little children, the evils of Slavery, and how he was stolen from his native land. My grandmother

From *A Narrative of the Life and Travels of Mrs. Nancy Prince. Written by Herself* (1850). Published by the Author (see Collected Black Women's Narrative, the Schomburg Library of Nineteenth-Century Black Women Writers (Oxford University Press)).

was an Indian of this country; she became a captive to the English, or their descendants. She served as a domestic in the Parsons family. My father, Thomas Gardner, was born in Nantucket; his parents were of African descent. He died in Newburyport, when I was three months old. My mother was thus a second time left a widow, with her two children, and she returned to Gloucester to her father. My mother married her third husband, by whom she had six children. My step-father was stolen from Africa, and while the vessel was at anchor in one of our Eastern ports, he succeeded in making his escape from his captors, by swimming ashore. I have often heard him tell the tale. Having some knowledge of the English language, he found no trouble to pass. There were two of them, and they found, from observation, that they were in a free State. I have heard my father describe the beautiful moon-light night when they two launched their bodies into the deep, for liberty. When they got upon soundings, their feet were pricked with a sea-plant that grew under water, they had to retreat, and, at last they reached the shore. When day began to break, they laid down under a fence, as naked as they were born—soon they heard a rattling sound, and trembling, they looked to see what it meant. In a few minutes, a man with a broad-brimed hat on, looked over the fence and cried out, "Halloo boys! you are from that ship at anchor?" Trembling, we answered, yes. He kindly took us by the hand, and told us not to fear, for we were safe. "Jump, boys," said he, "into my cart," which we readily did. He turned about, and soon entered a large yard—we were taken to his house and carried to an apartment, where he brought us clothes and food, and cheered us with every kindness. No search was made for us; it was supposed we were drowned, as many had jumped over-board on the voyage, thinking they could get home to Africa again. I have often heard my step-father boast how brave they were, and say they stood like men and saw the ship set sail with less than half they stole from Africa. He was selling his bamboo baskets, when he was seized by white men, and put in a boat, and taken on board the ship that lay off; many such ships there were! He was called "Money Vose," and his name may be found on the custom House books in Gloucester. His last voyage was with Captain Elias Davis, in the brig Romulus, belonging to Captain Fitz William Sargent, in whose employ he had been twelve years. During the war, the brig was taken by a British privateer, and he was pressed into their service. He was sick with the dropsy a long while, and died oppressed, in the English dominions. My mother was again left a widow, with an infant six weeks old, and seven other children. When she heard of her husband's death, she exclaimed, "I thought it; what shall I do with these children?" She was young, inexperienced, with no hope in God, and without the knowledge of her Saviour. Her grief, poverty, and responsibilities, were too much for her; she never again was the mother that she had been before. I was, at this time, in Captain F. W. Sargent's family. I shall never forget the feelings I experienced, on hearing of the decease of my father-in-law, although he was not kind to me or my sister; but, by industry a humble home was provided, for my mother and her younger children. Death had twice visited our family, in less than three months. My grandfather died before my father-in-law sailed. I thought I would go home a little while, and try and comfort my mother. The three oldest children were put into families.

My brother and myself stayed at home that Summer. We gathered berries and sold them in Gloucester; strawberries, raspberries, blackberries and whortleberries, were in abundance, in the stony environs, growing spontaneously. With the sale of these fruits, my brother and myself nearly supported my mother and her children, that Summer. My brother George, young as he was, caught fish and sold them, and run of errands, and was always watching for something to do, that he might help his mother. At one time he was missing; we expected he was drowned; a search was made for him in the water; the neighbors were all on the alert. Poor mother returning from a hard day's work, supposing the boy was lost, was like a lunatic. The lad was supposed to have fallen from the wharf, where he was fishing. Our friends had all given up the search—it was then eleven o'clock at night. Mother and I locked up the children and went round to the harbor, to one Captain Warner, who traded to the Eastward. Mrs. Warner informed us that my brother came there in the morning, with his bundle, and they supposed he was sent, as the Captain wished to take him with him. He went on board, and the vessel sailed that afternoon. In three weeks, he came home, to the comfort of his mother and all of us. He brought back, for his pay, four feet of wood and three dollars.

We stayed with our mother until every resource was exhausted; we then heard of a place eight miles out of town, where a boy and girl were wanted. We both went and were engaged. We often went home with our wages, and all the comforts we could get; but we could not approach our mother as we wished. God in mercy took one little boy of seven years, who had been in a consumption one year.

My oldest sister, Silvia, was seventy miles in the country, with the family that brought her up; so we were scattered all about. Soon as the war was over, I determined to get more for my labor. I left Essex and went to Salem, in the month of April, 1814, without a friend, without a guide. I first went to Gloucester, to bid my mother and the family adieu. George, my brother, I left with a promise to send for him when I should be settled. When I reached the Cove, about five miles from Gloucester, I stopped at a friend's, who urged me not to go, holding up obstacles. It rained and snowed, but I travelled along, following the guide-posts, until I reached Beverly bridge. I crossed it when the clock struck four, in the afternoon. I now wished to find a friend in Becket Street, Salem, but was afraid of the people that I met near the Bridge, they were so covered with rags and dirt. I kept on until I reached the Common; I then asked a woman who was neatly dressed, for the lady I wished to find. She did not know. I asked for another person, that I knew was not very good; she took me there, but I soon found my friend that I wished, and stopped there two weeks, and then went to live with a respectable colored family. My mother was not satisfied, and came after me. I would not go to Gloucester. She left me at a friend's, and this woman had a daughter, who came home from service, sick. I took her place, and thought myself fortunate to be with religious people, as I had enjoyed the happy privilege of religious instruction. My dear grandfather was a member of a Congregational Church, and a good man; he always attended meeting in the morning, and took his children with him. In the afternoon he took care of the smaller children, while my mother attended with her little group. He thought it was wrong for us to go to school where the teacher was not devoted to God. Thus I early knew the difference between right and wrong.

There were seven in the family, one sick with a fever, and another in a consumption; and of course, the work must have been very severe, especially the washings. Sabbath evening I had to prepare for the wash; soap the clothes and put them into the steamer, set the kettle of water to boiling, and then close in the steam, and let the pipe from the boiler into the steam box that held the clothes. At two o'clock, on the morning of Monday, the bell was rung for me to get up; but, that was not all, they said I was too slow, and the washing was not done well; I had to leave the tub to tend the door and wait on the family, and was not spoken kind to, at that.

Hard labor and unkindness was too much for me; in three months, my health and strength were gone. I often looked at my employers, and thought to myself, is this your religion? I did not wonder that the girl who had lived there previous to myself, went home to die. They had family prayers, morning and evening. Oh! yes, they were sanctimonious! I was a poor stranger, but fourteen years of age, imposed upon by these good people; but I must leave them. In the year 1814, they sent me to Gloucester in their chaise. I found my poor mother in bad health, and I was sick also; but, by the mercy of God, and the attention and skill of Dr. Dale, and the kindness of friends, I was restored, so that in a few months, I was able again to go to work, although my side afflicted me, which I attributed to overworking myself.

In the Spring of 1815, I returned to Salem, accompanied by my eldest sister, and we obtained good places. She took it into her head to go to Boston, as a nursery girl, where she lived a few months and was then deluded away. February 7th, 1816, a friend came to Salem and informed me of it. To have heard of her death, would not have been so painful to me, as we loved each other very much, and more particularly, as our step-father was not very kind to us. When little girls, she used to cry about it, and we used to say, when we were large enough we would go away.

It was very cold; but notwithstanding, I was so distressed about my sister that I started the next morning for Boston, on foot. A friend was with me. At Lynn Hotel we refreshed ourselves, and all seemed much interested about me; two women took me aside, and inquired how it was that I was with that woman. I told my reason; she was well known all about; she lived as a cook in Boston, she came after her son, a little child whom she held in her arms. By the time we were seven miles from Salem, cold and fatigued, I could walk no farther, and we hired a horse and sleigh, and a man to drive us to Boston, where we arrived at seven o'clock in the evening. The house where we stopped was in Green street, the lady kindly invited me to stop; I refused; I was suspicious the house was not good; the woman I came with took me to Belknap street, where I found an old friend; I would not stop, they went with me to Bedford street, where I intended to put up. The inmates received me very kindly; my feet, hands and ears were all frostbitten. I needed all the hospitality that was extended to me. I was young and inexperienced, but God knew that my object was good. "In wisdom he chooses the weak things of the earth." Without his aid, how could I ever have rescued my lost sister? Mr. Brown, when he learned my errand, kindly offered to assist me. He found where my sister resided, and taking with him a large cane, he accompanied me to the house, on Sabbath evening. My sister I found seated with a number of others round a fire, the mother of harlots at the head. My sister did not see me until I clasped her round the neck. The old woman flew at me, and bid me take my hands off of her; she opened a door that led down into a cellar kitchen, and told me to come down, she attempted to take my hands off of my sister. Mr. Brown defended me with his cane; there were many men and girls there, and all was confusion. When my sister came to herself, she looked upon me and said: "Nancy, O Nancy, I am ruined!" I said, "Silvia, my dear sister, what are you here for? Will you not go with me?" She seemed thankful to get away; the enraged old woman cried out, "she owes me, she cannot go." Silvia replied, "I will go." The old woman seized her to drag her down into the kitchen; I held on to her, while Mr. Brown at my side, used his great cane; he threatened her so that she was obliged to let my sister go, who, after collecting her things, accompanied Mr. Brown and myself.

Now while I write, I am near the spot that that was then the hold of all foul and unclean things. "The lips of a strange woman drop as an honey comb, and her mouth is smoother than oil; there she has slain her thousands; her end is bitter as wormwood, sharp as a two-edged sword, and lieth in wait at every corner, with an impudent face, saying, I have peace offerings, I have payed my vows. With her much fair speech, she flattereth: she hath cast down many wounded, yea, many strong have been slain by her; her house is the way to hell going down to the chambers of death." Even now, I cannot refrain my feelings, although death has long separated us; but her soul is precious; she was very dear to me; she was five years older than myself, and often protected me from the blows of an unkind step-father. She often said she was not fit to live, nor fit to die.

The next day, after breakfast, one of Mrs. Brown's daughters accompanied us to the stage office; we expected Mr. Low, the driver of the Gloucester stage, who knew us as his townspeople, would let us take passage with him without any difficulty; but he refused unless we would ride upon the top. It was very cold; I had sent my mother my wages the week before, and what money I had, I had taken in advance, of my employers. We were greatly embarrassed, when a colored man, unknown to us, penetrated our difficulty, and asked us if we had two dollars; we told him we had; he very kindly took us to the stage office, and we bargained for a horse and sleigh to carry us to Salem, where we arrived safely in about two hours and a half; and we gave up our conveyance to the same owners, with ten thousand thanks to our colored friend, and to our Heavenly Father; had we attempted to walk, we must have frozen by the way. The horse and sleigh belonged to the stage-office, so we had no more care for that. The man who let it to us was very humane, although a stranger. The price was two dollars, of which he not only gave us back fifty cents to pay our toll, but went with us as far as to Charlestown bridge.

I often thought of the contrast between our townsman, Mr. Low, and the stranger who was so kind to us. The lady I lived with, Mrs. John Deland, received us very kindly, and permitted my sister to remain with me awhile; then she returned to Gloucester, to the family who brought her up, and I thought we had gained a great victory.

My brother George and myself were very desirous to make our mother comfortable: he went to sea for that purpose; the next April, I came to Boston to get a higher price for my labor; for we had agreed to support my mother, and hoped she would take home our little brother and take care of him, who was supported by the town. George came home, and sailed again in the same employ, leaving mother a draw bill for half his wages. My sister returned to Boston to find me, and wished to procure a place to work out. I had just changed my place for one more retired, and engaged my sister with me as a chamber maid; she tried me much. I thought it a needy time, for I had not yielded my heart to the will of God, though I had many impressions, and formed many resolutions; but the situations that I had been placed in, (having left my mother's house at the age of eight,) had not permitted me to do as I wished, although the kind counsels of my dear grandfather and pious teachers followed me wherever I went. Care after care oppressed me—my mother wandered about like a Jew—the young children who were in families were dissatisfied; all hope but in God was lost. I resolved, in my mind, to seek an interest in my Savior, and put my trust in Him; and never shall I forget the place or time when God spake to my troubled conscience. Justified by faith I found peace with God, the forgiveness of sin through Jesus Christ my Lord. After living sixteen years without hope, and without a guide, May 6th, 1819, the Rev. Thomas Paul, baptized myself and seven others, in obedience to the great command.

We, on him our anchor cast—
Poor and needy, lean on him,
He will bring us through at last.

The same day, we received the right hand of fellowship from our then beloved pastor. After the absence of nine years, I had the happy privilege of meeting with two of the number, who were unshaken in the faith; they have since gone to join the spirits in glory. I had the happy privilege of attending them in sickness.

I now turn to the scenes of youth. George again returned home, and we again provided a home for mother and the little ones. He shipped in the same vessel again, and affairs now seemed to promise comfort and respectability; but mother chose to marry again; this was like death to us all. George returned home, but was so disappointed that he shipped again to return no more. Although a boy of sixteen, he was as steady as most men at twenty. My cares were consequently increased, having no one to share them with me. My next brother, who lived in South Essex, came to Salem to his mother's, but was

driven away by her husband, and came to me; I carried him to Gloucester and left him in the hands of the town; he stayed but three weeks, and returned to me again; I then boarded him out for one dollar a week, until I could procure suitable employment for him. When winter came, poor mother's health was declining. Little Samuel could do but little; my father-in-law was very cross, his disappointment was very great, for he expected to be supported by my brother George and myself. I could not see my mother suffer, therefore I left my place and went to Salem to watch over her and Samuel, and lived in the Rev. Dr. Bolle's family. In the Spring, I returned to Boston, and took my brother Samuel with me; soon after, my sister Lucy left her place and went to her mother, but was not permitted to stay; my mother wrote to me, requesting me to take care of her. I then determined, in my mind, to bring her to Boston, and if possible, procure a place for her; I then had Samuel and John on my hands; Lucy was not nine, and very small of her age, I could not easily get her a place, but fortunately obtained board for her and Samuel for one dollar a week. My brother John, whom I had boarded, at last got a place where he had wages. Soon the Lord opened the way for little Samuel; Dr. Phelps took him to bring up: so that I was left with one only to sustain; soon my hopes were blasted. John left his place, and was several months on my hands again; finally, he made up his mind to go to sea; I was so thankful that he had concluded to do something, that I took two months' wages in advance to fit him out for Liverpool, in five months he returned without a single thing but the clothes he had on. The ship brought passengers from Ireland. As soon as the vessel arrived, he came to seek me; I went with him for his things; but passengers and all were gone. His wages were small, not enough to make him comfortable: and, had not a friend given him a home, he would again have been dependent on my exertions; another friend took Lucy, with whom she stayed eleven months. She lived in different families until she was about twelve years old; I then put her in the Rev. Mr. Mann's family, at Westminster, for a certain time, thinking it would be best for her; and John I left to fight his own battles. My sister Silvia, was one of my greatest trials. Knowing she was in Boston, my mother, in one of her spells of insanity, got away from her home and travelled to Boston after her; she came where I lived, my employers were very kind to her, she tarried a few days, when I hired a horse and chaise and took them both back to Salem, and returned to my place in 1822, with a determination to do something for myself; I left my place after three months, and went to learn a trade; and after seven years of anxiety and toil, I made up my mind to leave my country. September 1st, 1823, Mr. Prince arrived from Russia. February 15th, 1824, we were married.

Maria W. Stewart (1803–1879)

On September 21, 1832, Maria W. Stewart spoke to men *and* women of the New England Anti-Slavery Society at Franklin Hall in Boston. This was the first time that an American woman formally addressed a mixed or what was called a "promiscuous audience." Born Maria Miller in Hartford, Connecticut, she was orphaned at the age of five and worked as a servant for a minister's family. In 1826 she married James W. Stewart, a shipping agent in the Boston fishing industry. Three years later, James died, and shortly thereafter, her friend and well-known antislavery activist, David Walker, died. To fill the void, Stewart worked more intensely as an abolitionist, writing for the *Liberator*, an antislavery newspaper. She wrote religious and antislavery tracts and worked as a schoolteacher in New York, Baltimore, and Washington. As an early advocate for black women's studies, Stewart's clarion call has resonated throughout several centuries: "O, ye daughters of Africa, awake! Awake! Arise!"

For sale at this office, a tract addressed to the people of color, by Mrs. Maria W. Steward [sic], a respectable colored lady of this city. Its title is, 'Religion And The Pure Principles of Morality, The Sure Foundation On Which We Must Build.' The production is most praiseworthy, and confers great credit on the talents and piety of its author. We hope she will have many patrons. Extracts of the paper hereafter. Price 6 cents.

THE LIBERATOR, 8 OCTOBER 1831

Religion and the Pure Principles of Morality, the Sure Foundation on Which We Must Build

Productions from the Pen of Mrs. Maria W. Steward [sic], Widow of the Late James W. Steward, of Boston

Introduction

Feeling a deep solemnity of soul, in view of our wretched and degraded situation, and sensible of the gross ignorance that prevails among us, I have thought proper thus publicly to express my sentiments before you. I hope my friends will not scrutinize these pages with too severe an eye, as I have not calculated to display either elegance or taste in their composition, but have merely written the meditations of my heart as far as my imagination led; and have presented them before you in order to arouse you to exertion, and to enforce upon your minds the great necessity of turning your attention to knowledge and improvement.

I was born in Hartford, Connecticut, in 1803; was left an orphan at five years of age; was bound out in a clergyman's family; had the seeds of piety and virtue early sown in my mind, but was deprived of the advantages of education, though my soul thirsted for knowledge. Left them at fifteen years of age; attended Sabbath schools until I was twenty; in 1826 was married to James W. Stewart; was left a widow in 1829; was, as I humbly hope and trust, brought to the knowledge of the truth, as it is in Jesus, in 1830; in 1831 made a public profession of my faith in Christ.

From the moment I experienced the change, I felt a strong desire, with the help and assistance of God, to devote the remainder of my days to piety and virtue, and now possess that spirit of independence that, were I called upon, I would willingly sacrifice my life for the cause of God and my brethren.

All the nations of the earth are crying out for liberty and equality. Away, away with tyranny and oppression! And shall Afric's sons be silent any longer? Far be it from me to recommend to you either to kill, burn, or destroy. But I would strongly recommend to you to improve your talents; let not one lie buried in the earth. Show forth your powers of mind. Prove to the world that

Though black your skins as shades of night,
your hearts are pure, your souls are white.

From "Religion and the Pure Principles of Morality" (1831).

This is the land of freedom. The press is at liberty. Every man has a right to express his opinion. Many think, because your skins are tinged with a sable hue, that you are an inferior race of beings; but God does not consider you as such. He hath formed and fashioned you in his own glorious image, and hath bestowed upon you reason and strong powers of intellect. He hath made you to have dominion over the beasts of the field, the fowls of the air, and the fish of the sea [Genesis 1:26]. He hath crowned you with glory and honor; hath made you but a little lower than the angels [Psalms 8:5]; and according to the Constitution of these United States, he hath made all men free and equal. Then why should one worm say to another, "Keep you down there, while I sit up yonder; for I am better than thou?" It is not the color of the skin that makes the man, but it is the principles formed within the soul.

Many will suffer for pleading the cause of oppressed Africa, and I shall glory in being one of her martyrs; for I am firmly persuaded, that the God in whom I trust is able to protect me from the rage and malice of mine enemies, and from them that will rise up against me; and if there is no other way for me to escape, he is able to take me to himself, as he did the most noble, fearless, and undaunted David Walker.

Never Will Virtue, Knowledge, And True Politeness Begin To Flow, Till The Pure Principles Of Religion And Morality Are Put Into Force.

My Respected Friends,

I feel almost unable to address you; almost incompetent to perform the task; and at times I have felt ready to exclaim, O that my head were waters, and mine eyes a fountain of tears, that I might weep day and night [Jeremiah 9:1], for the transgressions of the daughters of my people. Truly, my heart's desire and prayer is, that Ethiopia might stretch forth her hands unto God. But we have a great work to do. Never, no, never will the chains of slavery and ignorance burst, till we become united as one, and cultivate among ourselves the pure principles of piety, morality and virtue. I am sensible of my ignorance; but such knowledge as God has given to me, I impart to you. I am sensible of former prejudices; but it is high time for prejudices and animosities to cease from among us. I am sensible of exposing myself to calumny and reproach; but shall I, for fear of feeble man who shall die, hold my peace? Shall I for fear of scoffs and frowns, refrain my tongue? Ah, no! I speak as one that must give an account at the awful bar of God; I speak as a dying mortal to dying mortals. O, ye daughters of Africa, awake! Awake! Arise! No longer sleep nor slumber, but distinguish yourselves. Show forth to the world that ye are endowed with noble and exalted faculties. O, ye daughters of Africa! What have ye done to immortalize your names beyond the grave? What examples have ye set before the rising generation? What foundation have ye laid for generations yet unborn? Where are our union and love? And where is our sympathy, that weeps at another's woe, and hides the faults we see? And our daughters, where are they? Blushing in innocence and virtue? And our sons, do they bid fair to become crowns of glory to our hoary heads [Proverbs 16:31]? Where is the parent who is conscious of having faithfully discharged his duty, and at the last awful day of account, shall be able to say, here, Lord, is thy poor, unworthy servant, and the children thou hast given me? And where are the children that will arise and call them blessed? Alas, O God! Forgive me if I speak amiss; the minds of our tender babes are tainted as soon as they are born; they go astray, as it were, from the womb. Where is the maiden who will blush at vulgarity? And where is the youth who has written upon his manly brow a thirst for knowledge; whose ambitious mind soars above trifles, and longs for the time to come, when he shall redress the wrongs of his father and plead the cause of his brethren? Did the daughters of our land possess a delicacy of manners, combined with gentleness and dignity; did their pure minds hold vice in abhorrence and contempt, did they frown when their ears were polluted with its vile accents, would not their influence become powerful? Would not our brethren fall in love with their virtues? Their souls would become fired with a holy zeal for freedom's cause. They would become ambitious to distinguish themselves. They would become proud to display their talents. Able advocates would arise in our defence. Knowledge would begin to flow, and the chains of slavery and ignorance would melt like wax before the flames. I am but a feeble instrument. I am but as one particle of the small dust of the earth. You may frown or smile. After I am dead, perhaps before, God will surely rise up those who will more powerfully and eloquently plead the cause of virtue and the pure principles of morality than I am able to do. O virtue! How sacred is thy name! How pure are thy principles! Who can find a virtuous woman? For her price is far above rubies [Proverbs 31:10]. Blessed is the man who shall call her his wife; yea, happy is the child who shall call her mother. O woman, woman, would thou only strive to excel in merit and virtue; would thou only store thy mind with useful knowledge, great would be thine influence. Do you say you are too far advanced in life now to begin? You are not too far advanced to instil [sic] these principles into the minds of your tender infants. Let them by no means be neglected. Discharge your duty faithfully, in every point of view: leave the event with God. So shall your skirts become clear of their blood [Jeremiah 2:34].

When I consider how little improvement has been made the last eight years; the apparent cold and indifferent state of the children of God; how few have been hopefully brought to the knowledge of the truth as it is in Jesus; that our young men and maidens are fainting and drooping, as it were, by the way-side, for the want of knowledge; when I see how few care to distinguish themselves either in religious or moral improvement, and when I see the greater part of our community following the vain bubbles of life with so much eagerness, which will only prove to them like the serpent's sting upon the bed of death, I really think we are in as wretched and miserable a state as was the house of Israel in the days of Jeremiah.

I suppose many of my friends will say, "Religion is all your theme," I hope my conduct will ever prove me to be what I profess, a true follower of Christ; and it is the religion of Jesus alone that will constitute your happiness here, and support you in a dying hour. O then, do not trifle with God and your own souls any longer. Do not presume to offer him the very dregs of your lives; but now, whilst you are blooming in health and vigor, consecrate the remnant of your days to him. Do you wish to become useful in your day and generation? Do you wish to promote the welfare and happiness of your friends, as far as your circle extends? Have you one desire to become truly great? O then become truly pious and God will endow you with wisdom and knowledge from on high.

> Come, turn to God, who did thee make
> And at his presence fear and quake;
> Remember him now in thy youth,
> And let thy soul take hold of truth.
> The devil and his ways defy,
> Believe him not, he doth but lie;
> His ways seem sweet: but youth, beware!
> He for thy soul hath laid a snare.

Religion is pure; it is ever new; it is beautiful; it is all that is worth living for, it is worth dying for. O, could I but see the church built up in the most holy faith, could I but see men spiritually minded, walking in the fear of God, not given to filthy lucre, not holding religion in one hand and the world in the other, but diligent in business, fervent in spirit, serving the Lord, standing upon the walls of Zion, crying to passers by, "Ho, every one that thirsteth, come ye to the waters, and he that hath no money; yea, come and buy wine and milk without money and without price [Isaiah 55:1]." Turn ye, turn ye, for why will ye die [Ezekiel 33:11]? Could I but see mothers in Israel, chaste, keepers at home, not busy bodies, meddlers in other men's matters, whose adorning is of the inward man, possessing a meek and quiet spirit, whose sons were like olive-plants, and whose daughters were as polished corner-stones; could I but see young men and maidens turning their feet from impious ways, rather choosing to suffer affliction with the people of God than to enjoy the pleasures of sin for a season; could I but see the rising youth blushing in artless innocence, then could I say, now, Lord, let thine unworthy handmaiden depart in peace, for I have seen the desire of mine eyes, and am satisfied.

Prayer

O, Lord God, the watchmen of Zion have cried peace, peace, when there was no peace [Jeremiah 6:14]; they have been, as it were, blind leaders of the blind [Matthew 15:14]. Wherefore hast thou so long withheld from us the divine influences of thy Holy Spirit? Wherefore hast thou hardened our hearts and blinded our eyes? It is because we have honored thee with our lips, but our hearts were far from thee. We have polluted thy Sabbaths, and even our most holy things have been solemn mockery to thee. We have regarded iniquity in our hearts, therefore thou wilt not hear. Return again unto us. O Lord God, we beseech thee, and pardon this the iniquity of thy servants. Cause thy face to shine upon us, and we shall be saved. O visit us with thy salvation. Raise up sons and daughters unto Abraham, and grant that there might come a mighty shaking of dry bones among us, and a great ingathering of souls. Quicken thy professing children. Grant that the young may be constrained to believe that there is a reality in religion, and a beauty in the fear of the Lord. Have mercy on the benighted sons and daughters of Africa. Grant that we may soon become so distinguished for our moral and religious improvements, that the nations of the earth may take knowledge of us; and grant that our cries may come up before thy throne like holy incense. Grant that every daughter of Africa may consecrate her sons to thee from birth. And do thou, Lord, bestow upon them wise and understanding hearts. Clothe us with humility of soul, and give us a becoming dignity of manners: may we imitate the character of the meek and lowly Jesus; and do thou grant that Ethiopia may soon stretch forth her hands unto thee. And now, Lord, be pleased to grant that Satan's kingdom may be destroyed; that the kingdom of our Lord Jesus Christ may be built up; that all nations and kindreds and tongues and people might be brought to the knowledge of the truth, as it is in Jesus, and we at last meet around thy throne, and join in celebrating thy praises.

I have been taking a survey of the American people in my own mind, and I see them thriving in arts and sciences, and in polite literature. Their highest aim is to excel in political, moral and religious improvement. They early consecrate their children to God, and their youth indeed are blushing in artless innocence. They wipe the tears from the orphan's eyes, and they cause the widow's heart to sing for joy [Job 29:13]! And their poorest ones, who have the least wish to excel, they promote! And those that have but one talent they encourage.

But how very few are there among them that bestow one thought upon the benighted sons and daughters of Africa, who have enriched the soils of America with their tears and blood: few to promote their cause, none to encourage their talents. Under these circumstances, do not let our hearts be any longer discouraged; it is no use to murmur nor to repine: but let us promote ourselves and improve our own talents. And I am rejoiced to reflect that there are many able and talented ones among us, whose names might be recorded on the bright annals of fame. But "I can't," is a great barrier in the way. I hope it will soon be removed, and "I will," resume its place.

Righteousness exalteth a nation, but sin is a reproach to any people [Proverbs 14:34]. Why is it, my friends, that our minds have been blinded by ignorance, to the present moment? 'Tis on account of sin. Why is it that our church is involved in so much difficulty? It is on account of sin. Why is it that God has cut down, upon our right hand and upon our left, the most learned and intelligent of our men? O, shall I say, it is on account of sin! Why is it that thick darkness is mantled upon every brow, and we, as it were, look sadly upon one another? It is on account of sin. O, then, let us bow before the Lord our God, with all our hearts, and humble our very souls in the dust before him; sprinkling, as it were, ashes upon our heads, and awake to righteousness and sin not. The arm of the Lord is not shortened, that it cannot save; neither is his ear heavy, that it cannot hear; but it is your iniquities that have separated you from me, saith the Lord. Return, O ye backsliding children [Jeremiah 3:22], and I will return unto you, and ye shall be my people, and I will be your God.

O, ye mothers, what a responsibility rests on you! You have souls committed to your charge, and God will require a strict account of you. It is you that must create in the minds of your little girls and boys a thirst for knowledge, the love of virtue, the abhorrence of vice, and the cultivation of a pure heart. The seeds thus sown will grow with their growing years; and the love of virtue thus early formed in the soul will protect their inexperienced feet from many dangers. O, do not say you cannot make any thing of your children; but say, with the help and assistance of God, we will try. Do not indulge them in their little stubborn ways; for a child left to himself bringeth his mother to shame. Spare not for their crying; thou shalt beat them with a rod, and they shall not die [Proverbs 23:13]; and thou shalt save their souls from hell. When you correct them, do it in the fear of God, and for their own good. They will not thank you for your false and foolish indulgence; they will rise up, as it were, and curse you in this world and, in the world to come, condemn you. It is no use to say you can't do this, or you can't do that; you will not tell your Maker so, when you meet him at the great day of account. And you must be careful that you set an example

worthy of following, for you they will imitate. There are many instances, even among us now, where parents have discharged their duty faithfully, and their children now reflect honor upon their gray hairs.

Perhaps you will say that many parents have set pure examples at home, and they have not followed them. True, our expectations are often blasted; but let not this dishearten you. If they have faithfully discharged their duty, even after they are dead their works may live; their prodigal children may return to God and become heirs of salvation; if not, their children cannot rise and condemn them at the awful bar of God.

Perhaps you will say that you cannot send them to high schools and academies. You can have them taught in the first rudiments of useful knowledge, and then you can have private teachers who will instruct them in the higher branches; and their intelligence will become greater than ours, and their children will attain to higher advantages, and their children still higher; and then, though we are dead, our works shall live; though we are mouldering. our names shall not be forgotten.

Finally, my heart's desire and prayer to God is that there might come a thorough reformation among us. Our minds have too long grovelled in ignorance and sin. Come, let us incline our ears to wisdom, and apply our hearts to understanding; promote her, and she will exalt thee; she shall bring thee honor when thou dost embrace her. An ornament of grace shall she be to thy head, and a crown of glory shall she deliver to thee. Take fast hold of instruction: let her not go; keep her, for she is thy life [Proverbs 4:13]. Come, let us turn unto the Lord our God, with all our heart and soul, and put away every unclean and unholy thing from among us, and walk before the Lord our God, with a perfect heart, all the days of our lives: then we shall be a people with whom God shall delight to dwell; yea, we shall be that happy people whose God is the Lord.

I am of a strong opinion that the day on which we unite, heart and soul, and turn our attention to knowledge and improvement, that day the hissing and reproach among the nations of the earth against us will cease. And even those who now point at us with the finger of scorn, will aid and befriend us. It is of no use for us to sit with our hands folded, hanging our heads like bulrushes, lamenting our wretched condition; but let us make a mighty effort, and arise; and if no one will promote or respect us, let us promote and respect ourselves.

The American ladies have the honor conferred on them, that by prudence and economy in their domestic concerns, and their unwearied attention in forming the minds and manners of their children, they laid the foundation of their becoming what they now are. The good women of Wethersfield, Conn., toiled in the blazing sun, year after year, weeding onions, then sold the seed and procured enough money to erect them a house of worship; and shall we not imitate their examples, as far as they are worthy of imitation? Why cannot we do something to distinguish ourselves, and contribute some of our hard earnings that would reflect honor upon our memories, and cause our children to arise and call us blessed? Shall it any longer be said of the daughters of Africa, they have no ambition, they have no force? By no means. Let every female heart become united, and let us raise a fund ourselves; and at the end of one year and a half, we might be able to lay the corner stone for the building of a High School, that the higher branches of knowledge might be enjoyed by us; and God would raise us up, and enough to aid us in our laudable designs. Let each one strive to excel in good housewifery, knowing that prudence and economy are the road to wealth. Let us not say we know this, or we know that, and practise nothing; but let us practise what we do know.

How long shall the fair daughters of Africa be compelled to bury their minds and talents beneath a load of iron pots and kettles? Until union, knowledge and love begin to flow among us. How long shall a mean set of men flatter us with their smiles, and enrich themselves with our hard earnings; their wives' fingers sparkling with rings, and they themselves laughing at our folly? Until we begin to promote and patronize each other. Shall we be a by-word among the nations any longer? Shall they laugh us to scorn forever? Do you ask, what can we do? Unite and build a store of your own, if you cannot procure a license. Fill one side with dry goods, and the other with groceries. Do you ask where is the money? We have spent more than enough for nonsense, to do what building we should want. We have never had an opportunity of displaying our talents; therefore the world thinks we know nothing. And we have been possessed by far too mean and cowardly a disposition, though I highly disapprove of an insolent or impertinent one. Do you ask the disposition I would have you possess? Possess the spirit of independence. The Americans do, and why should not you? Possess the spirit of men, bold and enterprising, fearless and undaunted. Sue for your rights and privileges. Know the reason that you cannot attain them. Weary them with your importunities. You can but die if you make the attempt; and we shall certainly die if you do not. The Americans have practised nothing but head-work these 200 years, and we have done their drudgery. And is it not high time for us to imitate their examples, and practise head-work too, and keep what we have got, and get what we can? We need never to think that anybody is going to feel interested for us, if we do not feel interested for ourselves. That day we, as a people, hearken unto the voice of the Lord, our God, and walk in his ways and ordinances, and become distinguished for our ease, elegance and grace, combined with other virtues, that day the Lord

will raise us up, and enough to aid and befriend us, and we shall begin to flourish.

Did every gentleman in America realize, as one, that they had got to become bondmen, and their wives, their sons, and their daughters, servants forever, to Great Britain, their very joints would become loosened, and tremblingly would smite one against another: their countenance would be filled with horror, every nerve and muscle would be forced into action, their souls would recoil at the very thought, their hearts would die within them, and death would be far more preferable. Then why have not Afric's sons the right to feel the same? Are not their wives, their sons, and their daughters, as dear to them as those of the white man's? Certainly God has not deprived them of the divine influences of his Holy Spirit, which is the greatest of all blessings, if they ask him. Then why should man any longer deprive his fellow-man of equal rights and privileges? Oh, America, America, foul and indelible is thy stain! Dark and dismal is the cloud that hangs over thee, for thy cruel wrongs and injuries to the fallen sons of Africa. The blood of her murdered ones cries to heaven for vengeance against thee. Thou art almost become drunken with the blood of her slain; thou hast enriched thyself through her toils and labors; and now thou refuseth to make even a small return. And thou hast caused the daughters of Africa to commit whoredoms and fornications; but upon thee be their curse.

O, ye great and mighty men of America, ye rich and powerful ones, many of you will call for the rocks and mountains to fall upon you, and to hide you from the wrath of the Lamb [Revelation 6:16], and from him that sitteth upon the throne; whilst many of the sable-skinned Africans you now despise will shine in the kingdom of heaven as the stars forever and ever. Charity begins at home, and those that provide not for their own are worse than infidels. We know that you are raising contributions to aid the gallant Poles; we know that you have befriended Greece and Ireland; and you have rejoiced with France, for her heroic deeds of valor. You have acknowledged all the nations of the earth, except Hayti; and you may publish, as far as the East is from the West, that you have two millions of negroes, who aspire no higher than to bow at your feet, and to court your smiles. You may kill, tyrannize, and oppress as much as you choose, until our cry shall come up before the throne of God; for I am firmly persuaded, that he will not suffer you to quell the proud, fearless and undaunted spirits of the Africans forever; for in his own time, he is able to plead our cause against you, and to pour out upon you the ten plagues of Egypt. We will not come out against you with swords and staves, as against a thief [Matthew 26:55]; but we will tell you that our souls are fired with the same love of liberty and independence with which your souls are fired. We will tell you that too much of your blood flows in our veins, too much of your color in our skins, for us not to possess your spirits. We will tell you that it is our gold that clothes you in fine linen and purple, and causes you to fare sumptuously every day [Luke 16:19]; and it is the blood of our fathers, and the tears of our brethren that have enriched your soils. AND WE CLAIM OUR RIGHTS. We will tell you that we are not afraid of them that kill the body, and after that can do no more; but we will tell you whom we do fear. We fear Him who is able, after He hath killed, to destroy both soul and body in hell forever. Then, my brethren, sheath your swords, and calm your angry passions. Stand still and know that the Lord he is God. Vengeance is his, and he will repay. It is a long lane that has no turn. America has risen to her meridian. When you begin to thrive, she will begin to fall. God hath raised you up a Walker and a Garrison. Though Walker sleeps, yet he lives, and his name shall be had in everlasting remembrance. I, even I, who am but a child, inexperienced to many of you, am a living witness to testify unto you this day, that I have seen the wicked in great power, spreading himself like a green bay tree, and lo, he passed away; yea, I diligently sought him, but he could not be found [Psalms 37:35]; and it is God alone that has inspired my heart to feel for Afric's woes. Then fret not yourselves because of evil doers. Fret not yourselves because of the men who bring wicked devices to pass; for they shall be cut down as the grass, and wither as the green herb. Trust in the Lord, and do good; so shalt thou dwell in the land, and verily thou shalt be fed. Encourage the noble-hearted Garrison. Prove to the world that you are neither ourang-outangs, or a species of mere animals, but that you possess the same powers of intellect as the proud-boasting American.

I am sensible, my brethren and friends, that many of you have been deprived of advantages, kept in utter ignorance, and that your minds are now darkened; and if any one of you have attempted to aspire after high and noble enterprises, you have met with so much opposition that your souls have become discouraged. For this very cause, a few of us have ventured to expose our lives in your behalf, to plead your cause against the great; and it will be of no use, unless you feel for yourselves and then your little ones, and exhibit the spirits of men. Oh then, turn your attention to knowledge and improvement; for knowledge is power. And God is able to fill you with wisdom and understanding, and to dispel your fears. Arm yourselves with the weapons of prayer. Put your trust in the living God. Persevere strictly in the paths of virtue. Let nothing be lacking on your part; and in God's own time, and his time is certainly the best, he will surely deliver you with a mighty hand and with an outstretched arm.

I have never taken one step, my friends, with a design to raise myself in your esteem, or to gain applause. But what I have done, has been done with an eye single to the glory of God, and to promote the good of souls. I have neither kindred nor friends. I stand alone in your midst, exposed to the fiery darts of the devil, and to the assaults of wicked men. But though all the powers of earth and hell were to combine against me, though all nature should sink into decay, still I would trust in the Lord, and joy in the God of my salvation. For I am full persuaded that he will bring me off conqueror, yea, more than conqueror, through him who hath loved me and given himself for me.

Lecture Delivered at the Franklin Hall

Boston, September 21, 1832

[Franklin Hall, at No. 16 Franklin Street in Boston, was the site of regular monthly meetings of the New England Anti-Slavery Society.]

Why sit ye here and die? If we say we will go to a foreign land, the famine and the pestilence are there, and there we shall die. If we sit here, we shall die. Come let us plead our cause before the whites: if they save us alive, we shall live—and if they kill us, we shall but die.

Methinks I heard a spiritual interrogation—'Who shall go forward, and take off the reproach that is cast upon the people of color? Shall it be a woman?' And my heart made this reply—'If it is thy will, be it even so, Lord Jesus!'

I have heard much respecting the horrors of slavery; but may Heaven forbid that the generality of my color throughout these United States should experience any more of its horrors than to be a servant of servants, or hewers of wood and drawers of water [Joshua 9:23]! Tell us no more of southern slavery; for with few exceptions, although I may be very erroneous in my opinion, yet I consider our condition but little better than that. Yet, after all, methinks there are no chains so galling as those that bind the soul, and exclude it from the vast field of useful and scientific knowledge. O, had I received the advantages of an early education, my ideas would, ere now, have expanded far and wide; but, alas! I possess nothing but moral capability—no teachings but the teachings of the Holy Spirit.

I have asked several individuals of my sex, who transact business for themselves, if providing our girls were to give them the most satisfactory references, they would not be willing to grant them an equal opportunity with others? Their reply has been—for their own part, they had no objection; but as it was not the custom, were they to take them into their employ, they would be in danger of losing the public patronage.

And such is the powerful force of prejudice. Let our girls possess whatever amiable qualities of soul they may; let their characters be fair and spotless as innocence itself; let their natural taste and ingenuity be what they may; it is impossible for scarce an individual of them to rise above the condition of servants. Ah! why is this cruel and unfeeling distinction? Is it merely because God has made our complexion to vary? If it be, O shame to soft, relenting humanity! "Tell it not in Gath! publish it not in the streets of Askelon!" [2 Samuel 1:20]. Yet, after all, methinks were the American free people of color to turn their attention more assiduously to moral worth and intellectual improvement, this would be the result: prejudice would gradually diminish, and the whites would be compelled to say, unloose those fetters!

Though black their skins as shades of night
Their hearts are pure, their souls are white.

Few white persons of either sex, who are calculated for anything else, are willing to spend their lives and bury their talents in performing mean, servile labor. And such is the horrible idea that I entertain respecting a life of servitude, that if I conceived of their [sic] being no possibility of my rising above the condition of servant, I would gladly hail death as a welcome messenger. O, horrible idea, indeed! to possess noble souls aspiring after high and honorable acquirements, yet confined by the chains of ignorance and poverty to lives of continual drudgery and toil. Neither do I know of any who have enriched themselves by spending their lives as house domestics, washing windows, shaking carpets, brushing boots, or tending upon gentlemen's tables. I can but die for expressing my sentiments: and I am as willing to die by the sword as the pestilence; for I am a true born American; your blood flows in my veins, and your spirit fires my breast.

I observed a piece in the Liberator a few months since, stating that the colonizationists had published a work respecting us, asserting that we were lazy and idle. I confute them on that point. Take us generally as a people, we are neither lazy nor idle; and considering how little we have to excite or stimulate us, I am almost astonished that there are so many industrious and ambitious ones to be found; although I acknowledge, with extreme sorrow, that there are some who never were and never will be serviceable to society. And have you not a similar class among yourselves?

Again. It was asserted that we were "a ragged set, crying for liberty." I reply to it, the whites have so long and so loudly proclaimed the theme of equal rights and privileges, that our souls have caught the flame also, ragged as we are. As far as our merit deserves, we feel a common desire to rise above the condition of servants and drudges. I have learnt, by bitter experience, that continual hard labor deadens the energies of the soul, and benumbs the faculties of the mind; the ideas become confined, the mind barren, and, like the scorching sands of Arabia, produces nothing; or like the uncultivated soil, brings forth thorns and thistles.

Again, continual and hard labor irritates our tempers and sours our dispositions; the whole system becomes worn out with toil and fatigue; nature herself becomes almost exhausted, and we care but little whether we live or die. It is true, that the free people of color throughout these United States are neither bought nor sold, nor under the lash of the cruel driver; many obtain a comfortable support; but few, if any, have an opportunity of becoming rich and independent; and the enjoyments we most pursue are as unprofitable to us as the spider's web or the floating bubbles that vanish into air. As servants, we are respected; but let us presume to aspire any higher, our employer regards us no longer. And were it not that the King eternal has declared that Ethiopia shall stretch forth her hands unto God, I should indeed despair.

I do not consider it derogatory, my friends, for persons to live out to service. There are many whose inclination leads them to aspire no higher; and I would highly commend the performance of almost anything for an honest livelihood; but where constitutional strength is wanting, labor of this kind, in its mildest form, is painful. And doubtless many are the prayers that have ascended to Heaven from Afric's daughters for strength to perform their work. Oh, many are the tears that have been shed for the want of that strength! Most of our color have dragged out a miserable existence of servitude from the cradle to the grave. And what literary acquirement can be made, or useful knowledge derived, from either maps, books, or charts, by those who continually drudge from Monday morning until Sunday noon? O, ye fairer sisters, whose hands are never soiled, whose nerves and muscles are never strained, go learn by experience! Had we had the opportunity that you have had, to improve our moral and mental faculties, what would have hindered our intellects from being as bright, and our manners from being as dignified as yours? Had it been our lot to have been nursed in the lap of affluence and ease, and to have basked beneath the smiles and sunshine of fortune, should we not have naturally supposed that we were never made to toil? And why are not our forms as delicate, and our constitutions as slender, as yours? Is not the workmanship as curious and complete? Have pity upon us, have pity upon us, O ye who have hearts to feel for other's woes; for the hand of God has touched us. Owing to the disadvantages under which we labor, there are many flowers among us that are

. . . born to bloom unseen
And waste their fragrance on the desert air.

My beloved brethren, as Christ has died in vain for those who will not accept his offered mercy, so will it be vain for the advocates of freedom to spend their breath in our behalf, unless with united hearts and souls you make some mighty efforts to raise your sons and daughters from the horrible state of servitude and degradation in which they are placed. It is upon you that woman depends; she can do but little besides using her influence; and it is for her sake and yours that I have come forward and made myself a hissing and a reproach among the people [Jeremiah 29:18]; for I am also one of the wretched and miserable daughters of the descendants of fallen Africa. Do you ask, why are you wretched and miserable? I reply, look at many of the most worthy and most interesting of us doomed to spend our lives in gentlemen's kitchens. Look at our young men, smart, active and energetic, with souls filled with ambitious fire; if they look forward, alas! What are their prospects? They can be nothing but the humblest laborers, on account of their dark complexions; hence many of them lose their ambition, and become worthless. Look at our middle-aged men, clad in their rusty plaids and coats; in winter, every cent they earn goes to buy their wood and pay their rents; the poor wives also toil beyond their strength, to help support their families. Look at our aged sires, whose heads are whitened with the frosts of seventy winters, with their old wood-saws on their backs. Alas, what keeps us so? Prejudice, ignorance and poverty. But ah! methinks our oppression is soon to come to an end; yea, before the Majesty of heaven, our groans and cries have reached the ears of the Lord of Sabaoth [James 5:4]. As the prayers and tears of Christians will avail the finally impenitent nothing; neither will the prayers and tears of the friends of humanity avail us anything, unless we possess a spirit of virtuous emulation within our breasts. Did the pilgrims, when they first landed on these shores, quietly compose themselves and say. "The Britons have all the money and all the power, and we must continue their servants forever?" Did they sluggishly sigh and say, "Our lot is hard, the Indians own the soil, and we cannot cultivate it?" No; they first made powerful efforts to raise themselves, and then God raised up those illustrious patriots, WASHINGTON and LAFAYETTE, to assist and defend them. And, my brethren, have you made a powerful effort? Have you prayed the legislature for mercy's sake to grant you all the rights and privileges of free citizens, that your daughters may rise to that degree of respectability which true merit deserves, and your sons above the servile situations which most of them fill?

Harriet Jacobs (1813–1897)

"Slavery is terrible for men; but it is far more terrible for women. Superadded to the burden common to all, they have wrongs and sufferings, and mortifications peculiarly their own," writes Harriet Jacobs in *Incidents in the Life of a Slave Girl* (1861), the first slave narrative to be published by an African American woman. Using the pen name of Linda Brent, Jacobs thinly veils her life and escape from slavery. She was born in Edenton, North Carolina. Her mother died when Jacobs was six years old, so she and her brother went to live with a mistress who taught her how to read. Upon her death, the mistress bequeathed Jacobs to her three-year-old niece. Jacobs lived in the home of the little girl's father, a physician who sexually harassed her and would not permit her to marry a free black man. Rather than be raped by a man whom she did not feel would free their progeny, Jacobs exercised her limited choice by producing children with another white man, whom she felt would be more liberating. To escape slavery, Jacobs hid in a seven-by-nine foot crawlspace, three feet high, in her grandmother's attic for almost seven years. From this "loophole of retreat," she could see her children, but could not communicate with them. She fooled her master into thinking that she had escaped North long before she actually did so.

Many thought that *Incidents* was a novel written by a white author until critic Jean Fagan Yellin used correspondence from Jacobs to verify the autobiographical details of the narrative. *Incidents* is a gendered account of resistance and resourcefulness during the days of slavery.

Incidents in the Life of a Slave Girl, Seven Years Concealed

I. Childhood

I was born a slave; but I never knew it till six years of happy childhood had passed away. My father was a carpenter, and considered so intelligent and skilful in his trade, that, when buildings out of the common line were to be erected, he was sent for from long distances, to be head workman. On condition of paying his mistress two hundred dollars a year, and supporting himself, he was allowed to work at his trade, and manage his own affairs. His strongest wish was to purchase his children; but, though he several times offered his hard earnings for that purpose, he never succeeded. In complexion my parents were a light shade of brownish yellow, and were termed mulattoes. They lived together in a comfortable home, and, though we were all slaves, I was so fondly shielded that I never dreamed I was a piece of merchandise, trusted to them for safe keeping, and liable to be demanded of them at any moment. I had one brother, William, who was two years younger than myself—a bright, affectionate child. I had also a great treasure in my maternal grandmother, who was a remarkable woman in many respects. She was the daughter of a planter in South Carolina, who, at his death, left her mother and his three children free, with money to go to St. Augustine, where they had relatives. It was during the Revolutionary War; and they were captured on their passage, carried back, and sold to different purchasers. Such was the story my grandmother used to tell me, but I do not remember all the particulars. She was a little girl when she was captured and sold to the keeper of a large hotel. I have often heard her tell how hard she fared during childhood. But as she grew older she evinced so much intelligence, and was so faithful, that her master and mistress could not help seeing it was for their interest to take care of such a valuable piece of property. She became an indispensable personage in the household, officiating in all capacities, from cook and wet nurse to seamstress. She was much praised for her cooking, and her nice crackers became so famous in the neighborhood that many people were desirous of obtaining them. In consequence of numerous requests of this kind, she asked permission of her mistress to bake crackers at night, after all the household work was done; and she obtained leave to do it, provided she would clothe herself and her children from the profits. Upon these terms, after working hard all day for her mistress, she began her midnight bakings, assisted by her two oldest children. The business proved profitable; and each year she laid by a little, which was saved for a fund to purchase her children. Her master died, and the property was divided among his heirs. The widow had her dower in the hotel, which she continued to keep open. My grandmother remained in her service as a slave; but her children were divided among her master's children. As she had five, Benjamin, the youngest one, was sold, in order that each heir might have an equal portion of dollars and cents. There was so little difference in our ages that he seemed more like my brother than my uncle. He was a bright, handsome lad, nearly white: for he inherited the complexion my grandmother had derived from Anglo-Saxon ancestors. Though only ten years old, seven hundred and twenty dollars were paid for him. His sale was a terrible blow to my grandmother; but she was naturally hopeful, and she went to work with renewed energy, trusting in time to be able to purchase some of her children. She had laid up three hundred dollars, which her mistress one day begged as a loan, promising to pay her soon. The reader probably knows that no promise or writing given to a slave is legally binding; for, according to Southern laws, a slave, *being* property, can *hold* no property. When my grandmother lent her hard earnings to her mistress, she trusted solely to her honor. The honor of a slaveholder to a slave!

To this good grandmother I was indebted for many comforts. My brother Willie and I often received portions of the crackers, cakes, and preserves, she made to sell; and after we ceased to be children we were indebted to her for many more important services.

Such were the unusually fortunate circumstances of my early childhood. When I was six years old, my mother died; and then, for the first time, I learned, by the talk around me, that I was a slave. My mother's mistress was the daughter of my grandmother's mistress. She was the foster sister of my mother; they were both nourished at my grandmother's breast. In fact, my mother had been weaned at three months old, that the babe of the mistress might obtain sufficient food. They played together as children; and, when they became women, my mother was a most faithful servant to her whiter foster sister. On her death-bed her mistress promised that her children should never suffer for any thing; and during her lifetime she kept her word. They all spoke kindly of my dead mother, who had been a slave merely in name, but in nature was noble and womanly. I grieved for her, and my young mind was troubled with the thought who would now take care of me and my little brother. I was told that my home was now to be with her mistress; and I found it a happy one. No toilsome or disagreeable duties were imposed upon me. My mistress was so kind to me that I was always glad to do her bidding, and proud to labor for her as much as my young years would permit.

I would sit by her side for hours, sewing diligently, with a heart as free from care as that of any free-born white child. When she thought I was tired, she would send me out to run and jump; and away I bounded, to gather berries or flowers to decorate her room. Those were happy days—too happy to last. The slave child had no thought for the morrow; but there came that blight, which too surely waits on every human being born to be a chattel.

When I was nearly twelve years old, my kind mistress sickened and died. As I saw the cheek grow paler, and the eye more glassy, how earnestly I prayed in my heart that she might live! I loved her; for she had been almost like a mother to me. My prayers were not answered. She died, and they buried her in the little churchyard, where, day after day, my tears fell upon her grave.

I was sent to spend a week with my grandmother. I was now old enough to begin to think of the future; and again and again I asked myself what they would do with me. I felt sure I should never find another mistress so kind as the one who was gone. She had promised my dying mother that her children should never suffer for any thing, and when I remembered that, and recalled her many proofs of attachment to me, I could not help having some hopes that she had left me free. My friends were almost certain it would be so. They thought she would be sure to do it, on account of my mother's love and faithful service. But, alas! we all know that the memory of a faithful slave does not avail much to save her children from the auction block.

After a brief period of suspense, the will of my mistress was read, and we learned that she had bequeathed me to her sister's daughter, a child of five years old. So vanished our hopes. My mistress had taught me the precepts of God's Word: "Thou shalt love thy neighbor as thyself." "Whatsoever ye would that men should do unto you, do ye even so unto them." But I was her slave, and I suppose she did not recognize me as her neighbor. I would give much to blot out from my memory that one great wrong. As a child, I loved my mistress; and, looking back on the happy days I spent with her, I try to think with less bitterness of this act of injustice. While I was with her, she taught me to read and spell; and for this privilege, which so rarely falls to the lot of a slave, I bless her memory.

She possessed but few slaves; and at her death those were all distributed among her relatives. Five of them were my grandmother's children, and had shared the same milk that nourished her mother's children. Notwithstanding my grandmother's long and faithful service to her owners, not one of her children escaped the auction block. These God-breathing machines are no more, in the sight of their masters, than the cotton they plant, or the horses they tend.

Julia A. Foote (1823–1900)

A Brand Plucked from the Fire is the autobiography of a woman who, like Jarena Lee, felt that she was called to preach the Gospel. Born in Schenectady, New York, to former slaves, Foote grew up in the African Methodist Episcopal (AME) Church. Against the wishes of her parents and husband, George Foote, whom she married in 1841, she traveled throughout New England, the Midwest, the Mid-Atlantic States, and Canada preaching against racism and sexism. She became the first ordained deacon in the AME Church and the second woman to become an ordained elder. Foote saw herself as saved for some special service, "a brand plucked from the fire" (Zechariah 3:2).

From *A Brand Plucked in the Fire*

I

Birth and Parentage

I was born in 1823, in Schenectady, N.Y. I was my mother's fourth child. My father was born free, but was stolen, when a child, and enslaved. My mother was born a slave, in the State of New York. She had one very cruel master and mistress. This man, whom she was obliged to call master, tied her up and whipped her because she refused to submit herself to him, and reported his conduct to her mistress. After the whipping, he himself washed her quivering back with strong salt water. At the expiration of a week she was sent to change her clothing, which stuck fast to her back. Her mistress, seeing that she could not remove it, took hold of the rough tow-linen undergarment and pulled it off over her head with a jerk, which took the skin with it, leaving her back all raw and sore.

This cruel master soon sold my mother, and she passed from one person's hands to another's, until she found a comparatively kind master and mistress in Mr. and Mrs. Cheeseman, who kept a public house.

My father endured many hardships in slavery, the worst of which was his constant exposure to all sorts of weather. There being no railroads at that time, all goods and merchandise were moved from place to place with teams, one of which my father drove.

My father bought himself, and then his wife and their first child, at that time an infant. That infant is now a woman, more than seventy years old, and an invalid, dependent upon the bounty of her poor relatives.

I remember hearing my parents tell what first led them to think seriously of their sinful course. One night, as they were on their way home from a dance, they came to a stream of water, which, owing to rain the night previous, had risen and carried away the log crossing. In their endeavor to ford the stream, my mother made a misstep, and came very nearly being drowned, with her babe in her arms. This nearly fatal accident made such an impression upon their minds that they said, "We'll go to no more dances;" and they kept their word. Soon after, they made a public profession of religion and united with the M[ethodist] E[piscopal] Church. They were not treated as Christian believers, but as poor lepers. They were obliged to occupy certain seats in one corner of the gallery, and dared not come down to partake of the Holy Communion until the last white communicant had left the table.

One day my mother and another colored sister waited until all the white people had, as they thought, been served, when they started for the communion table. Just as they reached the lower door, two of the poorer class of white folks arose to go to the table. At this, a mother in Israel caught hold of my mother's dress and said to her, "Don't you know better than to go to the table when white folks are there?" Ah! she did know better than to do such a thing purposely. This was one of the fruits of slavery. Although professing to love the same God, members of the same church, and expecting to find the same heaven at last, they could not partake of the Lord's Supper until the lowest of the whites had been served. Were they led by the Holy Spirit? Who shall say? The Spirit of Truth can never be mistaken, nor can he inspire anything unholy. How many at the present day profess great spirituality, and even holiness, and yet are deluded by a spirit of error, which leads them to say to the poor and the colored ones among them, "Stand back a little—I am holier than thou."

My parents continued to attend to the ordinances of God as instructed, but knew little of the power of Christ to save; for their spiritual guides were as blind as those they led.

Printed for the author by Laver & Yost, Cleveland, Ohio; 1879.

It was the custom, at that time, for all to drink freely of wine, brandy and gin. I can remember when it was customary at funerals, as well as at weddings, to pass around the decanter and glasses, and sometimes it happened that the pall-bearers could scarcely move out with the coffin. When not handed round, one after another would go to the closet and drink as much as they chose of the liquors they were sure to find there. The officiating clergyman would imbibe as freely as any one. My parents kept liquor in the house constantly, and every morning sling was made, and the children were given the bottom of the cup, where the sugar and a little of the liquor was left, on purpose for them. It is no wonder, isn't it, that every one of my mother's children loved the taste of liquor?

One day, when I was but five years of age, I found the blue chest, where the black bottle was kept, unlocked—an unusual thing. Raising the lid, I took the bottle, put it to my mouth, and drained to the bottom. Soon after, the rest of the children becoming frightened at my actions, ran and told aunt Giney—an old colored lady living in a part of our house—who sent at once for my mother, who was away working. She came in great haste, and at once pronounced me DRUNK. And so I was—stupidly drunk. They walked with me, and blew tobacco smoke into my face, to bring me to. Sickness almost unto death followed, but my life was spared. I was like a "brand plucked from the burning" [Zech. 3:2].

Dear reader, have you innocent children, given you from the hand of God? Children, whose purity rouses all that is holy and good in your nature? Do not, I pray, give to these little ones of God the accursed cup which will send them down to misery and death. Listen to the voice of conscience, the woes of the drunkard, the wailing of poverty-stricken women and children, and touch not the accursed cup. From Sinai come the awful words of Jehovah, "No drunkard shall inherit the kingdom of heaven" [1 Cor. 6:10].

XVII

My Call to Preach the Gospel

For months I had been moved upon to exhort and pray with the people, in my visits from house to house; and in meetings my whole soul seemed drawn out for the salvation of souls. The love of Christ in me was not limited. Some of my mistaken friends said I was too forward, but a desire to work for the Master, and to promote the glory of his kingdom in the salvation of souls, was food to my poor soul.

When called of God, on a particular occasion, to a definite work, I said, "No, Lord, not me." Day by day I was more impressed that God would have me work in his vineyard. I thought it could not be that I was called to preach—I, so weak and ignorant. Still, I knew all things were possible with God, even to confounding the wise by the foolish things of this earth. Yet in me there was a shrinking.

I took all my doubts and fears to the Lord in prayer, when, what seemed to be an angel, made his appearance. In his hand was a scroll, on which were these words: "Thee have I chosen to preach my Gospel without delay." The moment my eyes saw it, it appeared to be printed on my heart. The angel was gone in an instant, and I, in agony, cried out, "Lord, I cannot do it!" It was eleven o'clock in the morning, yet everything grew dark as night. The darkness was so great that I feared to stir.

At last "Mam" Riley entered. As she did so, the room grew lighter, and I arose from my knees. My heart was so heavy I scarce could speak. Dear "Mam" Riley saw my distress, and soon left me.

From that day my appetite failed me and sleep fled from my eyes. I seemed as one tormented. I prayed, but felt no better. I belonged to a band of sisters whom I loved dearly, and to them I partially opened my mind. One of them seemed to understand my case at once, and advised me to do as God had bid me, or I would never be happy here or hereafter. But it seemed too hard—I could not give up and obey.

One night as I lay weeping and beseeching the dear Lord to remove this burden from me, there appeared the same angel that came to me before, and on his breast were these words: "You are lost unless you obey God's righteous commands." I saw the writing, and that was enough. I covered my head and awoke my husband, who had returned a few days before. He asked me why I trembled so, but I had not power to answer him. I remained in that condition until morning, when I tried to arise and go about my usual duties, but was too ill. Then my husband called a physician, who prescribed medicine, but it did me no good.

I had always been opposed to the preaching of women, and had spoken against it, though, I acknowledge, without foundation. This rose before me like a mountain, and when I thought of the difficulties they had to encounter, both from professors and non-professors, I shrank back and cried, "Lord, I cannot go!"

The trouble my heavenly Father has had to keep me out of the fire that is never quenched, he alone knoweth. My husband and friends said I would die or go crazy if something favorable did not take place soon. I expected to die and be lost, knowing I had been enlightened and had tasted the heavenly gift. I read again and again the sixth chapter of Hebrews.

Frances Ellen Watkins Harper (1825–1911)

Frances Ellen Watkins Harper's background includes a long list of notable achievements: first African American woman to be hired as an abolitionist lecturer, a founder of the American Woman Suffrage Association, member of the national board of the Women's Christian Temperance Union, executive officer of the Universal Peace Union, founding member of the National Association of Colored Women, Director of the American Association of Educators of Colored Youth, speaker at the women's Congress at the Columbian Exposition, and author of enough poems, novels, and essays to earn her the title of "bronze muse."

Although born to free parents in Baltimore, Maryland, Harper was orphaned by the age of three. Relatives took her in and had enough resources to send her to a prominent school founded by her uncle, thus providing her with a better education than that of most women of her day. She moved to Ohio where she was the first woman hired to teach at Union Seminary (Wilberforce University). Leaving Ohio for Pennsylvania, Harper became involved in the Philadelphia Underground Railroad and published essays in a number of newspapers and periodicals, including Frederick Douglass's antislavery paper, *Liberator*. In 1860 she married Fenton Harper, who had three children. They lived on a farm outside of Columbus, Ohio, and upon Fenton's death, Harper began a very full lecturing schedule. An advocate for gender and racial issues, Harper faced a dilemma when Elizabeth Cady Stanton, Susan B. Anthony, and others were fighting for women's suffrage as a priority over giving black men the right to vote. Harper formed her own suffrage association, emphasizing that black women ought to support the Fifteenth Amendment, giving black men the right to vote.

Harper's poems show her passion for freedom—a freedom that listened to the breaking heart of slave mothers, a freedom that asked for burial in a free land. Of the four novels that she wrote, her best-known one is *Iola Leroy* (1892), a novel about an octoroon heroine who is more empowered than conventional tragic mulatto characters.

The Slave Mother

Heard you that shriek? It rose
   So wildly on the air,
It seemed as if a burden'd heart
   Was breaking in despair.

Saw you those hands so sadly clasped—
   The bowed and feeble head—
The shuddering of that fragile form—
   That look of grief and dread?

Saw you the sad, imploring eye?
   Its every glance was pain,
As if a storm of agony
   Were sweeping through the brain.

She is a mother, pale with fear,
   Her boy clings to her side,
And in her kirtle vainly tries
   His trembling form to hide.

He is not hers, although she bore
   For him a mother's pains;
He is not hers, although her blood
   Is coursing through his veins!

He is not hers, for cruel hands
   May rudely tear apart
The only wreath of household love
   That binds her breaking heart.

His love has been a joyous light
   That o'er her pathway smiled,
A fountain gushing ever new,
   Amid life's desert wild.

His lightest word has been a tone
   Of music round her heart,

From *Poems on Miscellaneous Subjects*, 1854, 1857.

Their lives a streamlet blent in one—
 Oh, Father! must they part?

They tear him from her circling arms,
 Her last and fond embrace.
Oh! never more may her sad eyes
 Gaze on his mournful face.

No marvel, then, these bitter shrieks
 Disturb the listening air:
She is a mother, and her heart
 Is breaking in despair.

The Syrophenician Woman

Joy to my bosom! rest to my fear!
Judea's prophet draweth near!
Joy to my bosom! peace to my heart!
Sickness and sorrow before him depart!

Rack'd with agony and pain,
Writhing, long my child has lain;
Now the prophet draweth near,
All our griefs shall disappear.

"Lord!" she cried with mournful breath,
"Save! Oh, save my child from death!"
But as though she was unheard,
Jesus answered not a word.

With a purpose nought could move,
And the zeal of woman's love,
Down she knelt in anguish wild—
"Master! save, Oh! save my child!"

"'Tis not meet," the Saviour said,
"Thus to waste the children's bread;
I am only sent to seek
Israel's lost and scattered sheep."

"True," she said, "Oh gracious Lord!
True and faithful is thy word:
But the humblest, meanest, may
Eat the crumbs they cast away."

"Woman," said th' astonish'd Lord,
"Be it even as thy word!

By thy faith that knows no fail,
Thou hast ask'd, and shalt prevail."

Ethiopia

Yes! Ethiopia yet shall stretch
 Her bleeding hands abroad;
Her cry of agony shall reach
 The burning throne of God.

The tyrant's yoke from off her neck,
 His fetters from her soul,
The mighty hand of God shall break,
 And spurn the base control.

Redeemed from dust and freed from chains,
 Her sons shall lift their eyes;
From cloud-capt hills and verdant plains
 Shall shouts of triumph rise.

Upon her dark, despairing brow,
 Shall play a smile of peace;
For God shall bend unto her wo,
 And bid her sorrows cease.

'Neath sheltering vines and stately palms
 Shall laughing children play,
And aged sires with joyous psalms
 Shall gladden every day.

Secure by night, and blest by day,
 Shall pass her happy hours;
Nor human tigers hunt for prey
 Within her peaceful bowers.

Then, Ethiopia! stretch, oh! stretch
 Thy bleeding hands abroad;
Thy cry of agony shall reach
 And find redress from God.

Bury Me in a Free Land

Make me a grave where'er you will,
In a lowly plain or a lofty hill;
Make it among earth's humblest graves,
But not in a land where men are slaves.

I could not rest, if around my grave
I heard the steps of a trembling slave;
His shadow above my silent tomb
Would make it a place of fearful gloom.

I could not sleep, if I heard the tread
Of a coffle-gang to the shambles led,
And the mother's shriek of wild despair
Rise, like a curse, on the trembling air.

I could not rest, if I saw the lash
Drinking her blood at each fearful gash;
And I saw her babes torn from her breast,
Like trembling doves from their parent nest.

I'd shudder and start, if I heard the bay
Of a bloodhound seizing his human prey;
And I heard the captive plead in vain,
As they bound, afresh, his galling chain.

If I saw young girls from their mother's arms
Bartered and sold for their youthful charms,
My eye would flash with a mournful flame,
My death-pale cheek grow red with shame.

I would sleep, dear friends, where bloated Might
Can rob no man of his dearest right;
My rest shall be calm in any grave
Where none can call his brother a slave.

I ask no monument, proud and high,
To arrest the gaze of the passers by;
All that my yearning spirit craves
Is—*Bury me not in a land of slaves!*

The Two Offers

"What is the matter with you, Laura, this morning? I have been watching you this hour, and in that time you have commenced a half dozen letters and torn them all up. What matter of such grave moment is puzzling your dear little head, that you do not know how to decide?"

"Well, it is an important matter: I have two offers for marriage, and I do not know which to choose."

"I should accept neither, or to say the least, not at present."

"Why not?"

"Because I think a woman who is undecided between two offers, has not love enough for either to make a choice; and in that very hesitation, indecision, she has a reason to pause and seriously reflect, lest her marriage, instead of being an affinity of souls or a union of hearts, should only be a mere matter of bargain and sale, or an affair of convenience and selfish interest."

"But I consider them both very good offers, just such as many a girl would gladly receive. But to tell you the truth, I do not think that I regard either as a woman should the man she chooses for her husband. But then if I refuse, there is the risk of being an old maid, and that is not to be thought of."

"Well, suppose there is, is that the most dreadful fate that can befall a woman? Is there not more intense wretchedness in an ill-assorted marriage—more utter loneliness in a loveless home, than in the lot of the old maid who accepts her earthly mission as a gift from God, and strives to walk the path of life with earnest and unfaltering steps?"

"Oh! what a little preacher you are. I really believe that you were cut out for an old maid; that when nature formed you, she put in a double portion of intellect to make up for a deficiency of love; and yet you are kind and affectionate. But I do not think that you know anything of the grand, over-mastering passion, or the deep necessity of woman's heart for loving."

"Do you think so?" resumed the first speaker; and bending over her work she quietly applied herself to the knitting that had lain neglected by her side, during this brief conversation; but as she did so, a shadow flitted over her pale and intellectual brow, a mist gathered in her eyes, and a slight quivering of the lips, revealed a depth of feeling to which her companion was a stranger.

But before I proceed with my story, let me give you a slight history of the speakers. They were cousins, who had met life under different auspices. Laura Lagrange, was the only daughter of rich and indulgent parents, who had spared no pains to make her an accomplished lady. Her cousin, Janette Alston, was the child of parents, rich only in goodness and affection. Her father had been unfortunate in business, and dying before he could retrieve his fortunes, left his business in an embarrassed state. His widow was unacquainted with his business affairs, and when the estate was settled, hungry creditors had brought their claims and the lawyers had received their fees, she found herself homeless and almost penniless, and she who had been sheltered in the warm clasp of loving arms, found them too powerless to shield her from the pitiless pelting storms of adversity. Year after year she struggled with poverty and wrestled with want, till her toil-worn hands became too feeble to hold the shattered chords of existence, and her tear-dimmed eyes grew heavy with the slumber of death. Her daughter had watched over her with untiring devotion, had closed her eyes in death, and gone out into the busy, restless world, missing a precious tone from the voices of earth, a beloved step from the paths of life. Too self reliant to depend on the charity of relations, she endeavored to support herself by her own exertions, and she had succeeded. Her path for a while was marked with struggle and trial, but instead of uselessly repining, she met them bravely, and her life became not a thing of ease and indulgence, but of conquest, victory, and accomplishments. At the time when this conversation took place, the deep trials of her life had passed away. The achievements of her genius had won her a position in the literary world, where she shone as one of its bright particular stars. And with her fame came a competence of worldly means, which gave her leisure for improvement, and the riper development of her rare talents. And she, that pale intellectual woman, whose genius gave life and vivacity to the social circle, and whose presence threw a halo of beauty and grace around the charmed atmosphere in which she moved, had at one period of her life, known the mystic and solemn strength of an all-absorbing love. Years faded into the misty past, had seen the kindling of her eye, the quick flushing of her cheek, and the wild throbbing of her heart, at tones of a voice long since hushed to the stillness of death. Deeply, wildly, passionately, she had loved. Her whole life seemed like the pouring out of rich, warm and gushing affections. This love quickened her talents, inspired her genius, and threw over her life a tender and spiritual earnestness. And then came a fearful shock, a mournful waking from that "dream of beauty and delight." A shadow fell around her path; it came between her and the object of her heart's worship; first a few cold words, estrangement, and then a painful separation; the old story of woman's pride—digging the sepulchre of her happiness, and then a new-made grave, and her path over it to the spirit world; and thus faded out from that young heart her bright, brief and saddened dream of life. Faint and spirit-broken, she turned from the scenes associated with the memory of the loved and lost. She tried to break the chain of sad associations that bound her to the mournful past; and so, pressing back the bitter sobs from her almost breaking heart, like the dying dolphin, whose beauty is born of its death anguish, her genius gathered strength from suffering and wonderous power and brilliancy from the agony she hid within the desolate chambers of her soul. Men hailed her as one of earth's strangely gifted children, and wreathed the garlands of fame for her brow, when it was throbbing with a wild and fearful unrest. They breathed her name with applause, when through the lonely halls of her stricken spirit, was an earnest cry for peace, a deep yearning for sympathy and heart-support.

But life, with its stern realities, met her; its solemn responsibilities confronted her, and turning, with an earnest and shattered spirit, to life's duties and trials, she found a calmness and strength that she had only imagined in her dreams of poetry and song. We will now pass over a period of ten years, and the cousins have met again. In that calm and lovely woman, in whose eyes is a depth of tenderness, tempering the flashes of her genius, whose looks and tones are full of sympathy and love, we recognize the once smitten and stricken Janette Alston. The bloom of her girlhood had given way to a higher type of spiritual beauty, as if some unseen hand had been polishing and refining the temple in which her lovely spirit found its habitation; and this had been the fact. Her inner life had grown beautiful, and it was this that was constantly developing the outer. Never, in the early flush of womanhood, when an absorbing love had lit up her eyes and glowed in her life, had she appeared so interesting as when, with a countenance which seemed overshadowed with a spiritual light, she bent over the death-bed of a young woman, just lingering at the shadowy gates of the unseen land.

"Has he come?" faintly but eagerly exclaimed the dying woman. "Oh! how I have longed for his coming, and even in death he forgets me."

"Oh, do not say so, dear Laura, some accident may have detained him," said Janette to her cousin; for on that bed, from whence she will never rise, lies the once-beautiful and light-hearted Laura Lagrange, the brightness of whose eyes has long since been dimmed with tears, and whose voice had become like a harp whose every chord is tuned to sadness—whose faintest thrill and loudest vibrations are but the variations of agony. A heavy hand was laid upon her once warm and bounding heart, and a voice came whispering through her soul, that she must die. But, to her, the tidings was a message of deliverance—a voice, hushing her wild sorrows to the calmness of resignation and hope. Life had grown so weary upon her head—the future looked so hopeless—she had no wish to tread again the track where thorns had pierced her feet, and clouds overcast her sky; and she hailed the coming of death's angel as the footsteps of a welcome friend. And yet, earth had one object so very dear to her weary heart. It was her absent and recreant husband; for, since that conversation, she had accepted one of her offers, and become a wife. But, before she married, she learned that great lesson of human experience and woman's life, to love the man who bowed at her shrine, a willing worshipper. He had a pleasing address, raven hair, flashing eyes, a voice of thrilling sweetness, and lips of persuasive eloquence; and being well versed in the ways of the world, he won his way to her heart, and she became his bride, and he was proud of his prize. Vain and superficial in his character, he looked upon marriage not as a divine sacrament for the soul's development and human progression, but as the title-deed that gave him possession of the woman he thought he loved. But alas for her, the laxity of his principles had rendered him unworthy of the deep and undying devotion of a pure-hearted woman; but, for awhile, he hid from her his true character, and she blindly loved him, and for a short period was happy in the consciousness of being beloved;

though sometimes a vague unrest would fill her soul, when, overflowing with a sense of the good, the beautiful, and the true, she would turn to him, but find no response to the deep yearnings of her soul—no appreciation of life's highest realities—its solemn grandeur and significant importance. Their souls never met, and soon she found a void in her bosom, that his earth-born love could not fill. He did not satisfy the wants of her mental and moral nature—between him and her there was no affinity of minds, no intercommunion of souls.

Talk as you will of woman's deep capacity for loving, of the strength of her affectional nature. I do not deny it; but will the mere possession of any human love, fully satisfy all the demands of her whole being? You may paint her in poetry or fiction, as a frail vine, clinging to her brother man for support, and dying when deprived of it; and all this may sound well enough to please the imaginations of school-girls, or love-lorn maidens. But woman—the true woman—if you would render her happy, it needs more than the mere development of her affectional nature. Her conscience should be enlightened, her faith in the true and right established, and scope given to her Heaven-endowed and God-given faculties. The true aim of female education should be, not a development of one or two, but all the faculties of the human soul, because no perfect womanhood is developed by imperfect culture. Intense love is often akin to intense suffering, and to trust the whole wealth of a woman's nature on the frail bark of human love, may often be like trusting a cargo of gold and precious gems, to a bark that has never battled with the storm, or buffetted the waves. Is it any wonder, then, that so many life-barks go down, paving the ocean of time with precious hearts and wasted hopes? that so many float around us, shattered and dismasted wrecks? that so many are stranded on the shoals of existence, mournful beacons and solemn warnings for the thoughtless, to whom marriage is a careless and hasty rushing together of the affections? Alas that an institution so fraught with good for humanity should be so perverted, and that state of life, which should be filled with happiness, become so replete with misery. And this was the fate of Laura Lagrange. For a brief period after her marriage her life seemed like a bright and beautiful dream, full of hope and radiant with joy. And then there came a change—he found other attractions that lay beyond the pale of home influences. The gambling saloon had power to win him from her side, he had lived in an element of unhealthy and unhallowed excitements, and the society of a loving wife, the pleasures of a well-regulated home, were enjoyments too tame for one who had vitiated his tastes by the pleasures of sin. There were charmed houses of vice, built upon dead men's loves, where, amid a flow of song, laughter, wine, and careless mirth, he would spend hour after hour, forgetting the cheek that was

paling through his neglect, heedless of the tear-dimmed eyes, peering anxiously into the darkness, waiting, or watching his return.

The influence of old associations was upon him. In early life, home had been to him a place of ceilings and walls, not a true home, built upon goodness, love and truth. It was a place where velvet carpets hushed his tread, where images of loveliness and beauty invoked into being by painter's art and sculptor's skill, pleased the eye and gratified the taste, where magnificence surrounded his way and costly clothing adorned his person; but it was not the place for the true culture and right development of his soul. His father had been too much engrossed in making money, and his mother in spending it, in striving to maintain a fashionable position in society, and shining in the eyes of the world, to give the proper direction to the character of their wayward and impulsive son. His mother put beautiful robes upon his body, but left ugly scars upon his soul; she pampered his appetite, but starved his spirit. Every mother should be a true artist, who knows how to weave into her child's life images of grace and beauty, the true poet capable of writing on the soul of childhood the harmony of love and truth, and teaching it how to produce the grandest of all poems—the poetry of a true and noble life. But in his home, a love for the good, the true and right, had been sacrificed at the shrine of frivolity and fashion. That parental authority which should have been preserved as a string of precious pearls, unbroken and unscattered, was simply the administration of chance. At one time obedience was enforced by authority, at another time by flattery and promises, and just as often it was not enforced at all. His early associations were formed as chance directed, and from his want of home-training, his character received a bias, his life a shade, which ran through every avenue of his existence, and darkened all his future hours. Oh, if we would trace the history of all the crimes that have o'ershadowed this sin-shrouded and sorrow-darkened world of ours, how many might be seen arising from the wrong home influences, or the weakening of the home ties. Home should always be the best school for the affections, the birthplace of high resolves, and the altar upon which lofty aspirations are kindled, from whence the soul may go forth strengthened, to act its part aright in the great drama of life, with conscience enlightened, affections cultivated, and reason and judgment dominant. But alas for the young wife. Her husband had not been blessed with such a home. When he entered the arena of life, the voices from home did not linger around his path as angels of guidance about his steps; they were not like so many messages to invite him to deeds of high and holy worth. The memory of no sainted mother arose between him and deeds of darkness; the earnest prayers of no father arrested him in his downward course; and before a year of his married life had waned, his young wife had learned to wait and mourn his frequent and uncalled for absence. More than once had she seen him come home from his midnight haunts, the bright intelligence of his eye displaced by the drunkard's stare, and his manly gait changed to the inebriate's stagger; and she was beginning to know the bitter agony that is compressed in the mournful words, a drunkard's wife. And then there came a bright but brief episode in her experience; the angel of life gave to her existence a deeper meaning and loftier significance: she sheltered in the warm clasp of her loving arms, a dear babe, a precious child, whose love filled every chamber of her heart, and felt the fount of maternal love gushing so new within her soul. That child was hers. How overshadowing was the love with which she bent over its helplessness, how much it helped to fill the void and chasms in her soul. How many lonely hours were beguiled by its winsome ways, its answering smiles and fond caresses. How exquisite and solemn was the feeling that thrilled her heart when she clasped the tiny hands together and taught her dear child to call God "Our Father."

What a blessing was that child. The father paused in his headlong career, awed by the strange beauty and precocious intellect of his child; and the mother's life had a better expression through her ministrations of love. And then there came hours of bitter anguish, shading the sunlight of her home and hushing the music of her heart. The angel of death bent over the couch of her child and beaconed it away. Closer and closer the mother strained her child to her wildly heaving breast, and struggled with the heavy hand that lay upon its heart. Love and agony contended with death, and the language of the mother's heart was

"Oh, Death, away! that innocent is mine;
　I cannot spare him from my arms
To lay him, Death, in thine.
　I am a mother, Death; I gave that darling birth
I could not bear his lifeless limbs
　Should moulder in the earth."

But death was stronger than love and mightier than agony and won the child for the land of crystal founts and deathless flowers, and the poor, stricken mother sat down beneath the shadow of her mighty grief, feeling as if a great light had gone out from her soul, and that the sunshine had suddenly faded around her path. She turned in her deep anguish to the father of her child, the loved and cherished dead. For awhile his words were kind and tender, his heart seemed subdued, and his tenderness fell upon her worn and weary heart like rain on perishing flowers, or cooling waters to lips all parched with thirst and scorched with fever; but the change was evanescent, the influence of unhallowed associations and evil habits had vitiated and poisoned the springs of his existence.

They had bound him in their meshes, and he lacked the moral strength to break his fetters, and stand erect in all the strength and dignity of a true manhood, making life's highest excellence his ideal, and striving to gain it.

And yet moments of deep contrition would sweep over him, when he would resolve to abandon the wine-cup forever, when he was ready to forswear the handling of another card, and he would try to break away from the associations that he felt were working his ruin; but when the hour of temptation came his strength was weakness, his earnest purposes were cobwebs, his well-meant resolutions ropes of sand, and thus passed year after year of the married life of Laura Lagrange. She tried to hide her agony from the public gaze, to smile when her heart was almost breaking. But year after year her voice grew fainter and sadder, her once light and bounding step grew slower and faltering. Year after year she wrestled with agony, and strove with despair, till the quick eyes of her brother read, in the paling of her cheek and the dimming eye, the secret anguish of her worn and weary spirit. On that wan, sad face, he saw the death-tokens, and he knew the dark wing of the mystic angel swept coldly around her path. "Laura," said her brother to her one day, "you are not well, and I think you need our mother's tender care and nursing. You are daily losing strength, and if you will go I will accompany you." At first, she hesitated, she shrank almost instinctively from presenting that pale sad face to the loved ones at home. That face was such a tell-tale; it told of heart-sickness, of hope deferred, and the mournful story of unrequited love. But then a deep yearning for home sympathy woke within her a passionate longing for love's kind words, for tenderness and heart-support, and she resolved to seek the home of her childhood, and lay her weary head upon her mother's bosom, to be folded again in her loving arms, to lay that poor, bruised and aching heart where it might beat and throb closely to the loved ones at home. A kind welcome awaited her. All that love and tenderness could devise was done to bring the bloom to her cheek and the light to her eye; but it was all in vain; her's was a disease that no medicine could cure, no earthly balm would heal. It was a slow wasting of the vital forces, the sickness of the soul. The unkindness and neglect of her husband, lay like a leaden weight upon her heart, and slowly oozed away its life-drops. And where was he that had won her love, and then cast it aside as a useless thing, who rifled her heart of its wealth and spread bitter ashes upon its broken altars? He was lingering away from her when the death-damps were gathering on her brow, when his name was trembling on her lips! lingering away! when she was watching his coming, though the death films were gathering before her eyes, and earthly things were fading from her vision. "I think I hear him now," said the dying woman, "surely that is his step;" but the sound died away in the distance. Again she started from an uneasy slumber, "That is his voice! I am so glad he has come." Tears gathered in the eyes of the sad watchers by that dying bed, for they knew that she was deceived. He had not returned. For her sake they wished his coming. Slowly the hours waned away, and then came the sad, soul-sickening thought that she was forgotten, forgotten in the last hour of human need, forgotten when the spirit, about to be dissolved, paused for the last time on the threshold of existence, a weary watcher at the gates of death. "He has forgotten me," again she faintly murmured, and the last tears she would ever shed on earth sprung to her mournful eyes, and clasping her hands together in silent anguish, a few broken sentences issued from her pale and quivering lips. They were prayers for strength and earnest pleading for him who had desolated her young life, by turning its sunshine to shadows, its smiles to tears. "He has forgotten me," she murmured again, "but I can bear it, the bitterness of death is passed, and soon I hope to exchange the shadows of death for the brightness of eternity, the rugged paths of life for the golden streets of glory, and the care and turmoils of earth for the peace and rest of heaven." Her voice grew fainter and fainter, they saw the shadows that never deceive flit over her pale and faded face, and knew that the death angel waited to soothe their weary one to rest, to calm the throbbing of her bosom and cool the fever of her brain. And amid the silent hush of their grief the freed spirit, refined through suffering, and brought into divine harmony through the spirit of the living Christ, passed over the dark waters of death as on a bridge of light, over whose radiant arches hovering angels bent. They parted the dark locks from her marble brow, closed the waxen lids over the once bright and laughing eye, and left her to the dreamless slumber of the grave. Her cousin turned from that death-bed a sadder and wiser woman. She resolved more earnestly than ever to make the world better by her example, gladder by her presence, and to kindle the fires of her genius on the altars of universal love and truth. She had a higher and better object in all her writings than the mere acquisition of gold, or acquirement of fame. She felt that she had a high and holy mission on the battle-field of existence, that life was not given her to be frittered away in nonsense, or wasted away in trifling pursuits. She would willingly espouse an unpopular cause but not an unrighteous one. In her the down-trodden slave found an earnest advocate; the flying fugitive remembered her kindness as he stepped cautiously through our Republic, to gain his freedom in a monarchial land, having broken the chains on which the rust of centuries had gathered. Little children learned to name her with affection, the poor called her blessed, as she broke her bread to the pale lips of hunger. Her life was like a beautiful story, only it was clothed with the dignity of reality and invested with the sublimity of truth. True, she was an old maid, no husband brightened her life with his love, or shaded it with his neglect. No children nestling lovingly in her arms called her mother. No one appended Mrs. to her name; she was indeed an old maid, not vainly striving to keep up an appearance of girlishness, when departed was written on her youth. Not vainly pining at her loneliness and isolation: the world was full of warm, loving hearts, and her own beat in unison with them. Neither was she always sentimentally sighing for something to love, objects of affection were all around her, and the world was not so wealthy in love that it had no use for her's; in blessing others she made a life and benediction, and as old age descended peacefully and gently upon her, she had learned one of life's most precious lessons, that true happiness consists not so much in the fruition of our wishes as in the regulation of desires and the full development and right culture of our whole natures.

Our Greatest Want

Leading ideas impress themselves upon communities and countries. A thought is evolved and thrown out among the masses, they receive it and it becomes interwoven with their mental and moral life—if the thought be good the receivers are benefited, and helped onward to the truer life; if it is not, the reception of the idea is a detriment. A few earnest thinkers, and workers infuse into the mind of Great Britain, a sentiment of human brotherhood. The hue and cry of opposition is raised against it. Avarice and cupidity oppose it, but the great heart of the people throbs for it. A healthy public opinion dashes and surges against the British throne, the idea gains ground and progresses till hundreds of thousands of men, women and children arise, redeemed from bondage, and freed from chains, and the nation gains moral power by the act. Visions of dominion, proud dreams of conquest fill the soul of Napoleon Bonaparte, and he infuses them into the mind of France, and the peace of Europe is invaded. His bloodstained armies dazzled and misled, follow him through carnage and blood, to shake earth's proudest kingdoms to their base, and the march of a true progression is stayed by a river of blood. In America, where public opinion exerts such a sway, a leading is success. The politician who chooses for his candidate not the best man but the most available one.—The money getter, who virtually says let me make money, though I coin it from blood and extract it from tears—The minister, who stoops from his high position to the slave power, and in a word all who barter principle for expediency, the true and right for the available and convenient, are worshipers at the shrine of success. And we, or at least some of us, upon whose faculties the rust of centuries has lain, are beginning to awake and worship at the same altar, and bow to the idols. The idea if I understand it aright, that is interweaving itself with our thoughts, is that the greatest need of our people at present is money, and that as money is a symbol of power, the possession of it will gain for us the rights which power and prejudice now deny us.—And it may be true that the richer we are the nearer we are to social and political equality; but somehow, (and I may not fully comprehend the idea,) it does not seem to me that money, as little as we possess of it, is our greatest want. Neither do I think that the possession of intelligence and talent is our greatest want. If I understand our greatest wants aright they strike deeper than any want that gold or knowledge can supply. We want more soul, a higher cultivation of all our spiritual faculties. We need more unselfishness, earnestness and integrity. Our greatest need is not gold or silver, talent or genius, but true men and true women. We have millions of our race in the prison house of slavery, but have we yet a single Moses in freedom. And if we had who among us would be led by him?

I like the character of Moses. He is the first disunionist we read of in the Jewish Scriptures. The magnificence of Pharaoh's throne loomed up before his vision, its oriental splendors glittered before his eyes; but he turned from them all and chose rather to suffer with the enslaved, than rejoice with the free. He would have no union with the slave power of Egypt. When we have a race of men whom this blood stained government cannot tempt or flatter, who would sternly refuse every office in the nation's gift, from a president down to a tide-waiter, until she shook her hands from complicity in the guilt of cradle plundering and man stealing, then for us the foundations of an historic character will have been laid. We need men and women whose hearts are the homes of a high and lofty enthusiasm, and a noble devotion to the cause of emancipation, who are ready and willing to lay time, talent and money on the altar of universal freedom. We have money among us, but how much of it is spent to bring deliverance to our captive brethren? Are our wealthiest men the most liberal sustainers of the Anti-slavery enterprise? Or does the bare fact of their having money, really help mould public opinion and reverse its sentiments? We need what money cannot buy and what affluence is too beggarly to purchase. Earnest, self sacrificing souls that will stamp themselves not only on the present but the future. Let us not then defer all our noble opportunities till we get rich. And here I am not aiming to enlist a fanatical crusade against the desire for riches, but I do protest against chaining down the soul, with its Heaven endowed faculties and God given attributes to the one idea of getting money as stepping into power or even gaining our rights in common with others. The respect that is only bought by gold is not worth much. It is no honor to shake hands politically with men who whip women and steal babies. If this government has no call for our services, no aim for your children, we have the greater need of them to build up a true manhood and womanhood for ourselves. The important lesson we should learn and be able to teach, is how to make every gift, whether gold or talent, fortune or genius, subserve the cause of crushed humanity and carry out the greatest idea of the present age, the glorious idea of human brotherhood.

Woman's Political Future

If before sin had cast its deepest shadows or sorrow had distilled its bitterest tears, it was true that it was not good for man to be alone, it is no less true, since the shadows have deepened and life's sorrows have increased, that the world has need of all the spiritual aid that woman can give for the social advancement and moral development of the human race. The tendency of the present age, with its restlessness, religious upheavals, failures, blunders, and crimes, is toward broader freedom, an increase of knowledge, the emancipation of thought, and a recognition of the brotherhood of man; in this movement woman, as the companion of man, must be a sharer. So close is the bond between man and woman that you can not raise one without lifting the other. The world can not move without woman's sharing in the movement, and to help give a right impetus to that movement is woman's highest privilege.

If the fifteenth century discovered America to the Old World, the nineteenth is discovering woman to herself. Little did Columbus imagine, when the New World broke upon his vision like a lovely gem in the coronet of the universe, the glorious possibilities of a land where the sun should be our engraver, the winged lightning our messenger, and steam our beast of burden. But as mind is more than matter, and the highest ideal always the true real, so to woman comes the opportunity to strive for richer and grander discoveries than ever gladdened the eye of the Genoese mariner.

Not the opportunity of discovering new worlds, but that of filling this old world with fairer and higher aims than the greed of gold and the lust of power, is hers. Through weary, wasting years men have destroyed, dashed in pieces, and overthrown, but to-day we stand on the threshold of woman's era, and woman's work is grandly constructive. In her hand are possibilities whose use or abuse must tell upon the political life of the nation, and send their influence for good or evil across the track of unborn ages.

World's Congress of Representative Women, ed. May Write Sewell (Chicago: Rand, McNally and Co., 1894).

As the saffron tints and crimson flushes of morn herald the coming day, so the social and political advancement which woman has already gained bears the promise of the rising of the full-orbed sun of emancipation. The result will be not to make home less happy, but society more holy; yet I do not think the mere extension of the ballot a panacea for all the ills of our national life. What we need to-day is not simply more voters, but better voters. To-day there are red-handed men in our republic, who walk unwhipped of justice, who richly deserve to exchange the ballot of the freeman for the wristlets of the felon; brutal and cowardly men, who torture, burn, and lynch their fellow-men, men whose defenselessness should be their best defense and their weakness an ensign of protection. More than the changing of institutions we need the development of a national conscience, and the upbuilding of national character. Men may boast of the aristocracy of blood, may glory in the aristocracy of talent, and be proud of the aristocracy of wealth, but there is one aristocracy which must ever outrank them all, and that is the aristocracy of character; and it is the women of a country who help to mold its character, and to influence if not determine its destiny; and in the political future of our nation woman will not have done what she could if she does not endeavor to have our republic stand foremost among the nations of the earth, wearing sobriety as a crown and righteousness as a garment and a girdle. In coming into her political estate woman will find a mass of illiteracy to be dispelled. If knowledge is power, ignorance is also power. The power that educates wickedness may manipulate and dash against the pillars of any state when they are undermined and honeycombed by injustice.

I envy neither the heart nor the head of any legislator who has been born to an inheritance of privileges, who has behind him ages of education, dominion, civilization, and Christianity, if he stands opposed to the passage of a national education bill, whose purpose is to secure education to the children of those who were born under the shadow of institutions which made it a crime to read.

To-day women hold in their hands influence and opportunity, and with these they have already opened doors which have been closed to others. By opening doors of labor woman has become a rival claimant for at least some of the wealth monopolized by her stronger brother. In the home she is the priestess, in society the queen, in literature she is a power, in legislative halls law-makers have responded to her appeals, and for her sake have humanized and liberalized their laws. The press has felt the impress of her hand. In the pews of the church she constitutes the majority; the pulpit has welcomed her, and in the school she has the blessed privilege of teaching children and youth. To her is apparently coming the added responsibility of political power; and what she now possesses should only be the means of preparing her to use the coming power for the glory of God and the good of mankind; for power without righteousness is one of the most dangerous forces in the world.

Political life in our country has plowed in muddy channels, and needs the infusion of clearer and cleaner waters. I am not sure that women are naturally so much better than men that they will clear the stream by the virtue of their womanhood; it is not through sex but through character that the best influence of women upon the life of the nation must be exerted.

I do not believe in unrestricted and universal suffrage for either men or women. I believe in moral and educational tests. I do not believe that the most ignorant and brutal man is better prepared to add value to the strength and durability of the government than the most cultured, upright, and intelligent woman. I do not think that willful ignorance should swamp earnest intelligence at the ballot-box, not that educated wickedness, violence, and fraud should cancel the votes of honest men. The unsteady hands of a drunkard can not cast the ballot of a freeman. The hands of lynchers are too red with blood to determine the political character of the government for even four short years. The ballot in the hands of woman means power added to influence. How well she will use that power I can not foretell. Great evils stare us in the face that need to be throttled by the combined power of an upright manhood and an enlightened womanhood; and I know that no nation can gain its full measure of enlightenment and happiness if one-half of it is free and the other half is fettered. China compressed the feet of her women and thereby retarded the steps of her men. The elements of a nation's weakness must ever be found at the hearthstone.

More than the increase of wealth, the power of armies, and the strength of fleets is the need of good homes, of good fathers, and good mothers.

The life of a Roman citizen was in danger in ancient Palestine, and men had bound themselves with a vow that they would eat nothing until they had killed the Apostle Paul. Pagan Rome threw around that imperiled life a bulwark of living clay consisting of four hundred and seventy human hearts, and Paul was saved. Surely the life of the humblest American citizen should be as well protected in America as that of a Roman citizen was in heathen Rome. A wrong done to the weak should be an insult to the strong. Woman coming into her kingdom will find enthroned three great evils, for whose overthrow she should be as strong in a love of justice and humanity as the warrior is in his might. She will find intemperance sending its flood of shame, and death, and sorrow to the homes of men, a fretting leprosy in our politics, and a blighting curse in our social life; the social evil sending to our streets women whose laughter is sadder than their tears, who slide from the paths of sin and shame to the friendly shelter of the grave; and lawlessness enacting in our republic deeds over which angels might weep, if heaven knows sympathy.

How can any woman send petitions to Russia against the horrors of Siberian prisons if, ages after the Inquisition has ceased to devise its tortures, she has not done all she could by influence, tongue, and pen to keep men from making bonfires of the bodies of real or supposed criminals?

O women of America! into your hands God has pressed one of the sublimest opportunities that ever came into the hands of the women of any race or people. It is yours to create a healthy public sentiment; to demand justice, simple justice, as the right of every race; to brand with everlasting infamy the lawless and brutal cowardice that lynches, burns, and tortures your own countrymen.

To grapple with the evils which threaten to undermine the strength of the nation and to lay magazines of powder under the cribs of future generations is no child's play.

Let the hearts of the women of the world respond to the song of the herald angels of peace on earth and good will to men. Let them throb as one heart unified by the grand and holy purpose of uplifting the human race, and humanity will breathe freer, and the world grow brighter. With such a purpose Eden would spring up in our path, and Paradise be around our way.

A Double Standard

Do you blame me that I loved him?
    If when standing all alone
I cried for bread a careless world
    Pressed to my lips a stone.

Do you blame me that I loved him,
    That my heart beat glad and free,
When he told me in the sweetest tones
    He loved but only me?

Can you blame me that I did not see
    Beneath his burning kiss
The serpent's wiles, not even hear
    The deadly adder hiss?

Can you blame me that my heart grew cold
    That the tempted, tempter turned;
When he was feted and caressed
    And I was coldly spurned?

Would you blame him, when you draw from me
    Your dainty robes aside,
If he with gilded baits should claim
    Your fairest as his bride?

Would you blame the world if it should press
    On him a civic crown;
And see me struggling in the depth
    Then harshly press me down?

Crime has no sex and yet to-day
    I wear the brand of shame;
Whilst he amid the gay and proud
    Still bears an honored name.

Can you blame me if I've learned to think
    Your hate of vice a sham,
When you so coldly crushed me down
    And then excused the man?

Would you blame me if to-morrow
    The coroner should say,
A wretched girl, outcast, forlorn,
    Has thrown her life away?

Yes, blame me for my downward course,
    But oh! remember well,
Within your homes you press the hand
    That led me down to hell.

I'm glad God's ways are not our ways,
    He does not see as man;
Within His love I know there's room
    For those whom others ban.

I think before His great white throne,
    His throne of spotless light,
That whited sepulchres shall wear
    The hue of endless night.

That I who fell, and he who sinned,
    Shall reap as we have sown;
That each the burden of his loss
    Must bear and bear alone.

No golden weights can turn the scale
    Of justice in His sight;
And what is wrong in woman's life
    In man's cannot be right.

Harriet E. Wilson (1828c.–1863)

Although Harriet E. Wilson published *Our Nig: Or, Sketches from the Life of a Free Black* in 1859, it did not assume its place in the canon of African American literature until 1982 when critic Henry Louis Gates Jr. rediscovered and authenticated it. More recently, Gates has rediscovered another novel that was also written in the 1850s, *The Bondwoman's Narrative* by Hannah Crafts. Crafts's text is probably the first novel written by a black woman who was a slave, and Wilson's is the first novel written by a free black woman. *Our Nig* focuses on how racism in the North perpetuates its own peculiar brand of enslavement—indentured servitude. Frado, or "Nig," is the light-skinned daughter of a white mother and black father. She receives harsh treatment from the white family with whom she must live. Although she tries to make the best of her situation, when she becomes ill, she is told that she must leave. She eventually marries, but her husband goes off to sea, leaving Frado pregnant. The book chronicles Frado's efforts to support her child.

Similar to Frado's life, Wilson lived with a white family—the Boyles of Milford, New Hampshire. In 1851 she married Thomas Wilson, who left her and their baby, George, to go to sea. After a series of jobs, Wilson moved to Boston and decided to write a story based on her life to earn money to take care of her son. Shortly after *Our Nig* was published, George died.

From *Our Nig: Or, Sketches from the Life of a Free Black*

CHAPTER II

My Father's Death

Misery! we have known each other,
Like a sister and a brother,
Living in the same lone home
Many years—we must live some
Hours or ages yet to come.

SHELLEY

Jim, proud of his treasure,—a white wife,—tried hard to fulfil his promises; and furnished her with a more comfortable dwelling, diet, and apparel. It was comparatively a comfortable winter she passed after her marriage. When Jim could work, all went on well. Industrious, and fond of Mag, he was determined she should not regret her union to him. Time levied an additional charge upon him, in the form of two pretty mulattos, whose infantile pranks amply repaid the additional toil. A few years, and a severe cough and pain in his side

compelled him to be an idler for weeks together, and Mag had thus a reminder of by-gones. She cared for him only as a means to subserve her own comfort; yet she nursed him faithfully and true to marriage vows till death released her. He became the victim of consumption. He loved Mag to the last. So long as life continued, he stifled his sensibility to pain, and toiled for her sustenance long after he was able to do so.

A few expressive wishes for her welfare; a hope of better days for her; an anxiety lest they should not all go to the "good place;" brief advice about their children; a hope expressed that Mag would not be neglected as she used to be; the manifestation of Christian patience; these were *all* the legacy of miserable Mag. A feeling of cold desolation came over her, as she turned from the grave of one who had been truly faithful to her.

She was now expelled from companionship with white people; this last step—her union with a black—was the climax of repulsion.

Seth Shipley, a partner in Jim's business, wished her to remain in her present home; but she declined, and returned to her hovel again, with obstacles threefold more insurmountable than before. Seth accompanied her, giving her a weekly allowance which furnished most of the food necessary for the four inmates. After a time, work failed; their means were reduced.

How Mag toiled and suffered, yielding to fits of desperation, bursts of anger, and uttering curses too fearful to repeat.

From "Our Nig" (1859).

When both were supplied with work, they prospered; if idle, they were hungry together. In this way their interests became united; they planned for the future together. Mag had lived an outcast for years. She had ceased to feel the gushings of penitence; she had crushed the sharp agonies of an awakened conscience. She had no longings for a purer heart, a better life. Far easier to descend lower. She entered the darkness of perpetual infamy. She asked not the rite of civilization or Christianity. Her will made her the wife of Seth. Soon followed scenes familiar and trying.

"It's no use," said Seth one day; "we must give the children away, and try to get work in some other place."

"Who'll take the black devils?" snarled Mag.

"They're none of mine," said Seth; "what you growling about?"

"Nobody will want any thing of mine, or yours either," she replied.

"We'll make 'em, p'r'aps," he said. "There's Frado's six years old, and pretty, if she is yours, and white folks'll say so. She'd be a prize somewhere," he continued, tipping his chair back against the wall, and placing his feet upon the rounds, as if he had much more to say when in the right position.

Frado, as they called one of Mag's children, was a beautiful mulatto, with long, curly black hair, and handsome, roguish eyes, sparkling with an exuberance of spirit almost beyond restraint.

Hearing her name mentioned, she looked up from her play, to see what Seth had to say of her.

"Wouldn't the Bellmonts take her?" asked Seth.

"Bellmonts?" shouted Mag. "His wife is a right she-devil! and if—"

"Had n't they better be all together?" interrupted Seth, reminding her of a like epithet used in reference to her little ones.

Without seeming to notice him, she continued, "She can't keep a girl in the house over a week; and Mr. Bellmont wants to hire a boy to work for him, but he can't find one that will live in the house with her; she's so ugly, they can't."

"Well, we've got to make a move soon," answered Seth; "if you go with me, we shall go right off. Had you rather spare the other one?" asked Seth, after a short pause.

"One's as bad as t' other," replied Mag. "Frado is such a wild, frolicky thing, and means to do jest as she's a mind to; she won't go if she don't want to. I don't want to tell her she is to be given away."

"I will," said Seth. "Come here, Frado?"

The child seemed to have some dim foreshadowing of evil, and declined.

"Come here," he continued; "I want to tell you something."

She came reluctantly. He took her hand and said: "We're going to move, by-'m-bye; will you go?"

"No!" screamed she; and giving a sudden jerk which destroyed Seth's equilibrium, left him sprawling on the floor, while she escaped through the open door.

"She's a hard one," said Seth, brushing his patched coat sleeve. "I'd risk her at Bellmont's."

They discussed the expediency of a speedy departure. Seth would first seek employment, and then return for Mag. They would take with them what they could carry, and leave the rest with Pete Greene, and come for them when they were wanted. They were long in arranging affairs satisfactorily, and were not a little startled at the close of their conference to find Frado missing. They thought approaching night would bring her. Twilight passed into darkness, and she did not come. They thought she had understood their plans, and had, perhaps, permanently withdrawn. They could not rest without making some effort to ascertain her retreat. Seth went in pursuit, and returned without her. They rallied others when they discovered that another little colored girl was missing, a favorite playmate of Frado's. All effort proved unavailing. Mag felt sure her fears were realized, and that she might never see her again. Before her anxieties became realities, both were safely returned, and from them and their attendant they learned that they went to walk, and not minding the direction soon found themselves lost. They had climbed fences and walls, passed through thickets and marshes, and when night approached selected a thick cluster of shrubbery as a covert for the night. They were discovered by the person who now restored them, chatting of their prospects, Frado attempting to banish the childish fears of her companion. As they were some miles from home, they were kindly cared for until morning. Mag was relieved to know her child was not driven to desperation by their intentions to relieve themselves of her, and she was inclined to think severe restraint would be healthful.

The removal was all arranged; the few days necessary for such migrations passed quickly, and one bright summer morning they bade farewell to their Singleton hovel, and with budgets and bundles commenced their weary march. As they neared the village, they heard the merry shouts of children gathered around the schoolroom, awaiting the coming of their teacher.

"Halloo!" screamed one, "Black, white and yeller!" "Black, white and yeller," echoed a dozen voices.

It did not grate so harshly on poor Mag as once it would. She did not even turn her head to look at them. She had passed into an insensibility no childish taunt could penetrate, else she would have reproached herself as she passed familiar scenes, for extending the separation once so easily annihilated by steadfast integrity. Two miles beyond lived the Bellmonts, in a large, old fashioned, two-story white house, environed by fruitful acres, and embellished by shrubbery and shade trees. Years ago a youthful couple consecrated it as home; and after many little feet had worn paths to favorite fruit trees, and over its green hills, and mingled at last with brother man in the race which belongs neither to the swift or strong, the sire became grey-haired and decrepid, and went to his last repose. His aged consort soon followed him. The old homestead thus passed into the hands of a son, to whose wife Mag had applied the epithet "she-devil," as may be remembered. John, the son, had not in his family arrangements departed from the example of the father. The pastimes of his boyhood were ever freshly revived by witnessing the games of his own sons as they rallied about the same goal his youthful feet had often won; as well as by the amusements of his daughters in their imitations of maternal duties.

At the time we introduce them, however, John is wearing the badge of age. Most of his children were from home; some seeking employment; some were already settled in homes of their own. A maiden sister shared with him the estate on which he resided, and occupied a portion of the house.

Within sight of the house, Seth seated himself with his bundles and the child he had been leading, while Mag walked onward to the house leading Frado. A knock at the door brought Mrs. Bellmont, and Mag asked if she would be willing to let that child stop there while she went to the Reed's house to wash, and when she came back she would call and get her. It seemed a novel request, but she consented. Why the impetuous child entered the house, we cannot tell; the door closed, and Mag hastily departed. Frado waited for the close of day, which was to bring back her mother. Alas! it never came. It was the last time she ever saw or heard of her mother.

Hannah Crafts

As of this writing, Hannah Crafts is a mystery woman. Scholar Henry Louis Gates Jr., who previously rediscovered and authenticated Harriet Wilson's *Our Nig*, bought the 301-page clothbound, handwritten Crafts manuscript at an auction in 2001. Crafts's *The Bondwoman's Narrative* (1853–1861?) is the only known novel by a female slave and possibly the first novel written by a black woman anywhere. The novel is a gendered account of plantation life and resistance. As Gates explains in his introduction to the text, he has given us "the novel as it appeared in the original holograph." Therefore, the crossed-out words reflect Crafts's changes to the text.

From *The Bondswoman's Narrative*

A New Master

After exhausting a sleepless night in vain efforts to compose my mind and become reconciled to the fate that probably awaited me I arose in the morning really ill, nervous, and disheartened ~~with a despondency~~. The old man servant came with my breakfast. It was good, but I could not eat. Mental anxiety precluded the gratification of the senses, and I turned with loathing from the snowy bread and golden butter. It seemed like preparation for the sacrifice.

"You had much better eat" he said "as there's a long journey before you to[-]day.["]

"What kind of journey?" I inquired.

"Why you're sold" he answered in evident surprise that I was unaware of such an important change in my affairs.

"To whom?"

"Why to Saddler, the slave-trader but maybe I hadn't ought to tell you" he continued.

"Are you sure of this?"

"Surtin [certain] I am" and a grinning a sort of demoniacal smile he carried away the breakfast things.

In most cases there is something horrible in the idea of being bought and sold; it sent a thrill to my heart, a shiver through my brain. For a moment I felt dizzy, but a moment only. I had experienced too much trouble and anxiety to be overwhelmed by this. Then, too, I thought that though my perishable body was at their disposal, my soul was beyond their reach. They could never quench my immortality, shake my abiding faith and confidence in God, or destroy my living assurance in the efficacy of the dying Saviour's blood.

The old man, however, was mistaken. I was not sold, ~~though~~ though every thing was tending to that consummation. Towards noon I heard the roll of wheels and the tramp of horse's feet, evidently approaching the house. To these noises succeeded the echoing footsteps of a man, then there was a murmur of voices in an adjoining apartment and presently the door communicating with mine was thrown open; while some one said audibly "There she is." I knew the voice to be Mr Trappe's, but a stranger answered "Why Trappe I thought you said that she was beautiful; in my eye she's excessively homely."

"But you ~~haven't seen the good~~ haven't seen her good points yet" said Trappe "walk in and take a fair estimate of her attractions, they are neither small nor few."

Both men came in, while I shrunk into a distant corner.

"Nay: Hannah, that won't do" said Trappe. "Come out here and show yourself. I don't think Mr Saddler ever saw a better looking wench. Come out I say.["]

I obeyed reluctantly.

"Now I'll tell you what" said Trappe. "You won't find a nicer bit of woman's flesh to be bought for that money in old Virginia. Don't you see what a foot she has, so dainty and delicate, and what an ankle. I don't see how in conscience you can expect me to take any less. Why you'd make a small fortune of her at that rate."

"How you talk" said Saddler. "I've bought finer wenches often and often for less money. Then you see she's skittish which makes some difference. However as I'm making up a gang I wouldn't mind having her. But I think you told me that you wanted to dispose of two. Where is the other one?"

"Dead."

Saddler received this announcement with a look of profound surprise and repeated "dead."

"As a door nail" said Trappe.

"Why? how? what was the matter?" inquired Saddler. ["]If my memory serves me right you said that she was well only two or three days ago."

["]She did not die of disease. The truth is she broke a blood vessel. I reckon it a clear loss of one or two thousand."

"How unfortunate" said Saddler. "But these wenches will die. I have sometimes thought that accidents happened to them oftener than to others. I have lost much in that way myself, probably ten thousand dollars wouldn't cover the amount. If the business in general had not been so lucrative ~~it would have~~ such things would have broke me up long ago. You see my trade is altogether in the line of good-looking wenches, and these are a deal sight worse to manage than men—every way more skittish and skeery [scary]. Then it don't do to cross them much; or if you do they'll cut up the devil, and like as anyhow break their necks, or pine themselves to skeletons. I lost six in one season and out of one company. I had orders to fill at New Orleans and all for young and beautiful women without children. Now a woman of eighteen or twenty without a child, and a slave, is not so easy to find, to say nothing of looking for fifty or a hundred."

"Rather a difficulty I should think" said Trappe. ["]I've had some experience of that kind myself."

Trembling with fear I shrank back into the corner, while the gentlemen having seated themselves pursued the conversation. Mr Trappe meanwhile keeping his eye on me.

"At last I concluded" continued Saddler "to take the women with or without children, and get clear of the brats somehow, in any way that offered. But heavens, how they did carry on, and one, Louise by name, and the freshest and fairest in the gang, actually jumped into the river when she found that her child was irretrievably gone. Another one escaped and ran off to the place where she supposed her boy to have been carried. The overseer was the first to discover her, and knowing her to be a stranger, he lugged her off with the blood-hounds. They were real devils fierce, eager, and fiery—they tore her dreadfully, spoiled all her beauty, rendering her utterly unfit for my traffic; and so I sold her for a song. Now this one—what's her name?"

"Hannah."

"Thank you; now Hannah."

"Has no child" suggested Mr Trappe.

"Has no child" repeated Saddler "which is great advantage, but it seems that she's given to running away."

"Not at all" returned Trappe. "No one could be more peaceable and contented than she is. That running away was altogether the fault of the other one, and something Hannah would never have thought of had she been left alone."

"Is she good-tempered?"

"Lord love you, the best tempered in the world, kind trusty, and religious."

["]Bah: I hardly think that religion will do her much good, or make her more subservient to the wishes of my employers. On the whole I should prefer that she wasn't religious, ~~but I suppose that they can drive it out of her~~ because religion is so apt to make people stubborn; it gives them such notions of duty, and that one thing is right and another thing wrong; it sets them up so, you'll even hear them telling that all mankind are made of one blood, and equal in the sight of God."

"There may be something in that" said Mr Trappe.

"There is something in it, there's a great deal in it" pursued Saddler "give me a handsome wench, pleasant and good-tempered, willing to conform herself to circumstances, and anxious to please, without any notions of virtue, religion, or anything of that sort. Such are by far the most marketable, provided they have health, are young and show off to advantage."

"Well, Hannah does show off" answered Trappe. "Come out here again, and walk across the room. No disobedience, mind that."

I walked forth.

"There's a gait for you" said Trappe. "Few women can walk well, but Hannah does. She holds her head gracefully. Don't you think so?"

"Tolerable" said Saddler.

"She has a fine shape, good teeth, beautiful hair and fair complexion; is young; in high health; has good spirits and amiable disposition. Why fifteen hundred dollars is nothing, nothing at all put in the scale against such a woman. She'll bring you two thousand easy."

"I'm not so certain of that. She might possibly, provided I had her there, and she might not. It all depends on how she stands the journey. She may look old, worn and faded, and then I could scarcely ~~one thousand for her However at a risk I will give you twelve hundred~~ realize one half that sum. However I'll give you twelve hundred at a risk."

"Say thirteen and take her" said Trappe.

"Sorry that I can't" answered Saddler "but twelve hundred is really too much. Only think of my expense in getting her to the market, to say nothing of the risk. I think it would be a wise plan to have the lives of such wenches insured.["]

"Oh you'll have no risk with her on that score. Not a bit of it. Just get her into the wagon, put on the cuffs and she'll be safe enough."

"And you'll take twelve hundred?"

"Suppose I must though I am very certain it is not enough."

• • • •

The Reconstruction Period

Elizabeth Keckley (1824c.–1907)

Elizabeth Keckley held the unique position of dressmaker to Mary Todd Lincoln, President Lincoln's wife. *Behind the Scenes: or, Thirty Years a Slave, and Four Years in the White House* tells how Keckley, born to slaves in 1818 at Dinwiddie Court House in Virginia, used her sewing skills to buy her freedom and one day become Mrs. Lincoln's confidante. Keckley was born on the Burwell plantation to Agnes and George Pleasant. As a child and teenager, she was sold back and forth. Her first master sold her to a family in North Carolina where, while in her teens, she had a child by a local white man. Anne Burwell Garland, one of the daughters of her first master, repurchased Keckley, taking her and son George to live with the Garlands in St. Louis. One of Keckley's duties was to help the Garland family through her earnings as a seamstress. She did so well with dressmaking that in 1855, she was able to buy her freedom for $1,200. While in St. Louis, she married James Keckley, a slave masquerading as a freedman. She left him after eight years.

After learning to read and write, she moved to Baltimore and then to Washington, D.C. A number of prominent families noticed Keckley's skills, including the wives of Jefferson Davis and Stephen A. Douglas. Her sewing skills soon caught the attention of Mrs. Lincoln, who asked her to begin making her clothes. She made Mrs. Lincoln's inaugural outfit and worked for four years as a seamstress, traveling companion, and personal maid. During these years, her son, George, was killed while fighting as a Union soldier. In 1862, Keckley worked with other African American women to start an organization, the Contraband Relief Association, whose goal was to aid former slaves in the area. Immediately after President Lincoln's assassination, Mrs. Lincoln called Keckley to be at her side. Distraught over Lincoln's death, Keckley appealed to the African American community, including such friends as Frederick Douglass, to help her raise money for the widowed Mrs. Lincoln. Theirs was a very close friendship until, in part to help Mrs. Lincoln's reduced financial status, as well as her own, Keckley published *Behind the Scenes.* Mrs. Lincoln, her circle of friends, and members of the general public felt that the memoir was a breach of decorum. Keckley's business suffered and the friendship with Lincoln ended. As with Frances Watkins Harper, Keckley taught a few years at Wilberforce University in Ohio, but overall her life took a downward spiral. She became so poor that she died in a home for destitute women and girls in Washington, D.C., a home that she had help fund during her better years.

From *Behind the Scenes: or, Thirty Years as a Slave, and Four Years in the White House*

Preface

I have often been asked to write my life, as those who know me know that it has been an eventful one. At last I have acceded to the importunities of my friends, and have hastily sketched some of the striking incidents that go to make up my history. My life, so full of romance, may sound like a dream to the matter-of-fact reader, nevertheless everything I have written is strictly true; much has been omitted, but nothing has been exaggerated. In writing as I have done, I am well aware that I have invited criticism; but before the critic judges harshly, let my explanation be carefully read and weighed. If I have portrayed the dark side of slavery, I also have painted the bright side. The good that I have said of human servitude should be thrown into the scales with the evil that I have said of it. I have kind, true-hearted friends in the South as well as in the North, and I would not wound those Southern friends by sweeping condemnation, simply because I was once a slave. They were not so much responsible

From "Behind the Scenes: or, Thirty Years as a Slave, and Four Years in the White House."

for the curse under which I was born, as the God of nature and the fathers who framed the Constitution for the United States. The law descended to them, and it was but natural that they should recognize it, since it manifestly was their interest to do so. And yet a wrong was inflicted upon me; a cruel custom deprived me of my liberty, and since I was robbed of my dearest right, I would not have been human had I not rebelled against the robbery. God rules the Universe. I was a feeble instrument in His hands, and through me and the enslaved millions of my race, one of the problems was solved that belongs to the great problem of human destiny; and the solution was developed so gradually that there was no great convulsion of the harmonies of natural laws. A solemn truth was thrown to the surface, and what is better still, it was recognized *as a truth* by those who give force to moral laws. An act may be wrong, but unless the ruling power recognizes the wrong, it is useless to hope for a correction of it. Principles may be right, but they are not established within an hour. The masses are slow to reason, and each principle, to acquire moral force, must come to us from the fire of the crucible; the fire may inflict unjust punishment, but then it purifies and renders stronger the principle, not in itself, but in the eyes of those who arrogate judgment to themselves. When the war of the Revolution established the independence of the American colonies, an evil was perpetuated, slavery was more firmly established; and since the evil had been planted, it must pass through certain stages before it could be eradicated. In fact, we give but little thought to the plant of evil until it grows to such monstrous proportions that it overshadows important interests; then the efforts to destroy it become earnest. As one of the victims of slavery I drank of the bitter water; but then, since destiny willed it so, and since I aided in bringing a solemn truth to the surface *as a truth*, perhaps I have no right to complain. Here, as in all things pertaining to life, I can afford to be charitable.

It may be charged that I have written too freely on some questions, especially in regard to Mrs. Lincoln. I do not think so; at least I have been prompted by the purest motive. Mrs. Lincoln, by her own acts, forced herself into notoriety. She stepped beyond the formal lines which hedge about a private life, and invited public criticism. The people have judged her harshly, and no woman was ever more traduced in the public prints of the country. The people knew nothing of the secret history of her transactions, therefore they judged her by what was thrown to the surface. For an act may be wrong judged purely by itself, but when the motive that prompted the act is understood, it is construed differently. I lay it down as an axiom, that only that is criminal in the sight of God where crime is meditated. Mrs. Lincoln may have been imprudent, but since her intentions were good, she should be judged more kindly than she has been. But the world do not know what her intentions were; they have only been made acquainted with her acts without knowing what feeling guided her actions. If the world are to judge her as I have judged her, they must be introduced to the secret history of her transactions. The veil of mystery must be drawn aside; the origin of a fact must be brought to light with the naked fact itself. If I have betrayed confidence in anything I have published, it has been to place Mrs. Lincoln in a better light before the world. A breach of trust—if breach it can be called—of this kind is always excusable. My own character, as well as the character of Mrs. Lincoln, is at stake, since I have been intimately associated with that lady in the most eventful periods of her life. I have been her confidante, and if evil charges are laid at her door, they also must be laid at mine, since I have been a party to all her movements. To defend myself I must defend the lady that I have served. The world have judged Mrs. Lincoln by the facts which float upon the surface, and through her have partially judged me, and the only way to convince them that wrong was not meditated is to explain the motives that actuated us. I have written nothing that can place Mrs. Lincoln in a worse light before the world than the light in which she now stands, therefore the secret history that I publish can do her no harm. I have excluded everything of a personal character from her letters; the extracts introduced only refer to public men, and are such as to threw light upon her unfortunate adventure in New York. These letters were not written for publication, for which reason they are all the more valuable; they are the frank overflowings of the heart, the outcropping of impulse, the key to genuine motives. They prove the motive to have been pure, and if they shall help to stifle the voice of calumny, I am content. I do not forget, before the public journals vilified Mrs. Lincoln, that ladies who moved in the Washington circle in which she moved, freely canvassed her character among themselves. They gloated over many a tale of scandal that grew out of gossip in their own circle. If these ladies could say everything bad of the wife of the President, why should I not be permitted to lay her secret history bare, especially when that history plainly shows that her life, like all lives, has its good side as well as its bad side! None of us are perfect, for which reason we should heed the voice of charity when it whispers in our ears, "Do not magnify the imperfections of others." Had Mrs. Lincoln's acts never become public property, I should not have published to the world the secret chapters of her life. I am not the special champion of the widow of our lamented President; the reader of the pages which follow will discover that I have written with the utmost frankness in regard to her—have exposed her faults as well as given her credit for honest motives. I wish the world to judge her as she is, free from the exaggerations of praise or scandal, since I have been associated with her in so many things that have provoked hostile criticism; and the judgment that the world may pass upon her, I flatter myself, will present my own actions in a better light.

ELIZABETH KECKLEY

14 Carroll Place, New York, March 14, 1868.

Chapter I

Where I was Born

My life has been an eventful one. I was born a slave—was the child of slave parents—therefore I came upon the earth free in God-like thought, but fettered in action. My birthplace was Dinwiddie Court-House, in Virginia. My recollections of childhood are distinct, perhaps for the reason that many stirring incidents are associated with that period. I am now on the shady side of forty, and as I sit alone in my room the brain is busy, and a rapidly moving panorama brings scene after scene before me, some pleasant and others sad; and when I thus greet old familiar faces, I often find myself wondering if I am not living the past over again. The visions are so terribly distinct that I almost imagine them to be real. Hour after hour I sit while the scenes are being shifted; and as I gaze upon the panorama of the past, I realize how crowded with incidents my life has been. Every day seems like a romance within itself, and the years grow into ponderous volumes. As I cannot condense, I must omit many strange passages in my history. From such a wilderness of events it is difficult to make a selection, but as I am not writing altogether the history of myself, I will confine my story to the most important incidents which I believe influenced the moulding of my character. As I glance over the crowded sea of the past, these incidents stand forth prominently, the guide-posts of memory. I presume that I must have been four years old when I first began to remember; at least, I cannot now recall anything occurring previous to this period. My master, Col. A. Burwell, was somewhat unsettled in his business affairs, and while I was yet an infant he made several removals. While living at Hampton Sidney College, Prince Edward County, Va., Mrs. Burwell gave birth to a daughter, a sweet, black-eyed baby, my earliest and fondest pet. To take care of this baby was my first duty. True, I was but a child myself—only four years old—but then I had been raised in a hardy school—had been taught to rely upon myself, and to prepare myself to render assistance to others. The lesson was

not a bitter one, for I was too young to indulge in philosophy, and the precepts that I then treasured and practised I believe developed those principles of character which have enabled me to triumph over so many difficulties. Notwithstanding all the wrongs that slavery heaped upon me, I can bless it for one thing—youth's important lesson of self-reliance. The baby was named Elizabeth, and it was pleasant to me to be assigned a duty in connection with it, for the discharge of that duty transferred me from the rude cabin to the household of my master. My simple attire was a short dress and a little white apron. My old mistress encouraged me in rocking the cradle, by telling me that if I would watch over the baby well, keep the flies out of its face, and not let it cry, I should be its little maid. This was a golden promise, and I required no better inducement for the faithful performance of my task. I began to rock the cradle most industriously, when lo! out pitched little pet on the floor. I instantly cried out, "Oh! the baby is on the floor;" and, not knowing what to do, I seized the fire-shovel in my perplexity, and was trying to shovel up my tender charge, when my mistress called to me to let the child alone, and then ordered that I be taken out and lashed for my carelessness. The blows were not administered with a light hand, I assure you, and doubtless the severity of the lashing has made me remember the incident so well. This was the first time I was punished in this cruel way, but not the last. The black-eyed baby that I called my pet grew into a self-willed girl, and in after years was the cause of much trouble to me. I grew strong and healthy, and, notwithstanding I knit socks and attended to various kinds of work, I was repeatedly told, when even fourteen years old, that I would never be worth my salt. When I was eight, Mr. Burwell's family consisted of six sons and four daughters, with a large family of servants. My mother was kind and forbearing; Mrs. Burwell a hard task-master; and as mother had so much work to do in making clothes, etc., for the family, besides the slaves, I determined to render her all the assistance in my power, and in rendering her such assistance my young energies were taxed to the utmost. I was my mother's only child, which made her love for me all the stronger. I did not know much of my father, for he was the slave of another man, and when Mr. Burwell moved from Dinwiddie he was separated from us, and only allowed to visit my mother twice a year—during the Easter holidays and Christmas. At last Mr. Burwell determined to reward my mother, by making an arrangement with the owner of my father, by which the separation of my parents could be brought to an end. It was a bright day, indeed, for my mother when it was announced that my father was coming to live with us. The old weary look faded from her face, and she worked as if her heart was in every task. But the golden days did not last long. The radiant dream faded all too soon.

In the morning my father called me to him and kissed me, then held me out at arms' length as if he were regarding his child with pride. "She is growing into a large fine girl," he remarked to my mother. "I dun no which I like best, you or Lizzie, as both are so dear to me." My mother's name was Agnes, and my father delighted to call me his "Little Lizzie." While yet my father and mother were speaking hopefully, joyfully of the future, Mr. Burwell came to the cabin, with a letter in his hand. He was a kind master in some things, and as gently as possible informed my parents that they must part; for in two hours my father must join his master at Dinwiddie, and go with him to the West, where he had determined to make his future home. The announcement fell upon the little circle in that rude-log cabin like a thunderbolt. I can remember the scene as if it were but yesterday;—how my father cried out against the cruel separation; his last kiss; his wild straining of my mother to his bosom; the solemn prayer to Heaven; the tears and sobs—the fearful anguish of broken hearts. The last kiss, the last good-by; and he, my father, was gone, gone forever. The shadow eclipsed the sunshine, and love brought despair. The parting was eternal. The cloud had no silver lining, but I trust that it will be all silver in heaven. We who are crushed to earth with heavy chains, who travel a weary, rugged, thorny road, groping through midnight darkness on earth, earn our right to enjoy the sunshine in the great hereafter. At the grave, at least, we should be permitted to lay our burdens down, that a new world, a world of brightness, may open to us. The light that is denied us here should grow into a flood of effulgence beyond the dark, mysterious shadows of death. Deep as was the distress of my mother in parting with my father, her sorrow did not screen her from insult. My old mistress said to her: "Stop your nonsense; there is no necessity for you putting an airs. Your husband is not the only slave that has been sold from his family, and you are not the only one that has had to part. There are plenty more men about here, and if you want a husband so badly, stop your crying and go and find another." To these unfeeling words my mother made no reply. She turned away in stoical silence, with a curl of that loathing scorn upon her lips which swelled in her heart.

My father and mother never met again in this world. They kept up a regular correspondence for years, and the most precious mementoes of my existence are the faded old letters that he wrote, full of love, and always hoping that the future would bring brighter days. In nearly every letter is a message for me. "Tell my darling little Lizzie," he writes, "to be a good girl, and to learn her book. Kiss her for me, and tell her that I will come to see her some day." Thus he wrote time and again, but he never came. He lived in hope, but died without ever seeing his wife and child.

I note a few extracts from one of my father's letters to my mother, following copy literally:

"Shelbyvile, Sept. 6, 1833

"Mrs. Agnes Hobbs.

"Dear Wife: My dear biloved wife I am more than glad to meet with opportunty writee thes few lines to you by my Mistress who ar now about starterng to virginia, and sevl others of my old friends are with her; in compeney Mrs. Ann Rus the wife of master Thos Rus and Dan Woodiard and his family and I am very sorry that I havn the chance to go with them as I feele Determid to see you If life last again. I am now here and out at this pleace so I am not abble to get of at this time. I am write well and hearty and all the rest of masters family. I heard this eveng by Mistress that ar just from theree all sends love to you and all my old frends. I am a living in a town called Shelbyville and I have wrote a greate many letters since Ive beene here and almost been reeady to my selfe that its out of the question to write any more at tall: my dear wife I dont feell no whys like giving out writing to you as yet and I hope when you get this letter that you be Inncougege to write me a letter. I am well satisfied at my living at this place I am a making money for my own benifit and I hope that its to yours also If I live to see Nexct year I shall heve my own time from master by giving him 100 and twenty Dollars a year and I thinke I shall be doing good bisness at that and heve something more thean all that. I hope with gods helpe that I may be abble to rejoys with you on the earth and In heaven lets meets when will I am detemnid to nuver stope praying, not in this earth and I hope to praise god In glory there weel meet to part no more forever. So my dear wife I hope to meet you In paradase to prase god forever * * * * * I want Elizabeth to be a good girl and not to thinke that becasue I am bound so fare that gods not abble to open the way * * * *

"George Pleasant,
"Hobbs a servant of Grum."

The last letter that my mother received from my father was dated Shelbyville, Tennessee, March 20, 1839. He writes in a cheerful strain, and hopes to see her soon. Alas! he looked forward to a meeting in vain. Year after year the one great hope swelled in his heart, but the hope was only realized beyond the dark portals of the grave.

When I was about seven years old I witnessed, for the first time, the sale of a human being. We were living at Prince Edward, in Virginia, and master had just purchased his hogs for the winter, for which he was unable to pay in full. To escape from his embarrassment it was necessary to sell one of the slaves. Little Joe, the son of the cook, was selected as the victim. His mother was ordered to dress him up in his Sunday clothes, and send him to the house. He came in with a bright face, was placed in the scales, and was sold, like the hogs, at so much per pound. His mother was kept in ignorance of the transaction, but her suspicions were aroused. When her son started for Petersburgh in the wagon, the truth began to dawn upon her mind, and she pleaded piteously that her boy should not be taken from her; but master quieted her by telling her that he was simply going to town with the wagon, and would be back in the morning. Morning came, but little Joe did not return to his mother. Morning after morning passed, and the mother went down to the grave without ever seeing her child again. One day she was whipped for grieving for her lost boy. Colonel Burwell never liked to see one of his slaves wear a sorrowful face, and those who offended in this particular way were always punished. Alas! the sunny face of the slave is not always an indication of sunshine in the heart. Colonel Burwell at one time owned about seventy slaves, all of which were sold, and in a majority of instances wives were separated from husbands and children from their parents. Slavery in the Border States forty years ago was different from what it was twenty years ago. Time seemed to soften the hearts of master and mistress, and to insure kinder and more humane treatment to bondsmen and bondswomen. When I was quite a child, an incident occurred which my mother afterward impressed more strongly on my mind. One of my uncles, a slave of Colonel Burwell, lost a pair of plough-lines, and when the loss was made known the master gave him a new pair, and told him that if he did not take care of them he would punish him severely. In a few weeks the second pair of lines was stolen, and my uncle hung himself rather than meet the displeasure of his master. My mother went to the spring in the morning for a pail of water, and on looking up into the willow tree which shaded the bubbling crystal stream, she discovered the lifeless form of her brother suspended beneath one of the strong branches. Rather than be punished the way Colonel Burwell punished his servants, he took his own life. Slavery had its dark side as well as its bright side.

Chapter IX

Behind the Scenes

Some of the freedmen and freedwomen had exaggerated ideas of liberty. To them it was a beautiful vision, a land of sunshine, rest, and glorious promise. They flocked to Washington, and since their extravagant hopes were not realized, it was but natural that many of them should bitterly feel their disappointment. The colored people are wedded to associations, and when you destroy these you destroy half of the happiness of their lives. They make a home, and are so fond of it that they prefer it, squalid though it be, to the comparative ease and luxury of a shifting, roaming life. Well, the emancipated slaves, in coming North, left old associations behind them, and the love for the past was so strong that they could not find much beauty in the new life so suddenly opened to them. Thousands of the disappointed, huddled together in camps, fretted and pined like children for the "good old times." In visiting them in the interests of the Relief Society of which I was president, they would crowd around me with pitiful stories of distress. Often I heard them declare that they would rather go back to slavery in the South, and be with their old masters, than to enjoy the freedom of the North. I believe they were sincere in these declarations, because dependence had become a part of their second nature, and independence brought with it the cares and vexations of poverty.

I was very much amused one day at the grave complaints of a good old, simple-minded woman, fresh from a life of servitude. She had never ventured beyond a plantation until coming North. The change was too radical for her, and she could not exactly understand it. She thought, as many others thought, that Mr. and Mrs. Lincoln were the government, and that the President and his wife had nothing to do but to supply the extravagant wants of every one that applied to them. The wants of this old woman, however, were not very extravagant.

"Why, Missus Keckley," said she to me one day, "I is been here eight months, and Missus Lingom an't even give me one shife. Bliss God, children, if I had ar know dat de Government, and Mister and Missus Government, was going to do dat ar way, I neber would 've comed here in God's wurld. My old missus us't gib me two shifes eber year."

I could not restrain a laugh at the grave manner in which this good old woman entered her protest. Her idea of freedom was two or more old shifts every year. Northern readers may not fully recognize the pith of the joke. On the Southern plantation, the mistress, according to established custom, every year made a present of certain under-garments to her slaves, which articles were always anxiously looked forward to, and thankfully received. The old woman had been in the habit of receiving annually two shifts from her mistress, and she thought the wife of the President of the United States very mean for overlooking this established custom of the plantation.

While some of the emancipated blacks pined for the old associations of slavery, and refused to help themselves, others went to work with commendable energy, and planned with remarkable forethought. They built themselves cabins, and each family cultivated for itself a small patch of ground. The colored people are fond of domestic life, and with them domestication means happy children, a fat pig, a dozen or more chickens, and a garden. Whoever visits the Freedmen's Village now in the vicinity of Washington will discover all of these evidences of prosperity and happiness. The schools are objects of much interest. Good teachers, white and colored, are employed, and whole brigades of bright-eyed dusky children are there taught the common branches of education. These children are studious, and the teachers inform me that their advancement is rapid. I number among my personal friends twelve colored girls employed as teachers in the schools at Washington. The Colored Mission Sabbath School, established through the influence of Gen. Brown at the Fifteenth Street Presbyterian Church, is always an object of great interest to the residents of the Capital, as well as to the hundreds of strangers visiting the city.

In 1864 the receptions again commenced at the White House. For the first two years of Mr. Lincoln's administration, the President selected a lady to join in the promenade with him, which left Mrs. Lincoln free to choose an escort from among the distinguished gentlemen that always surrounded her on such occasions. This custom at last was discontinued by Mrs. Lincoln.

"Lizabeth!"—I was sewing in her room, and she was seated in a comfortable arm-chair—"Lizabeth, I have been thinking over a little matter. As you are well aware, the President, at every reception, selects a lady to lead the promenade with him. Now it occurs to me that this custom is an absurd one. On such occasions our guests recognize the position of the President as first of all; consequently, he takes the lead in everything; well, now, if they recognize his position they should also recognize mine. I am his wife, and should lead with him. And yet he offers his arm to any other lady in the room, making her first with him and placing me second. The custom is an absurd one, and I mean to abolish it. The dignity that I owe to my position, as Mrs. President, demands that I should not hesitate any longer to act."

Mrs. Lincoln kept her word. Ever after this, she either led the promenade with the President, or the President walked alone or with a gentleman. The change was much remarked, but the reason why it was made, I believe, was never generally known.

In 1864 much doubt existed in regard to the re-election of Mr. Lincoln, and the White House was besieged by all grades of politicians. Mrs. Lincoln was often blamed for having a certain class of men around her.

"I have an object in view, Lizabeth," she said to me in reference to this matter. "In a political canvass it is policy to cultivate every element of strength. These men have influence, and we require influence to re-elect Mr. Lincoln. I will

be clever to them until after the election, and then, if we remain at the White House, I will drop every one of them, and let them know very plainly that I only made tools of them. They are an unprincipled set, and I don't mind a little double-dealing with them."

"Does Mr. Lincoln know what your purpose is?" I asked.

"God! no; he would never sanction such a proceeding, so I keep him in the dark, and will tell him of it when all is over. He is too honest to take the proper care of his own interests, so I feel it to be my duty to electioneer for him."

Mr. Lincoln, as every one knows, was far from handsome. He was not admired for his graceful figure and finely moulded face, but for the nobility of his soul and the greatness of his heart. His wife was different. He was wholly unselfish in every respect, and I believe that he loved the mother of his children very tenderly. He asked nothing but affection from her, but did not always receive it. When in one of her wayward impulsive moods, she was apt to say and do things that wounded him deeply. If he had not loved her, she would have been powerless to cloud his thoughtful face, or gild it with a ray of sunshine as she pleased. We are indifferent to those we do not love, and certainly the President was not indifferent to his wife. She often wounded him in unguarded moments, but calm reflection never failed to bring regret.

Mrs. Lincoln was extremely anxious that her husband should be re-elected President of the United States. In endeavoring to make a display becoming her exalted position, she had to incur many expenses. Mr. Lincoln's salary was inadequate to meet them, and she was forced to run in debt, hoping that good fortune would favor her, and enable her to extricate herself from an embarrassing situation. She bought the most expensive goods on credit, and in the summer of 1864 enormous unpaid bills stared her in the face.

"What do you think about the election, Lizabeth?" she said to me one morning.

"I think that Mr. Lincoln will remain in the White House four years longer," I replied, looking up from my work.

"What makes you think so? Somehow I have learned to fear that he will be defeated."

"Because he has been tried, and has proved faithful to the best interests of the country. The people of the North recognize in him an honest man, and they are willing to confide in him, at least until the war has been brought to a close. The Southern people made his election a pretext for rebellion, and now to replace him by some one else, after years of sanguinary war, would look too much like a surrender of the North. So, Mr. Lincoln is certain to be re-elected. He represents a principle, and to maintain this principle the loyal people of the loyal States will vote for him, even if he had no merits to commend him."

"Your view is a plausible one, Lizabeth, and your confidence give me new hope. If he should be defeated, I do not know what would become of us all. To me, to him, there is more at stake in this election than he dreams of."

"What can you mean, Mrs. Lincoln? I do not comprehend."

"Simply this. I have contracted large debts, of which he knows nothing, and which he will be unable to pay if he is defeated."

"What are your debts, Mrs. Lincoln?"

"They consist chiefly of store bills. I owe altogether about twenty-seven thousand dollars; the principal portion at Stewart's, in New York. You understand, Lizabeth, that Mr. Lincoln has but little idea of the expense of a woman's wardrobe. He glances at my rich dresses, and is happy in the belief that the few hundred dollars that I obtain from him supply all my wants. I must dress in costly materials. The people scrutinize every article that I wear with critical curiosity. The very fact of having grown up in the West, subjects me to more searching observation. To keep up appearances, I must have money—more than Mr. Lincoln can spare for me. He is too honest to make a penny outside of his salary; consequently I had, and still have, no alternative but to run in debt."

"And Mr. Lincoln does not even suspect how much you owe?"

"God, no!"—this was a favorite expression of hers—"and I would not have him suspect. If he knew that his wife was involved to the extent that she is, the knowledge would drive him mad. He is so sincere and straightforward himself, that he is shocked by the duplicity of others. He does not know a thing about any debts, and I value his happiness, not to speak of my own, too much to allow him to know anything. This is what troubles me so much. If he is re-elected, I can keep him in ignorance of my affairs; but if he is defeated, then the bills will be sent in, and he will know all;" and something like a hysterical sob escaped her.

Mrs. Lincoln sometimes feared that the politicians would get hold of the particulars of her debts, and use them in the Presidential campaign against her husband; and when this thought occurred to her, she was almost crazy with anxiety and fear.

When in one of these excited moods, she would fiercely exclaim—

"The Republican politicians must pay my debts. Hundreds of them are getting immensely rich off the patronage of my husband, and it is but fair that they should help me out of my embarrassment. I will make a demand of them, and when I tell them the facts they cannot refuse to advance whatever money I require."

Charlotte L. Forten Grimké (1837–1914)

As the daughter in the well-to-do Forten family of Philadelphia, Charlotte L. Forten Grimké lived a life that was more privileged than most black women of her generation. Her grandfather, James Forten Sr., had been a prosperous sailmaker. Her parents, Robert Bridges Forten and Mary Woods Forten, were known for their participation in the arts and the abolitionist movement. During her early years, Grimké was privately tutored and later attended a school in Salem, Massachusetts. Following in the footsteps of family members who were active in the Philadelphia Female Anti-Slavery Society, she became a member of the Salem Female Anti-Slavery Society. She taught school in the all-white Epes Grammar School of Salem and at schools in Philadelphia and the South Carolina Sea Islands. Indeed, Grimké was the first black teacher hired to prepare the black Sea Island population for citizenship. After the Civil War, she served as secretary of the Freedmen's Relief Association and later became a clerk in the U.S. Treasury Department. In 1878 she married Francis J. Grimké, a Presbyterian minister and descendant of the famous abolitionists, the Grimké sisters of South Carolina. Although she published poems in many of the anti-slavery periodicals, her journals have been of more interest to today's readers. Typed by Anna Julia Cooper after Grimké's death from lung fever, the journals are an engaging record of the life of an upper-class, politically involved African American during the late 19th century.

From *The Journals of Charlotte L. Forten Grimké*

A wish to record the passing events of my life, which, even if quite unimportant to others, naturally possess great interest to myself, and of which it will be pleasant to have some remembrance, has induced me to commence this journal. I feel that keeping a diary will be a pleasant and profitable employment of my leisure hours, and will afford me much pleasure in after years, by recalling to my mind the memories of other days, thoughts of much-loved friends from whom I may then be separated, with whom I now pass many happy hours, in taking delightful walks, and holding 'sweet converse'; the interesting books that I read; and the different people, places, and things that I am permitted to see.

Besides this, it will doubtless enable me to judge correctly of the growth and improvement of my mind from year to year.

C.L.F.

Salem, May, 1854

Thursday, May 25, 1854. Did not intend to write this evening, but have just heard of something which is worth recording;—something which must ever rouse in the mind of every true friend of liberty and humanity, feelings of the deepest indignation and sorrow. Another fugitive from bondage has been arrested; a poor man, who for two short months has trod the soil and breathed the air of the "Old Bay State," was arrested like a criminal in the streets of her capital, and is now kept strictly guarded,—a double police force is required, the military are in readiness; and all this done to prevent a man, whom God has created in his own image, from regaining that freedom with which, he, in common with every other human being, is endowed. I can only hope and pray most earnestly that Boston will not again disgrace herself by sending him back to a bondage worse than death; or rather that she will redeem herself from the disgrace which his arrest alone has brought upon her. . . .

Friday, May 26, 1854. Had a conversation with Miss [Mary] Shepard about slavery; she is, as I thought, thoroughly opposed to it, but does not agree with me in thinking that the churches and ministers are generally supporters of the infamous system; I believe it firmly. Mr. Barnes, one of the most prominent of the Philadelphia clergy, who does not profess to be an abolitionist, has declared his belief that 'the American church is the bulwark of slavery.' Words cannot express all that I feel; all that is felt by the friends of Freedom, when thinking of this great obstacle to the removal of slavery from our land. Alas! that it should be so.—I was much disappointed in not seeing the eclipse, which, it was expected would be the most entire that has taken place for years; but the weather was rainy, and the sky obscured by clouds; so after spending half the

From the Francis Grimké Papers, courtesy of the Moorland-Springarm Research Center, Howard University, Washington, DC.

afternoon on the roof of the house in eager expectation, I saw nothing, heard since that the sun made his appearance for a minute or two, but I was not fortunate enough to catch even that momentary glimpse of him. . . .

Saturday, May 27.   . . . Returned home, read the Anti-Slavery papers, and then went down to the depot to meet father; he had arrived in Boston early in the morning, regretted very much that he had not reached there the evening before to attend the great meeting at Faneuil Hall. He says that the excitement in Boston is very great; the trial of the poor man takes place on Monday. We scarcely dare to think of what may be the result; there seems to be nothing too bad for these Northern tools of slavery to do.

Sunday, May 28.   A lovely day; in the morning I read in the Bible and wrote letters; in the afternoon took a quiet walk in Harmony Grove, and as I passed by many an 'unknown grave,' the question of 'who sleeps below?' rose often to my mind, and led to a long train of thoughts, of whose those departed ones might have been, how much beloved, how deeply regretted and how worthy of such love and such regret. I love to walk on the Sabbath, for all is so peaceful; the noise and labor of everyday life has ceased; and in perfect silence we can commune with Nature and with Nature's God. . . .

Tuesday, May 30.   Rose very early and was busy until nine o'clock; then, at Mrs. Putnam's urgent request, went to keep store for her while she went to Boston to attend the Anti-Slavery Convention. I was very anxious to go, and will certainly do so to-morrow; the arrest of the alleged fugitive will give additional interest to the meetings, I should think. His trial is still going on and I can scarcely think of anything else; read again to-day as most suitable to my feelings and to the times, "The Run-away Slave at Pilgrim's Point," by Elizabeth B. Browning; how powerfully it is written! how earnestly and touchingly does the writer portray the bitter anguish of the poor fugitive as she thinks over all the wrongs and sufferings that she has endured, and of the sin to which tryants have driven her but which they alone must answer for! It seems as if no one could read this poem without having his sympathies roused to the utmost in behalf of the oppressed.—After a long conversation with my friends on their return, on this all-absorbing subject, we separated for the night, and I went to bed, weary and sad.

Wednesday, May 31.   . . . Sarah [Remond] and I went to Boston in the morning. Everything was much quieter—outwardly than we expected, but still much real indignation and excitement prevail. We walked past the Court-House, which is now lawlessly converted into a prison, and filled with soldiers, some of whom were looking from the windows, with an air of insolent authority which made my blood boil, while I felt the strongest contempt for their cowardice and servility. We went to the meeting, but the best speakers were absent, engaged in the most arduous and untiring efforts in behalf of the poor fugitive; but though we missed the glowing eloquence of Philips, Garrison, and Parker, still there were excellent speeches made, and our hearts responded to the exalted sentiments of Truth and Liberty which were uttered. The exciting intelligence which occasionally came in relation to the trial, added fresh zeal to the speakers, of whom Stephen Foster and his wife were the principal. The latter addressed, in the most eloquent language, the women present, entreating them to urge their husbands and brothers to action, and also to give their aid on all occasions in our just and holy cause.—I did not see father the whole day; he, of course, was deeply interested in the trial.—Dined at Mr. Garrison's; his wife is one of the loveliest persons I have ever seen, worthy of such a husband. At the table, I watched earnestly the expression of that noble face, as he spoke beautifully in support of the non-resistant principles to which he has kept firm; his is indeed the very highest Christian spirit, to which I cannot hope to reach, however, for I believe in 'resistance to tyrants,' and would fight for liberty until death. We came home in the evening, and felt sick at heart as we passed through the streets of Boston on our way to the depot, seeing the military as they rode along, ready at any time to prove themselves the minions of the south.

Thursday, June 1st.   . . . The trial is over at last; the commissioner's decision will be given to-morrow. We are all in the greatest suspense; what will that decision be? Alas! that any one should have the power to decide the right of a fellow being to himself! It is thought by many that he will be acquitted of the *great crime* of leaving a life of bondage, as the legal evidence is not thought sufficient to convict him. But it is only too probable that they will sacrifice him to propitiate the South, since so many at the North dared oppose the passage of the infamous Nebraska Bill.—Miss Putnam was married this evening. Mr. Frothingham performed the ceremony, and in his prayer alluded touchingly to the events of this week; he afterwards in conversation with the bridegroom, (Mr. Gilliard), spoke in the most feeling manner about this case;—his sympathies are all on the right side. The wedding was a pleasant one; the bride looked very lovely; and we enjoyed ourselves as much as is possible in these exciting times. It is impossible to be happy now.

Friday, June 2.   Our worst fears are realized; the decision was against poor Burns, and he has been sent back to a bondage worse, a thousand times worse than death. Even an attempt at rescue was utterly impossible; the prisoner was completely surrounded by soldiers with bayonets fixed, a cannon loaded, ready to be fired at the slightest sign. To-day Massachusetts has again been disgraced; again has she shewed her submission to the Slave Power; and Oh! with what deep sorrow do we think of what will doubtless be the fate of that poor man, when he is again consigned to the horrors of Slavery. With what scorn must that government be regarded, which cowardly assembles thousands of soldiers to satisfy the demands of slaveholders; to deprive of his freedom a man, created in God's own image, whose sole offense is the color of his skin! And if resistance is offered to this outrage, these soldiers are to shoot down American citizens without mercy; and this by the express orders of a government which proudly boasts of being the freeest [*sic*] in the world; this on the very soil where the Revolution of 1776 began; in sight of the battle-field, were thousands of brave men fought and died in opposing British tyranny, which was nothing compared with the American oppression of to-day. In looking over my diary, I perceive that I did not mention that there was on the Friday night after the man's arrest, an attempt made to rescue him, but although it failed, on account of there not being men enough engaged in it, all honor should be given to those who bravely made the attempt. I can write no more. A cloud seems hanging over me, over all our persecuted race, which nothing can dispel.

Saturday, June 17.   A bad headache has prevented my enjoying the fine weather to-day, or taking as much exercise as I generally do. Did some sewing on my return from school.—Read the Liberator, then practiced a music lesson. . . . In the evening Miss [Sarah] Remond read aloud Mr. Frothingham's Sermon, whose stern truths shocked so many of his congregation. We, of course, were deeply interested in it, and felt grateful to this truly Christian minister for his eloquent defence of oppressed humanity. While Miss R[emond] was reading, Miss Osborne came in, and said she believed that we never talked or read anything but Anti-Slavery; she was quite tired of it. We assured her that she could never hear anything better; and said it was natural that we should speak and read much, on a subject so interesting to us. . . .

Sunday, June 25.   Have been writing nearly all day.— This afternoon went to an Anti-Slavery meeting in Danvers, from which I have just returned. Mr. Foss spoke eloquently, and with that warmth and sincerity which evidently come from the heart. He said he was rejoiced that the people at the North were beginning to feel that slavery is no longer confined to the black man alone, but that they too must wear the yoke; and they are becoming roused on the subject at last. He spoke of the objections made by many to the Abolitionists, on the plea of their using too violent language; they say that the slaveholders are driven by it to worse measures; what they need is mild entreaty, etc., etc. But the petition against the Nebraska Bill, couched in the very mildest terms by the clergymen of the North, was received even less favorably by the South, than the hardest sayings of the Abolitionists; and they were abused and denounced more severely than the latter have ever been.—As we walked home, Miss [Sarah] Remond and I were wishing that we could have an anti-slavery meeting in the neighborhood every Sunday, and as well attended as this was. . . .

Gertrude Bustill Mossell (1855–1948)

Born in Philadelphia to a prominent free Quaker family, Gertrude Bustill Mossell was an influential journalist and women's rights crusader. Like Charlotte Forten Grimké's family, Mossell was a member of the Philadelphia Female Anti-Slavery Society. Other well-known activists in Mossell's family included her cousin, activist and actor Paul Robeson. Three decades before Virginia Woolf wrote "A Room of One's Own" (1929), Mossell published "A Lofty Study," an essay that argues that women writers need space and money.

A Lofty Study

In these days of universal scribbling, when almost every one writes for fame or money, many people who are not reaping large pecuniary profits from their work do not feel justified in making any outlay to gratify the necessities of their labors in literature.

Every one engaged in literary work, even if but to a limited extent, feels greatly the need of a quiet nook to write in. Each portion of the home seems to have its clearly defined use, that will prevent their achieving the desired result. A few weeks ago, in the course of my travels, I came across an excellent idea carried into practical operation, that had accomplished the much-desired result of a quiet spot for literary work, without the disarrangement of a single portion of the household economy. In calling at the house of a member of the Society of Friends, I was ushered first into the main library on the first floor. Not finding in it the article sought, the owner invited me to walk upstairs to an upper library. I continued my ascent until we reached the attic. This had been utilized in such a way that it formed a comfortable and acceptable study. I made a mental note of my surroundings. The room was a large sloping attic chamber. It contained two windows, one opening on a roof; another faced the door: a skylight had been cut directly overhead, in the middle of the room. Around the ceiling on the side that was not sloping ran a line of tiny closets with glass doors. Another side had open shelves. On the sloping side, drawers rose from the floor a convenient distance. The remaining corner had a desk built in the wall; it was large and substantial, containing many drawers. Two small portable tables were close at hand near the centre.

An easy chair, an old-fashioned sofa with a large square cushion for a pillow, completed the furniture of this unassuming study. Neatness, order, comfort reigned supreme. Not a sound from the busy street reached us. It was so quiet, so peaceful, the air was so fresh and pure, it seemed like living in a new atmosphere.

I just sat down and wondered why I had never thought of this very room for a study. Almost every family has an unused attic, dark, sloping, given up to odds and ends. Now let it be papered with a creamy paper, with narrow stripes, giving the impression of height; a crimson velvety border. Paint the woodwork a darker shade of yellow, hang a buff and crimson portiére at the door. Put in an open grate; next widen the windowsills, and place on them boxes of flowering plants. Get an easy chair, a desk that suits your height, and place by its side a revolving bookcase, with the books most used in it. Let an adjustable lamp stand by its side, and with a nice old-fashioned sofa, well supplied with cushions, you will have a study that a queen might envy you. Bright, airy, cheerful, and almost noiseless, not easy of access to those who would come only to disturb, and far enough away to be cosy and inviting, conferring a certain privilege on the invited guest.

These suggestions can be improved upon, but the one central idea, a place to one's self without disturbing the household economy, would be gained.

Even when there is a library in the home, it is used by the whole family, and if the husband is literary in his tastes, he often desires to occupy it exclusively at the very time you have leisure, perhaps. Men are so often educated to work alone that even sympathetic companionship annoys. Very selfish, we say, but we often find it so—and therefore the necessity of a study of one's own.

If even this odd room cannot be utilized for your purposes, have at least your own corner in some cheerful room. A friend who edits a special department in a *weekly* has in her own chamber a desk with plenty of drawers and small separate compartments. The desk just fits in an alcove of the room, with a revolving-chair in front. What a satisfaction to put everything in order, turn the key, and feel that all is safe—no busy hands, no stray breeze can carry away or disarrange some choice idea kept for the future delectation of the public! Besides this, one who writes much generally finds that she can write best at some certain spot. Ideas come more rapidly, sentences take more lucid forms. Very often the least change from that position will break up the train of thought.

Anna Julia Cooper (1858–1964)

At a time when most African American women did well to finish high school, Anna Julia Cooper did teacher training at St. Augustine, the North Carolina school for ex-slaves; earned her A.B. and M.A. from Oberlin College, and earned a Ph.D. from the Sorbonne. Born in Raleigh, North Carolina, to a slave mother and her master, Cooper spent her life arguing for the rights of women. She made a special case for black women—"Only the Black Woman can say when and where I enter, in the quiet, undisputed dignity of my womanhood, without violence and without suing or special patronage, then and there the whole Negro race enters with me" ("Womanhood a Vital Element in the Regeneration and Progress of a Race"). Cooper published what is considered the first book-length black feminist text, *A Voice From the South*.

When Cooper entered St. Augustine's in 1867, she protested the fact that some classes, such as Greek, were for males only. She ended up marrying her Greek teacher, George A. C. Cooper, who died in 1879. Cooper went on to Oberlin College, where she eventually earned two degrees. During the course of her studies, she taught briefly at Wilberforce, as Frances Ellen Watkins Harper and Elizabeth Keckley had done. Later, Cooper became principal of the "M" Street High School in Washington, D.C., a popular school for African American leaders. Cooper lived over 105 years and had many notable achievements. Along with Frances Ellen Watkins Harper and two other African American women, she spoke at the Women's Congress during the Columbian Exposition in Chicago; she was the only woman elected to be a member of the American Negro Academy; she attended the first Pan-African Conference in London; she earned her doctorate at age 65, the fourth African American woman to do so, writing her dissertation in French on "The Attitude of France toward Slavery during the Revolution." For nearly a decade, she was a college president, spearheading the short-lived Frelinghuysen University in Washington, D.C. Throughout her life, Cooper fought for educational equality and was an extraordinary advocate for African American women.

From *A Voice From the South*

Womanhood a Vital Element in the Regeneration and Progress of a Race

The two sources from which, perhaps, modern civilization has derived its noble and ennobling ideal of woman are Christianity and the Feudal System.

In Oriental countries woman has been uniformly devoted to a life of ignorance, infamy, and complete stagnation. The Chinese shoe of to-day does not more entirely dwarf, cramp, and destroy her physical powers, than have the customs, laws, and social instincts, which from remotest ages have governed our Sister of the East, enervated and blighted her mental and moral life.

Mahomet makes no account of woman whatever in his polity. The Koran, which, unlike our Bible, was a product and not a growth, tried to address itself to the needs of Arabian civilization as Mahomet with his circumscribed powers saw them. The Arab was a nomad. Home to him meant his present camping place. That deity who, according to our western ideals, makes and sanctifies the home, was to him a transient bauble to be toyed with so long as it gave pleasure and then to be thrown aside for a new one. As a personality, an individual soul, capable of eternal growth and unlimited development, and destined to mould and shape the civilization of the future to an incalculable extent, Mahomet did not know woman. There was no hereafter, no paradise for her. The heaven of the Mussulman is peopled and made gladsome not by the departed wife, or sister, or mother, but by *houri* — a figment of Mahomet's brain, partaking of the ethereal qualities of angels, yet imbued with all the vices and inanity of

From *A Voice from the South*.

Oriental women. The harem here, and—"dust to dust" hereafter, this was the hope, the inspiration, the *summum bonum* of the Eastern woman's life! With what result on the life of the nation, the "Unspeakable Turk," the "sick man" of modern Europe can to-day exemplify.

Says a certain writer: "The private life of the Turk is vilest of the vile, unprogressive, unambitious, and inconceivably low." And yet Turkey is not without her great men. She has produced most brilliant minds; men skilled in all the intricacies of diplomacy and statesmanship; men whose intellects could grapple with the deep problems of empire and manipulate the subtle agencies which check-mate kings. But these minds were not the normal outgrowth of a healthy trunk. They seemed rather ephemeral excrescencies which shoot far out with all the vigor and promise, apparently, of strong branches; but soon alas fall into decay and ugliness because there is no soundness in the root, no life-giving sap, permeating, strengthening and perpetuating the whole. There is a worm at the core! The homelife is impure! and when we look for fruit, like apples of Sodom, it crumbles within our grasp into dust and ashes.

It is pleasing to turn from this effete and immobile civilization to a society still fresh and vigorous, whose seed is in itself, and whose very name is synonymous with all that is progressive, elevating and inspiring, viz., the European bud and the American flower of modern civilization.

And here let me say parenthetically that our satisfaction in American institutions rests not on the fruition we now enjoy, but springs rather from the possibilities and promise that are inherent in the system, though as yet, perhaps, far in the future.

"Happiness," says Madame de Stael, "consists not in perfections attained, but in a sense of progress, the result of our own endeavor under conspiring circumstances *toward* a goal which continually advances and broadens and deepens till it is swallowed up in the Infinite." Such conditions in embryo are all that we claim for the land of the West. We have not yet reached our ideal in American civilization. The pessimists even declare that we are not marching in that direction. But there can be no doubt that here in America is the arena in which the next triumph of civilization is to be won; and here too we find promise abundant and possibilities infinite.

Now let us see on what basis this hope for our country primarily and fundamentally rests. Can any one doubt that it is chiefly on the homelife and on the influence of good women in those homes? Says Macaulay: "You may judge a nation's rank in the scale of civilization from the way they treat their women." And Emerson, "I have thought that a sufficient measure of civilization is the influence of good women." Now this high regard for woman, this germ of a prolific idea which in our own day is bearing such rich and

varied fruit, was ingrafted into European civilization, we have said, from two sources, the Christian Church and the Feudal System. For although the Feudal System can in no sense be said to have originated the idea, yet there can be no doubt that the habits of life and modes of thought to which Feudalism gave rise, materially fostered and developed it; for they gave us chivalry, than which no institution has more sensibly magnified and elevated woman's position in society.

Tacitus dwells on the tender regard for woman entertained by these rugged barbarians before they left their northern homes to overrun Europe. Old Norse legends too, and primitive poems, all breathe the same spirit of love of home and veneration for the pure and noble influence there presiding—the wife, the sister, the mother.

And when later on we see the settled life of the Middle Ages "oozing out," as M. Guizot expresses it, from the plundering and pillaging life of barbarism and crystallizing into the Feudal System, the tiger of the field is brought once more within the charmed circle of the goddesses of his castle, and his imagination weaves around them a halo whose reflection possibly has not yet altogether vanished.

It is true the spirit of Christianity had not yet put the seal of catholicity on this sentiment. Chivalry, according to Bascom, was but the toning down and softening of a rough and lawless period. It gave a roseate glow to a bitter winter's day. Those who looked out from castle windows revelled in its "amethyst tints." But God's poor, the weak, the unlovely, the commonplace were still freezing and starving none the less in unpitied, unrelieved loneliness.

Respect for woman, the much lauded chivalry of the Middle Ages, meant what I fear it still means to some men in our own day—respect for the elect few among whom they expect to consort.

The idea of the radical amelioration of womankind, reverence for woman as woman regardless of rank, wealth, or culture, was to come from that rich and bounteous fountain from which flow all our liberal and universal ideas—the Gospel of Jesus Christ.

And yet the Christian Church at the time of which we have been speaking would seem to have been doing even less to protect and elevate woman than the little done by secular society. The Church as an organization committed a double offense against woman in the Middle Ages. Making of marriage a sacrament and at the same time insisting on the celibacy of the clergy and other religious orders, she gave an inferior if not an impure character to the marriage relation, especially fitted to reflect discredit on woman. Would this were all or the worst! but the Church by the licentiousness of its chosen servants invaded the household and established too often as vicious connections those relations which it forbade to assume openly and in good faith. "Thus," to use the words of our authority, "the religious corps became as numerous, as searching, and as unclean as the frogs of Egypt, which penetrated into all quarters, into the ovens and kneading troughs, leaving their filthy trail wherever they went." Says Chaucer with characteristic satire, speaking of the Friars:

'Women may now go safely up and doun
In every bush, and under every tree,
Ther is non other incubus but he,
And he ne will don hem no dishonour.'

Henry, Bishop of Liege, could unblushingly boast the birth of twenty-two children in fourteen years.

It may help us under some of the perplexities which beset our way in "the one Catholic and Apostolic Church" to-day, to recall some of the corruptions and incongruities against which the Bride of Christ has had to struggle in her past history and in spite of which she has kept, through many vicissitudes, the faith once delivered to the saints. Individuals, organizations, whole sections of the Church militant may outrage the Christ whom they profess, may ruthlessly trample under foot both the spirit and the letter of his precepts, yet not till we hear the voices audibly saying "Come let us depart hence," shall we cease to believe and cling to the promise, "*I am with you to the end of the world.*"

"Yet saints their watch are keeping,
The cry goes up 'How long!'
And soon the night of weeping
Shall be the morn of song."

However much then the facts of any particular period of history may seem to deny it, I for one do not doubt that the source of the vitalizing principle of woman's development and amelioration is the Christian Church, so far as that church is coincident with Christianity.

Christ gave ideals not formulæ. The Gospel is a germ requiring millennia for its growth and ripening. It needs and at the same time helps to form around itself a soil enriched in civilization, and perfected in culture and insight without which the embryo can neither be unfolded or comprehended. With all the strides our civilization has made from the first to the nineteenth century, we can boast not an idea, not a principle of action, not a progressive social force but was already mutely foreshadowed, or directly enjoined in that simple tale of a meek and lowly life. The quiet face of the Nazarene is ever seen a little way ahead, never too far to come down to and touch the life of the lowest in days the darkest, yet ever leading onward, still onward, the tottering childish feet of our strangely boastful civilization.

By laying down for woman the same code of morality, the same standard of purity, as for man; by refusing to countenance the shameless and equally guilty monsters who were gloating over her fall,—graciously stooping in all the majesty of his own spotlessness to wipe away the filth and grime of her guilty past and bid her go in peace and sin no more; and again in the moments of his own careworn and footsore dejection, turning trustfully and lovingly, away from the heartless snubbing and sneers, away from the cruel malignity of mobs and prelates in the dusty marts of Jerusalem to the ready sympathy, loving appreciation and unfaltering friendship of that quiet home at Bethany; and even at the last, by his dying bequest to the disciple whom he loved, signifying the protection and tender regard to be extended to that sorrowing mother and ever afterward to the sex she represented;—throughout his life and in his death he has given to men a rule and guide for the estimation of woman as an equal, as a helper, as a friend, and as a sacred charge to be sheltered and cared for with a brother's love and sympathy, lessons which nineteen centuries' gigantic strides in knowledge, arts, and sciences, in social and ethical principles have not been able to probe to their depth or to exhaust in practice.

It seems not too much to say then of the vitalizing, regenerating, and progressive influence of womanhood on the civilization of today, that, while it was foreshadowed among Germanic nations in the far away dawn of their history as a narrow, sickly and stunted growth, it yet owes its catholicity and power, the deepening of its roots and broadening of its branches to Christianity.

The union of these two forces, the Barbaric and the Christian, was not long delayed after the Fall of the Empire. The Church, which fell with Rome, finding herself in danger of being swallowed up by barbarism, with characteristic vigor and fertility of resources, addressed herself immediately to the task of conquering her conquerers. The means chosen does credit to her power of penetration and adaptability, as well as to her profound, unerring, all-compassing diplomacy; and makes us even now wonder if aught human can successfully and ultimately withstand her far-seeing designs and brilliant policy, or gainsay her well-earned claim to the word *Catholic*.

She saw the barbarian, little more developed than a wild beast. She forbore to antagonize and mystify his warlike nature by a full blaze of the heartsearching and humanizing tenets of her great Head. She said little of the rule "If thy brother smite thee on one cheek, turn to him the other also;" but thought it sufficient for the needs of those times, to establish the so-called "Truce of God" under which men were bound to abstain from butchering one another for three days of each week and on Church festivals. In other words, she respected their individuality: non-resistance pure and simple being for them an utter impossibility, she contented herself with less radical measures calculated to lead up finally to the full measure of the benevolence of Christ.

Next she took advantage of the barbarian's sensuous love of gaudy display and put all her magnificent garments on. She could not capture him by physical force, she would dazzle him by gorgeous spectacles. It is said that Romanism gained more in pomp and ritual during this trying period of the Dark Ages than throughout all her former history.

The result was she carried her point. Once more Rome laid her ambitious hand on the temporal power, and allied with Charlemagne, aspired to rule the world through a civilization dominated by Christianity and permeated by the traditions and instincts of those sturdy barbarians.

Here was the confluence of the two streams we have been tracing, which, united now, stretch before us as a broad majestic river. In regard to woman it was the meeting of two noble and ennobling forces, two kindred ideas the resultant of which, we doubt not, is destined to be a potent force in the betterment of the world.

Now after our appeal to history comparing nations destitute of this force and so destitute also of the principle of progress, with other nations among whom the influence of woman is prominent coupled with a brisk, progressive, satisfying civilization,—if in addition we find this strong presumptive evidence corroborated by reason and experience, we may conclude that these two equally varying concomitants are linked as cause and effect; in other words, that the position of woman in society determines the vital elements of its regeneration and progress.

Now that this is so on *a priori* grounds all must admit. And this not because woman is better or stronger or wiser than man, but from the nature of the case, because it is she who must first form the man by directing the earliest impulses of his character.

Byron and Wordsworth were both geniuses and would have stamped themselves on the thought of their age under any circumstances; and yet we find the one a savor of life unto life, the other of death unto death. "Byron, like a rocket, shot his way upward with scorn and repulsion, flamed out in wild, explosive, brilliant excesses and disappeared in darkness made all the more palpable."*

Wordsworth lent of his gifts to reinforce that "power in the Universe which makes for righteousness" by taking the harp handed him from Heaven and using it to swell the strains of angelic choirs. Two locomotives equally mighty stand facing opposite tracks; the one to rush headlong to destruction with all its precious freight, the other to toil grandly and gloriously up the steep embattlements to Heaven and to

God. Who—who can say what a world of consequences hung on the first placing and starting of these enormous forces!

Woman, Mother,—your responsibility is one that might make angels tremble and fear to take hold! To trifle with it, to ignore or misuse it, is to treat lightly the most sacred and solemn trust ever confided by God to human kind. The training of children is a task on which an infinity of weal or woe depends. Who does not covet it? Yet who does not stand awe-struck before its momentous issues! It is a matter of small moment, it seems to me, whether that lovely girl in whose accomplishments you take such pride and delight, can enter the gay and crowded salon with the ease and elegance of this or that French or English gentlewoman, compared with the decision as to whether her individuality is going to reinforce the good or the evil elements of the world. The lace and the diamonds, the dance and the theater, gain a new significance when scanned in their bearings on such issues. Their influence on the individual personality, and through her on the society and civilization which she vitalizes and inspires—all this and more must be weighed in the balance before the jury can return a just and intelligent verdict as to the innocence or banefulness of these apparently simple amusements.

Now the fact of woman's influence on society being granted, what are its practical bearings on the work which brought together this conference of colored clergy and laymen in Washington? "We come not here to talk." Life is too busy, too pregnant with meaning and far reaching consequences to allow you to come this far for mere intellectual entertainment.

The vital agency of womanhood in the regeneration and progress of a race, as a general question, is conceded almost before it is fairly stated. I confess one of the difficulties for me in the subject assigned lay in its obviousness. The plea is taken away by the opposite attorney's granting the whole question.

"Woman's influence on social progress"—who in Christendom doubts or questions it? One may as well be called on to prove that the sun is the source of light and heat and energy to this many-sided little world.

Nor, on the other hand, could it have been intended that I should apply the position when taken and proven, to the needs and responsibilities of the women of our race in the South. For is it not written, "Cursed is he that cometh after the king?" and has not the King already preceded me in "The Black Woman of the South"?*

They have had both Moses and the Prophets in Dr. Crummell and if they hear not him, neither would they be persuaded though one came up from the South.

I would beg, however, with the Doctor's permission, to add my plea for the *Colored Girls* of the South:—that large, bright, promising fatally beautiful class that stand shivering

---

*Bascom's Eng. Lit. p. 253 (Cooper's note).

*"Pamphlet published by Dr. Alex Crummell" (Cooper's note).

like a delicate plantlet before the fury of tempestuous elements, so full of promise and possibilities, yet so sure of destruction; often without a father to whom they dare apply the loving term, often without a stronger brother to espouse their cause and defend their honor with his life's blood; in the midst of pitfalls and snares, waylaid by the lower classes of white men, with no shelter, no protection nearer than the great blue vault above, which half conceals and half reveals the one Care-Taker they know so little of. Oh, save them, help them, shield, train, develop, teach, inspire them! Snatch them, in God's name, as brands from the burning! There is material in them well worth your while, the hope in germ of a staunch, helpful, regenerating womanhood on which, primarily, rests the foundation stones of our future as a race.

It is absurd to quote statistics showing the Negro's bank account and rent rolls, to point to the hundreds of newspapers edited by colored men and lists of lawyers, doctors, professors, D. D's, LL D's, etc., etc., etc., while the source from which the life-blood of the race is to flow is subject to taint and corruption in the enemy's camp.

True progress is never made by spasms. Real progress is growth. It must begin in the seed. Then, "first the blade, then the ear, after that the full corn in the ear." There is something to encourage and inspire us in the advancement of individuals since their emancipation from slavery. It at least proves that there is nothing irretrievably wrong in the shape of the black man's skull, and that under given circumstances his development, downward or upward, will be similar to that of other average human beings.

But there is no time to be wasted in mere felicitation. That the Negro has his niche in the infinite purposes of the Eternal, no one who has studied the history of the last fifty years in America will deny. That much depends on his own right comprehension of his responsibility and rising to the demands of the hour, it will be good for him to see; and how best to use his present so that the structure of the future shall be stronger and higher and brighter and nobler and holier than that of the past, is a question to be decided each day by every one of us.

The race is just twenty-one years removed from the conception and experience of a chattel, just at the age of ruddy manhood. It is well enough to pause a moment for retrospection, introspection, and prospection. We look back, not to become inflated with conceit because of the depths from which we have arisen, but that we may learn wisdom from experience. We look within that we may gather together once more our forces, and, by improved and more practical methods, address ourselves to the tasks before us. We look forward with hope and trust that the same God whose guiding hand led our fathers through and out of the gall and bitterness of oppression, will still lead and direct their children, to the honor of His name, and for their ultimate salvation.

But this survey of the failures or achievements of the past, the difficulties and embarrassments of the present, and the mingled hopes and fears for the future, must not degenerate into mere dreaming nor consume the time which belongs to the practical and effective handling of the crucial questions of the hour; and there can be no issue more vital and momentous than this of the womanhood of the race.

Here is the vulnerable point, not in the heel, but at the heart of the young Achilles; and here must the defenses be strengthened and the watch redoubled.

We are the heirs of a past which was not our fathers' moulding. "Every man the arbiter of his own destiny" was not true for the American Negro of the past: and it is no fault of his that he finds himself to-day the inheritor of a manhood and womanhood impoverished and debased by two centuries and more of compression and degradation.

But weaknesses and malformations, which to-day are attributable to a vicious schoolmaster and a pernicious system, will a century hence be rightly regarded as proofs of innate corruptness and radical incurability.

Now the fundamental agency under God in the regeneration, the re-training of the race, as well as the ground work and starting point of its progress upward, must be the *black woman*.

With all the wrongs and neglects of her past, with all the weakness, the debasement, the moral thralldom of her present, the black woman of to-day stands mute and wondering at the Herculean task devolving upon her. But the cycles wait for her. No other hand can move the lever. She must be loosed from her bands and set to work.

Our meager and superficial results from past efforts prove their futility; and every attempt to elevate the Negro, whether undertaken by himself or through the philanthropy of others, cannot but prove abortive unless so directed as to utilize the indispensable agency of an elevated and trained womanhood.

A race cannot be purified from without. Preachers and teachers are helps, and stimulants and conditions as necessary as the gracious rain and sunshine are to plant growth. But what are rain and dew and sunshine and cloud if there be no life in the plant germ? We must go to the root and see that that is sound and healthy and vigorous; and not deceive ourselves with waxen flowers and painted leaves of mock chlorophyll.

We too often mistake individuals' honor for race development and so are ready to substitute pretty accomplishments for sound sense and earnest purpose.

A stream cannot rise higher than its source. The atmosphere of homes is no rarer and purer and sweeter than are the mothers in those homes. A race is but a total of families. The nation is the aggregate of its homes. As the whole is sum of all its parts, so the character of the parts will determine the characteristics of the whole. These are all axioms and so evident that it seems gratuitous to remark it; and yet, unless I am greatly mistaken, most of the unsatisfaction from our past results arises from just such a radical and palpable error, as much almost on our own part as on that of our benevolent white friends.

The Negro is constitutionally hopeful and proverbially irrepressible; and naturally stands in danger of being dazzled by the shimmer and tinsel of superficials. We often mistake foliage for fruit and overestimate or wrongly estimate brilliant results.

The late Martin R. Delany, who was an unadulterated black man, used to say when honors of state fell upon him, that when he entered the council of kings the black race entered with him; meaning, I suppose, that there was no discounting his race identity and attributing his achievements to some admixture of Saxon blood. But our present record of eminent men, when placed beside the actual status of the race in America to-day, proves that no man can represent the race. Whatever the attainments of the individual may be, unless his home has moved on *pari passu*, he can never be regarded as identical with or representative of the whole.

Not by pointing to sun-bathed mountain tops do we prove that Phœbus warms the valleys. We must point to homes, average homes, homes of the rank and file of horny handed toiling men and women of the South (where the masses are) lighted and cheered by the good, the beautiful, and the true,—then and not till then will the whole plateau be lifted into the sunlight.

Only the BLACK WOMAN can say "when and where I enter, in the quiet, undisputed dignity of my womanhood, without violence and without suing or special patronage, then and there the whole *Negro race enters with me*." Is it not evident then that as individual workers for this race we must address ourselves with no half-hearted zeal to this feature of our mission. The need is felt and must be recognized by all. There is a call for workers, for missionaries, for men and women with the double consecration of a fundamental love of humanity and a desire for its melioration through the Gospel; but superadded to this we demand an intelligent and sympathetic comprehension of the interests and special needs of the Negro.

I see not why there should not be an organized effort for the protection and elevation of our girls such as the White Cross League in England. English women are strengthened and protected by more than twelve centuries of Christian influences, freedom and civilization; English girls are dispirited and crushed down by no such all-levelling prejudice as that supercilious caste spirit in America which cynically assumes "A Negro woman cannot be a lady." English womanhood is beset by no such snares and traps as betray the unprotected, untrained colored girl of the South, whose only crime and

dire destruction often is her unconscious and marvelous beauty. Surely then if English indignation is aroused and English manhood thrilled under the leadership of a Bishop of the English church to build up bulwarks around their wronged sisters, Negro sentiment cannot remain callous and Negro effort nerveless in view of the imminent peril of the mothers of the next generation. "*I am my Sister's keeper!*" should be the hearty response of every man and woman of the race, and this conviction should purify and exalt the narrow, selfish and petty personal aims of life into a noble and sacred purpose.

We need men who can let their interest and gallantry extend outside the circle of their æsthetic appreciation; men who can be a father, a brother, a friend to every weak, struggling unshielded girl. We need women who are so sure of their own social footing that they need not fear leaning to lend a hand to a fallen or falling sister. We need men and women who do not exhaust their genius splitting hairs on aristocratic distinctions and thanking God they are not as others; but earnest, unselfish souls, who can go into the highways and byways, lifting up and leading, advising and encouraging with the truly catholic benevolence of the Gospel of Christ.

As Church workers we must confess our path of duty is less obvious; or rather our ability to adapt our machinery to our conception of the peculiar exigencies of this work as taught by experience and our own consciousness of the needs of the Negro, is as yet not demonstrable. Flexibility and aggressiveness are not such strong characteristics of the Church to-day as in the Dark Ages.

As a Mission field for the Church the Southern Negro is in some aspects most promising; in others, perplexing. Aliens neither in language and customs, nor in associations and sympathies, naturally of deeply rooted religious instincts and taking most readily and kindly to the worship and teachings of the Church, surely the task of proselytizing the American Negro is infinitely less formidable than that which confronted the Church in the Barbarians of Europe. Besides, this people already look to the Church as the hope of their race. Thinking colored men almost uniformly admit that the Protestant Episcopal Church with its quiet, chaste dignity and decorous solemnity, its instructive and elevating ritual, its bright chanting and joyous hymning, is eminently fitted to correct the peculiar faults of worship—the rank exuberance and often ludicrous demonstrativeness of their people. Yet, strange to say, the Church, claiming to be missionary and Catholic, urging that schism is sin and denominationalism inexcusable, has made in all these years almost no inroads upon this semi-civilized religionism.

Harvests from this over ripe field of home missions have been gathered in by Methodists, Baptists, and not least by

Congregationalists, who were unknown to the Freedmen before their emancipation.

Our clergy numbers less than two dozen* priests of Negro blood and we have hardly more than one self-supporting colored congregation in the entire Southland. While the organization known as the A. M. E. Church has 14,063 ministers, itinerant and local, 4,069 self-supporting churches, 4,275 Sunday-schools, with property valued at $7,772,284, raising yearly for church purposes $1,427,000.

Stranger and more significant than all, the leading men of this race (I do not mean demagogues and politicians, but men of intellect, heart, and race devotion, men to whom the elevation of their people means more than personal ambition and sordid gain—and the men of that stamp have not all died yet) the Christian workers for the race, of younger and more cultured growth, are noticeably drifting into sectarian churches, many of them declaring all the time that they acknowledge the historic claims of the Church, believe her apostolicity, and would experience greater personal comfort, spiritual and intellectual, in her revered communion. It is a fact which any one may verify for himself, that representative colored men, professing that in their heart of hearts they are Episcopalians, are actually working in Methodist and Baptist pulpits; while the ranks of the Episcopal clergy are left to be filled largely by men who certainly suggest the propriety of a "*perpetual* Diaconate" if they cannot be said to have created the necessity for it.

Now where is the trouble? Something must be wrong. What is it?

A certain Southern Bishop of our Church reviewing the situation, whether in Godly anxiety or in "Gothic antipathy" I know not, deprecates the fact that the colored people do not seem *drawn* to the Episcopal Church, and comes to the sage conclusion that the Church is not adapted to the rude untutored minds of the Freedmen, and that they may be left to go to the Methodists and Baptists whither their racial proclivities undeniably tend. How the good Bishop can agree that all-foreseeing Wisdom, and Catholic Love would have framed his Church as typified in his seamless garment and unbroken body, and yet not leave it broad enough and deep enough and loving enough to seek and save and hold seven millions of God's poor, I cannot see.

But the doctors while discussing their scientifically conclusive diagnosis of the disease, will perhaps not think it presumptuous in the patient if he dares to suggest where at least the pain is. If this be allowed, a *Black woman of the South* would beg to

point out two possible oversights in this southern work which may indicate in part both a cause and a remedy for some failure. The first is *not calculating for the Black man's personality*; not having respect, if I may so express it, to his manhood or deferring at all to his conceptions of the needs of his people. When colored persons have been employed it was too often as machines or as manikins. There has been no disposition, generally, to get the black man's ideal or to let his individuality work by its own gravity, as it were. A conference of earnest Christian men have met at regular intervals for some years past to discuss the best methods of promoting the welfare and development of colored people in this country. Yet, strange as it may seem, they have never invited a colored man or even intimated that one would be welcome to take part in their deliberations. Their remedial contrivances are purely theoretical or empirical, therefore, and the whole machinery devoid of soul.

The second important oversight in my judgment is closely allied to this and probably grows out of it, and that is not developing Negro womanhood as an essential fundamental for the elevation of the race, and utilizing this agency in extending the work of the Church.

Of the first I have possibly already presumed to say too much since it does not strictly come within the province of my subject. However, Macaulay somewhere criticises the Church of England as not knowing how to use fanatics, and declares that had Ignatius Loyola been in the Anglican instead of the Roman communion, the Jesuits would have been schismatics instead of Catholics; and if the religious awakenings of the Wesleys had been in Rome, she would have shaven their heads, tied ropes around their waists, and sent them out under her own banner and blessing. Whether this be true or not, there is certainly a vast amount of force potential for Negro evangelization rendered latent, or worse, antagonistic by the halting, uncertain, I had almost said, *trimming* policy of the Church in the South. This may sound both presumptuous and ungrateful. It is mortifying, I know, to benevolent wisdom, after having spent itself in the execution of well conned theories for the ideal development of a particular work, to hear perhaps the weakest and humblest element of that work asking "what doest thou?"

Yet so it will be in life. The "thus far and no farther" pattern cannot be fitted to any growth in God's kingdom. The universal law of development is "onward and upward." It is God-given and inviolable. From the unfolding of the germ in the acorn to reach the sturdy oak, to the growth of a human soul into the full knowledge and likeness of its Creator, the breadth and scope of the movement in each and all are too grand, too mysterious, too like God himself, to be encompassed and locked down in human molds.

After all the Southern slave owners were right: either the very alphabet of intellectual growth must be forbidden and

---

*The published report of '91 shows 26 priests for the entire country, including one not engaged in work and one a professor in a non-sectarian school, since made Dean of an episcopal Annex to Howard University known as King Hall (Cooper's note).

the Negro dealt with absolutely as a chattel having neither rights nor sensibilities; or else the clamps and irons of mental and moral, as well as civil compression must be riven asunder and the truly enfranchised soul led to the entrance of that boundless vista through which it is to toil upwards to its beckoning God as the buried seed germ to meet the sun.

A perpetual colored diaconate, carefully and kindly superintended by the white clergy; congregations of shiny faced peasants with their clean white aprons and sunbonnets catechised at regular intervals and taught to recite the creed, the Lord's prayer and the ten commandments—duty towards God and duty towards neighbor, surely such well tended sheep ought to be grateful to their shepherds and content in that station of life to which it pleased God to call them. True, like the old professor lecturing to his solitary student, we make no provision here for irregularities. "Questions must be kept till after class," or dispensed with altogether. That some do ask questions and insist on answers, in class too, must be both impertinent and annoying. Let not our spiritual pastors and masters however be grieved at such self-assertion as merely signifies we have a destiny to fulfill and as men and women we must *be about our Father's business.*

It is a mistake to suppose that the Negro is prejudiced against a white ministry. Naturally there is not a more kindly and implicit follower of a white man's guidance than the average colored peasant. What would to others be an ordinary act of friendly or pastoral interest he would be more inclined to regard gratefully as a condescension. And he never forgets such kindness. Could the Negro be brought near to his white priest or bishop, he is not suspicious. He is not only willing but often longs to unburden his soul to this intelligent guide. There are no reservations when he is convinced that you are his friend. It is a saddening satire on American history and manners that it takes something to convince him.

That our people are not "drawn" to a church whose chief dignitaries they see only in the chancel, and whom they reverence as they would a painting or an angel, whose life never comes down to and touches theirs with the inspiration of an objective reality, may be "perplexing" truly (American caste and American Christianity both being facts) but it need not be surprising. There must be something of human nature in it, the same as that which brought about that "the Word was made flesh and dwelt among us" that He might "draw" us towards God.

Men are not "drawn" by abstractions. Only sympathy and love can draw, and until our Church in America realizes this and provides a clergy that can come in touch with our life and have a fellow feeling for our woes, without being imbedded and frozen up in their "Gothic antipathies," the good bishops are likely to continue "perplexed" by the sparsity of colored Episcopalians.

A colored priest of my acquaintance recently related to me, with tears in his eyes, how his reverend Father in God, the Bishop who had ordained him, had met him on the cars on his way to the diocesan convention and warned him, not unkindly, not to take a seat in the body of the convention with the white clergy. To avoid disturbance of their godly placidity he would of course please sit back and somewhat apart. I do not imagine that that clergyman had very much heart for the Christly (!) deliberations of that convention.

To return, however, it is not on this broader view of Church work, which I mentioned as a primary cause of its halting progress with the colored people, that I am to speak. My proper theme is the second oversight of which in my judgment our Christian propagandists have been guilty: or, the necessity of church training, protecting and uplifting our colored womanhood as indispensable to the evangelization of the race.

Apelles did not disdain even that criticism of his lofty art which came from an uncouth cobbler; and may I not hope that the writer's oneness with her subject both in feeling and in being may palliate undue obtrusiveness of opinions here. That the race cannot be effectually lifted up till its women are truly elevated we take as proven. It is not for us to dwell on the needs, the neglects, and the ways of succor, pertaining to the black woman of the South. The ground has been ably discussed and an admirable and practical plan proposed by the oldest Negro priest in America, advising and urging that special organizations such as Church Sisterhoods and industrial schools be devised to meet her pressing needs in the Southland. That some such movements are vital to the life of this people and the extension of the Church among them, is not hard to see. Yet the pamphlet fell still-born from the press. So far as I am informed the Church has made no motion towards carrying out Dr. Crummell's suggestion.

The denomination which comes next our own in opposing the proverbial emotionalism of Negro worship in the South, and which in consequence like ours receives the cold shoulder from the old heads, resting as we do under the charge of not "having religion" and not believing in conversion—the Congregationalists—have quietly gone to work on the young, have established industrial and training schools, and now almost every community in the South is yearly enriched by a fresh infusion of vigorous young hearts, cultivated heads, and helpful hands that have been trained at Fisk, at Hampton, in Atlanta University, and in Tuskegee, Alabama.

These young people are missionaries actual or virtual both here and in Africa. They have learned to love the methods and doctrines of the Church which trained and educated them; and so Congregationalism surely and steadily progresses.

Need I compare these well known facts with results shown by the Church in the same field and during the same or even a longer time.

The institution of the Church in the South to which she mainly looks for the training of her colored clergy and for the help of the "Black Woman" and "Colored Girl" of the South, has graduated since the year 1868, when the school was founded, *five young women*,* and while yearly numerous young men have been kept and trained for the ministry by the charities of the Church, the number of indigent females who have here been supported, sheltered and trained, is phenomenally small. Indeed, to my mind, the attitude of the Church toward this feature of her work is as if the solution of the problem of Negro missions depended solely on sending a quota of deacons and priests into the field, girls being a sort of *tertium quid* whose development may be promoted if they can pay their way and fall in with the plans *mapped out for the training of the other sex*. Now I would ask in all earnestness, does not this force potential deserve by education and stimulus to be made dynamic? Is it not a solemn duty incumbent on all colored churchmen to make it so? Will not the aid of the Church be given to prepare our girls in head, heart, and hand for the duties and responsibilities that await the intelligent wife, the Christian mother, the earnest, virtuous, helpful woman, at once both the lever and the fulcrum for uplifting the race.

As Negroes and churchmen we cannot be indifferent to these questions. They touch us most vitally on both sides. We believe in the Holy Catholic Church. We believe that however gigantic and apparently remote the consummation, the Church will go on conquering and to conquer till the kingdoms of this world, not excepting the black man and the black woman of the South, shall have become the kingdoms of the Lord and of his Christ.

That past work in this direction has been unsatisfactory we must admit. That without a change of policy results in the future will be as meagre, we greatly fear. Our life as a race is at stake. The dearest interests of our hearts are in the scales. We must either break away from dear old landmarks and plunge out in any line and every line that enables us to meet the pressing need of our people, or we must ask the Church to allow and help us, untrammelled by the prejudices and theories of individuals, to work agressively under her direction as we alone can, with God's help, for the salvation of our people.

The time is ripe for action. Self-seeking and ambition must be laid on the altar. The battle is one of sacrifice and hardship, but our duty is plain. We have been recipients of missionary bounty in some sort for twenty-one years. Not even the senseless vegetable is content to be a mere reservoir. Receiving without giving is an anomaly in nature. Nature's cells are all little workshops for manufacturing sunbeams, the product to be *given out* to earth's inhabitants in warmth, energy, thought, action. Inanimate creation always pays back an equivalent.

Now, *How much owest thou my Lord?* Will his account be overdrawn if he call for singleness of purpose and self-sacrificing labor for your brethren? Having passed through your drill school, will you refuse a general's commission even if it entail responsibility, risk and anxiety, with possibly some adverse criticism? Is it too much to ask you to step forward and direct the work for your race along those lines which you know to be of first and vital importance?

Will you allow these words of Ralph Waldo Emerson? "In ordinary," says he, "we have a snappish criticism which watches and contradicts the opposite party. We want the will which advances and dictates [acts]. Nature has made up her mind that what cannot defend itself, shall not be defended. Complaining never so loud and with never so much reason, is of no use. What cannot stand must fall; *and the measure of our sincerity and therefore of the respect of men is the amount of health and wealth we will hazard in the defense of our right.*"

The Status of Woman in America

Just four hundred years ago an obscure dreamer and castle builder, prosaically poor and ridiculously insistent on the reality of his dreams, was enabled through the devotion of a noble woman to give to civilization a magnificent continent.

What the lofty purpose of Spain's pure-minded queen had brought to the birth, the untiring devotion of pioneer women nourished and developed. The dangers of wild beasts and of wilder men, the mysteries of unknown wastes and unexplored forests, the horrors of pestilence and famine, of exposure and loneliness, during all those years of discovery and settlement, were braved without a murmur by women who had been most delicately constituted and most tenderly nurtured.

And when the times of physical hardship and danger were past, when the work of clearing and opening up was over and the struggle for accumulation began, again woman's inspiration and help were needed and still was she loyally at hand. A Mary Lyon, demanding and making possible equal advantages of education for women as for men, and, in the face of discouragement and incredulity, bequeathing to women the opportunities of Holyoke.

A Dorothea Dix, insisting on the humane and rational treatment of the insane and bringing about a reform in the

---

*Five have been graduated since '86, two in '91, two in '92 (Cooper's note).

lunatic asylums of the country, making a great step forward in the tender regard for the weak by the strong throughout the world.

A Helen Hunt Jackson, convicting the nation of a century of dishonor in regard to the Indian.

A Lucretia Mott, gentle Quaker spirit, with sweet insistence, preaching the abolition of slavery and the institution, in its stead, of the brotherhood of man; her life and words breathing out in tender melody the injunction

> "Have love. Not love alone for one
> But man as man thy brother call;
> And scatter, like the circling sun,
> Thy charities *on all.*"

And at the most trying time of what we have called the Accumulative Period, when internecine war, originated through man's love of gain and his determination to subordinate national interests and black men's rights alike to considerations of personal profit and loss, was drenching our country with its own best blood, who shall recount the name and fame of the women on both sides the senseless strife,—those uncomplaining souls with a great heart ache of their own, rigid features and pallid cheek their ever effective flag of truce, on the battle field, in the camp, in the hospital, binding up wounds, recording dying whispers for absent loved ones, with tearful eyes pointing to man's last refuge, giving the last earthly hand clasp and performing the last friendly office for strangers whom a great common sorrow had made kin, while they knew that somewhere—somewhere a husband, a brother, a father, a son, was being tended by stranger hands—or mayhap those familiar eyes were even then being closed forever by just such another ministering angel of mercy and love.

But why mention names? Time would fail to tell of the noble army of women who shine like beacon lights in the otherwise sordid wilderness of this accumulative period— prison reformers and tenement cleansers, quiet unnoted workers in hospitals and homes, among imbeciles, among outcasts—the sweetening, purifying antidotes for the poisons of man's acquisitiveness,—mollifying and soothing with the tenderness of compassion and love the wounds and bruises caused by his overreaching and avarice.

The desire for quick returns and large profits tempts capital ofttimes into unsanitary, well nigh inhuman investments,—tenement tinder boxes, stifling, stunting, sickening alleys and pestiferous slums; regular rents, no waiting, large percentages,—rich coffers coined out of the life-blood of human bodies and souls. Men and women herded together like cattle, breathing in malaria and typhus from an atmosphere seething with moral as well as physical impurity, revelling in vice as their native habitat and then, to drown the

whisperings of their higher consciousness and effectually to hush the yearnings and accusations within, flying to narcotics and opiates—rum, tobacco, opium, binding hand and foot, body and soul, till the proper image of God is transformed into a fit associate for demons,—a besotted, enervated, idiotic wreck, or else a monster of wickedness terrible and destructive.

These are some of the legitimate products of the unmitigated tendencies of the wealth-producing period. But, thank Heaven, side by side with the cold, mathematical, selfishly calculating, so-called practical and unsentimental instinct of the business man, there comes the sympathetic warmth and sunshine of good women, like the sweet and sweetening breezes of spring, cleansing, purifying, soothing, inspiring, lifting the drunkard from the gutter, the outcast from the pit. Who can estimate the influence of these "daughters of the king," these lend-a-hand forces, in counteracting the selfishness of an acquisitive age?

To-day America counts her millionaires by the thousand; questions of tariff and questions of currency are the most vital ones agitating the public mind. In this period, when material prosperity and well earned ease and luxury are assured facts from a national standpoint, woman's work and woman's influence are needed as never before; needed to bring a heart power into this money getting, dollar-worshipping civilization; needed to bring a moral force into the utilitarian motives and interests of the time; needed to stand for God and Home and Native Land *versus gain and greed and grasping selfishness.*

There can be no doubt that this fourth centenary of America's discovery which we celebrate at Chicago, strikes the keynote of another important transition in the history of this nation; and the prominence of woman in the management of its celebration is a fitting tribute to the part she is destined to play among the forces of the future. This is the first congressional recognition of woman in this country, and this Board of Lady Managers constitute the first women legally appointed by any government to act in a national capacity. This of itself marks the dawn of a new day.

Now the periods of discovery, of settlement, of developing resources and accumulating wealth have passed in rapid succession. Wealth in the nation as in the individual brings leisure, repose, reflection. The struggle with nature is over, the struggle with ideas begins. We stand then, it seems to me, in this last decade of the nineteenth century, just in the portals of a new and untried movement on a higher plain and in a grander strain than any the past has called forth. It does not require a prophet's eye to divine its trend and image its possibilities from the forces we see already at work around us; nor is it hard to guess what must be the status of woman's work under the new regime.

In the pioneer days her role was that of a camp-follower, an additional something to fight for and be burdened with, only repaying the anxiety and labor she called forth by her own incomparable gifts of sympathy and appreciative love; unable herself ordinarily to contend with the bear and the Indian, or to take active part in clearing the wilderness and constructing the home.

In the second or wealth producing period her work is abreast of man's, complementing and supplementing, counteracting excessive tendencies, and mollifying over rigorous proclivities.

In the era now about to dawn, her sentiments must strike the keynote and give the dominant tone. And this because of the nature of her contribution to the world.

Her kingdom is not over physical forces. Not by might, nor by power can she prevail. Her position must ever be inferior where strength of muscle creates leadership. If she follows the instincts of her nature, however, she must always stand for the conservation of those deeper moral forces which make for the happiness of homes and the righteousness of the country. In a reign of moral ideas she is easily queen.

There is to my mind no grander and surer prophecy of the new era and of woman's place in it, than the work already begun in the waning years of the nineteenth century by the W. C. T. U. in America, an organization which has even now reached not only national but international importance, and seems destined to permeate and purify the whole civilized world. It is the living embodiment of woman's activities and woman's ideas, and its extent and strength rightly prefigure her increasing power as a moral factor.

The colored woman of to-day occupies, one may say, a unique position in this country. In a period of itself transitional and unsettled, her status seems one of the least ascertainable and definitive of all the forces which make for our civilization. She is confronted by both a woman question and a race problem, and is as yet an unknown or an unacknowledged factor in both. While the women of the white race can with calm assurance enter upon the work they feel by nature appointed to do, while their men give loyal support and appreciative countenance to their efforts, recognizing in most avenues of usefulness the propriety and the need of woman's distinctive co-operation, the colored woman too often finds herself hampered and shamed by a less liberal sentiment and a more conservative attitude on the part of those for whose opinion she cares most. That this is not universally true I am glad to admit. There are to be found both intensely conservative white men and exceedingly liberal colored men. But as far as my experience goes the average man of our race is less frequently ready to admit the actual need among the sturdier forces of the world for woman's help or influence. That great social and economic questions await her interference, that she could throw any light on problems of national import, that her intermeddling could improve the management of school systems, or elevate the tone of public institutions, or humanize and sanctify the far reaching influence of prisons and reformatories and improve the treatment of lunatics and imbeciles,—that she has a word worth hearing on mooted questions in political economy, that she could contribute a suggestion on the relations of labor and capital, or offer a thought on honest money and honorable trade, I fear the majority of "Americans of the colored variety" are not yet prepared to concede. It may be that they do not yet see these questions in their right perspective, being absorbed in the immediate needs of their own political complications. A good deal depends on where we put the emphasis in this world; and our men are not perhaps to blame if they see everything colored by the light of those agitations in the midst of which they live and move and have their being. The part they have had to play in American history during the last twenty-five or thirty years has tended rather to exaggerate the importance of mere political advantage, as well as to set a fictitious valuation on those able to secure such advantage. It is the astute politician, the manager who can gain preferment for himself and his favorites, the demagogue known to stand in with the powers at the White House and consulted on the bestowal of government plums, whom we set in high places and denominate great. It is they who receive the hosannas of the multitude and are regarded as leaders of the people. The thinker and the doer, the man who solves the problem by enriching his country with an invention worth thousands or by a thought inestimable and precious is given neither bread nor a stone. He is too often left to die in obscurity and neglect even if spared in his life the bitterness of fanatical jealousies and detraction.

And yet politics, and surely American politics, is hardly a school for great minds. Sharpening rather than deepening, it develops the faculty of taking advantage of present emergencies rather than the insight to distinguish between the true and the false, the lasting and the ephemeral advantage. Highly cultivated selfishness rather than consecrated benevolence is its passport to success. Its votaries are never seers. At best they are but manipulators—often only jugglers. It is conducive neither to profound statesmanship nor to the higher type of manhood. Altruism is its *mauvais succes* and naturally enough it is indifferent to any factor which cannot be worked into its own immediate aims and purposes. As woman's influence as a political element is as yet nil in most of the commonwealths of our republic, it is not surprising that with those who place the emphasis on mere political capital she may yet seem almost a nonentity so far as it concerns the solution of great national or even racial perplexities.

There are those, however, who value the calm elevation of the thoughtful spectator who stands aloof from the heated scramble; and, above the turmoil and din of corruption and selfishness, can listen to the teachings of eternal truth and righteousness. There are even those who feel that the black man's unjust and unlawful exclusion temporarily from participation in the elective franchise in certain states is after all but a lesson "in the desert" fitted to develop in him insight and discrimination against the day of his own appointed time. One needs occasionally to stand aside from the hum and rush of human interests and passions to hear the voices of God. And it not unfrequently happens that the All-loving gives a great push to certain souls to thrust them out, as it were, from the distracting current for awhile to promote their discipline and growth, or to enrich them by communion and reflection. And similarly it may be woman's privilege from her peculiar coigne of vantage as a quiet observer, to whisper just the needed suggestion or the almost forgotten truth. The colored woman, then, should not be ignored because her bark is resting in the silent waters of the sheltered cove. She is watching the movements of the contestants none the less and is all the better qualified, perhaps, to weigh and judge and advise because not herself in the excitement of the race. Her voice, too, has always been heard in clear, unfaltering tones, ringing the changes on those deeper interests which make for permanent good. She is always sound and orthodox on questions affecting the well-being of her race. You do not find the colored woman selling her birthright for a mess of pottage. Nay, even after reason has retired from the contest, she has been known to cling blindly with the instinct of a turtle dove to those principles and policies which to her mind promise hope and safety for children yet unborn. It is notorious that ignorant black women in the South have actually left their husbands' homes and repudiated their support for what was understood by the wife to be race disloyalty, or "voting away," as she expresses it, the privileges of herself and little ones.

It is largely our women in the South to-day who keep the black men solid in the Republican party. The latter as they increase in intelligence and power of discrimination would be more apt to divide on local issues at any rate. They begin to see that the Grand Old Party regards the Negro's cause as an outgrown issue, and on Southern soil at least finds a too intimate acquaintanceship with him a somewhat unsavory recommendation. Then, too, their political wits have been sharpened to appreciate the fact that it is good policy to cultivate one's neighbors and not depend too much on a distant friend to fight one's home battles. But the black woman can never forget—however lukewarm the party may to-day appear—that it was a Republican president who struck the manacles from her own wrists and gave the possibilities of manhood to her helpless little ones; and to her mind a Democratic Negro is a traitor and a time-server. Talk as much as you like of venality and manipulation in the South, there

are not many men, I can tell you, who would dare face a wife quivering in every fiber with the consciousness that her husband is a coward who could be paid to desert her deepest and dearest interests.

Not unfelt, then, if unproclaimed has been the work and influence of the colored women of America. Our list of chieftains in the service, though not long, is not inferior in strength and excellence, I dare believe, to any similar list which this country can produce.

Among the pioneers, Frances Watkins Harper could sing with prophetic exaltation in the darkest days, when as yet there was not a rift in the clouds overhanging her people:

"Yes, Ethiopia shall stretch
Her bleeding hands abroad;
Her cry of agony shall reach the burning throne of God.
    Redeemed from dust and freed from chains
        Her sons shall lift their eyes,
    From cloud-capt hills and verdant plains
        Shall shouts of triumph rise."

Among preachers of righteousness, an unanswerable silencer of cavilers and objectors, was Sojourner Truth, that unique and rugged genius who seemed carved out without hand or chisel from the solid mountain mass; and in pleasing contrast, Amanda Smith, sweetest of natural singers and pleaders in dulcet tones for the things of God and of His Christ.

Sarah Woodson Early and Martha Briggs, planting and watering in the school room, and giving off from their matchless and irresistible personality an impetus and inspiration which can never die so long as there lives and breathes a remote descendant of their disciples and friends.

Charlotte Fortin Grimke, the gentle spirit whose verses and life link her so beautifully with America's great Quaker poet and loving reformer.

Hallie Quinn Brown, charming reader, earnest, effective lecturer and devoted worker of unflagging zeal and unquestioned power.

Fannie Jackson Coppin, the teacher and organizer, preeminent among women of whatever country or race in constructive and executive force.

These women represent all shades of belief and as many departments of activity; but they have one thing in common—their sympathy with the oppressed race in America and the consecration of their several talents in whatever line to the work of its deliverance and development.

Fifty years ago woman's activity according to orthodox definitions was on a pretty clearly cut "sphere," including primarily the kitchen and the nursery, and rescued from the barrenness of prison bars by the womanly mania for adorning every discoverable bit of china or canvass with forlorn looking cranes balanced idiotically on one foot. The woman of to-day finds herself in the presence of responsibilities which ramify through the profoundest and most varied interests of her country and race. Not one of the issues of this plodding, toiling, sinning, repenting, falling, aspiring humanity can afford to shut her out, or can deny the reality of her influence. No plan for renovating society, no scheme for purifying politics, no reform in church or in state, no moral, social, or economic question, no movement upward or downward in the human plane is lost on her. A man once said when told his house was afire: "Go tell my wife; I never meddle with household affairs." But no woman can possibly put herself or her sex outside any of the interests that affect humanity. All departments in the new era are to be hers, in the sense that her interests are in all and through all; and it is incumbent on her to keep intelligently and sympathetically *en rapport* with all the great movements of her time, that she may know on which side to throw the weight of her influence. She stands now at the gateway of this new era of American civilization. In her hands must be moulded the strength, the wit, the statesmanship, the morality, all the psychic force, the social and economic intercourse of that era. To be alive at such an epoch is a privilege, to be a woman then is sublime.

In this last decade of our century, changes of such moment are in progress, such new and alluring vistas are opening out before us, such original and radical suggestions for the adjustment of labor and capital, of government and the governed, of the family, the church and the state, that to be a possible factor though an infinitesimal in such a movement is pregnant with hope and weighty with responsibility. To be a woman in such an age carries with it a privilege and an opportunity never implied before. But to be a woman of the Negro race in America, and to be able to grasp the deep significance of the possibilities of the crisis, is to have a heritage, it seems to me, unique in the ages. In the first place, the race is young and full of the elasticity and hopefulness of youth. All its achievements are before it. It does not look on the masterly triumphs of nineteenth century civilization with that *blasé* world-weary look which characterizes the old washed out and worn out races which have already, so to speak, seen their best days.

Said a European writer recently: "Except the Sclavonic, the Negro is the only original and distinctive genius which has yet to come to growth—and the feeling is to cherish and develop it."

Everything to this race is new and strange and inspiring. There is a quickening of its pulses and a glowing of its self-consciousness. Aha, I can rival that! I can aspire to that! I can honor my name and vindicate my race! Something like this, it strikes me, is the enthusiasm which stirs the genius of young Africa in America; and the memory of past oppression and the fact of present attempted repression only serve to gather momentum for its irrepressible powers. Then again, a race in such a stage of growth is peculiarly sensitive to impressions. Not the photographer's sensitized plate is more delicately impressionable to outer influences than is this high strung people here on the threshold of a career.

What a responsibility then to have the sole management of the primal lights and shadows! Such is the colored woman's office. She must stamp weal or woe on the coming history of this people. May she see her opportunity and vindicate her high prerogative.

Pauline E. Hopkins (1859–1930)

A writer of many genres, Pauline E. Hopkins wrote seven short stories, three novels, and several plays and magazine articles. Her most popular novel is *Contending Forces*, a story about the effects of race, class, and caste issues on relationships. *Hagar's Daughter: A Story of Southern Caste Prejudice*, serialized at the turn of the century, is also gaining popularity. During her era, Hopkins was well-known for her work as founding member and editor of *The Colored American Magazine*. Born in Portland, Maine, to William and Sarah Allen Hopkins, great grandniece of poet James Whitfield, Hopkins attended elementary and high school in Boston. Before becoming a literary editor, she held jobs as a stenographer and returned to that work when she perceived her literary career was failing. Tragically, Hopkins died in a fire in her home. Today, her writings are receiving renewed attention.

From *Contending Forces*

Chapter VII

Friendship

What is so great as friendship? The only reward of virtue is virtue: the only way to have a friend is to be one.

—Emerson

After that evening the two girls were much together. Sappho's beauty appealed strongly to Dora's artistic nature; but hidden beneath the classic outlines of the face, the graceful symmetry of the form, and the dainty coloring of the skin, Dora's shrewd common sense and womanly intuition discovered a character of sterling worth—bold, strong and ennobling; while into Sappho's lonely self-suppressed life the energetic little Yankee girl swept like a healthful, strengthening breeze. Care was forgotten; there was new joy in living. It was the Southern girl's first experience of Northern life. True, the seductive skies of her nativitiy had a potent hold upon her affections, but truth demanded her to recognize the superiority of the vigrorous activity in the life all about her. The Negro, while held in comtempt by many, yet reflected the spirit of his surroundings in his upright carriage, his fearlessness in advancing his opinions, his self-reliance, his anxiety to obtain paying employment that would give to his family some few of the advantages enjoyed by the more favored classes of citizens, his love of liberty, which in its intensity recalled the memory of New England men who had counted all worldly gain as nothing if demanding the sacrifice of even one of the great principles of freedom. It was a new view of the possibilities and probabilities which the future might open to her people. Long she struggled with thoughts which represented to her but vaguely a life beyond anything of which she had ever dreamed.

Sappho generally carried her work home in the morning, but ten o'clock would find her seated at her desk and ready to begin her task anew. Some days she was unoccupied; but this did not happen very frequently. These free days were the gala days of her existence, when under Dora's guidance she explored various points of interest, and learned from observation the great plan of life as practiced in an intelligent, liberty-loving community. Here in the free air of New England's freest city, Sappho drank great draughts of freedom's subtle elixir. Dora was interested and amused in watching the changes on the mirror-like face of her friend whenever her attention was arrested by a new phenomenon. It was strange to see this girl, resembling nothing so much as a lily in its beautiful purity, shrink from entering a place of public resort for fear of insult. It was difficult to convince her that she might enter a restaurant frequented by educated whites and meet with nothing but the greatest courtesy; that she might take part in the glorious service at fashionable Trinity and be received with punctilious politeness. To this woman, denied association with the vast sources of information, which are heirlooms to the lowliest inhabitant of Boston, the noble piles, which represented the halls of learning, and the massive grandeur of the library, free to all, seemed to invite her to a full participation in their intellectual joys. She had seen nothing like them. Statuary, paintings, sculptures,—all appealed to her beauty-loving nature. The hidden springs of spirituality were satisfied and at rest, claiming kinship with the great minds of the past, whose

---

From *Contending Forces*.

never-dying works breathed perennial life in the atmosphere of the quiet halls.

Now was the beginning of the storm season in New England, and on stormy days the two girls would sit before the fire in Sappho's room and talk of the many things dear to women, while they embroidered or stitched. So they sat one cold, snowy day. The storm had started the afternoon before and had raged with unceasing fury all night,—snow and rain which the increasing cold quickly turned into cutting sleet. Morning had brought relief from the high winds, and the temperature had moderated somewhat; but the snow still fell steadily, drifting into huge piles, which made the streets impassable. It was the first great storm Sappho had seen. It was impossible for her to leave home, so she begged Dora to pass the day with her and play "company," like the children. Dora was nothing loathe; and as soon as her morning duties were finished, she told her mother that she was going visiting and would not be at home until tea time. By eleven o'clock they had locked the door of Sappho's room to keep out all intruders, had mended the fire until the little stove gave out a delicious warmth, and had drawn the window curtains close to keep out stray currents of air. Sappho's couch was drawn close beside the stove, while Dora's small person was most cosily bestowed in her favourite rocking-chair.

It was a very convenient stove that Sappho had in her room. The ornamental top could be turned back on its movable hinge, and there was a flat stove cover ready to hold any vessel and heat its contents to just the right temperature. Sappho was prouder of that stove than a daughter of Fortune would have been of the most expensive silver chafing-dish. It was very near lunch time, so the top was turned back, and the little copper teakettle was beginning to sing its welcome song. Dora had placed a small, round table between the couch and the rocker. A service for two was set out in dainty china dishes, cream and sugar looking doubly tempting as it gleamed and glistened in the delicate ware. One plate was piled with thinly cut slices of bread and butter, another held slices of pink ham.

Sappho lay back among her cushions, lazily stretching her little slippered feet toward the warm stove, where the fire burned so cheerily and glowed so invitingly as it shone through the isinglass door. She folded her arms above her head and turned an admiring gaze on the brown face of her friend, who swayed gently back and forth in her rocking-chair, her feet on a hassock, and a scarlet afghan wrapped about her knees. Dora was telling Sappho all about her engagement to John Langley and their plans for the future.

"I think you will be happy, Dora, if you love him. All things are possible if love is the foundation stone," said Sappho, after a slight pause, as she nestled among her pillows. Dora was sitting bolt upright with the usual business-like look upon her face.

"I like him well enough to marry him, but I don't believe there's enough sentiment in me to make love a great passion, such as we read of in books. Do you believe marriage is the beautiful state it is painted by writers?"

"Why, yes," laughed Sappho: "I wouldn't believe anything else for your sake, my little brownie."

"No joking, Sappho; this is dead earnest. Don't you ever expect to marry, and don't you speculate about the pros and cons and the maybes and perhaps of the situation?" asked Dora, as she filled the cups with steaming cocoa and passed one to her friend.

"Dora, you little gourmand, what have you got in the refrigerator?" A box ingeniously nailed to the window seat outside, and filled with shelves, and having a substantial door, was the ice-box, or refrigerator, where Sappho kept materials handy for a quick lunch. Dora closed the window and returned quickly to her seat, placing a glass dish on the table as she did so.

"It's only part of a cream pie that ma had left last night. I thought it would help out nicely with our lunch."

"What, again!" said Sappho significantly. "That's the fourth time this week, and here it is but Friday. You'll be as fat as a seal, and then John P. won't want you at any price. Take warning, and depart from the error of your ways before it is too late."

Dora laughed guiltily and said, as she drew a box from her apron pocked: "Well, here are John's chocolate bonbons that he brought last night. I suppose you won't want me to touch *them*, for fear of getting fat."

Sappho shook her head in mock despair. "And your teeth, your beautiful white teeth, where will they be shortly if you persist in eating a pound of bonbons every day? Think of your fate, Dora, and pause in your reckless career—forty inches about the waist and only scraggy snags to show me when you grin!"

"Thank heaven I'll never come to that while there's a dentist in the city of Boston! I'll eat all the bonbons I want in spite of you, Sappho, and if you don't hurry I'll eat your slice of cream pie, too." At this dire threat there ensued a scramble for the pie, mingled with peals of merry laughter, until all rosy and sparkling, Sappho emerged from the fray with the dish containing her share of the dainty held high in the air.

Presently lunch was over, and they resumed their old positions, prepared to "take comfort."

"You haven't answered my question yet, Sappho."

"To tell you the truth, I had forgotten your remark, Dora; what was it?"

"I suspect that is a bit of a fib to keep me from teasing you about getting maried. What I want to know is: Do you ever mean to marry, or are you going to pine in single blessedness on my hands and be a bachelor-maid to the end?"

"Well," replied Sappho, with a comical twist to her face, "in the words of Unc' Gulliver, 'I mote, an' then agin I moten't.'"

"What troubles me is having a man bothering around. Now I tell John P. that I'm busy, or something like that, and I'm rid of him; but after you marry a man, he's on your hands for good and all. I'm wondering if my love could stand the test."

"That's queer talk for an engaged girl, with a fine, handsome fellow to court her. Why, Dora, 'I'm s'prised at yer!'" laughed Sappho gaily.

"I'm not ashamed of John P.'s appearance in company; he looks all right; but when one is terribly in love one is supposed to want the dear object always near; but matches,—love matches,—my child, turn out so badly that a girl hesitates to 'git jined to eny man fer betterer or worserer,' as Dr. Peters says. Then I get tired of a man so soon! (This with a doleful sigh.) I dread to think of being tied to John for good and all; I know I'll be sick of him inside of a week. I do despair of ever being like other girls."

Sappho laughed outright at the woe-begone countenance before her.

"It is generally the other way: the men get tired of us first. A woman loves one man, and is true to him through all eternity."

"That's just what makes me feel so *unsexed*, so to speak; I like John's looks. He's the style among all the girls in our set. I like to know that I can claim him before them all. It's fun to see 'em fluttering around him, kindly trying to put my nose out of joint. I must say that I feel real *comfortable* to spoil sport by walking off with him just when they think they've got things running as they wish. Yes, it's real *comfortable* to know that they're all as jealous as can be. But for all that, I know I'll get tired of him."

"Let us hope not, if you have really made up your mind to marry him. Dora, sometimes I am afraid that you mean what you say. I notice that you call him 'John P.' What's the P for?"

"Pollock—John Pollock Langley. His grandfather was his father's master, and Pollock was his name," sang Dora, as she rocked gently to and fro. "Now, there's Arthur Lewis," she continued; "he's jolly fun. He isn't a fascinator, or anything of that sort; he's just good."

"Who is he?" asked Sappho, with languid interest.

"Properly speaking, he's Dr. Arthur Lewis. We were children together, although he is five years older than I. He's a fine scholar and a great business man. He has a large industrial school in Louisiana. He's gone up in the world, I tell you, since we made mud pies on the back doorsteps; but I never think of him except as old Arthur, who used to drag me to school on his sled."

There was a gleam of fun in Sappho's eyes, as she said demurely: "You seem to know all about him. Was he ever a lover of yours?"

"Lover! no, indeed!" Dora flushed vividly under her brown skin. "The idea of Arthur as my lover is too absurd."

"Excuse me, dear, for my mistake," said Sappho mischievously. "I didn't know but that he might be the mysterious link which would join love, marriage and the necessary man in a harmonious whole."

"Well," said Dora, after a slight pause, blushing furiously, "I don't say he wouldn't like the rôle. You'll see him soon; he's coming to Boston on business in a few weeks. Oh, we've had rare times together." She sighed and smiled, lost for the moment in pleasant memories. Sappho smiled, too, in sympathy with her mood

"Ah, yes; I think I understand. Poor John!"

"John's all right. Don't shed any tears over him," said Dora testily. They sat awhile in silence, listening to the sound of the whirling frozen flakes wind-driven against the window panes. It was scarce three o'clock, but darkness was beginning to envelop the city, and it was already a pleasant twilight in the room

"Tell me about Dr. Lewis and his work, Dora," said Sappho presently. "Do you know, he interests me exceedingly."

"I don't really understand Arthur's hobbies, but I believe that he is supposed to be doing a great work in the Black Belt. His argument is, as I understand it, that industrial education and the exclusion of politics will cure all our race troubles."

"I doubt it," returned Sappho quickly, with an impatient toss of the head. "That reasoning might be practically illustrated with benefit to us for a few years in the South, but to my mind would not effect a permanent cure for race troubles if we are willing to admit that human nature is the same in us as in others. The time will come when our men will grow away from the trammels of narrow prejudice, and desire the same treatment that is accorded to other men. Why, one can but see that any degree of education and development will not fail of such a result."

"I am willing to confess that the subject is a little deep for me," replied Dora. "I'm not the least bit of a politician, and I generally accept whatever the men tell me as right; but I know that there is something very wrong in our lives, and nothing seems to remedy the evils under which the colored man labors."

"But you can see, can't you, that if our men are deprived of the franchise, we become aliens in the very land of our birth?"

"Arthur says that would be better for us; the great loss of life would cease, and we should be at peace with the whites."

"Ah, how can he argue so falsely! I have lived beneath the system of oppression in the South. If we lose the franchise, at the same time we shall lose the respect of all other citizens. Temporizing will not benefit us; rather, it will leave us branded as cowards, not worthy a freeman's respect—an alien people, without a country and without a home."

Dora gazed at her friend with admiration, and wished that she had a kodak, so that she might catch just the expression that lighted her eyes and glowed in a bright color upon her cheeks.

"I predict some fun when you and Arthur meet. I'll just start you both out some night, and you'll be spitting at each other like two cats inside of five minutes. Arthur thinks that women should be seen and not heard, where politics is under discussion."

"Insufferable prig!" exclaimed Sappho, with snapping eyes.

"Oh, no he isn't; Arthur's all right. But you see he is living South; his work is there, and he must keep in with the whites of the section where his work lies, or all he has accomplished will go for naught, and perhaps his life might be forfeited, too."

"I see. The mess of pottage and the birthright."

"Bless you! not so bad as that; but money makes the mare go," returned Dora, with a wink at her friend, and a shrewd business look on her bright little Yankee face. "I say to you, as Arthur says to me when I tell him what I think of his system: 'If you want honey, you must have money.' I don't know anything about politics, as I said before, but my opinion won't cost you anything: when we can say that lots of our men are as rich as Jews, there'll be no question about the franchise, and my idea is that Arthur'll be one the Jews."

"Oh!" exclaimed Sappho disgustedly, as she resumed her lounging position.

"Sappho, how did you come to take up stenography? I should have thought you would have preferred teaching."

"I had to live, my dear; I could not teach school, because my education does not include a college course. I could not do housework, because my constitution is naturally weak."

It was noticeable in these confidential chats that Sappho never spoke of her early life. Dora had confided to her friend every event of importance that had occurred in her young life; and, in harmless gossip, had related the history of all the friends who visited the house intimately; but all this had begot no like unburdening to eager ears of the early history of her friend. Wonderful to relate, however, Dora did not resent this reserve, which she could see was studied. It spoke well for the sincerity of the love that had taken root in her heart for Sappho, that it subdued her inquisitiveness, and she gladly accepted her friendship without asking troublesome questions.

"How did you finally succeed in getting work? I have always heard that it was very difficult for colored girls to find employment in offices where your class of work is required."

"And so it is, my dear. I sometimes think that if I lose the work I am on, I shall not try for another position. I shall never forget the day I started out to find work: the first place that I visited was all right until the man found I was colored;

then he said that his wife wanted a nurse girl, and he had no doubt she would be glad to hire me, for I looked good-tempered. At the second place where I ventured to intrude the proprietor said: 'Yes; we want a stenographer, but we've no work for your kind.' However, that was preferable to the insulting familiarity which some men assumed. It was dreadful! I don't like to think about it. Father Andrew induced the man for whom I am working to employ me. I do not interfere with the other help, because I take my work home; many of the other clerks have never seen me, and so the proprietor runs no risk of being bothered with complaints from them. He treats me very well, too."

"I have heard many girls tell much the same tale about other lines of business," said Dora. "It makes me content to do the work of this house, and not complain."

"You ought to thank God every day for such a refuge as you have in your home."

"I cannot understand people. Here in the North we are allowed every privilege. There seems to be no prejudice until we seek employment; then every door is closed against us. Can you explain this?"

"No, I cannot; to my way of thinking the whole thing is a Chinese puzzle."

"Bless my soul! Just look at that clock!" exclaimed Dora, as she scrambled to her feet and began gathering up her scattered property. "Five o'clock, and tea to get. Sappho, you've been lazy enough for one day. Come downstairs and help me get tea. The boys will be here in no time, as hungry as bears."

Piloted by Dora, Sappho became well acquainted with ancient landmarks of peculiar interest to the colored people. They visited the home for aged women on M—— Street, and read and sang to the occupants. They visited St. Monica's Hospital, and carried clothes, flowers, and a little money saved from the cost of contemplated Easter finery. They scattered brightness along with charitable acts wherever a case of want was brought to their attention.

Dora had accepted the position of organist for a prominent colored church in the city. There was a small salary attached to the place, which she was glad to receive. Sappho usually went with her to choir rehearsals, and sitting in the shadows, well hidden from view, would think over the romantic history of the fine old edifice. The building, so the story ran, was the place of worship of a rich, white Baptist congregation in the years preceding the emancipation. Negroes were allowed in the galleries only. Believing this color-bar to be a stigma on the house of God, a few of the members protested, but finding their warnings unheeded, withdrew from the chruch, and finally found a Sabbath home in an old building long used as a theatre. These people prospered, and grew rich and powerful: colored people were always welcome in the congregation. The society in the old church, left to itself, had at last been glad to sell the building to its present occupants. Thus the despised people, who were not allowed a seat outside of the galleries, now owned and occupied the scene of their former humiliation. It was a solemn and wonderful dispensation of Providence, and filled the girl's heart with strong emotion.

During these evenings, when she waited for the close of the rehearsals, she became acquainted with many odd specimens of the race: men of brain and thought, but of unique expression and filled with quaint humor. One of these characters was known as Dr. Abraham Peters. Doctor Peters was a well-read man, greatly interested in scientific research, but who had lacked the opportunity to obtain information in his youth. He had been a slave when a boy, a few years before the Civil War. Now he was the church janitor, and to eke out his scanty income kept a little boot-black stand just around the corner from the church, and knowing something of medicine and nursing the sick, had advertised himself as a magnetic physician. He displayed much skill in practice, and had acquired something of a local reputation. Doctor Peters and Sappho were good friends, and he brought out all his store of knowledge, proudly displaying it for her approval.

"You see, Miss Sappho, I've knocked 'bout the worl' some consid'ble," he said one night, in his soft Southern tones and quaint Northernized dialect, as they sat in the cosy vestry waiting for the close of the rehearsal. "Ben po'rer than eny chuch mouse. But I've saved somethin', an' I know the worl'. Perhaps you's int'rest'd 'nuff in an ole man to want to hear how I come to 'vertis myself as a magnifyin' doctor, an' where I picked it up, eh?"

"Yes," replied Sappho, "I certainly am interested in your story."

"Well, while they're caterwaulin' on that Easter anthem in ten flats, I reckon I'll have time to tell you all 'bout it. Fust I knowed 'bout magnetics was brought to my 'tention down home. Some people said I had the evil eye, an' some said it was only a *strong* eye, but be that homsomever, it was a bad eye, an' a terror ter watermilyun thieves when it was my watch on the chickun houses. *Magnifyin'* an' *hoodooin'* is 'bout the same thing down thar, tho' sense the 'srender mos' all ol'-time doin's is done 'way. 'Bout the time I realized that I had this power I had 'sperinced ruligeon, an' had been jestified an' concentrated, so that I got the blessin'. Them days, too, I was a-sottin' out to court my Susie (that's my wife), an' all the young fellers 'roun' the county was a-sprucin' up to her jes' like crows 'roun' carr'on. Sunday was the day I had mos' on my mind, 'cause they'd ride up an' hitch thar mules in a line all along the ole man's fence (you see he had right smart prop'ty, an' I spec' that had a mighty drawin' infloonce on some of them shifless fellers who hadn't nuff skonsh to start that own mule team up a hill), an' thar they'd sot like so

many buzzards, waitin' fer a chance to sly Susie off to chuch under my nose. I had ter wurk lively, I tell you; Susie was kin' o' skittish an' res'less, an' it was fus' come, fus' sarved, with her, bein' she had her choice. Well, jes' at the time I got the blessin' I got the insurance that Susie was gwine ter have me. All the fellers was satisfied but Possum Tooit. Possum an' me was boys together, an' we'd both run each other purty hard strivin' to come through fust at the mourner's bench as well as to git the gal. Possum was beat when he found I had a full hand and had swept the pot."

"Oomhoo!" laughed Brother Jones, who was an interested listener to Doctor Peters' story. "Oomhoo, Brother Peters; done guv yerself 'way. What you know 'bout 'full hands an' pots?'"

"Who give himself 'way, Brother Jones? Ever hear me say Ise better'n enybody else in this chuch? I'm er man, sah, I'm er man! Ise done truspassed on the flesh-pots of Egypt as much as eny other man. Don't yer 'oomhoo' me, Brother Jones, no sah!"

"Tech a sore place, Brother Peters, tech a sore place," laughed the brother as he walked away, his shoulders shaking like great mounds of jelly. It was some minutes before Doctor Peters could recover his equilibrium and go on with his tale.

"Possum Tooit was so mad an' disapinted that he finally challenged me to fight a jewel. I wasn't in no state of mind to be killed by any of his hoodoo tricks. Possum bein' an export at puttin' spells an' sech like on enybody fer from twenty-five cents up to five dollars; neither did I want Susie to think I was 'fraid of Possum Tooit. So thar I was 'tween a hawk an' a buzzard. Well, I accepted the challenge, an' bein' the defendant in the matter, of course, I had the choice of weapins, an' I choose rifles. We kep' mighty secret 'bout the 'rangements, an' met at moonrise on a field jes' back of the graveyard. The seconds measured off ten spaces after we'd shooken hands, an' we each stepped to our places. Tho' it was a solemn 'casion, I wasn't skeered, but Possum was a rollin' up the whites of his eyes, an' you could hear his teeth chatter worse than dried corn shuks. Ike Watkins was head second, an' he stood 'tween us, holdin' his red bandanna in his han' waitin' to say the word. 'Gemplemen, is you ready?' he says 'Let her go, Ike,' says I. 'Take aim,' say he, an' I pinted the rifle at Possum, an' callin' up all the power in me I threw it along the body of the gun plumb 'tween Possum's eyes jes' above the bridge of his nose. An' that was a fair target, 'cause the bridge of Possum's nose was a miracle fer size. Possum gave a yell when he felt the strength of that eye, that would a splut yer year-pan in two. An' in two seconds he was in the worst alpaca fit you ever seen. The seconds acknowledged me the victor by a reckless invention of Providence, they bein' aware that the adversary wasn't hit by nary bullet, the rifles bein' loaded with salt fer fear of mischief. Possum owned up like a man that I was more powerful than him, because of the sufernatral strength in my bad eye.

"Well, I kep' on prayin' fer mo' faith until I got the power in my hands, an' by layin' em on a sick pusson I could 'lectrocute 'em instantly, an' thar bad feelin's would disappear. People got the notion I could pray a pusson right out the grave, an' my fame spread abroad until I began charging fer my services, explainin' to my patients that the dead might be raised, but not fer nuthin', after which I seed a fallin'off in my poperlarity. Business bein' purty brief jes' then, I took Susie an' moved up Norf, an' went ter cookin' on a steamboat. I've done mos' everythin' in this worl', honey, as I tol' you, to git an hones' livin' without stealin' it. An' I dunno," added the old man reflectively, as he stroked the gray, stubby fringe on his chin, "I dunno as I'm eny too good ef I got pushed, real hard to help myself out; humans is humans, an' I've seen many a well-'tentioned feller settin' in the caboose when times was hard, an' the mule mortgaged for full value to three men at once to buy meal an' bread, an' hog an' hominy, an' terbaccer. But mos' in ginerally, I've got along without silin' my hands with other people's prop'ty. Well, honey, they gave me fifteen dollars a munf an' found, fer bein' head cook, an' I paid ten dollars a munf house rent out of that. Things was purty brief, purty brief. Times was more an' more spurious, an' it was work yer wits, Abraham Peters, to git a livin'. I jes' didn't know whicher way to turn.

"One day I got a telegraph at the other end of the route that the baby was dead an' no money to pay the undertaker, an' the ole 'ooman sick in the bed from worryin'. The Lord jes' seemed to pour his blessin' down on us in a house full o' chillun. After Susie'd had twenty I used to pray the Lord to stop blessin' us that way, 'cause he could see fer himself that too many blessins was a gittin' to be a nuisance. I cooked the dinner myself that day, bein' the other cook was ashore, an' you believe me, I sung an' I prayed an' I wrastled for help in that ole steamboat kitchen down behin' my bigges' brass biler where I was kivered from pryin' eyes. All of a suddint I felt the power, an' the Lord spoke to me an' he said: 'Git up, Abraham Peters, an' go out an' hoodoo the fust man you meet'. Bless yo, chile, I riz up in a hurry an' started out, not knowin' no more than nuthin' what was meant by that. Fust man I saw when I got on deck was the cap'n; I went up to him, an' I smiled. I must have been a purty picture with my face all grease an' tears. I says, not thinkin' what wurds I was goin' ter utter: 'Mornin', Cap'n; how's yet corporosity seem to segashiate?' Cap'n he roared; you could a heard him holler up to Boston. He slapped me on the back, an' says he: 'Abe Peters, that's the gol darndest thing I ever heard.' With that he hauled out a five-dollar bill an' gave me, an' walked off laughin' fit to kill hisself. By night I had twenty dollars in my pocket, an' everybody on the boat was a callin' me 'corporosity

segashiate.' I've used that hoodoo ever since, an' I ain't found nary white gempleman can seem to git 'way from it without showing the color of his money.

"One of the owners of the boat took a great liking to me, an' he says to me one day, says he: 'Abe, how'd you like to wurk ashore so you could be nearer your family an' git better pay?' 'Like it?' says I. 'If you don't want to pulverize me, don' make me no sech an offer.' He laughed a bit, an' then he says: 'I've got a big buildin' up Washington Street, an' I want a trusty man to keep it clean an' look after the tenants. I'll give you ten dollars a week.'

"I took off my cap, an' I truly bowed down to that man, an' I says: 'The Lord's been a wurkin' on yer heart, Mr. Pierson.' 'Maybe he has,' says he; 'anyhow, you can pack up an' go ashore next trip; your place'll be waitin' fer yer.' Fust thing I knowed I was bossin' a big job of janitorin'. Mos' of the people in the buildin' was Christian Science. After they'd got a little bit acquainted with me they found out the power I had in my hands fer layin' on. 'Twant long before I was a pickin' up right smart nussin' nights. Don't suppose you know much 'bout this Science business, do you?" Sappho confessed her ignorance.

"Christian Science is a faith-cure; that is, it's usin' yet brains an' trainin' 'em to know that there's nuthin' 'tall the matter with you ef you only think there ain't. They argify that all sickness is a mistake, 'cause it's 'maginary. I don't b'lieve that, though, 'cause I had the rheumatism while I was there, an' the doctors started in to cure me by prayin' an' wurkin' on my body through my spirit, an' it warn't no more good than nuthin 'tall. I've got as much faith as eny livin' man, but rheumatism is one o' them things that'll convince you agin' your will; it will draw speech out of a deef mute an' make a blind man see, when them pains is a grindin' inter your bones an' jints worse than a saw cuttin' thro' knots in a cord wood stick. I'm free to say that curin' my mind didn't have no effect on my pain, an' I jes' kep' on seein' blue blazes an' swearin' like mad. I'll 'low that faith can move mountains, faith, as *leetle* as a mustard seed, an' that's mighty small. Ef you b'lieve you'll get what you wants an' asks fer, that's faith. That's good; that's all right. Trouble is we *don't b'lieve it 'cordin' to scripter*. We git mad when our prayers ain't answered, not thinkin' it's 'cause we ain't got horse sense nuff to use *discreetion* in puttin' our faith on subjects that is approvin' to the Lord, an' will fit in with his own idees 'bout runnin' the business of the universe. An' that's where faith-cure is weak, 'cause it's comin' in 'junction with God. Faith-cure won't operate on any man where it was *pre*ordinated that a *pre*tickler man was to die with a *pre* tickler complaint. No'm, we ain't up to comin' in 'junction with the Lord's business. There's a number of grand diversions to Christian Science. There's hypnism an' pessimism an' a number of other isms, but they all bear the same way—a sort of applostic healin' of sickness. The doctors kept after me 'bout my gifts of healin', an' very kindly showed me wherein I could make an hones' dollar, an' business bein' business I finally determined to adop' magnifyin' as a perfeshun. I've been in the business nigh upon ten years now, an' I've picked up as good a livin' as any colored gempleman who has wurked a sight harder an' had to take piles o' unregenerate sass from his boss."

That night they walked home together after the rehearsal: the four young people—Dora and John, Sappho and Will. Some one of the choir boys walking ahead of them was singing in a sweet, high tenor voice the refrain of an old love song: "Couldst thou but know how much I love thee." It suited Will's mood, and voiced his dream exquisitely. Across the heavens the Northern Lights streamed in radiance. Meteors bright and shooting stars added to the beauty of the night. The moon, at its full, shed the light of day about them. The wind whispered amidst the leafless branches of the huge old trees on the Common and Public Garden as they passed them on their homeward way. Once Will took her hand in his; she let it stay a moment while she made an incoherent little speech about clouds and trees. Will said nothing. It was not time yet, he told himself. He would wait a little longer.

Chapter VIII

The Sewing-Circle

Where village statesmen talked with looks profound,
Imagination fondly stoops to trace
The parlor splendors of that festive place.

Yes! let the rich decide, the proud disdain,
These simple blessings of the lowly train;
To me more dear,
One native charm than all the gloss of art.
—GOLDSMITH

Ma Smith was a member of the church referred to in the last chapter, the most prominent one of color in New England. It was situated in the heart of the West End, and was a very valuable piece of property. Every winter this church gave many entertainments to aid in paying off the mortgage, which at this time amounted to about eight thousand dollars. Mrs. Smith, as the chairman of the board of stewardesses, was inaugurating a fair—one that should eclipse anything of a similar nature ever attempted by the colored people, and

numerous sewing-circles were being held among the members all over the city. Parlor entertainments where an admission fee of ten cents was collected from every patron, were also greatly in vogue, and the money thus obtained was put into a fund to defray the expense of purchasing eatables and decorations, and paying for the printing of tickets, circulars, etc., for the fair. The strongest forces of the colored people in the vicinity were to combine and lend their aid in making a supreme effort to clear this magnificent property.

Boston contains a number of well-to-do families of color whose tax-bills show a most comfortable return each year to the city treasury. Strange as it may seem, these well-to-do people, in goodly numbers, distribute themselves and their children among the various Episcopal churches with which the city abounds, the government of which holds out the welcome hand to the brother in black, who is drawn to unite his fortunes with the members of this particular denomination. It may be true that the beautiful ritual of the church is responsible in some measure for this. Colored people are nothing if not beauty-lovers, and for such a people the grandeur of the service has great attractions. But in justice to this church one must acknowledge that it has been instrumental in doing much toward helping this race to help itself, along the lines of brotherly interest.

These people were well represented within the precincts of Mrs. Smith's pretty parlor one afternoon, all desirous of lending their aid to help along the great project.

As we have said, Mrs. Smith occupied the back parlor of the house as her chamber, and within this room the matrons had assembled to take charge of the cutting out of different garments; and here, too, the sewing machine was placed ready for use. In the parlor proper all the young ladies were seated ready to perform any service which might be required of them in the way of putting garments together.

By two o'clock all the members of the sewing-circle were in their places. The parlor was crowded. Mrs. Willis, the brilliant widow of a bright Negro politician, had charge of the girls, and after the sewing had been given out the first business of the meeting was to go over events of interest to the Negro race which had transpired during the week throughout the country. These facts had been previously tabulated upon a blackboard which was placed upon an easel, and occupied a conspicuous position in the room. Each one was supposed to contribute anything of interest that she had read or heard in that time for the benefit of all. After these points had been gone over, Mrs. Willis gave a talk upon some topic of interest. At six o'clock tea was to be served in the kitchen, the company taking refreshment in squads of five. At eight o'clock all unfinished work would be folded and packed away in the convenient little Boston bag, to be finished at home, and the male friends of the various ladies were expected to put in an appearance. Music and recitations were to be enjoyed for two hours, ice cream and cake being sold for the benefit of the cause.

Mrs. Willis was a good example of a class of women of color that came into existence at the close of the Civil War. She was not a *rara avis*, but one of many possibilities which the future will develop from among the colored women of New England. Every city or town from Maine to New York has its Mrs. Willis. Keen in her analysis of human nature, most people realized, after a short acquaintance, in which they ran the gamut of emotions from strong attraction to repulsion, that she had sifted them thoroughly, while they had gained nothing in return. Shrewd in business matters, many a subtle business man had been worsted by her apparent womanly weakness and charming simplicity. With little money, she yet contrived to live in quiet elegance, even including the little journeys from place to place, so adroitly managed as to increase her influence at home and her fame abroad. Well-read and thoroughly conversant with all current topics, she impressed one as having been liberally educated and polished by travel, whereas a high-school course more than covered all her opportunities.

Even today it is erroneously believed that all racial development among colored people has taken place since emancipation. It is impossible of belief for some, that little circles of educated men and women of color have existed since the Revolutionary War. Some of these people were born free, some have lost the memory of servitude in the dim past; a greater number by far were recruited from the energetic slaves of the South, who toiled when they should have slept, for the money that purchased their freedom, or else they boldly took the rights which man denied. Mrs. Willis was one from among these classes. The history of her descent could not be traced, but somewhere, somehow, a strain of white blood had filtered through the African stream. At sixty odd she was vigorous, well-preserved, broad and comfortable in appearance, with an aureole of white hair crowning a pleasant face.

She had loved her husband with a love ambitious for his advancement. His foot on the stairs mounting to the two-room tenement which constituted their home in the early years of married life, had sent a thrill to her very heart as she sat sewing baby clothes for the always expected addition to the family. But twenty years make a difference in all our lives. It brought many changes to the colored people of New England—social and business changes. Politics had become the open sesame for the ambitious Negro. A seat in the Legislature then was not a dream to this man, urged by the loving woman behind him. Other offices of trust were quickly offered him when his worth became known. He grasped his opportunity; grew richer, more polished, less social, and the family broadened out and overflowed from

old familiar "West End" environments across the River Charles into the aristocratic suburbs of Cambridge. Death comes to us all.

Money, the sinews of living and social standing, she did not possess upon her husband's death. Therefore she was forced to begin a weary pilgrimage—a hunt for the means to help her breast the social tide. The best opening, she decided after looking carefully about her, was in the great cause of the evolution of true womanhood in the work of the "Woman Question" as embodied in marriage and suffrage. She could talk dashingly on many themes, for which she had received much applause in by-gone days, when in private life she had held forth in the drawing-room of some Back Bay philanthropist who sought to use her talents as an attraction for a worthy charitable object, the discovery of a rare species of versatility in the Negro character being a sure drawing-card. It was her boast that she had made the fortunes of her family and settled her children well in life. The advancement of the colored woman should be the new problem in the woman question that should float her upon its tide into the prosperity she desired. And she succeeded well in her plans: conceived in selfishness, they yet bore glorious fruit in the formation of clubs of colored women banded together for charity, for study, for every reason under God's glorious heavens that can better the condition of mankind.

Trivialities are not to be despised. Inborn love implanted in a woman's heart for a luxurious, esthetic home life, running on well-oiled wheels amid flowers, sunshine, books and priceless pamphlets, easy chairs and French gowns, may be the means of developing a Paderewski or freeing a race from servitude. It was amusing to watch the way in which she governed societies and held her position. In her hands committees were as wax, and loud murmurings against the tyranny of her rule died down to judicious whispers. If a vote went contrary to her desires, it was in her absence. Thus she became the pivot about which all the social and intellectual life of the colored people of her section revolved. No one had yet been found with the temerity to contest her position, which, like a title of nobility, bade fair to descend to her children. It was thought that she might be eclipsed by the younger and more brilliant women students on the strength of their alma mater, but she still held her own by sheer force of will-power and indomitable pluck.

The subject of the talk at this meeting was: "The place which the virtuous woman occupies in upbuilding a race." After a few explanatory remarks, Mrs. Willis said:

"I am particularly anxious that you should think upon this matter seriously, because of its intrinsic value to all of us as race women. I am not less anxious because you represent the coming factors of our race. Shortly, you must fill the positions now occupied by your mothers, and it will rest with you and your children to refute the charges brought against us as to our moral irresponsibility, and the low moral standard maintained by us in comparison with other races."

"Did I understand you to say that the Negro woman in her native state is truly a virtuous woman?" asked Sappho, who had been very silent during the bustle attending the opening of the meeting.

"Travelers tell us that the native African woman is impregnable in her virtue," replied Mrs. Willis.

"So we have sacrificed that attribute in order to acquire civilization," chimed in Dora.

"No, not 'sacrificed,' but pushed one side by the force of circumstances. Let us thank God that it *is* an essential attribute peculiar to us—a racial characteristic which is slumbering but not lost," replied Mrs. Willis. "But let us not forget the definition of virtue—'Strength to do the right thing under all temptations.' Our ideas of virtue are too narrow. We confine them to that conduct which is ruled by our animal passions alone. It goes deeper than that—general excellence in every duty of life is what we may call virtue."

"Do you think, then, that Negro women will be held responsible for all the lack of virtue that is being laid to their charge today? I mean, do you think that God will hold us responsible for the *illegitimacy* with which our race has been obliged, as it were, to flood the world?" asked Sappho.

"I believe that we shall not be held responsible for wrongs which we have *unconsciously* committed, or which we have committed under *compulsion*. We are virtuous or non-virtuous only when we have a *choice* under temptation. We cannot by any means apply the word to a little child who has never been exposed to temptation, nor to the Supreme Being 'who cannot be tempted with evil.' So with the African brought to these shores against his will—the state of morality which implies willpower on his part does not exist, therefore he is not a responsible being. The sin and its punishment lies with the person *consciously* false to his *knowledge* of right. From this we deduce the truism that 'the civility of no race is perfect whilst another race is degraded.'"

"I shall never forget my feelings," chimed in Anna Stevens, a school teacher of a very studious temperament, "at certain remarks made by the Rev. John Thomas at one of his noonday lectures in the Temple. He was speaking on 'Different Races,' and had in his vigorous style been sweeping his audience with him at a high elevation of thought which was dazzling to the faculties, and almost impossible to follow in some points. Suddenly he touched upon the Negro, and with impressive gesture and lowered voice thanked God that the mulatto race was dying out, because it was a mongrel mixture which combined the worst elements of two races. Lo, the poor mulatto! despised by the blacks of his own race, scorned by the whites! Let him go out and hang himself!" In her indignation Anna forgot the scissors, and bit her thread off viciously with her little white teeth.

Mrs. Willis smiled as she said calmly: "My dear Anna, I would not worry about the fate of the mulatto, for the fate of the mulatto will be the fate of the entire race. Did you never think that today the black race on this continent has developed into a race of mulattoes?"

"Why, Mrs. Willis!" came in a chorus of voices.

"Yes," continued Mrs. Willis, still smiling. "It is an incontrovertible truth that there is no such thing as an unmixed black on the American continent. Just bear in mind that we cannot tell by a person's complexion whether he be dark or light in blood, for by the working of the natural laws the white father and black mother produce the mulatto offspring: the black father and white mother the mulatto offspring also, while the *black father* and *quadroon* mother produce the black child, which to the eye alone is a child of unmixed black blood. I will venture to say that out of a hundred apparently pure black men not one will be able to trace an unmixed flow of African blood since landing upon these shores! What an unhappy example of the frailty of all human intellects, when such a man and scholar as Doctor Thomas could so far allow his prejudices to dominate his better judgment as to add one straw to the burden which is popularly supposed to rest upon the unhappy mulattoes of a despised race," finished the lady, with a dangerous flash of her large dark eyes.

"Mrs. Willis," said Dora, with a scornful little laugh, "I am not unhappy, and I am a mulatto. I just enjoy my life, and I don't want to die before my time comes, either. There are lots of good things left on earth to be enjoyed even by mulattoes, and I want my share."

"Yes, my dear; and I hope you may all live and take comfort in the proper joys of your lives. While we are all content to accept life, and enjoy it along the lines which God has laid down for us as individuals as well as a race, we shall be happy and get the best out of life. Now, let me close this talk by asking you to remember one maxim written of your race by a good man: 'Happiness and social position are not to be gained by pushing.' Let the world, by its need of us along certain lines, and our intrinsic fitness for these lines, push us into the niche which God has prepared for us. So shall our lives be beautified and our race raised in the civilization of the future as we grow away from all these prejudices which have been the instruments of our advancement according to the intention of an All-seeing Omnipotence, from the beginning. Never mind our poverty, ignorance, and the slights and injuries which we bear at the hands of a higher race. With the thought ever before us of what the Master suffered to raise all humanity to its present degree of prosperity and intelligence, let us cultivate, while we go about our daily tasks, no matter how inferior they may seem to us, beauty of the soul and mind, which being transmitted to our children by the law of heredity, shall improve the race by eliminating *immorality* from our midst and raising *morality* and virtue to their true place. Thirty-five years of liberty have made us a new people. The marks of servitude and oppression are dropping slowly from us; let us hasten the transformation of the body by the nobility of the soul."

> For of the soul the body form doth take,
> For soul is form and doth the body make,

quoted Dora.

"Yes," said Mrs. Willis with a smile, "that is the idea exactly, and well expressed. Now I hope that through the coming week you will think of what we have talked about this afternoon, for it is of the very first importance to all people, but particularly so to young folks."

Sappho, who had been thoughtfully embroidering pansies on white linen, now leaned back in her chair for a moment and said: "Mrs. Willis, there is one thing which puzzles me— how are we to overcome the nature which is given us? I mean how can we eliminate passion from our lives, and emerge into the purity which marked the life of Christ? So many of us desire purity and think to have found it, but in a moment of passion, or under the pressure of circumstances which we cannot control, we commit some horrid sin, and the taint of it sticks and will not leave us, and we grow to loathe ourselves."

"Passion, my dear Miss Clark, is a state in which the will lies dormant, and all other desires become subservient to one. Enthusiasm for any one object or duty may become a passion. I believe that in some degree passion may be beneficial, but we must guard ourselves against a sinful growth of any appetite. All work of whatever character, as I look at it, needs a certain amount of absorbing interest to become successful, and it is here that the Christian life gains its greatest glory in teaching us how to keep ourselves from abusing any of our human attributes. We are not held responsible for compulsory sin, only for the sin that is pleasant to our thoughts and palatable to our appetites. All desires and hopes with which we are endowed are good in the sight of God, only it is left for us to discover their right uses. Do I cover your ground?"

"Yes and no," replied Sappho; "but perhaps at some future time you will be good enough to talk with me personally upon this subject."

"Dear child, sit here by me. It is a blessing to look at you. Beauty like yours is inspiring. You seem to be troubled; what is it? If I can comfort or strengthen, it is all I ask." She pressed the girl's hand in hers and drew her into a secluded corner. For a moment the flood-gates of suppressed feeling flew open in the girl's heart, and she longed to lean her head on that motherly breast and unburden her sorrows there.

"Mrs. Willis, I am troubled greatly," she said at length.

"I am *so* sorry; tell me, my love, what it is all about."

Just as the barriers of Sappho's reserve seemed about to be swept away, there followed, almost instantly, a wave of repulsion toward this woman and her effusiveness, so forced and insincere. Sappho was very impressionable, and yielded readily to the influence which fell like a cold shadow between them. She drew back as from an abyss suddenly beheld stretching before her.

"On second thoughts, I think I ought to correct my remarks. It is not really *trouble*, but more a desire to confirm me in my own ideas."

"Well, if you feel you are right, dear girl, stand for the uplifting of the race and womanhood. Do not shrink from duty."

"It was simply a thought raised by your remarks on morality. I once knew a woman who had sinned. No one in the community in which she lived knew it but herself. She married a man who would have despised her had he known her story; but as it is, she is looked upon as a pattern of virtue for all women."

"And then what?" asked Mrs. Willis, with a searching glance at the fair face beside her.

"Ought she not to have told her husband before marriage? Was it not her duty to have thrown herself upon his clemency?"

"I think not," replied Mrs. Willis dryly. "See here, my dear, I am a practical woman of the world, and I think your young woman builded wiser that she knew. I am of the opinion that most men are like the lower animals in many things—they don't always know what is for their best good. If the husband had been left to himself, he probably would not have married the one woman in the world best fitted to be his wife. I think in her case she did her duty."

"Ah, that word 'duty.' What is our duty?" queried the girl, with a sad droop to the sensitive mouth. "It is so hard to know our duty. We are told that all hidden things shall be revealed. Must repented and atoned-for sin rise at last to be our curse?"

"Here is a point, dear girl. God does not look upon the constitution of sin as we do. His judgement is not ours; ours is finite, his infinite. *Your* duty is not to be morbid, thinking these thoughts that have puzzled older heads than yours. *Your* duty is, also, to be happy and bright for the good of those about you. Just blossom like the flowers, have faith and *trust*." At this point the entrance of the men made an interruption, and Mrs. Willis disappeared in a crowd of other matrons. Sappho was impressed in spite of herself, by the woman's words. She sat buried in deep thought.

There was evidently more in this woman than appeared upon the surface. With all the centuries of civilization and culture that have come to this grand old world, no man has yet been found able to trace the windings of God's in-scrutable ways. There are men and women whose seeming uselessness fit perfectly into the warp and woof of Destiny's web. All things work together for good.

Supper being over, the elderly people began to leave. It was understood that after nine o'clock the night belonged to the young people. A committee had been formed from among them to plan for their enjoyment, and they consulted with Ma Smith, in the kitchen, as to the best plan of procedure.

"The case is this," said the chairman, who was also the church chorister: "Ma Smith has bought four gallons of ice cream, to be sold for the benefit of this fair. It's *got* to go, and it rests with us to devise ways and means of getting rid of it."

"Get up a dance," suggested Sam Washington, a young fellow who was the life of all social functions.

"Dance!" exclaimed Ma Smith, "not in this house."

The choir-master surreptitiously kicked Sam on the shins, as he said soothingly: "Under the circumstances I see no other way, as we've *got* to sell the cream, and there's no harm in dancing, anyway."

"You ain't going to object to our dancing, are you, Ma? It's all old fogyism about dancing being a sin," chimed in Sam.

"Oh, but my son, I've been a church member over thirty years, a consistent Christian, and I never was up before the board for behavior unbecoming a professor. Think of the dis-grace on me if the church took it up," she expostulated tearfully.

"Look here, Ma, the deacons and ministers are all fool-ing you. It's the style for church members to go to the theatre and the circus, to balls and everything you can mention. Why, I've seen our own pastor up to see the Black Crook, and laughing like all possessed at the sights. Fact!"

"Why, Samuel!" said Ma Smith, "how can you stand there and tell me such awful stories?"

"Not a bit of a story," declared the brazen-faced Sam, "it's as true as gospel. I'll find out what seat the minister gets next June when the circus comes into town, and I'll get a seat for you right behind him. If you've never been to the circus, Ma, and to see the seven-headed lady and the dancing mokes, you ought to go as soon as possible. Think of the fun you're missing."

"Oh!" groaned the good woman in holy horror, "how you do go on."

"But that ain't nothing to the ice cream," continued Sam, "and them girls in there have got to be warmed up, or the cream will be left, and there won't be a thing doing when the committee calls for the money."

"That's so," replied Ma Smith, beginning to weaken in her opposition.

"Well, mother," said Will, who had been an amused lis-tener to the dialogue, "we'll have the dance, and it shall be *my* dance for *my* company. No one shall trouble you; you will have nothing to do with it."

"Well, if you say so, Willie, it's all right," replied his mother with a fond smile; "you are master in this house."

In the meantime the furniture in the parlors had been moved out by other members of the committee, and in one corner a set of whist-players were enjoying themselves at ten cents a head for a thirty-minute game, which ended at the stroke of a small silver bell, their places being taken by others.

Already it was getting very warm in the crowded rooms. The doors leading into the entry had been thrown open, and couples were finding seats in convenient nooks waiting for dancing to begin. The girls were thinking of ice cream. Rev. Tommy James gravitated toward Mrs. Davis's corner. She had not gone out with the other matrons.

"I enjoy a real good time as much as anybody, children," she said; "and when it comes to dancing, you can't lose your Aunt Hannah."

The Reverend Tommy was always at his ease with Mrs. Davis. She led him along paths which caused him no embar-rassment. He knew that she looked up to him because of his education and his clerical dignity. On his side, he admired her rugged common-sense, which put him at his ease, and banished the last atom of his "ladylike" bashfulness. Early in the winter he had been brought to realize the nature of his feeling for Mrs. Davis, by seeing Brother Silas Hamm, re-cently left a widower, and having ten children, making a de-cided stampede in the widow's direction. Reverend Tommy was grieved. To be sure, she was old enough to be his mother, but she had many good points to be considered. She was a good worker, experienced in married life and ways of making a man comfortable. Then her savings must be considered. When Tommy reached this last point he always felt sure that she was the most desirable woman in the world for a young minister. He felt hopeful tonight, because he had seen Brother Hamm and his bride in church the Sunday before. Mrs. Davis opened the conversation by speaking of the bride and groom.

"Hamm and his bride looked mighty comfut'ble in chuch Sunday, didn't they?"

"*He* did. I'm glad he's settled again. It is not good for man to be alone."

"'Deed I'm glad, too."

"*You*—well, well, I'm real glad to hear *you* say it."

"What for?" asked the widow coyly, looking down and playing with her fan.

"I—I didn't know how you and Brother Hamm stood."

"Stood! Well, I never."

"I thought Brother Hamm had been trying to get you," whispered Tommy, sitting closer and putting his arm across the back of her chair.

"Law suz, Mr. Jeems, how nervous you does make me. Do take yer arm away, everybody'll be a-lookin' at yer, honey.

I'm 'sprised at yer thinkin' I'd look at Hamm an' all them chillun. Massy knows what the 'ooman he's got's gwine to do with 'em." But she looked so mild and smiling that Tommy went into the seventh heaven of delight, and so lost his head that when he heard the call "Another couple wanted here!" he took Mrs. Davis on his arm and stood up on the floor, forgetful of the fact that he was within a few months of his ordination. A good-natured matron not connected with the church had volunteered to supply the lack of an orchestra. Waltzing was soon in full blast, and the demand on the ice-cream cans was filling Ma Smith's heart with joy, tempered with inward stings of conscience and fear of the Steward's Board. Dora was dancing assiduously and eating ice cream at John's expense, he meantime saying that if she kept on she would turn into a frozen dainty, to say nothing of a frost in his pocket-book. Dora declared that it was for the good of the cause, and he'd "just got to stand it." She was wildly happy because of the tender familiarity between her brother and her friend. A long-stemmed rose that Will wore in his button-hole had been transferred to Sappho's corsage. Dora smiled as she caught the half-puzzled, half-wondering expression on her mother's face.

It was approaching twelve o'clock when it was proposed to wind up the festivities with the good old "Virginy" reel. Sam Washington was the caller, and did his work with the fancy touch peculiar to a poetic Southern temperament. He was shrewd and good-natured, and a bit of a wag. He knew all the secret sighings of the ladies and their attendant swains. A lively girl whom everyone called "Jinny," remarked to Sam, referring to the fact that Sam was on probation: "Your class-leader won't recommend you to the Board for membership after tonight."

"Now, Jinny," replied Sam, stopping in his business of arranging couples, "don't make yourself obnoxious bringing up unpleasant subjects. I'll take my medicine like a man when the time comes: but I'd bust, sho, if I didn't git loose tonight. I'm in good company, too," he grinned, nodding toward Reverend Tommy and Mrs. Davis, who were just taking their places on the floor. "If this is good for Tommy, it is good enough for me."

All reserve was broken down the instant the familiar strains of the Virginia reel were heard. The dance was soon in full swing—an up-and-down, dead-in-earnest seeking for a good time, and a determination to have it if it was to be got. It was a vehement rhythmic thump, thump, thumpity thump, with a great stamping of the feet and cutting of the pigeon wing. Sam had provided himself with the lively Jinny for a partner, and was cutting grotesque juba figures in the pauses of the music, to the delight of the company. His partner, in wild vivacity, fairly vied with him in his efforts at doing the hoedown and the heel-and-toe. Not to be outdone, the Rev. Tommy James and Mrs. Davis scored great hits in cutting pigeon wings and in reviving forgotten beauties of the "walk-'round." Tommy "allowed" he hadn't enjoyed himself so much since he came up North.

"Yes," said Sam, "this beats the cake-walk all holler. Now then, one more turn and we're done. Forward on the head; balance yer partner; swing the next gent; swing that lady. Now swing yer rose, yer pretty rose, yer yaller rose of Texas. All promen*ade*."

Everybody declared it had been a wonderful evening. "Thank the Lord it's over," said Ma Smith to Mrs. Sarah Ann White, who was helping her in the kitchen.

"Well," said the latter, pausing in her work with her arms akimbo, "sech sights as I've seen tonight I never would have believed. 'Phelia Davis, what ought ter be a mother in Jerusalem, kickin' up her heels in your parlor like a clot in a corn-field; and that Tommy Jeems, no more fittin' for a minister that a suckin' babe, a-traipsin' after her like a bald-headed rooster."

Ida B. Wells-Barnett (1862–1931)

A voice of reform and reason, Ida B. Wells-Barnett led the anti-lynching movement. In 1892 she expanded the column that she wrote for *The New York Age* and published it as a pamphlet, *Southern Horrors: Lynch Law in All Its Phases*. Three years later, she published *A Red Record: Tabulated Statistics and Alleged Causes of Lynching in the United States, 1892–1894*. Concerned with the causes and the occurrences of lynchings, Wells-Barnett argued that white women were making false allegations of rape. She stressed that political and economic reasons, as well as consensual sex, prompted most of the lynchings. She knew this to be true from her many years of research and from personal experience. In 1892 in Memphis, Thomas Moss, a friend of Wells-Barnett, and two other black men were lynched because their grocery store attracted black customers away from a white grocery store.

Born to slave parents in Holly Springs, Mississippi, Wells-Barnett had to take care of her seven siblings when her parents died during a yellow fever epidemic in 1878. To do so Wells-Barnett used the training that she had received at Shaw University (later Rust College) to become a teacher. She moved to Memphis where she began the activism for which she is best known. In 1884, she sat down in the ladies' coach, rather than the segregated coach for blacks, and white male passengers had to remove her. She sued, won her case, but a higher court reversed the decision. When she critiqued the condition of black schools in Memphis, she was fired from her teaching job. She began soliciting subscriptions to the Memphis *Free Speech and Headlight*, a newspaper she edited, becoming a full-time newspaperwoman. When her editorial on the Thomas Moss incident appeared in the paper, she was at a general conference meeting of the African Methodist Episcopal Church in Philadelphia. Mobs destroyed the office of *Free Speech* and threatened her life. Wells-Barnett then settled in New York where she began writing the columns for *New York Age* that would become *Southern Horrors*.

Because she was interested in a wide range of issues affecting the black community, Wells protested the exclusion of blacks from the Chicago World's Fair of 1893, publishing twenty thousand copies of her pamphlet, *The Reason Why the Colored American Is Not in the World's Columbian Exposition*. She stayed in Chicago, formed the Ida B. Wells Club, and married Ferdinand Barnett, a Chicago lawyer who had two children. The couple had four more children, and with her husband's support, Wells-Barnett was able to continue her activist agenda, founding the first black female suffrage club, the Alpha Suffrage Club, in 1913. When her white Illinois delegates refused to let her march in the national suffrage parade with them, she waited until the right moment and stepped in the front of the procession, thus integrating the suffrage movement. Wells-Barnett was a champion of issues of race and gender and a towering transition from the late 19th century to the Harlem Renaissance.

From *A Red Record*

Chapter I

The Case Stated

The student of American sociology will find the year 1894 marked by a pronounced awakening of the public conscience to a system of anarchy and outlawry which had grown during a series of ten years to be so common, that scenes of unusual brutality failed to have any visible effect upon the humane sentiments of the people of our land.

Beginning with the emancipation of the Negro, the inevitable result of unbridled power exercised for two and a half centuries, by the white man over the Negro, began to show itself in acts of conscienceless outlawry. During the slave regime, the Southern white man owned the Negro body and soul. It was to his interest to dwarf the soul and preserve the body. Vested with unlimited power over his slave, to subject

From *A Red Record*.

him to any and all kinds of physical punishment, the white man was still restrained from such punishment as tended to injure the slave by abating his physical powers and thereby reducing his financial worth. While slaves were scourged mercilessly, and in countless cases inhumanly treated in other respects, still the white owner rarely permitted his anger to go so far as to take a life, which would entail upon him a loss of several hundred dollars. The slave was rarely killed, he was too valuable; it was easier and quite as effective, for discipline or revenge, to sell him "Down South."

But Emancipation came and the vested interests of the white man in the Negro's body were lost. The white man had no right to scourge the emancipated Negro, still less has he a right to kill him. But the Southern white people had been educated so long in that school of practice, in which might makes right, that they disdained to draw strict lines of action in dealing with the Negro. In slave times the Negro was kept subservient and submissive by the frequency and severity of the scourging, but, with freedom, a new system of intimidation came into vogue; the Negro was not only whipped and scourged; he was killed.

Not all nor nearly all of the murders done by white men, during the past thirty years in the South, have come to light, but the statistics as gathered and preserved by white men, and which have not been questioned, show that during these years more than ten thousand Negroes have been killed in cold blood, without the formality of judicial trial and legal execution. And yet, as evidence of the absolute impunity with which the white man dares to kill a Negro, the same record shows that during all these years, and for all these murders only three white men have been tried, convicted, and executed. As no white man has been lynched for the murder of colored people, these three executions are the only instances of the death penalty being visited upon white men for murdering Negroes.

Naturally enough the commission of these crimes began to tell upon the public conscience, and the Southern white man, as a tribute to the nineteenth century civilization, was in a manner compelled to give excuses for his barbarism. His excuses have adapted themselves to the emergency, and are aptly outlined by that greatest of all Negroes, Frederick Douglass, in an article of recent date, in which he shows that there have been three distinct eras of Southern barbarism, to account for which three distinct excuses have been made.

The first excuse given to the civilized world for the murder of unoffending Negroes was the necessity of the white man to repress and stamp out alleged "race riots." For years immediately succeeding the war there was an appalling slaughter of colored people, and the wires usually conveyed to northern people and the world the intelligence, first, that an insurrection was being planned by Negroes, which, a few hours later, would prove to have been vigorously resisted by white men, and controlled with a resulting loss of several killed and wounded. It was always a remarkable feature in these insurrections and riots that only Negroes were killed during the rioting, and that all white men escaped unharmed.

From 1865 to 1872, hundreds of colored men and women were mercilessly murdered and the almost invariable reason assigned was that they met their death by being alleged participants in an insurrection or riot. But this story at last wore itself out. No insurrection ever materialized; no Negro rioter was ever apprehended and proven guilty, and no dynamite ever recorded the black man's protest against oppression and wrong. It was too much to ask thoughtful people to believe this transparent story, and the southern white people at last made up their minds that some other excuse must be had.

Then came the second excuse, which had its birth during the turbulent times of reconstruction. By an amendment to the Constitution the Negro was given the right of franchise, and, theoretically at least, his ballot became his invaluable emblem of citizenship. In a government "of the people, for the people, and by the people," the Negro's vote became an important factor in all matters of state and national politics. But this did not last long. The southern white man would not consider that the Negro had any right which a white man was bound to respect, and the idea of a republican form of government in the southern states grew into general contempt. It was maintained that "This is a white man's government," and regardless of numbers the white man should rule. "No Negro domination" became the new legend on the sanguinary banner of the sunny South, and under it rode the Ku Klux Klan, the Regulators, and the lawless mobs, which for any cause chose to murder one man or a dozen as suited their purpose best. It was a long, gory campaign; the blood chills and the heart almost loses faith in Christianity when one thinks of Yazoo, Hamburg, Edgefield, Copiah, and the countless massacres of defenseless Negroes, whose only crime was the attempt to exercise their right to vote.

But it was a bootless strife for colored people. The government which had made the Negro a citizen found itself unable to protect him. It gave him the right to vote, but denied him the protection which should have maintained that right. Scourged from his home; hunted through the swamps; hung by midnight raiders, and openly murdered in the light of day, the Negro clung to his right of franchise with a heroism which would have wrung admiration from the hearts of savages. He believed that in that small white ballot there was a subtle something which stood for manhood as well as citizenship, and thousands of brave black men went to their graves, exemplifying the one by dying for the other.

The white man's victory soon became complete by fraud, violence, intimidation and murder. The franchise vouchsafed to the Negro grew to be a "barren ideality," and regardless of numbers, the colored people found themselves voiceless in the councils of those whose duty it was to rule. With no longer the fear of "Negro Domination" before their eyes, the white man's second excuse became valueless. With the Southern governments all subverted and the Negro actually eliminated from all participation in state and national elections, there could be no longer an excuse for killing Negroes to prevent "Negro Domination."

Brutality still continued; Negroes were whipped, scourged, exiled, shot and hung whenever and wherever it pleased the white man so to treat them, and as the civilized world with increasing persistency held the white people of the South to account for its outlawry, the murderers invented the third excuse—that Negroes had to killed to avenge their assaults upon women. There could be framed no possible excuse more harmful to the Negro and more unanswerable if true in its sufficiency for the white man.

Humanity abhors the assailant of womanhood, and this charge upon the Negro at once placed him beyond the pale of human sympathy. With such unanimity, earnestness and apparent candor was this charge made and reiterated that the world has accepted the story that the Negro is a monster which the Southern white man has painted him. And to-day, the Christian world feels, that while lynching is a crime, and lawlessness and anarchy the certain precursors of a nation's fall, it can not by word or deed, extend sympathy or help to a race of outlaws, who might mistake their plea for justice and deem it an excuse for their continued wrongs.

The Negro has suffered much and is willing to suffer more. He recognizes that the wrongs of two centuries can not be righted in a day, and he tries to bear his burden with patience for to-day and be hopeful for to-morrow. But there comes a time when the veriest worm will turn, and the Negro feels to-day that after all the work he has done, all the sacrifices he has made, and all the suffering he has endured, if he did not, now, defend his name and manhood from this vile accusation, he would be unworthy even of the contempt of mankind. It is to this charge he how feels he must make answer.

If the Southern people in defense of their lawlessness, would tell the truth and admit that colored men and women are lynched for almost any offense, from murder to a misdemeanor, there would not now be the necessity for this defense. But when they intentionally, maliciously and constantly belie the record and bolster up these falsehoods by the words of legislators, preachers, governors and bishops, then the Negro must give to the world his side of the awful story.

A word as to the charge itself. In considering the third reason assigned by the Southern white people for the butchery of blacks, the question must be asked, what the white man means when he charges the black man with rape. Does he mean the crime which the statutes of the civilized states describe as such? Not by any means. With the Southern white man, any mesalliance existing between a white woman and a colored man is a sufficient foundation for the charge of rape. The Southern white man says that it is impossible for a voluntary alliance to exist between a white woman and a colored man, and therefore, the fact of an alliance is a proof of force. In numerous instances where colored men have been lynched on the charge of rape, it was positively known at the time of lynching, and indisputably proven after the victim's death, that the relationship sustained between the man and woman was voluntary and clandestine, and that in no court of law could even the charge of assault have successfully maintained.

It was for the assertion of this fact, in the defense of her own race, that the writer hereof became an exile; her property destroyed and her return to her home forbidden under penalty of death, for writing the following editorial which was printed in her paper, the Free Speech, in Memphis, Tenn., May 21, 1892:

"Eight Negroes lynched since last issue of the 'Free Speech' one at Little Rock, Ark., last Saturday morning where the citizens broke (?) into the penitentiary and got their man; three near Anniston, Ala., one near New Orleans; and three at Clarksville, Ga., the last three for killing a white man, and five on the same old racket—the new alarm about raping white women. The same programme of hanging, then shooting bullets into the lifeless bodies was carried out to the letter. Nobody in this section of the country believes the old threadbare lie that Negro men rape white women. If Southern white men are not careful, they will over-reach themselves and public sentiment will have a reaction; a conclusion will then be reached which will be very damaging to the moral reputation of their women."

But threats cannot suppress the truth, and while the Negro suffers the soul deformity, resultant from two and a half centuries of slavery, he is no more guilty of this vilest of all vile charges than the white man who would blacken his name.

During all the years of slavery, no such charge was ever made, not even during the dark days of the rebellion, when the white man, following the fortunes of war went to do battle for the maintenance of slavery. While the master was away fighting to forge the fetters upon the slave, he left his wife and children with no protectors save the Negroes themselves. And yet during those years of trust and peril, no Negro proved recreant to his trust and no white man returned to a home that had been dispoiled.

Likewise during the period of alleged "insurrection," and alarming "race riots," it never occurred to the white man, that his wife and children were in danger of assault. Nor in the

Reconstruction era, when the hue and cry was against "Negro Domination," was there ever a thought that the domination would ever contaminate a fireside or strike to death the virtue of womanhood. It must appear strange indeed, to every thoughtful and candid man, that more than a quarter of a century elapsed before the Negro began to show signs of such infamous degeneration.

In his remarkable apology for lynching, Bishop Haygood, of Georgia, says: "No race, not the most savage, tolerates the rape of woman, but it may be said without reflection upon any other people that the Southern people are now and always have been most sensitive concerning the honor of their women—their mothers, wives, sisters and daughters." It is not the purpose of this defense to say one word against the white women of the South. Such need not be said, but it is their misfortune that the chivalrous white men of that section, in order to escape the deserved execration of the civilized world, should shield themselves by their cowardly and infamously false excuse, and call into question that very honor about which their distinguished priestly apologist claims they are most sensitive. To justify their own barbarism they assume a chivalry which they do not possess. True chivalry respects all womanhood, and no one who reads the record, as it is written in the faces of the million mulattoes in the South, will for a minute conceive that the southern white man had a very chivalrous regard for the honor due the women of his own race or respect for the womanhood which circumstances placed in his power. That chivalry which is "most sensitive concerning the honour of women" can hope for but little respect from the civilized world, when it confines itself entirely to the women who happen to be white. Virtue knows no color line, and the chivalry which depends upon complexion of skin and texture of hair can command no honest respect.

When emancipation came to the Negroes, there arose in the northern part of the United States an almost divine sentiment among the noblest, purest and best white women of the North, who felt called to a mission to educate and Christianize the millions of southern ex-slaves. From every nook and corner of the North, brave young white women answered that call and left their cultured home, their happy associations and their lives of ease, and with heroic determination went to the South to carry light and truth to the benighted blacks. It was a heroism no less than that which calls for volunteers for India, Africa and the Isles of the sea. To educate their unfortunate charges; to teach them the Christian virtues and to inspire in them the moral sentiments manifest in their own lives, these young women braved dangers whose record reads more like fiction than fact. They became social outlaws in the South. The peculiar sensitiveness of the southern white men for women, never shed its protecting influence about them. No friendly word from their own race cheered them in their work; no hospitable doors gave them the companionship like that from which they had come. No chivalrous white man doffed his hat in honor or respect. They were "Nigger teachers"—unpardonable offenders in the social ethics of the South, and were insulted; persecuted and ostracised, not by Negroes, but by the white manhood which boasts of its chivalry toward women.

And yet these northern women worked on, year after year, unselfishly, with a heroism which amounted almost to martyrdom. Threading their way through dense forests, working in schoolhouse, in the cabin and in the church, thrown at all times and in all places among the unfortunate and lowly Negroes, whom they had come to find and to serve, these northern women, thousands of them, have spent more than a quarter of a century in giving to the colored people their splendid lessons for home and heart and soul. Without protection, save that which innocence gives to every good woman, they went about their work, fearing no assault and suffering none. Their chivalrous protectors were hundreds of miles away in their northern homes, and yet they never feared any "great dark faced mobs," they dared night or day to "go beyond their own roof trees." They never complained of assaults, and no mob was ever called into existence to avenge crimes against them. Before the world adjudges the Negro a moral monster, a vicious assailant of womanhood and a menace to the sacred precincts of home, the colored people ask the consideration of the silent record of gratitude, respect, protection and devotion of the millions of the race in the South, to the thousands of northern white women who have served as teachers and missionaries since the war.

The Negro may not have known what chivalry was, but he knew enough to preserve inviolate the womanhood of the South which was entrusted to his hands during the war. The finer sensibilities of his soul may have been crushed out by years of slavery, but his heart was full of gratitude to the white woman of the North, who blessed his home and inspired his soul in all these years of freedom. Faithful to his trust in both of these instances, he should now have the impartial ear of the civilized world, when he dares to speak for himself as against the infamy wherewith he stands charged.

It is his regret, that, in his own defense, he must disclose to the world that degree of dehumanizing brutality which fixes upon America the blot of a national crime. Whatever faults and failings other nations may have in their dealings with their own subjects or with other people, no other civilized nation stands condemned before the world with a series of crimes so peculiarly national. It becomes a painful duty of the Negro to reproduce a record which shows that a large portion of the American people avow anarchy, condone murder and defy the contempt of civilization.

These pages are written in no spirit of vindictiveness, for all who give the subject consideration must concede that far too serious is the condition of that civilized government in which the spirit of unrestrained outlawry constantly increases in violence, and casts its blight over a continually growing area of territory. We plead not for the colored people alone, but for all victims of the terrible injustice which puts men and women to death without form of law. During the year 1894, there were 132 person executed in the United States by due form of law, while in the same year, 197 persons were put to death by mobs who gave the victims no opportunity to make a lawful defense. No comment need be made upon a condition of public sentiment responsible for such alarming results.

The purpose of the pages which follow shall be to give the record which has been made, not by colored men, but that which is the result of compilations made by white men, of reports sent over the civilized world by white men in the South. Out of their own mouths shall the murderers be condemned. For a number of years the Chicago Tribune, admittedly one of the leading journals of America, has made a specialty of the compilation of statistics touching upon lynching. The data compiled by that journal and published to the world January 1st, 1894, up to the present time has not been disputed. In order to be safe from the charge of exaggeration, the incidents hereinafter reported have been confined to those vouched for by the Tribune.

Chapter X

The Remedy

It is a well established principle of law that every wrong has a remedy. Herein rests our respect for law. The Negro does not claim that all of the one thousand black men, women and children, who have been hanged, shot and burned alive during the past ten years, were innocent of the charges made against them. We have associated too long with the white man not to have copied his vices as well as his virtues. But we do insist that the punishment is not the same for both classes of criminals. In lynching, opportunity is not given the Negro to defend himself against the unsupported accusations of white men and women. The word of the accuser is held to be true and the excited blood-thirsty mob demands that the rule of law be reversed and instead of proving the accused to be guilty, the victim of their hate and revenge must prove himself innocent. No evidence he can offer will satisfy the mob; he is bound hand and foot and swung into eternity. Then to excuse its infamy, the mob almost invariably reports the monstrous falsehood that its victim made a full confession before he was hanged.

With all military, legal and political power in their hands, only two of the lynching States have attempted a check by exercising the power which is theirs. Mayor Trout, of Roanoke, Virginia, called out the militia in 1893, to protect a Negro prisoner, and in so doing nine men were killed and a number wounded. Then the mayor and militia withdrew, left the Negro to his fate and he was promptly lynched. The business men realized the blow to the town's financial interests, called the mayor home, [and] the grand jury indicted and prosecuted the ringleaders of the mob. They were given light sentences, the highest being one of twelve months in State prison. The day he arrived at the penitentiary, he was pardoned by the governor of the State.

The only other real attempt made by the authorities to protect a prisoner of the law, and which was more successful, was that of Gov. McKinley, of Ohio, who sent the militia to Washington Courthouse, O., in October, 1894, and five men were killed and twenty wounded in maintaining the principle that the law must be upheld.

In South Carolina, in April, 1893, Gov. Tillman aided the mob by yielding up to be killed, a prisoner of the law, who had voluntarily placed himself under the Governor's protection. Public sentiment by its representatives has encouraged Lynch Law, and upon the revolution of this sentiment we must depend for its abolition.

Therefore, we demand a fair trial by law for those accused of crime, and punishment by law after honest conviction. No maudlin sympathy for criminals is solicited, but we do ask that the law shall punish all alike. We earnestly desire those that control the forces which make public sentiment to join with us in the demand. Surely the humanitarian spirit of this country which reaches out to denounce the treatment of the Russian Jews, the Armenian Christians, the laboring poor of Europe, the Siberian exiles and the native women of India— will no longer refuse to lift its voice on this subject. If it were known that the cannibals or the savage Indians had burned three human beings alive in the past two years, the whole of Christendom would be roused, to devise ways and means to put a stop to it. Can you remain silent and inactive when such things are done in our own community and country? Is your duty to humanity in the United States less binding?

What can you do, reader, to prevent lynching, to thwart anarchy and promote law and order throughout our land?

1st. You can help disseminate the facts contained in this book by bringing them to the knowledge of every one with whom you come in contact, to the end that public sentiment may be revolutionized. Let the facts speak for themselves, with you as a medium.

2d. You can be instrumental in having churches, missionary societies, Y.M.C.A.'s, W.C.T.U.'s and all Christian and moral forces in connection with your religious and social life, pass resolutions of condemnation and protest every time a lynching takes place; and see that they are sent to the place where these outrages occur.

3d. Bring to the intelligent consideration of Southern people the refusal of capital to invest where lawlessness and mob violence hold sway. Many labor organizations have declared the resolution that they would avoid lynch infested localities as they would the pestilence when seeking new homes. If the South wishes to build up its waste places quickly, there is no better way than to uphold the majesty of the law by enforcing obedience to the same, and meting out the same punishment to all classes of criminals, white as well as black. "Equality before the law," must become a fact as well as a theory before America is truly the "land of the free and the home of the brave."

4th. Think and act on independent lines in this behalf, remembering that after all, it is the white man's civilization and the white man's government which are on trial. This crusade will determine whether that civilization can maintain itself by itself, or whether anarchy shall prevail; whether this Nation shall write itself down a success at self government, or in deepest humiliation admit its failure complete; whether the precepts and theories of Christianity are professed and practiced by American white people as Golden Rules of thought and action, or adopted as a system of morals to be preached to heathen until they attain to the intelligence which needs the system of Lynch Law.

5th. Congressman Blair offered a resolution in the House of Representatives, August, 1894. The organized life of the country can speedily make this a law by sending resolutions to Congress indorsing Mr. Blair's bill and asking Congress to create the commission. In no better way can the question be settled, and the Negro does not fear the issue. The following is the resolution:

"Resolved, By the House of Representatives and Senate in congress assembled, That the committee on labor be instructed to investigate and report the number, location and date of all alleged assaults by males upon females throughout the country during the ten years last preceding the passing of this joint resolution, for or on account of which organized but unlawful violence has been inflicted or attempted to be inflicted. Also to ascertain and report all facts of organized but unlawful violence to the person, with the attendant facts and circumstances, which have been inflicted upon accused persons alleged to have been guilty of crimes punishable by due process of law which have taken place in any part of the country within the ten years last preceding the passage of this resolution. Such investigation shall be made by the usual methods and agencies of the Department of Labor, and report made to Congress as soon as the work can be satisfactorily done, and the sum of $25,000, or so much thereof as may be necessary, is hereby appropriated to pay the expenses out of any money in the treasury not otherwise appropriated."

The belief has been constantly expressed in England that in the United States, which has produced Wm. Lloyd Garrison, Henry Ward Beecher, James Russell Lowell, John G. Whittier and Abraham Lincoln there must be those of their descendants who would take hold of the work of inaugurating an era of law and order. The colored people of this country who have been loyal to the flag believe the same, and strong in that belief have begun this crusade. To those who still feel they have no obligation in the matter, we commend the following lines of Lowell on "Freedom."

Men! whose boast it is that ye
Come of fathers brave and free,
If there breathe on earth a slave
Are ye truly free and brave?
If ye do not feel the chain,
When it works a brother's pain,
Are ye not base slaves indeed,
Slaves unworthy to be freed?

Women! who shall one day bear
Sons to breathe New England air,
If ye hear without a blush,
Deeds to make the roused blood rush
Like red lava through your veins,
For your sisters now in chains,—
Answer! are ye fit to be
Mothers of the brave and free?

Is true freedom but to break
Fetters for our own dear sake,
And, with leathern hearts, forget
That we owe mankind a debt?
No! true freedom is to share
All the chains our brothers wear,
And, with heart and hand, to be
Earnest to make others free!

There are slaves who fear to speak
For the fallen and the weak;
They are slaves who will not choose
Hatred, scoffing, and abuse,
Rather than in silence shrink
From the truth they needs must think;
They are slaves who dare not be
In the right with two or three.

A Field for Practical Work

The very frequent inquiry made after my lectures by interested friends is, "What can I do to help the cause?" The answer always is, "Tell the world the facts." When the Christian world knows the alarming growth and extent of outlawry in our land, some means will be found to stop it.

The object of this publication is to tell the facts, and friends of the cause can lend a helping hand by aiding in the distribution of these books. When I present our cause to a minister, editor, lecturer, or representative of any moral agency, the first demand is for facts and figures. Plainly, I can not then hand out a book with a twenty-five cent tariff on the information contained. This would be only a new method in the book agents' art. In all such cases it is a pleasure to submit this book for investigation, with the certain assurance of gaining a friend to the cause.

There are many agencies which may be enlisted in our cause by the general circulation of the facts herein contained. The preachers, teachers, editors and humanitarians of the white race, at home and abroad, must have facts laid before them, and it is our duty to supply these facts. The Central Anti-Lynching League, Room 9, 128 Clark st., Chicago, has established a Free Distribution Fund, the work of which can be promoted by all who are interested in this work.

Anti-lynching leagues, societies and individuals can order books from this fund at agents' rates. The books will be sent to their order, or, if desired, will be distributed by the League among those whose co-operative aid we so greatly need. The writer hereof assures prompt distribution of books according to order, and public acknowledgment of all orders through the public press.

Expansion, Experimentation, and Excellence:
20th- and 21st-Century African American Women's Writings

I f, as Jacqueline Jones Royster says in the opening essay to this volume, "the nineteenth century dawned as a world of danger and desire," the twentieth century ended as an era of expansion, experimentation, and excellence. Twentieth-century African American women writers have been instrumental in crafting an American literature informed by the nexus of race, gender, class, and other categories of difference. As a group of writers, they have been prolific, writing in all genres, spanning various literary movements, and garnering coveted prizes from the MacArthur to the Pulitzer, the American Book Award to the Nobel. The writers tackle vexing issues and create memorable characters: folk healers, conjure women, detectives, aliens, maids, models, slaves, saviors, and Christian grandmothers with devilish granddaughters. The writers have a story to tell, and they write their stories with pens dipped in the ink of their gendered and racialized lives.

The first distinct post-Reconstruction era of twentieth-century African American women's literature was the Harlem Renaissance, roughly the decade of the 1920s. This was the time when Harlem was in its glory as both a movement and a mecca. This was the age of "The New Negro"—a Negro very conscious of African roots deeply implanted in American soil. Political activist Marcus Garvey galvanized the hopeful with his plan to return to Africa. Langston Hughes fashioned characters and wrote poems that celebrated the resistance and resiliency of black life in Harlem. Claude McKay, Countee Cullen, W. E. B. DuBois, and a host of other male writers and thinkers did much to carve a cultural movement and a cultural site. Women writers, too, such as Jessie Fauset, Zora Neale Hurston, and Dorothy West flocked to Harlem. Yet, many of the women writers hosted alternative sites for the outpouring of the creative arts. Georgia Douglas Johnson's home in Washington, D.C., was one such site.

Along with a change of venue, women writers also changed the formula for writing some of the classic themes of African American literature. Rather than writing *Passing* (1929)[1] as a simple story of racial negotiation, Nella Larsen makes it a complicated story of black female sexuality. Rather than creating a protagonist who leaves the country for the city and marries a respectable husband, Zora Neale Hurston gives us Janie Crawford, who dares to marry a man twenty years her junior and lives with him in a place so countrified that it's called "the muck." Rather than hide behind a generic banner of blackness, Marita Bonner describes the particulars of being "young, a woman, and colored." The women of the Harlem Renaissance write about the intersectionality of their lives. They were aware of their various social classes and castes and did much to challenge an Anglo-beauty aesthetic. Jessie Fauset, as well as the other women fiction writers, gives us women characters who must negotiate a range of skin tones and hues.

---

[1]Because the full bibliographical information for primary texts is listed elsewhere in this volume, I do not repeat that information in this essay. The "Works Cited" page lists secondary texts only.

The Harlem Renaissance generated more women poets than women fiction writers. And as Maureen Honey points out, it is a misconception to think that the women poets wrote only pastoral and romantic lyrics: "In fact, much of their poetry exhibits the qualities of 'New Negro' writing: identification with the race, a militant proud spirit, anger at racism, determination to fight oppression, rejection of white culture, and an attempt to reconstruct an invisible heritage" (Honey 2). The poems by the women bring a specificity to their lives, as captured by Georgia Douglas Johnson when she speaks of "The Heart of a Woman," or Anne Spencer when she writes of "The Wife-Woman," or Gwendolyn Bennett when she speaks "To a Dark Girl."

On the heels of the Harlem Renaissance was the age of realism and naturalism. With its emphasis on environmental determinism, Richard Wright's *Native Son* (1940) established a different tone for African American literature in the 1940s and 1950s. Wright's Bigger Thomas quickly became a symbol of the way African American men led cornered and explosive lives. But Wright's heroes were not the only models for those who migrated to urban centers. Aptly typified by Ann Petry's *The Street* (1946), women experienced their own brand of alienation in a hostile environment. Rather than the Harlem of night clubs, rent parties, and the cultural arts, Petry's divorced mother, Lutie Johnson, struggles to make a life for herself and her son in a Harlem tenement. Lutie is not a female Bigger Thomas. Petry complicates Lutie's conflicts and gives her black women characters an agency not accorded the typical woman victim in a naturalistic text.

Nevertheless, Wright's *Native Son* did much to make Chicago an important geographical site in African American literature. By the time Lorraine Hansberry wrote *A Raisin in the Sun* (1959), Chicago was still a racially segregated area where the Younger family fights for their right to move despite restrictive housing covenants. Although the Younger family has more opportunities than the Southside Chicago family of Richard Wright's Bigger Thomas, they are still caught in material and psychological traps of an American dream that taunts them. It was not until Gwendolyn Brooks's *A Street in Bronzeville* (1945) and her many later poems about the urban poor that fuller pictures of black life in metropolitan areas began emerging. Brooks's well-crafted poems describe couples living in kitchenette buildings, preachers ruminating behind their sermons, funeral rites for relatives, and pool players who skip school. Respected by both earlier writers and the upcoming group of young black artists, Brooks became a transitional bridge between the first half of the 20th century and later decades.

With the dawning of the Black Arts Movement, African American women raised their voices in much more overt protest. As a literary aesthetic, the Black Arts Movement was "both inherently and overtly political in content . . . [and] the only American literary movement to advance 'social engagement' as a sine qua non of its aesthetic. The movement broke from the immediate past of protest and petition (civil rights) literature and dashed forward toward an alternative that initially seemed unthinkable and unobtainable: Black Power" (Salaam 70). The writers tried to define their roles in the midst of a cultural revolution. Alice Walker's *Meridian* (1976) asks: What is the role of a revolutionary? Are some roles more valued than others? How does one know when a racial debt has been paid?

Most of the African American women writers who responded to the identity and political issues of the 1960s and 1970s were poets. In "For Saundra," Nikki Giovanni explains that she "wanted to write a poem about trees," but writing about nature is a luxury that she cannot afford in the tense political climate. The titles of Sonia Sanchez's poetry collections announced a new era for the African American Woman artist: *We a BaddDDD People* (1970); *It's a New Day: Poems for Young Brothas and Sistuhs* (1971); *A Blues Book for Blue Black Magical Women* (1974); *I've Been a Woman: New and Selected Poems* (1979); *Homegirls and Handgrenades* (1984). Mari Evans announced, "I am a black woman. . . . look on me and be renewed" and June Jordan warned "I Must Become a Menace to my Enemies."

Although the poets led the way in heralding that "black is beautiful," novelists in the post–Civil Rights era and throughout the 1980s and 1990s have done much to challenge

Western notions of beauty and definitions of womanhood.[2] Each of the early works in Toni Morrison's canon deals with the changing community standards for black women's beauty and being. *The Bluest Eye* (1970) describes Pecola, a dark-skinned black girl whose dream is to have blue eyes. She becomes her community's scapegoat for all the ugliness of life. Morrison's Sula, "a heavy brown," helps her best friend Nel to see herself anew and not as "a custard-colored" imitation of her mother's lineage. In *Sula*, hotcombs to straighten the hair and clothespins to narrow the nose are items from a discriminatory past. In *Song of Solomon* (1977), the fair-skinned hues of Dr. Dead's daughters no longer give them the cultural currency they would have had during an earlier era. The daughters end up in their forties still making artificial roses, "sitting like big baby dolls before a table heaped with scraps of red velvet." In *Tar Baby* (1981) Morrison deconstructs notions of "good hair." Dreadlocks become "living hair," "foliage [that] from a distance . . . looked like nothing less than the crown of a deciduous tree." The book celebrates "wild," "aggressive hair."

Many other women writers have interrogated what it means to be a black woman with kinky hair and dark hues. Ntozake Shange celebrates coiled hair, naming her volume *Nappy Edges*. Audre Lorde raises the question, "Is Your Hair Still Political?" and in "homage to my hair" Lucille Clifton links nappy hair to tasty greens. Crucial to the empowerment of Alice Walker's Celie in *The Color Purple* (1982) is her appreciation of Shug: "She got the nattiest, shortest, kinkiest hair I ever saw, and I loves every strand of it" (57). Celie redefines beauty in terms of resiliency: "I'm pore, I'm black, I may be ugly and can't cook, a voice say to everything listening. But I'm here" (187). Gloria Naylor's *Mama Day* (1988) takes place in the Sea Islands, where an "ancient mother of pure black" sets the action rolling. Perhaps *The Women of Brewster Place* (1982) best describes the wide range of hues and features that black women have lobbied for in their creative works:

> Nutmeg arms leaned over windowsills, gnarled ebony legs carried groceries up double flights of steps, and saffron hands strung out wet laundry on back-yard lines. Their perspiration mingled with the steam from boiling pots of smoked pork and greens, and it curled on the edges of the aroma of vinegar douches and Evening in Paris cologne that drifted through the street where they stood together—hands on hips, straight-backed, round-bellied, high-behinded women who threw their heads back when they laughed and exposed strong teeth and dark gums (Naylor 5).

Having opened the way for a wide range of themes and protagonists, African American women in the late 1980s, 1990s, and the new Millennium have been freer to explore the possibilities of genres. Although black women always have experimented with the forms and conventions, the last several decades have seen a renaissance of such activity. Adrienne Kennedy writes plays that are avant-garde, surrealistic dreamscapes. Octavia Butler and Tananarive Due reconstruct the worlds of science fiction. Toni Morrison, Sherley Anne Williams, J. California Cooper, and others stretch the boundaries of slave narratives, while Bebe Moore Campbell, Michelle Cliff, Thulani Davis, and Tayari Jones rewrite pivotal historical moments. The writers challenge formal language codes (*Push, The Color Purple*), link words and music (*Muse-Echo Blues, Bailey's Café, Jazz*), and revitalize black autobiography through prose and poetry (*Every Goodbye Ain't Gone, Assata, Thomas and Beulah*).

Eschewing dichotomies between the vernacular and the academic, the folk and the formal, the writers are as at home with expressive culture as they are with stylized Western conventions. Alongside *Song of Solomon's* Greek and biblical myths are the African American myths of slaves who flew back home. In Julie Dash's *Daughters of the Dust* (1999), Ibo tales

[2]For a more extended version of this analysis of the changing beauty aesthetic in African American women's literature, see my book *Granny Midwives and Black Women Writers: Double-Dutched Readings* (New York: Routledge), 1996.

permeate the air. Interwoven in Ntozake Shange's *Sassafrass, Cypress, & Indigo* (1982) are recipes for "marvelous menstruating moments." Tina McElroy Ansa's *Baby of the Family* (1989) gives readers the lore behind babies born with a caul, while Gloria Naylor's *Mama Day* details the power of a woman born to the seventh son of a seventh son. Zora Neale Hurston would be proud of the way the writers have performed the interplay between lore and literature.

Paule Marshall's "Poets in the Kitchen" speaks of women who realize that "in this man world you got to take yuh mouth and make a gun!" (7). Twelve-year-old Betsy in Ntozake Shange's *Betsy Brown* (1985) gains a voice by repeating over and over again a line from a Paul Laurence Dunbar poem, " 'Speak up . . . an' 'spress yo'self.' " African American women have been speaking, preaching, and writing the word for centuries. As many have noted, they have cared enough to find each others' graves and work each other's gardens. And "because each had discovered years before that they were neither white nor male, and that all freedom and triumph was forbidden to them, they had set about creating something else to be" (*Sula* 52). In the 21st century, African American women writers are continuing this work of creation.

VALERIE LEE
Professor of English
The Ohio State University

Secondary Works Cited

Honey, Maureen, ed. *Shadowed Dreams: Women's Poetry of the Harlem Renaissance.* New Brunswick: Rutgers University Press, 1989.

Lee, Valerie. *Granny Midwives and Black Women Writers: Double-Dutched Readings.* New York: Routledge, 1996.

Salaam, Kalamu ya. "Black Arts Movement." *The Oxford Companion to African American Literature*, eds. William Andrews, Frances Smith Foster, & Trudier Harris. New York: Oxford University Press, 1997.

The Harlem Renaissance

Alice Moore Dunbar-Nelson (1875–1935)

Born of mixed parentage in New Orleans, Alice Moore Dunbar-Nelson wrote fiction, poetry, newspaper articles, and journal entries; she also played several musical instruments. She graduated from Straight University (now Dillard). At Cornell, she wrote a master's thesis on Milton and Wordsworth and published her first book, *Violets and Other Tales*, in 1895. Well-known poet Paul Laurence Dunbar saw the collection, began a correspondence with Alice, and married her in 1898. Unlike Paul, Alice did not write dialect poetry. Caste, class, demanding working and traveling schedules, and Paul's drinking caused problems within the marriage. When the marriage ended, Dunbar-Nelson returned to her teaching job and eventually married Robert Nelson. She was active in a number of political and social arenas.

I Sit and Sew

I sit and sew—a useless task it seems,
My hands grown tired, my head weighed down with
    dreams—
The panoply of war, the martial tread of men,
Grim-faced, stern-eyed, gazing beyond the ken
Of lesser souls, whose eyes have not seen Death
Nor learned to hold their lives but as a breath—
But—I must sit and sew.

I sit and sew—my heart aches with desire—
That pageant terrible, that fiercely pouring fire
On wasted fields, and writhing grotesque things
Once men. My soul in pity flings
Appealing cries, yearning only to go
There in that holocaust of hell, those fields of woe—
But—I must sit and sew.—

The little useless seam, the idle patch;
Why dream I here beneath my homely thatch,
When there they lie in sodden mud and rain,
Pitifully calling me, the quick ones and the slain?
You need me, Christ! It is no roseate dream
That beckons me—this pretty futile seam,
It stifles me—God, must I sit and sew?

"I Sit and Sew," "Snow in October," and "Une Femme Dit" by Alice Moore Dunbar-Nelson.

Snow in October

Today I saw a thing of arresting poignant beauty:
A strong young tree, brave in its Autumn finery
Of scarlet and burnt umber and flame yellow,
Bending beneath a weight of early snow,
Which sheathed the north side of its slender trunk,
And spread a heavy white chilly afghan
Over its crested leaves.

Yet they thrust through, defiant, glowing,
Claiming the right to live another fortnight,
Clamoring that Indian Summer had not come,
Crying "Cheat! Cheat!" because Winter had stretched
Long chill fingers into the brown, streaming hair
Of fleeing October.

The film of snow shrouded the proud redness of the tree,
As premature grief grays the strong head
Of a virile, red-haired man.

Une Femme Dit

February 20, 1926

The title of this column changes this week. It is to be regretted that it must be done. The writer is a peace-loving soul, with conservative tastes, and getting old enough to dislike change from comfortable well-known conditions to new things. But it had to be done. The title, "A Woman's Point of View" got to be so popular that it cropped up in all sorts of places and the writer found herself reading articles that bore her title, but not her imprint. That is regrettable. There are so many words in the English language, over a half-million, are there not? And so many phrase books. And thesauruses galore. But evidently not accessible to some editors. Am almost tempted to hunt up some of these battered old dictionaries and word books, left over from the crossword puzzle craze, and distribute them to the fraternity of the Fourth Estate. So, the English language not being large enough to accommodate all the female columnists extant, recourse must be made to the French. So—"One Woman Says" in French is the future caption of these burning thoughts.

Let us hope there will be no further need of change.

Never did like anyone to have a hat like mine. If someone did buy one—even though imitation may be the sincerest flattery—said imitated hat went promptly to the rummage sale—even though to go hatless was the alternative.

• • • •

Lulu Belle has come to Philadelphia; has been seen by the surrounding country, and has conquered. By now it is delighting New York.

And you can hear a howl go through the country like the wail of lost souls from the Man and Brother and the Woman and Sister over Lulu Belle.

"The worst side of Negro life depicted."

"Why did not Belasco and Sheldon pick out the best types of our race—our Washington and Cleveland and best New York and Philadelphia and Pittsburgh colored people and show them on the stage?"

"Why present the demi-monde and crap shooters, prize fighters, barbers and slum denizens to write a play around?"

"Why scenes in cabarets and saloons and bedrooms, instead of fashionable drawing rooms?"

"It will hurt us with the white people, who want to believe that what Octavius Roy Cohen says is true."

And in spite of all that, *Lulu Belle* is a wonderfully fine piece of production.

And why should a white man do our propaganda for us?

Our so-called "best people," our lovely drawing rooms and high types of men and women are uninteresting. Just as uninteresting as would be a pageant written around—well the Coolidge family for instance.

Lulu Belle, the play, is alive, vivid with color, action, romance, character study. Lulu Belle, the woman, is thoroughly detestable. She has not a single redeeming quality—except her vivid beauty, and the fact that she runs true to form. She is elemental, primordial, the Lilith of the ages, she is, in fact—Carmen.

Edward Sheldon and Charles MacArthur did not go far afield, when they conceived the plot of *Lulu Belle*. They simply took the old story, popularized by Merrimee, and set to music by Bizet, and now lately Russianized under the title of *Carmencita and the Soldier*. The old, old story, as old as the story of Adam and Eve. Transplanted now from Seville and the Pyrenees to Hell's Kitchen and Harlem and Paris. There is no detail of Bizet's opera missing. Lulu Belle swaggers into the noisome, picturesque, teeming streets of Hell's Kitchen, as Carmen swaggers into the streets of the Spanish town. Lulu Belle fights with one of her associate street gamins, as Carmen fights with one of the other girls in the cigar factory. Lulu Belle tempts the virtuous young barber, married and decent, into forgetting his respectability, as Carmen tempts Don Jose, the gentle young officer into forgetting his duty as a soldier. Lulu Belle is faithless to the barber, and he is cognizant of the fact, yet sinks so low that he aids and abets her in her plunder of the victims who come to her apartment in Harlem, even as Carmen is faithless to Don Jose, who deserting the army becomes a smuggler and a thief in her band of smugglers. The infatuated George is deaf to the entreaties of his uncle to return to his wife and suffering family, even as Don Jose is deaf to the pleadings of his erstwhile sweetheart, Michaela, who comes with a message from his dying mother. Lulu Belle deserts George when he is in dire trouble because of his love for her and goes with Vicompte de Viliars even as Carmen deserts Don Jose for the Toreador. And George, the beggar and ex-convict, finds Lulu Belle in Paris, and wreaks horrible vengeance on her, even as Don Jose finds Carmen in Seville, in the hour of her greatest triumph, and makes her pay the penalty of her falseness and cruelty.

There are no details lacking to make the parallel complete. Lulu Belle is superstitious, a believer in dreams and their interpretations, a gambler, who must rub her hands on the hump of her hunchback mascot before she goes into a friendly game of craps, even as Carmen is superstitious and helps the smugglers gamble, and reads her fortune in cards, and interprets dreams.

And neither seems to have a soul. They go from lover to lover with blithe abandon. The preferred man is the last one, and the one with money to spend for jewels. And the age-old law of retribution and compensation finds them both at last and fulfills itself upon their lovely, passionate, false, golden bodies.

Lulu Belle is Carmen, and Carmen is Lulu Belle, and both are ageless, eternal, universal, of no race, no clime, no color, no condition. They are in the jungles, and in the drawing rooms of the most exclusive Nordics. They are white and yellow and brown and black. They have always been and always will be.

So why rise and gibber at Sheldon and Belasco?

• • • •

The author and producer probably had no more idea of putting Lulu Belle forward as typifying Negro womanhood than Mr. Stribling had of making Peter in *Birthright* the typical young Negro college graduate. He was an individual, not a type. A reflection of his environment. Even the most ignorant Ku Klux Klanner must know how that Lulu Belle, while a type, is not a typical colored girl, or rather not all colored girls. High schools, colleges, Y.W.C.A., Christian Endeavors, B.Y.P.U., teachers, decent working girls, rural maidens—it is not in these groups that we find the Lulu Belles. Not even the most rabid Negro hater will fail to realize that. We need not concern ourselves about that idea becoming prevalent among our enemies.

• • • •

Rather let us look at the beauty of the play. Its sumptuous setting. Its vivid color. Its clash of personalities. Its tropic abandon. Its riot of color and sound. Its frank revelations. Its minute details. The richness of its blending of complexions, frankly natural and beautiful. In some spots the drama is so true that it hurts. In others, it is informative. And one can but marvel at the patient endeavor of the authors and producer to penetrate below the surface of the kind of Negro life which they depict in the play, and present to the audience the results of their painstaking studies.

• • • •

Of one thing we may be sure—our people will have something to discuss, argue about, get into heated controversies over, write bitter editorials about, denunciatory letters, diatribes from the pulpits, and long-winded papers from Uplift Societies for some weeks. Debates are forthcoming, whether Mr. Belasco means to insult the race, or merely to present a cross-section of metropolitan life. Resolutions—in spite of the conclusion at which we arrived a few weeks ago—will be drawn up, denouncing Mr. Belasco, Mr. Sheldon, Mr. McArthur, Miss Ulric and Mr. Hull for their slander against a race that has always proved loyal to the union, and the saviors of San Juan Hill (not in the play) and the Argonne Forest. We shall hear of Booker Washington and Du Bois, and Harriet Tubman and Lillian Evans, and Mrs. Bethune—all in one wild and hysterical outburst. See if we don't.

In the meanwhile, some of us would like to ask Miss Ulric, How did she find out about that darker brown streak down the middle of the spine of mulatto women?

February 27, 1926

Speaking of this month's Mercury, nearly everyone has had a fling at poor L. M. Hussy, with his "Aframerican, North and South," and since he is down, one kick more or less cannot do any harm. His idea of the isolation of the poor cultured Negro South is a weird one. Someone should take him gently by the hand and induct him into some of the communities where large numbers of cultured Negroes live—Durham, North Carolina, for instance, or Baltimore, or New Orleans, or Atlanta, or scores of like cities. He might change his ideas of what isolation means. Surely there were never happier or more self-satisfied groups to be found in any race anywhere than those above mentioned, especially in Durham.

But—why should all of us or any of us waste perfectly good time, type, paper, or energy frothing at the pen over what our white contemporaries think or write of us? We will rush into print and assert, deny, asseverate, fulminate, vociferate, and use up the dictionary, the thesaurus, and the encyclopedia with masses of statistics to prove that these statements made by the Nordics are all wrong. And to whom do we prove them? To our own dear selves. For said Nordic never sees our answers, or our papers or our statements. Wouldn't read them if he did. Having flung his bolt, he looks not to see who picks it up.

Someone should offer a prize, since prize awards are in the air for the most effective method of getting our answers over to the other side of the racial stream.

It must be admitted, however, that Hussy's dictum that "Great Cultures come only from assured peoples, from peoples of abounding self-esteem," is a splendid point. Grant him correct; then the African was a great race, a great people, and their art a great culture—or else his axiom is not true.

• • • •

H. L. Mencken, the great Iconoclast, and a god of the Iconoclasts, says that the inferiority complex got into everything Booker T. Washington said! That a Negro was almost as good as a white man, was the best he could think. In like manner, this inferiority complex is also in Du Bois, who is more intent on getting Negroes into Pullman cars, or in Kiwanis clubs, than in finding the Negro soul! Wow! Du Bois with an inferiority complex!

• • • •

Having duly celebrated Negro History Week in the same week with the birthdays of Lincoln, Douglass and St. Valentine, and in near juxtaposition to Washington's and Longfellow's birthdays and Ash Wednesday, let us hope the poor tired teachers will stop to take breath, and let the bewildered brains of their million charges recover from the shock and indigestion of so much knowledge, history, Negrophile history, literature, art and science; so much patriotism, Negro spirituals, cherry tree incidents, Gettysburg speech, Christ on the mountain with the Tempter, Children's Hour and Paul Revere, Second Inaugural, Farewell Address, Roland Hayes, Phyllis

Wheatley, Crispus Attucks, Hearts and Flowers, ground-hog day, Frederick Douglass mixed up with Stephen Douglass, the great debater, cupid, the first bluebird, snow storms, soft coal nuisance, end of longest strike in history, and Booker Washington, the Father of his Country; while George swept all over Hampton Institute. That is the way the poor youngsters' brains seem—an omelette of February data. What the little month lacks in chronological length, it amply makes up in historical depth.

Now they are saying that a certain well-known actress has colored blood in her veins, hence her understanding delineation of a mulatto gamin. Well, the accusation places her right in the ranks of the immortals. We claim them all; it is a sign that they have arrived, when we put forth our arresting hand and call them ours—Alexander Hamilton, Robert Browning, one of the Kings of Spain, Warren G. Harding, Charlie Chaplin, and there are still others. If the Germans can claim Shakespeare, what is to prevent us from claiming everything in sight? It's good politics.

March 6, 1926

"Will Uncle Sam Dishonor Our Women?" breathlessly says an esteemed contemporary, anent the marriage bill now up in Congress. Hardly. No one can dishonor a woman but herself, in the first place. She may be insulted, reviled, even raped, but dishonor can not be put upon her, except in so far as she is a consenting party to the aforementioned proceedings.

But—leaving quibbling out of the question—has not Uncle Sam been a silent party to the rape of black women for over three hundred years?

Think it over.

• • • •

About this time of the year some folks begin to wear a mysterious and harried look, and to talk in vague terms of income tax blank computations, helpful lawyers, difficulties in establishing exemptions, etc., etc.

And nine-tenths of those who are talking the loudest never had a blank to fill out.

Or an income large enough to be taxed.

And never will have.

But it sounds well to appear to be paying an income tax—even if it is like some of those $1.25 ones that were published last year in the list which we all read so carefully.

Watch out for the four-flusher who "was up all night figuring his income tax."

He might have been up all night, and he might have been figuring, but the chances are, that it was not on what he has to pay to the government, but how he could stretch that little hundred dollars a month to cover rent, groceries, clothes, insurance, shoes, and a trip to the movies on Saturday nights.

March 13, 1926

The dark nations are having a hard time. Poor little Liberia has been raped on a rubber proposition, and for the first time in its history will have a white minister from this country. Haiti, as usual, is in hot water; the Virgin Islands have had a cross-eyed decision handed down in Philadelphia, which out of its welter of word, affirms nothing, but leaves no doubt in the minds of the readers what the intent of this nation is concerning the freedom of the Islanders. Is it not true that the octopus is a white fish—reptile, creature of prey, what not? Its slimy white tentacles gripping, plunging, exploring, seizing, devouring all in its reach? Yes, surely, it is white.

• • • •

Lothrop Stoddard has found a mare's nest and cannot count the eggs. He does this once in a while. Now it's the Jews about whom he has made wonderful discoveries and announced them in the March *Forum*. He sets forth a "biological background," which will help them in uncovering the festering sore, of which the editor speaks in the foreward. Said festering sore being the whole discussion of the Jewish question.

For once Mr. Stoddard seems to have struck a fairly accurate, and for him, dispassioned presentment of the racial aspects of the case. Knowing his attitude on the darker races, we can infer that his love for the Jew is purely scientific. Grudgingly he admits what pseudo-scientists vehemently deny, that the ancient Egyptians belonged to the Hamitic race.

Angelina Weld Grimké (1880–1958)

Grimké's play, *Rachel*, was the first play staged by an African American woman. Although there had been a history of blacks reading dramas for abolitionist audiences, performed theater was not as common. Produced by the National Association of Colored People (NAACP), the play covers a wide range of issues central to black communities and reflects some of the despair that dominated Grimké's life, despite her privileged background. Her father, Archibald Grimké, was the well-known executive director of the NAACP and nephew of the popular abolitionists, the wealthy Grimké sisters, Sarah and Angelina, of South Carolina. Although white, the Grimké sisters acknowledged Archibald as their brother's child. An emancipated slave, Archibald attended Harvard Law School, married a well-to-do white woman, Sarah Stanley, and named their daughter after his Aunt Angelina. When Angelina was three, Sarah Stanley left Archibald, taking Angelina with her, but returned her to her father when she was seven years old. Angelina Grimké never saw her mother again. The sisters of South Carolina stepped in to help with Angelina's education. She attended Cushing Academy in Massachusetts, Carleton Academy in Minnesota, as well as Boston Normal School of Gymnastics. While a teacher at the Dunbar High School in Washington, D.C, she wrote plays, short stories, and poems about abandonment, isolation, and the loss of maternal and romantic love. Grimké's unpublished poetry speaks of a love affair with another woman.

The Closing Door

I was fifteen at the time, diffident and old far beyond my years from much knocking about from pillar to post, a yellow, scrawny, unbeautiful girl, when the big heart of Agnes Milton took pity upon me, loved me and brought me home to live with her in her tiny, sun-filled flat. We were only distantly related, very distantly, in fact, on my dead father's side. You can see then there was no binding blood-tie between us, that she [was] absolutely under no obligations to do what she did. I have wondered time and again how many women would have opened their hearts and their homes, as Agnes Milton did, to a forlorn, unattractive, homeless girl-woman. That one fine, free, generous act of hers alone shows the wonder-quality of her soul.

Just one little word to explain me. After my father had taken one last cup too many and they had carried him, for the last time, out of the house into which he had been carried so often, my mother, being compelled to work again, returned to the rich family with whom she had been a maid before her marriage. She regarded me as seriously I suppose as she did anything in this world; but as it was impossible to have me with her, I was passed along from one of her relatives to another. When one tired of me, on I went to the next. Well, I can say this for each and all of them, they certainly believed in teaching me how to work! Judging by the number of homes in which I lived until I was fifteen, my mother was rich in-deed in one possession—an abundance of relatives.

And then came Agnes Milton.

Have you ever, I wonder, known a happy person? I mean a really happy one? He is as rare as a white blackbird in this sombre-faced world of ours. I have known two and only two. They were Agnes Milton and her husband Jim. And their happiness did not last. Jim was a brown, good-natured giant with a slow, most attractive smile and gleaming teeth. He spoke always in a deep sad drawl and you would have thought him the most unhappy person imaginable until you glimpsed his black eyes fairly twinkling under their half-closed lids. He made money—what is called "easy money," by playing ragtime for dances. He was one of a troupe that are called "social entertainers." As far as Jim was concerned, it would have slipped away in just as easy a manner, if it hadn't been for Agnes. For she, in spite of all her seeming carefree joyousness was a thrifty soul. As long as Jim could have good food and plenty of it, now and then the theatre, a concert or a dance, and his gold-tipped cigarettes, he didn't care what became of his money.

Published in *Birth Control Review*, 1919.

"Oh, Ag!"

If I close my eyes I can hear his slow sad voice as clearly as though these ten long years had not passed by. I can hear the click of the patent lock as he closed the flat door. I can hear the bang of his hat as he hung it on the rack. I can get the whiff of his cigarette.

"Oh, Ag!"

"That you, Jim?" I can see Agnes' happy eyes and hear her eager, soft voice.

And then a pause, that sad voice:

"No, Ag!"

I can hear her delighted little chuckle. She very seldom laughed outright.

"Where are you, anyway?" It was the plaintive voice again.

"Here!"

And then he'd make believe he couldn't find her and go hunting her all over that tiny flat, searching for her in every room he knew she was not. And he'd stumble over things in pretended excitement and haste and grunt and swear all in that inimitable slow way of his. And she'd stand there, her eyes shining and every once in a while giving that dear little chuckle of hers.

Finally he'd appear in the door panting and disheveled and would look at her in pretended intense surprise for a second, and then he'd say in an aggrieved voice:

"'S not fair, Agnes! 'S not fair!"

She wouldn't say a word, just stand there smiling at him. After a little, slowly, he'd begin to smile too.

That smile of theirs was one of the most beautiful things I have ever seen and each meeting it was the same. Their joy and love seemed to gush up and bubble over through their lips and eyes.

Presently he'd say:

"Catch!" She'd hold up her little white apron by the corners and he'd put his hand in his pocket and bring out sometimes a big, sometimes a little wad of greenbacks and toss it to her and she'd catch it, too, I can tell you. And her eyes would beam and dance at him over it. Oh! she didn't love the money for itself but him for trusting her with it.

For fear you may not understand I must tell you no more generous soul ever lived than Agnes Milton. Look at what she did for me. And she was always giving a nickel or a dime to some child, flowers or fruit to a sick woman, money to tide over a friend. No beggar was ever turned away, empty, from her flat. But she managed, somehow, to increase her little horde in the bank against that possible rainy day.

Well, to return. At this juncture, Jim would say oh! so sadly his eyes fairly twinkling:

"Please, ma'm, do I get paid today too?"

And then she'd screw up her mouth and twist her head to the side and look at him and say in a most judicial manner:

"Well, now, I really can't say as to that. It strikes me you'll have to find that out for yourself."

Oh! they didn't mind me. He would reach her, it seemed, in one stride and would pick her up bodily, apron, money and all. After a space, she'd disentangle herself and say sternly, shaking the while her little forefinger before his delighted eyes:

"Jim Milton, you've overdrawn your wages again."

And then he'd look oh! so contrite and so upset and so shocked at being caught in such a gigantic piece of attempted fraud.

"No?" he'd say. If you only could have heard the mournful drawl of him.

"No? Now, is that so? I'm really at heart an honest, hardworking man. I'll have to pay it back."

He did. I can vouch for it.

Sometimes after this, he'd swing her up onto his shoulder and they'd go dashing and prancing and shrieking and laughing all over the little flat. I know the neighbors thought them mad. I can hardly blame them. Once after I had seen scared faces appearing at various windows, at times like these, I used to rush around and shut the windows down tight. Two happy children, that's what they were. Then—younger even than I.

There was just the merest suspicion of a cloud over their happiness, these days, they had been married five years and had no children.

It was the mother heart of Agnes that had yearned over me, had pity upon me, loved me and brought me to live in the only home I have ever known. I have cared for people. I care for Jim; but Agnes Milton is the only person I have ever really loved. I love her still. And before it was too late, I used to pray that in some way I might change places with her and go into that darkness where though still living, one forgets sun and moon and stars and flowers and winds—and love itself, and existence means dark, foul-smelling cages, hollow clanging doors, hollow monotonous days. But a month ago when Jim and I went to see her, she had changed—she had receded even from us. She seemed—how can I express it— blank, empty, a grey automation, a mere shell. No soul looked out at us through her vacant eyes.

We did not utter a word during our long journey homeward. Jim had unlocked the door before I spoke.

"Jim," I said, "they may still have the poor hush of her cooped up there but her soul, thank God, at least, for that! is free at last."

And Jim, I cannot tell of his face, said never a word but turned away and went heavily down the stairs. And I, I went into Agnes Milton's flat and closed the door. You would never have dreamed it was the same place. For a long time I stood amid all the brightness and mockery of her sun-drenched rooms. And I prayed. Night and day I have prayed since the same prayer—that God if he knows any pity at all may soon, soon, release the poor spent body of hers.

I wish I might show you Agnes Milton of those far off happy days. She wasn't tall and she wasn't short: she wasn't stout and she wasn't thin. Her back was straight and her head high. She was rather graceful, I thought. In coloring she was Spanish or Italian. Her hair was not very long but it was soft and silky and black. Her features were not too sharp, her eyes clear and dark, a warm leaf brown in fact. Her mouth was really beautiful. This doesn't give her I find. It was the shining beauty and gayety of her soul that lighted up her whole body and somehow made her her, and she was generally smiling or chuckling. Her eyes almost closed when she did so and there were the most delightful crinkles all about them. Under her left eye there was a small scar, a reminder of some childhood escapade, that became, when she smiled, the most adorable of dimples.

One day, I remember, we were standing at the window in the bright sunlight. Some excitement in the street below had drawn us. I turned to her—the reason has gone from me now—and called out suddenly:

"Agnes Milton!"

"Heavens! What is it!"

"Why, you're wrinkling!"

"Wrinkling! Where?" And she began inspecting the smooth freshness of her housedress.

"No, your face," I exclaimed. "Honest! Stand still there in that light. Now! Just look at them all around your eyes."

She chuckled.

"How you ever expect me to see them I don't know without a glass or something!"

And her face crinkled up into a smile.

"There! That's it!—That's how you get them."

"How?"

"Smiling too much."

"Oh, no! Lucy, child, that's impossible."

"How do you mean impossible! You didn't get them that way? Just wait till I get a glass."

"No, don't." And she stopped me with a detaining hand. "I'm not doubting you. What I mean is—it's absolutely impossible to smile too much."

I felt my eyes stretching with surprise.

"You mean," I said, "You don't mind being wrinkled? You, a woman?"

She shook her head at me many times, smiling and chuckling softly the while.

"Not the very littlest, tiniest bit—not this much," and she showed me just the fairest tip of her pink tongue between her white teeth. She smiled, then, and there was the dimple.

"And you only twenty-five?" I exclaimed.

She didn't answer for a moment and when she did she spoke quietly:

"Lucy, child, we've all got to wrinkle sometime, somehow, if we live long enough. I'd much rather know mine were smile ones than frown ones." She waited a second and then looked at me with her beautiful clear eyes and added, "Wouldn't you?"

For reply I leaned forward and kissed them. I loved them from that time on.

Here is another memory of her—perhaps the loveliest of them all and yet, as you will see, tinged with the first sadness. It came near the end of our happy days. It was a May dusk. I had been sewing all the afternoon and was as close to the window as I could get to catch the last of the failing light. I was trying to thread a needle—had been trying for several minutes, in fact, and was just in the very act of succeeding when two soft hands were clapped over my eyes.

"Oh, Agnes!" I said none too pleasantly. It was provoking. "There! You've made me lose my needle."

"Bother your old needle, cross patch!" She said close to my ear. She still held her hands over my eyes.

I waited a moment or so.

"Well," I said, "What's the idea?"

"Please don't be cross," came the soft voice still close to my ear.

"I'm not."

At that she chuckled.

"Well!" I said.

"I'm trying to tell you something. Sh! not so loud."

"Well, go ahead, then: and why must I sh!"

"Because you must."

I waited.

"Well!" I said a third time, but in a whisper to humor her. We were alone in the flat, there was no reason I could see for this tremendous secrecy.

"I'm waiting for you to be sweet to me."

"I am. But why I should have to lose my needle and my temper and be blinded and sweet just to hear something—is beyond me."

"Because I don't wish you to see me while I say it."

Her soft lips were kissing my ear.

"Well, I'm very sweet now. What is it?"

There was another little pause and during it her fingers over my eyes trembled a little. She was breathing quicker too.

"Agnes Milton, what *is* it?"

"Wait, I'm just trying to think of *how* to tell you. Are you sure you're very sweet?"

"Sure."

I loved the feel of her hands and sat very still.

"Lucy!"

"Yes."

"What do you think would be the loveliest, loveliest thing for you to know was—was—there—close—just under your heart?"

But I waited for no more. I took her hands from my eyes and turned to look at her. The beauty of her face made me catch my breath.

At last I said:

"You mean"—I didn't need to finish.

"Yes, Yes. And I'm so happy, happy, happy! and so is Jim."

"Agnes, Oh my dear, and so am I!" And I kissed her two dear eyes.

"But why mustn't I whoop. I've simply got to," I added.

"No! No! No! Oh, sh!" And for the very first time I saw fear in her eyes.

"Agnes," I said, "what is it?"

"I'm—I'm just a little afraid, I believe."

"Afraid!" I had cried out in surprise.

"Sh! Lucy!—Yes."

"But of what?" I spoke in a half whisper too. "You mean you're afraid you may die?"

"Oh, no, not that."

"What then?"

"Lucy," her answer came slowly a little abstractedly. "there's—such—a thing—as being—too happy,—too happy."

"Nonsense," I answered.

But she only shook her head at me slowly many times and her great wistful eyes came to mine and seemed to cling to them. It made my heart fairly ache and I turned my head away so that she couldn't see her fears were affecting me. And then quite suddenly I felt a disagreeable little chill run up and down my back.

"Lucy," she said after a little.

"Yes," I was looking out of the window and not at her.

"Do you remember Kipling's 'Without Benefit of Clergy'?" I did and I said so. Agnes had Kipling bound in ten beautiful volumes. She loved him. At first that had been enough for me and then I had come to love him for himself. I had read all of those ten volumes through from cover to cover, poetry and all.

"You haven't forgotten Ameera, then?"

"No." She was thoughtful a moment and then went on:

"Poor Ameera!" She knew what it was to be too happy. "Do you remember what she said once to Holden?"

Again I felt that queer little shiver.

"She said many things, as I remember her, Agnes. Which?"

"This was after Tota's death."

"Well!"

"They were on the roof—she and Holden—under the night."

Her eyes suddenly widened and darkened and then she went on:

"She turned to Holden and said: 'We must make no protestations of delight but go softly underneath the stars, lest God find us out.' " She paused. "Do you remember?"

"Yes," I answered; but I couldn't look at her.

"Well," she spoke slowly and quietly, "I have a feeling here, Lucy." And she placed her left hand against her heart, "Here, that Jim and you and I must go softly—very softly—underneath the stars."

Again I felt that unpleasant chill up and down my back.

She stood just where she was for a little space, her hand still against her heart and her eyes wide, dark and unseeing, fixed straight ahead of her. Then suddenly and without a sound she turned and went towards the door and opened it.

I started to follow her; but she put up her hand.

"No, Lucy, please.—I wish to be alone—for a little."

And with that she went out and shut the door very slowly, quite noiselessly behind her. The closing was so slow, so silent that I could not tell just when it shut. I found myself trembling violently. A sudden and inexplicable terror filled me as that door closed behind her.

We were to become accustomed to it, Jim and I, as much as it was possible to do so, in those terrible days that were to follow. We were to become used to entering a room in search of Agnes, only to find it empty and the door opposite closing, closing, almost imperceptibly noiselessly—and, yes, at last irrevocably between us. And each time it happened the terror was as fresh upon me as at the very first.

The days that immediately followed I cannot say were really unhappy ones. More to humor Agnes at first than anything else "we went softly." But as time passed even we became infected. Literally and figuratively we began to go "softly under the stars." We came to feel that each of us moved ever with a finger to his lips. There came to be also a sort of expectancy upon us, a listening, a waiting. Even the neighbors noticed the difference. Jim still played his ragtime and sang but softly; we laughed and joked but quietly. We got so we even washed the dishes and pots and pans quietly. Sometimes Jim and I forgot, but as certainly as we did there was Agnes in the door, dark-eyed, a little pale and her, "Oh! Jim!—Oh! Lucy! Sh!"

I haven't spoken of this before because it wasn't necessary. Agnes had a brother called Bob. He was her favorite of all her brothers and sisters. He was younger than she, five years, I think, a handsome, harum-scarum, happy-go-lucky, restless, reckless daredevil, but sweet-tempered and good hearted and lovable with all. I don't believe he knew what fear was. His home was in Mississippi, a small town there. It was the family home, in fact. Agnes had lived there, herself until she was seventeen or eighteen. He had visited us two or three times and you can imagine the pandemonium that reigned at such times, for he had come during our happy days. Well, he was very fond of Agnes and, as irresponsible as he seemed, one thing he never failed to do and that was to write her a letter every single week. Each Tuesday morning, just like clockwork, the very first mail there was his letter. Other mornings Agnes was not so particular but Tuesday mornings she always went herself to the mailbox in the hall.

It was a Tuesday morning about four months, maybe, after my first experience with the closing door. The bell rang three times, the postman's signal when he had left a letter, Agnes came to her feet, her eyes sparkling:

"My letter from Bob," she said and made for the door.

She came back slowly, I noticed, and her face was a little pale and worried. She had an opened and an unopened letter in her hand.

"Well, what does Bob say?" I asked.

"This—this isn't from Bob." she said slowly. "It's only a bill."

"Well, go ahead and open his letter," I said.

"There—there wasn't any, Lucy."

"What!" I exclaimed. I was surprised.

"No. I don't know what it means."

"It will come probably in the second mail," I said. "It has sometimes."

"Yes," she said, I thought rather listlessly.

It didn't come in the second mail nor in the third.

"Agnes," I said, "There's some good explanation. It's not like Bob to fail you."

"No."

"He's busy or got a girl maybe."

She was a little jealous of him and I hoped this last would rouse her but it didn't.

"Yes, maybe that's it," she said without any life.

"Well, I hope you're not going to let this interfere with your walk," I said.

"I had thought"—she began but I cut her off.

"You promised Jim you'd go out every single day," I reminded her.

"All right Agnes Milton's conscience," she said smiling a little. "I'll go, then."

She hadn't been gone fifteen minutes when the electric bell began shrilling continuously throughout the flat.

Somehow I knew it meant trouble. My mind immediately flew to Agnes. It took me a second or so to get myself together and then I went to the tube.

"Well," I called. My voice sounded strange and high.

A boy's voice answered.

"Lady here named Mrs. James Milton?"

"Yes." I managed to say.

"Telegram fo' youse."

It wasn't Agnes, after all. I drew a deep breath. Nothing else seemed to matter for a minute.

"Say!" the voice called up from below. "Wot's de mattah wid you'se up dere?"

"Bring it up." I said at last. "Third floor, front."

I opened the door and waited.

The boy was taking his time and whistling as he came.

"Here!" I called out as he reached our floor.

It was inside his cap and he had to take it off to give it to me.

I saw him eyeing me rather curiously.

"You Mrs. Milton?" he asked.

"No, but this is her flat. I'll sign for it. She's out. Where do I sign? There? Have you a pencil?"

With the door shut behind me again, I began to think out what I had better do. Jim was not to be home until late that night. Within five minutes I had decided. I tore open the yellow envelope and read the message.

It ran: "Bob died suddenly. Under no circumstances come. Father."

The rest of that day was a nightmare to me. I concealed the telegram in my waist. Agnes came home finally and was so alarmed at my appearance, I pleaded a frightful sick headache and went to bed. When Jim came home late that night Agnes was asleep. I caught him in the hall and gave him the telegram. She had to be told, we decided, because a letter from Mississippi might come at any time. He broke it to her the next morning. We were all hard hit, but Agnes from that time on was a changed woman.

Day after day dragged by and the letter of explanation did not come. It was strange to say the least.

The Sunday afternoon following we were all sitting, after dinner, in the littler parlor. None of us had been saying much.

Suddenly Agnes said:

"Jim!"

"Yes!"

"Wasn't it strange that Father never said how or when Bob died?"

"Would have made the telegram too long and expensive, perhaps," Jim replied.

We were all thinking, in the pause, that followed, the same thing, I dare say.

Agnes' father was not poor and it did seem he might have done that much.

"And why, do you suppose I was not to come under any circumstances?"

"And why don't they write?"

Just then the bell rang and there was no chance for a reply.

Jim got up in his leisurely way and went to the tube.

Agnes and I both listened—a little tensely, I remember.

"Yes!" we heard Jim say and then with spaces in between:

"Joe?—Joe who?—I think you must have made a mistake—can't say that I do know anyone called Joe—What?—Milton—Yes, that's my name!—What?—Oh! Brooks.—Joe Brooks?—

"Jim! Jim! It's my brother Joe."

"Look here! Are you Agnes' brother, Joe?" Jim called quietly at him. "Great Jehosaphet! Man! Come up! What a mess I've made of this."

For the first time I saw Jim move quickly. Within a second he was out of the flat and running down the stairs. Agnes followed to the stairs head and waited there. I went back into the little parlor for I had followed her into the hall, and sat down and waited.

They all came in presently. Joe was older than Agnes but looked very much like her. He was thin, his face really haggard and his hair quite grey. I found out afterward that he was in his early twenties but he appeared much older. He was smiling but it did not reach his eyes. They were strange aloof eyes. They rested on you and yet seemed to see something beyond. You felt as though they had looked upon something that could never be forgotten. When he was not smiling his face was grim, the chin firm and set. He was a man of very few words I found.

Agnes and Jim were both talking at once and he answered them now and then in monosyllables. Agnes introduced us. He shook hands, I thought in rather a perfunctory way without saying anything, and we all sat down.

We steered clear quite deliberately from the thought uppermost in all our minds. We spoke of his journey, when he left Mississippi, the length of time it had taken him to come and the weather. Suddenly Agnes jumped up:

"Joe, aren't you famished?"

"Well, I wouldn't mind a little something, Agnes," he answered, and then he added:

"I'm not as starved as I was traveling in the South; but I have kind of a hollow feeling."

"What do you mean?" she asked.

"Jim-Crow cars," he answered laconically.

"I'd forgotten," she said. "I've been away so long."

He made no reply.

"Aren't conditions any better at all?" she asked after a little.

"No, I can't say as they are."

None of us said anything. She stood there a minute or so, pulling away at the full on her apron. She stopped suddenly, drew a long breath, and said:

"I wish you all could move away, Joe, and come North."

For one second before he lowered his eyes I saw a strange gleam in them. He seemed to be examining his shoes carefully from all angles. His jaw looked grimmer than ever and I saw a flickering of the muscles in his cheeks.

"That would be nice," he said at last and then added, "but we can't, Agnes. I love my coffee strong, please."

"Joe," she said, going to the door. "I'm sorry, I was forgetting."

I rose up at that.

"Agnes, let me go. You stay here."

She hesitated, but Joe spoke up.

"No, Agnes, you go. I know your cooking."

You could have heard a pin drop for a minute. Jim looked queer and so did Agnes for a second and then she tried to laugh it off.

"Don't mind Joe. He doesn't mean anything. He always was like that."

And then she left us.

Well, I was hurt. Joe made no attempt to apologize or anything. He even seemed to have forgotten me. Jim looked at me and smiled his nice smile but I was really hurt. I came to understand, however, later. Presently Joe said:

"About Agnes! We hadn't been told anything!"

"Didn't she write about it?"

"No."

"Wanted to surprise you, I guess."

"How long?" Joe asked after a little.

"Before?"

"Yes."

"Four months, I should say."

"That complicates matters some."

I got up to leave. I was so evidently in the way.

Joe looked up quietly and said:

"Oh! don't go! It isn't necessary."

I sat down again.

"No, Lucy, stay." Jim added. "What do you mean 'complicates'?" ·

Joe examined his shoes for several moments and then looked up suddenly.

"Just where is Agnes?"

"In the kitchen, I guess"; Jim looked a trifle surprised.

"Where is that?"

"The other end of the flat near the door."

"She can't possibly hear anything, then?"

"No."

"Well, then listen, Jim, and you, what's your name? Lucy? Well Lucy, then. Listen carefully, you two, to every single word I am going to say." He frowned a few moments at his shoes and then went on: "Bob went out fishing in the woods near his shack; spent the night there; slept in wet clothes and it had been raining all day—; came home; contracted double pneumonia and died in two days time—Have you that?"

We both nodded. But that didn't satisfy him. He made us each repeat what he had said.

"Now," he said, "That's the story we are to tell Agnes."

Jim had his mouth open to ask something, when Agnes came in. She had very evidently not heard anything, however, for there was a little color in her face and it was just a little happy again.

"I've been thinking about you, Joe," said she, "What on earth are you getting so grey for?"

"Grey!" he exclaimed. "Am I grey?" There was no doubt about it. His surprise was genuine.

"Didn't you know it?" She chuckled a little. It was the first time in days.

"No, I didn't."

She made him get up, at that, and drew him to the oval glass over the mantel.

"Don't you ever look at yourself, Joe?"

"Not much, that's the truth." I could see his face in the mirror from where I sat. His eyes widened a trifle, I saw, and then he turned away abruptly and sat down again. He made no comment. Agnes broke the rather awkward little silence that followed.

"Joe!"

"Yes!"

"You haven't been sick or anything, have you?"

"No, why?"

"You seem so much thinner. When I last saw you you were almost stout."

"That's some years ago, Agnes."

"Yes, but one ought to get stouter not thinner with age."

Again I caught that strange gleam in his eyes before he lowered them. For a moment he sat perfectly still without answering.

"You can put it down to hard work, if you like, Agnes. Isn't that my coffee I smell boiling over?"

"Yes, I believe it is. I just ran in to tell you it'll be ready for you in about ten minutes."

She went out hastily but took time to pull the portiere across the door. I thought it strange at the time and looked at Jim. He didn't seem to notice it, however, but he waited, I saw, until he had heard Agnes' heel taps going into the kitchen.

"Now," he said, "what do you mean when you say that is the story we are to tell Agnes."

"Just that."

"You mean"—he paused, "that it isn't true?"

"No, it isn't true."

"Bob didn't die that way?"

"No."

I felt my-self stiffening in my chair and my two hands gripping the two arms of my chair tightly. I looked at Jim. I sensed the same tensioning in him. There was a long pause. Joe was examining his shoes again. The flickering in his cheeks I saw was more noticeable.

Finally Jim brought out just one word:

"How?"

"There was a little trouble," he began and then paused so long Jim said:

"You mean he was—injured in some way?"

Joe looked up suddenly at Jim, at that, and then down again. But his expression even in that fleeting glance set me to trembling all over. Jim, I saw, had been affected too. He sat stiffly bent forward. He had been in the act of raising his cigarette to his lips and his arm seemed as though frozen in mid-air.

"Yes," he said, "injured." But the way in which he said injured made me tremble all the more.

Again there was a pause and again Jim broke it with his one word:

"How?"

"You don't read the papers, I see," Joe said.

"Yes, I read them."

"It was in all the papers."

"I missed it, then."

"Yes."

It was quiet again for a little.

"Have you ever lived in the South?" Joe asked.

"No."

"Nice civilized place, the South." Joe said.

And again I found myself trembling violently. I had to fight with might and main to keep my teeth from chattering. And yet it was not what he had said but his tone again.

"I haven't so heard it described," Jim said after a little.

"No?—you didn't know, I suppose, that there is an un-written law in the South that when a colored and a white person meet on the sidewalk, the colored person must get off into the street until the white one passes?"

"No, I hadn't heard of it."

"Well, it's so. That was the little trouble."

"You mean—"

"Bob refused to get off the sidewalk."

"Well?"

"The white man pushed him off. Bob knocked him down. The white man attempted to teach the 'damned nig-ger' a lesson." Again he paused.

"Well?"

"The lesson didn't end properly. Bob all but killed him."

It was so still in that room that although Jim was sitting across the room I could hear his watch ticking distinctly in his vest pocket. I had been holding my breath and when I was forced to expel it the sound was so loud they both turned quickly towards me, startled for the second.

"That would have been Bob." It was Jim speaking.

"Yes."

"I suppose it didn't end there?"

"No."

"Go on, Joe." Even Jim's voice sounded strained and strange.

And Joe went on. He never raised his voice, never lowered it. Throughout, his tone was entirely colorless. And yet as though it had been seared into my very soul I remember, word for word everything he said.

"An orderly mob, in an orderly manner, on a Sunday morning—I am quoting the newspapers—broke into the jail, took him out, slung him up to the limb of a tree, riddled his body with bullets, saturated it with coal oil, lighted a fire underneath him, gouged out his eyes with red hot irons, burnt him to a crisp and then sold souvenirs of him, ears, fingers, toes. His teeth brought five dollars each." He ceased for a moment.

"He is still hanging on that tree.—We are not allowed to have even what is left."

There was a roaring in my ears. I seemed to be a long way off. I was sinking into a horrible black vortex that seemed to be sucking me down. I opened my eyes and saw Jim dimly. His nostrils seemed to be two black inch holes. His face was taut, every line set. I saw him draw a great deep breath. The blackness sucked me down still deeper. And then suddenly I found myself on my feet struggling against that hideous darkness and I heard my own voice as from a great distance calling out over and over again, "Oh, my God! Oh, my God! Oh, my God!"

They both came running to me, but I should have fainted for the first and only time in my life but that I heard suddenly above those strange noises in my ears a little choking, strangling sound. It revived me instantly. I broke from them and tried to get to the door.

"Agnes! Agnes!" I called out.

But they were before me. Jim tore the portiere aside. They caught her just as she was falling.

She lay unconscious for hours. When she did come to, she found all three of us about her bed. Her bewildered eyes went from Jim's face to mine and then to Joe's. They paused there; she frowned a little. And then we saw the whole thing slowly come back to her. She groaned and closed her eyes. Joe started to leave the room but she opened her eyes quickly and indicated he was not to go. He came back. Again she closed her eyes.

And then she began to grow restless.

"Agnes!" I asked, "Is there anything you want?"

"No," she said, "No."

Presently she opened her eyes again. They were very bright. She looked at each of us in turn a second time.

Then she said:

"I've had to live all this time to find out."

"Find out what, Agnes?" It was Jim's voice.

"Why I'm here—why I'm here."

"Yes, of course." Jim spoke oh so gently, humoring her. His hand was smoothing away the damp little curls about her forehead.

"It's no use your making believe you understand, you don't." It was the first time I had ever heard her speak even irritably to Jim. She moved her head away from his hand.

His eyes were a little hurt and took his hand away.

"No." His voice was as gentle as ever. "I don't understand, then."

There was a pause and then she said abruptly:

"I'm an instrument."

No one answered her.

"That's all—an instrument."

We merely watched her.

"One of the many."

And then Jim in his kindly blundering way made his second mistake.

"Yes, Agnes," he said, "Yes."

But at that, she took even me by surprise. She sat up in bed suddenly, her eyes wild and starey, and before we could stop her began beating her breasts.

"Agnes," I said, "Don't! Don't!"

"I shall," she said in a strange high voice.

Well, we let her alone. It would have meant a struggle.

And then amid little sobby breaths, beating her breasts the while she began to cry out: "Yes!—I!—I!—An instrument!—another one of the many! a colored woman—doomed!—cursed!—put here!—willing or unwilling! for what?—to bring children here—men children—for the sport—the lust—of possible orderly mobs—who go about things—in an orderly manner—on Sunday mornings!"

"Agnes," I cried out. "Agnes! Your child will be born in the North. He need never go South."

She had listened to me at any rate.

"Yes," she said, "In the North. In the North—And have there been no lynchings in the North?"

I was silenced.

"The North permits it too," she said. "The North is silent as well as the South."

And then as she sat there her eyes became less wild but more terrible. They became the eyes of a seeress. When she spoke again she spoke loudly, clearly, slowly:

"There is a time coming—and soon—when no colored man—no colored woman—no colored child, born or unborn—will be safe—in this country."

"Oh Agnes," I cried again, "Sh! sh!"

She turned her terrible eyes upon me.

"There is no more need for silence—in this house. God has found us out."

"Oh Agnes," the tears were frankly running down my cheeks. "We must believe that God is very pitiful. We must. He will find a way."

She waited a moment and said simply:

"Will He?"

"Yes, Agnes! Yes!"

"I will believe you, then. I will give Him one more chance. Then, if He is not pitiful, then if He is not pitiful"— But she did not finish. She fell back upon her pillows. She had fainted again.

Agnes did not die, nor did her child. She had kept her body clean and healthy. She was up and around again, but an Agnes that never smiled, never chuckled any more. She was a grey, pathetic shadow of herself. She who had loved joy so much cared more, it seemed, for solitude than anything else in the world. That was why, when Jim or I went looking for her we found so often only the empty room and that imperceptibly closing, slowly closing opposite door.

Joe went back to Mississippi and not one of us, ever again, mentioned Bob's name.

And Jim, poor Jim! I wish I could tell you of how beautiful he was those days. How he never complained, never was irritable, but was always so gentle, so full of understanding, that at times, I had to go out of the room for fear he might see my tears.

Only once I saw him when he thought himself alone. I had not known he was in his little den and entered it suddenly. I had made no sound, luckily, and he had not heard me. He was sitting leaning far forward, his head between his hands. I stood there five minutes at least, but not once did I see him stir. I silently stole out and left him.

It was a fortunate thing that Agnes had already done most of her sewing for the little expected stranger, for after Joe's visit, she never touched a thing.

"Agnes!" I said, one day, not without fear and trepidation it is true. "Isn't there something I can do?"

"Do?" she repeated rather vaguely.

"Yes. Some sewing?"

"Oh! sewing," she said. "No, I think not, Lucy."

"You've—You've finished?" I persisted.

"No."

"Then"—I began.

"I hardly think we shall need any of them." And then she added:

"I hope not."

"Agnes!" I cried out.

But she seemed to have forgotten me.

Well, time passed, it always does. And on a Sunday morning early Agnes' child was born. He was a beautiful, very grave baby with her great dark eyes.

As soon as they would let me, I went to her.

She was lying very still and straight, in the quiet, darkened room, her head turned on the pillow towards the wall. Her eyes were closed.

"Agnes!" I said in the barest whisper. "Are you asleep?"

"No." she said. And turned her head towards me and opened her eyes. I looked into a ravaged face. Agnes Milton had been down into Hell and back again.

Neither of us spoke for some time and then she said:

"Is he dead?"

"Your child?"

"Yes."

"I should say not, he's a perfect darling and so good."

No smile came into her face. It remained as expressionless as before. She paled a trifle more, I thought, if such a thing was possible.

"I'm sorry," she said finally.

"Agnes!" I spoke sharply. I couldn't help it.

But she closed her eyes and made no response.

I sat a long time looking at her. She must have felt my gaze for she slowly lifted her lids and looked at me.

"Well," she said, "what is it, Lucy?"

"Haven't you seen your child, Agnes?"

"No."

"Don't you wish to see it?"

"No."

Again it was wrung out of me.

"Agnes, Agnes, don't tell me you don't love it."

For the first and only time a spasm of pain went over her poor pinched face.

"Ah!" she said, "That's it." And she closed her eyes and her face was as expressionless as ever.

I felt as though my heart was breaking.

Again she opened her eyes.

"Tell me, Lucy," she began.

"What, Agnes?"

"Is he—healthy?"

"Yes."

"Quite strong?"

"Yes."

"You think he will live, then?"

"Yes, Agnes."

She closed her eyes once more. It was very still within the room.

Again she opened her eyes. There was a strange expression in them now.

"Lucy!"

"Yes."

"You were wrong."

"Wrong, Agnes?"

"Yes."

"How?"

"You thought your God was pitiful."

"Agnes, but I do believe it."

After a long silence she said very slowly:

"He—is—not."

This time, when she closed her eyes, she turned her head slowly upon the pillow to the wall. I was dismissed.

And again Agnes did not die. Time passed and again she was up and about the flat. There was a strange, stony stillness upon her, now, I did not like, though. If we only could have understood, Jim and I, what it meant. Her love for solitude, now, had become a passion. And Jim and I knew more and more that empty room and that silently slowly closing door.

She would have very little to do with her child. For some reason, I saw, she was afraid of it. I was its mother. I did for it, cared for it, loved it.

Twice only during these days I saw that stony stillness of hers broken.

The first time was one night. The baby was fast asleep. And she had stolen in to look at him, when she thought no one would know. I never wish to see such a tortured, hungry face again.

I was in the kitchen, the second time, when I heard strange sounds coming from my room. I rushed to it and there was Agnes, kneeling at the foot of the little crib, her head upon the spread. Great, terrible racking sobs were tearing her. The baby was lying there, all eyes, and beginning to whimper a little.

"Agnes! Oh, my dear! What is it?" The tears were streaming down my cheeks.

"Take him away! Take him away!" she gasped. "He's been cooing, and smiling and holding out his little arms to me. I can't stand it! I can't stand it."

I took him away. That was the only time I ever saw Agnes Milton weep.

The baby slept in my room, Agnes would not have him in hers. He was a restless little sleeper and I had to get up several times during the night to see that he was properly covered.

He was a noisy little sleeper as well. Many a night I have lain awake listening to the sound of his breathing. It is a lovely sound, a beautiful one—the breathing of a little baby in the dark.

This night, I remember, I had been up once and covered him over and had fallen off to sleep for the second time, when, for I had heard absolutely no sound, I awoke suddenly. There was upon me an overwhelming utterly paralyzing feeling not of fear but of horror. I thought, at first, I must have been having a nightmare, but strangely instead of diminishing the longer I lay awake, the more it seemed to increase.

It was a moonlight night and the light came in through the open window in a broad white steady stream.

A coldness seemed to settle all about my heart. What was the matter with me? I made a tremendous effort and sat up. Everything seemed peaceful and quiet enough.

The moonlight cut the room in two. It was dark where I was and dark beyond where the baby was.

One brass knob at the foot of the bed shone brilliantly, I remember, in that bright stream and the door that led into the hall stood out fully revealed. I looked at that door and then my heart suddenly seemed to stop beating! I grew deathly cold. The door was closing slowly, imperceptibly silently. Things were whirling around. I shut my eyes. When I opened them again the door was no longer moving: it had closed.

What had Agnes Milton wanted in my room? And the more I asked myself that question the deeper grew the horror.

And then slowly, by degrees, I began to realize there was something wrong within that room, something terribly wrong. But what was it?

I tried to get out of bed; but I seemed unable to move. I strained my eyes, but I could see nothing—only that bright knob, that stream of light, that closed white door.

I listened. It was quiet, very quiet, too quiet. But why too quiet? And then as though there had been a blinding flash of lightning I knew—the breathing wasn't there.

Agnes Milton had taken a pillow off of my bed and smothered her child.

One last word, Jim received word this morning. The door has finished closing for the last time—Agnes Milton is no more. God, I think, may be pitiful, after all.

The Black Finger

I have just seen a most beautiful thing
    Slim and still
  Against a gold, gold sky,
    A straight black cypress,
      Sensitive,
      Exquisite,
      A black finger
      Pointing upwards.
Why, beautiful still finger, are you black?
And why are you pointing upwards?

Originally published in *Opportunity*. Courtesy of the Moorland-Springarn Research Center, Howard University, Washington, D.C.

Anne Spencer (1882–1975)

Respected for her poetry and her garden, Anne Spencer was born in Henry County, Virginia. Her parents, Joel and Sarah, were former slaves. When her parents separated, Spencer went to live with her mother in Bramwell, West Virginia. She did not have any formal education until age eleven when she enrolled in Virginia Seminary and College in Lynchburg, Virginia. In 1901, she married Edward Spencer, her tutor while at the Seminary. Her poetry gained prominence when James Weldon Johnson visited her home. Johnson detected Spencer's talent, and she began publishing her poetry in various magazines and anthologies, including *Opportunity* and Countee Cullen's *Caroling Dusk*. With its carefully designed garden, now an historic landmark, Spencer's Lynchburg home was a gathering place for many of the Harlem Renaissance writers. Both her poems and her garden speak to Spencer's love for precision and beauty.

Before the Feast of Shushan

Garden of Shushan!
After Eden, all terrace, pool, and flower recollect thee:
Ye weavers in saffron and haze and Tyrian purple,
Tell yet what range in color wakes the eye;
Sorcerer, release the dreams born here when
Drowsy, shifting palm-shade enspells the brain;
And sound! ye with harp and flute ne'er essay
Before these star-noted birds escaped from paradise awhile to
Stir all dark, and dear, and passionate desire, till mine
Arms go out to be mocked by the softly kissing body of the
    wind—
Slave, send Vashti to her King!

The fiery wattles of the sun startle into flame
The marbled towers of Shushan:
So at each day's wane, two peers—the one in
Heaven, the other on earth—welcome with their
Splendor the peerless beauty of the Queen.

Cushioned at the Queen's feet and upon her knee
Finding glory for mine head,—still, nearly shamed
Am I, the King, to bend and kiss with sharp
Breath the olive-pink of sandaled toes between;
Or lift me high to the magnet of a gaze, dusky,
Like the pool when but the moon-ray strikes to its depth;
Or closer press to crush a grape 'gainst lips redder
Than the grape, a rose in the night of her hair;
Then—Sharon's Rose in my arms.

From *Time's Unfading Garden*, edited by J. Lee Green, © 1977. Used by permission of Louisiana State University Press.

And I am hard to force the petals wide;
And you are fast to suffer and be sad.
Is any prophet come to teach a new thing
Now in a more apt time?
Have him 'maze how you say love is sacrament;
How says Vashti, love is both bread and wine;
How to the altar may not come to break and drink,
Hulky flesh nor fleshly spirit!

I, thy lord, like not manna for meat as a Judahn;
I, thy master, drink, and red wine, plenty, and when
I thirst. Eat meat, and full, when I hunger.
I, thy King, teach you and leave you, when I list
No woman in all Persia sets out strange action
To confuse Persia's lord—
Love is but desire and thy purpose fulfillment;
I, thy King, so say!

The Wife-Woman

Maker-of-Sevens in the scheme of things
From earth to star;
Thy cycle holds whatever is fate, and
Over the border the bar.
Though rank and fierce the mariner
Sailing the seven seas,
He prays, as he holds his glass to his eyes,
Coaxing the Pleiades.

I cannot love them; and I feel your glad
Chiding from the grave,
That my all was only worth at all, what
Joy to you it gave,
These seven links the *Law* compelled
For the human chain—
I cannot love *them*; and *you,* oh,
Seven-fold months in Flanders slain!

A jungle there, a cave here, bred six
And a million years,
Sure and strong, mate for mate, such
Love as culture fears;
I gave you clear the oil and wine;
You saved me your hob and hearth—
See how *even* life may be ere the
Sickle comes and leaves a swath.

But I can wait the seven of moons,
Or years I spare,
Hoarding the heart's plenty, nor spend
A drop, nor share—
So long but outlives a smile and
A silken gown,
Then gayly I reach up from my shroud,
And you, glory-clad, reach down.

At the Carnival

Gay little Girl-of-the-Diving-Tank,
I desire a name for you,
Nice, as a right glove fits;
For you—who amid the malodorous
Mechanics of this unlovely thing,
Are darling of spirit and form.
I know you—a glance, and what you are
Sits-by-the-fire in my heart.
My Limousine-Lady knows you, or
Why does the slant-envy of her eye mark
Your straight air and radiant inclusive smile?
Guilt pins a fig-leaf; Innocence is its own adorning.
The bull-necked man knows you—this first time
His itching flesh sees form divine and vibrant health,
And thinks not of his avocation.
I came incuriously—
Set on no diversion save that my mind
Might safely nurse its brood of misdeeds

In the presence of a blind crowd.
The color of life was gray.
Everywhere the setting seemed right
For my mood!
Here the sausage and garlic booth
Sent unholy incense skyward;
There a quivering female-thing
Gestured assignations, and lied
To call it dancing;
There, too, were games of chance
With chances for none;
But oh! the Girl-of-the-Tank, at last!
Gleaming Girl, how intimately pure and free
The gaze you send the crowd,
As though you know the dearth of beauty
In its sordid life.
We need you—my Limousine-Lady,
The bull-necked man, and I.
Seeing you here brave and water-clean,
Leaven for the heavy ones of earth,
I am swift to feel that what makes
The plodder glad is good; and
Whatever is good is God.
The wonder is that you are here;
I have seen the queer in queer places,
But never before a heaven-fed
Naiad of the Carnival-Tank!
Little Diver, Destiny for you,
Like as for me, is shod in silence;
Years may seep into your soul
The bacilli of the usual and the expedient;
I implore Neptune to claim his child to-day!

Lady, Lady

Lady, Lady, I saw your face,
Dark as night withholding a star . . .
The chisel fell, or it might have been
You had borne so long the yoke of men.

Lady, Lady, I saw your hands,
Twisted, awry, like crumpled roots,
Bleached poor white in a sudsy tub,
Wrinkled and drawn from your rub-a-dub.

Lady, Lady, I saw your heart,
And altared there in its darksome place

Were the tongues of flame the ancients knew,
Where the good God sits to spangle through.

Letter to My Sister

It is dangerous for a woman to defy the gods;
To taunt them with the tongue's thin tip,
Or strut in the weakness of mere humanity,
Or draw a line daring them to cross;
The gods own the scaring lightning,
The drowning waters, tormenting fears
And anger of red sins.

Oh, but worse still if you mince timidly—
Dodge this way or that, or kneel or pray.
Be kind, or sweat agony drops
Or lay your quick body over your feeble young;
If you have beauty or none, if celibate
Or vowed—the gods are Juggernaut,
Passing over . . . over . . .

This you may do:
Lock your heart, then, quietly,
And lest they peer within,
Light no lamp when dark comes down
Raise no shade for sun;
Breathless must your breath come through
If you'd die and dare deny
The gods their god-like fun.

Jessie Redmon Fauset (1882–1961)

During the height of the Harlem Renaissance, Jessie Fauset wrote four novels: *There Is Confusion* (1924), *Plum Bun: A Novel Without a Moral* (1929), *The Chinaberry Tree: A Novel of American Life* (1931), and *Comedy: American Style* (1933). Additionally, she wrote many short stories, and W. E. B. Du Bois chose her for literary editor of *The Crisis*, publishing many of the works of the other Harlem Renaissance writers. Thus, she earned the title of "midwife" to the movement. The most common theme of her fiction was racial passing. Fauset was interested in the way caste and class affected the lives of middle-class African American women. She wrote racial up-lift narratives about African American genteel society.

Born in New Jersey to Reverend Redmon Fauset, an African Methodist Episcopal minister, and his wife, Annie, Fauset grew up in Philadelphia and experienced a racist educational system that would not allow her to teach there when she finished her education. Denied admission to Bryn Mawr, she graduated Phi Beta Kappa from Cornell, the first woman to graduate with that distinction. She received her master's degree in romance languages from the University of Pennsylvania. Like Anna Julia Cooper, she also studied at the Sorbonne in Paris, and like Angelina Weld Grimké and other writers, she taught at the Dunbar High School in Washington, D.C.

The Sleeper Wakes

Amy recognized the incident as the beginning of one of her phases. Always from a child she had been able to tell when "something was going to happen." She had been standing in Marshall's store, her young, eager gaze intent on the lovely little sample dress which was not from Paris, but quite as dainty as anything that Paris could produce. It was not the lines or even the texture that fascinated Amy so much, it was the grouping of colors—of shades. She knew the combination was just right for her.

"Let me slip it on, Miss," said the saleswoman suddenly. She had nothing to do just then, and the girl was so evidently charmed and so pretty—it was a pleasure to wait on her.

"Oh, no," Amy had stammered. "I haven't time." She had already wasted two hours at the movies, and she knew at home they were waiting for her.

The saleswoman slipped the dress over the girl's pink blouse, and tucked the linen collar under so as to bring the edge of the dress next to her pretty neck. The dress was apricot-color shading into a shell pink and the shell pink shaded off again into the pearl and pink whiteness of Amy's skin. The saleswoman beamed as Amy, entranced, surveyed herself naively in the tall looking-glass.

Then it was that the incident befell. Two men walking idly through the dress-salon stopped and looked—she made an unbelievably pretty picture. One of them with a short, soft brown beard,—"fuzzy" Amy thought to herself as she caught his glance in the mirror—spoke to his companion.

"Jove, how I'd like to paint her!" But it was the look on the other man's face that caught her and thrilled her. "My God! Can't a girl be beautiful!" he said half to himself. The pair passed on.

Amy stepped out of the dress and thanked the saleswoman half absently. She wanted to get home and think, think to herself about that look. She had seen it before in men's eyes, it had been in the eyes of the men in the moving-picture which she had seen that afternoon. But she had not thought *she* could cause it. Shut up in her little room she pondered over it. Her beauty,—she was really good-looking then—she could stir people—men! A girl of seventeen has no psychology, she does not go beneath the surface, she accepts. But she knew she was entering on one of her phases.

She was always living in some sort of story. She had started it when as a child of five she had driven with the tall, proud, white woman to Mrs. Boldin's home. Mrs. Boldin was a bride of one year's standing then. She was slender and very, very comely, with her rich brown skin and her hair that crinkled thick and soft above a low forehead. The house was still redolent of new furniture; Mr. Boldin was spick and span—he, unlike the furniture, remained so for that matter. The white woman had told Amy that this henceforth was to be her home.

Originally published in *The Crisis*, 1920.

Amy was curious, fond of adventure; she did not cry. She did not, of course, realize that she was to stay here indefinitely, but if she had, even at that age she would hardly have shed tears, she was always too eager, too curious to know, to taste what was going to happen next. Still since she had had almost no dealings with colored people and she knew absolutely none of the class to which Mrs. Boldin belonged, she did venture one question.

"Am I going to be colored now?"

The tall white woman had flushed and paled. "You—" she began, but the words choked her. "Yes, you are going to be colored now," she ended finally. She was a proud woman, in a moment she had recovered her usual poise. Amy carried with her for many years the memory of that proud head. She never saw her again.

When she was sixteen she asked Mrs. Boldin the question which in the light of that memory had puzzled her always. "Mrs. Boldin, tell me—am I white or colored?"

And Mrs. Boldin had told her and told her truly that she did not know.

"A—a—mee!" Mrs. Boldin's voice mounted on the last syllable in a shrill crescendo. Amy rose and went downstairs.

Down the comfortable, but rather shabby dining-room which the Boldins used after meals to sit in, and Mr. Boldin, a tall black man, with aristocratic features, sat practicing on a cornet, and Mrs. Boldin sat rocking. In all of their eyes was the manifestation of the light that Amy loved, but how truly she loved it, she was not to guess till years later.

"Amy," Mrs. Boldin paused in her rocking, "did you get the braid?" Of course she had not, though that was the thing she had gone to Marshall's for. Amy always forgot essentials. If she went on an errand, and she always went willingly, it was for the pure joy of going. Who knew what angels might meet one unawares? Not that Amy thought in biblical or in literary phrases. She was in the High School it is true, but she was simply passing through, "getting by" she would have said carelessly. The only reading that had ever made any impression on her had been fairy tales read to her in those long remote days when she had lived with the tall proud woman; and descriptions in novels or histories of beautiful, stately palaces tenanted by beautiful, stately women. She could pore over such pages for hours, her face flushed, her eyes eager.

At present she cast about for an excuse. She had so meant to get the braid. "There was a dress—" she began lamely, she was never deliberately dishonest.

Mr. Boldin cleared his throat and nervously fingered his paper. Cornelius ceased his awful playing and blinked at her short-slightedly through his thick glasses. Both of these, the man and the little boy, loved the beautiful, inconsequent creature with her airy, irresponsible ways. But Mrs. Boldin loved her too, and because she loved her she could not scold.

"Of course you forgot," she began chidingly. Then she smiled. "There was a dress that you looked at *perhaps*. But confess, didn't you go to the movies first?"

Yes, Amy confessed she had done just that. "And oh, Mrs. Boldin, it was the most wonderful picture—a girl—such a pretty one—and she was poor, awfully. And somehow she met the most wonderful people and they were so kind to her. And she married a man who was just tremendously rich and he gave her everything. I did so want Cornelius to see it."

"Huh!" said Cornelius who had been listening not because he was interested, but because he wanted to call Amy's attention to his playing as soon as possible. "Huh! I don't want to look at no pretty girl. Did they have anybody looping the loop in an airship?"

"You'd better stop seeing pretty girl pictures, Amy," said Mr. Boldin kindly. "They're not always true to life. Besides, I know where you can see all the pretty girls you want without bothering to pay twenty-five cents for it."

Amy smiled at the implied compliment and went on happily studying her lessons. They were all happy in their own way. Amy because she was sure of their love and admiration, Mr. and Mrs. Boldin because of her beauty and innocence and Cornelius because he knew he had in his foster-sister a listener whom his terrible practicing could never bore. He played brokenly a piece he had found in an old music-book. *"There's an aching void in every heart, brother."*

"Where do you pick up those old things, Neely?" said his mother fretfully. But Amy could not have her favorite's feelings injured.

"I think it's lovely," she announced defensively. "Cornelius, I'll ask Sadie Murray to lend me her brother's book. He's learning the cornet, too, and you can get some new pieces. Oh, isn't it awful to have to go to bed? Good-night, everybody." She smiled her charming, ever ready smile, the mere reflex of youth and beauty and content.

"You do spoil her, Mattie," said Mr. Boldin after she had left the room. "She's only seventeen—here, Cornelius, you go to bed—but it seems to me she ought to be more dependable about errands. Though she is splendid about some things," he defended her. "Look how willingly she goes off to bed. She'll be asleep before she knows it when most girls of her age would want to be up in the street."

But upstairs Amy was far from asleep. She lit one gas-jet and pulled down the shades. Then she stuffed tissue paper in the keyhole and under the doors, and lit the remaining gas-jets. The light thus thrown on the mirror of the ugly oak dresser was perfect. She slipped off the pink blouse and found two scarfs, a soft yellow and a soft pink,—she had had them in a scarf-dance for a school entertainment. She wound them and draped them about her pretty shoulders and loosened her hair. In the mirror she apostrophized the beautiful, glowing vision of herself.

"There," she said, "I'm like the girl in the picture. She had nothing but her beautiful face—and she did so want to be happy." She sat down on the side of the rather lumpy bed and stretched out her arms. "I want to be happy, too." She intoned it earnestly, almost like an incantation. "I want wonderful clothes, and people around me, men adoring me, and the world before me. I want—everything! It will come, it will all come because I want it so." She sat frowning intently as she was apt to do when very much engrossed. "And we'd all be so happy. I'd give Mr. and Mrs. Boldin money! And Cornelius—he'd go to college and learn all about his old airships. Oh, if I only knew how to begin!"

Smiling, she turned off the lights and crept to bed.

II

Quite suddenly she knew she was going to run away. That was in October. By December she had accomplished her purpose. Not that she was the least bit unhappy but because she must get out in the world,—she felt caged, imprisoned. "Trenton is stifling me," she would have told you, in her unconsciously adopted "movie" diction. New York she knew was the place for her. She had her plans all made. She had sewed steadily after school for two months—as she frequently did when she wanted to buy her season's wardrobe, so besides her carfare she had $25. She went immediately to a white Y.W.C.A., stayed there two nights, found and answered an advertisement for clerk and waitress in a small confectionery and bakery-shop, was accepted and there she was launched.

Perhaps it was because of her early experience when as a tiny child she was taken from that so different home and left at Mrs. Boldin's, perhaps it was some fault in her own disposition, concentrated and egotistic as she was, but certainly she felt no pangs of separation, no fear of her future. She was cold too,—unfired though so to speak rather than icy,—and fastidious. This last quality kept her safe where morality or religion, of neither of which had she any conscious endowment, would have availed her nothing. Unbelievably then she lived two years in New York, unspoiled, untouched, going to work on the edge of Greenwich Village early and coming back late, knowing almost no one and yet altogether happy in the expectation of some thing wonderful, which she knew some day must happen.

It was at the end of the second year that she met Zora Harrison. Zora used to come into lunch with a group of habitués of the place—all of them artists and writers Amy gathered. Mrs. Harrison (for she was married as Amy later learned) appealed to the girl because she knew so well how to afford the contrast to her blonde, golden beauty. Purple, dark and regal, enveloped in velvets and heavy silks, and strange marine blues she wore, and thus made Amy absolutely happy.

Singularly enough, the girl, intent as she was on her own life and experiences, had felt up to this time no yearning to know these strange, happy beings who surrounded her. She did miss Cornelius, but otherwise she was never lonely, or if she was she hardly knew it, for she had always lived an inner life to herself. But Mrs. Harrison magnetized her—she could not keep her eyes from her face, from her wonderful clothes. She made conjectures about her.

The wonderful lady came in late one afternoon—an unusual thing for her. She smiled at Amy invitingly, asked some banal questions and their first conversation began. The acquaintance once struck up progressed rapidly—after a few weeks Mrs. Harrison invited the girl to come to see her. Amy accepted quietly, unaware that anything extraordinary was happening. Zora noticed this and liked it. She had an apartment in 12th Street in a house inhabited only by artists—she was by no means one herself. Amy was fascinated by the new world into which she found herself ushered; Zora's surroundings were very beautiful and Zora herself was a study. She opened to the girl's amazed vision fields of thought and conjecture, phases of whose existence Amy, who was a builder of phases, had never dreamed. Zora had been a poor girl of good family. She had wanted to study art, she had deliberately married a rich man and as deliberately obtained in the course of four years a divorce, and she was now living in New York studying by means of her alimony and enjoying to its fullest the life she loved. She took Amy on a footing with herself—the girl's refinement, her beauty, her interest in colors (though this in Amy at that time was purely sporadic, never consciously encouraged), all this gave Zora a figure about which to plan and build romance. Amy had told her the truth, but not all about her coming to New York. She had grown tired of Trenton—her people were all dead—the folks with whom she lived were kind and good but not "inspiring" (she had borrowed the term from Zora and it was true, the Boldins, when one came to think of it, were not "inspiring"), so she had run away.

Zora had gone into raptures. "What an adventure! My dear, the world is yours. Why, with your looks and your birth, for I suppose you really belong to the Kildares who used to live in Philadelphia, I think there was a son who ran off and married an actress or someone—they disowned him I remember,—you can reach any height. You must marry a wealthy man—perhaps someone who is interested in art and who will let you pursue your studies." She insisted always that Amy had run away in order to study art. "But luck like that comes to few," she sighed, remembering her own plight, for Mr. Harrison had been decidedly unwilling to let her pursue her studies, at least to the extent she wished. "Anyway you must marry wealth,—one can always get a divorce," she ended sagely.

Amy—she came to Zora's every night now—used to listen dazedly at first. She had accepted willingly enough Zora's conjecture about her birth, came to believe it in fact—but she drew back somewhat at such wholesale exploitation of people to suit one's own convenience, still she did not probe too far into this thought—nor did she grasp at all the infamy of exploitation of self. She ventured one or two objections however, but Zora brushed everything aside.

"Everybody is looking out for himself," she said fairly. "I am interested in you, for instance, not for philanthropy's sake, not because I am lonely, and you are charming and pretty and don't get tired of hearing me talk. You'd better come and live with me awhile, my dear, six months or a year. It doesn't cost any more for two than for one, and you can always leave when we get tired of each other. A girl like you can always get a job. If you are worried about being dependent you can pose for me and design my frocks, and oversee Julienne"—her maid-of-all-work—"I'm sure she's a stupendous robber."

Amy came, not at all overwhelmed by the good luck of it—good luck was around the corner more or less for everyone, she supposed. Moreover, she was beginning to absorb some of Zora's doctrine—she, too, must look out for herself. Zora *was* lonely, she *did* need companionship, Julienne *was* careless about change and old blouses and left-over dainties. Amy had her own sense of honor. She carried out faithfully her share of the bargain, cut down waste, renovated Zora's clothes, posed for her, listened to her endlessly and bore with her fitfulness. Zora was truly grateful for this last. She was temperamental but Amy had good nerves and her strong natural inclination to let people do as they wanted stood her in good stead. She was a little stolid, a little unfeeling under her lovely exterior. Her looks at this time belied her—her perfect ivory-pink face, her deep luminous eyes,—very brown they were with purple depths that made one think of pansies—her charming, rather wide mouth, her whole face set in a frame of very soft, very live, brown hair which grew in wisps and tendrils and curls and waves back from her smooth, young forehead. All this made one look for softness and ingenuousness. The ingenuousness was there, but not the softness—except of her fresh, vibrant loveliness.

On the whole then she progressed famously with Zora. Sometimes the latter's callousness shocked her, as when they would go strolling through the streets south of Washington Square. The children, the people all foreign, all dirty, often very artistic, always immensely human, disgusted Zora except for "local color"—she really could reproduce them wonderfully. But she almost hated them for being what they were.

"Br-r-r, dirty little brats!" she would say to Amy. "Don't let them touch me." She was frequently amazed at her protégée's

utter indifference to their appearance, for Amy herself was the pink of daintiness. They were running from MacDougall into Bleecker Street one day and Amy had patted a child—dirty, but lovely—on the head.

"They are all people just like anybody else, just like you and me, Zora," she said in answer to her friend's protest.

"You *are* true democrat," Zora returned with a shrug. But Amy did not understand her.

Not the least of Amy's services was to come between Zora and the too pressing attention of the men who thronged about her.

"Oh, go and talk to Amy," Zora would say, standing slim and gorgeous in some wonderful evening gown. She was an extraordinarily attractive creature, very white and pink, with great ropes of dazzling gold hair, and that look of no-age which only American women possess. As a matter of fact she was thirty-nine, immensely sophisticated and selfish, even, Amy thought, a little cruel. Her present mode of living just suited her; she could not stand any condition that bound her, anything at all *exigeant*. It was useless for anyone to try to influence her. If she did not want to talk, she would not.

The men used to obey her orders and seek Amy sulkily at first, but afterwards with considerably more interest. She was so lovely to look at. But they really, as Zora knew, preferred to talk to the older woman, for while with Zora indifference was a role, second nature now but still a role—with Amy it was natural and she was also a trifle shallow. She had the admiration she craved, she was comfortable, she asked no more. Moreover she thought the men, with the exception of Stuart James Wynne, rather uninteresting—they were faddists for the most part, crazy not about art or music, but merely about some phase such as cubism or syncopation.

Wynne, who was much older than the older half-dozen men who weekly paid Zora homage—impressed her by his suggestion of power. He was a retired broker, immensely wealthy (Zora, who had known him since childhood, informed her), very set and purposeful and polished. He was perhaps fifty-five, widely traveled, of medium height, very white skin and clear, frosty blue eyes, with sharp, proud features. He liked Amy from the beginning, her childishness touched him. In particular he admired her pliability—not knowing it was really indifference. He had been married twice; one wife had divorced him, the other had died. Both marriages were unsuccessful owing to his dominant, rather unsympathetic nature. But he had softened considerably with years, though he still had decided views, [and] was glad to see that Amy, in spite of Zora's influence, neither smoked nor drank. He liked her shallowness—she fascinated him.

Zora had told him much—just the kind of romantic story to appeal to the rich, powerful man. Here was beauty forlorn, penniless, of splendid birth,—for Zora once having connected Amy with the Philadelphia Kildares never swerved from that belief. Amy seemed to Wynne everything a girl should be—she was so unspoiled, so untouched. He asked her to marry him. If she had tried she could not have acted more perfectly. She looked at him with her wonderful eyes.

"But I am poor, ignorant—a nobody," she stammered. "I'm afraid I don't love you either," she went on in her pretty troubled voice, "though I do like you very, very much."

He liked her honesty and her self-depreciation, even her coldness. The fact that she was not flattered seemed to him an extra proof of her native superiority. He, himself, was a representative of one of the South's oldest families, though he had lived abroad lately.

"I have money and influence," he told her gravely, "but I count them nothing without you." And as for love—he would teach her that, he ended, his voice shaking a little. Underneath all his chilly, polished exterior he really cared.

"It seems an unworthy thing to say," he told her wistfully, for she seemed very young beside his experienced fifty-five years, "but anything you wanted in this world could be yours. I could give it to you—clothes, houses and jewels."

"Don't be an idiot," Zora had said when Amy told her. "Of course, marry him. He'll give you a beautiful home and position. He's probably no harder to get along with than anybody else, and if he is, there is always the divorce court."

It seemed to Amy somehow that she was driving a bargain—how infamous a one she could not suspect. But Zora's teachings had sunk deep. Wynne loved her, and he could secure for her what she wanted. "And after all," she said to herself once, "it really is my dream coming true."

She resolved to marry him. There were two weeks of delirious, blissful shopping. Zora was very generous. It seemed to Amy that the whole world was contributing largely to her happiness. She was to have just what she wanted and as her taste was perfect she afforded almost as much pleasure to the people from whom she bought as to herself. In particular she brought rapture to an exclusive modiste in Forty-second Street who exclaimed at her "so perfect taste."

"Mademoiselle is of a marvelous, of an absolute correctness," she said.

Everything whirled by. After the shopping there was the small, impressive wedding. Amy stumbled somehow through the service, struck by its awful solemnity. Then later there was the journey and the big house waiting them in the small town, fifty miles south of Richmond. Wynne was originally from Georgia, but business and social interests had made it necessary for him to be nearer Washington and New York.

Amy was absolute mistress of himself and his home, he said, his voice losing its coldness. "Ah, my dear, you'll never realize what you mean to me—I don't envy any other man in this world. You are so beautiful, so sweet, so different!"

III

From the very beginning *he* was different from what she had supposed. To start with he was far, far wealthier, and he had, too, a tradition, a family-pride which to Amy was inexplicable. Still more inexplicably he had a race-pride. To his wife this was not only strange but foolish. She was as Zora had once suggested, the true democrat. Not that she preferred the company of her maids, though the reason for this did not lie *per se* in the fact that they were maids. There was simply no common ground. But she was uniformly kind, a trait which had she been older would have irritated her husband. As it was, he saw in it only an additional indication of her freshness, her lack of worldliness which seemed to him the attributes of an inherent refinement and goodness untouched by experience.

He, himself, was intolerant of all people of inferior birth or standing and looked with contempt on foreigners, except the French and English. All the rest were variously "guineys," "niggers," and "wops," and all of them he genuinely despised and hated, and talked of them with the huge intolerant carelessness characteristic of occidental civilization. Amy was never able to understand it. People were always first and last, just people to her. Growing up as the average colored American girl does grow up, surrounded by types of every hue, color and facial configuration she had had no absolute ideal. She was not even aware that there was one. Wynne, who in his grim way had a keen sense of humor, used to be vastly amused at the artlessness with which she let him know that she did not consider him to be good-looking. She never wanted him to wear anything but dark blue, or sombre mixtures always.

"They take away from that awful whiteness of your skin," she used to tell him, "and deepen the blue of your eyes."

In the main she made no attempt to understand him, as indeed she made no attempt to understand anything. The result, of course, was that such ideas as seeped into her mind stayed there, took growth and later bore fruit. But just at this period she was like a well-cared for, sleek, house-pet, delicately nurtured, velvety, content to let her days pass by. She thought almost nothing of her art just now except as her sensibilities were jarred by an occasional disharmony. Likewise, even to herself, she never criticized Wynne, except when some act or attitude of his stung. She could never understand why he, so fastidious, so versed in elegance of word and speech, so careful in his surroundings, even down to the last detail of glass and napery, should take such evident pleasure in literature of a certain prurient. He fairly revelled in the realistic novels which to her depicted sheer badness. He would get her to read to him, partly because he liked to be read to, mostly because he enjoyed the realism and in a slighter degree because he enjoyed seeing her shocked. Her point of view amused him.

"What funny people," she would say naively, "to do such things." She could not understand the liaisons and intrigues of women in the society novels, such infamy was stupid and silly. If one starved, it was conceivable that one might steal; if one were intentionally injured, one might hit back, even murder; but deliberate nastiness she could not envisage. The stories, after she had read them to him, passed out of her mind as completely as though they had never existed.

Picture the two of them spending three years together with practically no friction. To his dominance and intolerance she opposed a soft and unobtrusive indifference. What she wanted she had, ease, wealth, adoration, love, too, passionate and imperious, but she had never known any other kind. She was growing cleverer also, her knowledge of French was increasing, she was acquiring a knowledge of politics, of commerce and of the big social questions, for Wynne's interests were exhaustive and she did most of his reading for him. Another woman might have yearned for a more youthful companion, but her native coldness kept her content. She did not love him, she had never really loved anybody, but little Cornelius Boldin—he had been such an enchanting, such a darling baby, she remembered,—her heart contracted painfully when she thought as she did very often of his warm softness.

"He must be a big boy now," she would think almost maternally, wondering—once she had been so sure!—if she would ever see him again. But she was very fond of Wynne, and he was crazy over her just as Zora had predicted. He loaded her with gifts, dresses, flowers, jewels—she amused him because none but colored stones appealed to her.

"Diamonds are so hard, so cold, and pearls are dead," she told him.

Nothing ever came between them, but his ugliness, his hatefulness to dependents. It hurt her so, for she was naturally kind in her careless, uncomprehending way. True, she had left Mrs. Boldin without a word, but she did not guess how completely Mrs. Boldin loved her. She would have been aghast had she realized how stricken her flight had left them. At twenty-two, Amy was still as good, as unspoiled, as pure as a child. Of course with all this she was too unquestioning, too selfish, too vain, but they were all faults of her lovely, lovely flesh. Wynne's intolerance finally got on her nerves. She used to blush for his unkindness. All the servants were colored, but she had long since ceased to think that perhaps she, too, was colored, except when he, by insult toward an employee, overt, always at least implied, made her realize his contemptuous dislike and disregard for a dark skin or Negro blood.

"Stuart, how can you say such things?" she would expostulate. "You can't expect a man to stand such language as that." And Wynne would sneer, "A man—you don't consider a nigger a man, do you? Oh, Amy, don't be such a fool. You've got to keep them in their places."

Some innate sense of the fitness of things kept her from condoling outspokenly with the servants, but they knew she was ashamed of her husband's ways. Of course, they left—it seemed to Amy that Peter, the butler, was always getting new "help,"—but most of the upper servants stayed, for Wynne paid handsomely and although his orders were meticulous and insistent the retinue of employees was so large that the individual's work was light.

Most of the servants who did stay on in spite of Wynne's occasional insults had a purpose in view. Callie, the cook, Amy found out, had two children at Howard University—of course she never came in contact with Wynne. The chauffeur had a crippled sister. Rose, Amy's maid and purveyor of much outside information, was the chief support of the family. About Peter, Amy knew nothing: he was a striking, taciturn man, very competent, who had left the Wynnes' service years before and had returned in Amy's third year. Wynne treated him with comparative respect. But Stephen, the new valet, met with entirely different treatment. Amy's heart yearned toward him, he was like Cornelius, with short-sighted, patient eyes, always willing, a little over-eager. Amy recognized him for what he was: a boy of respectable, ambitious parentage, striving for the means for an education; naturally far above his present calling, yet willing to pass through all this as a means to an end. She questioned Rosa about him.

"Oh, Stephen," Rosa told her, "yes'm, he's workin' for fair. He's got a brother at the Howard's and a sister at the Smith's. Yes'm, it do seem a little hard on him, but Stephen, he say, they're both goin' to turn roun' and help him when they get through. That blue silk has a rip in it, Miss Amy, if you was thinkin' of wearin' that. Yes'm, somehow I don't think Steve's very strong, kinda worries like. I guess he's sorta nervous."

Amy told Wynne, "He's such a nice boy, Stuart," she pleaded, "it hurts me to have you so cross with him. Anyway don't call him names." She was both surprised and frightened at the feeling in her that prompted her to interfere. She had held so aloof from other people's interests all these years.

"I *am* colored," she told herself that night. "I feel it inside of me. I must be or I couldn't care so about Stephen. Poor boy, I suppose Cornelius is just like him. I wish Stuart would let him alone. I wonder if all white people are like that. Zora was hard, too, on unfortunate people." She pondered over it a bit. "I wonder what Stuart would say if he knew I was colored?" She lay perfectly still, her smooth brow knitted, thinking hard. "But he loves me," she said to herself still silently. "He'll always love my looks," and she fell to thinking that all the wonderful happenings in her sheltered, pampered life had come to her through her beauty. She reached out an exquisite arm, switched on a light, and picking up a hand-mirror from a dressing-table, fell to studying her face. She was right. It was her chiefest asset. She forgot Stephen and fell asleep.

But in the morning her husband's voice, issuing from his dressing-room across the hall, awakened her. She listened drowsily. Stephen, leaving the house the day before, had been met by a boy with a telegram. He had taken it, slipped it into his pocket, (he was just going to the mailbox) and had forgotten to deliver it until now, nearly twenty-four hours later. She could hear Stuart's storm of abuse—it was terrible, made up as it was of oaths and insults to the boy's ancestry. There was a moment's lull. Then she heard him again.

"If your brains are a fair sample of that black wench of a sister of yours—"

She sprang up then thrusting her arms as she ran into her pink dressing-gown. She got there just in time. Stephen, his face quivering, was standing looking straight into Wynne's smoldering eyes. In spite of herself, Amy was glad to see the boy's bearing. But he did not notice her.

"You devil!" he was saying. "You white-faced devil! I'll make you pay for that!" He raised his arm. Wynne did not blench.

With a scream she was between them. "Go, Stephen, go,—get out of the house. Where do you think you are? Don't you know you'll be hanged, lynched, tortured?" Her voice shrilled at him.

Wynne tried to thrust aside her arms that clung and twisted. But she held fast till the door slammed behind the fleeing boy.

"God, let me by, Amy!" As suddenly as she had clasped him she let him go, ran to the door, fastened it and threw the key out the window.

He took her by the arm and shook her. "Are you mad? Didn't you hear him threaten me, me, a nigger threaten me?" His voice broke with nigger, "And you're letting him get away! Why, I'll get him. I'll set bloodhounds on him, I'll have every white man in this town after him! He'll be hanging so high by midnight—" he made for the other door, cursing, half-insane.

How, *how* could she keep him back! She hated her weak arms with their futile beauty! She sprang toward him. "Stuart, wait," she was breathless and sobbing. She said the first thing that came into her head. "Wait, Stuart, you cannot do this thing." She thought of Cornelius—suppose it had been he—"Stephen,—that boy,—he is my brother."

He turned on her. "What!" he said fiercely, then laughed a short laugh of disdain. "You are crazy," he said roughly. "My God, Amy! How can you even in jest associate yourself with these people? Don't you suppose I know a white girl when I see one? There's no use in telling a lie like that."

Well, there was no help for it. There was only one way. He had turned back for a moment, but she must keep him many moments—an hour. Stephen must get out of town.

She caught his arm again. "Yes," she told him, "I did lie. Stephen is not my brother, I never saw him before." The light of relief that crept into his eyes did not escape her, it only nerved her. "But I *am* colored," she ended.

Before he could stop her she had told him all about the tall white woman. "She took me to Mrs. Boldin's and gave me to her to keep. She would never have taken me to her if I had been white. If you lynch this boy, I'll let the world, your world, know that your wife is a colored woman."

He sat down like a man suddenly sticken old, his face ashen. "Tell me about it again," he commanded. And she obeyed, going mercilessly into every damning detail.

IV

Amazingly her beauty availed her nothing. If she had been an older woman, if she had had Zora's age and experience, she would have been able to gauge exactly her influence over Wynne. Though even then in similar circumstances she would have taken the risk and acted in just the same manner. But she was a little bewildered at her utter miscalculation. She had thought he might not want his friends—his world by which he set such store—to know that she was colored, but she had not dreamed it could make any real difference to him. He had chosen her, poor and ignorant, but of a host of women, and had told her countless times of his love. To herself Amy Wynne was in comparison with Zora for instance, stupid and uninteresting. But his constant, unsolicited iterations had made her accept his idea.

She was just the same woman she told herself, she had not changed, she was still beautiful, still charming, still "different." Perhaps, that very difference had its being in the fact of her mixed blood. She had been his wife—there were memories—she could not see how he could give her up. The suddenness of the divorce carried her off her feet. Dazedly she left him—though almost without a pang for she had only liked him. She had been perfectly honest about this, and he, although consumed by the fierceness of his emotion toward her, had gradually forced himself to be content, for at least she had never made him jealous.

She was to live in a small house of his in New York, up town in the 80's. Peter was in charge and there was a new maid and a cook. The servants, of course, knew of the separation, but nobody guessed why. She was living on a much smaller basis than the one to which she had become so accustomed in the last three years. But she was very comfortable. She felt, at any rate she manifested, no qualms at receiving alimony from Wynne. That was the way things happened, she supposed when she thought of it at all. Moreover, it seemed to her perfectly in keeping with Wynne's former attitude toward her; she did not see how he could do less. She expected people to be consistent. That was why she was so amazed that he in spite of his oft iterated love, could let her go. If she had felt half the love for him which he had professed for her, she would not have sent him away if he had been a leper.

"Why I'd stay with him," she told herself, "if he were one, even as I feel now."

She was lonely in New York. Perhaps it was the first time in her life that she had felt so. Zora had gone to Paris the first year of her marriage and had not come back.

The days dragged on emptily. One thing helped her. She had gone one day to the modiste from whom she had brought her trousseau. The woman remembered her perfectly—"The lady with the exquisite taste for colors—ah, madame, but you have the rare gift." Amy was grateful to be taken out of her thoughts. She bought one or two daring but altogether lovely creations and let fall a few suggestions:

"That brown frock, Madame,—you say it has been on your hands a long time? Yes? But no wonder. See, instead of that dead white you should have a shade of ivory, that white cheapens it." Deftly she caught up a bit of ivory satin and worked out her idea. Madame was ravished.

"But yes, Madame Ween is correct,—as always. Oh, what a pity that the Madame is so wealthy. If she were only a poor girl—Mlle. Antoine with the best eye for color in the place has just left, gone back to France to nurse her brother— this World War is of such a horror! If someone like Madame, now, could be found, to take little Antoine's place!"

Some obscure impulse drove Amy to accept the half proposal: "Oh! I don't know, I have nothing to do just now. My husband is abroad." Wynne had left her with that impression. "I could contribute the money to the Red Cross or to charity."

The work was the best thing in the world for her. It kept her from becoming too introspective, though even then she did more serious, connected thinking than she had done in all the years of her varied life.

She missed Wynne definitely, chiefly as a guiding influence for she had rarely planned even her own amusements. Her dependence on him had been absolute. She used to picture him to herself as he was before the trouble—and his changing expressions as he looked at her, of amusement, interest, pride, a certain little teasing quality that used to come into his eyes, which always made her adopt her "spoiled child air" as he used to call it. It was the way he liked her best. Then last, there was that look he had given her the morning she had told him she was colored—it had depicted so many emotions, various and yet distinct. There were dismay, disbelief, coldness, a final aloofness.

There was another expression, too, that she thought of sometimes—the look on the face of Mr. Packard, Wynne's lawyer. She, herself, had attempted no defense.

"For God's sake why did you tell him, Mrs. Wynne?" Packard asked her. His curiosity got the better of him. "You couldn't have been in love with that yellow rascal," he blurted out. "She's too cold really, to love anybody," he told himself. "If you didn't care about the boy why should you have told?"

She defended herself feebly. "He looked so like Cornelius Boldin," she replied vaguely, "and he couldn't help being colored." A clerk came in then and Packard said no more. But into his eyes had crept a certain reluctant respect. She remembered the look, but could not define it.

She was so sorry about the trouble now, she wished it had never happened. Still if she had it to repeat she would act in the same way again. "There was nothing else for me to do," she used to tell herself.

But she missed Wynne unbelievably.

If it had not been for Peter, her life would have been almost that of a nun. But Peter, who read the papers and kept abreast of times, constantly called her attention, with all due respect, to the meetings, the plays, the sights which she ought to attend or see. She was truly grateful to him. She was very kind to all three of the servants. They had the easiest "places" in New York, the maids used to tell their friends. As she never entertained, and frequently dined out, they had a great deal of time off.

She had been separated from Wynne for ten months before she began to make any definite plans for her future. Of course, she could not go on like this always. It came to her suddenly that probably she would go to Paris and live there— why or how she did not know. Only Zora was there and lately she had begun to think that her life was to be like Zora's. They had been amazingly parallel up to this time. Of course she would have to wait until after the war.

She sat musing about it one day in the big sitting-room which she had had fitted over into a luxurious studio. There was a sewing-room off to the side from which Peter used to wheel into the room waxen figures of all colorings and contours so that she could drape the various fabrics about them to be sure of the best results. But today she was working out a scheme for one of Madame's customers, who was of her own color and size and she was her own lay-figure. She sat in front of the huge pier glass, a wonderful soft yellow silk draped about her radiant loveliness.

"I could do some serious work in Paris," she said half aloud to herself. "I suppose if I really wanted to, I could be very successful along this line."

Somewhere downstairs an electric bell buzzed, at first softly, then after a slight pause, louder, and more insistently.

"If Madame sends me that lace today," she was thinking, idly, "I could finish this and start on the pink. I wonder why Peter doesn't answer the bell."

She remembered then that Peter had gone to New Rochelle on business and she had sent Ellen to Altman's to find a certain rare velvet and had allowed Mary to go with her. She would dine out, she told them, so they need not hurry. Evidently she was alone in the house.

Well she could answer the bell. She had done it often enough in the old days at Mrs. Boldin's. Of course it was the lace. She smiled a bit as she went downstairs thinking how surprised the delivery boy would be to see her arrayed thus early in the afternoon. She hoped he wouldn't go. She could see him through the long, thick panels of glass in the vestibule and front door. He was just turning about as she opened the door.

This was no delivery-boy, this man whose gaze fell on her hungry and avid. This was Wynne. She stood for a second leaning against the doorjamb, a strange figure surely in the sharp November weather. Some leaves—brown, skeleton shapes—rose and swirled unnoticed about her head. A passing letter-carrier looked at them curiously.

"What are you doing answering the door?" Wynne asked her roughly. "Where is Peter? Go in, you'll catch cold."

She was glad to see him. She took him into the drawing room—a wonderful study in browns—and looked at him and looked at him.

"Well," he asked her, his voice eager in spite of the commonplace words, "are you glad to see me? Tell me what you do with yourself."

She could not talk fast enough, her eyes clinging to his face. Once it struck her that he had changed in some indefinable way. Was it a slight coarsening of that refined aristocratic aspect? Even in her subconsciousness she denied it.

He had come back to her.

"So I design for Madame when I feel like it, and send the money to the Red Cross and wonder when you are coming back to me." For the first time in their acquaintanceship she was conscious deliberately of trying to attract, to hold him. She put on her spoiled child air which had once been so successful.

"It took you long enough to get here," she pouted. She was certain of him now. His mere presence assured her.

They sat silent a moment, the late November sun bathing her head in an austere glow of chilly gold. As she sat there in the big brown chair she was, in her yellow dress, like some mysterious emanation, some wraith-like aura developed from the tone of her surroundings.

He rose and came toward her, still silent. She grew nervous, and talked incessantly with sudden unusual gestures. "Oh, Stuart, let me give you tea. It's right there in the pantry

off the dining-room. I can wheel the table in." She rose, a lovely creature in her yellow robe. He watched her intently.

"Wait," he bade her.

She paused almost on tiptoe, a dainty golden butterfly.

"You are coming back to live with me?" he asked her hoarsely.

For the first time in her life she loved him.

"Of course I am coming back," she told him softly. "Aren't you glad? Haven't you missed me? I didn't see how you *could* stay away. Oh! Stuart, what a wonderful ring!"

For he had slipped on her finger a heavy dull gold band, with an immense sapphire in an oval setting—a beautiful thing of Italian workmanship.

"It is so like you to remember," she told him gratefully. "I love colored stones." She admired it, turning it around and around on her slender finger.

How silent he was, standing there watching her with his sombre yet eager gaze. It made her troubled, uneasy. She cast about for something to say.

"You can't think how I've improved since I saw you, Stuart. I've read all sorts of books—Oh! I'm learned," she smiled at him. "And Stuart," she went a little closer to him, twisting the button on his perfect coat, "I'm so sorry about it all,—about Stephen, that boy, you know. I just couldn't help interfering. But when we're married again, if you'll just remember how it hurts me to have you so cross—"

He interrupted her. "I wasn't aware that I spoke of our marrying again," he told her, his voice steady, his blue eyes cold.

She thought he was teasing. "Why you just asked me to. You said 'aren't you coming back to live with me—'"

Still she didn't comprehend. "But what do you mean?" She asked bewildered.

"What do you suppose a man means," he returned deliberately, "when he asks a woman to live with him but not to marry him?"

She sat down heavily in the brown chair, all glowing ivory and yellow against its sombre depths.

"Like the women in those awful novels?" she whispered. "Not like those women!—Oh Stuart! you don't mean it!" Her very heart was numb.

"But you must care a little—" she was amazed at her own depth of feeling. "Why I care—there are all those memories back of us—you must want me really—"

"I do want you," he told her tensely. "I want you damnably. But—well—I might as well out with it—A white man like me simply doesn't marry a colored woman. After all what difference need it make to you? We'll live abroad—you'll travel, have all the things you love. Many a white woman would envy you." He stretched out an eager hand.

She evaded it, holding herself aloof as though his touch were contaminating. Her movement angered him.

"Oh, hell!" he snarled at her roughly. "Why don't you stop posing? What do you think you are anyway? Do you suppose I'd take you for my wife—what do you think can happen to you? What man of your race could give you what you want? You don't suppose I am going to support you this way forever, do you? The court imposed no alimony. You've got to come to it sooner or later—you're bound to fall to some white man. What's the matter—I'm not rich enough?"

Her face flamed at that—"As though it were *that* that mattered!"

He gave her a deadly look. "Well, isn't it? Ah, my girl, you forget you told me you didn't love me when you married me. You sold yourself to me then. Haven't I reason to suppose you are waiting for a higher bidder?"

At these words something in her died forever, her youth, her illusions, her happy, happy blindness. She saw life leering mercilessly in her face. It seemed to her that she would give all her future to stamp out, to kill the contempt in his frosty insolent eyes. In a sudden rush of savagery she struck him, struck him across his hateful sneering mouth with the hand which wore his ring.

As *she* fell, reeling under the fearful impact of his brutal but involuntary blow, her mind caught at, registered two things. A little thin stream of blood was trickling across his chin. She had cut him with the ring, she realised with a certain savage satisfaction. And there was something else which she must remember, which she *would* remember if only she could fight her way out of this dreadful clinging blackness, which was bearing down upon her—closing her in.

When she came to she sat up holding her bruised, aching head in her palms, trying to recall what it was that had impressed her so.

Oh yes, her very mind ached with the realization. She lay back again on the floor, prone, anything to relieve that intolerable pain. But her memory, her thoughts went on.

"Nigger," he had called her as she fell, "nigger, nigger," and again, "nigger."

"He despised me absolutely," she said to herself wonderingly, "because I was colored. And yet he wanted me."

V

Somehow she reached her room. Long after the servants had come in, she lay face downward across her bed, thinking. How she hated Wynne, how she hated herself! And for ten months she had been living off his money although in no way had she a claim on him. Her whole body burned with the shame of it.

In the morning she rang for Peter. She faced him, white and haggard, but if the man noticed her condition, he made no sign. He was, if possible, more imperturbable than ever.

"Peter," she told him, her eyes and voice very steady, "I am leaving this house today and shall never come back."

"Yes, Miss."

"And, Peter, I am very poor now and shall have no money besides what I can make for myself."

"Yes, Miss."

Would nothing surprise him, she wondered dully. She went on, "I don't know whether you knew it or not, Peter, but I am colored, and hereafter I mean to live among my own people. Do you think you could find a little house or little cottage not too far from New York?"

He had a little place in New Rochelle, he told her, his manner altering not one whit, or better yet his sister had a four-room house in Orange, with a garden, if he remembered correctly. Yes, he was sure there was a garden. It would be just the thing for Mrs. Wynne.

She had four hundred dollars of her very own which she had earned by designing for Madame. She paid the maids a month in advance—they were to stay as long as Peter needed them. She, herself, went to a small hotel in Twenty-eighth Street, and here Peter came for her at the end of ten days, with the acknowledgement of the keys and receipts from Mr. Packard. Then he accompanied her to Orange and installed her in her new home.

"I wish I could afford to keep you, Peter," she said a little wistfully, "but I am very poor. I am heavily in debt and I must get that off my shoulders at once."

Mrs. Wynne was very kind, he was sure; he could think of no one with whom he would prefer to work. Furthermore, he often ran down from New Rochelle to see his sister; he would come in from time to time, and in the spring would plant the garden if she wished.

She hated to see him go, but she did not dwell long on that. Her only thought was to work and work and work and save until she could pay Wynne back. She had not lived very extravagantly during those ten months and Peter was a perfect manager—in spite of her remonstrances he had given her every month an account of his expenses. She had made arrangements with Madame to be her regular designer. The French woman guessing that more than whim was behind this move drove a very shrewd bargain, but even then the pay was excellent. With care, she told herself, she could be free within two years, three at most.

She lived a dull enough existence now, going to work steadily every morning and getting home late at night. Almost it was like those early days when she had first left Mrs. Boldin, except that now she had no high sense of adventure, no expectation of great things to come, which might buoy her up. She no longer thought of phases and the proper setting for her beauty. Once indeed catching sight of her face late one night in the mirror in her tiny work-room in Orange, she stopped and scanned herself, loathing what she saw there.

"You *thing!*" she said to the image in the glass, "if you hadn't been so vain, so shallow!" And she had struck herself violently again and again across the face until her head ached.

But such fits of passion were rare. She had a curious sense of freedom in these days, a feeling that at last her brain, her sense were liberated from some hateful clinging thrall-dom. Her thoughts were always busy. She used to go over that last scene with Wynne again and again trying to probe the inscrutable mystery which she felt was at the bottom of the affair. She groped her way toward a solution, but always something stopped her. Her impulse to strike, she realized, and his brutal rejoinder had been actuated by something more than mere sex antagonism, there was *race* antagonism there—two elements clashing. That much she could fathom. But that he despising her, hating her for not being white should yet desire her! It seemed to her that his attitude to-ward her—hate and yet desire, was the attitude in microcosm of the whole white world toward her own, toward that world to which those few possible strains of black blood so tenu-ously and yet so tenaciously linked her.

Once she got hold of a big thought. Perhaps there *was* some root, some racial distinction woven in with the stuff of which she was formed which made her persistently kind and unexacting. And perhaps in the same way this difference, helplessly, inevitably operated in making Wynne and his kind, cruel or at best indifferent. Her reading for Wynne re-acted to her thought—she remembered the grating insolence of white exploiters in foreign lands, the wrecking of African villages, the destruction of homes in Tasmania. She couldn't imagine where Tasmania was, but wherever it was, it had been the realest thing in the world to its crude inhabitants.

Gradually she reached a decision. There were two divi-sions of people in the world—on the one hand insatiable de-sire for power; keenness, mentality; a vast and cruel pride. On the other there was ambition, it is true, but modified, a cer-tain humble sweetness, too much inclination to trust, an un-thinking, unswerving loyalty. All the advantages in the world accrued to the first division. But without bitterness she chose the second. She wanted to be colored, she hoped she was col-ored. She wished even that she did not have to take advantage of her appearance to earn a living. But that was to meet an end. After all she had contracted her debt with a white man, she would pay him with a white man's money.

The years slipped by—four of them. One day a letter came from Mr. Packard. Mrs. Wynne had sent him the last penny of the sum received from Mr. Wynne from February to November, 1914. Mr. Wynne had refused to touch the money, it was and would be indefinitely at Mrs. Wynne's disposal.

She never even answered the letter. Instead she dismissed the whole incident,—Wynne and all,—from her mind and began to plan for her future. She was free, free! She had paid back her sorry debt with labor, money and anguish. From now on she could do as she pleased. Almost she caught her-self saying "something is going to happen." But she checked herself, she hated her old attitude.

But something *was* happening. Insensibly from the mo-ment she knew of her deliverance, her thoughts turned back to a stifled hidden longing, which had lain, it seemed to her, and eternity in her heart. Those days with Mrs. Boldin! At night,—on her way to New York,—in the work-rooms,—her mind was busy with little intimate pictures of that happy, wholesome, unpretentious life. She could see Mrs. Boldin, clean and portly, in a lilac chambray dress, upbraiding her for some trifling, yet exasperating fault. And Mr. Boldin, immac-ulate and slender, with his noticeably polished air—how kind he had always been, she remembered. And lastly, Cornelius: Cornelius in a thousand attitudes and engaged in a thousand occupations, brown and near-sighted and sweet—devoted to his pretty sister, as he used to call her; Cornelius, who used to come to her as a baby as willingly as to his mother; Cornelius spelling out colored letters on his blocks, pointing to them stickily with a brown, perfect finger; Cornelius singing like an angel in his breathy, sexless voice and later murdering everything possible on his terrible corner. How had she ever been able to leave them all and the dear shabbiness of that home! Nothing, she realized, in all these years had touched her inmost being, had penetrated to the core of her cold heart like the memories of those early, misty scenes.

One day she wrote a letter to Mrs. Boldin. She, the writer, Madame A. Wynne, had come across a young woman, Army Kildare, who said that as a girl she had run away from home and now she would like to come back. But she was ashamed to write. Madame Wynne had questioned the girl closely and she was quite sure that this Miss Kildare had in no way incurred shame or disgrace. It had been some time since Madame Wynne had seen the girl but if Mrs. Boldin wished, she would try to find her again—perhaps Mrs. Boldin would like to get in touch with her. The letter ended on a tentative note.

The answer came at once.

My Dear Madame Wynne:

My mother told me to write you this letter. She says even if Amy Kildare had done something terrible, she would want her to come home again. My father says so too. My mother says, please find her as soon as you can and tell her to come back. She still misses her. We all miss her. I was a little boy when she left, but though I am in the High School now and play in the school orchestra, I would rather see her than do anything I know. If you see her, be sure to tell her to come right away. My mother says thank you.

Yours respectfully,
Cornelius Boldin

The letter came to the modiste's establishment in New York. Amy read it and went with it to Madame. "I must go away immediately. I can't come back—you may have these last two weeks for nothing." Madame, who had surmised long since the separation, looked curiously at the girl's flushed cheeks, and decided that "Monsieur Ween" had returned. She gave her fatalistic shrug. All Americans were crazy.

"But, yes, Madame, if you must go, absolument."

When she reached the ferry, Amy looked about her searchingly. "I hope I'm seeing you for the last time. I'm going home!" Oh, the unbelievable kindness! She had left them without a word and they still wanted her back!

Eventually she got to Orange and to the little house. She sent a message to Peter's sister and set about her packing. But first she sat down in the little house and looked about her. She would go home, home—how she loved the world, she would stay there a while, but always there was life, still beckoning. It would beckon forever she realized to her adventurousness. Afterwards she would set up an establishment of her own,—she reviewed possibilities—in a rich suburb, where white women would pay her expertness, caring nothing for realities, only for externals.

"As I myself used to care," she sighed. Her thoughts flashed on. "Then some day I'll work and help with colored people—the only ones who have really cared for and wanted me." Her eyes blurred.

She would never make any attempt to find out who or what she was. If she were white, there would always be people urging her to keep up the silliness of racial prestige. How she hated it all!

"Citizen of the world, that's what I'll be. And now I'll go home."

Peter's sister's little girl came over to be with the pretty lady whom she adored.

"You sit here, Angel, and watch me pack," Amy said, placing her in a little arm-chair. And the baby sat there in silent observation, one tiny leg crossed over the other, surely the quaintest, gravest bit of bronze, Amy thought, that ever lived.

"Miss Amy cried," the child told her mother afterwards.

Perhaps Amy did cry, but if so she was unaware. Certainly she laughed more happily, more spontaneously than she had done for years. Once she got down on her knees in front of the little arm-chair and buried her face in the baby's tiny bosom.

"Oh Angel, Angel," she whispered, "do you suppose Cornelius still plays on that cornet?"

From *Plum Bun: A Novel Without a Moral*

Chapter 1 [Passing]

Opal Street, as streets go, is no jewel of the first water. It is merely an imitation, and none too good at that. Narrow, unsparkling, uninviting, it stretches meekly off from dull Jefferson Street to the dingy, drab market which forms the north side of Oxford Street. It has no mystery, no allure, either of exclusiveness or of downright depravity; its usages are plainly significant,—an unpretentious little street lined with unpretentious little houses, inhabited for the most part by unpretentious little people.

The dwellings are three stories high, and contain six boxes called by courtesy, rooms—a "parlour," a midget of a dining-room a larger kitchen and, above, a front bedroom seemingly large only because it extends for the full width of the house, a mere shadow of a bathroom, and another back bedroom with windows whose possibilities are spoiled by their outlook on sad and diminutive back-yards. And above these two, still two others built in similar wise.

In one of these houses dwelt a father, a mother and two daughters. Here, as often happens in a home sheltering two generations, opposite, unevenly matched emotions faced each other. In the houses of the rich the satisfied ambition of the older generation is faced by the overwhelming ambition of the younger. Or the elders may find themselves brought in opposition to the blank indifference and ennui of youth engendered by the realization that there remain no more worlds to conquer; their fathers having already taken all. In houses on Opal Street these niceties of distinction are hardly to be found; there is a more direct and concrete contrast. The satisfied ambition of maturity is a foil for the restless despair of youth.

Affairs in the Murray household were advancing towards this stage; yet not a soul in that family of four could have foretold its coming. To Junius and Mattie Murray, who had known poverty and homelessness, the little house on Opal Street represented the *ne plus ultra* of ambition; to their daughter Angela it seemed the dingiest, drabbest chrysalis that had ever fettered the wings of a brilliant butterfly. The stories which Junius and Mattie told of difficulties overcome, of the arduous learning of trades, of the pitiful scraping together of infinitesimal savings, would have made a latter-day Iliad, but to Angela they were merely a description of a life which she at any cost would avoid living. Somewhere in the world were paths which lead to broad thoroughfares, large, bright houses, delicate niceties of existence. Those paths Angela meant to find and frequent. At a very early age she had observed that the good things of life are unevenly distributed; merit is not always rewarded; hard labour does not necessarily entail adequate recompense. Certain fortuitous endowments, great physical beauty, unusual strength, a certain unswerving singleness of mind,—gifts bestowed quite blindly and disproportionately by the forces which control life,—these were the qualities which contributed toward a glowing and pleasant existence.

Angela had no high purpose in life; unlike her sister Virginia, who meant some day to invent a marvellous method for teaching the pianoforte, Angela felt no impulse to discover, or to perfect. True she thought she might become eventually a distinguished painter, but that was because she felt within herself an ability to depict which as far as it went was correct and promising. Her eye for line and for expression was already good and she had a nice feeling for colour. Moreover she possessed the instinct for self-appraisal which taught her that she had much to learn. And she was sure that the knowledge once gained would flower in her case to perfection. But her gift was not for her the end of existence; rather it was an adjunct to a life which was to know light, pleasure, gaiety and freedom.

Freedom! That was the note which Angela heard oftenest in the melody of living which was to be hers. With a wildness that fell just short of unreasonableness she hated restraint. Her father's earlier days as coachman in a private family, his later successful, independent years as boss carpenter, her mother's youth spent as maid to a famous actress, all this was to Angela a manifestation of the sort of thing which happens to those enchained it might be by duty, by poverty, by weakness or by colour.

Colour or rather the lack of it seemed to the child the one absolute prerequisite to the life of which she was always dreaming. One might break loose from a too hampering sense of duty; poverty could be overcome; physicians conquered weakness; but colour, the mere possession of a black or a white skin, that was clearly one of those fortuitous endowments of the gods. Gratitude was no strong ingredient in this girl's nature, yet very often early she began thanking Fate for the chance which in that household of four had bestowed on her the heritage of her mother's fair skin. She might so easily have been, like her father, black, or have received the melange which had resulted in Virginia's rosy bronzeness and her deeply waving black hair. But Angela had received not only her mother's creamy complexion and her soft cloudy, chestnut hair, but she had taken from Junius the aquiline nose, the gift

of some remote Indian ancestor which gave to his face and his eldest daughter's that touch of chiselled immobility.

• • • •

It was from her mother that Angela learned the possibilities for joy and freedom which seemed to her inherent in mere whiteness. No one would have been more amazed than that same mother if she could gave guessed how her daughter interpreted her actions. Certainly Mrs. Murray did not attribute what she considered her happy, busy, sheltered life on tiny Opal Street to the accident of her colour; she attributed it to her black husband whom she had been glad and proud to marry. It is equally certain that that white skin of hers had not saved her from occasional contumely and insult. The famous actress for whom she had worked was aware of Mattie's mixed blood and, boasting temperament rather than refinement, had often dubbed her "white nigger."

Angela's mother employed her colour very much as she practised certain winning usages of smile and voice to obtain indulgences which meant much to her and which took nothing from anyone else. Then, too, she was possessed of a keener sense of humour than her daughter; it amused her when by herself to take lunch at an exclusive restaurant whose patrons would have been panic-stricken if they had divined the presence of a "coloured" woman no matter how little her appearance differed from theirs. It was with no idea of disclaiming her own that she sat in orchestra seats which Philadelphia denied to coloured patrons. But when Junius or indeed any other dark friend accompanied her she was the first to announce that she liked to sit in the balcony or gallery, as indeed she did; her infrequent occupation of orchestra seats was due merely to a mischievous determination to flout a silly and unjust law.

Her years with the actress had left their mark, a perfectly harmless and rather charming one. At least so it seemed to Junius, whose weakness was for the qualities known as "essentially feminine." Mrs. Murray loved pretty clothes, she liked shops devoted to the service of women; she enjoyed being even on the fringe of a fashionable gathering. A satisfaction that was almost ecstatic seized her when she drank tea in the midst of modishly gowned women in a stylish tea-room. It pleased her to stand in the foyer of a great hotel or of the Academy of Music and to be part of the whirling, humming, palpitating gaiety. She had no desire to be of these people, but she liked to look on; it amused and thrilled and kept alive some unquenchable instinct for life which thrived within her. To walk through Wanamaker's on Saturday, to stroll from Fifteenth to Ninth Street on Chestnut, to have her tea in the Bellevue Stratford, to stand in the lobby of the St. James' fitting on immaculate gloves; all innocent, childish pleasures pursued without malice or envy contrived to cast a glamour over Monday's washing and Tuesday's ironing, the scrubbing of kitchen and bathroom and the fashioning of children's clothes. She was endowed with a humorous and pungent method of presentation; Junius, who had had the wit not to interfere with these little excursions and the sympathy to take them at their face value, preferred one of his wife's sparkling accounts of a Saturday's adventure in "passing" to all the tall stories told by cronies at his lodge.

Much of this pleasure, harmless and charming though it was, would have been impossible with a dark skin.

In these first years of marriage, Mattie, busied with the house and the two babies had given up those excursions. Later, when the children had grown and Junius had reached the stage where he could afford to give himself a half-holiday on Saturdays, the two parents inaugurated a plan of action which eventually became a fixed programme. Each took a child, and Junius went off to a beloved but long since suspended pastime of exploring old Philadelphia, whereas Mattie embarked once more on her social adventures. It is true that Mattie accompanied by brown Virginia could not move quite as freely as when with Angela. But her maternal instincts were sound; her children, their feelings and their faith in her meant much more than the pleasure which she would have been first to call unnecessary and silly. As it happened the children themselves quite unconsciously solved the dilemma; Virginia found shopping tiring and stupid, Angela returned from her father's adventuring worn and bored. Gradually the rule was formed that Angela accompanied her mother and Virginia her father.

• • • •

On such fortuities does life depend. Little Angela Murray, hurrying through Saturday morning's scrubbing of steps in order that she might have her bath at one and be with her mother on Chestnut Street at two, never realized that her mother took her pleasure among all these pale people because it was there that she happened to find it. It never occurred to her that the delight which her mother obviously showed in meeting friends on Sunday morning when the whole united Murray family came out of church was the same as she showed on Chestnut Street the previous Saturday, because she was finding the qualities which her heart craved, bustle, excitement and fashion. The daughter could not guess that if the economic status or the racial genius of coloured people had permitted them to run modish hotels or vast and popular department stores her mother would have been there. She drew for herself certain clearly formed conclusions which her subconscious mind thus codified:

First, that the great rewards of life—riches, glamour, pleasure,—are for white-skinned people only. Secondly, that Junius and Virginia were denied these privileges because they were dark; here her reasoning bore at least an element of verisimilitude but she missed the essential fact that her father

and sister did not care for this type of pleasure. The effect of her fallaciousness was to cause her to feel a faint pity for her unfortunate relatives and also to feel that coloured people were to be considered fortunate only in the proportion in which they measured up to the physical standards of white people.

One Saturday excursion left a far-reaching impression. Mrs. Murray and Angela had spent a successful and interesting afternoon. They had browsed among the contents of the small exclusive shops in Walnut Street; they had had soda at Adams' on Broad Street and they were standing finally in the portico of the Walton Hotel deciding with fashionable and idle elegance what they should be next. A thin stream of people constantly passing threw an occasional glance at the quietly modish pair, the well-dressed, assured woman and the refined and no less assured daughter. The door-man knew them; it was one of Mrs. Murray's pleasures to proffer him a small tip, much appreciated since it was uncalled for. This was the atmosphere which she loved. Angela had put on her gloves and was waiting for her mother, who was drawing on her own, with great care, when she glimpsed in the laughing, hurrying Saturday throng the figures of her father and of Virginia. They were close enough for her mother, who saw them too, to touch them by merely descending a few steps and stretching out her arm. In a second the pair had vanished. Angela saw her mother's face change—with trepidation she thought. She remarked: "It's a good thing Papa didn't see us, you'd have had to speak to him, wouldn't you?" But her mother, giving her a distracted glance, made no reply.

That night, after the girls were in bed, Mattie, perched on the arm of her husband's chair, told him about it. "I was at my old game of play-acting again to-day, June, passing you know, and darling, you and Virginia went by within arm's reach and we never spoke to you. I'm so ashamed."

But Junius consoled her. Long before their marriage he had known of his Mattie's weakness and its essential harmlessness. "My dear girl, I told you long ago that where no principle was involved, your passing means nothing to me. It's just a little joke; I don't think you'd be ashamed to acknowledge your old husband anywhere if it were necessary."

"I'd do that if people were mistaking me for a queen," she assured him fondly. But she was silent, not quite satisfied. "After all," she said with her charming frankness, "it isn't you, dear, who make me feel guilty. I really am ashamed to think that I let Virginia pass by without a word. I think I should feel very badly if she were to know it. I don't believe I'll ever let myself be quite as silly as that again."

But of this determination Angela, dreaming excitedly of Saturdays spent in turning her small olive face firmly away from peering black countenances was, unhappily, unaware.

Mary Effie Lee Newsome (1885–1979)

Many of the writers during the Harlem Renaissance wrote for both children and adults. One venue for such writings was the *Brownies' Book*, a publication targeted to African American children with contributions from such writers as Jessie Fauset, Langston Hughes, and Nella Larsen. The *Brownies' Book* was short-lived. Mary Effie Lee Newsome carried on the tradition by writing a column for children in *The Crisis* from 1925 to 1929. She also wrote short fiction. Newsome was born in Philadelphia and raised in Wilberforce, Ohio, where her father, Dr. Benjamin Franklin Lee, was president of Wilberforce University. In addition to Wilberforce, Newsome attended Oberlin and the University of Pennsylvania.

The Bronze Legacy
(To a Brown Boy)

'Tis a noble gift to be brown, all brown,
    Like the strongest things that make up this earth,
Like the mountains grave and grand,
    Even like the trunks of trees—
    Even oaks, to be like those!
God builds His strength in bronze.

To be brown like thrush and lark!
    Like the subtle wren so dark!
Nay, the king of beasts wears brown;
    Eagles are of this same hue.
I thank God, then, I am brown.
    Brown has might things to do.

Morning Light

(The Dew-Drier)

Brother to the firefly—
For as the firefly lights the night,

So lights he the morning—
Bathed in the dank dews as he goes forth
Through heavy menace and mystery
Of half-waking tropic dawn,
Behold a little boy,
A naked black boy,
Sweeping aside with his slight frame
Night's pregnant tears,
And making a morning path to the light
For the tropic traveler!

2

Bathed in the blood of battle,
Treading toward a new morning,
May not his race—
Its body long bared to the world's disdain,
Its face schooled to smile for a light to come—
May not his race, even as the Dew Boy leads,
Bear onward the world to a time
When tolerance, forbearance,
Such as reigned in the heart of ONE
Whose heart was gold
Shall shape the world for that fresh dawning
After the dews of blood?

Originally published in Brownies' Book, 1928.

Georgia Douglas Johnson (1886–1966)

Harlem was not the only site for the Harlem Renaissance. The "S" Street NW, Washington, D.C. home of Georgia Douglas Johnson for over 50 years was another prominent site. Serving as a literary salon, Johnson's home was a place where many of the writers met. Known best for her poems about women in their roles as lovers and mothers, Douglas also wrote several plays, including *Plumes* (1927), a play that uses a mother's love for her child to contrast folk and scientific knowledge.

Born Georgia Blanche Douglas in Atlanta, she attended Oberlin Conservatory of Music after her graduation from Atlanta University. In 1903, she married Henry Lincoln Johnson, a prominent Republican attorney whose parents were ex-slaves. In 1912, President Taft appointed Henry Johnson Recorder of Deeds for Washington, D.C. After Henry Johnson's death, Taft appointed Georgia Douglas Johnson a position as a commissioner for the Department of Labor. As a writer of several genres, Johnson was prolific. In addition to her most prominent poetry collections, *The Heart of a Woman* (1918), *Bronze* (1922), and her folk and historical dramas, she wrote a newspaper column, "Homely Philosophy," which was syndicated to twenty newspapers.

The Heart of a Woman

The heart of a woman goes forth with the dawn,
As a lone bird, soft winging, so restlessly on,
Afar o'er life's turrets and vales does it roam
In the wake of those echoes the heart calls home.

The heart of a woman falls back with the night,
And enters some alien cage in its plight,
And tries to forget it has dreamed of the stars
While it breaks, breaks, breaks on the sheltering bars.

Your World

Your world is as big as you make it
I know, for I used to abide
In the narrowest nest in a corner
My wings pressing close to my side.

But I sighted the distant horizon
Where the sky-line encircled the sea
And I throbbed with a burning desire
To travel this immensity.

I battered the cordons around me
And cradled my wings on the breeze
Then soared to the uttermost reaches
With rapture, with power, with ease!

Motherhood

Don't knock on my door, little child,
I cannot let you in;
You know not what a world this is
Of cruelty and sin.
Wait in the still eternity
Until I come to you.
The world is cruel, cruel, child,
I cannot let you through.

Don't knock at my heart, little one,
I cannot bear the pain
Of turning deaf ears to your call,
Time and time again.
You do not know the monster men
Inhabiting the earth.
Be still, be still, my precious child,
I cannot give you birth.

From *The Heart of a Woman*, 1918.

From *Bronze*, 1922.

Wishes

I'm tired of pacing the petty round of the ring of the thing I
  know—
I want to stand on the daylight's edge and see where the
  sunsets go.

I want to sail on a swallow's tail and peep through the sky's
  blue glass.
I want to see if the dreams in me shall perish or come to pass.

I want to look through the moon's pale crook and gaze on
  the moon-man's face.
I want to keep all the tears I weep and sail to some unknown
  place.

I Want to Die While You Love Me

I want to die while you love me,
  While yet you hold me fair,
While laughter lies upon my lips
  And lights are in my hair.

I want to die while you love me
  And bear to that still bed
Your kisses—turbulent, unspent,
  To warm me when I'm dead.

I want to die while you love me
  Oh, who would care to live,
'Til love has nothing more to ask
  And nothing more to give.

From *An Autumn Love Cycle*, 1928.

Plumes: A Folk Tragedy

CHARACTERS

CHARITY BROWN, the mother
EMMERLINE BROWN, the daughter
TILDY, the friend
DOCTOR SCOTT, physician

Published in 1920.

Scene: A poor cottage in the South.
Time: Contemporary.

SCENE: THE KITCHEN *of a two-room cottage. A window over-looking the street. A door leading to street, one leading to the back yard and one to the inner room. A stove, a table with shelf over it, a washtub. A rocking-chair, a cane-bottom chair. Needle, thread, scissors, etc. on table.*

> *Scene opens with* CHARITY BROWN *heating a poultice over the stove. A groaning is heard from the inner room.*

CHARITY. Yes, honey, mamma is fixing somethin' to do you good. Yes, my baby, jus' you wait—I'm a-coming. (*Knock is heard at door. It is gently pushed open and* TILDY *comes in cautiously.*)

TILDY. (*Whispering*) How is she?

CHARITY. Poorly, poorly. Didn't rest last night none hardly. Move that dress and set in th' rocker. I been trying to snatch a minute to finish it but don't seem like I can. She won't have nothing to wear if she—she——

TILDY. I understands. How near done is it?

CHARITY. Ain't so much more to do.

TILDY. (*Takes up dress from chair; looks at it*) I'll do some on it.

CHARITY. Thank you, sister Tildy. Whip that torshon on and turn down the hem in the skirt.

TILDY. (*Measuring dress against herself*) How deep?

CHARITY. Let me see, now (*Studies a minute with finger against lip*) I tell you—jus' baste it, 'cause you see— she wears 'em short, but—it might be—— (*Stops.*)

TILDY. (*Bowing her head comprehendingly*) Huh-uh, I see exzackly. (*Sighs*) You'd want it long—over her feet then.

CHARITY. That's it, sister Tildy. (*Listening*) She's some easy now! (*Stirring poultice*) Jest can't get this poltis' hot enough somehow this morning.

TILDY. Put some red pepper in it. Got any?

CHARITY. Yes. There ought to be some in one of them boxes on the shelf there. (*Points.*)

TILDY. (*Goes to shelf, looks about and gets the pepper*) Here, put a-plenty of this in.

CHARITY. (*Groans are heard from the next room*) Good Lord, them pains got her again. She suffers so, when she's 'wake.

TILDY. Poor little thing. How old is she now, sister Charity?

CHARITY. Turning fourteen this coming July.

TILDY. (*Shaking her head dubiously*) I sho' hope she'll be mended by then.

CHARITY. It don't look much like it, but I trusts so—— (*Looking worried*) That doctor's mighty late this morning.

TILDY. I expects he'll be 'long in no time. Doctors is mighty onconcerned here lately.

CHARITY. (*Going toward inner room with poultice*) They surely is and I don't have too much confidence in none of 'em. (*You can hear her soothing the child.*)

TILDY. (*Listening*) Want me to help you put it on, sister Charity?

CHARITY. (*From inner room*) No, I can fix it. (*Coming back from sick room shaking her head rather dejectedly.*)

TILDY. How is she, sister Charity?

CHARITY. Mighty feeble. Gone back to sleep now. My poor little baby. (*Bracing herself*) I'm going to put on some coffee now.

TILDY. I'm sho' glad. I feel kinder low-spirited.

CHARITY. It's me that low-sperited. The doctor said last time he was here he might have to oparate—said, she mought have a chance then. But I tell you the truth, I've got no faith a-tall in 'em. They takes all your money for nothing.

TILDY. They sho' do and don't leave a cent for putting you away decent.

CHARITY. That's jest it. They takes all you got and then you dies jest the same. It ain't like they was sure.

TILDY. No, they ain't sure. That's it exzactly. But they takes your money jest the same, and leaves you flat.

CHARITY. I been thinking 'bout Zeke these last few days—how he was put away——

TILDY. I wouldn't worry 'bout him now. He's out of his troubles.

CHARITY. I know. But it worries me when I think about how he was put away . . . that ugly pine coffin, jest one shabby old hack and nothing else to show—to show—what we thought about him.

TILDY. Hush, sister! Don't you worry over him. He's happy now, anyhow.

CHARITY. I can't help it! Then little Bessie. We all jest scrooged in one hack and took her little coffin in our lap all the way out to the graveyard. (*Breaks out crying.*)

TILDY. Do hush, sister Charity. You done the best you could. Poor folks got to make the best of it. The Lord understands——

CHARITY. I know that—but I made up my mind the time Bessie went that the next one of us what died would have a shore nuff funeral, everything grand,—with plumes!—I saved and saved and now—this yah doctor——

TILDY. All they think about is cuttin' and killing and taking your money. I got nothin' to put 'em doing.

CHARITY. (*Goes over to washtub and rubs on clothes*) Me neither. These clothes got to get out somehow, I needs every cent.

TILDY. How much that washing bring you?

CHARITY. Dollar and a half. It's worth a whole lot more. But what can you do?

TILDY. You can't do nothing—Look there, sister Charity, ain't that coffee boiling?

CHARITY. (*Wipes hands on apron and goes to stove*) Yes it's boiling good fashioned. Come on, drink some.

TILDY. There ain't nothing I'd rather have than a good strong cup of coffee. (CHARITY *pours* TILDY's *cup.*) (*Sweetening and stirring hers*) Pour you some. (CHARITY *pours her own cup*) I'd been dead, too, long ago if it hadn't a been for my coffee.

CHARITY. I love it, but it don't love me—gives me the shortness of breath.

TILDY. (*Finishing her cup, taking up sugar with spoon*) Don't hurt me. I could drink a barrel.

CHARITY. (*Drinking more slowly—reaching for coffeepot*) Here, drink another cup.

TILDY. I shore will, that cup done me a lot of good.

CHARITY. (*Looking into her empty cup thoughtfully*) I wish Dinah Morris would drop in now. I'd ask her what these grounds mean.

TILDY. I can read 'em a little myself.

CHARITY. You can? Well, for the Lord's sake, look here and tell me what this cup says! (*Offers cup to* TILDY. TILDY *wards it off.*)

TILDY. You got to turn it 'round in your saucer three times first.

CHARITY. Yes, that's right, I forgot. (*Turns cup 'round, counting*) One, two, three. (*Starts to pick it up.*)

TILDY. Huhudh. (*Meaning no*) Let it set a minute. It might be watery. (*After a minute, while she finishes her own cup*) Now let me see. (*Takes cup and examines it very scrutinizingly.*)

CHARITY. What you see?

TILDY. (*Hesitatingly*) I ain't seen a cup like this one for many a year. Not since—not since——

CHARITY. When?

TILDY. Not since jest before ma died. I looked in the cup then and saw things and— I stopped looking . . .

CHARITY. Tell me what you see, I want to know.

TILDY. I don't like to tell no bad news——

CHARITY. Go on. I can stan' anything after all I been thru'.

TILDY. Since you're bound to know I'll tell you. (CHARITY *draws nearer*) I sees a big gethering!

CHARITY. Gethering, you say?

TILDY. Yes, a big gethering. People all crowded together. Then I see 'em going one by one and two by two. Long line stretching out and out and out!

CHARITY. (*In a whisper*) What you think it is?

TILDY. (*Awed like*) Looks like (*Hesitates*) a possession!

CHARITY. (*Shouting*) You sure!

TILDY. I know it is. (*Just then the toll of a church bell is heard and then the steady and slow tramp, tramp, of horses' hoofs. Both women look at each other.*)

TILDY. (*In a hushed voice*) That must be Bell Gibson's funeral coming 'way from Mt. Zion (*Gets up and goes to window*) Yes, it sho' is.

CHARITY. (*Looking out of the window also*) Poor Bell suffered many a year; she's out of the pain now.

TILDY. Look, here comes the hearse now!

CHARITY. My Lord! ain't it grand! Look at them horses—look at their heads—plumes—how they shake 'em! Land o' mighty! It's fine sight, sister Tildy.

TILDY. That must be Jer'miah in that first carriage, bending over like; he shorely is putting her away grand.

CHARITY. No mistake about it. That's Pickett's best funeral turnout he's got.

TILDY. I'll bet is cost a lot.

CHARITY. Fifty dollars, so Matilda Jenkins told me. She had it for Bud. The plumes is what cost.

TILDY. Look at the hacks—— (*Counts*) I believe to my soul there's eight.

CHARITY. Got somebody in all of 'em too—and flowers—She shore got a lot of 'em. (*Both women's eyes follow the tail end of the procession, horses' hoofs die away as they turn away from window. The two women look at each other significantly.*)

TILDY. (*Significantly*) Well!—— (*They look at each other without speaking for a minute.* CHARITY *goes to the washtub*) Want these cups washed up?

CHARITY. No don't mind 'em. I'd rather you get that dress done. I got to get these clothes out.

TILDY. (*Picking up dress*) Shore, there ain't so much more to do on it now. (*Knock is heard on the door.* CHARITY *answers knock and admits* Dr. Scott.)

DR. SCOTT. Good morning. How's the patient today?

CHARITY. Not so good, doctor. When she ain't 'sleep she suffers so; but she sleeps mostly.

DR. SCOTT. Well, let's see, let's see. Just hand me a pan of warm water and I'll soon find out just what's what.

CHARITY. All right, doctor. I'll bring it to you right away. (*Bustles about fixing water—looking toward dress* Tildy *is working on*) Poor little Emmerline's been wanting a white dress trimmed with torshon a long time—now she's got it and it looks like—well—— (*Hesitates*) t'warn't made to wear.

TILDY. Don't take on so, sister Charity—The Lord giveth and the Lord taketh.

CHARITY. I know—but it's hard—hard—— (*Goes into inner room with water. You can hear talking with the doctor after a minute and the doctor expostulating with her—in a minute she appears at the door, being led from the room by the doctor.*)

DR. SCOTT. No, my dear Mrs. Brown. It will be much better for you to remain outside.

CHARITY. But doctor——

DR. SCOTT. NO. You stay outside and get your mind on something else. You can't possibly be of any service. Now be calm, will you?

CHARITY. I'll try, doctor.

TILDY. The doctor's right. You can't do no good in there.

CHARITY. I knows, but I thought I could hold the pan or somethin'. (*Lowering her voice*) Says he got to see if her heart is all right or somethin'. I tell you—nowadays——

TILDY. I know.

CHARITY. (*Softly to* TILDY) Hope he won't come out here saying he got to operate. (*Goes to washtub.*)

TILDY. I hope so, too. Won't it cost a lot?

CHARITY. That's jest it. It would take all I got saved up.

TILDY. Of course, if he's goin' to get her up—but I don't believe in 'em. I don't believe in 'em.

CHARITY. He didn't promise tho'—even if he did, he said maybe it wouldn't do no good.

TILDY. I'd think a long time before I'd let him operate on my chile. Taking all yuh money, promising nothing and ten to one killing her to boot.

CHARITY. This is a hard world.

TILDY. Don't you trus' him. Coffee grounds don't lie!

CHARITY. I don't trust him. I jest want to do what's right by her. I ought to put these clothes on the line while you're settin' in here, but I jes hate to go outdoors while he's in there.

TILDY. (*Getting up*) I'll hang 'em out. You stay here. Where your clothespins at?

CHARITY. Hanging right there by the back door in the bag. They ought to dry before dark and then I can iron to-night.

TILDY. (*Picking up tub*) They ought to blow dry in no time. (*Goes toward back door.*)

CHARITY. Then I can shore rub 'em over to-night. Say, sister Tildy, hist 'em up with that long saplin' prop leaning in the fence corner.

TILDY. (*Going out*) All right.

CHARITY. (*Standing by the table beating nervously on it with her fingers—listens—and then starts to bustling about the kitchen*) (*Enter*) DOCTOR (*from inner room.*)

DR. SCOTT. Well, Mrs. Brown, I've decided I'll have to operate.

CHARITY. MY Lord! Doctor—don't say that!

DR. SCOTT. It's the only chance.

CHARITY. You mean she'll get well if you do?

DR. SCOTT. No, I can't say that——It's just a chance——a last chance. And I'll do just what I said, cut the price of the operation down to fifty dollars. I'm willing to do that for you. (CHARITY *throws up her hands in dismay.*)

CHARITY. Doctor, I was so in hopes you wouldn't operate—I—I—— And yo' say ain't a bit sure she'll get well—even then?

DR. SCOTT. No. I can't be sure. We'll just have to take the chance. But I'm sure you want to do everything——

CHARITY. Sure, doctor, I do want to—do—everything I can do to—to—— Doctor, look at this cup. (*Picks up fortune cup and shows the doctor*) My fortune's jes' been told this very morning—look at these grounds—they says—— (*Softly*) it ain't no use, no use a-tall.

DR. SCOTT. Why, my good woman, don't you believe in such senseless things! That cup of grounds can't show you anything. Wash them out and forget it.

CHARITY. I can't forget it. I feel like it ain't no use; I'd just be spendin' the money that I needs—for nothing— nothing.

DR. SCOTT. But you won't though—— You'll have a clear conscience. You'd know that you did everything you could.

CHARITY. I know that, doctor. But there's things you don't know 'bout—there's other things I got to think about. If she goes—if she must go . . . I had plans—I been getting ready—now—— Oh, doctor, I jest can't see how I can have this operation—you say you can't promise—nothing?

DR. SCOTT. I didn't think you'd hesitate about it—I imagined your love for your child——

CHARITY. (*Breaking in*) I do love my child. My God. I do love my child. You don't understand . . . but . . . but—can't I have a little time to think about it, doctor? It means so much—to her—and—me!

DR. SCOTT. I tell you. I'll go on over to the office. I'd have to get my—(*Hesitates*) my things, anyhow. And as soon as you make up your mind, get one of the neighbors to run over and tell me. I'll come right back. But don't waste any time now, Mrs. Brown, every minute counts.

CHARITY. Thank you, doctor, thank you. I'll shore send you word as soon as I can. I'm so upset and worried I'm half crazy.

DR. SCOTT. I know you are . . . but don't take too long to make up your mind . . . . It ought to be done to-day. Remember—it may save her. (*Exits.*)

CHARITY. (*Goes to door of sick room—looks inside for a few minutes, then starts walking up and down the little kitchen,*

first holding a hand up to her head and then wringing them. Enter TILDY *from yard with tub under her arm.*)

TILDY. Well, they're all out, sister Charity—— (*Stops*) Why, what's the matter?

CHARITY. The doctor wants to opearte.

TILDY. (*Softly*) Where he—gone?

CHARITY. Yes—he's gone, but he's coming back—if I send for him.

TILDY. You going to? (*Puts down tub and picks up white dress and begins sewing.*)

CHARITY. I dunno—I got to think.

TILDY. I can't see what's the use myself. He can't save her with no operation—— Coffee grounds don't lie.

CHARITY. It would take all the money I got for the operation and then what about puttin' her away? He can't save her—don't even promise ter. I know he can't—I feel it . . . I feel it . . .

TILDY. It's in the air . . . . (*Both women sit tense in the silence.* TILDY *has commenced sewing again. Just then a strange, strangling noise comes from the inner room.*)

TILDY. What's that?

CHARITY. (*Running toward and into inner room*) Oh, my God! (*From inside*) Sister Tildy—Come here—No,—some water, quick. (*TILDY with dress in hand starts towards inner room. Stops at door, sighs and then goes hurriedly back for the water pitcher.* CHARITY *is heard moaning softly in the next room, then she appears at doorway and leans against jamb of door*) Rip the hem out, sister Tildy.

CURTAIN

Zora Neale Hurston (1891–1960)

Probably the most widely read novel in colleges today from the Harlem Renaissance is Zora Neale Hurston's *Their Eyes Were Watching God*. The novel reflects the background of a writer who was also an anthropologist and folklorist. Hurston's story of how Janie Crawford comes to understand herself and her desires is set in an all-black town where folks swap stories on their porches at dusk and where storytelling is an art. In 1973 when Alice Walker found Hurston's unmarked grave, she started a literary revival that continues to swell.

Born to Reverend John Hurston and Lucy Potts Hurston, Zora was the fifth of eight children. The Hurstons lived in Eatonville, Florida, an all-black town, that would later figure prominently in Hurston's fiction. When Hurston's mother died and her father remarried shortly thereafter, Hurston left her home and began working as a maid to a white actress, a job that took her to various places. While in Baltimore, she attended Morgan Academy (Morgan State University). After finishing high school at Morgan, she attended Howard University. While in Washington, D.C., Hurston met other writers and intellectuals of the Harlem Renaissance, including Alain Locke who encouraged her to take her talent to Harlem. Upon her arrival in New York, Hurston became the personal secretary to novelist Fannie Hurst who helped her secure a scholarship to Barnard College where Hurston did graduate work under the famous anthropologist, Franz Boas. Hurston was also able to secure the patronage of Charlotte Mason, a wealthy white woman who supported Hurston's fieldwork.

In total, Hurston wrote four novels, *Jonah's Gourd Vine* (1934), *Their Eyes Were Watching God* (1937), *Moses, Man of the Mountain* (1939), and *Seraph on the Suwanee* (1948). Additionally, Hurston wrote short stories, a play (with Langston Hughes), several collections of folklore, and an autobiography, *Dust Tracks on a Road* (1942). Although Hurston's later life was marked by poverty and false accusations of criminal activity involving a minor, her reputation today is that of one of the most beloved writers of the Harlem Renaissance.

Sweat

It was eleven o'clock of a Spring night in Florida. It was Sunday. Any other night, Delia Jones would have been in bed for two hours by this time. But she was a washwoman, and Monday morning meant a great deal to her. So she collected the soiled clothes on Saturday when she returned the clean things. Sunday night after church, she sorted them and put the white things to soak. It saved her almost a half day's start. A great hamper in the bedroom held the clothes that she brought home. It was so much neater than a number of bundles lying around.

She squatted in the kitchen floor beside the great pile of clothes, sorting them into small heaps according to color, and humming a song in a mournful key, but wondering through it all where Sykes, her husband, had gone with her horse and buckboard.

Just then something long, round, limp and black fell upon her shoulders and slithered to the floor beside her. A great terror took hold of her. It softened her knees and dried her mouth so that it was a full minute before she could cry out or move. Then she saw that it was the big bull whip her husband liked to carry when he drove.

She lifted her eyes to the door and saw him standing there bent over with laughter at her fright. She screamed at him.

"Sykes, what you throw dat whip on me like dat? You know it would skeer me—looks just like a snake, an' you knows how skeered Ah is of snakes."

"Course Ah knowed it! That's how come Ah done it." He slapped his leg with his hand and almost rolled on the ground in his mirth. "If you such a big fool dat you got to have a fit over a earth worm or a string, Ah don't keer how bad Ah skeer you."

"You aint got no business doing it. Gawd knows it's a sin. Some day Ah'm gointuh drops dead from some of yo' foolishness. 'Nother thing, where you been wid mah rig? Ah feeds dat pony. He aint fuh you to be drivin' wid no bull whip."

"Yo sho is one aggravatin' nigger woman!" he declared and stepped into the room. She resumed her work and did not answer him at once. "Ah done tole you time and again to keep them white folks' clothes outa dis house."

He picked up the whip and glared down at her. Delia went on with her work. She went out into the yard and returned with a galvanized tub and set it on the washbench. She saw that Sykes had kicked all of the clothes together again, and now stood in her way truculently, his whole manner hoping, *praying*, for an argument. But she walked calmly around him and commenced to re-sort the things.

"Next time, Ah'm gointer to kick 'em outdoors," he threatened as he struck a match along the leg of his corduroy breeches.

Delia never looked up from her work, and her thin, stooped shoulders sagged further.

"Ah aint for no fuss t'night Sykes. Ah just come from taking sacrament at the church house."

He snorted scornfully. "Yeah, you just come from de church house on a Sunday night, but heah you is gone to work on them clothes. You ain't nothing but a hypocrite. One of them amen-corner Christians—sing, whoop, shout, then come home and wash white folks clothes on the Sabbath."

He stepped roughly upon the whitest pile of things, kicking them helterskelter as he crossed the room. His wife gave a little scream of dismay, and quickly gathered them together again.

"Sykes, you quit grindin dirt into these clothes! How can Ah git through by Sat'day if Ah don't start on Sunday?"

"Ah don't keer if you never git through. Anyhow, Ah done promised Gawd and a couple of other men, Ah aint gointer have it in mah house. Don't gimme no lip neither, else Ah'll throw 'em out and put mah fist up side yo' head to boot."

Delia's habitual meekness seemed to slip from her shoulders like a blown scarf. She was on her feet; her poor little body, her bare knuckly hands bravely defying the strapping bulk before her.

"Looka heah, Sykes, you done gone too far. Ah been married to you fur fifteen years, and Ah been takin' in washin' for fifteen years. Sweat, sweat, sweat! Work and sweat, cry and sweat, pray and sweat!"

"What's that got to do with me?" he asked brutally.

"What's it got to do with you, Sykes? Mah tub of suds is filled yo' belly with vittles more times than yo' hands is filled it. Mah sweat is done paid for this house and Ah reckon Ah kin keep on sweatin' in it."

She seized the iron skillet from the stove and struck a defensive pose, which act surprised him greatly, coming from her. It cowed him and he did not strike her as he usually did.

"Naw you won't," she panted, "that ole snaggle-toothed black woman you runnin' with aint comin' heah to pile up on

mah sweat and blood. You aint paid for nothin' on this place, and Ah'm gointer stay right heah till Ah'm toted out foot foremost."

"Well, you better quit gittin' me filed up, else they'll be totin' you out sooner than you expect. Ah'm so tired of you Ah don't know what to do. Gawd! how Ah hates skinny wimmen!"

A little awed by this new Delia, he sidled out of the door and slammed the back gate after him. He did not say where he had gone, but she knew too well. She knew very well that he would not return until nearly daybreak also. Her work over, she went on to bed but not to sleep at once. Things had come to a pretty pass!

She lay awake, gazing upon the debris that cluttered their matrimonial trail. Not an image left standing along the way. Anything like flowers had long ago been drowned in the salty stream that had been pressed from her heart. Her tears, her sweat, her blood. She had brought love to the union and he had brought a longing for the flesh. Two months after the wedding, he had given her the first brutal beating. She had the memory of numerous trips to Orlando with all of his wages when he had returned to her penniless, even before the first year had passed. She was young and soft then, but now she thought of her knotty, muscled limbs, her harsh knuckly hands, and drew herself up into an unhappy little ball in the middle of the big feather bed. Too late now to hope for love, even if it were not Bertha it would be someone else. This case differed from the others only in that she was bolder than the others. Too late for everything except her little home. She had built it for her old days, and planted one by one the trees and flowers there. It was lovely to her, lovely.

Somehow before sleep came, she found herself saying aloud: "Oh well, whatever goes over the Devil's back, is got to come under his belly. Sometime or ruther, Sykes, like everybody else, is gointer reap his sowing." After that she was able to build a spiritual earthworks against her husband. His shells could no longer reach her. *Amen.* She went to sleep and slept until he announced his presence in bed by kicking her feet and rudely snatching the cover away.

"Gimme some kivah heah, an' git yo' damn foots over on yo' own side! Ah oughter mash you in yo' mouf fuh drawing dat skillet on me."

Delia went clear to the rail without answering him. A triumphant indifference to all that he was or did.

The week was as full of work for Delia as all other weeks, and Saturday found her behind her little pony, collecting and delivering clothes.

It was a hot, hot day near the end of July. The village men on Joe Clarke's porch even chewed cane listlessly. They did not hurt the caneknots as usual. They let them dribble over the edges of the porch. Even conversation had collapsed under the heat.

"Heah comes Delia Jones," Jim Merchant said, as the shaggy pony came round the bend of the road toward them. The rusty backboard was heaped with baskets of crisp, clean laundry.

"Yep," Joe Lindsay agreed. "Hot or col', rain or shine, jes' cz reg'lar cz de wccks roll roun' Delia carries 'em an' fetches 'em on Sat'day."

"She better if she wanter eat," said Moss. "Syke Jones aint wuth de shot an powder hit would tek tuh kill 'em. Not to *huh* he aint."

"He sho' aint," Walter Thomas chimed in. "It's too bad, too, cause she wuz a right pritty lil trick when he got huh. Ah'd uh mah'ied huh mahseff if he hadnter beat me to it."

Delia nodded briefly at the men as she drove past.

"Too much knockin' will ruin *any* 'oman. He done beat huh 'nough tuh kill three women, let 'lone change they looks," said Elijah Mosely. "How Syke kin stommuck dat big black greasy Mogul he's layin' roun' wid, gets me. Ah swear dat eight-rock couldn't kiss a sardine can Ah done thowed out de back do' 'way las' yeah."

"Aw, she's fat, thass how come. He's allus been crazy 'bout fat women," put in Merchant. "He'd a'been tied up wid one long time ago if he could a' found one tuh have him. Did Ah tell yuh 'bout him come sidlin' round *mah* wife—bringin' her a basket uh pee-cans outa his yard fuh a present? Yes-sir, mah wife! She tol' him tuh take 'em right straight back home, cause Delia works so hard ovah dat washtub she reckon everything on de place taste lak sweat an' soapsuds. Ah jus' wisht Ah'd a' caught 'im roun' dere! Ah'd a' made his hips ketch on fiah down dat shell road."

"Ah know he done it, too. Ah sees 'im grinnin' at every 'oman dat passes," Walter Thomas said. "But even so, he useter eat some mighty big hunks uh humble pie tuh git dat lil' 'oman he got. She wuz ez pritty ez a speckled pup! Dat wuz fifteen years ago. He useter be so skeered uh losin' huh, she could make him do some parts of a hushand's duty. Dey never wuz de same in de mind."

"There oughter be a law about him," said Lindsay. "He aint fit tuh carry guts tuh a bear."

Clarke spoke for the first time. "Taint no law on earth dat kin make a man be decent if it aint in 'im. There's plenty men dat takes a wife lak dey do a joint uh sugar-cane. It's round, juicy an' sweet when dey gits it. But dey squeeze an' grind, squeeze an' grind an' wring tell day wring every drop uh pleasure dat's in 'em out. When dey's satisfied dat dey is wrung dry, dey treats 'em jes lak dey do a cane-chew. Dey throws 'em away. Dey knows what dey is doin' while dey is at it, an' hates theirselves fuh it but they keeps on hangin' after huh tell she's empty. Den dey hates huh fuh bein' a cane-chew an' in de way."

"We oughter take Syke an' dat stray 'oman uh his'n down in Lake Howell swamp an' lay on de rawhide till they

cain't say 'Lawd a' mussy.' He allus wuz uh ovahbearin' niggah, but since dat white 'oman from up north done teached 'im how to run a automobile, he done got too biggety to live—an' we oughter kill 'im," Old Man Anderson advised.

A grunt of approval went around the porch. But the heat was melting their civic virtue and Elijah Moseley began to bait Joe Clarke.

"Come on, Joe, git a melon outa dere an' slice it up for yo' customers. We'se all sufferin' wid de heat. De bear's done got *me*!"

"Thass right, Joe, a watermelon is jes' whut Ah needs tuh cure de eppizudicks," Walter Thomas joined forces with Moseley. "Come on dere, Joe. We all is steady customers an' you aint set us up in a long time. Ah chooses dat long, bow-legged Floridy favorite."

"A god, an' be dough. You all gimme twenty cents and slice away," Clarke retorted. "Ah needs a col' slice m'self. Heah, everybody chip in. Ah'll lend y'll mah meat knife."

The money was quickly subscribed and the huge melon brought forth. At that moment, Sykes and Bertha arrived. A determined silence fell on the porch and the melon was put away again.

Merchant snapped down the blade of his jackknife and moved toward the store door.

"Come on in, Joe, an' gimme a stab uh sow belly an' uh pound uh coffee—almost fuhgot 'twas Sat'day. Got to git on home." Most of the men left also.

Just then Delia drove past on her way home, as Sykes was ordering magnificently for Bertha. It pleased him for Delia to see.

"Git whutsoever yo' heart desires, Honey. Wait a minute. Joe. Give huh two botles uh strawberry soda-water, uh quart uh parched ground-peas, an' block uh chewin' gum."

With all this they left the store, with Sykes reminding Bertha that this was his town and she could have it if she wanted it.

The men returned soon after they left, and held their watermelon feast. "Where did Syke Jones git dat 'oman from nohow?" Lindsay asked.

"Ova Apopka. Guess dey musta been cleanin' out de town when she lef. She don't look lak a thing but a hunk uh liver wid hair on it."

"Well, she sho' kin squall." Dave Carter contributed. "When she gits ready tuh laff, she jes' opens huh mouf an' latches it back tuh de las' notch. No ole grandpa alligator down in Lake Bell ain't got nothin' on huh."

Bertha had been in town three months now. Sykes was still paying her room rent at Della Lewis'—the only house in town that would have taken her in. Sykes took her frequently to Winter Park to "stomps." He still assured her that he was the swellest man in the state.

"Sho' you kin have dat lil' ole house soon's Ah kin git dat 'oman oota dere. Everything b'longs tuh me an' you sho' kin have it. Ah sho'.'bominates uh skinny 'oman. Lawdy, you sho' is got one portly shape on you! You kin git *anything* you wants. Dis is *mah* town an' you sho 'kin have it."

Delta's work-worn knees crawled over the earth in Gethsemane and up the rocks of Calvary many, many times during these months. She avoided the villagers and meeting places in her efforts to be blind and deaf. But Bertha nullified this to a degree, by coming to Delia's house to call Sykes out to her at the gate.

Delia and Sykes fought all the time now with no peaceful interludes. They slept and ate in silence. Two or three times Delia had attempted a timid friendliness, but she was repulsed each time. It was plain that the breaches must remain agape.

The sun had burned July to August. The heat streamed down like a million hot arrows, smiting all things living upon the earth. Grass withered, leaves browned, snakes went blind in shedding and men and dogs went mad. Dog days!

Delia came home one day and found Sykes there before her. She wondered, but started to go on into the house without speaking, even though he was standing in the kitchen door and she must either stoop under his arm or ask him to move. He made no room for her. She noticed a soap box beside the steps, but paid no particular attention to it, knowing that he must have brought it there. As she was stooping to pass under his outstretched arm, he suddenly pushed her backward, laughingly.

"Look in de box dere Delia, Ah done brung yuh somethin'!"

She nearly fell upon the box in her stumbling, and when she saw what it held, she all but fainted outright.

"Syke! Syke, mah Gawd! You take dat rattlesnake 'way from heah! You *gottuh*. Oh, Jesus, have mussy!"

"Ah aint gut tuh do nothin' uh de kin'—fact is Ah aint got tuh do nothin' but die. Taint no use uh you puttin' on airs makin' out lak you skeered uh dat snake—he's gointer stay right heah tell he die. He wouldn't bite me cause Ah knows how tuh handle 'im. Nohow he wouldn't risk breakin' out his fangs 'gin *yo*' skinny laigs."

"Naw, now Syke, don't keep dat thing 'roun' heath tuh skeer me tuh death. You knows Ah'm even feared uh earth worms. Thass de biggest snake Ah evah did see. Kill 'im Syke, please."

"Doan ast me tuh do nothin' fuh yuh. Goin' 'roun' tryin' to be so damn asterperious. Naw, Ah aint gonna kill it. Ah think uh damn sight mo' uh him dan you! Dat's a nice snake an' anybody doan lak 'im kin jes' hit de grit."

The village soon heard that Sykes had the snake, and came to see and ask questions.

"How de hen-fire did you ketch dat six-root rattler, Syke?" Thomas asked.

"He's full uh frogs so he caint hardly move, thass how Ah eased up on 'm. But Ah'm a snake charmer an' knows how tuh handle 'em. Shux, dat aint nothin'. Ah could ketch on eve'y day if Ah so wanted tuh."

"What he needs is a heavy hick'ry club learned real heavy on his head. Dat's de bes 'way tuh charm a rattlesnake."

"Naw, Walt, y'll jes' don't understand dese diamon' backs lak Ah do," said Syke in a superior tone of voice.

The village agreed with Walter, but the snake stayed on. His box remained by the kitchen door with its screen wire covering. Two or three days later it had digested its meal of frogs and literally came to life. It rattled at every movement in the kitchen or the yard. One day as Delia came down the kitchen steps she saw his chalky-white fangs curved like scimitars hung in the wire meshes. This time she did not run away with averted eyes as usual. She stood for a long time in the doorway in a red fury that grew bloodier for every second that she regarded the creature that was her torment.

That night she broached the subject as soon as Sykes sat down to the table.

"Syke, Ah wants you tuh take dat snake 'way fum heah. You done starved me an' An put up widcher, you done beat me an Ah took dat, but you done kilt all mah insides bringin' dat varmint heah."

Sykes poured out a saucer full of coffee and drank it deliberately before he answered her.

"A whole lot Ah keer 'bout how you feels inside uh out. Dat snake aint goin' no damn wheah till Ah gits ready fuh 'im tuh so. So fur as beatin' is concerned, yuh aint look near all dat you gointer take ef yuh stay 'roun' me."

Delia pushed back her plate and got up from the table. "Ah hates you, Sykes," she said calmly. "Ah hates you tuh de same degree dat Ah useter love yuh. Ah done took an' took till mah belly is full up tuh mah neck. Dat's de reason Ah got mah letter fum de church an' moved mah membership tuh Woodbridge—so Ah don't haftuh take no sacrament wid yuh. Ah don't wantuh see yuh 'round' me atall. Lay 'round' wid dat 'oman all yuh wants tuh, but gwan 'way fum me an' mah house. Ah hates yuh lak uh suck-egg dog."

Sykes almost let the huge wad of corn bread and collard greens he was chewing fall out of his mouth in amazement. He had a hard time whipping himself to the proper fury to try to answer Delia.

"Well, Ah'm glad you does hate me. Ah'm sho' tiahed uh you hangin' ontuh me. Ah don't want yuh. Look at yuh stringey ole neck! Yo' raw-bony laigs an' arms is enough tuh cut uh man tuh death. You looks jes' lak de devvul's doll-baby tuh *me*. You caint hate me no worse dan Ah hates you. Ah been hatin' *you* fuh years."

"Yo' ole black hide don't look lak nothin' tuh me, but uh passle uh wrinkled up rubber, wid yo' big ole yeahs flappin' on each side lak up paih uh buzzard wings. Don't think Ah'm gointuh be run 'way fum mah house neither. Ah'm goin' tuh de white folks about *you*, mah young man, de very nex' time yo lay yo' hand's on me. Mah cup is done run ovah." Delia said this with no signs of fear and Sykes departed from the house, threatening her, but made not the slightest move to carry out any of them.

That night he did not return at all, and the next day being Sunday, Delia was glad that she did not have to quarrel before she hitched up her pony and drove the four miles to Woodbridge.

She stayed to the night service—"love feast"—which was very warm and full of spirit. In the emotional winds her domestic trials were borne far and wide so that she sang as she drove homeward,

"Jurden water, black an' col'
Chills de body, not de soul
An' Ah wantah cross Jurden in uh calm time."

She came from the barn to the kitchen door and stopped.

"Whut's de mattah, ol' satan, you aint kickin' up yo' racket?" She addressed the snake's box. Complete silence. She went on into the house with a new hope in its birth struggles. Perhaps her threat to go to the white folks had frightened Sykes! Perhaps he was sorry! Fifteen years of misery and suppression had brought Delia to the place where she would hope *anything* that looked towards a way over or through her wall of inhibitions.

She felt in the match safe behind the stove at once for a match. There was only one there.

"Dat niggah wouldn't fetch nothin' heah tuh save his rotten neck, but he kin run thew whut Ah brings quick enough. Now he done toted off nigh on tuh haff uh box uh matches. He done had dat 'oman heah in mah house, too."

Nobody but a woman could tell how she knew this even before she struck the match. But she did and it put her into a new fury.

Presently she brought in the tubs to put the white things to soak. This time she decided she need not bring the hamper out of the bedroom; she would go in there and do the sorting. She picked up the pot-bellied lamp and went in. The room was small and the hamper stood hard by the foot of the white iron bed. She could sit and reach through the bedposts—resting as she worked.

"Ah wantah cross Jurden in uh calm time." She was singing again. The mood of the "love feast" had returned. She threw back the lid of the basket almost gaily. Then, moved by both horror and terror, she sprang back toward the door. *There lay the snake in the basket!* He moved sluggishly at first, but even as she turned round and round, jumped up and down in an insanity of fear, he began to stir vigorously. She saw him pouring his awful beauty from the basket upon the bed, then she seized the lamp and ran as fast as she could to the kitchen. The wind from the open door blew out the light and the darkness added to her terror. She sped to the darkness of the yard, slamming the door after her before she thought to set down the lamp. She did not feel safe even on the ground, so she climbed up in the hay barn.

There for an hour or more she lay sprawled upon the hay a gibbering wreck.

Finally she grew quiet, and after that, coherent thought. With this, stalked through her a cold, blood rage. Hours of this. A period of introspection, a space of retrospection, then a mixture of both. Out of this an awful calm.

"Well, Ah done de bes' Ah could. If things aint right, Gawd knows taint mah fault."

She went to sleep—a twitchy sleep—and woke up to a faint gray sky. There was a loud hollow sound below. She peered out. Sykes was at the wood-pile, demolishing a wire-covered box.

He hurried to the kitchen door, but hung outside there some minutes before he entered, and stood some minutes more inside before he closed it after him.

The gray in the sky was spreading. Delia descended without fear now, and crouched beneath the low bedroom window. The drawn shade shut out the dawn, shut in the night. But the thin walls held back no sound.

"Dat ol' scratch is woke up now!" She mused at the tremendous whirr inside, which every woodsman knows, is one of the sound illusions. The rattler is a ventriloquist. His whirr sounds to the right, to the left, straight ahead, behind, close under foot—everywhere but where it is. Woe to him who guesses wrong unless he is prepared to hold up his end of the argument! Sometimes he strikes without rattling at all.

Inside, Sykes heard nothing until he knocked a pot lid off the stove while trying to reach the match safe in the dark. He had emptied his pockets at Bertha's.

The snake seemed to wake up under the stove and Sykes made a quick leap into the bedroom. In spite of the gin he had had, his head was clearing now.

"Mah Gawd!" he chattered, "ef Ah could on'y strack uh light!"

The rattling ceased for a moment as he stood paralyzed. He waited. It seemed that the snake waited also.

"Oh, fuh de light! Ah thought he'd be too sick"—Sykes was muttering to himself when the whirr began again, closer, right underfoot this time. Long before this, Sykes' ability to think had been flattened down to primitive instinct and he leaped—onto the bed.

Outside Delia heard a cry that might have come from a maddened chimpanzee, a stricken gorilla. All the terror, all the horror, all the rage that man possibly could express, without a recognizable human sound.

A tremendous stir inside there, another series of animal screams, the intermittent whirr of the reptile. The shade torn violently down from the window, letting in the red dawn, a huge brown hand seizing the window stick, great dull blows upon the wooden floor punctuating the gibberish of sound long after the rattle of the snake had abruptly subsided. All this Delia could see and hear from her place beneath the window, and it made her ill. She crept over to the four-o'clocks and stretched herself on the cool earth to recover.

She lay there. "Delia, Delia!" She could hear Sykes callings in a most despairing tone as one who expected no answer. The sun crept on up, and he called. Delia could not move—her legs were gone flabby. She never moved, he called, and the sun kept rising.

"Mah Gawd!" She heard him moan, "Mah Gawd fum Heben!" She heard him stumbling about and got up from her flower-bed. The sun was growing warm. As she approached the door she heard him call out hopefully, "Delia, is dat you Ah heah?"

She saw him on his hands and knees as soon as she reached the door. He crept an inch or two toward her—all that he was able, and she saw his horribly swollen neck and his one open eye shining with hope. A surge of pity too strong to support bore her away from that eye that must, could not, fail to see the tubs. He would see the lamp. Orlando with its doctors was too far. She could scarcely reach the Chinaberry tree, where she waited in the growing heat while inside she knew the cold river was creeping up and up to extinguish that eye which must know by now that she knew.

The Gilded Six-Bits

It was a Negro yard around a Negro house in a Negro settlement that looked to the payroll of the G and G Fertilizer works for its support.

But there was something happy about the place. The front yard was parted in the middle by a sidewalk from gate

to door-step, a sidewalk edged on either side by quart bottles driven neck down into the ground on a slant. A mess of homey flowers planted without a plan but blooming cheerily from their helter-skelter places. The fence and house were whitewashed. The porch and steps scrubbed white.

The front door stood open to the sunshine so that the floor of the front room could finish drying after its weekly scouring. It was Saturday. Everything clean from the front gate to the privy house. Yard raked so that the strokes of the rake would make a pattern. Fresh newspaper cut in fancy edge on the kitchen shelves.

Missie May was bathing herself in the galvanized washtub in the bedroom. Her dark-brown skin glistened under the soapsuds that skittered down from her wash rag. Her stiff young breasts thrust forward aggressively like broad-based cones with the lips lacquered in black.

She heard men's voices in the distance and glanced at the dollar clock on the dresser.

"Humph! Ah'm way behind time t'day! Joe gointer be heah 'fore Ah git mah clothes on if Ah don't make haste."

She grabbed the clean meal sack at hand and dried herself hurriedly and began to dress. But before she could tie her slippers, there came the ring of singing metal on wood. Nine times.

Missie May grinned with delight. She had not seen the big tall man come stealing in the gate and creep up the walk grinning happily at the joyful mischief he was about to commit. But she knew that it was her husband throwing silver dollars in the door for her to pick up and pile beside her plate at dinner. It was this way every Saturday afternoon. The nine dollars hurled into the open door, he scurried to a hiding place behind the cape jasmine bush and waited.

Missie May promptly appeared at the door in mock alarm.

"Who dat chunkin' money in mah do'way?" She demanded. No answer from the yard. She leaped off the porch and began to search the shrubbery.

She peeped under the porch and hung over the gate to look up and down the road. While she did this, the man behind the jasmine darted to the chinaberry tree. She spied him and gave chase.

"Nobody ain't gointer be chuckin' money at me and Ah not do 'em nothin'," she shouted in mock anger. He ran around the house with Missie May at his heels. She overtook him at the kitchen door. He ran inside but could not close it after him before she crowded in and locked with him in a rough and tumble. For several minutes the two were a furious mass of male and female energy. Shouting, laughing, twisting, turning, tussling, tickling each other in the ribs; Missie May clutching onto Joe and Joe trying, but not too hard, to get away.

"Missie May, take yo' hand out mah pocket!" Joe shouted out between laughs.

"Ah ain't, Joe, not lessen you gwine gimme whateve' it is good you got in yo' pocket. Turn it go, Joe, do Ah'll tear yo' clothes."

"Go on tear 'em. You de one dat pushes de needles round heah. Move yo' hand Missie May."

"Lemme git dat paper sack out yo' pocket. Ah bet its candy kisses."

"'Tain't. Move yo' hand. Woman ain't go no business in a man's clothes nohow. Go way."

Missie May gouged way down and gave an upward jerk and triumphed.

"Unhhunh! Ah got it. It 'tis so candy kisses. Ah knowed you had somethin' for me in yo' clothes. Now Ah got to see whut's in every pocket you got."

Joe smiled indulgently and let his wife go through all of his pockets and take out the things that he had hidden there for her to find. She bore off the chewing gum, the cake of sweet soap, the pocket handkerchief as if she had wrested them from him, as if they had not been bought for the sake of this friendly battle.

"Whew! dat play-fight done got me all warmed up." Joe exclaimed. "Got me some water in de kittle?"

"Yo' water is on de fire and yo' clean things is cross de bed. Hurry up and wash yo'self and git changed so we kin eat. Ah'm hongry." As Missie said this, she bore the steaming kettle into the bedroom.

"You ain't hongry, sugar," Joe contradicted her. "Youse jes' a little empty. Ah'm de one whut's hongry. Ah could eat up camp meetin', back off 'ssociation, and drink Jurdan dry. Have it on de table when Ah git out de tub."

"Don't you mess wid mah business, man. You git in yo' clothes. Ah'm a real wife, not no dress and breath. Ah might not look lak one, but if you burn me, you won't git a thing but wife ashes."

Joe splashed in the bedroom and Missie May fanned around in the kitchen. A fresh red and white checked cloth on the table. Big pitcher of buttermilk beaded with pale drops of butter from the churn. Hot fried mullet, crackling bread, ham hock atop a mound of string beans and new potatoes, and perched on the window-sill a pone of spicy potato pudding.

Very little talk during the meal but that little consisted of banter that pretended to deny affection but in reality flaunted it. Like when Missie May reached for a second helping of the tater pone. Joe snatched it out of her reach.

After Missie May had made two or three unsuccessful grabs at the pan, she begged, "Aw, Joe gimme some mo' dat tater pone."

"Nope, sweetenin' is for us men-folks. Y'all pretty lil frail eels don't need nothin' lak dis. You too sweet already."

"Please, Joe."

"Naw, naw. Ah don't want you to git no sweeter than whut you is already. We goin' down de road a lil piece t'night so you go put on yo' Sunday-go-to-meetin' things."

Missie May looked at her husband to see if he was playing some prank.

"Sho nuff, Joe?"

"Yeah. We goin' to de ice cream parlor."

"Where de ice cream parlor at, Joe?"

"A new man done come heah from Chicago and he done got a place and took and opened it up for a ice cream parlor, and bein' as it's real swell, Ah wants you to be one de first ladies to walk in dere and have some set down."

"Do Jesus, Ah ain't knowed nothin' 'bout it. Who de man done it?"

"Mister Otis D. Slemmons, of spots and places—Memphis, Chicago, Jacksonville, Philadelphia and so on."

"Dat heavy-set man wid his mouth full of gold teethes?"

"Yeah. Where did you see 'im at?"

"Ah went down to de sto' tuh git a box of lye and Ah seen 'im standin' on de corner talkin' to some of de mens, and Ah come on back and went to scrubbin' de floor, and he passed and tipped his hat whilst Ah was scourin' de steps. Ah thought Ah never seen *him* befo'."

Joe smiled pleasantly. "Yeah, he's up to date. He got de finest clothes Ah ever seen on a colored man's back."

"Aw, he don't look no better in his clothes than you do in yourn. He got a puzzlegut on 'im and he so chuckle-headed, he got a pone behind his neck."

Joe looked down at his own abdomen and said wistfully, "Wisht Ah had a build on me lak he got. He ain't puzzle-gutted, honey. He jes' got a corperation. Dat make 'm look lak a rich white man. All rich mens is got some belly on 'em."

"Ah seen de pitchers of Henry Ford and he's a spare-built man and Rockefeller look lak he ain't got but one gut. But Ford and Rockefeller and dis Slemmons and all de rest kin be as many-gutted as dey please, Ah'm satisfied wid you jes' lak you is, baby. God took pattern after a pine tree and built you noble. Youse a pritty man, and if Ah knowed any way to make you mo' pritty still Ah'd take and do it."

Joe reached over gently and toyed with Missie May's ear. "You jes' say dat cause you love me, but Ah can't hold no light to Otis D. Slemmons. Ah ain't never been nowhere and Ah ain't got nothin' but you."

Missie May got his lap and kissed him and he kissed back in kind. Then he went on. "All de womens is crazy 'bout 'im everywhere he go."

"How you know dat, Joe?"

"He tole us so hisself."

"Dat don't make it so. His mouf is cut cross-ways, ain't it? Well, he kin lie jes' lak anybody else."

"Good Lawd, Missie! You womens sho is hard to sense into things. He's got a five-dollar gold piece for a stick-pin and he got a ten-dollar gold piece on his watch chain and his mouf is jes' crammed full of gold teethes. Sho wisht it wuz mine. And whut make it so cool, he got money 'cumulated. And womens give it all to 'im."

"Ah don't see whut de womens see on 'im. Ah wouldn't give 'im a wink if de sheriff wuz after 'im."

"Well, he tole us how de white womens in Chicago give 'im all dat gold money. So he don't 'low nobody to touch it all. Not even put dey finger on it. Dey tole 'im not to. You kin make 'miration at it, but don't tetch it."

"Whyn't he stay up dere where dey so crazy 'bout 'im?"

"Ah reckon dey done made 'im vast-rich and he wants to travel some. He say dey wouldn't leave 'im hit a lick of work. He got mo' lady people crazy 'bout him than he kin shake a stick at."

"Joe, Ah hates to see you so dumb. Dat stray nigger jes' tell y'all anything and y'all b'lieve it."

"Go 'head on now, honey and put on yo' clothes. He talkin' 'bout his pritty womens—Ah want 'im to see *mine*."

Missie May went off to dress and Joe spent the time trying to make his stomach punch out like Slemmons' middle. He tried the rolling swagger of the stranger, but found that his tall bone-and-muscle stride fitted ill with it. He just had time to drop back into his seat before Missie May came in dressed to go.

On the way home that night Joe was exultant. "Didn't Ah say ole Otis was swell? Can't he talk Chicago talk? Wuzn't dat funny whut he said when great big fat ole Ida Armstrong come in? He asted me, 'Who is dat broad wid de forte shake?' Dat's a new word. Us always thought forty was a set of figgers but he showed us where it means a whole heap of things. Sometimes he don't say forty, he jes' say thirty-eight and two and dat mean de same thing. Know whut he tole me when Ah wuz payin' for our ice cream? He say, 'Ah have to hand it to you, Joe. Dat wife of yours is jes' thirty-eight and two. Yessuh, she's forte!' Ain't he killin'?"

"He'll do in case of a rush. But he sho is got uh heap uh gold on 'im. Dat's de first time Ah ever seed gold money. It looked good on him sho nuff, but it'd look a whole heap better on you."

"Who, me? Missie May youse crazy! Where would a po' man lak me git gold money from?"

Missie May was silent for a minute, then she said, "Us might find some goin' long de road some time. Us could."

"Who would be losin' gold money round heah? We ain't even seen none dese white folks wearin' no gold money on

dey watch chain. You must be figgerin' Mister Packard or Mister Cadillac goin' pass through heah."

"You don't know whut been lost 'round heah. Maybe somebody way back in memorial times lost they gold money and went on off and it ain't never been found. And then if we wuz to find it, you could wear some 'thout havin' no gang of womens lak dat Slemmons say he got."

Joe laughed and hugged her. "Don't be so wishful 'bout me. Ah'm satisfied de way Ah is. So long as Ah be yo' husband, Ah don't keer 'bout nothin' else. Ah'd ruther all de other womens in de world to be dead than for you to have de toothache. Less we go to bed and git our night rest."

It was Saturday night once more before Joe could parade his wife in Slemmons' ice cream parlor again. He worked the night shift and Saturday was his only night off. Every other evening around six o'clock he left home, and dying dawn saw him hustling home around the lake where the challenging sun flung a flaming sword from east to west across the trembling water.

That was the best part of life—going home to Missie May. Their whitewashed house, the mock battle on Saturday, the dinner and ice cream parlor afterwards, church on Sunday nights when Missie outdressed any woman in town—all, everything was right.

One night around eleven the acid ran out at the G. and G. The foreman knocked off the crew and let the steam die down. As Joe rounded the lake on his way home, a lean moon rode the lake in a silver boat. It anybody had asked Joe about the moon on the lake, he would have said he hadn't paid it any attention. But he saw it with his feelings. It made him yearn painfully for Missie. Creation obsessed him. He thought about children. They had been married for more than a year now. They had money put away. They ought to be making little feet for shoes. A little boy child would be about right.

He saw a dim light in the bedroom and decided to come in through the kitchen door. He could wash the fertilizer dust off himself before presenting himself to Missie May. It would be nice for her not to know that he was there until he slipped into his place in bed and hugged her back. She always liked that.

He eased the kitchen door open slowly and silently, but when he went to set his dinner bucket on the table he bumped it into a pile of dishes, and something crashed to the floor. He heard his wife gasp in fright and hurried to reassure her.

"Iss me, honey. Don't get skeered."

There was a quick, large movement in the bedroom. A rustle, a thud, and a stealthy silence. The light went out.

What? Robbers? Murderers? Some varmint attacking his helpless wife, perhaps. He struck a match, threw himself on guard and stepped over the door-sill into the bedroom.

The great belt on the wheel of Time slipped and eternity stood still. By the match light he could see the man's legs fighting with his breeches in his frantic desire to get them on. He had both chance and time to kill the intruder in his helpless condition—half in and half out of his pants—but he was too weak to take action. The shapeless enemies of humanity that live in the hours of Time had waylaid Joe. He was assaulted in his weakness. Like Samson awakening after his haircut. So he just opened his mouth and laughed.

The match went out and he struck another and lit the lamp. A howling wind raced across his heart, but underneath its fury he heard his wife sobbing and Slemmons pleading for his life. Offering to buy it with all that he had. "Please, suh, don't kill me. Sixty-two dollars at de sto'. Cold money."

Joe just stood, Slemmons looked at the window, but it was screened. Joe stood out like a rough-backed mountain between him and the door. Barring him from escape, from sunrise, from life.

He considered a surprise attack upon the big clown that stood there laughing like a chessy cat. But before his fist could travel an inch, Joe's own rushed out to crush him like a battering ram. Then Joe stood over him.

"Git into yo' damn rags, Slemmons, and dat quick."

Slemmons scrambled to his feet and into his vest and coat. As he grabbed his hat, Joe's fury overrode his intentions and he grabbed at Slemmons with his left hand and struck at him with his right. The right landed. The left grazed the front of his vest. Slemmons was knocked a somersault into the kitchen and fled through the open door. Joe found himself alone with Missie May, with the golden watch charm clutched in his left fist. A short bit of broken chain dangled between his fingers.

Missie May was sobbing. Wails of weeping without words. Joe stood, and after awhile he found out that he had something in his hand. And then he stood and felt without thinking and without seeing with his natural eyes. Missie May kept on crying and Joe kept on feeling so much and not knowing what to do with all his feelings, he put Slemmons' watch charm in his pants pocket and took a good laugh and went to bed.

"Missie May, whut you cryin' for?"

"Cause Ah love you so hard and Ah know you don't love *me* no mo'."

Joe sank his face into the pillow for a spell then he said huskily, "You don't know de feelings of dat yet, Missie May."

"Oh Joe, honey, he said he wuz gointer give me dat gold money and he jes' kept on after me—"

Joe was very still and silent for a long time. Then he said, "Well, don't cry no mo', Missie May. Ah got yo' gold piece for you."

The hours went past on their rusty ankles. Joe still quiet on one bedrail and Missie May wrung dry of sobs on the other. Finally the sun's tide crept upon the shore of night and drowned all its hours. Missie May with her face stiff and streaked towards the window saw the dawn come into her yard. It was day. Nothing more, Joe wouldn't be coming home as usual. No need to fling open the front door and sweep off the porch, making it nice for Joe. Never no more breakfast to cook; no more washing and starching of Joe's jumper-jackets and pants. No more nothing. So why get up?

With this strange man in her bed, she felt embarrasssed to get up and dress. She decided to wait till he had dressed and gone. Then she would get up, dress quickly and be gone forever beyond reach of Joe's looks and laughs. But he never moved. Red light turned to yellow, then white.

From beyond the no-man's land between them came a voice. A strange voice that yesterday had been Joe's.

"Missie May, ain't you gonna fix me no breakfus'?"

She sprang out of bed. "Yeah, Joe. Ah didn't reckon you wuz hongry."

No need to die today. Joe needed her for a few more minutes anyhow.

Soon there was a roaring fire in the cook stove. Water bucket full and two chickens killed. Joe loved fried chicken and rice. She didn't deserve a thing and good Joe was letting her cook him some breakfast. She rushed hot biscuits to the table as Joe took his seat.

He ate with his eyes on his plate. No laughter, no banter.

"Missie May, you ain't eatin' yo' breakfus'."

"Ah don't choose none, Ah thank yuh."

His coffee cup was empty. She sprang to refill it. When she turned from the stove and bent to set the cup beside Joe's plate, she saw the yellow coin on the table between them.

She slumped into her seat and wept into her arms.

Presently Joe said calmly, "Missie May, you cry too much. Don't look back lak Lot's wife and turn to salt."

The sun, the hero of every day, the impersonal old man that beams as brightly on death as on birth, came up every morning and raced across the blue dome and dipped into the sea of fire every evening. Water ran down hill and birds nested.

Missie knew why she didn't leave Joe. She couldn't. She loved him too much, but she could not understand why Joe didn't leave her. He was polite, even kind at times, but aloof.

There were no more Saturday romps. No ringing silver dollars to stack beside her plate. No pockets to rifle. In fact the yellow coin in his trousers was like a monster hiding in the cave of his pockets to destroy her.

She often wondered if he still had it, but nothing could have induced her to ask nor yet to explore his pockets to see for herself. Its shadow was in the house whether or no.

One night Joe came home around midnight and complained of pains in the back. He asked Missie to rub him down with liniment. It had been three months since Missie had touched his body and it all seemed strange. But she rubbed him. Grateful for the chance. Before morning, youth triumphed and Missie exulted. But the next day, as she joyfully made up their bed, beneath her pillow she found the piece of money with the bit of chain attached.

Alone to herself, she looked at the thing with loathing, but look she must. She took it into her hands with trembling and saw first thing that it was no gold piece. It was a gilded half dollar. Then she knew why Slemmons had forbidden anyone to touch his gold. He trusted village eyes at a distance not to recognize his stick-pin as a gilded quarter, and his watch charm as a four-bit piece.

She was glad at first that Joe had left it there. Perhaps he was through with her punishment. They were man and wife again. Then another thought came clawing at her. He had come home to buy from her as if she were any woman in the long house. Fifty cents for her love. As if to say that he could pay as well as Slemmons. She slid the coin into his Sunday pants pocket and dressed herself and left his house.

Halfway between her house and the quarters she met her husband's mother, and after a short talk she turned and went back home. Never would she admit defeat to that woman who prayed for it nightly. If she had not the substance of marriage she had the outside show. Joe must leave *her*. She let him see she didn't want his old gold four-bits too.

She saw no more of the coin for some time though she knew that Joe could not help finding it in his pocket. But his health kept poor, and he came home at least every ten days to be rubbed.

The sun swept around the horizon, trailing its robes of weeks and days. One morning as Joe came in from work, he found Missie May chopping wood. Without a word he took the ax and chopped a huge pile before he stopped.

"You ain't got no business choppin' wood, and you know it."

"How come? Ah been choppin' it for de last longest."

"Ah ain't blind. You makin' feet for shoes."

"Won't you be glad to have a lil baby chile, Joe?"

"You know dat 'thout astin' me."

"Iss gointer be a boy chile and de very spit of you." "You reckon, Missie May?"

"Who else could it look lak?"

Joe said nothing, but he thrust his hand deep into his pocket and fingered something there.

It was almost six months later Missie May took to bed and Joe went and got his mother to come wait on the house.

Missie May delivered a fine boy. Her travail was over when Joe came in from work one morning. His mother and the old women were drinking great bowls of coffee around the fire in the kitchen.

The minute Joe came into the room his mother called him aside.

"How did Missie May make out?" he asked quickly.

"Who, dat gal? She strong as a ox. She gointer have plenty mo'. We done fixed her wid de sugar and lard to sweeten her for de nex' one."

Joe stood silent awhile.

"You ain't ast 'bout de baby, Joe. You oughter be mighty proud cause he sho is de spittin' image of yuh, son. Dat's yourn all right, if you never git another one, dat un is yourn. And you know Ah'm mighty proud too, son, cause Ah never thought well of you marryin' Missie May cause her ma used tuh fan her foot round right smart and Ah been mighty skeered dat Missie May was gointer git misput on her road."

Joe said nothing. He fooled around the house till late in the day then just before he went to work, he went and stood at the foot of the bed and asked his wife how she felt. He did this every day during the week.

On Saturday he went to Orlando to make his market. It had been a long time since he had done that.

Meat and lard, meal and flour, soap and starch. Cans of corn and tomatoes. All the staples. He fooled around town for awhile and bought bananas and apples. Way after while he went around to the candy store.

"Hellow, Joe." the clerk greeted him. "Ain't seen you in a long time."

"Nope, Ah ain't been heah. Been round in spots and places."

"Want some of them molasses kisses you always buy?"

"Yessuh," He threw the gilded half dollar on the counter. "Will dat spend?"

"Whut is it, Joe? Well, I'll be doggone! A gold-plated four-bit piece. Where'd you git it, Joe?"

"Offen a stray nigger dat come through Eatonville. He had it on his watch chain for a charm—goin' round making out iss gold money. Ha ha! He had a quarter on his tie pin and it wuz all golded up too. Tryin' to fool people. Makin' out he so rich and everything. Ha! Ha! Tryin' to tole off folkses wives from home."

"How did you git it, Joe? Did he fool you, too?"

"Who, me? Naw suh! He ain't fooled me none. Know whut Ah done? He come round me wid his smart talk. Ah hauled off and knocked 'im down and took his old four-bits way from 'im. Gointer buy my wife some good ole lasses kisses wid it. Gimme fifty cents worth of dem candy kisses."

"Fifty cents buys a mighty lot of candy kisses, Joe. Why don't you split it up and take some chocolate bars too. They eat good, too."

"Yessuh, dey do, but Ah wants all dat in kisses. Ah got a lil boy chile home now. Tain't a week old yet, but he kin suck a sugar tit and maybe eat one them kisses hisself."

Joe got his candy and left the store. The clerk turned to the next customer. "Wisht I could be like these darkies. Laughin' all the time. Nothin' worries 'em."

Back in Eatonville, Joe reached his own front door. There was the ring of singing metal on wood. Fifteen times, Missie May couldn't run to the door, but she crept there as quickly as she could.

"Joe Banks, Ah hear you chunkin' money in mah do'way. You wait till Ah got mah strength back and Ah'm gointer fix you for dat."

Nella Larsen (1891–1964)

Racial passing has been a theme of many African American writers. Exploring the risky behavior of living life on the other side of the color line dominated 19th-century and early-20th-century African American literature. Few authors, however, have captured the gendered nuances of passing as well as Nella Larsen. By adding issues of sexuality, *Passing* (1929) interweaves another layer to the typical passing narrative.

Larsen's biography has been a bit of a mystery. She was born in Chicago to a Danish mother and black father. Accounts vary as to whether the father was African American or West Indian. While Nella was still young, her mother divorced her father and married a white man by whom she had a white daughter. Larsen was no longer welcomed in the home. Investigative work by critic Thadious Davis raises the possibility that Larsen's black biological father and the new "white" father might have been the same man, the black father passing as white. Larsen includes some autobiographical details about the trauma and entrapment of her early and later life in her novel *Quicksand* (1928). Larsen attended Fisk University, spent some time in Copenhagen, and worked as a nurse in New York City. She married Elmer S. Imes, a Fisk physicist, but the marriage ended with Larsen devastated over his affair with a white woman. Although Larsen's later life was riddled by other crises, including a charge of plagiarism for one of her stories, her two novels and the winning of the first Guggenheim Fellowship awarded to an African American woman have secured her place in history.

PASSING

For Carl Van Vechten and Fania Marinoff

> One three centuries removed
> From the scenes his fathers loved,
> Spicy grove, cinnamon tree,
> What is Africa to me?
> —COUNTÉE CULLEN

Part One

Encounter

One

It was the last letter in Irene Redfield's little pile of morning mail. After her other ordinary and clearly directed letters the long envelope of thin Italian paper with its almost illegible scrawl seemed out of place and alien. And there was, too, something mysterious and slightly furtive about it. A thin sly thing which bore no return address to betray the sender. Not that she hadn't immediately known who its sender was. Some two years ago she had one very like it in outward appearance. Furtive, but yet in some peculiar, determined way a little flaunting. Purple ink. Foreign paper of extraordinary size.

It had been, Irene noted, postmarked in New York the day before. Her brows came together in a tiny frown. The frown, however, was more from perplexity than from annoyance; though there was in her thoughts an element of both. She was wholly unable to comprehend such an attitude towards danger as she was sure the letter's contents would reveal; and she disliked the idea of opening and reading it.

This, she reflected, was of a piece with all that she knew of Clare Kendry. Stepping always on the edge of danger. Always aware, but not drawing back or turning aside. Certainly not because of any alarms or feeling of outrage on the part of others.

And for a swift moment Irene Redfield seemed to see a pale small girl sitting on a ragged blue sofa, sewing pieces of bright red cloth together, while her drunken father, a tall, powerfully built man, raged threateningly up and down the shabby room, bellowing curses and making spasmodic lunges at her which were not the less frightening because they were, for the most part, ineffectual. Sometimes he did manage to reach her. But only the fact that the child had edged herself

---

From *Passing* (1929).

and her poor sewing over to the farthermost corner of the sofa suggested that she was in any way perturbed by this menace to herself and her work.

Clare had known well enough that it was unsafe to take a portion of the dollar that was her weekly wage for the doing of many errands for the dressmaker who lived on the top floor of the building of which Bob Kendry was janitor. But that knowledge had not deterred her. She wanted to go to her Sunday school's picnic, and she had made up her mind to wear a new dress. So, in spite of certain unpleasantness and possible danger, she had taken the money to buy the material for that pathetic little red frock.

There had been, even in those days, nothing sacrificial in Clare Kendry's idea of life, no allegiance beyond her own immediate desire. She was selfish, and cold, and hard. And yet she had, too, a strange capacity of transforming warmth and passion, verging sometimes almost on theatrical heroics.

Irene, who was a year or more older than Clare, remembered the day that Bob Kendry had been brought home dead, killed in a silly saloon-fight. Clare, who was at that time a scant fifteen years old, had just stood there with her lips pressed together, her thin arms folded across her narrow chest, staring down at the familiar pasty-white face of her parent with a sort of disdain in her slanting black eyes. For a very long time she had stood like that, silent and staring. Then, quite suddenly, she had given way to a torrent of weeping, swaying her thin body, tearing at her bright hair, and stamping her small feet. The outburst had ceased as suddenly as it had begun. She glanced quickly about the bare room, taking everyone in, even the two policemen, in a sharp look of flashing scorn. And, in the next instant, she had turned and vanished through the door.

Seen across the long stretch of years, the thing had more the appearance of an outpouring of pent-up fury than of an overflow of grief for her dead father; though she had been, Irene admitted, fond enough of him in her own rather catlike way.

Catlike. Certainly that was the word which best described Clare Kendry, if any single word could describe her. Sometimes she was hard and apparently without feeling at all; sometimes she was affectionate and rashly impulsive. And there was about her an amazing soft malice, hidden well away until provoked. Then she was capable of scratching, and very effectively too. Or, driven to anger, she would fight with a ferocity and impetuousness that disregarded or forgot any danger; superior strength, numbers, or other unfavourable circumstances. How savagely she had clawed those boys the day they had hooted her parent and sung a derisive rhyme, of their own composing, which pointed out certain eccentricities in his careening gait! And how deliberately she had—

Irene brought her thoughts back to the present, to the letter from Clare Kendry that she still held unopened in her hand. With a little feeling of apprehension, she very slowly cut the envelope, drew out the folded sheets, spread them, and began to read.

It was, she saw at once, what she had expected since learning from the postmark that Clare was in the city. An extravagantly phrased wish to see her again. Well, she needn't and wouldn't, Irene told herself, accede to that. Nor would she assist Clare to realize her foolish desire to return for a moment to that life which long ago, and of her own choice, she had left behind her.

She ran through the letter, puzzling out, as best she could, the carelessly formed words or making instinctive guesses at them.

". . . For I am lonely, so lonely . . . cannot help longing to be with you again, as I have never longed for anything before; and I have wanted many things in my life. . . . You can't know how in this pale life of mine I am all the time seeing the bright pictures of that other that I once thought I was glad to be free of. . . . It's like an ache, a pain that never ceases. . . ." Sheets upon thin sheets of it. And ending finally with, "and it's your fault, 'Rene dear. At least partly. For I wouldn't now, perhaps, have this terrible, this wild desire if I hadn't seen you that time in Chicago. . . ."

Brilliant red patches flamed in Irene Redfield's warm olive cheeks.

"That time in Chicago." The words stood out from among the many paragraphs of other words, bringing with them a clear, sharp remembrance, in which even now, after two years, humiliation, resentment, and rage were mingled.

Two

This is what Irene Redfield remembered.

Chicago, August. A brilliant day, hot, with a brutal staring sun pouring down rays that were like molten rain. A day on which the very outlines of the buildings shuddered as if in protest at the heat. Quivering lines sprang up from baked pavements and wriggled along the shining car-tracks. The automobiles parked at the kerbs were a dancing blaze, and the glass of the shop-windows threw out a blinding radiance. Sharp particles of dust rose from the burning sidewalks, stinging the seared or dripping skins of wilting pedestrians. What small breeze there was seemed like the breath of a flame fanned by slow bellows.

It was on that day of all others that Irene set out to shop for the things which she had promised to take home from Chicago to her two small sons, Brian junior and Theodore. Characteristically, she had put it off until only a few crowded days remained of her long visit. And only this sweltering one was free of engagements till the evening.

Without too much trouble she had got the mechanical aeroplane for Junior. But the drawing-book, for which Ted had so gravely and insistently given her precise directions, had sent her in and out of five shops without success.

It was while she was on her way to a sixth place that right before her smarting eyes a man toppled over and became an inert crumpled heap on the scorching cement. About the lifeless figure a little crowd gathered. Was the man dead, or only faint? someone asked her. But Irene didn't know and didn't try to discover. She edged her way out of the increasing crowd, feeling disagreeably damp and sticky and soiled from contact with so many sweating bodies.

For a moment she stood fanning herself and dabbing at her moist face with an inadequate scrap of handkerchief. Suddenly she was aware that the whole street had a wobbly look, and realized that she was about to faint. With a quick perception of the need for immediate safety, she lifted a wavering hand in the direction of a cab parked directly in front of her. The perspiring driver jumped out and guided her to his car. He helped, almost lifted her in. She sank down on the hot leather seat.

For a minute her thoughts were nebulous. They cleared.

"I guess," she told her Samaritan, "it's tea I need. On a roof somewhere."

"The Drayton, ma'am?" he suggested. "They do say as how it's always a breeze up there."

"Thank you. I think the Drayton'll do nicely," she told him.

There was that little grating sound of the clutch being slipped in as the man put the car in gear and slid deftly out into the boiling traffic. Reviving under the warm breeze stirred up by the moving cab, Irene made some small attempts to repair the damage that the heat and crowds had done to her appearance.

All too soon the rattling vehicle shot towards the sidewalk and stood still. The driver sprang out and opened the door before the hotel's decorated attendant could reach it. She got out, and thanking him smilingly as well as in a more substantial manner for his kind helpfulness and understanding, went in through the Drayton's wide doors.

Stepping out of the elevator that had brought her to the roof, she was led to a table just in front of a long window whose gently moving curtains suggested a cool breeze. It was, she thought, like being wafted upward on a magic carpet to another world, pleasant, quiet, and strangely remote from the sizzling one that she had left below.

The tea, when it came, was all that she had desired and expected. In fact, so much was it what she had desired and expected that after the first deep cooling drink she was able to forget it, only now and then sipping, a little absently, from the tall green glass, while she surveyed the room about her or looked out over some lower buildings at the bright unstirred blue of the lake reaching away to an undetected horizon.

She had been gazing down for some time at the specks of cars and people creeping about in streets, and thinking how silly they looked, when on taking up her glass she was surprised to find it empty at last. She asked for more tea and while she waited, began to recall the happenings of the day and to wonder what she was to do about Ted and his book. Why was it that almost invariably he wanted something that was difficult or impossible to get? Like his father. For ever wanting something that he couldn't have.

Presently there were voices, a man's booming one and a woman's slightly husky. A waiter passed her, followed by a sweetly scented woman in a fluttering dress of green chiffon whose mingled pattern of narcissuses, jonquils, and hyacinths was a remainder of pleasantly chill spring days. Behind her there was a man, very red in the face, who was mopping his neck and forehead with a big crumpled handkerchief.

"Oh dear!" Irene groaned, rasped by annoyance, for after a little discussion and commotion they had stopped at the very next table. She had been alone there at the window and it had been so satisfyingly quiet. Now, of course, they would chatter.

But no. Only the woman sat down. The man remained standing, abstractedly pinching the knot of his bright blue tie. Across the small space that separated the two tables his voice carried clearly.

"See you later, then," he declared, looking down at the woman. There was pleasure in his tones and a smile on his face.

His companion's lips parted in some answer, but her words were blurred by the little intervening distance and the medley of noises floating up from the streets below. They didn't reach Irene. But she noted the peculiar caressing smile that accompanied them.

The man said: "Well, I suppose I'd better," and smiled again, and said good-bye, and left.

An attractive-looking woman, was Irene's opinion, with those dark, almost black, eyes and that wide mouth like a scarlet flower against the ivory of her skin. Nice clothes too, just right for the weather, thin and cool without being mussy, as summer things were so apt to be.

A waiter was taking her order. Irene saw her smile up at him as she murmured something—thanks, maybe. It was an odd sort of smile. Irene couldn't quite define it, but she was sure that she would have classed it, coming from another woman, as being just a shade too provocative for a waiter. About this one, however, there was something that made her hesitate to name it that. A certain impression of assurance, perhaps.

The waiter came back with the order. Irene watched her spread out her napkin, saw the silver spoon in the white hand slit the dull gold of the melon. Then, conscious that she had been staring, she looked quickly away.

Her mind returned to her own affairs. She had settled, definitely, the problem of the proper one of two frocks for the bridge party that night, in rooms whose atmosphere would be so thick and hot that every breath would be like breathing soup. The dress decided, her thoughts had gone back to the snag of Ted's book, her unseeing eyes far away on the lake, when by some sixth sense she was acutely aware that someone was watching her.

Very slowly she looked around, and into the dark eyes of the woman in the green frock at the next table. But she evidently failed to realized that such intense interest as she was showing might be embarrassing, and continued to stare. Her demeanour was that of one who with utmost singleness of mind and purpose was determined to impress firmly and accurately each detail of Irene's features upon her memory for all time, nor showed the slightest trace of disconcertment at having been detected in her steady scrutiny.

Instead, it was Irene who was put out. Feeling her colour heighten under the continued inspection, she slid her eyes down. What, she wondered, could be the reason for such persistent attention? Had she, in her haste in the taxi, put her hat on backwards? Guardedly she felt at it. No. Perhaps there was a streak of powder somewhere on her face. She made a quick pass over it with her handkerchief. Something wrong with her dress? She shot a glance over it. Perfectly all right. *What* was it?

Again she looked up, and for a moment her brown eyes politely returned the stare of the other's black ones, which never for an instant fell or wavered. Irene made a little mental shrug. Oh well, let her look! She tried to treat the woman and her watching with indifference, but she couldn't. All her efforts to ignore her, it, were futile. She stole another glance. Still looking. What strange languorous eyes she had!

And gradually there rose in Irene a small inner disturbance, odious and hatefully familiar. She laughed softly, but her eyes flashed.

Did that woman, could that woman, somehow know that here before her very eyes on the roof of the Drayton sat a Negro?

Absurd! Impossible! White people were so stupid about such things for all that they usually asserted that they were able to tell; and by the most ridiculous means, finger-nails, palms of hands, shapes of ears, teeth, and other equally silly rot. They always took her for an Italian, a Spaniard, a Mexican, or a gipsy. Never, when she was alone, had they even remotely seemed to suspect that she was a Negro. No, the woman sitting there staring at her couldn't possibly know.

Nevertheless, Irene felt, in turn, anger, scorn, and fear slide over her. It wasn't that she was ashamed of being a Negro, or even of having it declared. It was the idea of being ejected from any place, even in the polite and tactful way in which the Drayton would probably do it, that disturbed her.

But she looked, boldly this time, back into the eyes still frankly intent upon her. They did not seem to her hostile or resentful. Rather, Irene had the feeling that they were ready to smile if she would. Nonsense, of course. The feeling passed, and she turned away with the firm intention of keeping her gaze on the lake, the roofs of the buildings across the way, the sky, anywhere but on that annoying woman. Almost immediately, however, her eyes were back again. In the midst of her fog of uneasiness she had been seized by a desire to outstare the rude observer. Suppose the woman did know or suspect her race. She couldn't prove it.

Suddenly her small fright increased. Her neighbor had risen and was coming towards her. What was going to happen now?

"Pardon me," the woman said pleasantly, "but I think I know you." Her slightly husky voice held a dubious note.

Looking up at her, Irene's suspicions and fears vanished. There was no mistaking the friendliness of that smile or resisting its charm. Instantly she surrendered to it and smiled too, as she said: "I'm afraid you're mistaken."

"Why, of course, I know you!" the other exclaimed. "Don't tell me you're not Irene Westover. Or do they still call you 'Rene?"

In the brief second before her answer, Irene tried vainly to recall where and when this woman could have known her. There, in Chicago. And before her marriage. That much was plain. High school? College? Y.W.C.A. committees? High school, most likely. What white girls had she known well enough to have been familiarly addressed as 'Rene by them? The woman before her didn't fit her memory of any of them. Who was she?

"Yes, I'm Irene Westover. And though nobody calls me 'Rene any more, it's good to hear the name again. And you—" She hesitated, ashamed that she could not remember, and hoping that the sentence would be finished for her.

"Don't you know me? Not really, 'Rene?"

"I'm sorry, but just at the minute I can't seem to place you."

Irene studied the lovely creature standing beside her for some clue to her identity. Who could she be? Where and when had they met? And through her perplexity there came the thought that the trick which her memory had played her was for some reason more gratifying than disappointing to her old acquaintance, that she didn't mind not being recognized.

And, too, Irene felt that she was just about to remember her. For about the woman was some quality, an intangible something, too vague to define, too remote to seize, but which was, to Irene Redfield, very familiar. And that voice. Surely she'd heard those husky tones somewhere before. Perhaps before time, contact, or something had been at them, making them into a voice remotely suggesting England. Ah! could it have been in Europe that they had met? 'Rene. No.

"Perhaps," Irene began, "you—"

The woman laughed, a lovely laugh, a small sequence of notes that was like a trill and also like ringing of a delicate bell fashioned of a precious metal, a tinkling.

Irene drew a quick sharp breath. "Clare!" she exclaimed, "not really Clare Kendry?"

So great was her astonishment that she had started to rise.

"No, no don't get up," Clare Kendry commanded, and sat down herself. "You've simply got to stay and talk. We'll have something more. Tea? Fancy meeting you here! It's simply too, too lucky!"

"It's awfully surprising," Irene told her, and, seeing the change in Clare's smile, knew that she had revealed a corner of her own thoughts. But she only said: "I'd never in this world have known you if you hadn't laughed. You are changed, you know. And yet, in a way, you're just the same."

"Perhaps," Clare replied, "Oh, just a second."

She gave her attention to the waiter at her side. "M-mm, let's see. Two teas. And bring some cigarettes. Y-es, they'll be all right. Thanks." Again that odd upward smile. Now, Irene was sure that it was too provocative for a waiter.

While Clare had been giving the order, Irene made a rapid mental calculation. It must be, she figured, all of twelve years since she, or anybody that she knew, had laid eyes on Clare Kendry.

After her father's death she'd gone to live with some relatives, aunts or cousins two or three times removed, over on the west side: relatives that nobody had known the Kendry's possessed until they had turned up at the funeral and taken Clare away with them.

For about a year or more afterwards she would appear occasionally among her old friends and acquaintances on the south side for short little visits that were, they understood, always stolen from the endless domestic tasks in her new home. With each succeeding one she was taller, shabbier, and more belligerently sensitive. And each time the look on her face was more resentful and brooding. "I'm worried about Clare, she seems so unhappy," Irene remembered her mother saying. The visits dwindled, becoming shorter, fewer, and further apart until at last they ceased.

Irene's father, who had been fond of Bob Kendry, made a special trip over to the west side about two months after the last time Clare had been to see them and returned with the bare information that he had seen the relatives and that Clare had disappeared. What else he had confided to her mother, in the privacy of their own room, Irene didn't know.

But she had something more than a vague suspicion of its nature. For there had been rumours. Rumours that were, to girls of eighteen and nineteen years, interesting and exciting.

There was the one about Clare Kendry's having been seen at the dinner hour in a fashionable hotel in company with another woman and two men, all of them white. And *dressed*! And there was another which told of her driving in Lincoln Park with a man, unmistakably white, and evidently rich. Packard limousine, chauffeur in livery, and all that. There had been others whose context Irene could no longer recollect, but all pointing in the same glamorous direction.

And she could remember quite vividly how, when they used to repeat and discuss these tantalizing stories about Clare, the girls would always look knowingly at one another and then, with little excited giggles, drag away their eager shining eyes and say with lurking undertones of regret or disbelief some such thing as: "Oh, well, maybe she's got a job or something," or "After all, it mayn't have been Clare," or "You can't believe all you hear."

And always some girl, more matter-of-fact or more frankly malicious than the rest, would declare: "Of course it was Clare! Ruth said it was and so did Frank, and they certainly know her when they see her as well as we do." And someone else would say: "Yes, you can bet it was Clare all right." And then they would all join in asserting that there could be no mistake about its having been Clare, and that such circumstances could mean only one thing. Working indeed! People didn't take their servants to the Shelby for dinner. Certainly not all dressed up like that. There would follow insincere regrets, and somebody would say: "Poor girl, I suppose it's true enough, but what can you expect. Look at her father. And her mother, they say, would have run away if she hadn't died. Besides, Clare always had a—a—having way with her."

Precisely that! The words came to Irene as she sat there on the Drayton roof, facing Clare Kendry. "A having way." Well, Irene acknowledged, judging from her appearance and manner, Clare seemed certainly to have succeeded in having a few of the things that she wanted.

It was, Irene repeated, after the interval of the waiter, a great surprise and a very pleasant one to see Clare again after all those years, twelve at least.

"Why, Clare, you're the last person in the world I'd have expected to run into. I guess that's why I didn't know you."

Clare answered gravely: "Yes. It is twelve years. But I'm not surprised to see you, 'Rene. That is, not so very. In fact, ever since I've been here, I've more or less hoped that I should, or someone. Preferably you, though. Still, I imagine that's because I've thought of you often and often, while you—I'll wager you've never given me a thought."

It was true, of course. After the first speculations and indictments, Clare had gone completely from Irene's thoughts. And from the thoughts of others too—if their conversation was any indication of their thoughts.

Besides, Clare had never been exactly one of the group, just as she'd never been merely the janitor's daughter, but the daughter of Mr. Bob Kendry, who, it was true, was a janitor, but who also, it seemed, had been in college with some of their fathers. Just how or why he happened to be a janitor, and a very inefficient one at that, they none of them quite knew. One of Irene's brothers, who had put the question to their father, had been told: "That's something that doesn't concern you," and given him the advice to be careful not to end in the same manner as "poor Bob."

No, Irene hadn't thought of Clare Kendry. Her own life had been too crowded. So, she supposed, had the lives of other people. She defended her—their—forgetfulness. "You know how it is. Everybody's so busy. People leave, drop out, maybe for a little while there's talk about them, or questions; then, gradually they're forgotten."

"Yes, that's natural," Clare agreed. And what, she inquired, had they said of her for that little while at the beginning before they'd forgotten her altogether?

Irene looked away. She felt the telltale colour rising in her cheeks. "You can't," she evaded. "expect me to remember trifles like that over twelve years of marriages, births, deaths, and the war."

There followed that trill of notes that was Clare Kendry's laugh, small and clear and the very essence of mockery.

"Oh, 'Rene!" she cried, "of course you remember! But I won't make you tell me, because I know just as well as if I'd been there and heard every unkind word. Oh, I know, I know. Frank Danton saw me in the Shelby one night. Don't tell me he didn't broadcast that, and with embroidery. Others may have seen me at other times. I don't know. But once I met Margaret Hammer in Marshall Field's. I'd have spoken, was on the very point of doing it, but she cut me dead. My dear 'Rene, I assure you that from the way she looked through me, even I was uncertain whether I was actually there in the flesh or not. I remember it clearly, too clearly. It was that very thing which, in a way, finally decided me not to go out and see you one last time before I went away to stay. Somehow, good as all of you, the whole family, had always been to the poor forlorn child that was me, I felt I shouldn't be able to bear that. I mean if any of you, your mother or the boys or—Oh, well, I just felt I'd rather not known it if you did. And so I stayed away. Silly, I suppose. Sometimes I've been sorry I didn't go."

Irene wondered if it was tears that made Clare's eyes so luminous.

"And now 'Rene, I want to hear all about you and everybody and everything. You're married, I s'pose?"

Irene nodded.

"Yes," Clare said knowingly, "you would be. Tell me about it."

And so for an hour or more they had sat there smoking and drinking tea and filling in the gap of twelve years with talk. That is, Irene did. She told Clare about her marriage and removal to New York, about her husband, and about her two sons, who were having their first experience of being separated from their parents at a summer camp, about her mother's death, about the marriages of her two brothers. She told of the marriages, births and deaths in other families that Clare had known, opening up, for her, new vistas on the lives of old friends and acquaintances.

Clare drank it all in, these things which for so long she had wanted to know and hadn't been able to learn. She sat motionless, her bright lips slightly parted, her whole face lit by the radiance of her happy eyes. Now and then she put a question, but for the most part she was silent.

Somewhere outside, a clock struck. Brought back to the present, Irene looked down at her watch and exclaimed: "Oh, I must go, Clare!"

A moment passed during which she was the prey of uneasiness. It had suddenly occurred to her that she hadn't asked Clare anything about her own life and that she had a very definite unwillingness to do so. And she was quite well aware of the reason for that reluctance. But, she asked herself, wouldn't it, all things considered, be the kindest thing not to ask? If things with Clare were as she—as they all—had suspected, wouldn't it be more tactful to seem to forget to inquire how she had spent those twelve years?

If? It was that "if" which bothered her. It might be, it might just be, in spite of all gossip and even appearances to the contrary, that there was nothing, had been nothing, that couldn't be simply and innocently explained. Appearances, she knew now, had a way sometimes of not fitting facts, and if Clare hadn't—Well, if they had all been wrong, then certainly she ought to express some interest in what had happened to her. It would seem queer and rude if she didn't. But how was she to know? There was, she at last decided, no way; so she merely said again. "I must go, Clare."

"Please, not so soon, 'Rene," Clare begged, not moving.

Irene thought: "She's really almost too good-looking. It's hardly any wonder that she—"

"And now, 'Rene dear, that I've found you, I mean to see lots and lots of you. We're here for a month at least. Jack, that's my husband, is here on business. Poor dear! in this heat. Isn't it beastly? Come to dinner with us tonight, won't you?" And she gave Irene a curious little sidelong glance and a sly, ironical smile peeped out on her full red lips, as if she had been in the secret of the other's thoughts and was mocking her.

Irene was conscious of a sharp intake of breath, but whether it was relief or chagrin that she felt, she herself could not have told. She said hastily: "I'm afraid I can't, Clare. I'm filled up. Dinner and bridge. I'm so sorry."

"Come tomorrow instead, to tea," Clare insisted. "Then you'll see Margery—she's just ten—and Jack too, maybe, if he hasn't got an appointment or something."

From Irene came an uneasy little laugh. She had an engagement for tomorrow also and she was afraid that Clare would not believe it. Suddenly, now, that possibility disturbed her. Therefore it was with a half-vexed feeling at the sense of undeserved guilt that had come upon her that she explained that it wouldn't be possible because she wouldn't be free for tea, or for luncheon or dinner either. "And the next day's Friday when I'll be going away for the week-end, Idlewild, you know. It's quite the thing now." And then she had an inspiration.

"Clare!" she exclaimed, "why don't you come up with me? Our place is probably full up—Jim's wife has a way of collecting mobs of the most impossible people—but we can always manage to find room for one more. And you'll see absolutely everybody."

In the very moment of giving the invitation she regretted it. What a foolish, what an idiotic impulse to have given way to! She groaned inwardly as she thought of the endless explanations in which it would involve her, of the curiosity, and the talk, and the lifted eye-brows. It wasn't she assured herself, that she was a snob, that she cared greatly for the petty restrictions and distinctions with which what called itself Negro society chose to hedge itself about; but that she had a natural and deeply rooted aversion to the kind of front-page notoriety that Clare Kendry's presence in Idlewild, as her guest, would expose her to. And here she was, perversely and against all reason, inviting her.

But Clare shook her head. "Really, I'd love to, 'Rene," she said, a little mournfully. "There's nothing I'd like better. But I couldn't. I mustn't, you see. It wouldn't do at all. I'm sure you understand. I'm simply crazy to go, but I can't." The dark eyes glistened and there was a suspicion of a quaver in the husky voice. "And believe me, 'Rene, I do thank you for asking me. Don't think I've entirely forgotten just what it would mean for you if I went. That is, if you still care about such things."

All indication of tears had gone from her eyes and voice, and Irene Redfield, searching her face, had an offended feeling that behind what was now only an ivory mask lurked a scornful amusement. She looked away, at the wall far beyond Clare. Well, she deserved it, for, as she acknowledged to herself, she *was* relieved. And for the very reason at which Clare had hinted. The fact Clare had guessed her perturbation did not, however, in any degree lessen that relief. She was

annoyed at having been detected in what might seem to be an insincerity; but that was all.

The waiter came with Clare's change. Irene reminded herself that she ought immediately to go. But she didn't move.

The truth was, she was curious. There were things that she wanted to ask Clare Kendry. She wished to find out about this hazardous business of "passing," this breaking away from all that was familiar and friendly to take one's chances in another environment, not entirely strange, perhaps, but certainly not entirely friendly. What, for example, one did about background, how one accounted for oneself. And how one felt when one came into contact with other Negroes. But she couldn't. She was unable to think of a single question that in its context or its phrasing was not too frankly curious, if not actually impertinent.

As if aware of her desire and her hesitation, Clare remarked, thoughtfully: "You know, 'Rene, I've often wondered why more coloured girls, girls like you and Margaret Hammer and Esther Dawson and—oh, lots of others—never 'passed' over. It's such a frightfully easy thing to do. If one's the type, all that's needed is a little nerve."

"What about background? Family, I mean. Surely you can't just drop down on people from nowhere and expect them to receive you with open arms, can you?"

"Almost," Clare asserted. "You'd be surprised, 'Rene, how much easier that is with white people than with us. Maybe because there are so many more of them, or maybe because they are secure and so don't have to bother. I've never quite decided."

Irene was inclined to be incredulous. "You mean that you didn't have to explain where you came from? It seems impossible."

Clare cast a glance of repressed amusement across the table at her. "As a matter of fact, I didn't. Though I suppose under any other circumstances I might have had to provide some plausible tale to account for myself. I've a good imagination, so I'm sure I could have done it quite creditably, and credibly. But it wasn't necessary. There were my aunts, you see, respectable and authentic enough for anything or anybody."

"I see. They were 'passing' too."

"No. They weren't. They were white."

"Oh!" And in the next instant it came back to Irene that she had heard this mentioned before; by her father, or, more likely, her mother. They were Bob Kendry's aunts. He had been a son of their brother's, on the left hand. A wild oat.

"They were nice old ladies," Clare explained, "very religious and as poor as church mice. That adored brother of theirs, my grandfather, got through every penny they had after he'd finished his own little bit."

Clare paused in her narrative to light another cigarette. Her smile, her expression, Irene noticed, was faintly resentful.

"Being good Christians," she continued, "when dad came to his tipsy end, they did their duty and gave me a home of sorts. I was, it was true, expected to earn my keep by doing all the housework, and most of the washing. But do you realize, 'Rene, that if it hadn't been for them, I shouldn't have had a home in the world?"

Irene's nod and little murmur were comprehensive, understanding.

Clare made a small mischievous grimace and proceeded. "Besides to their notion, hard labour was good for me. I had Negro blood and they belonged to the generation that had written and read long articles headed: 'Will the Blacks Work?' Too, they weren't quite sure that the good God hadn't intended the sons and daughters of Ham to sweat because he had poked fun at old man Noah once when he had taken a drop too much. I remember the aunts telling me that that old drunkard had cursed Ham and his sons for all time."

Irene laughed. But Clare remained quite serious.

"It was more than a joke, I assure you, 'Rene. It was a hard life for a girl of sixteen. Still, I had a roof over my head, and food, and clothes—such as they were. And there were the Scriptures, and talks on morals and thrift and industry and the loving-kindness of the good Lord."

"Have you ever stopped to think, Clare," Irene demanded, "how much unhappiness and downright cruelty are laid to the loving-kindness of the Lord? And always by His most ardent followers, it seems."

"Have I?" Clare exclaimed. "It, they, made me what I am today. For, of course, I was determined to get away, to be a person and not a charity or a problem, or even a daughter of the indiscreet Ham. Then, too, I wanted things. I knew I wasn't bad-looking and that I could 'pass.' You can't know, 'Rene, how, when I used to go over to the south side, I used almost to hate all of you. You had all the things I wanted and never had had. It made me all the more determined to get them, and others. Do you, can you understand what I felt?"

She looked up with a pointed and appealing effect, and, evidently finding the sympathetic expression on Irene's face sufficient answer, went on. "The aunts were queer. For all their Bibles and praying and ranting about honesty, they didn't want anyone to know that their darling brother had seduced—ruined, they called it—a Negro girl. They could excuse the ruin, but they couldn't forgive the tar-brush. They forbade me to mention Negroes to the neighbours, or even to mention the south side. You may be sure that I didn't. I'll bet they were good and sorry afterwards."

She laughed and the ringing bells in her laugh had a hard metallic sound.

"When the chance to get away came, that omission was of great value to me. When Jack, a schoolboy acquaintance of some people in the neighbourbood, turned up from South America with untold gold, there was no one to tell him that I was coloured, and many to tell him about the severity and the religiousness of Aunt Grace and Aunt Edna. You can guess the rest. After he came, I stopped slipping off to the south side and slipped off to meet him instead. I couldn't manage both. In the end I had no great difficulty in convincing him that it was useless to talk marriage to the aunts. So on the day that I was eighteen, we went off and were married. So that's that. Nothing could have been easier."

"Yes, I do see that for you it was easy enough. By the way! I wonder why they didn't tell father that you were married. He went over to find out about you when you stopped coming over to see us. I'm sure they didn't tell him. Not that you were married."

Clare Kendry's eyes were bright with tears that didn't fall. "Oh, how lovely! To have cared enough about me to do that. The dear sweet man! Well, they couldn't tell him because they didn't know it. I took care of that, for I couldn't be sure that those consciences of theirs wouldn't begin to work on them afterwards and make them let the cat out of the bag. The old things probably thought I was living in sin, wherever I was. And it would be about what they expected."

An amused smile lit the lovely face for the smallest fraction of a second. After a little silence she said soberly: "But I'm sorry if they told your father so. That was something I hadn't counted on."

"I'm not sure that they did," Irene told her. "He didn't say so, anyway."

"He wouldn't, 'Rene dear. Not your father."

"Thanks, I'm sure he wouldn't."

"But you've never answered my question. Tell me, honestly, haven't you ever thought of 'passing'?"

Irene answered promptly: "No. Why should I?" And so disdainful was her voice and manner that Clare's face flushed and her eyes glinted. Irene hastened to add: "You see, Clare, I've everything I want. Except, perhaps, a little more money."

At that Clare laughed, her spark of anger vanished as quickly as it had appeared. "Of course," she declared, "that's what everybody wants, just a little more money, even the people who have it. And I must say I don't blame them. Money's awfully nice to have. In fact, all things considered, I think, 'Rene, that it's even worth the price."

Irene could only shrug her shoulders. Her reason partly agreed, her instinct wholly rebelled. And she could not say why. And though conscious that if she didn't hurry away, she was going to be late to dinner, she still lingered. It was as if the woman sitting on the other side of the table, a girl that she had known, who had done this rather dangerous and, to Irene Redfield, abhorrent thing successfully and had announced herself well satisfied, had for her a fascination, strange and compelling.

Clare Kendry was still leaning back in the tall chair, her sloping shoulders against the carved top. She sat with an air of indifferent assurance, as if arranged for, desired. About her clung that dim suggestion of polite insolence with which a few women are born and which some acquire with the coming of riches or importance.

Clare, it gave Irene a little prick of satisfaction to recall, hadn't got that by passing herself off as white. She herself had always had it.

Just as she'd always had that pale gold hair, which, unsheared still, was drawn loosely back from a broad brow, partly hidden by the small close hat. Her lips, painted a brilliant geranium-red, were sweet and sensitive and a little obstinate. A tempting mouth. The face across the forehead and cheeks was a trifle too wide, but the ivory skin had a peculiar soft lustre. And the eyes were magnificent! dark, sometimes absolutely black, always luminous, and set in long, black lashes. Arresting eyes, slow and mesmeric, and with, for all their warmth, something withdrawn and secret about them.

Ah! Surely! They were Negro eyes! mysterious and concealing. And set in that ivory face under that bright hair, there was about them something exotic.

Yes, Clare Kendry's loveliness was absolute, beyond challenge, thanks to those eyes which her grandmother and later her mother and father had given her.

Into those eyes there came a smile and over Irene the sense of being petted and caressed. She smiled back.

"Maybe," Clare suggested, "you can come Monday, if you're back. Or, if you're not, then Tuesday."

With a small regretful sigh, Irene informed Clare that she was afraid she wouldn't be back by Monday and that she was sure she had dozens of things for Tuesday, and that she was leaving Wednesday. It might be, however, that she could get out of something Tuesday.

"Oh, do try. Do put somebody else off. The others can see you any time, while I—Why, I may never see you again! Think of that, 'Rene! You'll have to come. You'll simply have to! I'll never forgive you if you don't."

At that moment it seemed a dreadful thing to think of never seeing Clare Kendry again. Standing there under the appeal, the caress, of her eyes, Irene had the desire, the hope, that this parting wouldn't be the last.

"I'll try, Clare," she promised gently. "I'll call you—or will you call me?"

"I think, perhaps, I'd better call you. Your father's in the book, I know, and the address is the same. Sixty-four eighteen. Some memory, what? Now remember, I'm going to expect you. You've got to be able to come."

Again that peculiar mellowing smile.

"I'll do my best, Clare."

Irene gathered up her gloves and bag. They stood up. She put out her hand. Clare took it and held it.

"It has been nice seeing you again, Clare. How pleased and glad father'll be to hear about you!"

"Until Tuesday, then," Clare Kendry replied. "I'll spend every minute of the time from now on looking forward to seeing you again. Goodbye, 'Rene dear. My love to your father, and this kiss for him."

The sun had gone from overhead, but the streets were still like fiery furnaces. The languid breeze was still hot. And the scurrying people looked even more wilted than before Irene had fled from their contact.

Crossing the avenue in the heat, far from the coolness of the Drayton's roof, away from the seduction of Clare Kendry's smile, she was aware of a sense of irritation with herself because she had been pleased and a little flattered at the other's obvious gladness at their meeting.

With her perspiring progress homeward this irritation grew, and she began to wonder just what had possessed her to make her promise to find time, in the crowded days that remained of her visit, to spend another afternoon with a woman whose life had so definitely and deliberately diverged from hers; and whom, as had been pointed out, she might never see again.

Why in the world had she made such a promise?

As she went up the steps to her father's house, thinking with what interest and amazement he would listen to her story of the afternoon's encounter, it came to her that Clare had omitted to mention her marriage name. She had referred to her husband as Jack. That was all. Had that, Irene asked herself, been intentional?

Clare had only to pick up the telephone to communicate with her, or to drop her a card, or to jump into a taxi. But she couldn't reach Clare in any way. Nor could anyone else to whom she might speak of their meeting.

"As if I should!"

Her key turned in the lock. She went in. Her father, it seemed, hadn't come in yet.

Irene decided that she wouldn't, after all, say anything to him about Clare Kendry. She had, she told to herself, no inclination to speak of a person who held so low an opinion of her loyalty, or her discretion. And certainly she had no desire or intention of making the slightest effort about Tuesday. Nor any other day for that matter.

She was through with Clare Kendry.

Three

On Tuesday morning a dome of grey sky rose over the parched city, but the stifling air was not relieved by the silvery mist that seemed to hold a promise of rain, which did not fall.

To Irene Redfield this soft foreboding fog was another reason for doing nothing about seeing Clare Kendry that afternoon.

But she did see her.

The telephone. For hours it had rung like something possessed. Since nine o'clock she had been hearing its insistent jangle. Awhile she was resolute, saying firmly each time: "Not in, Liza, take the message." And each time the servant returned with the information. "It's the same lady, ma'am; she says she'll call again."

But at noon, her nerves frayed and her conscience smiting her at the reproachful look on Liza's ebony face as she withdrew for another denial, Irene weakened.

"Oh, never mind. I'll answer this time, Liza."

"It's her again."

"Hello. . . . Yes."

"It's Clare, 'Rene. . . . Where *have* you been? . . . Can you be here around four? . . . What? But, 'Rene, you promised! Just for a little while . . . You can if you want to . . . I am *so* disappointed. I had counted so on seeing you . . . Please be nice and come. Only for a minute. I'm sure you can manage it if you try. . . . I won't beg you to stay. . . . Yes. . . . I'm going to expect you. . . . It's the Morgan. . . . Oh, yes! The name's Bellew, Mrs. John Bellew. . . . About four, then. . . . I'll be so happy to see you! . . . Goodbye."

"Damn!"

Irene hung up the receiver with an emphatic bang, her thoughts immediately filled with self-reproach. She'd done it again. Allowed Clare Kendry to persuade her into promising to do something for which she had neither time nor any special desire. What was it about Clare's voice that was so appealing, so very seductive?

Clare met her in the hall with a kiss. She said: "You're good to come, 'Rene. But, then, you always were nice to me." And under her potent smile a part of Irene's annoyance with herself fled. She was even a little glad that she had come.

Clare led the way, stepping lightly, towards a room whose door was standing partly open, saying: "There's a surprise. It's a real party. See."

Entering, Irene found herself in a sitting-room, large and high, at whose windows hung startling blue draperies which triumphantly dragged attention from the gloomy chocolate-coloured furniture. And Clare was wearing a thin floating dress of the same shade of blue, which suited her and the rather difficult room to perfection.

For a minute Irene thought the room was empty, but turning her head, she discovered, sunk deep in the cushions of a huge sofa, a woman staring up at her with such intense concentration that her eyelids were drawn as though the strain of that upward glance had paralysed them. At first Irene took her to be a stranger, but in the next instant she

said in an unsympathetic, almost harsh voice: "And how are you, Gertrude?"

The woman nodded and forced a smile to her pouting lips. "I'm all right," she replied. "And you're just the same, Irene. Not changed a bit."

"Thank you." Irene responded, as she chose a seat. She was thinking: "Great goodness! Two of them."

For Gertrude too had married a white man, though it couldn't be truthfully said that she was "passing." Her husband—what was his name?—had been in school with her and had been quite well aware, as had his family and most of his friends, that she was a Negro. It hadn't, Irene knew, seemed to matter to him then. Did it now, she wondered? Had Fred—Fred Martin, that was it—had he ever regretted his marriage because of Gertrude's race? Had Gertrude?

Turning to Gertrude, Irene asked: "And Fred, how is he? It's unmentionable years since I've seen him."

"Oh, he's all right," Gertrude answered briefly.

For a full minute no one spoke. Finally out of the oppressive little silence Clare's voice came pleasantly, conversationally: "We'll have tea right away. I know that you can't stay long, 'Rene. And I'm sorry you won't see Margery. We went up the lake over the week end to see some of Jack's people, just out of Milwaukee. Margery wanted to stay with the children. It seemed a shame not to let her, especially since it's so hot in town. But I'm expecting Jack any second."

Irene said briefly: "That's nice."

Gertrude remained silent. She was, it was plain, a little ill at ease. And her presence there annoyed Irene, roused in her a defensive and resentful feeling for which she had at the moment no explanation. But it did seem to her odd that the woman that Clare was now should have invited the woman that Gertrude was. Still, of course, Clare couldn't have known. Twelve years since they had met.

Later, when she examined her feeling of annoyance, Irene admitted, a shade reluctantly, that it arose from a feeling of being outnumbered, a sense of aloneness, in her adherence to her own class and kind; not merely in the great thing of marriage, but in the whole pattern of her life as well.

Clare spoke again, this time at length. Her talk was of the change that Chicago presented to her after her long absence in European cities. Yes, she said in reply to some question from Gertrude, she'd been back to America a time or two, but only as far as New York and Philadelphia, and once she had spent a few days in Washington. John Bellew, who, it appeared, was some sort of international banking agent, hadn't particularly wanted her to come with him on this trip, but as soon as she had learned that it would possibly take him as far as Chicago, she made up her mind to come anyway.

"I simply had to. And after I once got here, I was determined to see someone I knew and find out what had happened to everybody. I didn't quite see how I was going manage it, but I meant to. Somehow. I'd just about decided to take a chance and go out to your house, 'Rene, or call up and arrange a meeting, when I ran into you. What luck!"

Irene agreed that it was luck. "It's the first time I've been home for five years, and now I'm about to leave. A week later and I'd have been gone. And how in the world did you find Gertrude?"

"In the book. I remembered about Fred. His father still has the meat market."

"Oh, yes," said Irene, who had only remembered it as Clare had spoken, "on Cottage Grove near—"

Gertrude broke in. "No. It's moved. We're on Maryland Avenue—used to be Jackson—now. Near Sixty-third Street. And the market's Fred's. His name's the same as his father's."

Gertrude, Irene thought, looked as if her husband might be a butcher. There was left of her youthful prettiness, which had been so much admired in their high-school days, no trace. She had grown broad, fat almost, and though there were no lines on her large white face, its very smoothness was somehow prematurely ageing. Her black hair was clipt, and by some unfortunate means all the live curliness had gone from it. Her over-trimmed Georgette *crêpe* dress was too short and showed an appalling amount of leg, stout legs in sleazy stockings of a vivid rose-beige shade. Her plump hands were newly and not too competently manicured—for the occasion, probably. And she wasn't smoking.

Clare said—and Irene fancied that her husky voice held a slight edge—"Before you came, Irene, Gertrude was telling me about her two boys. Twins. Think of it! Isn't too marvellous for words?"

Irene felt a warmness creeping into her cheeks. Uncanny, the way Clare could divine what one was thinking. She was a little put out, but her manner was entirely easy as she said: "That is nice. I've two boys myself, Gertrude. Not twins, though. It seems that Clare's rather behind, doesn't it?"

Gertrude, however, wasn't sure that Clare hadn't the best of it. "She's got a girl. I wanted a girl. So did Fred."

"Isn't it a bit unusual?" Irene asked. "Most men want sons. Egotism, I suppose."

"Well, Fred didn't."

The tea-things had been placed on a low table at Clare's side. She gave them her attention now, pouring the rich amber fluid from the tall glass pitcher into stately slim glasses, which she handed to the guests, and then offered them lemon or cream and tiny sandwiches or cakes.

After taking up her own glass she informed them: "No, I have no boys and I don't think I'll ever have any. I'm afraid. I nearly died of terror the whole nine months before Margery was born for fear that she might be dark. Thank goodness, she turned out all right. But I'll never risk it again. Never! The strain is simply too—too hellish."

Gertrude Martin nodded in complete comprehension.

This time it was Irene who said nothing.

"You don't have to tell me!" Gertrude said fervently. "I know what it is all right. Maybe you don't think I wasn't scared to death too. Fred said I was silly, and so did his mother. But, of course, they thought it was just a notion I'd gotten into my head and they blamed it on my condition. They don't know like we do, how it might go way back, and turn out dark no matter what colour the father and mother are."

Perspiration stood out on her forehead. Her narrow eyes rolled first in Clare's, then in Irene's direction. As she talked she waved her heavy hands about.

"No," she went on, "no more for me either. Not even a girl. It's awful the way it skips generations and then pops out. Why, he actually said he didn't care what colour it turned out, if I would only stop worrying about it. But, of course, nobody wants a dark child." Her voice was earnest and she took for granted that her audience was in entire agreement with her.

Irene, whose head had gone up with a quick little jerk, now said in a voice of whose even tones she was proud: "One of my boys is dark."

Gertrude jumped as if she had been shot at. Her eyes goggled. Her mouth flew open. She tried to speak, but could not immediately get the words out. Finally she managed to stammer: "Oh! And your husband, is he—is he—er—dark, too?"

Irene, who was struggling with a flood of feelings, resentment, anger, and contempt, was, however, still able to answer as coolly as if she had not that sense of not belonging to and of despising the company in which she found herself drinking iced tea from tall amber glasses on that hot August afternoon. Her husband, she informed them quietly, couldn't exactly "pass."

At that reply Clare turned on Irene her seductive caressing smile and remarked a little scoffingly: "I do think that coloured people—we—are too silly about some things. After all, the thing's not important to Irene or hundreds of others. Not awfully, even to you, Gertrude. It's only deserters like me who have to be afraid of freaks of the nature. As my inestimable dad used to say, 'Everything must be paid for.' Now, please one of you tell me what ever happened to Claude Jones. You know, the tall, lanky specimen who used to wear that comical little moustache that the girls used to laugh at so. Like a thin streak of soot. The moustache, I mean."

At that Gertrude shrieked with laughter. "Claude Jones!" and launched into the story of how he was no longer a Negro or a Christian but had become a Jew.

"A Jew!" Clare exclaimed.

"Yes, a Jew. A black Jew, he calls himself. He won't eat ham and goes to the synagogue on Saturday. He's got a beard now as well as a moustache. You'd die laughing if you saw him. He's really too funny for words. Fred says he's crazy and I guess he is. Oh, he's scream all right, a regular scream!" And she shrieked again.

Clare's laugh tinkled out. "It certainly sounds funny enough. Still, it's his own business. If he gets along better by turning—"

At that, Irene, who was still laughing her unhappy don't-care feeling of rightness, broke in, saying bitingly: "It evidently doesn't occur to either you or Gertrude that he might possibly be sincere in changing his religion. Surely everyone doesn't do everything for gain."

Clare Kendry had no need to search for the full meaning of that utterance. She reddened slightly and retorted seriously: "Yes, I admit that might be possible—his being sincere, I mean. It just didn't happen to occur to me, that's all. I'm surprised," and the seriousness changed to mockery, "that you should have expected it to. Or did you really?"

"You don't, I'm sure, imagine that that is a question that I can answer," Irene told her. "Not here and now."

Gertrude's face expressed complete bewilderment. However, seeing that little smiles had come out on the faces of the two other women and not recognizing them for the smiles of mutual reservations which they were, she smiled too.

Clare began to talk, steering carefully away from anything that might lead towards race or other thorny subjects. It was the most brilliant exhibition of conversational weight-lifting that Irene had ever seen. Her words swept over them in charming well-modulated streams. Her laughs tinkled and pealed. Her little stories sparkled.

Irene contributed a bare "Yes" or "No" here and there. Gertrude, a "You don't say!" less frequently.

For a while the illusion of general conversation was nearly perfect. Irene felt her resentment changing gradually to a silent, somewhat grudging admiration.

Clare talked on, her voice, her gestures, colouring all she said of wartime in France, of after-the-wartime in Germany, of the excitement at the time of the general strike in England, of dressmakers' openings in Paris, of the new gaiety of Budapest.

But it couldn't last, this verbal feat. Gertrude shifted in her seat and fell to fidgeting with her fingers. Irene, bored at last by all this repetition of the selfsame things that she had read all too often in papers, magazines, and books, set down her glass and collected her bag and handkerchief. She was smoothing out the tan fingers of her gloves preparatory to putting them on when she heard the sound of the outer door being opened and saw Clare spring up with an expression of relief saying: "How lovely! Here's Jack at exactly the right minute. You can't go now, 'Rene dear."

John Bellew came into the room. The first thing that Irene noticed about him was that he was not the man that she had seen with Clare Kendry on the Drayton roof. This man, Clare's husband, was a tallish person, broadly made. His age she guessed to be somewhere between thirty-five and forty. His hair was dark brown and waving, and he had a soft mouth, somewhat womanish, set in an unhealthy-looking dough-coloured face. His steel-grey opaque eyes were very much alive, moving ceaselessly between thick bluish lids. But there was, Irene decided, nothing unusual about him, unless it was an impression of latent physical power.

"Hello, Nig," was his greeting to Clare.

Gertrude who had started slightly, settled back and looked covertly towards Irene, who had caught her lip between her teeth and sat gazing at husband and wife. It was hard to believe that even Clare Kendry would permit this ridiculing of her race by an outsider, though he chanced to be her husband. So he knew, then, that Clare was a Negro? From her talk the other day Irene had understood that he didn't. But how rude, how positively insulting, for him to address her in that way in the presence of guests!

In Clare's eyes, as she presented her husband, was a queer gleam, a jeer, it might be. Irene couldn't define it.

The mechanical professions that attend an introduction over, she inquired: "Did you hear what Jack called me?"

"Yes," Gertrude answered, laughing with a dutiful eagerness.

Irene didn't speak. Her gaze remained level on Clare's smiling face.

The black eyes fluttered down. "Tell them, dear, why you call me that."

The man chuckled, crinkling up his eyes, not, Irene was compelled to acknowledge, unpleasantly. He explained: "Well, you see, it's like this. When we were first married, she was as white as—as—well as white as a lily. But I declare she's gettin' darker and darker. I tell her if she don't look out, she'll wake up one of these days and find she's turned into a nigger."

He roared with laughter. Clare's ringing bell-like laugh joined his. Gertrude after another uneasy shift in her seat added her shrill one. Irene, who had been sitting with lips tightly compressed, cried out: "That's good!" and gave way to gales of laughter. She laughed and laughed and laughed. Tears ran down her cheeks. Her sides ached. Her throat hurt. She laughed on and on and on, long after the others had subsided. Until, catching sight of Clare's face, the need for a more quiet enjoyment of this priceless joke, and for caution, struck her. At once she stopped.

Clare handed her husband his tea and laid her hand on his arm with an affectionate little gesture. Speaking with confidence as well as with amusement, she said: "My goodness, Jack! What difference would it make if, after all these years, you were to find out that I was one or two per cent coloured?"

Bellew put out his hand in a repudiating fling, definite and final. "Oh, no, Nig," he declared, "nothing like that with me. I know you're no nigger, so it's all right. You can get as black as you please as far as I'm concerned, since I know you're no nigger. I draw the line at that. No niggers in my family. Never have been and never will be."

Irene's lips trembled almost uncontrollably, but she made a desperate effort to fight back her disastrous desire to laugh again, and succeeded. Carefully selecting a cigarette from the lacquered box on the tea-table before her, she turned an oblique look on Clare and encountered her peculiar eyes fixed on her with an expression so dark and deep and unfathomable that she had for a short moment the sensation of gazing into the eyes of some creature utterly strange and apart. A faint sense of danger brushed her, like the breath of a cold fog. Absurd, her reason told her, as she accepted Bellew's proffered light for her cigarette. Another glance at Clare showed her smiling. So, as one always ready to oblige, was Gertrude.

An on-looker, Irene reflected, would have thought it a most congenial tea-party, all smiles and jokes and hilarious laughter. She said humorously: "So you dislike Negroes, Mr. Bellew?" But her amusement was at her thought, rather than her words.

John Bellew gave a short denying laugh. "You got me wrong there, Mrs. Redfield. Nothing like that at all. I don't dislike them, I hate them. And so does Nig, for all she's trying to turn into one. She wouldn't have a nigger maid around her for love nor money. Not that I'd want her to. They give me the creeps. The black scrimy devils."

This wasn't funny. Had Bellew, Irene inquired, ever known any Negroes? The defensive tone of her voice brought another start from the uncomfortable Gertrude, and, for all her appearance of serenity, a quick apprehensive look from Clare.

Bellew answered: "Thank the Lord, no! And never expect to! But I know people who've known them, better than they know their black selves. And I read in the papers about them. Always robbing and killing people. And," he added darkly, "worse."

From Gertrude's direction came a queer little suppressed sound, a snort or a giggle. Irene couldn't tell which. There was a brief silence, during which she feared that her self-control was about to prove too frail a bridge to support her mounting anger and indignation. She had a leaping desire to shout at the man beside her: "And you're sitting here surrounded by three black devils, drinking tea."

The impulse passed, obliterated by her consciousness of the danger in which such rashness would involve Clare, who remarked with a gentle reprovingness: "Jack dear, I'm sure 'Rene doesn't care to hear all about your pet aversions. Nor Gertrude either. Maybe they read the papers too, you know." She smiled on him, and her smile seemed to transform him, to soften and mellow him, as the rays of the sun does a fruit.

"All right, Nig, old girl. I'm sorry," he apologized. Reaching over, he playfully touched his wife's pale hands, then turned back to Irene. "Didn't mean to bore you, Mrs. Redfield. Hope you'll excuse me," he said sheepishly. "Clare tells me you're living in New York. Great city, New York. The city of the future."

In Irene, rage had not retreated, but was held by some dam of caution and allegiance to Clare. So, in the best casual voice she could muster, she agreed with Bellew. Though, she reminded him, it was exactly what Chicagoans were apt to say of their city. And all the while she was speaking, she was thinking how amazing it was that her voice did not tremble, that outwardly she was calm. Only her hands shook slightly. She drew them inward from their rest in her lap and pressed the tips of her fingers together to still them.

"Husband's a doctor, I understand. Manhattan, or one of the other boroughs?"

Manhattan, Irene informed him, and explained the need for Brian to be within easy reach of certain hospitals and clinics.

"Interesting life, a doctor's."

"Ye-es. Hard, though. And, in a way, monotonous. Nerve-racking too."

"Hard on the wife's nerves at least, eh? So many lady patients." He laughed, enjoying, with a boyish heartiness, the hoary joke.

Irene managed a momentary smile, but her voice was sober as she said: "Brian doesn't care for ladies, especially sick ones. I sometimes wish he did. It's South America that attracts him."

"Coming place, South America, if they ever get the niggers out of it. It's run over—"

"Really, Jack!" Clare's voice was on the edge of temper.

"Honestly, Nig, I forgot." To the others he said: "You see how henpecked I am." And to Gertrude: "You're still in Chicago, Mrs.—er—Mrs. Martin?"

He was, it was plain, doing his best to be agreeable to these old friends of Clare's. Irene had to concede that under other conditions she might have liked him. A fairly good-looking man of amiable disposition, evidently, and in easy circumstances. Plain and with no nonsense about him.

Gertrude replied that Chicago was good enough for her. She'd never been out of it and didn't think she ever should. Her husband's business was there.

"Of course, of course. Can't jump up and leave a business."

There followed a smooth surface of talk about Chicago, New York, their differences and their recent spectacular changes.

It was, Irene, thought, unbelievable and astonishing that four people could sit so unruffled, so ostensibly friendly, while they were in reality seething with anger, mortification, shame. But no, on second thought she was forced to amend her opinion. John Bellew, most certainly, was as undisturbed within as without. So, perhaps, was Gertrude Martin. At least she hadn't the mortification and shame that Clare Kendry must be feeling, or, in such full measure, the rage and rebellion that she, Irene, was repressing.

"More tea, 'Rene," Clare offered.

"Thanks, no. And I must be going. I'm leaving tomorrow, you know, and I've still got packing to do."

She stood up. So did Gertrude, and Clare, and John Bellew.

"How do you like the Drayton, Mrs. Redfield?" the latter asked.

"The Drayton? Oh, very much. Very much indeed," Irene answered, her scornful eyes on Clare's unrevealing face.

"Nice place, all right. Stayed there a time or two myself," the man informed her.

"Yes, it is nice," Irene agreed. "Almost as good as our best New York places." She had withdrawn her look from Clare and was searching in her bag for some non-existent something. Her understanding was rapidly increasing, as was her pity and her contempt. Clare was so daring, so lovely, and so "having."

They gave their hands to Clare with appropriate murmurs. "So good to have seen you." . . . "I do hope I'll see you again soon."

"Good-bye," Clare returned. "It was good of you to come, 'Rene dear. And you too, Gertrude."

"Good-bye, Mr. Bellew." . . . "So glad to have met you." It was Gertrude who had said that. Irene couldn't, she absolutely couldn't bring herself to utter the polite fiction or anything approaching it.

He accompanied them out into the hall, summoned the elevator.

"Good-bye," they said again, stepping in.

Plunging downward they were silent.

They made their way through the lobby without speaking.

But as soon as they had reached the street Gertrude, in the manner of one unable to keep bottled up for another minute that which for the last hour she had had to retain, burst out: "My God! What an awful chance! She must be plumb crazy."

"Yes, it certainly seems risky," Irene admitted.

"Risky! I should say it was. Risky! My God! What a world! And the mess she's liable to get herself into!"

"Still, I imagine she's pretty safe. They don't live here, you know. And there's a child. That's a certain security."

"It's an awful chance, just the same," Gertrude insisted. "I'd never in the world have married Fred without him knowing. You can't tell what will turn up."

"Yes, I do agree that it's safer to tell. But then Bellew wouldn't have married her. And, after all, that's what she wanted."

Gertrude shook her head. "I wouldn't be in her shoes for all the money she's getting out of it, when he finds out. Not with him feeling the way he does. Gee! Wasn't it awful? For a minute I was so mad I could have slapped him."

It had been, Irene acknowledged, a distinctly trying experience, as well as a very unpleasant one. "I was more than a little angry myself."

"And imagine her not telling us about him feeling that way! Anything might have happened. We might have said something."

That, Irene pointed out, was exactly like Clare Kendry. Taking a chance, and not at all considering anyone else's feelings.

Gertrude said: "Maybe she thought we'd think it a good joke. And I guess you did. The way you laughed. My land! I was scared to death he might catch on."

"Well, it was rather a joke," Irene told her, "on him and us and maybe on her."

"All the same, it's an awful chance. I'd hate to be her."

"She seems satisfied enough. She's got what she wanted, and the other day she told me it was worth it."

But about that Gertrude was sceptical. "She'll find out different," was her verdict. "She'll find out different all right."

Rain had begun to fall, a few scattered large drops.

The end-of-the-day crowds were scurrying in the directions of street-cars and elevated roads.

Irene said: "You're going south? I'm sorry. I've got an errand. If you don't mind, I'll just say good-bye here. It has been nice seeing you, Gertrude. Say hello to Fred for me, and to your mother if she remembers me. Good-bye."

She had wanted to be free of the other woman, to be alone; for she was still sore and angry.

What right, she kept demanding of herself, had Clare Kendry to expose her, or even Gertrude Martin, to such humiliation, such downright insult?

And all the while, on the rushing ride out to her father's house, Irene Redfield was trying to understand the look on Clare's face as she had said good-bye. Partly mocking, it had seemed, and partly menacing. And something else for which she could find no name. For an instant a recrudescence of that sensation of fear which she had had while looking into Clare's eyes that afternoon touched her. A slight shiver ran over her.

"It's nothing," she told herself. "Just somebody walking over my grave, as the children say." She tried a tiny laugh and was annoyed to find that it was close to tears.

What a state she had allowed that horrible Bellew to get her into!

And late that night, even, long after the last guest had gone and the old house was quiet, she stood at her window frowning out into the dark rain and puzzling again over that look on Clare's incredibly beautiful face. She couldn't, however, come to any conclusion about its meaning, try as she might. It was unfathomable, utterly beyond any experience or comprehension of hers.

She turned away from the window, at last, with a still deeper frown. Why, after all, worry about Clare Kendry? She was well able to take care of herself, had always been able. And there were, for Irene, other things, more personal and more important to worry about.

Besides, her reason told her, she had only herself to blame for her disagreeable afternoon and its attendant fears and questions. She ought never to have gone.

Four

The next morning, the day of her departure for New York, had brought a letter, which, at first glance, she had instinctively known came from Clare Kendry, though she couldn't remember ever having had a letter from her before. Ripping it open and looking at the signature, she saw that she had been right in her guess. She wouldn't, she told herself, read it. She hadn't the time. And, besides, she had no wish to be reminded of the afternoon before. As it was, she felt none too fresh for her journey; she had had a wretched night. And all because of Clare's innate lack of consideration for the feelings of others.

But she did read it. After father and friends had waved good-bye, and she was being hurled eastward, she became possessed of an uncontrollable curiosity to see what Clare had said about yesterday. For what, she asked, as she took it out of her bag and opened it, could she, what could anyone, say about a thing like that?

Clare Kendry had said:

'Rene Dear:

However am I to thank you for your visit? I know you are feeling that under the circumstances I ought not to have asked you to come, or, rather, insisted. But if you could know how glad, how excitingly happy, I was to meet you and how I ached to see more of you (to see everybody and couldn't), you would understand my wanting to see you again, and maybe forgive me a little.

My love to you always and always and to your dear father, and all my poor thanks.

CLARE

And there was a postscript which said:

It may be, 'Rene dear, it may just be, that, after all, your way may be the wiser and infinitely happier one. I'm not sure just now. At least not so sure as I have been.

C.

But the letter hadn't conciliated Irene. Her indignation was not lessened by Clare's flattering reference to her wiseness. As if, she thought wrathfully, anything could take away the humiliation, or any part of it, of what she had gone through yesterday afternoon for Clare Kendry.

With an unusual methodicalness she tore the offending letter into tiny ragged squares that fluttered down and made a small heap in her black *crêpe de Chine* lap. The destruction completed, she gathered them up, rose, and moved to the train's end. Standing there, she dropped them over the railing and watched them scatter, on tracks, on cinders, on forlorn grass, in rills of dirty water.

And that, she told herself, was that. The chances were one in a million that she would ever again lay eyes on Clare Kendry. If, however, that millionth chance should turn up, she had only to turn away her eyes, to refuse her recognition.

She dropped Clare out of her mind and turned her thoughts to her own affairs. To home, to the boys, to Brian. Brian, who in the morning would be waiting for her in the great clamourous station. She hoped that he had been comfortable and not too lonely without her and the boys. Not so lonely that that old, queer, unhappy restlessness had begun again within him; that craving for some place strange and different, which at the beginning of her marriage she had had to make such strenuous efforts to repress, and which yet faintly alarmed her, though it now sprang up at gradually lessening intervals.

Part Two

Re-Encounter

One

Such were Irene Redfield's memories as she sat there in her room, a flood of October sun-light streaming in upon her, holding that second letter of Clare Kendry's.

Laying it aside, she regarded with an astonishment that had in it a mild degree of amusement the violence of the feelings which is stirred in her.

It wasn't the great measure of anger that surprised and slightly amused her. That, she was certain, was justified and reasonable, as was the fact that it could hold, still strong and unabated, across the stretch of two years' time entirely removed from any sight or sound of John Bellew, or of Clare. That even at this remote date the memory of the man's words and manner had power to set her hands to trembling and to send the blood pounding against her temples did not seem to her extraordinary. But that she should retain that dim sense of fear, of panic, was surprising, silly.

That Clare should have written, should, even all things considered, have expressed a desire to see her again, did not so much amaze her. To count as nothing the annoyances, the bitterness, or the suffering of others, that was Clare.

Well—Irene's shoulders went up—one thing was sure: that she needn't, and didn't intend to, lay herself open to any repetition of a humiliation as galling and outrageous as that which, for Clare Kendry's sake, she had borne "that time in Chicago." Once was enough.

If, at the time of choosing, Clare hadn't precisely reckoned the cost, she had, nevertheless, no right to expect others to help make up the reckoning. The trouble with Clare was, not only that she wanted to have her cake and eat it too, but that she wanted to nibble at the cakes of other folk as well.

Irene Redfield found it hard to sympathize with this new tenderness, this avowed yearning of Clare's for "my own people."

The letter which she just put out of her hand was, to her taste, a bit too lavish in its wordiness, a shade too unreserved in the manner of its expression. It roused again that old suspicion that Clare was acting, not consciously, perhaps—that is, not too consciously—but, none the less, acting. Nor was Irene inclined to excuse what she termed Clare's downright selfishness.

And mingled with her disbelief and resentment was another feeling, a question. Why hadn't she spoken that day? Why, in the face of Bellew's ignorant hate and aversion, had she concealed her own origin? Why had she allowed him to make his assertions and express his misconceptions undisputed? Why, simply because of Clare Kendry, who had exposed her to such torment, had she failed to take up the defence of the race to which she belonged?

Irene asked these questions, felt them. They were, however, merely rhetorical, as she herself was well aware. She knew their answers, every one, and it was the same for them all. The irony of it! She couldn't betray Clare, couldn't even run the risk of appearing to defend a people that were being maligned, for fear that that defence might in some infinitesimal degree lead the way to final discovery of her secret. She had to Clare Kendry a duty. She was bound to her by those very ties of race, which, for all her repudiation of them, Clare had been unable to completely sever.

And it wasn't, as Irene knew, that Clare cared at all about the race or what was to become of it. She didn't. Or that she had for any of its members great, or even real, affection, though she professed undying gratitude for the small kindnesses which the Westover family had shown her when she was a child. Irene doubted the genuineness of it, seeing herself only as a means to an end where Clare was concerned. Nor could it be said that she had even the slight artistic or sociological interest in the race that some members of other races displayed. She hadn't. No, Clare Kendry cared nothing for the race. She only belonged to it.

"Not another damned thing!" Irene declared aloud as she drew a fragile stocking over a pale beige-coloured foot.

"Aha! Swearing again, are you, madam? Caught you in the act that time."

Brian Redfield had come into the room in that noiseless way which, in spite of the years of their life together, still had the power to disconcert her. He stood looking down on her with that amused smile of his, which was just the faintest bit supercilious and yet was somehow very becoming to him.

Hastily Irene pulled on the other stocking and slipped her feet into the slippers besides her chair.

"And what brought on this particular outburst of profanity? That is, if an indulgent but perturbed husband may inquire. The mother of sons too! The times, alas, the times!"

"I've had this letter," Irene told him. "And I'm sure that anybody'll admit it's enough to make a saint swear. The nerve of her!"

She passed the letter to him, and in the act made a little mental frown. For, with a nicety of perception, she saw that she was doing it instead of answering his question with words, so that he might be occupied while she hurried through her dressing. For she was late again, and Brian, she well knew, detested that. Why, oh why, could't she ever manage to be on time? Brian had been up for ages, had made some calls for all she knew, besides having taken the boys downtown to school. And she wasn't dressed yet; had only begun. Damn Clare! This morning it was her fault.

Brian sat down and bent his head over the letter, puckering his brows slightly in his effort to make out Clare's scrawl.

Irene, who had risen and was standing before the mirror, ran a comb through her black hair, then tossed her head with a light characteristic gesture, in order to disarrange a little the set locks. She touched a powder-puff to her warm olive skin, and then put on her frock with a motion so hasty that it was with some difficulty properly adjusted. At last she was ready, though she didn't immediately say so, but stood, instead, looking with a sort of curious detachment at her husband across the room.

Brian, she was thinking, was extremely good-looking. Not, of course, pretty or effeminate; the slight irregularity of his nose saved him from the prettiness, and the rather marked heaviness of his chin saved him from the effeminacy. But he was, in a pleasant masculine way, rather handsome. And yet, wouldn't he, perhaps, have been merely ordinarily good-looking but for the richness, the beauty of his skin, which was of an exquisitely fine texture and deep copper colour.

He looked up and said: "Clare? That must be the girl you told me about meeting the last time you were out home. The one you went to tea with?"

Irene's answer to that was an inclination of the head.

"I'm ready," she said.

They were going downstairs, Brian deftly, unnecessarily, piloting her round the two short curved steps, just before the centre landing.

"You're not," he asked, "going to see her?"

His words, however, were in reality not a question, but, as Irene was aware, an admonition.

Her front teeth just touched. She spoke through them, and her tones held a thin sarcasm. "Brian, darling, I'm really not such an idiot that I don't realize that if a man calls me a nigger, it's his fault the first time, but mine if he has the opportunity to do it again."

They went into the dining-room. He drew back her chair and she sat down behind the fat-bellied German coffee-pot, which sent out its morning fragrance, mingled with the smell of crisp toast and savoury bacon, in the distance. With his long, nervous fingers he picked up the morning paper from his own chair and sat down.

Zulena, a small mahogany-coloured creature, brought in the grapefruit.

They took up their spoons.

Out of the silence Brian spoke. Blandly. "My dear, you misunderstand me entirely. I simply meant that I hope you're not going to let her pester you. She will, you know, if you give her half a chance and she's anything at all like your description of her. Anyway, they always do. Besides," he corrected, "the man, her husband, didn't call you a nigger. There's a difference, you know."

"No, certainly he didn't. Not actually. He couldn't, not very well, since he didn't know. But he would have. It amounts to the same thing. And I'm sure it was just as unpleasant."

"U-mm, I don't know. But it seems to me," he pointed out, "that you, my dear, had all the advantage. You knew what his opinion of you was, while he—well, 'twas ever thus. We know, always have. They don't. Not quite. It has, you will admit, its humorous side, and, sometimes, its conveniences."

She poured the coffee.

"I can't see it. I'm going to write Clare. Today, if I can find a minute. It's a thing we might as well settle definitely, and immediately. Curious, isn't it, that knowing, as she does, his unqualified attitude, she still—"

Brian interrupted: "It's always that way. Never known it to fail. Remember Albert Hammond, how he used to be for ever haunting Seventh Avenue, and Lenox Aveune, and the dancing-places, until some 'shine' took a shot at him for casting an eye towards his 'sheba?' They always come back. I've seen it happen time and time again."

"But why?" Irene wanted to know. "Why?"

"If I knew that, I'd know what race is."

"But wouldn't you think that having got the thing, or things, they were after, and at such risk, they'd be satisfied? Or afraid?"

"Yes," Brian agreed, "you certainly would think so. But, the fact remains, they aren't. Not satisfied, I mean. I think they're scared enough most of the time, when they give way to the urge and slip back. Not scared enough to stop them, though. Why, the good God only knows."

Irene leaned forward, speaking, she was aware, with a vehemence absolutely unnecessary, but which she could not control.

"Well, Clare can just count me out. I've no intention of being the link between her and her poorer darker brethren. After that scene in Chicago too! To calmly expect me—" She stopped short, suddenly too wrathful for words.

"Quite right. The only sensible thing to do. Ler her miss you. It's an unhealthy business, the whole affair. Always is."

Irene nodded. "More coffee," she offered.

"Thanks, no." He took up his paper again, spreading it open with a little rattling noise.

Zulena came in bringing more toast. Brian took a slice and bit into it with that audible crunching sound that Irene disliked so intensely, and turned back to his paper.

She said: "It's funny about 'passing.' We disapprove of it and at the same time condone it. It excites our contempt and yet we rather admire it. We shy away from it with an odd kind of revulsion, but we protect it."

"Instinct of the race to survive and expand."

"Rot! Everything can't be explained by some general biological phrase."

"Absolutely everything can. Look at the so-called whites, who've left bastards all over the known earth. Same thing in them. Instinct of the race to survive and expand."

With that Irene didn't at all agree, but many arguments in the past had taught her the futility of attempting to combat Brian on ground where he was more nearly at home than she. Ignoring his unqualified assertion, she slid away from the subject entirely.

"I wonder," she asked, "if you'll have time to run me down to the printing-office. It's on a Hundred and Sixteenth Street. I've got to see about some handbills and some more tickets for the dance."

"Yes, of course. How's it going? Everything all set?"

"Ye-es. I guess so. The boxes are all sold and nearly all the first batch of tickets. And we expect to take in almost as much again at the door. Then, there's all that cake to sell. It's a terrible lot of work, though."

"I'll bet it is. Uplifting the brother's no easy job. I'm as busy as a cat with fleas, myself." And over his face there came a shadow. "Lord! how I hate sick people, and their stupid, meddling families, and smelly, dirty rooms, and climbing filthy steps in dark hallways."

"Surely," Irene began, fighting back the fear and irritation that she felt, "surely—"

Her husband silenced her, saying sharply: "Let's not talk about it, please." And immediately, in his usual, slightly mocking tone he asked: "Are you ready to go now? I haven't a great deal of time to wait."

He got up. She followed him out into the hall without replying. He picked up his soft brown hat from the small table and stood a moment whirling it round on his long tea-coloured fingers.

Irene, watching him, was thinking: "It isn't fair, it isn't fair." After all these years to still blame her like this. Hadn't his success proved that she'd been right in insisting that he stick to his profession right there in New York? Couldn't he see, even now, that it *had* been best? Not for her, oh no, not for her—she had never really considered herself—but for him and the boys. Was she never to be free of it, that fear which crouched, always, deep down within her, stealing away the sense of security, the feeling of permanence, from the life which she had so admirably arranged for them all, and desired so ardently to have remain as it was? That strange, and to her fantastic, notion of Brian's of going off to Brazil, which, though unmentioned, yet lived within him; how it frightened her, and—yes, angered her!

"Well?" he asked lightly.

"I'll just get my things. One minute," she promised and turned upstairs.

Her voice had been even and her step was firm, but in her there was no slackening of the agitation, of the alarms, which Brian's expression of discontent had raised. He had never spoken of his desire since that long-ago time of storm and strain, of hateful and nearly disastrous quarrelling, when she had so firmly opposed him, so sensibly pointed out its utter impossibility and its probable consequences to her and the boys, and had even hinted at a dissolution of their marriage in the event of his persistence in his idea. No, there had been, in all the years that they had lived together since then, no other talk of it, no more than there had been any other quarrelling or any other threats. But because, so she insisted, the bond of flesh and spirit between them was so strong, she knew, had always known, that his dissatisfaction had continued, as had his dislike and disgust for his profession and his country.

A feeling of uneasiness stole upon her at the inconceivable suspicion that she might have been wrong in her estimate of her husband's character. But she squirmed away from it. Impossible! She couldn't have been wrong. Everything proved that she had been right. More than right, if such a

thing could be. And all, she assured herself, because she understood him so well, because she had, actually, a special talent for understanding him. It was, as she saw it, the one thing that had been the basis of the success which she had made of a marriage that had threatened to fail. She knew him as well as he knew himself, or better.

Then why worry? The thing, this discontent which had exploded into words, would surely die, flicker out, at last. True, she had in the past often been tempted to believe that it had died, only to become conscious, in some instinctive, subtle way, that she had been merely deceiving herself for a while and that it still lived. But it *would* die. Of that she was certian. She had only to direct and guide her man, to keep him going in the right direction.

She put on her coat and adjusted her hat.

Yes, it would die, as long ago she had made up her mind that it should. But in the meantime, while it was still living and still had the power to flare up and alarm her, it would have to be banked, smothered, and something offered in its stead. She would have to make some plan, some decision, at once. She frowned, for it annoyed her intensely. For, though temporary, it would be important and perhaps disturbing. Irene didn't like changes, particularly changes that affected her smooth routine of her household. Well, it couldn't be helped. Something would have to be done. And immediately.

She took up her purse and drawing on her gloves, ran down the steps and out through the door which Brian held open for her and stepped into the waiting car.

"You know," she said, settling herself into the seat beside him, "I'm awfully glad to get his minute alone with you. It does seem that we're always so busy—I do hate that—but what can we do? I've had something on my mind for ever so long, something that needs talking over and really serious consideration."

The car's engine rumbled as it moved out from the kerb and into the scant traffic of the street under Brian's expert guidance.

She studied his profile.

They turned into Seventh Avenue. Then he said: "Well, let's have it. No time like the present for the settling of weighty matters."

"It's about Junior. I wonder if he isn't going too fast in school? We do forget that he's not eleven yet. Surely it can't be good for him to—well, if he is, I mean. Going too fast, you know. Of course, you know more about these things than I do. You're better able to judge. That is, if you've noticed or thought about it at all."

"I do wish, Irene, you wouldn't be for ever fretting about those kids. They're all right. Perfectly all right. Good, strong, healthy boys, especially Junior. Most especially Junior."

"We-ll, I s'pose you're right. You're expected to know about things like that, and I'm sure you wouldn't make a mistake about your own boy." (Now, why had she said that?) "But that isn't all. I'm terribly afraid he's picked up some queer ideas about things—some things—from the older boys, you know."

Her manner was consciously light. Apparently she was intent on the maze of traffic, but she was still watching Brian's face closely. On it was a peculiar expression. Was it, could it possibly be, a mixture of scorn and distaste?

"Queer ideas?" he repeated. "D'you mean ideas about sex, Irene?"

"Ye-es. Not quite nice ones. Dreadful jokes, and things like that."

"Oh, I see," he threw at her. For a while there was silence between them. After a moment he demanded bluntly: "Well, what of it? If sex isn't a joke, what is it? And what is a joke?"

"As you please, Brian. He's your son, you know." Her voice was clear, level, disapproving.

"Exactly! And you're trying to make a molly-coddle out of him. Well, just let me tell you, I won't have it. And you needn't think I'm going to let you change him to some nice kindergarten kind of a school because he's getting a little necessary education. I won't! He'll stay right where he is. The sooner and the more he learns about sex, the better for him. And most certainly if he learns that it's a grand joke, the greatest in the world. It'll keep him from lots of disappointments later on."

Irene didn't answer.

They reached the printing-shop. She got out, emphatically slamming the car's door behind her. There was a piercing agony of misery in her heart. She hadn't intended to behave like this, but her extreme resentment at his attitude, the sense of having been wilfully misunderstood and reproved, drove her to fury.

Inside the shop, she stilled the trembling of her lips and drove back her rising anger. Her business transacted, she came back to the car in a chastened mood. But against the armour of Brian's stubborn silence she heard herself saying in a calm, metallic voice: "I don't belive I'll go back just now. I've remembered that I've got to do something about getting something decent to wear. I haven't a rag that's fit to be seen. I'll take the bus downtown."

Brian merely doffed his hat in that maddening polite way which so successfully curbed and yet revealed his temper.

"Good-bye," she said bitingly. "Thanks for the lift," and turned towards the avenue.

What, she wondered contritely, was she to do next? she was vexed with herself for having chosen, as it had turned out, so clumsy an opening for what she had intended to suggest: some European school for Junior next year, and Brian to

take him over. If she had been able to present her plan, and he had accepted it, as she was sure that he would have done, with other more favourable opening methods, he would have had that to look forward to as a break in the easy monotony that seemed, for some reason she was wholly unable to grasp, so hateful to him.

She was even more vexed at her own explosion of anger. What could have got into her to give way to it in such a moment?

Gradually her mood passed. She drew back from the failure of her first attempt at substitution, not so much discouraged as disappointed and ashamed. It might be, she reflected, that, in addition to her ill-timed loss of temper, she had been too hasty in her eagerness to distract him, had rushed too closely on the heels of his outburst, and had thus aroused his suspicions and his obstinacy. She had but to wait. Another more appropriate time would come, tomorrow, next week, next month. It wasn't now, as it had been once, that she was afraid that he would throw everything aside and rush off to that remote place of his heart's desire. He wouldn't, she knew. He was fond of her, loved her, in his slightly undemonstrative way.

And there were the boys.

It was only that she wanted him to be happy, resenting, however, his inability to be so with things as they were, and never acknowledging that though she did want him to be happy, it was only in her own way and by some plan of hers for him that she truly desired him to be so. Nor did she admit that all other plans, all other ways, she regarded as menaces, more or less indirect, to that security of place and substance which she insisted upon for her sons and in a lesser degree for herself.

Two

Five days had gone by since Clare Kendry's appealing letter. Irene Redfield had not replied to it. Nor had she had any other word from Clare.

She had not carried out her first intention of writing at once because on going back to the letter for Clare's address, she had come upon something which, in the rigour of her determination to maintain unbroken between them the wall that Clare had raised, she had forgotten, or not fully noted. It was the fact that Clare had requested her to direct her answer to the post officer's general delivery.

That had angered Irene, and increased her disdain and contempt for the other.

Tearing the letter across, she had flung it into the scarp-basket. It wasn't so much Clare's carefulness and her desire for secrecy in their relations—Irene understood the need for that—as that Clare should have doubted her discretion, implied that she might not be cautious in the wording of her reply and the choice of a posting-box. Having always had complete confidence in her own good judgment and tact, Irene couldn't bear to have anyone seem to question them. Certainly not Clare Kendry.

In another, calmer moment she decided that it was, after all, better to answer nothing, to explain nothing, to refuse nothing; to dispose of the matter simply by not writing at all. Clare, of whom it couldn't be said that she was stupid, would not mistake the implication of that silence. She might—and Irene was sure that she would—choose to ignore it and write again, but that didn't matter. The whole thing would be very easy. The basket for all letters, silence for their answers.

Most likely she and Clare would never meet again. Well, she, for one, could endure that. Since childhood their lives had never really touched. Actually they were strangers. Strangers in their ways and means of living. Strangers in their desires and ambitions. Strangers even in their racial consciousness. Between them the barrier was just as high, just as broad, and just as firm as if in Clare did not run that strain of black blood. In truth, it was higher, broader, and firmer; because for her there were perils, not known, or imagined, by those others who had no such secrets to alarm or endanger them.

The day was getting on toward evening. It was past the middle of October. There had been a week of cold rain, drenching the rotting leaves which had fallen from the poor trees that lined the street on which the Redfields' house was located, and sending a damp air of penetrating chill into the house, with a hint of cold days to come. In Irene's room a low fire was burning. Outside, only a dull grey light was left of the day. Inside, lamps had already been lighted.

From the floor above there was the sound of young voices. Sometimes Junior's serious and positive; again, Ted's deceptively gracious one. Often there was laughter, or the noise of commotion, tussling, or toys being slammed down.

Junior, tall for his age, was almost incredibly like his father in feature and colouring; but his temperament was hers, practical and determined, rather than Brian's. Ted, speculative and withdrawn, was, apparently, less positive in his ideas and desires. About him there was a deceiving air of candour that was, Irene knew, like his father's show of reasonable acquiescence. If, for the time being, and with a charming appearance of artlessness, he submitted to the force of superior strength, or some other immovable condition or circumstance, it was because of his intense dislike of scenes and unpleasant argument. Brian over again.

Gradually Irene's thought slipped away from Junior and Ted, to become wholly absorbed in their father.

The old fear, with strength increased, the fear for the future, had again laid its hand on her. And, try as she might, she could not shake it off. It was as if she had admitted to herself that against that easy surface of her husband's concordance with her wishes, which had, since the war had given him back to her physically unimpaired, covered an increasing inclination to tear himself and his possessions loose from their proper setting, she was helpless.

The chagrin which she had felt at her first failure to subvert this latest manifestation of his discontent had receded, leaving in its wake an uneasy depression. Were all her efforts, all her labours, to make up to him that one loss, all her silent striving to prove to him that her way had been best, all her ministrations to him, all her outward sinking of self, to count for nothing in some unperceived sudden moment? And if so, what, then, would be the consequences to the boys? To her? To Brian himself? Endless searching had brought no answer to these questions. There was only an intense weariness from their shuttle-like procession in her brain.

The noise and commotion from above grew increasingly louder. Irene was about to go to the stairway and request the boys to be quieter in their play when she heard the doorbell ringing.

Now, who was that likely to be? She listened to Zulena's heels, faintly tapping on their way to the door, then to the shifting sound of her feet on the steps, then to her light knock on the bedroom door.

"Yes. Come in," Irene told her.

Zulena stood in the doorway. She said: "Someone to see you, Mrs. Redfield." Her tone was discreetly regretful, as if to convey that she was reluctant to disturb her mistress at that hour, and for a stranger. "A Mrs. Bellew."

Clare!

"Oh dear! Tell her, Zulena," Irene began, "that I can't— No. I'll see her. Please bring her up here."

She heard Zulena pass down the hall, down the stairs, then stood up, smoothing out the tumbled green and ivory draperies of her dress with light stroking pats. At the mirror she dusted a little powder on her nose and brushed out her hair.

She meant to tell Clare Kendry at once, and definitely, that it was of no use, her coming, that she couldn't be responsible, that she'd talked it over with Brian, who had agreed with her that it was wiser, for Clare's own sake, to refrain—

But that was as far as she got in her rehearsal. For Clare had come softly into the room without knocking, and before Irene could greet her, had dropped a kiss on her dark curls.

Looking at the woman before her, Irene Redfield had a sudden inexplicable onrush of affectionate feeling. Reaching out, she grasped Clare's two hands in her own and cried with something like awe in her voice: "Dear God! But aren't you lovely, Clare!"

Clare tossed that aside. Like the furs and small blue hat which she threw on the bed before seating herself slantwise in Irene's favourite chair, with one foot curled under her.

"Didn't you mean to answer my letter, 'Rene?" she asked gravely.

Irene looked away. She had that uncomfortable feeling that one has when one has not been wholly kind or wholly true.

Clare went on: "Every day I went to that nasty little post-office place. I'm sure they were all beginning to think that I'd been carrying on an illicit love-affair and that the man had thrown me over. Every morning the same answer: 'Nothing for you.' I got into an awful fright, thinking that something might have happened to your letter, or to mine. And half the nights I would lie awake looking out at the watery stars—hopeless things, the stars—worrying and wondering. But at last it soaked in, that you hadn't written and didn't intend to. And then—well, as soon as ever I'd seen Jack off for Florida, I came straight here. And now, 'Rene, please tell me quite frankly why you didn't answer my letter."

"Because, you see—" Irene broke off and kept Clare waiting while she lit a cigarette, blew out the match, and dropped it into a tray. She was trying to collect her arguments, for some sixth sense warned her that it was going to be harder than she thought to convince Clare Kendry of the folly of Harlem for her. Finally she proceeded: "I can't help thinking that you ought not to come up here, ought not to run the risk of knowing Negroes."

"You mean you don't want me, 'Rene?"

Irene hadn't supposed that anyone could look so hurt. She said, quite gently, "No Clare, it's not that. But even you must see that it's terribly foolish, and not just the right thing."

The tinkle of Clare's laugh rang out, while she passed her hands over the bright sweep of her hair. "Oh, 'Rene!" she cried, "you're priceless! And you haven't changed a bit. The right thing!" Leaning forward, she looked curiously into Irene's disapproving brown eyes. "You don't, you really can't mean exactly that! Nobody could. It's simply unbelievable."

Irene was on her feet before she realized that she had risen. "What I really mean," she retorted, "is that it's dangerous and that you ought not to run such silly risks. No one ought to. You least of all."

Her voice was brittle. For into her mind had come a thought, strange and irrelevant, a suspicion, that had surprised and shocked her and driven her to her feet. It was that in spite of her determined selfishness the woman before her was yet capable of heights and depths of feeling that she, Irene Redfield, had never known. Indeed, never cared to know. The thought, the suspicion, was gone as quickly as it had come.

Clare said: "Oh, me!"

Irene touched her arm caressingly, as if in contrition for that flashing thought. "Yes, Clare, you. It's not safe. Not safe at all."

"Safe!"

It seemed to Irene that Clare had snapped her teeth down on the word and then flung it from her. And for another flying second she had that suspicion of Clare's ability for a quality of feeling that was to her strange, and even repugnant. She was aware, too, of a dim premonition of some impending disaster. It was as if Clare Kendry had said to her, for whom safety, security, were all-important: "Safe! Damn being safe!" and mean it.

With a gesture of impatience she sat down. In a voice of cool formality, she said: "Brian and I have talked the whole thing over carefully and decided that it isn't wise. He says it's always a dangerous business, this coming back. He's seen more than one come to grief because of it. And, Clare, considering everything—Mr. Bellew's attitude and all that—don't you think you ought to be as careful as you can?"

Clare's deep voice broke the small silence that had followed Irene's speech. She said, speaking almost plaintively: "I ought to have known. It's Jack. I don't blame you for being angry, though I must say you behaved beautifully that day. But I did think you'd understand, 'Rene. It was that, partly, that has made me want to see other people. It just swooped down and changed everything. If it hadn't been for that, I'd have gone on to the end, never seeing any of you. But that did something to me, and I've been so lonely since! You can't know. Not close to a single soul. Never anyone to really talk to."

Irene pressed out her cigarette. While doing so, she saw again the vision of Clare Kendry staring disdainfully down at the face of her father, and thought that it would be like that that she would look at her husband if he lay dead before her.

Her own resentment was swept aside and her voice held an accent of pity as she exclaimed: "Why, Clare! I didn't know. Forgive me. I feel like seven beasts. It was stupid of me not to realize."

"No. Not at all. You couldn't. Nobody, none of you, could," Clare moaned. The black eyes filled with tears that ran down her cheeks and spilled into her lap, ruining the priceless velvet of her dress. Her long hands were a little uplifted and clasped tightly together. Her effort to speak moderately was obvious, but not successful. "How could you know? How could you? You're free. You're happy. And," with faint derision, "safe."

Irene passed over that touch of derision, for the poignant rebellion of the other's words had brought the tears to her own eyes, though she didn't allow them to fall. The truth was that she knew weeping did not become her. Few women, she imagined, wept as attractively as Clare. "I'm beginning to believe," she murmured, "that no one is ever completely happy, or free, or safe."

"Well, then, what does it matter? One risk more or less, if we're not safe anyway, if even you're not, it can't make all the difference in the world. It can't to me. Besides, I'm used to risks. And this isn't such a big one as you're trying to make it."

"Oh, but it is. And it can make all the difference in the world. There's your little girl, Clare. Think of the consequences to her."

Clare's face took on a startled look, as though she were totally unprepared for this new weapon with which Irene had assailed her. Seconds passed, during which she sat with stricken eyes and compressed lips. "I think," she said at last, "that being a mother is the cruellest thing in the world." Her clasped hands swayed forward and back again, and her scarlet mouth trembled irrepressibly.

"Yes," Irene softly agreed. For a moment she was unable to say more, so accurately had Clare put into words that which, not so definitely defined, was so often in her own heart of late. At the same time she was conscious that here, to her hand, was a reason which could not be lightly brushed aside. "Yes," she repeated, "and the most responsible, Clare. We mothers are all responsible for the security and happiness of our children. Think of what it would mean to your Margery if Mr. Bellew should find out. You'd probably lose her. And even if you didn't, nothing that concerned her would ever be the same again. He'd never forget that she had Negro blood. And if she should learn—Well, I believe that after twelve it is too late to learn a thing like that. She'd never forgive you. You may be used to risks, but this one you mustn't take, Clare. It's selfish whim, an unnecessary and—"

"Yes, Zulena, what is it?" she inquired, a trifle tartly, of the servant who had silently materialized in the doorway.

"The telephone's for you, Mrs. Redfield. It's Mr. Wentworth."

"All right. Thank you. I'll take it here." And, with a muttered apology to Clare, she took up the instrument.

"Hello. . . . Yes, Hugh. . . . Oh, quite. . . . And you? . . . I'm sorry, every single thing's gone. . . . Oh, too bad. . . . Ye-es, I s'pose you could. Not very pleasant, though. . . . Yes, of course, in a pinch everything goes. . . . Wait! I've got it! I'll change mine with whoever's next to you, and you can have that. . . . No. . . . I mean it. . . . I'll be so busy I shan't know whether I'm sitting or standing. . . . As long as Brian has a place to drop down now and then. . . . Not a single soul. . . . No, don't. . . . That's nice. . . . My love to Bianca. . . . I'll see to it right away and call you back. . . . Good-bye."

She hung up and turned back to Clare, a little frown on her softly chiselled features. "It's the N.W.L. dance," she explained, "the Negro Welfare League, you know. I'm on the ticket committee, or, rather, I *am* the committee. Thank heaven it comes off tomorrow night and doesn't happen again for a year. I'm about crazy, and now I've got to persuade somebody to change boxes with me."

"That wasn't," Clare asked, "Hugh Wentworth? Not *the* Hugh Wentworth?"

Irene inclined her head. On her face was a tiny triumphant smile. "Yes, *the* Hugh Wentworth. D'you know him?"

"No. How should I? But I do know about him. And I've read a book or two of his."

"Awfully good, aren't they?"

U-umm, I s'pose so. Sort of contemptuous, I thought. As if he more or less despised everything and everybody."

"I shouldn't be a bit surprised if he did. Still he's about earned the right to. Lived on the edges of nowhere in at least three continents. Been through every danger in all kinds of savage places. It's no wonder he thinks the rest of us are a lazy self-pampering lot. Hugh's a dear, though, generous as one of the twelve disciples; give you the shirt off his back. Bianca—that's his wife—is nice too."

"And he's coming up here to your dance?"

Irene asked why not.

"It seems rather curious, a man like that, going to a Negro dance."

This, Irene told her, was the year 1927 in the city of New York, and hundreds of white people of Hugh Wentworth's type came to affairs in Harlem, more all the time. So many that Brian had said: "Pretty soon the coloured people won't be allowed in at all, or will have to sit in Jim Crowed sections."

"What do they come for?"

"Same reason you're here, to see Negroes."

"But why?"

"Various motives," Irene explained. "A few purely and frankly to enjoy themselves. Others to get material to turn into shekels. More, to gaze on these great and near great while they gaze on the Negroes."

Clare clapped her hand. " 'Rene, suppose I come too! It sounds terribly interesting and amusing. And I don't see why I shouldn't."

Irene, who was regarding her through narrowed eyelids, had the same thought that she had had two years ago on the roof of the Drayton, that Clare Kendry was just a shade too good-looking. Her tone was on the edge of irony as she said: "You mean because so many other white people go?"

A pale rose-colour came into Clare's ivory cheeks. She lifted a hand in protest. "Don't be silly! Certainly not! I mean that in a crowd of that kind I shouldn't be noticed."

On the contrary, was Irene's opinion. It might be even doubly dangerous. Some friend or acquaintance of John Bellew or herself might see and recognize her.

At that, Clare laughed for a long time, little musical trills following one another in sequence after sequence. It was as if the thought of any friend of John Bellew's going to a Negro dance was to her the most amusing thing in the world.

"I don't think," she said, when she had done laughing, "we need worry about that."

Irene, however, wasn't so sure. But all her efforts to dissuade Clare were useless. To her, "You never can tell whom you're likely to meet there," Clare's rejoinder was: "I'll take my chance on getting by."

"Besides, you won't know a soul and I shall be too busy to look after you. You'll be bored stiff."

"I won't, I won't. If nobody asks me to dance, not even Dr. Redfield, I'll just sit and gaze on the great and the near great, too. Do, 'Rene, be polite and invite me."

Irene turned away from the caress of Clare's smile, saying promptly and positively: "I will not."

"I mean to go anyway," Clare retorted, and her voice was no less positive than Irene's.

"Oh, no. You couldn't possibly go there alone. It's a public thing. All sorts of people go, anybody who can pay a dollar, even ladies of easy virtue looking for trade. If you were to go there alone, you might be mistaken for one of them, and that wouldn't be too pleasant."

Clare laughed again. "Thanks. I never have been. It might be amusing. I'm warning you, 'Rene, that if you're not going to be nice and take me, I'll still be among those present. I suppose, my dollar's as good as anyone's."

"Oh, the dollar! Don't be a fool, Clare. I don't care where you go, or what you do. All I'm concerned with is the unpleasantness and possible danger which your going might incur, because of your situation. To put it frankly, I shouldn't like to be mixed up in any row of the kind." She had risen again as she spoke and was standing at the window lifting and spreading the small yellow chrysanthemums in the grey stone jar on the sill. Her hands shook slightly, for she was in a near rage of impatience and exasperation.

Clare's face looked strange, as if she wanted to cry again. One of her satin-covered feet swung restlessly back and forth. She said vehemently, violently almost: "Damn Jack! He keeps me out of everything. Everything I want. I could kill him! I expect I shall, some day."

"I wouldn't," Irene advised her, "you see, there's still capital punishment, in this state at least. And really, Clare, after everything's said, I can't see that you've a right to put all the blame on him. You've got to admit that there's his side to the thing. You didn't tell him you were coloured, so he's got no way of knowing about this hankering of yours after Negroes, or that it galls you to fury to hear them called niggers and black devils. As far as I can see, you'll just have to endure some things and give up others. As we've said before, everything must be paid for. Do, please, be reasonable."

But Clare, it was plain, had shut away reason as well as caution. She shook her head. "I can't, I can't," she said. "I would if I could, but I can't. You don't know, you can't realize how I want to see Negroes, to be with them again, to talk with them, to hear them laugh."

And in the look she gave Irene, there was something groping, and hopeless, and yet so absolutely determined that it was like an image of her futile searching and the firm resolution in Irene's own soul, and increased the feeling of doubt and compunction that had been growing within her about Clare Kendry.

"Oh, come if you want to. I s'pose you're right. Once can't do such a terrible lot of harm."

Pushing aside Clare's extravagant thanks, for immediately she was sorry that she had consented, she said briskly: "Should you like to come up and see my boys?"

"I'd love to."

They went up, Irene thinking that Brian would consider that she'd behaved like a spineless fool. And he would be right. She certainly had.

Clare was smiling. She stood in the doorway of the boys' playroom, her shadowy eyes looking down on Junior and Ted, who had sprung apart from their tussling. Junior's face had a funny look of resentment. Ted's was blank.

Clare said: "Please don't be cross. Of course, I know I've gone and spoiled everything. But maybe, if I promise not to get too much in the way, you'll let me come in, just the same."

"Sure, come in if you want to," Ted told her. "We can't stop you, you know." He smiled and made her a little bow and then turned away to a shelf that held his favorite books. Taking one down, he settled himself in a chair and began to read.

Junior said nothing, did nothing, merely stood there waiting.

"Get up, Ted! That's rude. This is Theodore, Mrs. Bellew. Please excuse his bad manners. He does know better. And this is Brian junior. Mrs. Bellew is an old friend of mother's. We used to play together when we were little girls."

Clare had gone and Brian had telephoned that he'd been detained and would have his dinner downtown. Irene was a little glad for that. She was going out later herself, and that meant she wouldn't, probably, see Brian until morning and so could put off for a few more hours speaking of Clare and the N.W.L. dance.

She was angry with herself and with Clare. But more with herself, for having permitted Clare to tease her into doing something that Brian had, all but expressly, asked her not to do. She didn't want him ruffled, not just then, not while he was possessed of that unreasonable restless feeling.

She was annoyed, too, because she was aware that she had consented to something which, if it went beyond the dance, would involve her in numerous petty inconveniences and evasions. And not only at home with Brian, but outside with friends and acquaintances. The disagreeable possibilities in connection with Clare Kendry's coming among them loomed before her in endless irritating array.

Clare, it seemed, still retained her ability to secure the thing that she wanted in the face of any opposition, and in utter disregard of the convenience and desire of others. About her there was some quality, hard and persistent, with the strength and endurance of rock, that would not be beaten or ignored. She couldn't, Irene thought, have had an entirely serene life. Not with that dark secret for ever crouching in the background of her consciousness. And yet she hadn't the air of a woman whose life had been touched by uncertainty of suffering. Pain, fear, and grief were things that left their mark on people. Even love, that exquisite torturing emotion, left its subtle traces on the countenance.

But Clare—she had remained almost what she had always been, an attractive, somewhat lonely child—selfish, willful, and disturbing.

Three

The things which Irene Redfield remembered afterward about the Negro Welfare League dance seemed, to her, unimportant and unrelated.

She remembered the not quite derisive smile with which Brian had cloaked his vexation when she informed him—oh, so apologetically—that she had promised to take Clare, and related the conversation of her visit.

She remembered her own little choked exclamation of admiration, when, on coming downstairs a few minutes later than she had intended, she had rushed into the living-room where Brain was waiting and had found Clare there too. Clare, exquisite, golden, fragrant, flaunting, in a stately gown of shining black taffeta, whose long, full skirt lay in graceful folds about her slim golden feet; her glistening hair drawn smoothly back into a small twist at the nape of her neck; her eyes sparkling like dark jewels. Irene, with her new rose-coloured chiffon frock ending at the knees, and her cropped curls, felt dowdy and commonplace. She regretted that she hadn't counselled Clare to wear something ordinary and inconspicuous. What on earth would Brian think of deliberate courting of attention? But if Clare Kendry's appearance had in it anything that was, to Brain Redfield, annoying or displeasing, the fact was not discernible to his wife as, with an uneasy feeling of guilt, she stood there looking into his face while Clare explained that she and he had made their own introductions, accompanying her words with a little deferential smile for Brian, and receiving in return one of his amused, slightly mocking smiles.

She remembered Clare's saying, as they sped northward: "You know, I feel exactly as I used to on the Sunday we went to the Christmas-tree celebration. I knew there was to be a

surprise for me and couldn't quite guess what it was to be. I am *so* excited. You can't possibly imagine! It's marvellous to be really on the way! I can hardly believe it!"

At her words and tone a chilly wave of scorn had crept through Irene. All those superlatives! She said, taking care to speak indifferently: "Well, maybe in some ways you will be surprised, more, probably, than you anticipate."

Brain, at the wheel, had thrown back: "And then again, she won't be so very surprised after all, for it'll no doubt be about what she expects. Like the Christmas-tree."

She remembered rushing around here and there, consulting with this person and that one, and now and then snatching a part of a dance with some man whose dancing she particularly liked.

She remembered catching glimpses of Clare in the whirling crowd, dancing, sometimes with a white man, more often with a Negro, frequently with Brian. Irene was glad that he was being nice to Clare, and glad that Clare was having the opportunity to discover that some coloured men were superior to some white men.

She remembered a conversation she had with Hugh Wentworth in a free half-hour when she had dropped into a chair in an emptied box and let her gaze wander over the bright crowd below.

Young men, old men, white men, black men; youthful women, older women, pink women, golden women; fat men, thin men, tall men, short men; stout women, slim women, stately women, small women moved by. An old nursery rhyme popped into her head. She turned to Wentworth, who had just taken a seat beside her, and recited it:

"Rich men, poor man,
Beggar man, thief,
Doctor, lawyer,
Indian chief."

"Yes," Wentworth said, "that's it. Everybody seems to be here and a few more. But what I'm trying to find out is the name, status, and race of the blonde beauty out of the fairy-tale. She's dancing with Ralph Hazelton at the moment. Nice study in contrasts, that."

It was. Clare fair and golden, like a sunlit day. Hazelton dark, with gleaming eyes, like a moonlight night.

"She's a girl I used to know a long time ago in Chicago. And she wanted especially to meet you."

"'S awfully good of her, I'm sure. And now, alas! the usual thing's happened. All these others, these—er—'gentlemen of colour' have driven a mere Nordic from her mind."

"Stuff!"

"'S a fact, and what happens to all the ladies of my superior race who're lured up here. Look at Bianca. Have I laid eyes on her tonight except in spots, here and there, being twirled about by some Ethiopian? I have not."

"But, Hugh, you've got to admit that the average coloured man is a better dancer than the average white man—that is, if the celebrities and 'butter and egg' men who find their way up here are fair specimens of white Terpsichorean art."

"Not having tripped the light fantastic with any of the males, I'm not in a position to argue the point. But I don't think it's merely that. 'S something else, some other attraction. They're always raving about the good looks of some Negro, preferably an unusually dark one. Take Hazelton there, for example. Dozens of women have declared him to be fascinatingly handsome. How about you, Irene? Do you think he's—er—ravishingly beautiful?"

"I do not! And I don't think the others do either. Not honestly, I mean. I think that what they feel is—well, a kind of emotional excitement. You know, the sort of thing you feel in the presence of something strange, and even, perhaps, a bit repugnant to you; something so different that it's really at the opposite end of the pole from all your accustomed notions of beauty."

"Damned if I don't think you're half-way right!"

"I'm sure I am. Completely. (Except, of course, when it's just patronizing kindness on their part.) And I know coloured girls who've experienced the same thing—the other way round, naturally."

"And the men? You don't subscribe to the general opinion about their reason for coming up here. Purely predatory. Or, do you?"

"N-no. More curious, I should say."

Wentworth, whose eyes were a clouded amber colour, had given her a long, searching look that was really a stare. He said: "All this is awfully interestin', Irene. We've got to have a long talk about it some time soon. There's your friend from Chicago, first time up here and all that. A case in point."

Irene's smile had only just lifted the corners of her painted lips. A match blazed in Wentworth's broad hands as he lighted her cigarette and his own, and flickered out before he asked: "Or isn't she?"

Her smile changed to a laugh. "Oh, Hugh! You're so clever. You usually know everything. Even how to tell the sheep from the goats. What do you think? Is she?"

He blew a long contemplative wreath of smoke. "Damned if I know! I'll be as sure as anything that I've learned the trick. And then in the next minute I'll find I couldn't pick some of 'em if my life depended on it."

"Well, don't let that worry you. Nobody can. Not by looking."

"Not by looking, eh? Meaning?"

"I'm afraid I can't explain. Not clearly. There are ways. But they're not definite or tangible."

"Feeling of kinship, or something like that?"

"Good heavens, no! Nobody has that, except for their in-laws."

"Right again! But go on about the sheep and the goats."

"Well, take my own experience with Dorothy Thompkins. I'd met her four or five times, in groups and crowds of people, before I knew she wasn't a Negro. One day I went to an awful tea, terribly dicty. Dorothy was there. We got talking. In less than five minutes, I knew she was 'fay.' Not from anything she did or said or anything in her appearance. Just—just something. A thing that couldn't be registered."

"Yes, I understand what you mean. Yet lots of people 'pass' all the time."

"Not on our side, Hugh. It's easy for a Negro to 'pass' for white. But I don't think it would be so simple for a white person to 'pass' for coloured."

"Never thought of that."

"No, you wouldn't. Why should you?"

He regarded her critically through mists of smoke. "Slippin' me, Irene?"

She said soberly: "Not you, Hugh. I'm too fond of you. And you're too sincere."

And she remembered that towards the end of the dance Brian had come to her and said: "I'll drop you first and then run Clare down." And that he had been doubtful of her discretion when she had explained to him that he wouldn't have to bother because she had asked Bianca Wentworth to take her down with them. Did she, he had asked, think it had been wise to tell them about Clare?

"I told them nothing," she said sharply, for she was unbearably tired, "except that she was at the Walsingham. It's on their way. And, really, I haven't thought anything about the wisdom of it, but now that I do, I'd say it's much better for them to take her than you."

"As you please. She's your friend, you know," he had answered, with a disclaiming shrug of his shoulders.

Except for these few unconnected things the dance faded to a blurred memory, its outlines mingling with those of other dances of its kind that she had attended in the past and would attend in the future.

Four

But undistinctive as the dance had seemed, it was, nevertheless, important. For it marked the beginning of a new factor in Irene Redfield's life, something that left its trace on all the future years of her existence. It was the beginning of a new friendship with Clare Kendry.

She came to them frequently after that. Always with a touching gladness that welled up and overflowed on all the Redfield household. Yet Irene could never be sure whether her comings were a joy or a vexation.

Certainly she was no trouble. She had not to be entertained, or even noticed—if anyone could ever avoid noticing Clare. If Irene happened to be out or occupied, Clare could very happily amuse herself with Ted and Junior, who had conceived for her an admiration that verged on adoration, especially Ted. Or, lacking the boys, she would descend to the kitchen and, with—to Irene—an exasperating childlike lack of perception, spend her visit in talk and merriment with Zulena and Sadie.

Irene, while secretly resenting these visits to the playroom and kitchen, for some obscure reason which she shied away from putting into words, never requested that Clare make an end of them, or hinted that she wouldn't have spoiled her own Margery so outrageously, nor been so friendly with white servants.

Brian looked on these things with the same tolerant amusement that marked his entire attitude toward Clare. Never since his faintly derisive surprise at Irene's information that she was to go with them the night of the dance, had he shown any disapproval of Clare's presence. On the other hand, it couldn't be said that her presence seemed to please him. It didn't annoy or disturb him, so far as Irene could judge. That was all.

Didn't he, she once asked him, think Clare was extraordinarily beautiful?

"No," he had answered. "That is, not particularly."

"Brain, you're fooling!"

"No, honestly. Maybe I'm fussy. I s'pose she'd be an unusually good-looking white woman. I like my ladies darker. Beside an A-number-one sheba, she simply hasn't got 'em."

Clare went, sometimes with Irene and Brian, to parties and dances, and on a few occasions when Irene hadn't been able or inclined to go out, she had gone alone with Brian to some bridge party or benefit dance.

Once in a while she came formally to dine with them. She wasn't, however, in spite of her poise and air of worldliness, the ideal dinner-party guest. Beyond the aesthetic pleasure one got from watching her, she contributed little, sitting for the most part silent, an odd dreaming look in her hypnotic eyes. Though she could for some purpose of her own—the desire to be included in some party being made up to go cabareting, or an invitation to a dance or a tea—talk fluently and entertainingly.

She was generally liked. She was so friendly and responsive, and so ready to press the sweet food of flattery on all. Nor did she object to appearing a bit pathetic and ill-used, so that people could feel sorry for her. And, no matter how often she came among them, she still remained someone apart, a little mysterious and strange, someone to wonder about and to admire and to pity.

Her visits were undecided and uncertain, being, as they were, dependent on the presence or absence of John Bellew in the city. But she did, once in a while, manage to steal uptown for an afternoon even when he was not away. As time went on without any apparent danger of discovery, even Irene ceased to be perturbed about the possibility of Clare's husband's stumbling on her racial identity.

The daughter, Margery, had been left in Switzerland in school, for Clare and Bellew would be going back in early spring. In March, Clare thought. "And how I do hate to think of it!" she would say, always with a suggestion of leashed rebellion; "but I can't see how I'm going to get out of it. Jack won't hear of my staying behind. If I could have just a couple of months more in New York, alone I mean, I'd be the happiest thing in the world."

"I imagine you'll be happy enough, once you get away," Irene told her one day when she was bewailing her approaching departure. "Remember, there's Margery. Think how glad you'll be to see her after all this time."

"Children aren't everything," was Clare Kendry's answer to that. "There are other things in the world, though I admit some people don't seem to suspect it." And she laughed, more, it seemed, at some secret joke of her own than at her words.

Irene replied: "You know you don't mean that, Clare. You're only trying to tease me. I know very well that I take being a mother rather seriously. I *am* wrapped up in my boys and the running of my house. I can't help it. And, really, I don't think it's anything to laugh at." And though she was aware of the slight primness in her words and attitude, she had neither power nor wish to efface it.

Clare, suddenly very sober and sweet, said: "You're right. It's no laughing matter. It's shameful of me to tease you, 'Rene. You are so good." And she reached out and gave Irene's hand an affectionate little squeeze. "Don't think," she added, "whatever happens, that I'll ever forget how good you've been to me."

"Nonsense!"

"Oh, but you have, you have. It's just that I haven't any proper morals or sense of duty, as you have, that makes me act as I do."

"Now you are talking nonsense."

"But it's true, 'Rene. Can't you realize that I'm not like you a bit? Why, to get the things I want badly enough, I'd do anything, hurt anybody, throw anything away. Really, 'Rene, I'm not safe." Her voice as well as the look on her face had a beseeching earnestness that made Irene vaguely uncomfortable.

She said: "I don't believe it. In the first place what you're saying is so utterly, so wickedly wrong. And as for your giving up things—" She stopped, at a loss for an acceptable term to express her opinion of Clare's "having" nature.

But Clare Kendry had begun to cry, audibly, with no effort at restraint, and for no reason that Irene could discover.

Part Three

Finale

One

The year was getting on towards its end. October, November had gone. December had come and brought with it a little snow and then a freeze and after that a thaw and some soft pleasant days that had in them a feeling of spring.

It wasn't, this mild weather, a bit Christmasy, Irene Redfield was thinking, as she turned out of Seventh Avenue into her own street. She didn't like it to be warm and springy when it should have been cold and crisp, or grey and cloudy as if snow was about to fall. The weather, like people, ought to enter into the spirit of the season. Here the holidays were almost upon them, and the streets through which she had come were streaked with rills of muddy water and the sun shone so warmly that children had taken off their hats and scarfs. It was all as soft, as like April, as possible. The kind of weather for Easter. Certainly not for Christmas.

Though, she admitted, reluctantly, she herself didn't feel the proper Christmas spirit this year, either. But that couldn't be helped, it seemed, any more than the weather. She was weary and depressed. And for all her trying, she couldn't be free of that dull, indefinite misery which with increasing tenaciousness had laid hold of her. The morning's aimless wandering through the teeming Harlem streets, long after she had ordered the flowers which had been her excuse for setting out, was but another effort to tear herself loose from it.

She went up the cream stone steps, into the house, and down to the kitchen. There were to be people in to tea. But that, she found, after a few words with Sadie and Zulena, need give her no concern. She was thankful. She didn't want to be bothered. She went upstairs and took off her things and got into bed.

She thought: "Bother those people coming to tea!"

She thought: "If I could only be sure that at bottom it's just Brazil."

She thought: "Whatever it is, if I only knew what it was, I could manage it."

Brian again. Unhappy, restless, withdrawn. And she, who had prided herself on knowing his moods, their causes and their remedies, had found it first unthinkable, and then intolerable, that this, so like and yet so unlike those other spasmodic restlessnesses of his, should be to her incomprehensible and elusive.

He was restless and he was not restless. He was discontented, yet there were times when she felt he was possessed of some intense secret satisfaction, like a cat who had stolen the cream. He was irritable with the boys, especially Junior, for

Ted, who seemed to have an uncanny knowledge of his father's periods of off moods, kept out of his way when possible. They got on his nerves, drove him to violent outbursts of temper, very different from his usual gently sarcastic remarks that constituted his idea of discipline for them. On the other hand, with her he was more than customarily considerate and abstemious. And it had been weeks since she had felt the keen edge of his irony.

He was like a man marking time, waiting. But what was he waiting for? It was extraordinary that, after all these years of accurate perception, she now lacked the talent to discover what that appearance of waiting meant. It was the knowledge that, for all her watching, all her patient study, the reason for his humour still eluded her which filled her with foreboding dread. That guarded reserve of his seemed to her unjust, inconsiderate, and alarming. It was as if he had stepped out beyond her reach into some section, strange and walled, where she could not get at him.

She closed her eyes, thinking what a blessing it would be if she could get a little sleep before the boys came in from school. She couldn't, of course, though she was so tired, having had, of late, so many sleepless nights. Nights filled with questionings and premonitions.

But she did sleep—several hours.

She wakened to find Brian standing at her bedside looking down at her, an unfathomable expression in his eyes.

She said: "I must have dropped off to sleep," and watched a slender ghost of his old amused smile pass over his face.

"It's getting on to four," he told her, meaning, she knew, that she was going to be late again.

She fought back the quick answer that rose to her lips and said instead: "I'm getting right up. It was good of you to think to call me." She sat up.

He bowed. "Always the attentive husband, you see."

"Yes indeed. Thank goodness, everything's ready."

"Except you. Oh, and Clare's downstairs."

"Clare! What a nuisance! I didn't ask her. Purposely."

"I see. Might a mere man ask why? Or is the reason so subtly feminine that it wouldn't be understood by him?"

A little of his smile had come back. Irene, who was beginning to shake off some of her depression under his familiar banter, said, almost gaily: "Not at all. It just happens that this party happens to be for Hugh, and that Hugh happens not to care a great deal for Clare; therefore I, who happen to be giving the party, didn't happen to ask her. Nothing could be simpler. Could it?"

"Nothing. It's so simple that I can easily see beyond your simple explanation and surmise that Clare, probably, just never happened to pay Hugh the admiring attention that he happens to consider no more than his just due. Simplest thing in the world."

Irene exclaimed in amazement: "Why, I thought you liked Hugh! You don't, you can't, believe anything so idiotic!"

"Well, Hugh does think he's God, you know."

"That," Irene declared, getting out of bed, "is absolutely not true. He thinks ever so much better of himself than that, as you, who know and have read him, ought to be able to guess. If you remember what a low opinion he has of God, you won't make such a silly mistake."

She went into the closet for her things and, coming back, hung her frock over the back of a chair and placed her shoes on the floor beside it. Then she sat down before her dressing-table.

Brian didn't speak. He continued to stand beside the bed, seeming to look at nothing in particular. Certainly not at her. True, his gaze was on her, but in it there was some quality that made her feel that at that moment she was no more to him than a pane of glass through which he stared. At what? She didn't know, couldn't guess. And this made her uncomfortable. Piqued her.

She said: "It just happens that Hugh prefers intelligent women."

Plainly he was startled. "D'you mean that you think Clare is stupid?" he asked, regarding her with lifted eyebrows, which emphazied the disbelief of his voice.

She wiped the cold cream from her face, before she said: "No, I don't. She isn't stupid. She's intelligent enough in a purely feminine way. Eighteenth-century France would have been a marvellous setting for her, or the old South if she hadn't made the mistake of being born a Negro."

"I see. Intelligent enough to wear a tight bodice and keep bowing swains whispering compliments and retrieving dropped fans. Rather a pretty picture. I take it, though, as slightly feline in its implication."

"Well, then, all I can say is that you take it wrongly. Nobody admires Clare more than I do, for the kind of intelligence she has, as well as for her decorative qualities. But she's not—She isn't—She hasn't—Oh, I can't explain it. Take Bianca, for example, or, to keep to the race, Felise Freeland. Looks and brains. Real brains that can hold their own with anybody. Clare has got brains of a sort, the kind that are useful too. Acquisitive, you know. But she'd bore a man like Hugh to suicide. Still, I never thought that even Clare would come to a private party to which she hadn't been asked. But, it's like her."

For a minute there was silence. She completed the bright red arch of her full lips. Brian moved towards the door. His hand was on the knob. He said: "I'm sorry, Irene. It's my fault entirely. She seemed so hurt at being left out that I told her I was sure you'd forgotten and to just come along."

Irene cried out: "But, Brian, I—" and stopped, amazed at the fierce anger that had blazed up in her.

Brian's head came round with a jerk. His brows lifted in an odd surprise.

Her voice, she realized, *had* gone queer. But she had an instinctive feeling that it hadn't been the whole cause of his attitude. And that little straightening motion of the shoulders. Hadn't it been like that of a man drawing himself up to receive a blow? Her fright was like a scarlet spear of terror leaping at her heart.

Clare Kendry! So that was it! Impossible. It couldn't be.

In the mirror before her she saw that he was still regarding her with that air of slight amazement. She dropped her eyes to the jars and bottles on the table and began to fumble among them with hands whose fingers shook slightly.

"Of course," she said carefully. "I'm glad you did. And in spite of my recent remarks, Clare does add to any party. She's so easy on the eyes."

When she looked again, the surprise had gone from his face and the expectancy from his bearing.

"Yes," he agreed. "Well, I guess I'll run along. One of us ought to be down, I s'pose."

"You're right. One of us ought to." She was surprised that it was in her normal tones she spoke, caught as she was by the heart since that dull indefinite fear had grown suddenly into sharp panic. "I'll be down before you know it," she promised.

"All right," But he still lingered. "You're quite certain. You don't mind my asking her? Not awfully, I mean? I see now that I ought to have spoken to you. Trust women to have their reasons for everything."

She made a little pretence at looking at him, managed a tiny smile, and turned away. Clare! How sickening!

"Yes, don't they?" she said, striving to keep her voice casual. Within her she felt a hardness from feeling, not absent, but repressed. And that hardness was rising, swelling. Why didn't he go? Why didn't he?

He had opened the door at last. "You won't be long?" he asked, admonished.

She shook her head, unable to speak, for there was a choking in her throat, and the confusion in her mind was like the beating of wings. Behind her she heard the gentle impact of the door as it closed behind him, and knew that he had gone. Down to Clare.

For a long minute she sat in strained stiffness. The face in the mirror vanished from her sight, blotted out by this thing which had so suddenly flashed across her groping mind. Impossible for her to put it immediately into words or give it outline, for, prompted by some impulse of self-protection, she recoiled from exact expression.

She closed her unseeing eyes and clenched her fists. She tried not to cry. But her lips tightened and no effort could check the hot tears of rage and shame that sprang into her eyes and flowed down her cheeks; so she laid her face in her arms and wept silently.

When she was sure that she had done crying, she wiped away the warm remaining tears and got up. After bathing her swollen face in cold, refreshing water and carefully applying a stinging splash of toilet water, she went back to the mirror and regarded herself gravely. Satisfied that there lingered no betraying evidence of weeping, she dusted a little powder on her dark-white face and again examined it carefully, and with a kind of ridiculing contempt.

"I do think," she confided to it, "that you've been something—oh, very much—of a damned fool."

Downstairs the ritual of tea give her some busy moments, and that, she decided, was a blessing. She wanted no empty spaces of time in which her mind would immediately return to that horror which she had not yet gathered sufficient courage to face. Pouring tea properly and nicely was an occupation that required a kind of well-balanced attention.

In the room beyond, a clock chimed. A single sound. Fifteen minutes past five o'clock. That was all! And yet in the short space of half an hour all of life had changed, lost its colour, its vividness, its whole meaning. No, she reflected, it wasn't that that had happened. Life about her, apparently, went on exactly as before.

"Oh, Mrs. Runyon. . . . So nice to see you. . . . Two? . . . Really? . . . How exciting! . . . Yes, I think Tuesday's all right. . . ."

Yes, life went on precisely as before. It was only she that had changed. Knowing, stumbling on this thing, had changed her. It was as if in a house long dim, a match had been struck, showing ghastly shapes where had been only blurred shadows.

Chatter, chatter, chatter. Someone asked her a question. She glanced up with what she felt was a rigid smile.

"Yes . . . Brian picked it up last winter in Haiti. Terribly weird, isn't it? . . . It *is* rather marvellous in its own hideous way. . . . Practically nothing, I believe. A few cents. . . ."

Hideous. A great weariness came over her. Even the small exertion of pouring golden tea into thin old cups seemed almost too much for her. She went on pouring. Made repetitions of her smile. Answered questions. Manufactured conversation. She thought: "I feel like the oldest person in the world with the longest stretch of life before me."

"Josephine Baker? . . . No. I've never seen her. . . . Well, she might have been in *Shuffle Along* when I saw it, but if she was, I don't remember her. . . . Oh, but you're wrong! . . . I do think Ethel Waters is awfully good. . . ."

There were the familiar little tinkling sounds of spoons striking against frail cups, the soft running sounds of inconsequential talk, punctuated now and then with laughter. In irregular small groups, disintegrating, coalescing, striking just the right note of disharmony, disorder in the big room, which Irene had furnished with a sparingness that was almost chaste, moved the guests with that slight familiarity that makes a party a success. On the floor and the walls the sinking sun threw long, fantastic shadows.

So like many other tea-parties she had had. So unlike any of those others. But she mustn't think yet. Time enough for that after. All the time in the world. She had a second's flashing knowledge of what those words might portend. Time with Brian. Time without him. It was gone, leaving in its place an almost uncontrollable impulse to laugh, to scream, to hurl things about. She wanted, suddenly, to shock people, to hurt them, to make them notice her, to be aware of her suffering.

"Hello, Dave. . . . Felise. . . . Really your clothes are the despair of half the women in Harlem. . . . How do you do it? . . . Lovely, is it Worth or Lanvin? . . . Oh, a mere Babani. . . ."

"Merely that," Felise Freeland acknowledged. "Come out of it, Irene, whatever it is. You look like the second gravedigger."

"Thanks, for the hint, Felise. I'm not feeling quite up to par. The weather, I guess."

"Buy yourself an expensive new frock, child. It always helps. Any time this child gets the blues, it means money out of Dave's pocket. How're those boys of yours?"

The boys! For once she'd forgotten them.

They were, she told Felise, very well. Felise mumbled something about that being awfully nice, and said she'd have to fly, because for a wonder she saw Mrs. Bellew sitting by herself, "and I've been trying to get her alone all afternoon. I want her for a party. Isn't she stunning today?"

Clare was. Irene couldn't remember ever having seen her look better. She was wearing a superlatively simple cinnamon-brown frock which brought out all her vivid beauty, and a little golden bowl of a hat. Around her neck hung a string of amber beads that would easily have made six or eight like one Irene owned. Yes, she was stunning.

The ripple of talk flowed on. The fire roared. The shadows stretched longer.

Across the room was Hugh. He wasn't, Irene hoped, being too bored. He seemed as he always did, a bit aloof, a little amused, and somewhat weary. And as usual he was hovering before the book-shelves. But he was not, she noticed, looking at the book he had taken down. Instead, his dull amber eyes were held by something across the room. They were a little scornful. Well, Hugh had never cared for Clare Kendry. For a minute Irene hesitated, then turned her head, though she knew what it was that held Hugh's gaze. Clare, who had suddenly clouded all her days. Brian, the father of Ted and Junior.

Clare's ivory face was what it always was, beautiful and caressing. Or maybe today a little masked. Unrevealing.

Unaltered and undisturbed by any emotion within or without. Brian's seemed to Irene to be pitiably bare. Or was it too as it always was? That half-effaced seeking look, did he always have that? Queer, that now she didn't know, couldn't recall. Then she saw him smile, and the smile made his face all eager and shining. Impelled by some inner urge of loyalty to herself, she glanced away. But only for a moment. And when she turned towards them again, she thought that the look in his face was the most melancholy and yet the most scoffing that she had ever seen upon it.

In the next quarter of an hour she promised herself to Bianca Wentworth in Sixty-second Street, Jane Tenant at Seventh Avenue and a Hundred and Fiftieth Street, and the Dashields in Brooklyn for dinner all on the same evening and at almost the same hour.

Oh well, what did it matter? She had no thoughts at all now, and all she felt was a great fatigue. Before her tired eyes Clare Kendry was talking to Dave Freeland. Scraps of their conversation, in Clare's husky voice, floated over to her: ". . . always admired you . . . so much about you long ago . . . everybody says so . . . no one but you. . . ." And more of the same. The man hung rapt on her words, though he was the husband of Felise Freeland, and the author of novels that revealed a man of perception and a devastating irony. And he fell for such pish-posh! And all because Clare had a trick of sliding down ivory lids over astonishing black eyes and then lifting them suddenly and turning on a caressing smile. Men like Dave Freeland fell for it. And Brian.

Her mental and physical languor receded. Brian. What did it mean? How would it affect her and the boys? The boys! She had a surge of relief. It ebbed, vanished. A feeling of absolute unimportance followed. Actually, she didn't count. She was, to him, only the mother of his sons. That was all. Alone she was nothing. Worse. An obstacle.

Rage boiled up in her.

There was a slight crash. On the floor at her feet lay the shattered cup. Dark stains dotted the bright rug. Spread. The chatter stopped. Went on. Before her, Zulena gathered up the white fragments.

As from a distance Hugh Wentworth's clipt voice came to her, though he was, she was aware, somehow miraculously at her side. "Sorry," he apologized. "Must have pushed you. Clumsy of me. Don't tell me it's priceless and irreplaceable."

It hurt. Dear God! How the thing hurt! But she couldn't think of that now. Not with Hugh sitting there mumbling apologies and lies. The significance of his words, the power of his discernment, stirred in her a sense of caution. Her pride revolted. Damn Hugh! Something would have to be done about him. Now. She couldn't, it seemed, help his knowing. It was too late for that. But she could and would keep him from knowing that she knew. She could, she would bear it.

She'd have to. There were the boys. Her whole body went taut. In the second she saw that she could bear anything, but only if no one knew that she had anything to bear. It hurt. It frightened her, but she could bear it.

She turned to Hugh. Shook her head. Raised innocent dark eyes to his concerned pale ones. "Oh, no," she protested, "you didn't push me. Cross your heart, hope to die, and I'll tell you how it happened."

"Done!"

"Did you notice that cup? Well, you're lucky. It was the ugliest thing that your ancestors, the charming Confederates ever owned. I've forgotten how many thousands of years ago it was that Brian's great-great-grand-uncle owned it. But it has, or had, a good old hoary history. It was brought North by way of the subway. Oh, all right! Be English if you want to and call it the underground. What I'm coming to is the fact that I've never figured out a way of getting rid of it until about five minutes ago. I had an inspiration. I had only to break it, and I was rid of it for ever. So simple! And I'd never thought of it before."

Hugh nodded and his frosty smile spread over his features. Had she convinced him?

"Still," she went on with a little laugh that didn't, she was sure, sound the least bit forced, "I'm perfectly willing for you to take the blame and admit that you pushed me at the wrong moment. What are friends for, if not to help bear our sins? Brian will certainly be told that it was your fault."

"More tea, Clare? . . . I haven't had a minute with you. . . . Yes, it is a nice party. . . . You'll stay to dinner, I hope. . . . Oh, too bad! . . . I'll be alone with the boys. . . . They'll be sorry. Brian's got a medical meeting, or something. . . . Nice frock you're wearing. . . . Thanks. . . . Well, good-bye; see you soon, I hope."

The clock chimed. One. Two. Three. Four. Five. Six. Was it, could it be, only a little over an hour since she had come down to tea? One little hour.

"Must you go? . . . Good-bye. . . . Thank you so much. . . . So nice to see you. . . . Yes, Wednesday. . . . My love to Madge. . . . Sorry, but I'm filled up for Tuesday. . . . Oh, really? . . . Yes. . . . Good-bye. . . . Good-bye. . . ."

It hurt. It hurt like hell. But it didn't matter, if no one knew. If everything could go on as before. If the boys were safe.

It did hurt.

But it didn't matter.

Two

But it did matter. It mattered more than anything had ever mattered before.

What bitterness! That the one fear, the one uncertainty, that she had left, Brian's ache to go somewhere else, should have dwindled to a childish triviality! And with it the quality of the courage and resolution with which she had met it. From the visions and dangers which she now perceived she shrank away. For them she had no remedy or courage. Desperately she tried to shut out the knowledge from which had risen this turmoil, which she had no power to moderate or still, within her. And half succeeded.

For, she reasoned, what was there, what had there been, to show that she was even half correct in her tormenting notion? Nothing. She had seen nothing, heard nothing. She had no facts or proofs. She was only making herself unutterably wretched by an unfounded suspicion. It had been a case of looking for trouble and finding it in good measure. Merely that.

With this self-assurance that she had no real knowledge, she redoubled her efforts to drive out of her mind the distressing thought of faiths broken and trusts betrayed which every mental vision of Clare, of Brian, brought with them. She could not, she would not, go again through the tearing agony that lay just behind her.

She must, she told herself, be fair. In all their married life she had had no slightest cause to suspect her husband of any infidelity, of any serious flirtation, even. If—and she doubted it—he had had his hours of outside erratic conduct, they were unknown to her. Why begin now to assume them? And on nothing more concrete than an idea that had leapt into her mind because he had told her that he had invited a friend, a friend of hers, to a party in his own house. And at a time when she had been, it was likely, more asleep than awake. How could she without anything done or said, or left undone or unsaid, so easily believe him guilty? How be so ready to renounce all confidence in the worth of their life together?

And if, perchance, there were some small something— well, what could it mean? Nothing. There were the boys. There was John Bellew. The thought of these three gave her some slight relief. But she did not look the future in the face. She wanted to feel nothing, to think nothing; simply to believe that it was all silly invention on her part. Yet she could not. Not quite.

Christmas, with its unreality, its hectic rush, its false gaiety, came and went. Irene was thankful for the confused unrest of the season. Its irksomeness, its crowds, its inane and insincere repetitions of genialities, pushed between her and the contemplation of her growing unhappiness.

She was thankful, too, for the continued absence of Clare, who, John Bellew having returned from a long stay in Canada, had withdrawn to that other life of hers, remote and inaccessible. But beating against the walled prison of Irene's thoughts was the shunned fancy that, though absent, Clare Kendry was still present, that she was close.

Brian, too, had withdrawn. The house contained his outward self and his belongings. He came and went with his usual noiseless irregularity. He sat across from her at table. He slept in his room next to hers at night. But he was remote and inaccessible. No use pretending that he was happy, that things were the same as they had always been. He wasn't and they weren't. However, she assured herself, it needn't necessarily be because of anything that involved Clare. It was, it must be, another manifestation of the old longing.

But she did wish it were spring, March, so that Clare would be sailing, out of her life and Brian's. Though she had come almost to believe that there was nothing but generous friendship between those two, she was very tired of Clare Kendry. She wanted to be free of her, and of her furtive comings and goings. If something would only happen, something that would make John Bellew decide on an earlier departure, or that would remove Clare. Anything. She didn't care what. Not even if it were that Clare's Margery were ill, or dying. Not even if Bellew should discover—

She drew a quick, sharp breath. And for a long time sat staring down at the hands in her lap. Strange, she had not before realized how easily she could put Clare out of her life! She had only to tell John Bellew that his wife—No. Not that! But if he should somehow learn of these Harlem visits—why should she hesitate? Why spare Clare?

But she shrank away from the idea of telling that man, Clare Kendry's white husband, anything that would lead him to suspect that his wife was a Negro. Nor could she write it, or telephone it, or tell it to someone else who would tell him.

She was caught between two allegiances, different, yet the same. Herself. Her race. Race! The thing that bound and suffocated her. Whatever steps she took, or if she took none at all, something would be crushed. A person or the race. Clare, herself, or the race. Or, it might be, all three. Nothing, she imagined, was ever more completely sardonic.

Sitting alone in the quiet living-room in the pleasant firelight, Irene Redfield wished, for the first time in her life, that she had not been born a Negro. For the first time she suffered and rebelled because she was unable to disregard the burden of race. It was, she cried silently, enough to suffer as a woman, an individual, on one's own account, without having to suffer for the race as well. It was a brutality, and undeserved. Surely, no other people so cursed as Ham's dark children.

Nevertheless, her weakness, her shrinking, her own inability to compass the thing, did not prevent her from wishing fervently that, in some way with which she had no concern, John Bellew would discover, not that his wife had a touch of the tar-brush—Irene didn't want that—but that she was spending all the time that he was out of the city in black Harlem. Only that. It would be enough to rid her forever of Clare Kendry.

Three

As if in answer to her wish, the very next day Irene came face to face with Bellew.

She had gone downtown with Felise Freeland to shop. The day was an exceptionally cold one, with a strong wind that had whipped a dusky red into Felise's smooth golden cheeks and driven moisture into Irene's soft brown eyes.

Clinging to each other, with heads bent against the wind, they turned out of the Avenue into Fifty-seventh Street. A sudden bluster flung them around the corner with unexpected quickness and they collided with a man.

"Pardon," Irene begged laughingly, and looked up into the face of Clare Kendry's husband.

"Mrs. Redfield!"

His hat came off. He held out his hand, smiling genially.

But the smile faded at once. Surprise, incredulity, and—was it understanding?—passed over his features.

He had, Irene knew, become conscious of Felise, golden, with curly black Negro hair, whose arm was still linked in her own. She was sure, now, of the understanding in his face, as he looked at her again and then back at Felise. And displeasure.

He didn't, however, withdraw his outstretched hand. Not at once.

But Irene didn't take it. Instinctively, in the first glance of recognition, her face had become a mask. Now she turned on him a totally uncomprehending look, a bit questioning. Seeing that he still stood with hand outstretched, she gave him the cool appraising stare which she reserved for mashers, and drew Felise on.

Felise drawled: "Aha! Been 'passing,' have you? Well, I've queered that."

"Yes, I'm afraid you have."

"Why, Irene Redfield! You sound as if you cared terribly. I'm sorry."

"I do, but not for the reason you think. I don't believe I've ever gone native in my life except for the sake of convenience, restaurants, theatre tickets, and things like that. Never socially I mean, except once. You've just passed the only person that I've ever met disguised as a white woman."

"Awfully sorry. Be sure your sin will find you out and all that. Tell me about it."

"I'd like to. It would amuse you. But I can't."

Felise's laughter was as languidly nonchalant as her cool voice. "Can it be possible that the honest Irene has—Oh, do look at that coat! There. The red one. Isn't it a dream?"

Irene was thinking: "I had my chance and didn't take it. I had only to speak and to introduce him to Felise with the casual remark that he was Clare's husband. Only that. Fool. Fool." That instinctive loyalty to a race. Why couldn't she get free of it? Why should it include Clare? Clare, who'd shown little enough consideration for her, and hers. What she felt was not so much resentment as a dull despair because she could not change herself in this respect, could not separate individuals from the race, herself from Clare Kendry.

"Let's go home, Felise. I'm so tired I could drop."

"Why, we haven't done half the things we planned."

"I know, but it's too cold to be running all over town. But you stay down if you want to."

"I think I'll do that, if you don't mind."

AND NOW another problem confronted Irene. She must tell Clare of this meeting. Warn her. But how? She hadn't seen her for days. Writing and telephoning were equally unsafe. And even if it was possible to get in touch with her, what good would it do? If Bellew hadn't concluded that he'd made a mistake, if he was certain of her identity—and he was nobody's fool—telling Clare wouldn't avert the results of the encounter. Besides, it was too late. Whatever was in store for Clare Kendry had already overtaken her.

Irene was conscious of a feeling of relieved thankfulness at the thought that she was probably rid of Clare, and without having lifted a finger or uttered a word.

But she did mean to tell Brian about meeting John Bellew.

But that, it seemed, was impossible. Strange. Something held her back. Each time she was on the verge of saying: "I ran into Clare's husband on the street downtown today. I'm sure he recognized me, and Felise was with me," she failed to speak. It sounded too much like the warning she wanted it to be. Not even in the presence of the boys at dinner could she make the bare statement.

The evening dragged. At last she said good-night and went upstairs, the words unsaid.

She thought: "Why didn't I tell him? Why didn't I? If trouble comes from this, I'll never forgive myself. I'll tell him when he comes up."

She took up a book, but she could not read, so oppressed was she by a nameless foreboding.

What if Bellew should divorce Clare? Could he? There was the Rhinelander case. But in France, in Paris, such things were very easy. If he divorced her—If Clare were free—But of all the things that could happen, that was the one she did not want. She must get her mind away from that possibility. She must.

Then came a thought which she tried to drive away. If Clare should die! Then—Oh, it was vile! To think, yes, to wish that! She felt faint and sick. But the thought stayed with her. She could not get rid of it.

She heard the outer door open. Close. Brian had gone out. She turned her face into her pillow to cry. But no tears came.

She lay there awake, thinking of things past. Of her courtship and marriage and Junior's birth. Of the time they had bought the house in which they had lived so long and so happily. Of the time Ted had passed his pneumonia crisis and they knew he would live. And of other sweet painful memories that would never come again.

Above everything else she had wanted, had striven, to keep undisturbed the pleasant routine of her life. And now Clare Kendry had come into it, and with her the menace of impermanence.

"Dear God," she prayed, "make March come quickly."

By and by she slept.

Four

The next morning brought with it a snowstorm that lasted throughout the day.

After a breakfast, which had been eaten almost in silence and which she was relieved to have done with, Irene Redfield lingered for a little while in the downstairs hall, looking out at the soft flakes fluttering down. She was watching them immediately fill some ugly irregular gaps left by the feet of hurrying pedestrians when Zulena came to her, saying: "The telephone, Mrs. Redfield, It's Mrs. Bellew."

"Take the message, Zulena, please."

Though she continued to stare out of the window, Irene saw nothing now, stabbed as she was by fear—and hope. Had anything happened between Clare and Bellew? And if so, what? And was she to be freed at last from the aching anxiety of the past weeks? Or was there to be more, and worse? She had wrestling moment, in which it seemed that she must rush after Zulena and hear for herself what it was that Clare had to say. But she waited.

Zulena, when she came back, said. "She says, ma'am, that she'll be able to go to Mrs. Freeland's tonight. She'll be here some time between eight and nine."

"Thank you, Zulena."

The day dragged on to its end.

At dinner Brian spoke bitterly of a lynching that he had been reading about in the evening paper.

"Dad, why is it that they only lynch colored people?" Ted asked.

"Because they hate 'em, son."

"Brian!" Irene's voice was a plea and a rebuke.

Ted said: "Oh! And why do they hate 'em?"

"Because they are afraid of them."

"But what makes them afraid of 'em?"

"Because—"

"Brian!"

"It seems, son, that is a subject we can't go into at the moment without distressing the ladies of our family," he told the boy with mock seriousness, "but we'll take it up some time when we're alone together."

Ted nodded in his engaging grave way. "I see. Maybe we can talk about it tomorrow on the way to school."

"That'll be fine."

"Brian!"

"Mother," Junior remarked, "that's the third time you've said 'Brian' like that."

"But not the last, Junior, never you fear," his father told him.

After the boys had gone up to their own floor, Irene said suavely: "I do wish, Brian, that you wouldn't talk about lynching before Ted and Junior. It was really inexcusable for you to bring up a thing like that at dinner. There'll be time enough for them to learn about such horrible things when they're older."

"You're absolutely wrong! If, as you're so determined, they've got to live in this damned country, they'd better find out what sort of thing they're up against as soon as possible. The earlier they learn it, the better prepared they'll be."

"I don't agree. I want their childhood to be happy and as free from the knowledge of such things as it possibly can be."

"Very laudable," was Brian's sarcastic answer. "Very laudable indeed, all things considered. But can it?"

"Certainly it can. If you'll only do your part."

"Stuff! You know as well as I do, Irene, that it can't. What was the use of our trying to keep them from learning the word 'nigger' and its connotation? They found out, didn't they? And how? Because somebody called Junior a dirty nigger."

"Just the same you're not to talk to them about the race problem. I won't have it."

They glared at each other.

"I tell you, Irene, they've got to know these things, and it might as well be now as later."

"They do not!" she insisted, forcing back the tears of anger that were threatening to fall.

Brian growled: "I can't understand how anybody as intelligent as you like to think you are can show evidences of such stupidity." He looked at her in a puzzled harassed way.

"Stupid!" she cried. "Is it stupid to want my children to be happy?" Her lips were quivering.

"At the expense of proper preparation for life and their future happiness, yes. And I'd feel I hadn't done my duty by them if I didn't give them some inkling of what's before them. It's the least I can do. I wanted to get them out of this hellish place years ago. You wouldn't let me. I gave up the idea, because you objected. Don't expect me to give up everything."

Under the lash of his words she was silent. Before any answer came to her, he had turned and gone from the room.

Sitting there alone in the forsaken dining-room, unconsciously pressing the hands lying in her lap, tightly together, she was seized by a convulsion of shivering. For, to her, there had been something ominous in the scene that she had just had with her husband. Over and over in her mind his last words: "Don't expect me to give up everything," repeated themselves. What had they meant? What could they mean? Clare Kendry?

Surely, she was going mad with fear and suspicion. She must not work herself up. She must not! Where were all the self-control, the common sense, that she was so proud of? Now, if ever, was the time for it.

Clare would soon be there. She must hurry or she would be late again, and those two would wait for her downstairs together, as they had done so often since that first time, which now seemed so long ago. Had it been really only last October? Why, she felt years, not months, older.

Drearily she rose from her chair and went upstairs to set about the business of dressing to go out when she would far rather have remained at home. During the process she wondered, for the hundredth time, why she hadn't told Brian about herself and Felise running into Bellew the day before, and for the hundredth time she turned away from acknowledging to herself the real reason for keeping back the information.

When Clare arrived, radiant in a shining red gown, Irene had not finished dressing. But her smile scarcely hesitated as she greeted her, saying: "I always seem to keep C.P. time, don't I? We hardly expected you to be able to come. Felise will be pleased. How nice you look."

Clare kissed a bare shoulder, seeming not to notice a slight shrinking.

"I hadn't an idea in the world, myself, that I'd be able to make it; but Jack had to run down to Philadelphia unexpectedly. So here I am."

Irene looked up, a flood of speech on her lips. "Philadelphia. That's not very far, is it? Clare, I—?"

She stopped, one of her hands clutching the side of her stool, the other lying clenched on the dressing-table. Why didn't she go on and tell Clare about meeting Bellew? Why couldn't she?

But Clare didn't notice the unfinished sentence. She laughed and said lightly: "It's far enough for me. Anywhere, away from me, is far enough. I'm not particular."

Irene passed a hand over her eyes to shut out the accusing face in the glass before her. With one corner of her mind she wondered how long she had looked like that, drawn and haggard and—yes, frightened. Or was it only imagination?

"Clare," she asked, "have you ever seriously thought what it would mean if he should find you out?"

"Yes."

"Oh! You have! And what you'd do in that case?"

"Yes." And having said it, Clare Kendry smiled quickly, a smile that came and went like a flash, leaving untouched the gravity of her face.

That smile and the quiet resolution of that one word, "yes," filled Irene with a primitive paralysing dread. Her hands were numb, her feet like ice, her heart like a stone weight. Even her tongue was like a heavy dying thing. There were long spaces between the words as she asked: "And what should you do?"

Clare, who was sunk in a deep chair, her eyes far away, seemed wrapped in some pleasant impenetrable reflection. To Irene, sitting expectantly upright, it was an interminable time before she dragged herself back to the present to say calmly: "I'd do what I want to do more than anything else right now. I'd come up here to live. Harlem, I mean. Then I'd be able to do as I please, when I please."

Irene leaned forward, cold and tense. "And what about Margery?" Her voice was a strained whisper.

"Margery?" Clare repeated, letting her eyes flutter over Irene's concerned face. "Just this, 'Rene. If it wasn't for her, I'd do it anyway. She's all that holds me back. But if Jack finds out, if our marriage is broken, that lets me out. Doesn't it?"

Her gentle resigned tone, her air of innocent candour, appeared, to her listener, spurious. A conviction that the words were intended as a warning took possession of Irene. She remembered that Clare Kendry had always seemed to know what other people were thinking. Her compressed lips grew firm and obdurate. Well, she wouldn't know this time.

She said: "Do go downstairs and talk to Brian. He's got a mad on."

Though she had determined that Clare should not get at her thoughts and fears, the words had sprung, unthought of, to her lips. It was as if they had come from some outer layer of callousness that had no relation to her tortured heart. And they had been, she realized, precisely the right words for her purpose.

For as Clare got up and went out, she saw that that arrangement was as good as her first plan of keeping her waiting up there while she dressed—or better. She would only have hindered and rasped her. And what matter if those two spent one hour, more or less, alone together, one or many, now that everything had happened between them?

Ah! The first time that she had allowed herself to admit to herself that everything had happened, had not forced herself to believe, to hope, that nothing irrevocable had been consummated! Well, it had happened. She knew it, and knew that she knew it.

She was surprised that, having thought the thought, conceded the fact, she was no more hurt, cared no more, than during her previous frenzied endeavours to escape it. And this absence of acute, unbearable pain seemed to her unjust, as if she had been denied some exquisite solace of suffering which the full acknowledgment should have given her.

Was it, perhaps, that she had endured all that a woman could endure of tormenting humiliation and fear? Or was it that she lacked the capacity for the acme of suffering? "No, no!" she denied fiercely. "I'm human like everybody else. It's just that I'm so tired, so worn out, I can't feel any more." But she did not really believe that.

Security. Was it just a word? If not, then was it only by the sacrifice of other things, happiness, love, or some wild ecstasy that she had never known, that it could be obtained? And did too much striving, too much faith in safety and permanence, unfit one for these other things?

Irene didn't know, couldn't decide, though for a long time she sat questioning and trying to understand. Yet all the while, in spite of her searchings and feeling of frustration, she was aware that, to her, security was the most important and desired thing in life. Not for any of the others, or for all of them, would she exchange it. She wanted only to be tranquil. Only, unmolested, to be allowed to direct for their own best good the lives of her sons and her husband.

Now that she had relieved herself of what was almost like a guilty knowledge, admitted that which by some sixth sense she had long known, she could again reach out for plans. Could think again of ways to keep Brian by her side, and in New York. For she would not go to Brazil. She belonged in this land of rising towers. She was an American. She grew from this soil, and she would not be uprooted. Not even because of Clare Kendry, or a hundred Clare Kendrys.

Brian, too, belonged here. His duty was to her and to his boys.

Strange, that she couldn't now be sure that she had ever truly known love. Not even for Brian. He was her husband and the father of her sons. But was he anything more? Had she ever wanted or tried for more? In that hour she thought not.

Nevertheless, she meant to keep him. Her freshly painted lips narrowed to a thin straight line. True, she had left off trying to believe that he and Clare loved and yet did not love, but she still intended to hold fast to the outer shell of her marriage, to keep her life fixed, certain. Brought to the edge of distasteful reality, her fastidious nature did not recoil. Better, far better, to share him than to lose him completely. Oh, she could close her eyes, if need be. She could bear it. She could bear anything. And there was March ahead. March and the departure of Clare.

Horribly clear, she could now see the reason for her instinct to withhold—omit, rather—her news of the encounter with Bellew. If Clare was freed, anything might happen.

She paused in her dressing, seeing with perfect clearness that dark truth which she had from that first October afternoon felt about Clare Kendry and of which Clare herself had once warned her—that she got the things she wanted because she met the great conditions of conquest, sacrifice. If she wanted Brian, Clare wouldn't revolt from the lack of money or place. It was as she had said, only Margery kept her from

throwing all that away. And if things were taken out of her hands—Even if she was only alarmed, only suspected that such a thing was to occur, anything might happen. Anything.

No! At all costs, Clare was not to know of that meeting with Bellew. Nor was Brian. It would only weaken her own power to keep him.

They would never know from her that he was on his way to suspecting the truth about his wife. And she would do anything, risk anything, to prevent him from finding out that truth. How fortunate that she had obeyed her instinct and omitted to recognize Bellew!

"*EVER GO* up to the sixth floor, Clare?" Brian asked as he stopped the car and got out to open the door for them.

"Why, of course! We're on the seventeenth."

"I mean, did you ever go up by nigger-power?"

"That's good!" Clare laughed. "Ask 'Rene. My father was a janitor, you know, in the good old days before every ramshackle flat had its elevator. But you can't mean we've got to walk up? Not here!"

"Yes, here. And Felise lives at the very top," Irene told her.

"What on earth for?"

"I believe she claims it discourages the casual visitor."

"And she's probably right. Hard on herself, though."

Brian said "Yes, a bit. But she says she'd rather be dead than bored."

"Oh, a garden! And how lovely with that undisturbed snow!"

"Yes, isn't it? But keep to the walk with those foolish thin shoes. You too, Irene."

Irene walked beside them on the cleared cement path that split the whiteness of the courtyard garden. She felt a something in the air, something that had been between those two and would be again. It was like a live thing pressing against her. In a quick furtive glance she saw Clare clinging to Brian's other arm. She was looking at him with that provocative upward glance of hers, and his eyes were fastened on her face with what seemed to Irene an expression of wistful eagerness.

"It's this entrance, I believe," she informed them in quite her ordinary voice.

"Mind," Brian told Clare, "you don't fall by the wayside before the fourth floor. They absolutely refuse to carry anyone up more that the last two flights."

"Don't be silly!" Irene snapped.

THE PARTY began gaily.

Dave Freeland was at his best, brilliant, crystal clear, and sparkling. Felise, too, was amusing, and not so sarcastic as usual, because she liked the dozen or so guests that dotted the long, untidy living-room. Brian was witty, though, Irene noted, his remarks were somewhat more barbed than was customary even with him. And there was Ralph Hazelton, throwing nonsensical shining things into the pool of talk, which the others, even Clare, picked up and flung back with fresh adornment.

Only Irene wasn't merry. She sat almost silent, smiling now and then, that she might appear amused.

"What's the matter, Irene?" someone asked. "Taken a vow never to laugh, or something? You're as sober as a judge."

"No. It's simply that the rest of you are so clever that I'm speechless, absolutely stunned."

"No wonder," Dave Freeland remarked, "that you're on the verge of tears. You haven't a drink. What'll you take?"

"Thanks. If I must take something, make it a glass of ginger-ale and three drops of Scotch. The Scotch first, please. Then the ice, then the ginger ale."

"Heavens! Don't attempt to mix that yourself, Dave darling. Have the butler in," Felise mocked.

"Yes, do. And the footman." Irene laughed a little, then said: "It seems dreadfully warm in here. Mind if I open this window?" With that she pushed open one of the long casement-windows of which the Freelands were so proud.

It had stopped snowing some two or three hours back. The moon was just rising, and far behind the tall buildings a few stars were creeping out. Irene finished her cigarette and threw it out, watching the tiny sparks drop slowly down to the white ground below.

Someone in the room had turned on the phonograph. Or was it the radio? She didn't know which she disliked more. And nobody was listening to its blare. The talking, the laughter never for a minute ceased. Why must they have more noise?

Dave came with her drink. "You ought not," he told her, "to stand there like that. You'll take cold. Come along and talk to me, or listen to me gabble." Taking her arm, he led her across the room. They had just found seats when the door-bell rang and Felise called over to him to go and answer it.

In the next moment Irene heard his voice in the hall, carelessly polite: "Your wife? Sorry. I'm afraid you're wrong. Perhaps next—"

Then the roar of John Bellew's voice above all the other noises of the room: "I'm *not* wrong! I've been to the Redfields and I know she's with them. You'd better stand out of my way and save yourself trouble in the end."

"What is it, Dave?" Felise ran out to the door.

And so did Brian. Irene heard him saying: "I'm Redfield. What the devil's the matter with you?"

But Bellew didn't heed him. He pushed past them all into the room and strode towards Clare. They all looked at her as she got up from her chair, backing a little from his approach.

"So you're a nigger, a damned dirty nigger!" His voice was a snarl and a moan, an expression of rage and of pain.

Everything was in confusion. The men had sprung forward. Felise had leapt between them and Bellew. She said quickly: "Careful. You're the only white man here." And the silver chill of her voice, as well as her words, was a warning.

Clare stood at the window, as composed as if everyone were not staring at her in curiosity and wonder, as if the whole structure of her life were not lying in fragments before her. She seemed unaware of any danger or uncaring. There was even a faint smile on her full, red lips, and in her shining eyes.

It was that smile that maddened Irene. She ran across the room, her terror tinged with ferocity, and laid a hand on Clare's bare arm. One thought possessed her. She couldn't have Clare Kendry cast aside by Bellew. She couldn't have her free.

Before them stood John Bellew, speechless now in his hurt and anger. Beyond them the little huddle of other people, and Brian stepping out from among them.

What happened next, Irene Redfield never afterwards allowed herself to remember. Never clearly.

One moment Clare had been there, a vital glowing thing, like a flame of red and gold. The next she was gone.

There was a gasp of horror, and above it a sound not quite human, like a beast in agony. "Nig! My God! Nig!"

A frenzied rush of feet down long flights of stairs. The slamming of distant doors. Voices.

Irene stayed behind. She sat down and remained quite still, staring at a ridiculous Japanese print on the wall across the room.

Gone! The soft white face, the bright hair, the disturbing scarlet mouth, the dreaming eyes, the caressing smile, the whole torturing loveliness that had been Clare Kendry. That beauty that had torn at Irene's placid life. Gone! The mocking daring, the gallantry of her pose, the ringing bells of her laughter.

Irene wasn't sorry. She was amazed, incredulous almost.

What would the others think? That Clare had fallen? That she had deliberately leaned backward? Certainly one or the other. Not—

But she mustn't, she warned herself, think of that. She was too tired, and too shocked. And, indeed, both were true. She was utterly weary, and she was violently staggered. But her thoughts reeled on. If only she could be as free of mental as she was of bodily vigour; could only put from her memory the vision of her hand on Clare's arm!

"It was an accident, a terrible accident," she muttered fiercely. "It *was*."

People were coming up the stairs. Through the still open door their steps and talk sounded nearer, nearer.

Quickly she stood up and went noiselessly into the bedroom and closed the door softly behind her.

Her thoughts raced. Ought she to have stayed? Should she go back out there to them? But there would be questions.

She hadn't thought of them, of afterwards, of this. She had thought of nothing in that sudden moment of action.

It was cold. Icy chills ran up her spine and over her bare neck and shoulders.

In the room outside there were voices. Dave Freeland's and others that she did not recognize.

Should she put on her coat? Felise had rushed down without any wrap. So had all the others. So had Brian. Brian! He mustn't take cold. She took up his coat and left her own. At the door she paused for a moment, listening fearfully. She heard nothing. No voices. No footsteps. Very slowly she opened the door. The room was empty. She went out.

In the hall below she heard dimly the sound of feet going down the steps, of a door being opened and closed, and of voices far away.

Down, down, she went, Brian's great coat clutched in her shivering arms and trailing a little on each step behind her.

What was she to say to them when at last she had finished going down those endless stairs? She should have rushed out when they did. What reason could she give for her dallying behind? Even she didn't know why she had done that. And what else would she be asked? There had been her hand reaching out towards Clare. What about that?

In the midst of her wonderings and questionings came a thought so terrifying, so horrible, that she had had to grasp hold of the banister to save herself from pitching downwards. A cold perspiration drenched her shaking body. Her breath came short in sharp and painful gasps.

What if Clare was not dead?

She felt nauseated, as much at the idea of the glorious body mutilated as from fear.

How she managed to make the rest of the journey without fainting she never knew. But at last she was down. Just at the bottom she came on the others, surrounded by a little circle of strangers. They were all speaking in whispers, or in the awed, discreetly lowered tones adapted to the presence of disaster. In the first instant she wanted to turn and rush back up the way she had come. Then a calm desperation came over her. She braced herself physically and mentally.

"Here's Irene now," Dave Freeland announced, and told her that, having only just missed her, they had concluded that she had fainted or something like that, and were on the way to find out about her. Felise, she saw, was holding on to his arm, all the insolent nonchalance gone out of her, and the golden brown of her handsome face changed to a queer mauve colour.

Irene made no indication that she had heard Freeland, but went straight to Brian. His face looked aged and altered, and his lips were purple and trembling. She had a great longing to comfort him, to charm away his suffering and horror. But she was helpless, having so completely lost control of his mind and heart.

She stammered: "Is she—is she—?"

It was Felise who answered. "Instantly, we think."

Irene struggled against the sob of thankfulness that rose in her throat. Chocked down, it turned to a whimper, like a hurt child's. Someone laid a hand on her shoulder in a soothing gesture. Brian wrapped his coat about her. She began to cry rackingly, her entire body heaving with convulsive sobs. He made a slight perfunctory attempt to comfort her.

"There, there, Irene. You mustn't. You'll make yourself sick. She's—" His voice broke suddenly.

As from a long distance she heard Ralph Hazelton's voice saying. "I was looking right at her. She just tumbled over and was gone before you could say 'Jack Robinson.' Fainted, I guess. Lord! It was quick. Quickest thing I ever saw in all my life."

"It's impossible, I tell you! Absolutely impossible!"

It was Brian who spoke in that frenzied hoarse voice, which Irene had never heard before. Her knees quaked under her.

Dave Freeland said: "Just a minute, Brian. Irene was there beside her. Let's hear what she has to say."

She had a moment of stark craven fear. "Oh God," she thought, prayed, "help me."

A strange man, official and authoritative, addressed her. "You're sure she fell? Her husband didn't give her a shove or anything like that, as Dr. Redfield seems to think?"

For the first time she was aware that Bellew was not in the little group shivering in the small hallway. What did that mean? As she began to work it out in her numbed mind, she was shaken with another hideous trembling. Not that! Oh, not that!

"No, no!" she protested. "I'm quite certain that he didn't. I was there, too. As close as he was. She just fell, before anybody could stop her. I—"

Her quaking knees gave way under her. She moaned and sank down, moaned again. Through the great heaviness that submerged and drowned her she was dimly conscious of strong arms lifting her up. Then everything was dark.

Marita Bonner (1899–1971)

As with a number of other women associated with the Harlem Renaissance, Marita Bonner never actually lived in Harlem. She was one of four children born to Joseph Andrew and Mary Anne Bonner and grew up near Boston. She majored in English and Comparative Literature at Radcliffe College, graduating in 1922. After graduation, she taught at the Bluefield Colored Institute in Bluefield, West Virginia. Later she moved to Washington, D.C., where she joined such writers as Langston Hughes, Countee Cullen, and Jessie Fauset, who met in the famous "S" Street home of Georgia Douglas Johnson. In 1930, she married William Almy Occomy, moved to Chicago, and raised three children. She wrote plays, short stories, and music. Her essay, "On Being Young—a Woman—and Colored" (1925) won first place in the *Crisis* Literary Contest.

On Being Young—a Woman—and Colored

You start out after you have gone from kindergarten to sheepskin covered with sundry Latin phrases.

At least you know what you want life to give you. A career as fixed and as calmly brilliant as the North Star. The one real thing that money buys. Time. Time to do things. A house that can be as delectably out of order and as easily put in order as the doll-house of "playing-house" days. And of course, a husband you can look up to without looking down on yourself.

Somehow you feel like a kitten in a sunny catnip field that sees sleek plump brown field mice and yellow baby chicks sitting coyly, side by side, under each leaf. A desire to dash three or four ways seizes you.

That's Youth.

But you know that things learned need testing—acid testing—to see if they are really after all, an interwoven part of you. All your life you have heard of the debt you owe "Your People" because you have managed to have things they have not largely had.

So you find a spot where there are hordes of them—of course below the Line—to be your catnip field while you close your eyes to mice and chickens alike.

If you have never lived among your own, you feel prodigal. Some warm untouched current flows through them—through you—and drags you out into the deep waters of a new sea of human foibles and mannerisms: of a peculiar psychology and prejudices. And one day you find yourself entangled—enmeshed—pinioned in the seaweed of a Black Ghetto.

Not a Ghetto, placid like the Strasse that flows, outwardly unperturbed and calm in a stream of religious belief, but a peculiar group. Cut off, flung together, shoved aside in a bundle because of color and with no more in common.

Unless color is, after all, the real bond.

Milling around like live fish in a basket. Those at the bottom crushed into a sort of stupid apathy by the weight of those on top. Those on top leaping, leaping; leaping to scale the sides, to get out.

There are two "colored" movies, innumerable parties—and cards. Cards played so intensely that it fascinates and repulses at once.

Movies.

Movies worthy and worthless—but not even a low-caste spoken stage.

Parties, plentiful. Music and dancing and much that is wit and color and gaiety. But they are like the richest chocolate; stuffed costly chocolates that make the taste go stale if you have too many of them. That make plain whole bread taste like ashes.

There are all the earmarks of a group within a group. Cut off all around from ingress from or egress to other groups. A sameness of type. The smug self-satisfaction of an inner measurement; a measurement by standards known within a limited group and not those of an unlimited, seeing, world. . . . Like the blind, blind mice. Mice whose eyes have been blinded.

Strange longing seizes hold of you. You wish yourself back where you can lay your dollar down and sit in a dollar seat to hear voices, strings, reeds that have lifted the World out, up, beyond things that have bodies and walls. Where you can marvel at new marbles and bronzes and flat colors that will make men forget that things exist in a flesh more

From *Frye Street and Environs: The Collected Works of Marita Bonner* by Joyce Flynn © 1987 by Joyce Flynn and Joyce Occomy Stricklin. Reprinted by permission of Beacon Press, Boston.

often than in spirit. Where you can sink your body in a cushioned seat and sink your soul at the same time into a section of life set before you on the boards for a few hours.

You hear that up at New York this is to be seen, that, to be heard.

You decide the next train will take you there.

You decide the next second that that train will not take you, nor the next—nor the next for some time to come.

For you know that—being a woman—you cannot twice a month or twice a year, for that matter, break away to see or hear anything in a city that is supposed to see and hear too much.

That's being a woman. A woman of any color.

You decide that something is wrong with a world that stifles and chokes; that cuts off and stunts; hedging in, pressing down on eyes, ears and throat. Somehow all wrong.

You wonder how it happens there that—say five hundred miles from the Bay State—Anglo Saxon intelligence is so warped and stunted.

How judgement and discernment are bred out of the race. And what has become of discrimination? Discrimination of the right sort. Discrimination that the best minds have told you weighs shadows and nuances and spiritual differences before it catalogues. The kind they have taught you all of your life was best: that looks clearly past generalization and past appearance to dissect, to dig down to the real heart of matters. That casts aside rapid summary conclusions, drawn from primary inference, as Daniel did the spiced meats.

Why can't they then perceive that there is a difference in the glance from a pair of eyes that look, mildly docile, at "white ladies" and those that, impersonally and perceptively—aware of distinctions—see only women who happen to be white?

Why do they see a colored woman only as a gross collection of desires, all uncontrolled, reaching out for their Apollos and the Quasimodos with avid indiscrimination?

Why unless you talk in staccato squawks—brittle as seashells—unless you "champ" gum—unless you cover two yards square when you laugh—unless your taste runs to violent colors—impossible perfumes and more impossible clothes—are you a feminine Caliban craving to pass for Ariel?

An empty imitation of an empty invitation. A mime; a sham; a copy cat. A hollow re-echo. A froth, a foam. A fleck of the ashes of superficiality?

Everything you touch or taste now is like the flesh of an unripe persimmon.

. . . Do you need to be told what that is being . . . ?

Old ideas, old fundamentals seem worm-eaten, outgrown, worthless, bitter; fit for the scrap-heap of Wisdom.

What you had thought tangible and practical has turned out to be a collection of "blue-flower" theories.

If they have not discovered how to use their accumulation of facts, they are useless to you in Their world.

Every part of you becomes bitter.

But—"In Heaven's name, do not grow bitter. Be bigger than they are"—exhort white friends who have never had to draw breath in a Jim-Crow train. Who have never had petty putrid insult dragged over them—drawing blood—like pebbled sand on your body where the skin is tenderest. On your body where the skin is thinnest and tenderest.

You long to explode and hurt everything white; friendly; unfriendly. But you know that you cannot live with a chip on your shoulder even if you can manage a smile around your eyes—without getting steely and brittle and losing the softness that makes you a woman.

For chips make you bend your body to balance them. And once you bend, you lose your poise, your balance, and the chip gets into you. The real you. You get hard.

. . . And many things in you can ossify. . . .

And you know, being a woman, you have to go about it gently and quietly, to find out and to discover just what is wrong. Just what can be done.

You see clearly that they have acquired things.

Money; money. Money to build with, money to destroy. Money to swim in. Money to drown in. Money.

An ascendancy of wisdom. An incalculable hoard of wisdom in all fields, in all things collected from all quarters of humanity.

A stupendous mass of things.

Things.

So, too, the Greeks . . . Things.

And the Romans. . . .

And you wonder and wonder why they have not discovered how to handle deftly and skillfully, Wisdom, stored up for them—like the honey for the Gods on Olympus—since time unknown.

You wonder and you wonder until you wander out into Infinity, where—if it is to be found anywhere—Truth really exists.

The Greeks had possessions, culture. They were lost because they did not understand.

The Romans owned more than anyone else. Trampled under the heel of Vandals and Civilization, because they would not understand.

Greeks. Did not understand.

Romans. Would not understand.

"They." Will not understand.

So you find they have shut Wisdom up and have forgotten to find the key that will let her out. They have trapped, trammeled, lashed her to themselves with thews and thongs and theories. They have ransacked sea and earth and air to bring every treasure to her. But she sulks and will not work for a world with a whitish hue because it has snubbed her twin sister, Understanding.

You see clearly—off there is Infinity—Understanding. Standing alone, waiting for someone to really want her.

But she is so far our there is no way to snatch at her and really drag her in.

So—being a woman—you can wait.

You must sit quietly without a chip. Not sodden—and weighted as if your feet were cast in the iron of your soul. Not wasting strength in enervating gestures as if two hundred years of bonds and whips had really tricked you into nervous uncertainty.

But quiet; quiet. Like Buddha—who brown like I am—sat entirely at ease, entirely sure of himself; motionless and knowing, a thousand years before the white man knew there was so very much difference between feet and hands.

Motionless on the outside. But on the inside?

Silent.

Still . . . "Perhaps Buddha is a woman."

So you too. Still; quiet; with a smile, ever so slight, at the eyes so that Life will flow into and not by you. And you can gather, as it passes, the essences, the overtones, the tints, the shadows; draw understanding to yourself.

And then you can, when Time is ripe, swoop to your feet—at your full height—at a single gesture.

Ready to go where?

Why . . . Wherever God motions.

Gwendolyn B. Bennett (1902–1981)

Gwendolyn B. Bennett's poetry and artwork appeared in *The Crisis* and *Opportunity* journals. Her poems "Heritage" (1923) and "To a Dark Girl" (1927) are representative of her major concern: negotiating race and gender in the New World. Born in Giddings, Texas, Bennett was the only child of Joshua, an attorney, and Maime Bennett, a teacher. When her parents divorced, the courts granted her mother custody, so her father kidnapped her, taking Bennett to live with him in Pennsylvania and various other places. Bennett attended the School of Fine Arts at Columbia University and graduated from the Pratt Institute in 1924. She took a job as assistant professor of art at Howard University. It was during these years that she again saw her mother. Also, while at Howard she had the opportunity to study art in Paris. In 1927, she was fired from Howard for marrying. She married a medical student. After teaching elsewhere and working for community organizations, Bennett spent the final years of her life with her second husband working as an antique collector in Kutztown, Pennsylvania. Along with her poetry, her legacy includes "The Ebony Flute" fine arts column in *Opportunity*.

Heritage

I want to see the slim palm-trees,
Pulling at the clouds
With little pointed fingers. . . .

I want to see lithe Negro girls
Etched dark against the sky
While sunset lingers.

I want to hear the silent sands,
Singing to the moon
Before the Sphinx-still face. . . .

I want to hear the chanting
Around a heathen fire
Of a strange black race.

I want to breathe the Lotus flow'r,
Sighing to the stars
With tendrils drinking at the Nile. . . .

I want to feel the surging
Of my sad people's soul,
Hidden by a minstrel-smile.

To a Dark Girl

I love you for your brownness
And the rounded darkness of your breast.
I love you for the breaking sadness in your voice
And shadows where your wayward eye-lids rest.

Something of old forgotten queens
Lurks in the lithe abandon of your walk
And something of the shackled slave
Sobs in the rhythm of your talk.

Oh, little brown girl, born for sorrow's mate,
Keep all you have of queenliness,
Forgetting that you once were slave,
And let your full lips laugh at Fate!

Helene Johnson (1907–1995)

Along with her cousin and fellow author, Dorothy West, Helene Johnson was born and raised in Boston, attended Boston University, and was a member of the Boston Quill Club, which published the *Saturday Evening Quill* from 1928 to 1930. Helene's grandfather, who had been a slave in South Carolina, bought property in Martha's Vineyard where both she and Dorothy West lived in a large house. It was Dorothy West's mother who added the –e to Helene's name, making it sound higher class. Johnson's mother was a domestic for well-to-do, educated Bostonians. In addition to Boston literary circles, Johnson made her home in New York City and published in the major journal and anthologies of her day, including *Opportunity*, *The Crisis*, the one issue of *Fire!!*, and Countee Cullen's *Caroling Dusk* (1927).

Sonnet to a Negro in Harlem

You are disdainful and magnificent—
Your perfect body and your pompous gait,
Your dark eyes flashing solemnly with hate,
Small wonder that you are incompetent
To imitate those whom you so despise—
Your shoulders towering high above the throng.
Your head thrown back in rich, barbaric song,
Palm trees and mangoes stretched before your eyes.
Let others toil and sweat for labor's sake
And wring from grasping hands their meed of gold.
Why urge ahead your supercilious feet?
Scorn will efface each footprint that you make.
I love your laughter arrogant and bold
You are too splendid for this city street.

My Race

Ah, my race,
Hungry race,
Throbbing and young—
Ah, my race,
Wonder race,
Sobbing with song—
Ah, my race,
Laughing race,
Careless in mirth—

Ah, my veiled
Unformed race,
Fumbling in birth.

Magalu

Summer comes.
The ziczac hovers
'Round the greedy-mouthed crocodile.
A vulture bears away a foolish jackal.
The flamingo is a dash of pink
Against dark green mangroves,
Her slender legs rivalling her slim neck.
The laughing lake gurgles delicious music in its throat
And lulls to sleep the lazy lizard,
A nebulous being on a sun-scorched rock.
In such a place,
In this pulsing, riotous gasp of color,
I met Magalu, dark as a tree at night,
Eager-lipped, listening to a man with a white collar
And a small black book with a cross on it.
Oh Magalu, come! Take my hand and I will read you poetry,
Chromatic words,
Seraphic symphonies,
Fill up your throat with laughter and your heart with song.
Do not let him lure you from your laughing waters,
Lulling lakes, lissome winds.
Would you sell the colors of your sunset and the fragrance
Of your flowers, and the passionate wonder of your forest
For a creed that will not let you dance?

Fom *Shadowed Dreams: Women's Poetry of the Harlem Renaissance*, ed. Maureen Honey, Rutgers UP, 1989. Reprinted by arrangement with Abigail McGrath.

Dorothy West (1907–1998)

In the late 1990s, Dorothy West was the last surviving writer from the Harlem Renaissance. In 1934, she founded the Harlem Renaissance literary magazine, *Challenge*, and in 1948 published *The Living Is Easy*, a novel that takes place in the Boston black society that she knew so well. As late as 1995, she would publish yet another novel about upper-class blacks on Martha's Vineyard. That novel, *The Wedding*, became a bestseller and a television movie. West was born in Boston to Isaac West and Rachel Benson West. An ex-slave from Virginia, Isaac West became a prosperous seller of bananas and was known as the Black Banana King. Rachel Benson West was a light-skinned woman whose family sent her North to avoid becoming the victim of white southern men's sexual desires. Dorothy attended the Girls' Latin School, Boston University, and the Columbia School of Journalism. When just eighteen, she published her first short story, "The Typewriter." West's major emphases are race, class, gender, and geography.

The Typewriter

It occurred to him, as he eased past the bulging knees of an Irish wash lady and forced an apologetic passage down the aisle of the crowded car, that more than anything in all the world he wanted not to go home. He began to wish passionately that he had never been born, that he had never been married, that he had never been the means of life's coming into the world. He knew quite suddenly that he hated his flat and his family and his friends. And most of all the incessant thing that would "clatter clatter" until every nerve screamed aloud, and the words of the evening paper danced crazily before him, and the insane desire to crush and kill set his fingers twitching.

He shuffled down the street, an abject little man of fifty-odd years, in an ageless overcoat that flapped in the wind. He was cold, and he hated the North, and particularly Boston, and saw suddenly a barefoot pickaninny sitting on a fence in the hot, Southern sun with a piece of steaming corn bread and a piece of fried salt pork in either grimy hand.

He was tired, and he wanted his supper, but he didn't want the beans, and frankfurters, and light bread that Net would undoubtedly have. That Net had had every Monday night since that regrettable moment fifteen years before when he had told her—innocently—that such a supper tasted "right nice. Kinda change from what we always has."

He mounted the four brick steps leading to his door and pulled at the bell; but there was no answering ring. It was broken again, and in a mental flash he saw himself with a multitude of tools and a box of matches shivering in the vestibule after supper. He began to pound lustily on the door and wondered vaguely if his hand would bleed if he smashed the glass. He hated the sight of blood. It sickened him.

Someone was running down the stairs. Daisy probably. Millie would be at that infernal thing, pounding, pounding. . . . He entered. The chill of the house swept him. His child was wrapped in a coat. She whispered solemnly, "Poppa, Miz Hicks an' Miz Berry's orful mad. They gointa move if they can't get more heat. The furnace's bin out all day. Mama couldn't fix it." He said hurriedly, "I'll go right down. I'll go right down." He hoped Mrs. Hicks wouldn't pull open her door and glare at him. She was large and domineering, and her husband was a bully. If her husband ever struck him it would kill him. He hated life, but he didn't want to die. He was afraid of God, and in his wildest flights of fancy couldn't imagine himself an angel. He went softly down the stairs.

He began to shake the furnace fiercely. And he shook into it every wrong, mumbling softly under his breath. He began to think back over his uneventful years, and it came to him as rather a shock that he had never sworn in all his life. He wondered uneasily if he dared say "damn." It was taken for granted that a man swore when he tended a stubborn furnace. And his strongest interjection was "Great balls of fire!"

The cellar began to warm, and he took off his inadequate overcoat that was streaked with dirt. Well, Net would have to clean that. He'd be damned—! It frightened him and thrilled him. He wanted suddenly to rush upstairs and tell Mrs. Hicks if she didn't like the way he was running things, she could get out. But he heaped another shovelful of coal on the fire and sighed. He would never be able to get away from himself and the routine of years.

He thought of that eager Negro lad of seventeen who had come North to seek his fortune. He had walked jauntily down Boylston Street, and even his own kind had laughed at the incongruity of him. But he had thrown up his head and promised himself. "You'll have an office here some day. With plate-glass windows and a real mahogany desk." But, though he didn't know it then, he was not the progressive type. And he became successively, in the years, bell boy, porter, waiter, cook, and finally janitor in a downtown office building.

He had married Net when he was thirty-three and a waiter. He had married her partly because—though he might not have admitted it—there was no one to eat the expensive delicacies the generous cook gave him every night to bring home. And partly because he dared hope there might be a son to fulfill his dreams. But Millie had come, and after her, twin girls who had died within two weeks, then Daisy, and it was tacitly understood that Net was done with childbearing.

Life, though flowing monotonously, had flowed peacefully enough until that sucker of sanity became a sitting room fixture. Intuitively at the very first he had felt its undesirability. He had suggested hesitatingly that they couldn't afford it. Three dollars the eighth of every month. Three dollars: food and fuel. Times were hard, and the twenty dollars apiece the respective husbands of Miz Hicks and Miz Berry irregularly paid was only five dollars more than the thirty-five a month he paid his own Hebraic landlord. And the Lord knew his salary was little enough. At which point Net spoke her piece, her voice rising shrill. "God knows I never complain 'bout nothin'. Ain't no other woman got less than me. I bin wearin' this same dress here five years, an' I'll wear it another five. But I don't want nothin'. I ain't never wanted nothin'. An' when I does as', it's only for my children. You're a poor sort of father if you can't give that child jes' three dollars a month to rent that typewriter. Ain't 'nother girl in school ain't got one. An' mos' of 'ems bought an paid for. You know yourself how Millie is. She wouldn't as' me for it till she had to. An' I ain't going to disappoint her. She's goin' to get that typewriter Saturday, mark my words."

On a Monday then it had been installed. And in the months that followed, night after night he listened to the murderous "tack, tack, tack" that was like a vampire slowly drinking his blood. If only he could escape. Bar a door against the sound of it. But tied hand and foot by the economic fact that "Lord knows we can't afford to have fires burnin' an' lights lit all over the flat. You'all gotta set in one room. An' when y'get tired setting y'c'n go to bed. Gas bill was somep'n scandalous last month."

He heaped a final shovelful of coal on the fire and watched the first blue flames. Then, his overcoat under his arm, he mounted the cellar stairs. Mrs. Hicks was standing in her kitchen door, arms akimbo. "It's warmin'," she volunteered.

"Yeh," he was conscious of his grime-streaked face and hands, "it's warmin'. I'm sorry 'bout all day."

She folded her arms across her ample bosom. "Tending a furnace ain't a woman's work. I don't blame you wife none 'tall."

Unsuspecting, he was grateful. "Yeh, it's pretty hard for a woman. I always look after it 'fore I goes to work, but some days it jes' ac's up."

"Y'oughta have a janitor, that's what y'ought," she flung at him. "The same cullud man that tends them apartments would be willin'. Mr. Taylor has him. It takes a man to run a furnace, and when the man's away all day—"

"I know," he interrupted, embarrassed and hurt. "I know. Tha's right, Miz Hicks, tha's right. But I ain't in a position to make no improvements. Times is hard."

She surveyed him critically. "Your wife called down 'bout three times while you was in the cellar. I reckon she wants you for supper."

"Thanks," he mumbled and escaped up the back stairs.

He hung up his overcoat in the closet, telling himself, a little lamely, that it wouldn't take him more than a minute to clean it up himself after supper. After all, Net was tired and probably worried what with Mrs. Hicks and all. And he hated men who made slaves of their womenfolk. Good old Net.

He tidied up in the bathroom, washing his face and hands carefully and cleanly so as to leave no—or very little—stain on the roller towel. It was hard enough for Net, God knew.

He entered the kitchen. The last spirals of steam were rising from his supper. One thing about Net, she served a full plate. He smiled appreciatively at her unresponsive back, bent over the kitchen sink. There was no one who could bake beans just like Net's. And no one who could find a market with frankfurters quite so fat.

He sat down at his place. "Evenin', hon."

He saw her back stiffen. "If your supper's cold, 'tain't my fault. I called and called."

He said hastily, "It's fine, Net, fine. Piping."

She was the usual tired housewife. "Y'oughta et your supper 'fore you fooled with that furnace. I ain't bothered 'bout them niggers. I got all my dishes washed 'cept yours. An' I hate to mess up my kitchen after I once get it straightened up."

He was humble. "I'll give that old furnace an extra lookin' after in the mornin'. It'll last all day tomorrow, hon."

"An' on top of that," she continued, unheeding him and giving a final wrench to her dish towel, "that confounded bell don't ring. An'—"

"I'll fix it after supper," he interposed quickly.

She hung up her dish towel and came to stand before him looming large and yellow. "An' that old Miz Berry, she claim she was expectin' comp'ny. An' she know they must 'a come an' gone while she was in her kitchen an' couldn't be at her winder to watch for 'em. Old liar." She brushed back a lock of naturally straight hair. "She wasn't expectin' nobody."

"Well, you know how some folks are—"

"Fools! Half the world," was her vehement answer. "I'm goin' in the front room an' set down a spell. I bin on my feet all day. Leave them dishes on the table. God knows I'm tired, but I'll come back an' wash 'em." But they both knew, of course, that he, very clumsily, would.

At precisely quarter past nine when he, strained at last to the breaking point, uttering an inhuman, strangled cry, flung down his paper, clutched at his throat, and sprang to his feet, Millie's surprised young voice, shocking him to normalcy, heralded the first of that series of great moments that every humble little middle-class man eventually experiences.

"What's the matter, Poppa? You sick? I wanted you to help me."

He drew out his handkerchief and wiped his hot hands. "I declare I must 'a' fallen asleep an' had a nightmare. No, I ain't sick. What you want, hon?"

"Dictate me a letter, Poppa. I c'n do sixty words a minute. You know, like a business letter. You know, like those men in your building dictate to their stenographers. Don't you hear 'em sometimes?"

"Oh sure, I know, hon. Poppa'll help you. Sure. I hear that Mr. Browning. Sure."

Net rose, "Guess I'll put this child to bed. Come on now, Daisy, without no fuss. Then I'll run up to Pa's. He ain't bin well all week."

When the door closed behind them, he crossed to his daughter, conjured the image of Mr. Browning in the process of dictating, so arranged himself, and coughed importantly.

"Well, Millie—"

"Oh, Poppa, is that what you'd call your stenographer?" she teased. "And anyway pretend I'm really one—and you're really my boss, and this letter's real important."

A light crept into his dull eyes. Vigor through his thin blood. In a brief moment the weight of years fell from him like a cloak. Tired, bent, little old man that he was, he smiled, straightened, tapped impressively against his teeth with a toil-stained finger, and became that enviable emblem of American life: a businessman.

"You be Miz Hicks, huh, honey? Course we can't both use the same name. I'll be J. Lucius Jones. J. Lucius. All them real big men use their middle names. Jus' kinda looks big doin', doncha think, hon? Looks like, money, huh? J. Lucius." He uttered a sound that was like the proud cluck of a strutting hen. "J. Lucius." It rolled like oil from his tongue.

His daughter twisted impatiently. "Now, Poppa—I mean Mr. Jones, sir—please begin. I am ready for dictation, sir."

He was in that office on Boylston Street, looking with visioning eyes through its plate-glass windows, tapping with impatient fingers on its real mahogany desk.

"Ah—Beaker Brothers, Park Square Building, Boston, Mass. Ah—Gentlemen: In reply to yours of the seventh instant would state—"

Every night thereafter in the weeks that followed, with Daisy packed off to bed, and Net "gone up to Pa's" or nodding unobtrusively in her corner, there was the chameleon change of a Court Street janitor to J. Lucius Jones, dealer in stocks and bonds. He would stand, posturing, importantly flicking imaginary dust from his coat lapel, or, his hands locked behind his back, he would stride up and down, earnestly and seriously debating the advisability of buying copper with the market in such a fluctuating state. Once a week, too, he stopped in at Jerry's, and after a preliminary purchase of cheap cigars, bought the latest trade papers, mumbling an embarrassed explanation: "I got a little money. Think I'll invest it in reliable stock."

The letters Millie typed and subsequently discarded, he rummaged for later, and under cover of writing to his brother in the South, laboriously, with a great many fancy flourishes, signed each neatly typed sheet with the exalted J. Lucius Jones.

Later, when he mustered the courage, he suggested tentatively to Millie that it might be fun—just fun, of course—to answer his letters. One night—he laughed a good deal louder and longer than necessary—he'd be J. Lucius Jones, and the next night—here he swallowed hard and looked a little frightened—Rockefeller or Vanderbilt or Morgan—just for fun, y'understand! To which Millie gave consent. It mattered little to her one way or the other. It was practice, and that was what she needed. Very soon now she'd be in the hundred class. Then maybe she could get a job!

He was growing very careful of his English. Occasionally—and it must be admitted, ashamedly—he made surreptitious ventures into the dictionary. He had to, of course. J. Lucius Jones would never say "Y'got to" when he meant "It is expedient." And, old brain though he was, he learned quickly and easily, juggling words with amazing facility.

Eventually, he bought stamps and envelopes—long, important-looking envelopes—and stammered apologetically to Millie, "Honey, Poppa thought it'd help you if you learned to type envelopes, too. Reckon you'll have to do that, too, when y'get a job. Poor old man," he swallowed painfully, "came round selling these envelopes. You know how 'tis. So I had to buy 'em." Which was satisfactory to Millie. If she saw through her father, she gave no sign. After all, it was practice, and Mr. Hennessey had promised the smartest girl in the class a position in the very near future. And she, of course, was smart as a steel trap. Even Mr. Hennessey had said that—though not in just those words.

He had gotten in the habit of carrying those self-addressed envelopes in his inner pocket where they bulged impressively. And occasionally he would take them out—on the car usually—and smile upon them. This one might be from J. P. Morgan. This one from Henry Ford. And a million-dollar deal involved in each. That narrow, little spinster who, upon his sitting down, had drawn herself away from his contact, was shunning J. Lucius Jones!

Once, led by some sudden, strange impulse, as an outgoing car rumbled up out of the subway, he got out a letter, darted a quick shamed glance about him, dropped it in an adjacent box, and swung aboard the car, feeling, dazedly, as if he had committed a crime. And the next night he sat in the sitting room quite on edge until Net said suddenly, "Look here, a real important letter come today for you, Pa. Here 'tis. What you s'pose it says?" And he reached out a hand that trembled. He made brief explanation. "Advertisement, hon. Thassal."

They came quite frequently after that, and despite the fact that he knew them by heart, he read them quite slowly and carefully, rustling the sheet, and making inaudible, intelligent comments. He was, in these moments, pathetically earnest.

Monday, as he went about his janitor's duties, he composed in his mind the final letter from J. P. Morgan that would consummate a big business deal. For days now, letters had passed between them. J. P. had been at first quite frankly uninterested. He had written tersely and briefly. Which was meat to J. Lucius. The compositions of his brain were really the work of an artist. He wrote glowingly of the advantages of a pact between them. Daringly he argued in terms of billions. And at last J. P. had written his next letter would be decisive. Which next letter, this Monday, as he trailed about the office building, was writing itself in his brain.

That night Millie opened the door for him. Her plain face was transformed. "Poppa—Poppa, I got a job! Twelve dollars a week to start with! Isn't that swell!"

He was genuinely pleased. "Honey, I'm glad. Right glad," and went upstairs, unsuspecting.

He ate his supper hastily, went down into the cellar to see about his fire, returned and carefully tidied up, informing his reflection in the bathroom mirror, "Well, J. Lucius, you c'n expect that final letter any day now."

He entered the sitting room. The phonograph was playing. Daisy was singing lustily. Strange. Net was talking animatedly to Millie, busy with needle and thread over a neat, little frock. His wild glance darted to the table. The pretty little centerpiece of the bowl and wax flowers all neatly

arranged: the typewriter gone from its accustomed place. It seemed an hour before he could speak. He felt himself trembling. Went hot and cold.

"Millie—your typewriter's—gone!"

She made a deft little in-and-out movement with her needle. "It's the eighth, you know. When the man came today for the money, I sent it back. I won't need it no more—now! The money's on the mantelpiece, Poppa."

"Yeh," he muttered. "All right."

He sank down in his chair, fumbled for the paper, found it.

Net said, "Your poppa wants to read. Stop your noise, Daisy."

She obediently stopped both her noise and the phonograph, took up her book, and became absorbed. Millie went on with her sewing in placid anticipation of the morrow. Net immediately began to nod, gave a curious snort, slept.

Silence. That crowded in on him, engulfed him. That blurred his vision, dulled his brain. Vast, white, impenetrable. . . . His ears strained for the old, familiar sound. And silence beat upon them. . . . The words of the evening paper jumbled together. He read: "J. P. Morgan goes—"

It burst upon him. Blinded him. His hands groped for the bulge beneath his coat. Why this—this was the end! The end of those great moments—the end of everything! Bewildering pain tore through him. He clutched at his heart and felt, almost, the jagged edges drive into his hand. A lethargy swept down upon him. He could not move, nor utter a sound. He could not pray, nor curse.

Against the wall of that silence. J. Lucius Jones crashed and died.

The Richer, The Poorer

Over the years Lottie had urged Bess to prepare for her old age. Over the years Bess had lived each day as if there were no other. Now they were both past sixty, the time for summing up. Lottie had a bank account that had never grown lean. Bess had the clothes on her back, and the rest of her worldly possessions in a battered suitcase.

Lottie had hated being a child, hearing her parents' skimping and scraping. Bess had never seemed to notice. All she ever wanted was to go outside and play. She learned to skate on borrowed skates. She rode a borrowed bicycle. Lottie couldn't wait to grow up and buy herself the best of everything.

As soon as anyone would hire her, Lottie put herself to work. She minded babies, she ran errands for the old.

She never touched a penny of her money, though her child's mouth watered for ice cream and candy. But she could not bear to share with Bess, who never had anything to share with her. When the dimes began to add up to dollars, she lost her taste for sweets.

By the time she was twelve, she was clerking after school in a small variety store. Saturdays she worked as long as she was wanted. She decided to keep her money for clothes. When she entered high school, she would wear a wardrobe that neither she nor anyone else would be able to match.

But her freshman year found her unable to indulge so frivolous a whim, particularly when her admiring instructors advised her to think seriously of college. No one in her family had ever gone to college, and certainly Bess would never get there. She would show them all what she could do, if she put her mind to it.

She began to bank her money, and her bank became her most private and precious possession.

In her third year she found a job in a small but expanding restaurant, where she cashiered from the busy hour until closing. In her last year the business increased so rapidly that Lottie was faced with the choice of staying in school or working full-time.

She made her choice easily. A job in hand was worth two in the future.

Bess had a beau in the school band, who had no other ambition except to play a horn. Lottie expected to be settled with a home and family while Bess was still waiting for Harry to earn enough to buy a marriage license.

That Bess married Harry straight out of high school was not surprising. That Lottie never married at all was not really surprising either. Two or three times she was halfway persuaded, but to give up a job that paid well for a home-making job that paid nothing was a risk she was incapable of taking.

Bess's married life was nothing for Lottie to envy. She and Harry lived like gypsies, Harry playing in second-rate bands all over the country, even getting himself and Bess stranded in Europe. They were often in rags and never in riches.

Bess grieved because she had no child, not having sense enough to know she was better off without one. Lottie was certainly better off without nieces and nephews to feel sorry for. Very likely Bess would have dumped them on her doorstep.

That Lottie had a doorstep they might have been left on was only because her boss, having bought a second house, offered Lottie his first house at a price so low and terms so reasonable that it would have been like losing money to refuse.

She shut off the rooms she didn't use, letting them go to rack and ruin. Since she ate her meals out, she had no food at home, and did not encourage callers, who always expected a cup of tea.

Her way of life was mean and miserly, but she did not know it. She thought she lived frugally in her middle years so that she could live in comfort and ease when she most needed peace of mind.

The years, after forty, began to race. Suddenly Lottie was sixty, and retired from her job by her boss's son, who had no sentimental feeling about keeping her on until she was ready to quit.

She made several attempts to find other employment, but her dowdy appearance made her look old and inefficient. For the first time in her life Lottie would gladly have worked for nothing, to have some place to go, something to do with her day.

Harry died abroad, in a third-rate hotel, with Bess weeping as hard as if he had left her a fortune. He had left her nothing but his horn. There wasn't even money for her passage home.

Lottie, trapped by the blood tie, knew she would not only have to send for her sister, but take her in when she returned. It didn't seem fair that Bess should reap the harvest of Lottie's lifetime of self-denial.

It took Lottie a week to get a bedroom ready, a week of hard work and hard cash. There was everything to do, everything to replace or paint. When she was through the room looked so fresh and new that Lottie felt she deserved it more than Bess.

She would let Bess have her room, but the mattress was so lumpy, the carpet so worn, the curtains so threadbare that Lottie's conscience pricked her. She supposed she would have to redo that room, too, and went about doing it with an eagerness that she mistook for haste.

When she was through upstairs, she was shocked to see how dismal downstairs looked by comparison. She tried to ignore it, but with nowhere to go to escape it, the contrast grew more intolerable.

She worked her way from kitchen to parlor, persuading herself she was only putting the rooms to right to give herself something to do. At night she slept like a child after a long and happy day of playing house. She was having more fun than she had ever had in her life. She was living each hour for itself.

There was only a day now before Bess would arrive. Passing her gleaming mirrors, at first with vague awareness, then with painful clarity, Lottie saw herself as others saw her, and could not stand the sight.

She went on a spending spree from specialty shops to beauty salon, emerging transformed into a woman who believed in miracles.

She was in the kitchen basting a turkey when Bess rang the bell. Her heart raced, and she wondered if the heat from the oven was responsible.

She went to the door, and Bess stood before her. Stiffly she suffered Bess's embrace, her heart racing harder, her eyes suddenly smarting from the onrush of cold air.

"Oh, Lottie, it's good to see you," Bess said, but saying nothing about Lottie's splendid appearance. Upstairs Bess, putting down her shabby suitcase, said, "I'll sleep like a rock tonight," without a word of praise for her lovely room. At the lavish table, top-heavy with turkey, Bess said, "I'll take light and dark both," with no marveling at the size of the bird, or that there was turkey for two elderly women, one of them too poor to buy her own bread.

With the glow of good food in her stomach, Bess began to spin stories. They were rich with places and people, most of them lowly, all of them magnificent. Her face reflected her telling, the joys and sorrows of her remembering, and above all, the love she lived by that enhanced the poorest place, the humblest person.

Then it was that Lottie knew why Bess had made no mention of her finery, or the shining room, or the twelve-pound turkey. She had not even seen them. Tomorrow she would see the room as it really looked, and Lottie as she really looked, and the warmed-over turkey in its second-day glory.

Tonight she saw only what she had come seeking, a place in her sister's home and heart.

She said, "That's enough about me. How have the years used you?"

"It was me who didn't use them," said Lottie wistfully. "I saved for them. I forgot the best of them would go without my ever spending a day or a dollar enjoying them. That's my life story in those few words, a life never lived.

"Now it's too near the end to try."

Bess said, "To know how much there is to know is the beginning of learning to live. Don't count the years that are left us. At our time of life it's the days that count. You've too much catching up to do to waste a minute of a waking hour feeling sorry for yourself."

Lottie grinned, a real wide open grin, "Well, to tell the truth I felt sorry for you. Maybe if I had any sense I'd feel sorry for myself, after all. I know I'm too old to kick up my heels, but I'm going to let you show me how. If I land on my head, I guess it won't matter. I feel giddy already, and I like it."

Ann Petry (1908–1997)

Ann Petry wrote short stories, children's literature, and three novels: *The Street* (1946), *Country Place* (1947), and *The Narrows* (1953). She was born in Old Saybrook, Connecticut, to one of the few black families living there at the time. Her middle-class family included a father, Peter Lane, who was a licensed pharmacist and owner of a drugstore, and her mother, Bertha Lane, who was a licensed podiatrist. Petry's sister was a graduate of Brown University, and Petry graduated from the School of Pharmacy at what is now the University of Connecticut. When she married George Petry in 1938, she moved to Harlem and decided to become a writer. "Like a Winding Sheet" was published in *Crisis* in 1945. Houghton Mifflin awarded her a literary fellowship that helped her to complete *The Street*, a well-received novel that depicts the entrapped life of Lutie Johnson who must deal with issues of race, class, and gender.

Like a Winding Sheet

He had planned to get up before Mae did and surprise her by fixing breakfast. Instead he went back to sleep and she got out of bed so quietly he didn't know she wasn't there beside him until he woke up and heard the queer soft gurgle of water running out of the sink in the bathroom.

He knew he ought to get up but instead he put his arms across his forehead to shut the afternoon sunlight out of his eyes, pulled his legs up close to his body, testing them to see if the ache was still in them.

Mae had finished in the bathroom. He could tell because she never closed the door when she was in there and now the sweet smell of talcum powder was drifting down the hall and into the bedroom. Then he heard her coming down the hall.

"Hi, babe," she said affectionately.

"Hum," he grunted, and moved his arms away from his head, opened one eye.

"It's a nice morning."

"Yeah." He rolled over and the sheet twisted around him, outlining his thighs, his chest. "You mean afternoon, don't ya?"

Mae looked at the twisted sheet and giggled. "Looks like a winding sheet," she said. "A shroud—" Laughter tangled with her words and she had to pause for a moment before she could continue. "You look like a huckleberry—in a winding sheet—"

"That's no way to talk. Early in the day like this," he protested.

He looked at his arms silhouetted against the white of the sheets. They were inky black by contrast and he had to smile in spite of himself and he lay there smiling and savoring the sweet sound of Mae's giggling.

"Early?" She pointed a finger at the alarm clock on the table near the bed and giggled again. "It's almost four o'clock. And if you don't spring up out of there, you're going to be late again."

"What do you mean 'again'?"

"Twice last week. Three times the week before. And once the week before and—"

"I can't get used to sleeping in the daytime," he said fretfully. He pushed his legs out from under the covers experimentally. Some of the ache had gone out of them but they weren't really rested yet. "It's too light for good sleeping. And all that standing beats the hell out of my legs."

"After two years you oughta be used to it," Mae said.

He watched her as she fixed her hair, powdered her face, slipped into a pair of blue denim overalls. She moved quickly and yet she didn't seem to hurry.

"You look like you'd had plenty of sleep," he said lazily. He had to get up but he kept putting the moment off, not wanting to move, yet he didn't dare let his legs go completely limp because if he did he'd go back to sleep. It was getting later and later but the thought of putting his weight on his legs kept him lying there.

When he finally got up he had to hurry, and he gulped his breakfast so fast that he wondered if his stomach could possibly use food thrown at it at such a rate of speed. He was still wondering about it as he and Mae were putting their coats on in the hall.

Mae paused to look at the calendar. "It's the thirteenth," she said. Then a faint excitement in her voice, "Why, it's Friday the thirteenth." She had one arm in her coat sleeve and she held it there while she stared at the calendar. "I oughta stay home," she said. "I shouldn't go outa the house."

"Aw, don't be a fool," he said. "Today's payday. And payday is a good luck day everywhere, any way you look at it." And as she stood hesitating he said, "Aw, come on."

And he was late for work again because they spent fifteen minutes arguing before he could convince her she ought to go to work just the same. He had to talk persuasively, urging her gently, and it took time. But he couldn't bring himself to talk to her roughly or threaten to strike her like a lot of men might have done. He wasn't made that way.

So when he reached the plant he was late and he had to wait to punch the time clock because the day-shift workers were streaming out in long lines, in groups and bunches that impeded his progress.

Even now just starting his workday his legs ached. He had to force himself to struggle past the outgoing workers, punch the time clock, and get the little cart he pushed around all night, because he kept toying with the idea of going home and getting back in bed.

He pushed the cart out on the concrete floor, thinking that if this was his plant he'd make a lot of changes in it. There were too many standing-up jobs for one thing. He'd figure out some way most of 'em could be done sitting down and he'd put a lot more benches around. And this job he had—this job that forced him to walk ten hours a night, pushing this little cart, well, he'd turn it into a sitting-down job. One of those little trucks they used around railroad stations would be good for a job like this. Guys sat on a seat and the thing moved easily, taking up little room and turning in hardly any space at all, like on a dime.

He pushed the cart near the foreman. He never could remember to refer to her as the forelady even in his mind. It was funny to have a white woman for a boss in a plant like this one.

She was sore about something. He could tell by the way her face was red and her eyes were half-shut until they were slits. Probably been out late and didn't get enough sleep. He avoided looking at her and hurried a little, head down, as he passed her though he couldn't resist stealing a glance at her out of the corner of his eyes. He saw the edge of the light-colored slacks she wore and the tip end of a big tan shoe.

"Hey, Johnson!" the woman said.

The machines had started full blast. The whirr and the grinding made the building shake, made it impossible to hear conversations. The men and women at the machines talked to each other but looking at them from just a little distance away, they appeared to be simply moving their lips because you couldn't hear what they were saying. Yet the woman's voice cut across the machine sounds—harsh, angry.

He turned his head slowly. "Good evenin', Mrs. Scott," he said, and waited.

"You're late again."

"That's right. My legs were bothering me."

The woman's face grew redder, angrier looking. "Half this shift comes in late," she said. "And you're the worst one of all. You're always late. Whatsa matter with ya?"

"It's my legs," he said. "Somehow they don't ever get rested. I don't seem to get used to sleeping days. And I just can't get started."

"Excuses. You guys always got excuses," her anger grew and spread. "Every guy comes in here late always has an excuse. His wife's sick or his grandmother died or somebody in the family had to go to the hospital," she paused, drew a deep breath. "And the niggers is the worse. I don't care what's wrong with your legs. You get in here on time. I'm sick of you niggers—"

"You got the right to get mad," he interrupted softly. "You got the right to cuss me four ways to Sunday but I ain't letting nobody call me a nigger."

He stepped closer to her. His fists were doubled. His lips were drawn back in a thin narrow line. A vein in his forehead stood out swollen, thick.

And the woman backed away from him, not hurriedly but slowly—two, three steps back.

"Aw, forget it," she said. "I didn't mean nothing by it. It slipped out. It was an accident." The red of her face deepened until the small blood vessels in her cheeks were purple. "Go on and get to work," she urged. And she took three more slow backward steps.

He stood motionless for a moment and then turned away from the sight of the red lipstick on her mouth that made him remember that the foreman was a woman. And he couldn't bring himself to hit a woman. He felt a curious tingling in his fingers and he looked down at his hands. They were clenched tight, hard, ready to smash some of those small purple veins in her face.

He pushed the cart ahead of him, walking slowly. When he turned his head, she was staring in his direction, mopping her forehead with a dark blue handkerchief. Their eyes met and then they both looked away.

He didn't glance in her direction again but moved past the long work benches, carefully collecting the finished parts, going slowly and steadily up and down, back and forth the length of the building, and as he walked he forced himself to swallow his anger, get rid of it.

And he succeeded so that he was able to think about what had happened without getting upset about it. An hour went by but the tension stayed in his hands. They were clenched and knotted on the handles of the cart as though ready to aim a blow.

And he thought he should have hit her anyway, smacked her hard in the face, felt the soft flesh of her face give under the hardness of his hands. He tried to make his hands relax by offering them a description of what it would have been like to strike her because he had the queer feeling that his hands were not exactly a part of him anymore—they had developed a separate life of their own over which he had no control. So he dwelt on the pleasure his hands would have felt—both of them cracking at her, first one and then the other. If he had done that his hands would have felt good now—relaxed, rested.

And he decided that even if he'd lost his job for it, he should have let her have it and it would have been a long time, maybe the rest of her life, before she called anybody else a nigger.

The only trouble was he couldn't hit a woman. A woman couldn't hit back the same way a man did. But it would have been a deeply satisfying thing to have cracked her narrow lips wide open with just one blow, beautifully timed and with all his weight in back of it. That way he would have gotten rid of all the energy and tension his anger had created in him. He kept remembering how his heart had started pumping blood so fast he had felt it tingle even in the tips of his fingers.

With the approach of night, fatigue nibbled at him. The corners of his mouth drooped, the frown between his eyes deepened, his shoulders sagged; but his hands stayed tight and tense. As the hours dragged by he noticed that the women workers had started to snap and snarl at each other. He couldn't hear what they said because of the sound of machines but he could see the quick lip movements that sent words tumbling from the sides of their mouths. They gestured irritably with their hands and scowled as their mouths moved.

Their violent jerky motions told him that it was getting close on to quitting time but somehow he felt that the night still stretched ahead of him, composed of endless hours of steady walking on his aching legs. When the whistle finally blew he went on pushing the cart, unable to believe that it had sounded. The whirring of the machines died away to a murmur and he knew then that he'd really heard the whistle. He stood still for a moment, filled with a relief that made him sigh.

Then he moved briskly, putting the cart in the storeroom, hurrying to take his place in the line forming before the paymaster. That was another thing he'd change, he thought. He'd have the pay envelopes handed to the people right at their benches so there wouldn't be ten or fifteen minutes lost waiting for the pay. He always got home about fifteen minutes late on payday. They did it better in the plant where Mae worked, brought the money right to them at their benches.

He stuck his pay envelope in his pants' pocket and followed the line of workers heading for the subway in a slow-moving stream. He glanced up at the sky. It was a nice night, the sky looked packed full to running over with stars. And he thought if he and Mae would go right to bed when they got home from work they'd catch a few hours of darkness for

sleeping. But they never did. They fooled around—cooking and eating and listening to the radio and he always stayed in a big chair in the living room and went almost but not quite to sleep and when they finally got to bed it was five or six in the morning and daylight was already seeping around the edges of the sky.

He walked slowly, putting off the moment when he would have to plunge into the crowd hurrying toward the subway. It was a long ride to Harlem and tonight the thought of it appalled him. He paused outside an all-night restaurant to kill time, so that some of the first rush of workers would be gone when he reached the subway.

The lights in the restaurant were brilliant, enticing. There was life and motion inside. And as he looked through the window he thought that everything within range of his eyes gleamed—the long imitation marble counter, the tall stools, the white porcelain-topped tables and especially the big metal coffee urn right near the window. Steam issued from its top and a gas flame flickered under it—a lively, dancing, blue flame.

A lot of the workers from his shift—men and women—were lining up near the coffee urn. He watched them walk to the porcelain-topped tables carrying steaming cups of coffee and he saw that just the smell of the coffee lessened the fatigue lines in their faces. After the first sip their faces softened, they smiled, they began to talk and laugh.

On a sudden impulse he shoved the door open and joined the line in front of the coffee urn. The line moved slowly. And as he stood there the smell of the coffee, the sound of the laughter and of the voices, helped dull the sharp ache in his legs.

He didn't pay any attention to the white girl who was serving the coffee at the urn. He kept looking at the cups in the hands of the men who had been ahead of him. Each time a man stepped out of the line with one of the thick white cups the fragrant steam got in his nostrils. He saw that they walked carefully so as not to spill a single drop. There was a froth of bubbles at the top of each cup and he thought about how he would let the bubbles break against his lips before he actually took a big deep swallow.

Then it was his turn. "A cup of coffee," he said, just as he had heard the others say.

The white girl looked past him, put her hands up to her head and gently lifted her hair away from the back of her neck, tossing her head back a little. "No more coffee for a while," she said.

He wasn't certain he'd heard her correctly and he said, "What?" blankly.

"No more coffee for a while," she repeated.

There was silence behind him and then uneasy movement. He thought someone would say something, ask why or protest, but there was only silence and then a faint shuffling sound as though the men standing behind him had simultaneously shifted their weight from one foot to the other.

He looked at the girl without saying anything. He felt his hands begin to tingle and the tingling went all the way down to his finger tips so that he glanced down at them. They were clenched tight, hard, into fists. Then he looked at the girl again. What he wanted to do was hit her so hard that the scarlet lipstick on her mouth would smear and spread over her nose, her chin, out toward her cheeks, so hard that she would never toss her head again and refuse a man a cup of coffee because he was black.

He estimated the distance across the counter and reached forward, balancing his weight on the balls of his feet, ready to let the blow go. And then his hands fell back down to his sides because he forced himself to lower them, to unclench them and make them dangle loose. The effort took his breath away because his hands fought against him. But he couldn't hit her. He couldn't even now bring himself to hit a woman, not even this one, who had refused him a cup of coffee with a toss of her head. He kept seeing the gesture with which she had lifted the length of her blond hair from the back of her neck as expressive of her contempt for him.

When he went out the door he didn't look back. If he had he would have seen the flickering blue flame under the shiny coffee urn being extinguished. The line of men who had stood behind him lingered a moment to watch the people drinking coffee at the tables and then they left just as he had without having had the coffee they wanted so badly. The girl behind the counter poured water in the urn and swabbed it out and as she waited for the water to run out, she lifted her hair gently from the back of her neck and tossed her head before she began making a fresh lot of coffee.

But he had walked away without a backward look, his head down, his hands in his pockets, raging at himself and whatever it was inside of him that had forced him to stand quiet and still when he wanted to strike out.

The subway was crowded and he had to stand. He tried grasping an overhead strap and his hands were too tense to grip it. So he moved near the train door and stood there swaying back and forth with the rocking of the train. The roar of the train beat inside his head, making it ache and throb, and the pain in his legs clawed up into his groin so that he seemed to be bursting with pain and he told himself that it was due to all that anger-born energy that had piled up in him and not been used and so it had spread through him like a poison—from his feet and legs all the way up to his head.

Mae was in the house before he was. He knew she was home before he put the key in the door of the apartment. The radio was going. She had it turned up loud and she was singing along with it.

"Hello, babe," she called out, as soon as he opened the door.

He tried to say 'hello' and it came out half grunt and half sigh.

"You sure sound cheerful," she said.

She was in the bedroom and he went and leaned against the doorjamb. The denim overalls she wore to work were carefully draped over the back of a chair by the bed. She was standing in front of the dresser, tying the sash of a yellow housecoat around her waist and chewing gum vigorously as she admired her reflection in the mirror over the dresser.

"Whatsa matter?" she said. "You get bawled out by the boss or somep'n?"

"Just tired," he said slowly. "For God's sake, do you have to crack that gum like that?"

"You don't have to lissen to me," she said complacently. She patted a curl in place near the side of her head and then lifted her hair away from the back of her neck, ducking her head forward and then back.

He winced away from the gesture. "What you got to be always fooling with your hair for?" he protested.

"Say, what's the matter with you anyway?" She turned away from the mirror to face him, put her hands on her hips. "You ain't been in the house two minutes and you're picking on me."

He didn't answer her because her eyes were angry and he didn't want to quarrel with her. They'd been married too long and got along too well and so he walked all the way into the room and sat down in the chair by the bed and stretched his legs out in front of him, putting his weight on the heels of his shoes, leaning way back in the chair, not saying anything.

"Lissen," she said sharply. "I've got to wear those overalls again tomorrow. "You're going to get them all wrinkled up leaning against them like that."

He didn't move. He was too tired and his legs were throbbing now that he had sat down. Besides the overalls were already wrinkled and dirty, he thought. They couldn't help but be for she'd worn them all week. He leaned farther back in the chair.

"Come on, get up," she ordered.

"Oh, what the hell," he said wearily, and got up from the chair. "I'd just as soon live in a subway. There'd be just as much place to sit down."

He saw that her sense of humor was struggling with her anger. But her sense of humor won because she giggled.

"Aw, come on and eat," she said. There was a coaxing note in her voice. "You're nothing but an old hungry nigger trying to act tough and—" she paused to giggle and then continued, "You—"

He had always found her giggling pleasant and deliberately said things that might amuse her and then waited, listening for the delicate sound to emerge from her throat.

This time he didn't even hear the giggle. He didn't let her finish what she was saying. She was standing close to him and that funny tingling started in his finger tips, went fast up his arms and sent his fist shooting straight for her face.

There was the smacking sound of soft flesh being struck by a hard object and it wasn't until she screamed that he realized he had hit her in the mouth—so hard that the dark red lipstick had blurred and spread over her full lips, reaching up toward the tip of her nose, down toward her chin, out toward her cheeks.

The knowledge that he had struck her seeped through him slowly and he was appalled but he couldn't drag his hands away from her face. He kept striking her and he thought with horror that something inside him was holding him, binding him to this act, wrapping and twisting about him so that he had to continue it. He had lost all control over his hands. And he groped for a phrase, a word, something to describe what this thing was like that was happening to him and he thought it was like being enmeshed in a winding sheet—that was it—like a winding sheet. And even as the thought formed in his mind, his hands reached for her face again and yet again.

Margaret Walker (Alexander) (1915–1998)

Margaret Walker's poem "For My People" aptly summarizes the tenor of her life and writings. Very much engaged in reconstructing the history of her people, she wrote a number of poems about African American heritage, as well as *Jubilee* (1966), the fictional retelling of her own life history based on decades of research. In *Jubilee*, she recounts the story of her great-grandmother's escape from slavery. Born in Birmingham, Alabama, to Reverend Sigismund Walker and Marion Dozier Walker, Walker received a B.A. from Northwestern University and her M.A. and Ph.D. from the University of Iowa. In 1942, she married Firnist James Alexander and taught at various colleges.

In *How I Wrote Jubilee* (1972), Walker chronicles the long history and many avenues of research that she uses to retell the story of her ancestors. Very much associated with Walker is Jackson State where she taught for over thirty years, directing Jackson State University's Institute for the Study of the History, Life, and Culture of Black People. Walker's close friendship with Richard Wright was the source of her biography *Richard Wright: Daemonic Genius* (1988). Among her many honors, the one recognition that jump-started her career was the Yale Series of Younger Poets Award that she received in 1942 for the volume, *For My People*.

Ex-Slave

When I see you bending over something rare
   Like music, or a painting, or a book,
   And see within your eyes that vacant stare
   And halfway understand that pleading look;
   I cannot help but bitterly detest
   The age and men who made you what you are,
   Who robbed you of your all—your ample best—
   And left you seeking life across a hateful bar,
   And left you vainly searching for a star
   Your soul appreciates but cannot understand.

For My People

For my people everywhere singing their slave songs repeatedly:
   their dirges and their ditties and their blues and jubilees,
   praying their prayers nightly to an unknown god, bending
   their knees humbly to an unseen power;

For my people lending their strength to the years, to the gone
   years and the now years and the maybe years, washing
   ironing cooking scrubbing sewing mending hoeing
   plowing digging planting pruning patching dragging
   along never gaining never reaping never knowing and
   never understanding;

For my playmates in the clay and dust and sand of Alabama
   backyards playing baptizing and preaching and doctor
   and jail and soldier and school and mama and cooking
   and playhouse and concert and store and hair and Miss
   Choomby and company;

For the cramped bewildered years we went to school to learn
   to know the reasons why and the answers to and the
   people who and the places where and the days when, in
   memory of the bitter hours when we discovered we were
   black and poor and small and different and nobody cared
   and nobody wondered and nobody understood;

For the boys and girls who grew in spite of these things to be
   man and woman, to laugh and dance and sing and play
   and drink their wine and religion and success, to marry
   their playmates and bear children and then die of
   consumption and anemia and lynching;

For my people thronging 47th Street in Chicago and Lenox
   Avenue in New York and Rampart Street in New Orleans,

lost disinherited dispossessed and happy people filling the cabarets and taverns and other people's pockets needing bread and shoes and milk and land and money and something—something all our own;

For my people walking blindly spreading joy, losing time being lazy, sleeping when hungry, shouting when burdened, drinking when hopeless, tied, and shackled and tangled among ourselves by the unseen creatures who tower over us omnisciently and laugh;

For my people blundering and groping and floundering in the dark of churches and schools and clubs and societies, associations and councils and committees and conventions, distressed and disturbed and deceived and devoured by money-hungry glory-craving leeches, preyed on by facile force of state and fad and novelty, by false prophet and holy believer;

For my people standing staring trying to fashion a better way from confusion, from hypocrisy and misunderstanding, trying to fashion a world that will hold all the people, all the faces, all the adams and eves and their countless generations;

Let a new earth rise. Let another world be born. Let a bloody peace be written in the sky. Let a second generation full of courage issue forth; let a people loving freedom come to growth. Let a beauty full of healing and a strength of final clenching be the pulsing in our spirits and our blood. Let the martial songs be written, let the dirges disappear. Let a race of men now rise and take control.

Lineage

My grandmothers were strong.
They followed plows and bent to toil.
They moved through fields sowing seed.
They touched earth and grain grew.
They were full of sturdiness and singing.
My grandmothers were strong.

My grandmothers are full of memories
Smelling of soap and onions and wet clay
With veins rolling roughly over quick hands
They have many clean words to say.
My grandmothers were strong.
Why am I not as they?

Gwendolyn Brooks (1917–2000)

As a bridge between the earlier writers of the 1940s and 1950s and the emerging black protest writers of the 1960s and 1970s, Brooks won the respect of both groups. Her finely crafted poems earned her the honor of being the first African American woman to receive the Pulitzer Prize for poetry, which she won in 1950 for *Annie Allen*. Her other collections of poetry include *A Street in Bronzeville* (1945), *The Bean Eaters* (1962), *In the Mecca* (1968), *Riot* (1969), *Aloneness* (1971), *Family Pictures* (1971), *The Tiger Who Wore White Gloves* (1974), and *Beckonings* (1975). Whether composing a sonnet or a ballad, Brooks writes with a crispness and precision that catapulted African American women's poetry to the forefront of American letters. In addition to her poetry, she wrote two autobiographical narratives, *Maud Martha* (1953) and *Report from Part One* (1972).

Although born in Topeka, Kansas, Brooks is very much associated with Chicago where she grew up. Her parents, David Anderson Brooks, a janitor, and her mother, Keziah Wims, a schoolteacher, moved their two children to Chicago shortly after Brooks was born. In her poetry Brooks writes of streets in brown urban meccas. She wrote for the *Chicago Defender*, graduated from Wilson Junior College, and married Henry Blakely II, a man who she met when she joined Chicago's NAACP Youth Council. Committed to a number of race-related causes, Brooks made a political decision that had financial implications when she moved her work from the publishing giant of Harper & Row to emerging, urban, black presses: Broadside in Detroit and Third World Press in Chicago.

Kitchenette Building

We are things of dry hours and the involuntary plan,
Grayed in, and gray. "Dreams" makes a giddy sound, not
   strong
Like "rent," "feeding a wife," "satisfying a man."

But could a dream send up through onion fumes
Its white and violet, fight with fried potatoes
And yesterday's garbage ripening in the hall,
Flutter, or sing an aria down these rooms

Even if we were willing to let it in,
Had time to warm it, keep it very clean,
Anticipate a message, let it begin?

We wonder. But not well! not for a minute!
Since Number Five is out of the bathroom now,
We think of lukewarm water, hope to get in it.

The Mother

Abortions will not let you forget.
You remember the children you got that you did not get,
The damp small pulps with a little or with no hair,
The singers and workers that never handled the air.
You will never neglect or beat
Them, or silence or buy with a sweet.
You will never wind up the sucking-thumb
Or scuttle off ghosts that come.
You will never leave them, controlling your luscious sigh,
Return for a snack of them, with gobbling mother-eye.

I have heard in the voices of the wind the voices of my
   dim killed children.
I have contracted. I have eased
My dim dears at the breasts they could never suck.
I have said, Sweets, if I sinned, if I seized
Your luck
And your lives from your unfinished reach,
If I stole your births and your names,
Your straight baby tears and your games,
Your stilted or lovely loves, your tumults, your marriages,
   aches, and your deaths,
If I poisoned the beginnings of your breaths,

Believe that even in my deliberateness I was not deliberate.
Though why should I whine,
Whine that the crime was other than mine?—
Since anyhow you are dead.
Or rather, or instead,
You were never made.
But that too, I am afraid,
Is faulty: oh, what shall I say, how is the truth to be
    said?
You were born, you had body, you died.
It is just that you never giggled or planned or
    cried.

Believe me, I loved you all.
Believe me, I knew you, though faintly, and I loved, I
    loved you
All.

We Real Cool

The pool players.
Seven at the golden shovel.

We real cool. We
Left school. We

Lurk late. We
Strike straight. We

Sing sin. We
Thin gin. We

Jazz June. We
Die soon.

Lorraine Hansberry (1930–1965)

Lorraine Hansberry's reputation rests largely on the success of *A Raisin in the Sun*, the play that was first performed on March 11, 1959, and earned the New York Drama Critics Circle Award for Best Play of the Year. Hansberry was the first black playwright to receive the award. Her middle-class background began in Chicago where her father, Carl Hansberry, was a real estate broker and her mother, Nannie Perry Hansberry, a schoolteacher. Their circle of friends included Duke Ellington, Joe Louis, Paul Robeson, Langston Hughes, and other well-known African Americans. When their family decided to move to a white neighborhood, they encountered restrictive covenants preventing them from doing so. Carl Hansberry challenged these covenants, winning a landmark Supreme Court case. The animosity that the family faced, however, took its toll. Lorraine was eight years old at the time when the family moved and someone threw a brick through the window, almost hitting Lorraine in the head.

Hansberry went to college at the University of Wisconsin. While doing civil rights work, she met her husband Robert Nemiroff, a Jewish activist and intellectual. After their divorce, Hansberry disclosed her sexual orientation in several gay magazines. Her relationship with Nemiroff remained amicable. Upon Hansberry's death at thirty-four years of age, Nemiroff compiled her writings in a collection that he named *To Be Young, Gifted and Black*, terms Hansberry coined in a speech.

A Raisin in the Sun builds on the experiences of Hansberry's family. Like the Hansberrys, the family in the play, the Youngers, saved their money to move to a better neighborhood. Their dreams collide with the economic and social attitudes of whites in the community. The black family asks the same question that Langston Hughes asks in his famous poem, "Harlem"—Do dreams "dry up like a raisin in the sun?" Although Hansberry wrote other plays, including *The Drinking Gourd* (1960), *The Sign in Sidney Brustein's Window* (1964), and *Les Blancs* (1972), *A Raisin in the Sun*, as a play on Broadway and as a movie with Sidney Poitier, Ruby Dee, Ossie Davis, and Claudia McNeil, remains an American classic.

A Raisin in the Sun

CHARACTERS

RUTH YOUNGER

TRAVIS YOUNGER

WALTER LEE YOUNGER (BROTHER)

BENEATHA YOUNGER

LENA YOUNGER (MAMA)

JOSEPH ASAGAI

GEORGE MURCHISON

KARL LINDNER

BOBO

MOVING MEN

The action of the play is set in Chicago's Southside sometime between World War II and the present.

ACT 1

SCENE 1: *Friday morning.*

SCENE 2: *The following morning.*

ACT 2

SCENE 1: *Later, the same day.*

SCENE 2: *Friday night, a few weeks later.*

SCENE 3: *Moving day, one week later.*

ACT 3

An hour later.

ACT 1

SCENE 1

The YOUNGER *living room would be a comfortable and well-ordered room if it were not for a number of indestructible contradictions to this state of being. Its furnishings are typical and undistinguished and their primary feature now is that they have clearly had to accommodate the living of too many people for too many years—and they are tired. Still, we can see that at some time, a time probably no longer remembered by the family (except perhaps for* MAMA*), the furnishings of this room were actually selected with care and love and even hope and brought to this apartment and arranged with taste and pride.*

That was long time ago. Now the once loved pattern of the couch upholstery has to fight to show itself from under acres of crocheted doilies and couch covers which have themselves finally come to be more important than the upholstery. And here a table or a chair has been moved to disguise the worn places in the carpet; but the carpet has fought back by showing its weariness, with depressing uniformity, elsewhere on its surface.

Weariness has, in fact, won in this room. Everything has been polished, washed, sat on, used, scrubbed too often. All pretenses but living itself have long since vanished from the very atmosphere of this room.

Moreover, a section of this room, for it is not really a room unto itself, though the landlord's lease would make it seem so, slopes backward to provide a small kitchen area, where the family prepares the meals that are eaten in the living room proper, which must also serve as dining room. The single window that has been provided for these "two" rooms is located in this kitchen area. The sole natural light the family may enjoy in the course of a day is only that which fights its way through this little window.

At Left, a door leads to a bedroom which is shared by MAMA *and her daughter,* BENEATHA. *At Right, opposite, is a second room (which in the beginning of the life of this apartment was probably a breakfast room) which serves as a bedroom for* WALTER *and his wife,* RUTH.

TIME:
Sometime between World War II and the present.

PLACE:
Chicago's Southside.

AT RISE:
It is morning dark in the living room. TRAVIS *is asleep on the make-down bed at Center. An* ALARM CLOCK *sounds from within the bedroom at Right, and presently* RUTH *enters from that room and closes the door behind her. She crosses sleepily toward the window. As she passes her sleeping son she reaches down and shakes him a little. At the window she raises the shade and a dusky Southside morning light comes in feebly. She fills a pot with water and puts it on to boil. She calls to the boy, between yawns, in a slightly muffled voice.*

RUTH *is about thirty. We can see that she was a pretty girl, even exceptionally so, but now it is apparent that life has been little that she expected, and disappointment has already begun to hang in her face. In a few years, before thirty-five even, she will be known among her people as a "settled woman."*
She crosses to her son and gives him a good, final, rousing shake.

RUTH: Come on now, boy, it's seven thirty!

(Her son sits up at last, in a stupor of sleepiness.)

I say hurry up, Travis! You ain't the only person in the world got to use a bathroom.

(The child, a sturdy, handsome little boy of ten or eleven, drags himself out of the bed and almost blindly takes his towels and "today's clothes" from drawers and a closet and goes out to the bathroom, which is in an outside hall and which is shared by another family or families on the same floor.)

*(*RUTH *crosses to the bedroom door at Right and opens it and calls in to her husband.)*

Walter Lee! . . . It's after seven thirty! Lemme see you do some waking up in there now! *(She waits.)* You better get up from there, man! It's after seven thirty I tell you. *(She waits again.)* All right, you just go ahead and lay there and next thing you know Travis be finished and Mr. Johnson'll be in there and you'll be fussing and cussing round here like a madman! And be late too! *(She waits, at the end of patience.)* Walter Lee—it's time for you to get up! *(She waits another second and then starts to go into the bedroom, but is apparently satisfied that her husband has begun to get up. She stops, pulls the door to, and returns to the kitchen area. She wipes her face with a moist cloth and runs her fingers through her sleep-disheveled hair in a vain effort and ties an apron around her housecoat.)*

(The bedroom door at Right opens and her husband stands in the doorway in his pajamas, which are rumpled and mis-mated. He is a lean, intense young man in his middle thirties, inclined to quick nervous movements and erratic speech habits—and always in his voice there is a quality of indictment.)

WALTER: Is he out yet?

RUTH: What do you mean *out*? He ain't hardly got in there good yet.

WALTER: *(Wandering in, still more oriented to sleep than to a new day.)* Well, what was you doing all that yelling for if I can't even get in there yet? *(Stopping and thinking.)* Check coming today?

RUTH: They *said* Saturday and this is just Friday and I hopes to God you ain't going to get up here first thing this morning and start talking to me 'bout no money— 'cause I 'bout don't want to hear it.

WALTER: Something the matter with you this morning?

RUTH: No—I'm just sleepy as the devil. What kind of eggs you want?

WALTER: Not scrambled.

(RUTH *starts to scramble eggs.*)

Paper come?

(RUTH *points impatiently to the rolled-up* Tribune *on the table, and he gets it and spreads it out and vaguely reads the front page.*)

Set off another bomb yesterday.

RUTH: (*Maximum indifference.*) Did they?

WALTER: (*Looking up.*) What's the matter with you?

RUTH: Ain't nothing the matter with me. And don't keep asking me that this morning.

WALTER: Ain't nobody bothering you. (*Reading the news of the day absently again.*) Say Colonel McCormick is sick.

RUTH: (*Affecting tea-party interest.*) Is he now? Poor thing.

WALTER: (*Sighing and looking at his watch.*) Oh, me. (*He waits.*) Now what is that boy doing in that bathroom all this time? He just going to have to start getting up earlier. I can't be being late to work on account of him fooling around in there.

RUTH: (*Turning on him.*) Oh, no he ain't going to be getting up no earlier no such thing! It ain't his fault that he can't get to bed no earlier nights 'cause he got a bunch of crazy good-for-nothing clowns sitting up running their mouths in what is supposed to be his bedroom after ten o'clock at night. . . .

WALTER: That's what you mad about, ain't it? The things I want to talk about with my friends just couldn't be important in your mind, could they? (*He rises and finds a cigarette in her handbag on the table and crosses to the little window and looks out, smoking and deeply enjoying this first one.*)

RUTH: (*Almost matter of factly, a complaint too automatic to deserve emphasis.*) Why you always got to smoke before you eat in the morning?

WALTER: (*At the window.*) Just look at 'em down there . . . running and racing to work . . . (*He turns and faces his wife and watches her a moment at the stove, and then, suddenly.*) You look young this morning, baby.

RUTH: (*Indifferently.*) Yeah?

WALTER: Just for a second—stirring them eggs. It's gone now—just for a second it was—you looked real young again. (*Then, drily.*) It's gone now—you look like yourself again.

RUTH: Man, if you don't shut up and leave me alone.

WALTER: (*Looking out to the street again.*) First thing a man ought to learn in life is not to make love to no colored woman first thing in the morning. You all some evil people at eight o'clock in the morning.

(TRAVIS *appears in the hall doorway, almost fully dressed and quite wide awake now, his towels and pajamas across his shoulders. He opens the door and signals for his father to make the bathroom in a hurry.*)

TRAVIS: (*Watching the bathroom.*) Daddy, come on!

(WALTER *gets his bathroom utensils and flies out to the bathroom.*)

RUTH: Sit down and have your breakfast, Travis.

TRAVIS: Mama, this is Friday. (*Gleefully.*) Check coming tomorrow, huh?

RUTH: You get your mind off money and eat your breakfast.

TRAVIS: (*Eating.*) This is the morning we supposed to bring the fifty cents to school.

RUTH: Well, I ain't got no fifty cents this morning.

TRAVIS: Teacher say we have to.

RUTH: I don't care what teacher say. I ain't got it. Eat your breakfast, Travis.

TRAVIS: I *am* eating.

RUTH: Hush up now and just eat!

(*The boy gives her an exasperated look for her lack of understanding, and eats grudgingly.*)

TRAVIS: You think Grandmama would have it?

RUTH: No! And I want you to stop asking your grandmother for money, you hear me?

TRAVIS: (*Outraged.*) Gaaaleee! I don't ask her, she just gimme it sometimes!

RUTH: Travis Willard Younger—I got too much on me this morning to be—

Travis. Maybe Daddy—

RUTH: TRAVIS!

(*The boy hushes abruptly. They are both quiet and tense for several seconds.*)

TRAVIS: (*Presently.*) Could I maybe go carry some groceries in front of the supermarket for a little while after school then?

RUTH: Just hush, I said.

(TRAVIS *jabs his spoon into his cereal bowl viciously, and rests his head in anger upon his fists.*)

If you through eating, you can get over there and make up your bed.

(*The boy obeys stiffly and crosses the room, almost mechanically, to the bed and more or less carefully folds the covering. He carries the bedding into his mother's room and returns with his books and cap.*)

TRAVIS: (*Sulking and standing apart from her unnaturally.*) I'm gone.

RUTH: *Looking up from the stove to inspect him automatically.*) Come here. (*He crosses to her and she studies his head.*) If you don't take this comb and fix this here head, you better!

(TRAVIS *puts down his books with a great sigh of oppression, and crosses to the mirror. His mother mutters under her breath about his "slubbornness."*)

'Bout to march out of here with that head looking just like chickens slept in it! I just don't know where you get your slubborn ways. . . . And get your jacket, too. Looks chilly out this morning.

TRAVIS: (*With conspicuously brushed hair and jacket.*) I'm gone.

RUTH: Get carfare and milk money—*(Waving one finger.)* — and not a single penny for no caps, you hear me?

TRAVIS: *(With sullen politeness.)* Yes'm. *(He turns in outrage to leave.)*

(His mother watches after him as in his frustration he approaches the door almost comically. When she speaks to him, her voice has become a very gentle tease.)

RUTH: *(Mocking; as she thinks he would say it.)* Oh, Mama makes me so mad sometimes, I don't know what to do! *(She waits and continues to his back as he stands stock still in front of the door.)* I wouldn't kiss that woman good-bye for nothing in this world this morning!

(The boy finally turns around and rolls his eyes at her, knowing the mood has changed and he is vindicated; he does not, however, move toward her yet.)

Not for nothing in this world! *(She finally laughs aloud at him and holds out her arms to him and we see that it is a way between them, very old and practiced.)*

(He crosses to her and allows her to embrace him warmly but keeps his face fixed with masculine rigidity. She holds him back from her presently and looks at him and runs her fingers over the features of his face.)

(With utter gentleness.) Now—whose little old angry man are you?

TRAVIS: *(The masculinity and gruffness start to fade at last.)* Aw gaalee—Mama . . .

RUTH: *(Mimicking.)* Aw—gaaaaalleeeee, Mama! *(She pushes him, with rough playfulness and finality, toward the door.)* Get on out of here or you going to be late.

TRAVIS: *(In the face of love, new aggressiveness.)* Mama, could I *please* go carry groceries.

RUTH: Honey, it's starting to get so cold evenings.

WALTER: *(Coming in from the bathroom and drawing a make-believe gun from a make-believe bolster and shooting at his son.)* What is it he wants to do?

RUTH: Go carry groceries after school at the supermarket.

WALTER: Well, let him go. . . .

TRAVIS: *(Quickly, to the ally.)* I have to—she won't gimme the fifty cents. . . .

WALTER: *(To his wife only.)* Why not?

RUTH: *(Simply, and with flavor.)* 'Cause we don't have it.

WALTER: *(To RUTH only.)* What you tell the boy things like that for? *(Reaching down into his pants with a rather important gesture.)* Here, son—*(He bands the boy the coin, but his eyes are directed to his wife's.)*

(TRAVIS takes the money happily.)

TRAVIS: Thanks, Daddy. *(He starts out.)*

(RUTH watches both of them with murder in her eyes. WALTER stands and stares back at her with defiance, and suddenly reaches into his pocket again on an afterthought.)

WALTER: *(Without even looking at his son, still staring hard at his wife.)* In fact, here's another fifty cents. . . . Buy yourself some fruit today—or take a taxicab to school or something!

TRAVIS: Whoopee—*(He leaps up and clasps his father around the middle with his legs, and they face each other in mutual appreciation.)*

(Slowly WALTER LEE peeks around the boy to catch the violent rays from his wife's eyes and draws his head back as if shot.)

WALTER: You better get down now—and get to school, man.

TRAVIS: *(At the door.)* O.K. Good-bye. *(He exits.)*

WALTER: *(After him, pointing with pride.)* That's *my* boy.

(She looks at him in disgust and turns back to her work.)

You know what I was thinking 'bout in the bathroom this morning?

RUTH: No.

WALTER: How come you always try to be so pleasant!

RUTH: What is there to be pleasant 'bout!

WALTER: You want to know what I was thinking 'bout in the bathroom or not!

RUTH: I know what you thinking 'bout!

WALTER: *(Ignoring her.)* 'Bout what me and Willy Harris was talking about last night.

RUTH: *(Immediately—a refrain.)* Willy Harris is a good-for-nothing loud mouth.

WALTER: Anybody who talks to me has got to be a good-for-nothing loud mouth, ain't he? And what you know about who is just a good-for-nothing loud mouth? Charlie Atkins was just a "good-for-nothing" loud mouth too, wasn't he! When he wanted me to go in the dry-cleaning business with him. And now—he's grossing a hundred thousand a year. A hundred thousand dollars a year! You still call *him* a loud mouth!

RUTH: *(Bitterly.)* Oh, Walter Lee. . . . *(She folds her head on her arms over the table.)*

WALTER: *(Rising and coming to her and standing over her.)* You tired, ain't you? Tired of everything. Me, the boy, the way we live—this beat-up hole—everything. Ain't you?

(She doesn't look up, doesn't answer.)

So tired—moaning and groaning all the time, but you wouldn't do nothing to help, would you? You couldn't be on my side that long for nothing, could you?

RUTH: Walter, please leave me alone.

WALTER: A man needs for a woman to back him up . . .

RUTH: Walter—

WALTER: Mama would listen to you. You know she listen to you more than she do me and Bennie. She think more of you. All you have to do is just sit down with her when you drinking your coffee one morning and talking 'bout things like you do and—*(He sits down beside her and demonstrates graphically what he thinks her methods and tone should be.)* —you just sip your coffee, see, and say easy like that you been thinking 'bout that deal Walter Lee is so interested in, 'bout the store and all, and sip some more coffee, like what you saying ain't really that important to you—and the next thing you know, she be listening good and asking you questions and when I come home— I can tell her the details. This ain't no fly-by-night proposition, baby. I mean we figured it out, me and Willy and Bobo.

RUTH: *(With a frown.)* Bobo?

WALTER: Yeah. You see, this little liquor store we got in mind cost seventy-five thousand and we figured the initial investment on the place be 'bout thirty thousand, see. That be ten thousand each. Course, there's a couple of hundred you got to pay so's you don't spend your life just waiting for them clowns to let your license get approved—

RUTH: You mean graft?

WALTER: *(Frowning impatiently.)* Don't call it that. See there, that just goes to show you what women understand about the world. Baby, don't *nothing* happen for you in this world 'less you pay *somebody* off!

RUTH: Walter, leave me alone! *(She raises her head and stares at him vigorously—then says, more quietly.)* Eat your eggs, they gonna be cold.

WALTER: *(Straightening up from her and looking off.)* That's it. There you are. Man say to his woman: I got me a dream. His woman say: Eat your eggs. *(Sadly, but gaining in power.)* Man say: I got to take hold of this here world, baby! And a woman will say: Eat your eggs and go to work. *(Passionately now.)* Man say: I got to change my life, I'm choking to death, baby! And his woman say—*(In utter anguish as he brings his fists down on his thighs.)*—Your eggs is getting cold!

RUTH: *(Softly.)* Walter, that ain't none of our money.

WALTER: *(Not listening at all or even looking at her.)* This morning, I was lookin' in the mirror and thinking about it . . . I'm thirty-five years old; I been married eleven years and I got a boy who sleeps in the living room— *(Very, very quietly.)*—and all I got to give him is stories about how rich white people live. . . .

RUTH: Eat your eggs, Walter.

WALTER: DAMN MY EGGS . . . DAMN ALL THE EGGS THAT EVER WAS!

RUTH: Then go to work.

WALTER: *(Looking up at her.)* See—I'm trying to talk to you 'bout myself—*(Shaking his head with the repetition.)*—and all you can say is eat them eggs and go to work.

RUTH: *(Wearily.)* Honey, you never say nothing new. I listen to you every day, every night and every morning, and you never say nothing new. *(Shrugging.)* So you would rather *be* Mr. Arnold than be his chauffeur. So—I would *rather* be living in Buckingham Palace.

WALTER: That is just what is wrong with the colored woman in this world . . . don't understand about building their

men up and making 'em feel like they somebody. Like they can do something.

RUTH: *(Drily, but to hurt.)* There *are* colored men who do things.

WALTER: No thanks to the colored woman.

RUTH: Well, being a colored woman, I guess I can't help myself none. *(She rises and gets the ironing board and sets it up and attacks a huge pile of rough-dried clothes, sprinkling them in preparation for the ironing and then rolling them into tight fat balls.)*

WALTER: *(Mumbling.)* We one group of men tied to a race of women with small minds.

(His sister BENEATHA enters. She is about twenty, as slim and intense as her brother. She is not as pretty as her sister-in-law, but her lean, almost intellectual face has a handsomeness of its own. She wears a bright-red flannel nightie, and her thick hair stands wildly about her head. Her speech is a mixture of many things; it is different from the rest of the family's in so far as education has permeated her sense of English—and perhaps the Midwest rather than the South has finally—at last—won out in her inflection; but not altogether; because over all of it is a soft slurring and transformed use of vowels which is the decided influence of the Southside. She passes through the room without looking at either RUTH or WALTER and goes to the outside door and looks, a little blindly, out to the bathroom. She sees that it has been lost to the Johnsons. She closes the door with a sleepy vengeance and crosses to the table and sits down a little defeated.)

BENEATHA: I am going to start timing those people.

WALTER: You should get up earlier.

BENEATHA: *(Her face in her hands. She is still fighting the urge to go back to bed.)* Really—would you suggest dawn? Where's the paper?

WALTER: *(Pushing the paper across the table to her as he studies her almost clinically, as though he has never seen her before.)* You a horrible-looking chick at this hour.

BENEATHA: *(Drily.)* Good morning, everybody.

WALTER: *(Senselessly.)* How is school coming?

BENEATHA: *(In the same spirit.)* Lovely. Lovely. And you know, biology is the greatest. *(Looking up at him.)* I dissected something that looked just like you yesterday.

WALTER: I just wondered if you've made up your mind and everything.

BENEATHA: *(Gaining in sharpness and impatience.)* And what did I answer yesterday morning—and the day before that?

RUTH: *(From the ironing board, like someone disinterested and old.)* Don't be so nasty, Bennie.

BENEATHA: *(Still to her brother.)* And the day before that and the day before that!

WALTER: *(Defensively.)* I'm interested in you. Something wrong with that? Ain't many girls who decide—

WALTER *and* BENEATHA: *(In unison.)*—To be a doctor.

(Silence.)

WALTER: Have we figured out yet just exactly how much medical school is going to cost?

RUTH: Walter Lee, why don't you leave that girl alone and get out of here to work?

BENEATHA: *(Exits to the bathroom and bangs on the door.)* Come on out of there, please! *(She comes back into the room.)*

WALTER: *(Looking at his sister intently.)* You know the check is coming tomorrow.

BENEATHA: *(Turning on him with a sharpness all her own.)* That money belongs to Mama, Walter, and it's for her to decide how she wants to use it. I don't care if she wants to buy a house or a rocket ship or just nail it up somewhere and look at it. It's hers. Not ours—*hers.*

WALTER: *(Bitterly.)* Now ain't that fine! You just got your mother's interest at heart, ain't you, girl? You such a nice girl—but if Mama got that money she can always take a few thousand and help you through school too—can't she?

BENEATHA: I have never asked anyone around here to do anything for me!

WALTER: No! And the line between asking and just accepting when the time comes is big and wide—ain't it!

BENEATHA: *(With fury.)* What do you want from me, Brother—that I quit school or just drop dead, which!

WALTER: I don't want nothing but for you to stop acting holy 'round here. Me and Ruthie done made some sacrifices for you—why can't you do something for the family?

RUTH: Walter, don't be dragging me in it.

WALTER: You are in it—don't you get up and go to work in somebody's kitchen for the last three years to help put clothes on her back?

RUTH: Oh, Walter—that's not fair. . . .

WALTER: It ain't that nobody expects you to get on your knees and say thank you, Brother; thank you, Ruth; thank you, Mama—and thank you, Travis, for wearing the same pair of shoes for two semesters—

BENEATHA: *(Dropping to her knees.)* Well—I *do*—all right?—thank everybody . . . and forgive me for ever wanting to be anything at all . . . forgive me, forgive me!

RUTH: Please stop it! Your mama'll hear you.

WALTER: Who the hell told you you had to be a doctor? If you so crazy 'bout messing 'round with sick people—then go be a nurse like other women—or just get married and be quiet. . . .

BENEATHA: Well—you finally got it said. . . . It took you three years but you finally got it said. Walter, give up; leave me alone—it's Mama's money.

WALTER: HE WAS MY FATHER, TOO!

BENEATHA: So what? He was mine, too—and Travis' grandfather—but the insurance money belongs to Mama.

Picking on me is not going to make her give it to you to invest in any liquor stores—*(Under breath, dropping into a chair.)*—and I for one say, God bless Mama for that!

WALTER: *(To RUTH.)* See—did you hear? Did you hear!

RUTH: Honey, please go to work.

WALTER: Nobody in this house is ever going to understand me.

BENEATHA: Because you're a nut.

WALTER: Who's a nut?

BENEATHA: You—you are a nut. Thee is mad, boy.

WALTER: *(Looking at his wife and sister from the door, very sadly.)* The world's most backward race of people, and that's a fact.

BENEATHA: *(Turning slowly in her chair.)* And then there are all those prophets who would lead us out of the wilderness—(WALTER *slams out of the house.)*—into the swamps!

RUTH: Bennie, why you always gotta be pickin' on your brother? Can't you be a little sweeter sometimes?

(Door opens. WALTER *walks in.)*

WALTER: *(To RUTH.)* I need some money for carfare.

RUTH: *(Looks at him, then warms; teasing, but tenderly.)* Fifty cents? *(She goes to her bag and gets money.)* Here, take a taxi.

(WALTER exits. MAMA enters. She is a woman in her early sixties, full-bodied and strong. She is one of those women of a certain grace and beauty who wear it so unobtrusively that it takes a while to notice. Her dark-brown face is surrounded by the total whiteness of her hair, and, being a woman who has adjusted to many things in life and overcome many more, her face is full of strength. She has, we can see, wit and faith of a kind that keep her eyes lit and full of interest and expectancy. She is, in a word, a beautiful woman. Her bearing is perhaps most like the noble bearing of the women of the Hereros of Southwest Africa—rather as if she imagines that as she walks she still bears a basket or a vessel upon her head. Her speech, on the other hand, is as careless as her carriage is precise—she is inclined to slur everything—but her voice is perhaps not so much quiet as simply soft.)

MAMA: Who that 'round here slamming doors at this hour? *(She crosses through the room, goes to the window, opens it, and brings in a feeble little plant growing doggedly in a small pot on the window sill. She feels the dirt and puts it back out.)*

RUTH: That was Walter Lee. He and Bennie was at it again.

MAMA: My children and they tempers. Lord, if this little old plant don't get more sun than it's been getting it ain't never going to see spring again. *(She turns from the window.)* What's the matter with you this morning, Ruth? You looks right peaked, You aiming to iron all them things? Leave some for me. I'll get to 'em this afternoon. Bennie honey, it's too drafty for you to be sitting 'round half dressed. Where's your robe?

BENEATHA: In the cleaners.

MAMA: Well, go get mine and put it on.

BENEATHA: I'm not cold, Mama, honest.

MAMA: I know—but you so thin. . . .

BENEATHA: (Irritably.) Mama, I'm not cold.

MAMA: (Seeing the make-down bed as TRAVIS has left it.) Lord have mercy, look at that poor bed. Bless his heart—he tries, don't he? (She moves to the bed TRAVIS has sloppily made up.)

RUTH: No—he don't half try at all 'cause he knows you going to come along behind him and fix everything. That's just how come he don't know how to do nothing right now—you done spoiled that boy so.

MAMA: Well—he's a little boy. Ain't supposed to know 'bout housekeeping. My baby, that's what he is. What you fix for his breakfast this morning?

RUTH: (Angrily.) I feed my son, Lena!

MAMA: I ain't meddling—(Under breath; busy-bodyish.) I just noticed all last week he had cold cereal, and when it starts getting this chilly in the fall a child ought to have some hot grits or something when he goes out in the cold—

RUTH: (Furious.) I gave him hot oats—is that all right!

MAMA: I ain't meddling. (Pause.) Put a lot of nice butter on it? (RUTH shoots her an angry look and does not reply.) He likes lots of butter.

RUTH: (Exasperated.) Lena—

MAMA: To BENEATHA. MAMA is inclined to wander conversationally sometimes.) What was you and your brother fussing 'bout this morning?

BENEATHA: It's not important, Mama. (She gets up and goes to look out at the bathroom, which is apparently free, and she picks up her towels and rushes out.)

MAMA: What was they fighting about?

RUTH: Now you know as well as I do.

MAMA: (Shaking her head.) Brother still worrying hisself sick about that money?

RUTH: You know he is.

MAMA: You had breakfast?

RUTH: Some coffee.

MAMA: Girl, you better start eating and looking after yourself better. You almost thin as Travis.

RUTH: Lena—

MAMA: Un-hunh?

RUTH: What are you going to do with it?

MAMA: Now don't you start, child. It's too early in the morning to be talking about money. It ain't Christian.

RUTH: It's just that he got his heart set on that store—

MAMA: You mean that liquor store that Willy Harris want him to invest in?

RUTH: Yes—

MAMA: We ain't no business people, Ruth. We just plain working folks.

RUTH: Ain't nobody business people till they go into business. Walter Lee say colored people ain't never going to start getting ahead till they start gambling on some different kinds of things in the world—investments and things.

MAMA: What done got into you, girl? Walter Lee done finally sold you on investing.

RUTH: No, Mama, something is happening between Walter and me. I don't know what it is—but he needs something—something I can't give him any more. He needs this chance, Lena.

MAMA: (Frowning deeply.) But liquor, honey—

RUTH: Well—like Walter say—I 'spec' people going to always be drinking themselves some liquor.

MAMA: Well—whether they drinks it or not ain't none of my business. But whether I go into business selling it to 'em is, and I don't want that on my ledger this late in life. (Stopping suddenly and studying her daughter-in-law.) Ruth Younger, what's the matter with you today? You look like you could fall over right there.

RUTH: I'm tired.

MAMA: Then you better stay home from work today.

RUTH: I can't stay home. She'd be calling up the agency and screaming at them, "My girl didn't come in today—send me somebody! My girl didn't come in!" Oh, she just have a fit. . . .

MAMA: Well, let her have it. I'll just call her up and say you got the flu—

RUTH: (Laughing.) Why the flu?

MAMA: 'Cause it sounds respectable to 'em. Something white people get, too. They know 'bout the flu. Otherwise they think you been cut up or something when you tell 'em you sick.

RUTH: I got to go in. We need the money.

MAMA: Somebody would of thought my children done all but starved to death the way they talk about money here late. Child, we got a great big old check coming tomorrow.

RUTH: (Sincerely, but also self-righteously.) Now that's your money. It ain't got nothing to do with me, We all feel like that—Walter and Bennie and me—even Travis.

MAMA: (Thoughtfully, and suddenly very far away.) Ten thousand dollars—

RUTH: Sure is wonderful.

MAMA: Ten thousand dollars.

RUTH: You know what you should do, Miss Lena? You should take yourself a trip somewhere. To Europe or South America or someplace—

MAMA: (Throwing up her hands at the thought.) Oh, child!

RUTH: I'm serious. Just pack up and leave! Go on away and enjoy yourself some. Forget about the family and have yourself a ball for once in your life—

MAMA: *(Drily.)* You sound like I'm just about ready to die. Who'd go with me? What I look like wandering 'round Europe by myself?

RUTH: Shoot—these here rich white women do it all the time. They don't think nothing of packing up they suitcases and piling on one of them big steamships and—swoosh!—they gone, child.

MAMA: Something always told me I wasn't no rich white woman.

RUTH: Well—what are you going to do with it then?

MAMA: I ain't rightly decided. *(Thinking. She speaks now with emphasis.)* Some of it got to be put away for Beneatha and her schoolin'—and ain't nothing going to touch that part of it. Nothing. *(She waits several seconds, trying to make up her mind about something, and looks at* RUTH *a little tentatively before going on.)* Been thinking that we maybe could meet the notes on a little old two-story somewhere, with a yard where Travis could play in the summertime, if we use part of the insurance for a down payment and everybody kind of pitch in. I could maybe take on a little day work again, few days a week—

RUTH: *(Studying her mother-in-law furtively and concentrating on her ironing, anxious to encourage without seeming to.)* Well, Lord knows, we've put enough rent into this here rat trap to pay for four houses by now. . . .

MAMA: *(Looking up at the words "rat trap" and then looking around and leaning back and sighing, in a suddenly reflective mood.)* "Rat trap"—yes, that's all it is. *(Smiling.)* I remember just as well the day me and Big Walter moved in here. Hadn't been married but two weeks and wasn't planning on living here no more than a year. *(She shakes her head at the dissolved dream.)* We was going to set away, little by little, don't you know, and buy a little place out in Morgan Park. We had even picked out the house. *(Chuckling a little.)* Looks right dumpy today. But Lord, child, you should know all the dreams I had 'bout buying that house and fixing it up and making me a little garden in the back—*(She waits and stops smiling.)* And didn't none of it happen. *(Dropping her hands in a futile gesture.)*

RUTH: *(Keeps her head down, ironing.)* Yes, life can be a barrel of disappointments, sometimes.

MAMA: Honey, Big Walter would come in here some nights back then and slump down on that couch there and just look at the rug, and look at me and look at the rug and then back at me—and I'd know he was down then . . . really down. *(After a second very long and thoughtful pause; she is seeing back to times that only she can see.)* And then, Lord, when I lost that baby—little Claude—I almost thought I was going to lose Big Walter too. Oh, that man grieved hisself! He was one man to love his children.

RUTH: Ain't nothin' can tear at you like losin' your baby.

MAMA: I guess that's how come that man finally worked hisself to death like he done. Like he was fighting his own war with this here world that took his baby from him.

RUTH: He sure was a fine man, all right. I always liked Mr. Younger.

MAMA: Crazy 'bout his children! God knows there was plenty wrong with Walter Younger—hard-headed, mean, kind of wild with women—plenty wrong with him. But he sure loved his children. Always wanted them to have something—be something. That's where Brother gets all these notions, I reckon. Big Walter used to say, he'd get right wet in the eyes sometimes, lean his head back with the water standing in his eyes and say, "Seem like God don't see fit to give the black man nothing but dreams—but He did give us children to make them dreams seem worthwhile." *(She smiles.)* He could talk like that, don't you know.

RUTH: Yes, he sure could. He was a good man, Mr. Younger.

MAMA: Yes, a fine man—just couldn't never catch up with his dreams, that's all.

*(*BENEATHA *comes in, brushing her hair and looking up at the ceiling, where the sound of a vacuum cleaner has started up.)*

BENEATHA: What could be so dirty on that woman's rugs that she has to vacuum them every single day?

RUTH: I wish certain young women 'round here who I could name would take inspiration about certain rugs in a certain apartment I could also mention.

BENEATHA: *(Shrugging.)* How much cleaning can a house need, for Christ's sakes.

MAMA: *(Not liking the Lord's name used thus.)* Bennie!

RUTH: Just listen to her—just listen!

BENEATHA: Oh, God!

MAMA: If you use the Lord's name just one more time—

BENEATHA: *(A bit of a whine.)* Oh, Mama—

RUTH: Fresh—just fresh as salt, this girl!

BENEATHA: *(Drily.)* Well—if the salt loses its savor—

MAMA: Now that will do. I just ain't going to have you 'round here reciting the scriptures in vain—you hear me?

BENEATHA: How did I manage to get on everybody's wrong side by just walking into a room?

RUTH: If you weren't so fresh—

BENEATHA: Ruth, I'm twenty years old.

MAMA: What time you be home from school today?

BENEATHA: Kind of late. *(With enthusiasm.)* Madeline is going to start my guitar lessons today.

*(*MAMA *and* RUTH *look up with the same expression.)*

MAMA: Your *what* kind of lessons?

BENEATHA: Guitar.

RUTH: Oh, Father!

MAMA: How come you done taken it in your mind to learn to play the guitar?

BENEATHA: I just want to, that's all.

MAMA: (Smiling.) Lord, child, don't you know what to do with yourself? How long it going to be before you get tired of this now—like you got tired of that little play-acting group you joined last year? (Looking at RUTH.) And what was it the year before that?

RUTH: The horseback-riding club for which she bought that fifty-five-dollar riding habit that's been hanging in the closet ever since!

MAMA: (To BENEATHA.) Why you got to flit so from one thing to another, baby?

BENEATHA: (Sharply.) I just want to learn to play the guitar. Is there anything wrong with that?

MAMA: Ain't nobody trying to stop you. I just wonders sometimes why you has to flit so from one thing to another all the time. You ain't never done nothing with all that camera equipment you brought home—

BENEATHA: I don't flit! I—I experiment with different forms of expression—

RUTH: Like riding a horse?

BENEATHA: People have to express themselves one way or another.

MAMA: What is it you want to express?

BENEATHA: (Angrily.) Me!

(MAMA and RUTH look at each other and burst into raucous laughter.)

Don't worry—I don't expect you to understand.

MAMA: (To change the subject.) Who you going out with tomorrow night?

BENEATHA: (With displeasure.) George Murchison again.

MAMA: (Pleased.) Oh—you getting a little sweet on him?

RUTH: You ask me, this child ain't sweet on nobody but herself. (Under breath.) Express herself!

(They laugh.)

BENEATHA: Oh—I like George all right, Mama. I mean I like him enough to go out with him and stuff, but—

RUTH: (For devilment.) What does and stuff mean?

BENEATHA: Mind your own business.

MAMA: Stop picking at her now, Ruth. (A thoughtful pause, and then a suspicious sudden look at her daughter as she turns in her chair for emphasis.) What does it mean?

BENEATHA: (Wearily.) Oh, I just mean I couldn't ever really be serious about George. He's—he's so shallow.

RUTH: Shallow—what do you mean he's shallow? He's RICH!

MAMA: Hush, Ruth.

BENEATHA: I know he's rich. He knows he's rich, too.

RUTH: Well—what other qualities a man got to have to satisfy you, little girl?

BENEATHA: You wouldn't even begin to understand. Anybody who married Walter could not possibly understand.

MAMA: (Outraged.) What kind of way is that to talk about your brother?

BENEATHA: Brother is a flip—let's face it.

MAMA: (To RUTH, helplessly.) What's a flip?

RUTH: (Glad to add kindling.) She's saying he's crazy.

BENEATHA: Not crazy. Brother isn't really crazy yet—he—he's an elaborate neurotic.

MAMA: Hush your mouth!

BENEATHA: As for George. Well. George looks good—he's got a beautiful car and he takes me to nice places and, as my sister-in-law says, he is probably the richest boy I will ever get to know and I even like him sometimes—but if the Youngers are sitting around waiting to see if their little Bennie is going to tie up the family with the Murchisons, they are wasting their time.

RUTH: You mean you wouldn't marry George Murchison if he asked you someday? That pretty, rich thing? Honey, I knew you was odd—

BENEATHA: No I would not marry him if all I felt for him was what I feel now. Besides, George's family wouldn't really like it.

MAMA: Why not?

BENEATHA: Oh, Mama—the Murchisons are honest-to-God-real-live-rich colored people, and the only people in the world who are more snobbish than rich white people are rich colored people. I thought everybody knew that. I've met Mrs. Murchison. She's a scene!

MAMA: You must not dislike people 'cause they well off, honey.

BENEATHA: Why not? It makes just as much sense as disliking people 'cause they are poor, and lots of people do that.

RUTH: (A wisdom-of-the-ages manner. To MAMA.) Well, she'll get over some of this—

BENEATHA: Get over it? What are you talking about, Ruth? Listen, I'm going to be a doctor. I'm not worried about who I'm going to marry yet—if I ever get married.

MAMA and RUTH: IF!

MAMA: Now, Bennie—

BENEATHA: Oh, I probably will . . . but first I'm going to be a doctor, and George, for one, still thinks that's pretty funny. I couldn't be bothered with that. I am going to be a doctor and everybody around here better understand that!

MAMA: (Kindly.) 'Course you going to be a doctor, honey, God willing.

BENEATHA: (Drily.) God hasn't got a thing to do with it.

MAMA: Beneatha—that just wasn't necessary.

BENEATHA: Well—neither is God. I get sick of hearing about God.

MAMA: Beneatha!

BENEATHA: I mean it! I'm just tired of hearing about God all the time. What has He got to do with anything? Does he pay tuition?

MAMA: You 'bout to get your fresh little jaw slapped!

RUTH: That's just what she needs, all right!

BENEATHA: Why? Why can't I say what I want to around here, like everybody else?

MAMA: It don't sound nice for a young girl to say things like that—you wasn't brought up that way. Me and your father went to trouble to get you and Brother to church every Sunday.

BENEATHA: Mama, you don't understand. It's all a matter of ideas, and God is just one idea I don't accept. It's not important. I am not going out and be immoral or commit crimes because I don't believe in God. I don't even think about it. It's just that I get tired of Him getting credit for all things the human race achieves through its own stubborn effort. There simply is no blasted God—there is only man and it is he who makes miracles!

(MAMA absorbs this speech, studies her daughter and rises slowly and crosses to BENEATHA and slaps her powerfully across the face. After, there is only silence and the daughter drops her eyes from her mother's face, and MAMA is very tall before her.)

MAMA: Now—you say after me, in my mother's house there is still God.

(There is a long pause and BENEATHA stares at the floor wordlessly. MAMA repeats the phrase with precision and cool emotion.)

In my mother's house there is still God.

BENEATHA: In my mother's house there is still God.

(A long pause.)

MAMA: *(Walking away from BENEATHA, too disturbed for triumphant posture. Stopping and turning back to her daughter.)* There are some ideas we ain't going to have in this house. Not long as I am at the head of this family.

BENEATHA: Yes, ma'am.

(MAMA walks out of the room.)

RUTH: *(Almost gently, with profound understanding.)* You think you a woman, Bennie—but you still a little girl. What you did was childish—so you got treated like a child.

BENEATHA: I see. *(Quietly.)* I also see that everybody think it's all right for Mama to be a tyrant. But all the tyranny in the world will never put a God in the heavens! *(She picks up her books and goes out.)*

RUTH: *(Goes to MAMA's door.)* She said she was sorry.

MAMA: *(Coming out, going to her plant.)* They frightens me, Ruth. My children,

RUTH: You got good children, Lena. They just a little off sometimes—but they're good.

MAMA: No—there's something come down between me and them that don't let us understand each other and I don't know what it is. One done almost lost his mind thinking 'bout money all the time and the other done commence to talk about thing I can't seem to understand in no form or fashion. What is it that's changing, Ruth?

RUTH: *(Soothingly, older than her years.)* Now . . . you taking it all too seriously. You just got strong-willed children and it takes a strong woman like you to keep 'em in hand.

MAMA: *(Looking at her plant and sprinkling a little water on it.)* They spirited all right, my children. Got to admit they got spirit—Bennie and Walter. Like this little old plant that ain't never had enough sunshine or nothing— and look at it. . . .

(She has her back to RUTH, who has had to stop ironing and lean against something and put the back of her hand to her forehead.)

RUTH: *(Trying to keep MAMA from noticing.)* You . . . sure . . . loves that little old thing, don't you? . . .

MAMA: Well, I always wanted me a garden like I used to see sometimes at the back of the houses down home. This plant is close as I ever got to having one. *(She looks out of the window as she replaces the plant.)* Lord, ain't nothing as dreary as the view from this window on a dreary day, is there? Why ain't you singing this morning, Ruth? Sing that "No Ways Tired." That song always lifts me up so— *(She turns at last to see that RUTH has slipped quietly into a chair, in a state of semiconsciousness.)* Ruth! Ruth honey— what's the matter with you . . . Ruth!

CURTAIN

ACT 1

SCENE 2

It is the following morning; a Saturday morning, and house cleaning is in progress at the YOUNGERS. Furniture has been shoved hither and yon and MAMA is giving the kitchen-area walls a washing down. BENEATHA, in dungarees, with a handkerchief tied around her face, is spraying insecticide into the cracks in the walls. As they work, the RADIO is on and a Southside disc-jockey program is inappropriately filling the house with a rather exotic saxophone blues. TRAVIS, the sole idle one, is leaning on his arms, looking out of the window.

TRAVIS: Grandmama, that stuff Bennie is using smells awful. Can I go downstairs, please?

MAMA: Did you get all them chores done already? I ain't seen you doing much.

TRAVIS: Yes'm—finished early. Where did Mama go this morning?

MAMA: *(Looking at BENEATHA.)* She had to go on a little errand.

TRAVIS: Where?

MAMA: To tend to her business.

TRAVIS: Can I go outside then?

MAMA: Oh, I guess so. You better stay right in front of the house, though . . . and keep a good lookout for the postman.

TRAVIS: Yes'm. (*He starts out and decides to give his* AUNT BENEATHA *a good swat on the legs as he passes her.*) Leave them poor little old cockroaches alone, they ain't bothering you none. (*He runs as she swings the spray gun at him both viciously and playfully.*)

(WALTER *enters from the bedroom and goes to the phone.*)

MAMA: Look out there, girl, before you be spilling some of that stuff on that child!

TRAVIS: (*Teasing.*) That's right—look out now! (*He exits.*)

BENEATHA: (*Drily.*) I can't imagine that it would hurt him—it has never hurt the roaches.

MAMA: Well, little boys' hides ain't as tough as Southside roaches.

WALTER: (*Into phone.*) Hello—Let me talk to Willy Harris.

MAMA: You better get over there behind the bureau. I seen one marching out of there like Napoleon yesterday.

WALTER: Hello, Willy? It ain't come yet. It'll be here in a few minutes. Did the lawyer give you the papers?

BENEATHA: There's really only one way to get rid of them, Mama—

MAMA: How?

BENEATHA: Set fire to this building.

WALTER: Good. Good. I'll be right over.

BENEATHA: Where did Ruth go, Walter?

WALTER: I don't know. (*He exits abruptly.*)

BENEATHA: Mama, where did Ruth go?

MAMA: (*Looking at her with meaning.*) To the doctor, I think.

BENEATHA: The doctor? What's the matter? (*They exchange glances.*) You don't think—

MAMA: (*With her sense of drama.*) Now I ain't saying what I think. But I ain't never been wrong 'bout a woman neither.

(*The phone rings.*)

BENEATHA: (*At the phone.*) Hay-lo. . . . (*Pause, and a moment of recognition.*) Well—when did you get back! . . . And how was it? . . . Of course I've missed you—in my way. . . . This morning? No . . . house cleaning and all that and Mama hates it if I let people come over when the house is like this. . . . You *have?* Well, that's different . . . What is it—oh, what the hell, come on over. . . . Right, see you then. (*She hangs up.*)

MAMA: (*Who has listened vigorously, as is her habit.*) Who is that you inviting over here with this house looking like this? You ain't got the pride you was born with!

BENEATHA: Asagai doesn't care how houses look, Mama—he's an intellectual.

MAMA: WHO?

BENEATHA: Asagai—Joseph Asagai. He's an African boy I met on campus. He's been studying in Canada all summer.

MAMA: What's his name?

BENEATHA: Asagai, Joseph. Ah-sah-guy. . . . He's from Nigeria.

MAMA: Oh, that's the little country that was founded by slaves way back. . . .

BENEATHA: No, Mama—that's Liberia.

MAMA: I don't think I never met no African before.

BENEATHA: Well, do me a favor and don't ask him a whole lot of ignorant questions about Africans. I mean, do they wear clothes and all that—

MAMA: Well, now, I guess if you think we so ignorant 'round here maybe you shouldn't bring your friends here—

BENEATHA: It's just that people ask such crazy things. All anyone seems to know about when it comes to Africa is Tarzan—

MAMA: (*Indignantly.*) Why should I know anything about Africa?

BENEATHA: Why do you give money at church for the missionary work?

MAMA: Well, that's to help save people.

BENEATHA: You mean save them from *heathenism*—

MAMA: (*Innocently.*) Yes.

BENEATHA: I'm afraid they need more salvation from the British and the French.

(RUTH *comes in forlornly and pulls off her coat with dejection. They both turn to look at her.*)

RUTH: (*Dispiritedly.*) Well, I guess from all the happy faces—everybody knows.

BENEATHA: You pregnant?

MAMA: Lord have mercy, I sure hope it's a little old girl. Travis ought to have a sister.

(BENEATHA *and* RUTH *give her a hopeless look for this grandmotherly enthusiasm.*)

BENEATHA: How far along are you?

RUTH: Two months.

BENEATHA: Did you mean to? I mean did you plan it or was it an accident?

MAMA: What do you know about planning or not planning?

BENEATHA: Oh, Mama.

RUTH: (*Wearily.*) She's twenty years old, Lena.

BENEATHA: Did you plan it, Ruth?

RUTH: Mind your own business.

BENEATHA: It is my business—where is he going to live, on the *roof?*

(*There is silence following the remark as the three women react to the sense of it.*)

Gee—I didn't mean that, Ruth, honest. Gee, I don't feel like that at all, I—I think it is wonderful.

RUTH: (*Dully.*) Wonderful.

BENEATHA: Yes—really.

MAMA: *(Looking at* RUTH, *worried.)* Doctor say everything going to be all right?

RUTH: *(Far away.)* Yes—she says everything is going to be fine. . . .

MAMA: *(Immediately suspicious.)* "She"? What doctor you went to?

*(*RUTH *folds over, near hysteria.)*

MAMA: *(Worriedly hovering over* RUTH.) Ruth honey—what's the matter with you—you sick?

*(*RUTH *has her fists clenched on her thighs and is fighting hard to suppress a scream that seems to be rising in her.)*

BENEATHA: What's the matter with her, Mama?

MAMA: *(Working her fingers in* RUTH's *shoulder to relax her.)* She be all right. Women gets right depressed sometimes when they get her way. *(Speaking softly, expertly, rapidly.)* Now you just relax. That's right . . . just lean back, don't think 'bout nothing at all . . . nothing at all—

RUTH: I'm all right. *(The glassy-eyed look melts and then she collapses into a fit of heavy sobbing.)*

(The BELL *rings.)*

BENEATHA: Oh, my God—that must be Asagai.

MAMA: *(To* RUTH.) Come on now, honey. You need to lie down and rest awhile . . . then have some nice hot food.

(They exit, RUTH's *weight on her mother-in-law.* BENEATHA, *herself profoundly disturbed, opens the door to admit a rather dramatic-looking young man with a large package.)*

ASAGAI: Hello, Alaiyo—

BENEATHA: *(Holding the door open and regarding him with pleasure.)* Hello. . . . *(Long pause.)* Well—come in. And please excuse everything. My mother was very upset about my letting anyone come here with the place like this.

ASAGAI: *(Coming into the room.)* You look disturbed too. . . . Is something wrong?

BENEATHA: *(Still at the door, absently.)* Yes . . . we've all got acute ghetto-itis. *(She smiles and comes toward him, finding a cigarette and sitting.)* So—sit down! How was Canada?

ASAGAI: *(A sophisticate.)* Canadian.

BENEATHA: *(Looking at him.)* I'm very glad you are back.

ASAGAI: *(Looking back at her in turn.)* Are you really?

BENEATHA: Yes—very.

ASAGAI: Why—you were quite glad when I went away. What happened?

BENEATHA: You went away.

ASAGAI: Ahhhhhhhh.

BENEATHA: Before—you wanted to be so serious before there was time.

ASAGAI: How much time must there be before one knows what one feels?

BENEATHA: *(Stalling this particular conversation. Her hands pressed together, in a deliberately childish gesture.)* What did you bring me?

ASAGAI: *(Handing her the package.)* Open it and see.

BENEATHA: *(Eagerly opening the package and drawing out some records and the colorful robes of a Nigerian woman.)* Oh, Asagai! . . . You got them for me! . . . How beautiful . . . and the records too! *(She lifts out the robes and runs to the mirror with them and holds the drapery up in front of herself.)*

ASAGAI: *(Coming to her at the mirror.)* I shall have to teach you how to drape it properly. *(He flings the material about her for the moment and stands back to look at her.)* Ah—*Oh-pay-gay-day, oh-ghah-mu-shay. (A Yoruba exclamation for admiration.)* You wear it well . . . very well . . . mutilated hair and all.

BENEATHA: *(Turning suddenly.)* My hair—what's wrong with my hair?

ASAGAI: *(Shrugging.)* Were you born with it like that?

BENEATHA: *(Reaching up to touch it.)* No . . . of course not. *(She looks back to the mirror, disturbed.)*

ASAGAI: *(Smiling.)* How then?

BENEATHA: You know perfectly well how . . . as crinkly as yours . . . that's how.

ASAGAI: And it is ugly to you that way?

BENEATHA: *(Quickly.)* Oh, no—not ugly . . . *(More slowly, apologetically.)* but it's so hard to manage when it's, well—raw.

ASAGAI: And so to accommodate that—you mutilate it every week?

BENEATHA: It's not mutilation!

ASAGAI: *(Laughing aloud at her seriousness.)* Oh . . . please! I am only teasing you because you are so very serious about these things. *(He stands back from her and folds his arms across his chest as he watches her pulling at her hair and frowning in the mirror.)* Do you remember the first time you met me at school? . . . *(He laughs.)* You came up to me and you said—and I thought you were the most serious little thing I had ever seen—you said: *(He imitates her.)* "Mr. Asagai—I want very much to talk with you. About Africa. You see, Mr. Asagai, I am looking for my *identity!*" *(He laughs.)*

BENEATHA: *(Turning to him, not laughing.)* Yes—*(Her face is quizzical, profoundly disturbed.)*

ASAGAI: *(Still teasing and reaching out and taking her face in his hands and turning her profile to him.)* Well . . . it is true that this is not so much a profile of a Hollywood queen as perhaps a queen of the Nile—*(A mock dismissal of the importance of the question.)*—but what does it matter? Assimilationism is so popular in your country.

BENEATHA: *(Wheeling, passionately, sharply.)* I am not an assimilationist!

ASAGAI: *(The protest hangs in the room for a moment and* ASAGAI *studies her, his laughter fading.)* Such a serious one. *(There is a pause.)* So—you like the robes? You must take excellent care of them—they are from my sister's personal wardrobe.

BENEATHA: *(With incredulity.)* You—you sent all the way home—for me?

ASAGAI: *(With charm.)* For you—I would do much more. . . . Well, that is what I came for. I must go.

BENEATHA: Will you call me Monday?

ASAGAI: Yes . . . we have a great deal to talk about. I mean about identity and time and all that.

BENEATHA: Time?

ASAGAI: Yes. About how much time one needs to know what one feels.

BENEATHA: You never understood that there is more than one kind of feeling which can exist between a man and a woman—or, at least, there should be.

ASAGAI: *(Shaking his head negatively but gently.)* No. Between a man and a woman there need be only one kind of feeling. I have that for you . . . now even . . . right this moment . . .

BENEATHA: I know—and by itself—it won't do. I can find that anywhere.

ASAGAI: For a woman it should be enough.

BENEATHA: I know—because that's what it says in all the novels that men write. But it isn't. Go ahead and laugh—but I'm not interested in being someone's little episode in America or—*(With feminine vengeance.)*—one of them!

(ASAGAI has burst into laughter again.)

That's funny as hell, huh!

ASAGAI: It's just that every American girl I have known has said that to me. White—black—in this you are all the same. And the same speech, too!

BENEATHA: *(Angrily.)* Yuk, yuk, yuk!

ASAGAI: It's how you can be sure that the world's most liberated women are not liberated at all. You all talk about it too much!

(MAMA enters and is immediately all social charm because of the presence of a guest.)

BENEATHA: Oh—Mama—this is Mr. Asagai.

MAMA: How do you do?

ASAGAI: *(Total politeness to an elder.)* How do you do, Mrs. Younger. Please forgive me for coming at such an outrageous hour on a Saturday.

MAMA: Well, you are quite welcome. I just hope you understand that our house don't always look like this. *(Chatterish.)* You must come again. I would love to hear all about—*(Not sure of the name.)*—your country. I think it's so sad the way our American Negroes don't know nothing about Africa 'cept Tarzan and all that. And all that money they pour into these churches when they ought to be helping you people over there drive out them French and Englishmen done taken away your land. *(The mother flashes a slightly superior look at her daughter upon completion of the recitation.)*

ASAGAI: *(Taken aback by this sudden and acutely unrelated expression of sympathy.)* Yes . . . yes. . . .

MAMA: *(Smiling at him suddenly and relaxing and looking him over.)* How many miles is it from here to where you come from?

ASAGAI: Many thousands.

MAMA: *(Looking at him as she would* WALTER.*)* I bet you don't half look after yourself, being away from your mama either. I 'spec' you better come 'round here from time to time and get yourself some decent home-cooked meals. . . .

ASAGAI: *(Moved.)* Thank you. Thank you very much. *(They are all quiet, then—)* Well . . . I must go. I will call you Monday, Alaiyo.

MAMA: What's that he call you?

ASAGAI: Oh—"Alaiyo." I hope you don't mind. It is what you would call a nickname, I think. It is a Yoruba word. I am a Yoruba.

MAMA: *(Looking at* BENEATHA.*)* I—I thought he was from—

ASAGAI: *(Understanding.)* Nigeria is my country. Yoruba is my tribal origin—

BENEATHA: You didn't tell us what Alaiyo means. . . for all I know, you might be calling me Little Idiot or something. . . .

ASAGAI: Well . . . let me see . . . I do not know just to explain it. . . . The sense of a thing can be so different when it changes languages.

BENEATHA: You're evading.

ASAGAI: No—really it is difficult . . . *(Thinking.)* It means . . . it means One for Whom Bread—Food—Is Not Enough. *(He looks at her.)* Is that all right?

BENEATHA: *(Understanding, softly.)* Thank you.

MAMA: *(Looking from one to the other and not understanding any of it.)* Well . . . that's nice. . . . You must come see us again—Mr.—

ASAGAI: Ah-sah-guy.

MAMA: Yes . . . do come again.

ASAGAI: Good-bye. *(He exits.)*

MAMA: *(After him.)* Lord, that's a pretty thing just went out here! *(Insinuatingly, to her daughter.)* Yes, I guess I see why we done commence to get so interested in Africa 'round here. Missionaries my aunt Jenny! *(She exits.)*

BENEATHA: Oh, Mama! . . . *(She picks up the Nigerian dress and holds it up to her in front of the mirror again. She sets the headdress on haphazardly and then notices her hair again and clutches at it and then replaces the headdress and frowns at herself. Then she starts to wriggle in front of the mirror as she thinks a Nigerian woman might.)*

(TRAVIS *enters and regards her.*)

TRAVIS: You cracking up?

BENEATHA: Shut up. (*She pulls the headdress off and looks at herself in the mirror and clutches at her hair again and squinches her eyes as if trying to imagine something. Then, suddenly, she gets her raincoat and kerchief and hurriedly prepares for going out.*)

MAMA: (*Coming back into the room.*) She's resting now. Travis, baby, run next door and ask Miss Johnson to please let me have a little kitchen cleanser. This here can is empty as Jacob's kettle.

TRAVIS: I just came in.

MAMA: Do as you told. (*He exits and she looks at her daughter.*) Where are you going?

BENEATHA: (*Halting at the door.*) To become a queen of the Nile! (*She exits in a breathless blaze of glory.*)

(RUTH *appears in the bedroom doorway.*)

MAMA: Who told you to get up?

RUTH: Ain't nothing wrong with me to be lying in no bed for. Where did Bennie go?

MAMA: (*Drumming her fingers.*) Far as I could make out—to Egypt.

(RUTH *just looks at her.*)

What time is it getting to?

RUTH: Ten twenty. And the mailman going to ring that bell this morning just like he done every morning for the last umpteen years.

(TRAVIS *comes in with the cleanser can.*)

TRAVIS: She say to tell you that she don't have much.

MAMA: (*Angrily.*) Lord, some people I could name sure is tight-fisted! (*Directing her grandson.*) Mark two cans of cleanser down on the list there. If she that hard up for kitchen cleanser, I sure don't want to forget to get her none!

RUTH: Lena—maybe the woman is just short on cleanser—

MAMA: (*Not listening.*) Much baking powder as she done borrowed from me all these years, she could of done gone into the baking business!

(*The* BELL *sounds suddenly and sharply and all three are stunned—serious and silent—mid-speech. In spite of all the other conversations and distractions of the morning, this is what they have been waiting for, even* TRAVIS, *who looks helplessly from his mother to his grandmother.* RUTH *is the first to come to life again.*)

RUTH: (*To* TRAVIS.) GET DOWN THEM STEPS, BOY!

(TRAVIS *snaps to life and flies out to get the mail.*)

MAMA: (*Her eyes wide, her hand to her breast.*) You mean it done really come?

RUTH: (*Excited.*) Oh, Miss Lena!

MAMA: (*Collecting herself.*) Well . . . I don't know what we all so excited about 'round here. We known it was coming for months.

RUTH: That's a whole lot different from having it come and being able to hold it in your hands . . . a piece of paper worth ten thousand dollars. . . .

(TRAVIS *bursts back into the room. He holds the envelope high above his head, like a little dancer, his face is radiant and he is breathless. He moves to his grandmother with sudden slow ceremony and puts the envelope into her hands. She accepts it, and then merely holds it and looks at it.*)

Come on! Open it . . . Lord have mercy, I wish Walter Lee was here!

TRAVIS: Open it, Grandmama!

MAMA: (*Staring at it.*) Now you all be quiet. It's just a check.

RUTH: Open it. . . .

MAMA: (*Still staring at it.*) Now don't act silly. . . . We ain't never been no people to act silly 'bout no money—

RUTH: (*Swiftly.*) We ain't never had none before—OPEN IT!

(MAMA *finally makes a good strong tear and pulls out the thin blue slice of paper and inspects it closely. The boy and his mother study it raptly over* MAMA's *shoulders.*)

MAMA: TRAVIS! (*She is counting off with doubt.*) Is that the right number of zeros?

TRAVIS: Yes'm . . . ten thousand dollars. Gaalee, Grandmama, you rich.

MAMA: (*She holds the check away from her, still looking at it. Slowly her face sobers into a mask of unhappiness.*) Ten thousand dollars. (*She hands it to* RUTH.) Put it away somewhere, Ruth. (*She does not look at* RUTH; *her eyes seem to be seeing something somewhere very far off.*) Ten thousand dollars they give you. Ten thousand dollars.

TRAVIS: (*To his mother, sincerely.*) What's the matter with Grandmama—don't she want to be rich?

RUTH: (*Distractedly.*) You go on out and play now, baby.

(TRAVIS *exits.* MAMA *starts wiping dishes absently, humming intently to herself.*)

(RUTH *turns to her, with kind exasperation.*) You've gone and got yourself upset.

MAMA: (*Not looking at her.*) I 'spec' if it wasn't for you all . . . I would just put that money away or give it to the church or something.

RUTH: Now what kind of talk is that. Mr. Younger would just be plain mad if he could hear you talking foolish like that.

MAMA: (*Stopping and staring off.*) Yes . . . he sure would. (*Sighing.*) We got enough to do with that money, all right. (*She halts then, and turns and looks at her daughter-in-law hard;* RUTH *avoids her eyes and* MAMA *wipes her hands with finality and starts to speak firmly to* RUTH.) Where did you go today, girl?

RUTH: To the doctor.

MAMA: (*Impatiently.*) Now, Ruth . . . you know better than that. Old Doctor Jones is strange enough in his way but there ain't nothing 'bout him make somebody slip and call him "she"—like you done this morning.

RUTH: Well, that's what happened—my tongue slipped.

MAMA: You went to see that woman, didn't you?

RUTH: (Defensively, giving herself away.) What woman you talking about?

MAMA: (Angrily.) That woman who—

(WALTER enters in great excitement.)

WALTER: Did it come?

MAMA: (Quietly.) Can't you give people a Christian greeting before you start asking about money?

WALTER: (To RUTH.) Did it come?

(RUTH unfolds the check and lays it quietly before him, watching him intently with thoughts of her own.)

(WALTER sits down and grasps it close and counts off the zeros.) Ten thousand dollars. (He turns suddenly, frantically to his mother and draws some papers out of his breast pocket.) Mama—look. Old Willy Harris put everything on paper—

MAMA: Son—I think you ought to talk to your wife . . . I'll go on out and leave you alone if you want—

WALTER: I can talk to her later—Mama, look—

MAMA: Son—

WALTER: WILL SOMEBODY PLEASE LISTEN TO ME TODAY?

MAMA: (Quietly.) I don't 'low no yellin' in this house, Walter Lee, and you know it—

(WALTER stares at them in frustration and starts to speak several times.)

—and there ain't going to be no investing in no liquor stores. I don't aim to have to speak on that again.

(A long pause.)

WALTER: Oh—so you don't aim to have to speak on that again? So you have decided. . . . (Crumpling his papers.) Well, you tell that to my boy tonight when you put him to sleep on the living-room couch . . . (Turning to MAMA and speaking directly to her.) yeah—and tell it to my wife, Mama, tomorrow when she has to go out of here to look after somebody else's kids. And tell it to me, Mama, every time we need a new pair of curtains and I have to watch you go out and work in somebody's kitchen. Yeah, you tell me then! (WALTER starts out.)

RUTH: Where you going?

WALTER: I'm going out!

RUTH: Where?

WALTER: Just out of this house somewhere—

RUTH: (Getting her coat.) I'll come too.

WALTER: I don't want you to come!

RUTH: I got something to talk to you about, Walter.

WALTER: That's too bad.

MAMA: (Still quietly.) Walter Lee—(She waits and he finally turns and looks at her)—sit down.

WALTER: I'm a grown man, Mama.

MAMA: Ain't nobody said you wasn't grown. But you still in my house and my presence. And as long as you are—you'll talk to your wife civil. Now sit down.

RUTH: (Suddenly.) Oh, let him go on out and drink himself to death! He makes me sick to my stomach! (She flings her coat against him.)

WALTER: (Violently.) And you turn mine too, baby! (RUTH goes into their bedroom and slams the door behind her.) That was my greatest mistake—

MAMA: (Still quietly.) Walter, what is the matter with you?

WALTER: Matter with me? Ain't nothing the matter with me!

MAMA: Yes there is. Something eating you up like a crazy man. Something more than me not giving you this money. The past few years I been watching it happen to you. You get all nervous acting and kind of wild in the eyes—

(WALTER jumps up impatiently at her words.)

I said sit there now, I'm talking to you!—

WALTER: Mama—I don't need no nagging at me today.

MAMA: Seem like you getting to a place where you always tied up in some kind of knot about something. But if anybody ask you 'bout it you just yell at 'em and bust out the house and go out and drink somewheres. Walter Lee, people can't live with that. Ruth's a good, patient girl in her way—but you getting to be too much. Boy, don't make the mistake of driving that girl away from you.

WALTER: Why—what she do for me?

MAMA: She loves you.

WALTER: Mama—I'm going out. I want to go off somewhere and be by myself for a while.

MAMA: I'm sorry 'bout your liquor store, son. It just wasn't the thing for us to do. That's what I want to tell you about—

WALTER: I got to go out, Mama—(He rises.)

MAMA: It's dangerous, son.

WALTER: What's dangerous?

MAMA: When a man goes outside his home to look for peace.

WALTER: (Beseechingly.) Then why can't there never be no peace in this house then?

MAMA: You done found it in some other house?

WALTER: No—there ain't no woman! Why do women always think there's a woman somewhere when a man gets restless. (Coming to her.) Mama—Mama—I want so many things . . .

MAMA: Yes, son—

WALTER: I want so many things that they are driving me kind of crazy . . . Mama—look at me.

MAMA: I'm looking at you. You a good-looking boy. You got a job, a nice wife, a fine boy and—

WALTER: A job. (*Looks at her.*) Mama, a job? I open and close car doors all day long. I drive a man around in his limousine and I say, "Yes sir; no, sir; very good, sir; shall I take the Drive, sir?" Mama, that ain't no kind of job . . . that ain't nothing at all. (*Very quietly.*) Mama, I don't know if I can make you understand.

MAMA: Understand what, baby?

WALTER: (*Quietly.*) Sometimes it's like I can see the future stretched out in front of me—just plain as day. The future, Mama. Hanging over there at the edge of my days. Just waiting for me—a big, looming blank space—full of *nothing*. Just waiting for *me*. (*Pause.*) Mama—sometimes when I'm downtown and I pass them cool, quiet-looking restaurants where them white boys are sitting back and talking 'bout things . . . sitting there turning deals worth millions of dollars . . . sometimes I see guys don't look much older than me—

MAMA: Son—how come you talk so much 'bout money?

WALTER: (*With immense passion.*) Because it is life, Mama!

MAMA: (*Quietly.*) Oh—(*Very quietly.*)—so now it's life. Money is life. Once upon a time freedom used to be life—now it's money. I guess the world really do change . . .

WALTER: No—it was always money, Mama. We just didn't know about it.

MAMA: No . . . something has changed. (*She looks at him.*) You something new, boy. In my time we was worried about not being lynched and getting to the North if we could and how to stay alive and still have a pinch of dignity too. . . . Now here come you and Beneatha—talking 'bout things we ain't never even thought about hardly, me and your daddy. You ain't satisfied or proud of nothing we done. I mean that you had a home; that we kept you out of trouble till you was grown; that you don't have to ride to work on the back of nobody's streetcar—you my children—but how different we done become.

WALTER: You just don't understand, Mama, you just don't understand.

MAMA: Son—do your know your wife is expecting another baby?

(WALTER *stands, stunned, and absorbs what his mother has said.*) That's what she wanted to talk to you about.

(WALTER *sinks down into a chair.*)

This ain't for me to be telling—but you ought to know. (*She waits.*) I think Ruth is thinking 'bout getting rid of that child.

WALTER: (*Slowly understanding.*) No—no—Ruth wouldn't do that.

MAMA: When the world gets ugly enough—a woman will do anything for her family. *The part that's already living.*

WALTER: You don't know Ruth, Mama, if you think she would do that.

(RUTH *opens the bedroom door and stands there a little limp.*)

RUTH: (*Beaten.*) Yes I would too, Walter. (*Pause.*) I gave her a five-dollar down payment.

(*There is total silence as the man stares at his wife and the mother stares at her son.*)

MAMA: (*Presently.*) Well—(*Tightly.*)—well—son, I'm waiting to hear you say something . . . I'm waiting to hear how you be your father's son. Be the man he was . . . (*Pause.*) Your wife say she going to destroy your child. And I'm waiting to hear you talk like him and say we a people who give children life, not who destroys them—(*She rises.*)—I'm waiting to see you stand up and look like your daddy and say we done give up one baby to poverty and that we ain't going to give up nary another one. . . . I'm waiting.

WALTER: Ruth—

MAMA: If you a son of mine, tell her!

(WALTER *turns, looks at her and can say nothing.*)

(*She continues, bitterly.*) You . . . you are a disgrace to your father's memory. Somebody get me my hat.

CURTAIN

ACT 2

SCENE 1

TIME:
Later the same day.
AT RISE:
RUTH *is ironing again. She has the* RADIO *going. Presently* BENEATHA*'s bedroom door opens and* RUTH*'s mouth falls and she puts down the iron in fascination.*

RUTH: What have we got on tonight!

BENEATHA: (*Emerging grandly from the doorway so that we can see her thoroughly robed in the costume Asagai brought.*) You are looking at what a well-dressed Nigerian woman wears—(*She parades for* RUTH, *her hair completely hidden by the headdress; she is coquettishly fanning herself with an ornate oriental fan, mistakenly more like Butterfly than any Nigerian that ever was.*)—isn't it beautiful? (*She promenades to the radio and, with an arrogant flourish, turns off the good loud blues that is playing.*) Enough of this assimilationist junk! (RUTH *follows her with her eyes as she goes to the phonograph and puts on a record and turns and waits ceremoniously for the music to come up. Then, with a shout—*) OCOMOGOSIAY!

(RUTH *jumps. The music comes up, a lovely Nigerian melody.* BENEATHA *listens, enraptured, her eyes far away—"back to the past." She begins to dance.* RUTH *is dumbfounded.*)

RUTH: What kind of dance is that?

BENEATHA: A folk dance.

RUTH: *(Pearl Bailey.)* What kind of folks do that, honey?

BENEATHA: It's from Nigeria. It's a dance of welcome.

RUTH: Who you welcoming?

BENEATHA: The men back to the village.

RUTH: Where they been?

BENEATHA: How should I know—out hunting or something. Anyway, they are coming back now. . . .

RUTH: Well, that's good.

BENEATHA: *(With the record.)*

Alundi, alundi
Alundi alunya
Jop pu a jeepua
Ang gu soooooooooo

Ai yai yae . . .
Ayehaye—alundi . . .

(WALTER comes in during this performance; he has obviously been drinking. He leans against the door heavily and watches his sister, at first with distaste. Then his eyes look off—"back to the past"—as he lifts both his fists to the roof, screaming.)

WALTER: YEAH . . . AND ETHIOPIA STRETCH FORTH HER HANDS AGAIN! . . .

RUTH: *(Drily, looking at him.)* Yes—and Africa sure is claiming her own tonight. *(She gives them both up and starts ironing again.)*

WALTER: *(All in a drunken, dramatic shout.)* Shut up! . . . I'm digging them drums . . . them drums move me! . . . *(He makes his weaving way to his wife's face and leans in close to her.)* In my *heart of hearts*—*(He thumps his chest.)*—I am much warrior!

RUTH: *(Without even looking up.)* In your heart of hearts you are much drunkard.

WALTER: *(Coming away from her and starting to wander around the room, shouting.)* Me and Jomo . . . *(Intently, in his sister's face. She has stopped dancing to watch him in this unknown mood.)* that's my man, Kenyatta. *(Shouting and thumping his chest.)* FLAMING SPEAR! HOT DAMN! *(He is suddenly in possession of an imaginary spear and actively spearing enemies all over the room.)* OCOMOGOSIAY . . . THE LION IS WAKING . . . OWIMOWEH! *(He pulls his shirt open and leaps up on a table and gestures with his spear. The bell rings.* RUTH *goes to answer.)*

BENEATHA: *(To encourage* WALTER, *thoroughly caught up with this side of him.)* OCOMOGOSIAY, FLAMING SPEAR!

WALTER: *(On the table, very far gone, his eyes pure glass sheets. He sees what we cannot, that he is a leader of his people, a great chief, a descendant of Chaka, and that the hour to march has come.)* Listen, my black brothers—

BENEATHA: OCOMOGOSIAY!

WALTER: —Do you hear the waters rushing against the shores of the coastlands—

BENEATHA: OCOMOGOSIAY!

WALTER: —Do you hear the screeching of the cocks in yonder hills beyond where the chiefs meet in council for the coming of the mighty war—

BENEATHA: OCOMOGOSIAY!

WALTER: —Do you hear the beating of the wings of the birds flying low over the mountains and the low places of our land—

(RUTH opens the door. GEORGE MURCHISON *enters.)*

BENEATHA: OCOMOGOSIAY!

WALTER: —Do you hear the singing of the women, singing the war songs of our fathers to the babies in the great houses . . . singing the sweet war songs? OH, DO YOUR HEAR, MY BLACK BROTHERS!

BENEATHA: *(Completely gone.)* We hear you, Flaming Spear—

WALTER: Telling us to prepare for the greatness of the time— *(To* GEORGE.*)* Black Brother! *(He extends his hand for the fraternal clasp.)*

GEORGE: Black Brother, hell!

RUTH: *(Having had enough, and embarrassed for the family.)* Beneatha, you got company—what's the matter with you? Walter Lee Younger, get down off that table and stop acting like a fool . . .

(WALTER comes down off the table suddenly and makes a quick exit to the bathroom.)

RUTH: He's had a little to drink . . . I don't know what her excuse is.

GEORGE: *(To* BENEATHA.*)* Look honey, we're going *to* the theater—we're not going to be *in* it . . . so go change, huh?

RUTH: You expect this boy to go out with you looking like that?

BENEATHA: *(Looking at* GEORGE.*)* That's up to George. If he's ashamed of his heritage—

GEORGE: Oh, don't be so proud of yourself, Bennie—just because you look eccentric.

BENEATHA: How can something that's natural be eccentric?

GEORGE: That's what being eccentric means—being natural. Get dressed.

BENEATHA: I don't like that, George.

RUTH: Why must you and your brother make an argument out of everything people say?

BENEATHA: Because I hate assimilationist Negroes!

RUTH: Will somebody please tell me what assimila-whoever means!

GEORGE: Oh, it's just a college girl's way of calling people Uncle Toms—but that isn't what it means at all.

RUTH: Well, what does it mean?

BENEATHA: *(Cutting* GEORGE *off and staring at him as she replies to* RUTH.*)* It means someone who is willing to give up his own culture and submerge himself completely in the dominant, and in this case, *oppressive* culture!

GEORGE: Oh, dear, dear, dear! Here we go! A lecture on the African past! On our Great West African Heritage! In one second we will hear all about the great Ashanti empires; the great Songhay civilizations; and the great sculpture of Benin—and then some poetry in the Bantu—and the whole monologue will end with the word *heritage!* (*Nastily.*) Let's face it, baby, your heritage is nothing but a bunch of raggedy-assed spirituals and some grass huts!

BENEATHA: *Grass huts!*

(RUTH *crosses to her and forcibly pushes her toward the bedroom.*) See there . . . you are standing there in your splendid ignorance talking about people who were the first to smelt iron on the face of the earth!

(RUTH *is pushing her through the door.*)

The Ashanti were performing surgical operations when the English—

(RUTH *pulls the door to, with* BENEATHA *on the other side, and smiles graciously at* GEORGE.)

(BENEATHA *opens the door and shouts the end of the sentence defiantly at* GEORGE.)—were still tattooing themselves with blue dragons. . . . (*She goes back inside.*)

RUTH: Have a seat, George. (*They both sit.* RUTH *folds her hands rather primly on her lap, determined to demonstrate the civilization of the family.*) Warm, ain't it? I mean for September. (*Pause.*) Just like they always say about Chicago weather: If it's too hot or cold for you, just wait a minute and it'll change. (*She smiles happily at this clichè of clichès.*) Everybody say it's got to do with them bombs and things they keep setting off. (*Pause.*) Would you like a nice cold beer?

GEORGE: No, thank you. I don't care for beer. (*He looks at his watch.*) I hope she hurries up.

RUTH: What time is the show?

GEORGE: It's an eight-thirty curtain. That's just Chicago, though. In New York standard curtain times is eight forty. (*He is rather proud of this knowledge.*)

RUTH: (*Properly appreciating it.*) You get to New York a lot?

GEORGE: (*Offhand.*) Few times a year.

RUTH: Oh—that's nice. I've never been to New York.

(WALTER *enters. We feel he has relieved himself, but the edge of unreality is still with him.*)

WALTER: New York ain't got nothing Chicago ain't. Just a bunch of hustling people all squeezed up together—being "Eastern." (*He turns his face into a screw of displeasure.*)

GEORGE: Oh—you've been?

WALTER: *Plenty* of times.

RUTH: (*Shocked at the lie.*) Walter Lee Younger!

WALTER: (*Staring her down.*) Plenty! (*Pause.*) What we got to drink in this house? Why don't you offer this man some refreshment. (*To* GEORGE.) They don't know how to entertain people in this house, man.

GEORGE: Thank you—I don't really care for anything.

WALTER: (*Feeling his head; sobriety coming.*) Where's Mama?

RUTH: She ain't come back yet.

WALTER: (*Looking* GEORGE *over from head to toe, scrutinizing his carefully casual tweed sports jacket over cashmere V-neck sweater over soft eyelet shirt and tie, and soft slacks, finished off with white buckskin shoes.*) Why all you college boys wear them fairyish-looking white shoes?

RUTH: Walter Lee!

(GEORGE *ignores the remark.*)

WALTER: (*To* RUTH.) Well, they look crazy as hell—white shoes, cold as it is.

RUTH: (*Crushed.*) You have to excuse him—

WALTER: No he don't! Excuse me for what? What you always excusing me for! I'll excuse myself when I needs to be excused! (*A pause.*) They look as funny as them black knee socks Beneatha wears out of here all the time.

RUTH: It's the college *style*, Walter.

WALTER: Style, hell. She looks like she got burnt legs or something!

RUTH: Oh, Walter—

WALTER: (*An irritable mimic.*) Oh, Walter! Oh, Walter! (*To* MURCHISON.) How's your old man making out? I understand you all going to buy that big hotel on the Drive? (*He finds a beer in the refrigerator, wanders over to* MURCHISON, *sipping and wiping his lips with the back of his hand, and straddling a chair backwards to talk to the other man.*) Shrewd move. Your old man is all right, man. (*Tapping his head and half winking for emphasis.*) I mean he knows how to operate. I mean he thinks *big*, you known what I mean, I mean for a *home*, you know? But I think he's kind of running out of ideas now. I'd like to talk to him. Listen, man, I got some plans that could turn this city upside down. I mean I think like he does. *Big.* Invest big, gamble big, hell, lose *big* if you have to, you know what I mean. It's hard to find a man on this whole southside who understand my kind of thinking—you dig? (*He scrutinizes* MURCHISON *again, drinks his beer, squints his eyes and leans in close, confidential, man to man.*) Me and you ought to sit down and talk sometimes, man. Man, I got me some ideas. . . .

GEORGE: (*With boredom.*) Yeah—sometimes we'll have to do that, Walter.

WALTER: (*Understanding the indifference, and offended.*) Yeah—well, when you get the time, man. I know you a busy little boy.

RUTH: Walter, please—

WALTER: (*Bitterly, hurt.*) I know ain't nothing in this world as busy as you colored college boys with your fraternity pins and white shoes. . . .

RUTH: (*Covering her face with humiliation.*) Oh, Walter Lee—

WALTER: I see you all all the time—with the books tucked under your arms—going to your *(British A—a mimic.)* "clahsses." And for what! What the hell you learning over there? Filling up your heads—*(Counting off on his fingers.)*—with the sociology and the psychology—but they teaching you how to be a man? How to take over and run the world? They teaching you how to run a rubber plantation or a steel mill? Naw—just to talk proper and read books and wear white shoes. . . .

GEORGE: *(Looking at him with distaste, a little above it all.)* You're all wacked up with bitterness, man.

WALTER: *(Intently, almost quietly, between the teeth, glaring at the boy.)* And you—ain't you bitter, man? Ain't you just about had it yet? Don't you see no stars gleaming that you can't reach out and grab? You happy?—you contented son-of-a-bitch—you happy? You got it made? Bitter? Man, I'm a volcano. Bitter? Here I am a giant—surrounded by ants! Ants who can't even understand what it is the giant is talking about.

RUTH: *(Passionately and suddenly.)* Oh, Walter—ain't you with nobody!

WALTER: *(Violently.)* No! 'Cause ain't nobody with me! Not even my own mother!

RUTH: Walter, that's a terrible thing to say!

(BENEATHA enters, dressed for the evening in a cocktail dress and earrings.)

GEORGE: Well—hey, you look great.

BENEATHA: Let's go, George. See you all later.

RUTH: Have a nice time.

GEORGE: Thanks. Good night. *(To WALTER, sarcastically.)* Good night, *Prometheus.*

(BENEATHA and GEORGE exit.)

WALTER: *(To RUTH.)* Who is Prometheus?

RUTH: I don't know. Don't worry about it.

WALTER: *(In fury, pointing after GEORGE.)* See there—they get to a point where they can't insult you man to man—they got to go talk about somethings ain't nobody never heard of!

RUTH: How do you know it was an insult? *(To humor him.)* May be Prometheus is a nice fellow.

WALTER: Prometheus! I bet there ain't even no such thing! I bet that simple-minded clown—

RUTH: Walter—*(She stops what she is doing and looks at him.)*

WALTER: *(Yelling.)* Don't start!

RUTH: Start what?

WALTER: Your nagging! Where was I? Who was I with? How much money did I spend?

RUTH: *(Plaintively.)* Walter Lee—why don't we just try to talk about it. . . .

WALTER: *(Not listening.)* I been out talking with people who understand me. People who care about the things I got on my mind.

RUTH: *(Wearily.)* I guess that means people like Willy Harris.

WALTER: Yes, people like Willy Harris.

RUTH: *(With a sudden flash of impatience.)* Why don't you all just hurry up and go into the banking business and stop talking about it!

WALTER: Why? You want to know why? 'Cause we all tied up in a race of people that don't know how to do nothing but moan, pray and have babies! *(The line is too bitter even for him and he looks at her and sits down.)*

RUTH: Oh, Walter . . . *(Softly.)* honey, why can't you stop fighting me?

WALTER: *(Without thinking.)* Who's fighting you? Who even cares about you? *(This line begins the retardation of his mood.)*

RUTH: Well—*(She waits a long time, and then with resignation, starts to put away her things.)* —I guess I might as well go on bed . . . *(More or less to herself.)* I don't know where we lost it . . . but we have . . . *(Then, to him.)* I—I'm sorry about this new baby, Walter. I guess maybe I better go on and do what I started . . . I guess I just didn't realize how bad things was with us . . . I guess I just didn't really realize—*(She starts out to the bedroom and stops.)*—you want some hot milk?

WALTER: Hot milk?

RUTH: Yes—hot milk.

WALTER: Why hot milk?

RUTH: 'Cause after all that liquor you come home with you ought to have something hot in your stomach.

WALTER: I don't want no milk.

RUTH: You want some coffee then?

WALTER: No, I don't want no coffee. I don't want nothing hot to drink. *(Almost plaintively.)* Why you always trying to give me something to eat?

RUTH: *(Standing and looking at him helplessly.)* What else can I give you, Walter Lee Younger? *(She stands and looks at him and presently turns to go out again.)*

(He lifts his head and watches her going away from him in a new mood which began to emerge when he asked her "Who cares about you?")

WALTER: It's been rough, ain't it, baby? *(She hears and stops but does not turn around and he continues to her back.)* I guess between two people there ain't never as much understood as folks generally thinks there is. I mean like between me and you—*(She turns to face him.)*—how we gets to the place where we scared to talk softness to each other. *(He waits, thinking hard himself.)* Why you think it got to be like that? *(He is thoughtful, almost as a child would be.)* Ruth, what is it gets into people ought to be close?

RUTH: I don't know, honey. I think about it a lot.

WALTER: On account of you and me, you mean? The way things are with us. The way something done come down between us.

RUTH: There ain't so much between us, Walter . . . not when you come to me and try to talk to me. Try to be with me . . . a little even.

WALTER: *(Total honesty.)* Sometimes . . . sometimes . . . I don't even know how to try.

RUTH: Walter—

WALTER: Yes?

RUTH: *(Coming to him, gently and with misgiving, but coming to him.)* Honey . . . life don't have to be like this. I mean sometimes people can do things so that things are better. . . . You remember how we used to talk when Travis was born . . . about the way we were going to live . . . the kind of house . . . *(She is stroking his head.)* Well, it's all starting to slip away from us. . . .

(MAMA enters, and WALTER jumps up and shouts at her.)

WALTER: Mama, where have you been?

MAMA: My—them steps is longer than they used to be. Whew! *(She sits down and ignores him.)* How you feeling this evening, Ruth?

(RUTH shrugs, disturbed some at having been prematurely interrupted and watching her husband knowingly.)

WALTER: Mama, where you been all day?

MAMA: *(Still ignoring him and learning on the table and changing to more comfortable shoes.)* Where's Travis?

RUTH: I let him go out earlier and he ain't come back yet. Boy, is he going to get it!

WALTER: Mama!

MAMA: *(As if she has heard him for the first time.)* Yes, son?

WALTER: Where did you go this afternoon?

MAMA: I went downtown to tend to some business that I had to tend to.

WALTER: What kind of business?

MAMA: You know better than to question me like a child, Brother.

WALTER: *(Rising and bending over the table.)* Where were you, Mama? *(Bringing his fists down and shouting.)* Mama, you didn't go do something with that insurance money, something crazy?

(The front door opens slowly, interrupting him, and TRAVIS peeks his head in, less than hopefully.)

TRAVIS: *(To his mother.)* Mama, I—

RUTH: "Mama I" nothing! You're going to get it, boy! Get on in that bedroom and get yourself ready!

TRAVIS: But I—

MAMA: Why don't you all never let the child explain hisself.

RUTH: Keep out of it now, Lena.

(MAMA clamps her lips together, and RUTH advances toward her son menacingly.)

RUTH: A thousand times I have told you not to go off like that—

MAMA: *(Holding out her arms to her grandson.)* Well—at least let me tell him something. I want him to be the first one to hear. . . . Come here, Travis.

(The boy obeys, gladly.)

Travis—*(She takes him by the shoulder and looks into his face.)* —you know that money we got in the mail this morning?

TRAVIS: Yes'm—

MAMA: Well—what do you think your grandmama gone and done with that money?

TRAVIS: I don't know, Grandmama.

MAMA: *(Putting her finger on his nose for emphasis.)* She went out and she bought you a house!

(The explosion comes from WALTER at the end of the revelation and he jumps up and turns away from all of them in a fury.)

(MAMA continues, to TRAVIS). You glad about the house? It's going to be yours when you get to be a man.

TRAVIS: Yeah—I always wanted to live in a house.

MAMA: All right, gimme some sugar then—*(TRAVIS puts his arms around her neck as she watches her son over the boy's shoulder. Then, to TRAVIS, after the embrace.)*—now when you say your prayers tonight, you thank God and your grandfather—'cause it was him who give you the house—in his way.

RUTH: *(Taking the boy from MAMA and pushing him toward the bedroom.)* Now you get out of here and get ready for your beating.

TRAVIS: Aw, Mama—

RUTH: Get on in there. *(Closing the door behind him and turning radiantly to her mother-in-law.)* So you went and did it!

MAMA: *(Quietly, looking at her son with pain.)* Yes, I did.

RUTH: *(Raising both arms classically.)* PRAISE GOD! *(Looks at WALTER a moment, who says nothing. She crosses rapidly to her husband.)* Please, honey—let me be glad . . . you be glad too. *(She has laid her hands on his shoulders, but he shakes himself free of her roughly, without turning to face her.)* Oh, Walter . . . a home . . . a home. *(She comes back to MAMA.)* Well—where is it? How big is it? How much it going to cost?

MAMA: Well—

RUTH: When we moving?

MAMA: *(Smiling at her.)* First of the month.

MAMA: *(Throwing back her head with jubilance.)* PRAISE GOD!

MAMA: *(Tentatively, still looking at her son's back turned against her and RUTH.)* It's—it's a nice house too . . . *(She cannot help speaking directly to him. An imploring quality in her voice, her manner, makes her almost like a girl now.)* Three bedrooms—nice big one for you and Ruth. . . . Me and Beneatha still have to share our room, but Travis have one of this own—and *(With difficulty.)* I figure if the—new baby—is a boy, we could get one of them double-decker outfits. . . . And there's a yard with a little patch of dirt where I could maybe get to grow me a few flowers . . . and a nice big basement . . .

RUTH: Walter honey, be glad—

MAMA: (*Still to his back, fingering things on the table.*) 'Course I don't want to make it sound fancier than it is. . . . It's just a plain little old house—but it's made good and solid—and it will be *ours*. Walter Lee—it makes a difference in a man when he can walk on floors that belong to him. . . .

RUTH: Where is it?

MAMA: (*Frightened at this telling.*) Well—well—it's out there in Clybourne Park—

(RUTH's *radiance fades abruptly, and* WALTER *finally turns slowly to face his mother with incredulity and hostility.*)

RUTH: Where?

MAMA: (*Matter-of-factly.*) Four o six Clybourne street, Clybourne Park.

RUTH: Clybourne Park? Mama, there ain't no colored people living in Clybourne Park.

MAMA: (*Almost idiotically.*) Well, I guess there's going to be some now.

WALTER: (*Bitterly.*) So that's the peace and comfort you went out and bought for us today!

MAMA: (*Raising her eyes to meet his finally.*) Son—I just tried to find the nicest place for the least amount of money for my family.

RUTH: (*Trying to recover from the shock.*) Well—well—'course I ain't one never been 'fraid of no crackers, mind you—but—well, wasn't there no other houses nowhere?

MAMA: Them houses they put up for colored in them areas way out all seem to cost twice as much as other houses. I did the best I could.

RUTH: (*Struck senseless with the news, in its various degrees of goodness and trouble, she sits a moment, her fists propping her chin in thought, and then she starts to rise, bringing her fists down with vigor, the radiance spreading from cheek to cheek again.*) Well—well!—All I can say is—if this is my time in life—my time—to say good-bye—(*And she builds with momentum as she starts to circle the room with an exuberant, almost tearfully happy release.*)—to these God-damned cracking walls!—(*She pounds the walls.*)—and these marching roaches!—(*She wipes at an imaginary army of marching roaches.*)—and this cramped little closet which ain't now or never was no kitchen! . . . then I say it loud and good, HALLELUJAH! AND GOOD-BYE MISERY . . . I DON'T NEVER WANT TO SEE YOUR UGLY FACE AGAIN! (*She laughs joyously, having practically destroyed the apartment, and flings her arms up and lets them come down happily, slowly, reflectively, over her abdomen, aware for the first time perhaps that the life therein pulses with happiness and not despair.*) Lena?

MAMA: (*Moved, watching her happiness.*) Yes, honey?

RUTH: (*Looking off.*) Is there—is there a whole lot of sunlight?

MAMA: (*Understanding.*) Yes, child, there's a whole lot of sunlight?

(*Long pause.*)

RUTH: (*Collecting herself and going to the door of the room* TRAVIS *is in.*) Well—I guess I better see 'bout Travis. (*To* MAMA.) Lord, I sure don't feel like whipping nobody today! (*She exits.*)

(*The mother and son are left alone now and the mother waits a long time, considering deeply, before she speaks.*)

MAMA: Son—you—you understand what I done, don't you?

(WALTER *is silent and sullen.*)

I—I just seen my family falling apart today . . . just falling to pieces in front of my eyes. . . . We couldn't of gone on like we was today. We was going backwards 'stead of forwards—talking 'bout killing babies and wishing each other was dead. . . . When it gets like that in life—you just got to do something different, push on out and do something bigger. . . . (*She waits.*) I wish you say something, son. . . . I wish you'd say how deep inside you you think I done the right thing—

WALTER: (*Crossing slowly to his bedroom door and finally turning there and speaking measuredly.*) What you need me to say you done right for? *You* the head of this family. You run our lives like you want to. It was your money and you did what you wanted with it. So what you need for me to say it was all right for? (*Bitterly, to hurt her as deeply as he knows is possible.*) So you butchered up a dream of mine—you—who always talking 'bout your children's dreams . . .

MAMA: Walter Lee—

(*He just closes the door behind him.* MAMA *sits alone, thinking heavily.*)

CURTAIN

ACT 2

SCENE 2

TIME:
Friday night. A few weeks later.

AT RISE:
Packing crates mark the intention of the family to move. BENEATHA *and* GEORGE *come in, presumably from an evening out again.*

GEORGE: O.K. . . . O.K., whatever you say. . . .

(*They both sit on the couch. He tries kiss her. She moves away.*)

Look, we've had a nice evening; let's not spoil it, huh? . . .

(*He again turns her head and tries to nuzzle in and she turns away from him, not with distaste but with momentary lack of interest; in a mood to pursue what they were talking about.*)

BENEATHA: I'm *trying* to talk to you.

GEORGE: We always talk.

BENEATHA: Yes—and I love to talk.

GEORGE: (*Exasperated; rising.*) I know it and I don't mind it sometimes . . . I want you to cut it out, see—the moody stuff, I mean. I don't like it. You're a nice-looking girl . . . all over. That's all you need, honey, forget the atmosphere. Guys aren't going to go for the atmosphere—they're going to go for what they see. Be glad for that. Drop the Garbo routine. It doesn't go with you. As for myself, I want a nice—(*Groping.*)—simple (*Thoughtfully.*)—sophisticated girl . . . not a poet—O.K.?

(*She rebuffs him again and he starts to leave.*)

BENEATHA: Why are you angry?

GEORGE: Because this is stupid! I don't go out with you to discuss the nature of "quiet desperation" or to hear all about your thoughts—because the world will go on thinking what it thinks regardless—

BENEATHA: Then why read books? Why go to school?

GEORGE: (*With artificial patience, counting on his fingers.*) It's simple. You read books—to learn facts—to get grades—to pass the course—to get a degree. That's all—it has nothing to do with thoughts.

(*A long pause.*)

BENEATHA: I see.

(*A longer pause as she looks at him.*)

Good night, George.

(GEORGE *looks at her a little oddly, and starts to exit. He meets* MAMA *coming in.*)

GEORGE: Oh—hello, Mrs. Younger.

MAMA: Hello, George, how you feeling?

GEORGE: Fine—fine, how are you?

MAMA: Oh, a little tired. You know them steps can get you after a day's work. You all have a nice time tonight?

GEORGE: Yes—a fine time. Well, good night.

MAMA: Good night.

(*He exits.*)

(MAMA *closes the door behind her.*) Hello, honey. What you sitting like that for?

BENEATHA: I'm just sitting.

MAMA: Didn't you have a nice time?

BENEATHA: No.

MAMA: No? What's the matter?

BENEATHA: Mama, George is a fool—honest. (*She rises.*)

MAMA: (*Hustling around unloading the packages she has entered with. She stops.*) Is he, baby?

BENEATHA: Yes. (BENEATHA *makes up* TRAVIS' *bed as she talks.*)

MAMA: You sure?

BENEATHA: Yes.

MAMA: Well—I guess you better not waste your time with no fools.

(BENEATHA *looks up at her mother, watching her put groceries in the refrigerator. Finally she gathers up her things and starts into the bedroom. At the door she stops and looks back at her mother.*)

BENEATHA: Mama—

MAMA: Yes, baby—

BENEATHA: Thank you.

MAMA: For what?

BENEATHA: For understanding me this time.

(*She exits quickly and the mother stands, smiling a little, looking at the place where* BENEATHA *just stood.* RUTH *enters.*)

RUTH: Now don't you fool with any of this stuff, Lena—

MAMA: Oh, I just thought I'd sort a few things out.

(*The phone rings.* RUTH *answers.*)

RUTH: (*At the phone.*) Hello—just a minute. (*Goes to the door.*) Walter, it's Mrs. Arnold. (*Waits. Goes back to the phone. Tense.*) Hello. Yes, this is his wife speaking . . . he's lying down now. Yes . . . well, he'll be in tomorrow. He's been very sick. Yes—I know we should have called, but we were so sure he'd be able to come in today. Yes—yes, I'm very sorry. Yes . . . thank you very much. (*She hangs up.*)

(WALTER *is standing in the doorway of the bedroom behind her.*)

That was Mrs. Arnold.

WALTER: (*Indifferently.*) Was it?

RUTH: She said if you don't come in tomorrow that they are getting a new man . . .

WALTER: Ain't that sad—ain't that crying sad.

RUTH: She said Mr. Arnold has had to take a cab for three days . . . Walter, you ain't been to work for three days! (*This is a revelation to her.*) Where you been, Walter Lee Younger?

(WALTER *looks at her and starts to laugh.*)

You're going to lose your job.

WALTER: That's right . . .

RUTH: Oh, Walter, and with your mother working like a dog every day—

WALTER: That's sad too—everything is sad.

MAMA: What you been doing for these three days, son?

WALTER: Mama—you don't know all the things a man what got leisure can find to do in this city. . . . What's this—Friday night? Well—Wednesday I borrowed Willy Harris' car and I went for a drive . . . just me and myself and I drove and drove . . . way out . . . way past South Chicago, and I parked the car and I sat and looked at the steel mills all day long. I just sat in the car and looked at them big black chimneys for hours. Then I drove back and I went to the Green Hat. (*Pause.*) And Thursday—Thursday I borrowed the car again and I got in and I pointed it the other way and I drove other way—for hours—way, way up to Wisconsin, and I looked at the farms. I just drove and looked at the farms. Then I drove back and I went to the Green Hat. (*Pause*) And today—today I didn't get the car. Today I just walked. All over the Southside. And

I looked at the Negroes and they looked at me and finally I just sat down on the curb at Thirty-ninth and South Parkway and I just sat there and watched the Negroes go by. And then I went to the Green Hat. You all sad? You all depressed? And you know where I am going right now—

(RUTH *goes out quietly.*)

MAMA: Oh, Big Walter, is this the harvest of our days?

WALTER: You know what I like about the Green Hat? *(He turns the* RADIO *on and a steamy, deep blues pours into the room.)* I like this little cat they got there who blows a sax . . . he blows. He talks to me. He ain't but 'bout five feet tall and he's got a conked head and his eyes is always closed and he's all music—

MAMA: *(Rising and getting some papers out of her handbag.)* Walter—

WALTER: And there's this other guy who plays the piano . . . and they got a sound. I mean they can work on some music . . . they got the best little combo in the world in the Green Hat . . . you can just sit there and drink and listen to them three men play and you realize that don't nothing matter worth a damn, but just being there—

MAMA: I've helped do it to you, haven't I, son? Walter, I been wrong.

WALTER: Naw—you ain't never been wrong about nothing, Mama.

MAMA: Listen to me, now. I say I been wrong, son. That I been doing to you what the rest of the world been doing to you. *(She stops and he looks up slowly at her and she meets his eyes pleadingly.)* Walter—what you ain't never understood is that I ain't got nothing, don't own nothing, ain't never really wanted nothing that wasn't for you. There ain't nothing as precious to me. . . . There ain't nothing worth holding on to, money, dreams, nothing else—if it means—if it means it's going to destroy my boy. *(She puts her papers in front of him and he watches her without speaking or moving.)* I paid the man thirty-five hundred dollars down on the house. That leaves sixty-five hundred dollars. Monday morning I want you to take this money and take three thousand dollars and put it in a savings account for Beneatha's medical schooling. The rest you put in a checking account—with your name on it. And from now on any penny that come out of it or that go in it is for you to look after. For you to decide. *(She drops her hands a little helplessly.)* It ain't much, but it's all I got in this world and I'm putting it in your hands. I'm telling you to be the head of this family from now on like you supposed to be.

WALTER: *(Stares at the money.)* You trust me like that, Mama?

MAMA: I ain't never stop trusting you. Like I ain't never stop loving you.

(She goes out, and WALTER *sits looking at the money on the table as the* MUSIC *continues in its idiom, pulsing in the room. Finally,* in a decisive gesture, he gets up, and, in mingled joy and desperation, picks up the money. At the same moment, TRAVIS *enters for bed.)*

TRAVIS: What's the matter, Daddy? You drunk?

WALTER: *(Sweetly, more sweetly than we have ever known him.)* No, Daddy ain't drunk. Daddy ain't going to never be drunk again . . .

TRAVIS: Well, good night, Daddy.

(The father has come from behind the couch and leans over, embracing his son.)

WALTER: Son, I feel like talking to you tonight.

TRAVIS: About what?

WALTER: Oh, about a lot of things. About you and what kind of man you going to be when you grow up. . . . Son— son, what do you want to be when you grow up?

TRAVIS: A bus driver.

WALTER: *(Laughing a little.)* A what? Man, that ain't nothing to want to be!

TRAVIS: Why not?

WALTER: 'Cause, man—it ain't big enough—you know what I mean.

TRAVIS: I don't know then. I can't make up my mind. Sometimes Mama asks me that too. And sometimes when I tell her I want to be like you—she says she don't want me to be like that and sometimes she says she does. . . .

WALTER: *(Gathering him up in his arms.)* You know what, Travis? In seven years you going to be seventeen years old. And things is going to be very different with us in seven years, Travis. . . . One day when you are seventeen I'll come home—home from my office downtown somewhere—

TRAVIS: You don't work in no office, Daddy.

WALTER: No—but after tonight. After what your daddy gonna do tonight, there's going to be offices—a whole lot of offices. . . .

TRAVIS: What you gonna do tonight, Daddy?

WALTER: You wouldn't understand yet, son, but your daddy's gonna make a transaction . . . a business transaction that's going to change our lives. . . . That's how come one day when you 'bout seventeen years old I'll come come home and I'll be pretty tired, you known what I mean, after a day of conferences and secretaries getting things wrong the way they do . . . 'cause an executive's life is hell, man—*(The more he talks the farther away he gets.)* And I'll pull the car up on the driveway . . . just a plain black Chrysler, I think, with white walls—no—black tires. More elegant. Rich people don't have to be flashy . . . though I'll have to get something a little sportier for Ruth—maybe a Cadillac convertible to do her shopping in. . . . And I'll come up the steps to the house and the gardener will be clipping away at the hedges and he'll say, "Good evening, Mr. Younger." And I'll say, "Hello, Jefferson, how are you this evening?" And I'll go inside and Ruth will come downstairs and meet me at the door and we'll kiss each other and she'll take my arm and we'll go up to your room to see you sitting on the floor with the catalogues of all the great schools in America around you. . . . All the great schools in the world! And—and I'll say, all right, son—it's your seventeenth birthday, what is it you've decided? . . . Just tell me where you want to go to school and you'll *go*. Just tell me, what it is you want to be—*and* you'll *be* it. . . . Whatever you want to be—Yessir! *(He holds his arms open for* TRAVIS.*)* You just name it, son . . .

*(*TRAVIS *leaps into them.)*

and I hand you the world! (WALTER's *voice has risen in pitch and hysterical promise and on the last line he lifts* TRAVIS *high.)*

BLACKOUT

ACT 2

SCENE 3

TIME:

Saturday, moving day, one week later.

Before the Curtain rises, RUTH'S *VOICE, a strident, dramatic church alto, cuts through the silence.*

It is, in the darkness, a triumphant surge, a penetrating statement of expectation: "Oh, Lord, I don't feel no ways tired! Children, oh, glory hallelujah!"

As the Curtain rises we see that RUTH *is alone in the living room, finishing up the family's packing. It is moving day. She is nailing crates and tying cartons.* BENEATHA *enters, carrying a guitar case, and watches her exuberant sister-in-law.*

RUTH: Hey!

BENEATHA: *(Putting away the case.)* Hi.

RUTH: *(Pointing at a package.)* Honey—look in that package there and see what I found on sale this morning at the South Center. (RUTH *gets up and moves to the package and draws out some curtains.)* Lookahere—hand-turned hems!

BENEATHA: How do you know the window size out there?

RUTH: *(Who hadn't thought of that.)* Oh—well, they bound to fit something in the whole house. Anyhow, they was too good a bargain to pass up.*(*RUTH *slaps her head, suddenly remembering something.)* Oh, Bennie—I meant to put a special note on that carton over there. That's your mama's good china and she wants 'em to be very careful with it.

BENEATHA: I'll do it. *(*BENEATHA *finds a piece of paper and starts to draw large letter on it.)*

RUTH: You know what I'm going to do soon as I get in that new house?

BENEATHA: What?

RUTH: Honey—I'm going to run me a tub of water up to here . . . *(With her fingers practically up to her nostrils.)* and I'm going to get in it—and I am going to sit . . . and sit . . . and sit in that hot water and the first person who knocks to tell *me* to hurry up and come out—

BENEATHA: Gets shot at sunrise.

RUTH: *(Laughing happily.)* You said it, sister! *(Noticing how large* BENEATHA *is absent-mindedly making the note.)* Honey, they ain't going to read that from no airplane.

BENEATHA: *(Laughing herself.)* I guess I always think things have more emphasis if they are big, somehow.

RUTH: *(Looking up at her and smiling.)* You and your brother seem to have that as a philosophy of life. Lord, that man—done changed so 'round here. You know—you know what we did last night? Me and Walter Lee?

BENEATHA: What?

RUTH: *(Smiling to herself.)* We went to the movies. *(Looking at* BENEATHA *to see if she understands.)* We went to the movies. You know the last time me and Walter went to the movies together?

BENEATHA: No.

RUTH: Me neither. That's how long it been. *(Smiling again.)* But we went last night. The picture wasn't much good, but that didn't seem to matter. We went—and we held hands.

BENEATHA: Oh, Lord!

RUTH: We held hands—and you know what?

BENEATHA: What?

RUTH: When we come out of the show it was late and dark and all the stores and things was closed up . . . and it was kind of chilly and there wasn't many people on the streets . . . and we was still holding hands, me and Walter.

BENEATHA: You're killing me.

*(*WALTER *enters with a large package. His happiness is deep in him; he cannot keep still with his new-found exuberance. He is singing and wiggling and snapping his fingers. He puts his package in a corner and puts a phonograph record, which he has brought in with him, on the record player. As the* MUSIC *comes he dances over to* RUTH *and tries to get her to dance with him. She gives in at last to his raunchiness and in a fit of giggling, allows herself to be drawn into his mood and together they deliberately burlesque an old social dance of their youth.)*

BENEATHA: *(Regarding them a long time as they dance, then drawing in her breath for a deeply exaggerated comment which she does not particularly mean.)* Talk about—olddddddddddd-fashioneddddddddd—Negroes!

WALTER: *(Stopping momentarily.)* What kind of Negroes? *(He says this in fun. He is not angry with her today, nor with anyone. He starts to dance with his wife again.)*

BENEATHA: Old-fashioned.

WALTER: (*As he dances with* RUTH.) You know, when these *New Negroes* have their convention—(*Pointing at his sister.*)—that is going to be the chairman of the Committee on Unending Agitation. (*He goes on dancing, then stops.*) Race, race, race! . . . Girl, I do believe you are the first person in the history of the entire human race to successfully brainwash yourself. (BENEATHA *breaks up and he goes on dancing. He stops again, enjoying his tease.*) Damn, even the N double A C P takes a holiday sometimes!

(BENEATHA *and* RUTH *laugh.*)

(*He dances with* RUTH *some more and starts to laugh and stops and pantomimes someone over an operating table.*) I can just see that chick someday looking down at some poor cat on an operating table before she starts to slice him, saying . . . (*Pulling his sleeves back maliciously.*) "By the way, what are your views on civil rights down there? . . ." (*He laughs at her again and starts to dance happily.*)

(*The* BELL *sounds.*)

BENEATHA: Sticks and stones may break my bones . . . but words will never hurt me! (BENEATHA *goes to the door and opens it as* WALTER *and* RUTH *go on with the clowning.* BENEATHA *is somewhat surprised to see a quiet-looking middle-aged* WHITE MAN *in a business suit holding his hat and a briefcase in his hand and consulting a small piece of paper.*)

MAN: Uh—how do you do, miss. I am looking for a Mrs.—(*He looks at the slip of paper.*) Mrs. Lena—Younger?

BENEATHA: (*Smoothing her hair with slight embarrassment.*) Oh—yes, that's my mother. Excuse me. (*She closes the door and turns to quiet the other two.*) Ruth! Brother! Somebody's here. (*Then she opens the door.*)

(*The* MAN *casts a curious glance at all of them.*)

Uh—come in please.

Man. (*Coming in.*) Thank you.

BENEATHA: My mother isn't here just now. Is it business?

MAN: Yes . . . well, of a sort.

WALTER: (*Freely, the Man of the House.*) Have a seat. I'm Mrs. Younger's son. I look after most of her business matters.

(RUTH *and* BENEATHA *exchange amused glances.*)

MAN: (*Regarding* WALTER, *and sitting.*) Well—my name is Karl Lindner . . .

WALTER: (*Stretching out his hand.*) Walter Younger. This is my wife—(RUTH *nods politely.*)—and my sister.

LINDNER: How do you do.

WALTER: (*Amiably, as he sits himself easily on a chair, leaning with interest forward on his knees and looking expectantly into the newcomer's face.*) What can we do for you, Mr. Lindner!

LINDNER: (*Some minor shuffling of the hat and briefcase on his knees.*) Well—I am a representative of the Clybourne Park Improvement Association—

WALTER: (*Pointing.*) Why don't you sit your things on the floor?

LINDNER: Oh—yes. Thank you. (*He slides the briefcase and hat under the chair.*) And as I was saying—I am from the Clybourne Park Improvement Association and we have had it brought to our attention at the last meeting that you people—or at least your mother—has bought a piece of residential property at—(*He digs for the slip of paper again.*)—four o six Clybourne Street. . . .

WALTER: That's right. Care for something to drink? Ruth, get Mr. Lindner a beer.

LINDNER: (*Upset for some reason.*) Oh—no, really. I mean thank you very much, but no thank you.

RUTH: (*Innocently.*) Some coffee?

LINDNER: Thank you, nothing at all.

(BENEATHA *is watching the man carefully.*)

LINDNER: Well, I don't know how much you folks know about our organization. (*He is a gentle man; thoughtful and somewhat labored in his manner.*) It is one of these community organizations set up to look after—oh, you know, things like block upkeep and special projects and we also have what we call our New Neighbors Orientation Committee. . . .

BENEATHA: (*Drily.*) Yes—and what do they do?

LINDNER: (*Turning a little to her and then returning the main force to* WALTER.) Well—it's what you might call a sort of welcoming committee, I guess. I mean they, we, I'm the chairman of the committee—go around and see the new people who move into the neighborhood and sort of give them the lowdown on the way we do things out in Clybourne Park.

BENEATHA: (*With appreciation of the two meanings, which escape* RUTH *and* WALTER) Un-huh.

LINDNER: And we also have the category of what the association calls—(*He looks elsewhere.*)—uh—special community problems. . . .

BENEATHA: Yes—and what are some of those?

WALTER: Girl, let the man talk.

LINDNER: (*With understated relief.*) Thank you. I would sort of like to explain this thing in my own way. I mean I want to explain to you in a certain way.

WALTER: Go ahead.

LINDNER: Yes. Well. I'm going to try to get right to the point. I'm sure we'll all appreciate that in the long run.

BENEATHA: Yes.

WALTER: Be still now!

LINDNER: Well—

RUTH: (*Still innocently.*) Would you like another chair—you don't look comfortable.

LINDNER: (*More frustrated than annoyed.*) No, thank you very much. Please. Well—to get right to the point I—(*A great breath, and he is off at last.)*—I am sure you people must be aware of some of the incidents which have happened in various parts of the city when colored people have moved into certain areas—

(BENEATHA *exhales heavily and starts tossing a piece of fruit up and down in the air.)*

—well—because we have what I think is going to be a unique type of organization in American community life—not only do we deplore that kind of thing—but we are trying to do something about it.

(BENEATHA *stops tossing and turns with a new and quizzical interest to the man.)*

We feel—*(gaining confidence in his mission because of the interest in the faces of the people he is talking to.)*—we feel that most of the trouble in this world, when you come right down to it—*(He hits his knee for emphasis.)*—most of the trouble exists because people just don't sit down and talk to each other.

RUTH: *(Nodding as she might in church, pleased with the remark.)* You can say that again, mister.

LINDNER: *(More encouraged by such affirmation.)* That we don't try hard enough in this world to understand the other fellow's problem. The other guy's point of view.

RUTH: Now that's right.

(BENEATHA *and* WALTER *merely watch and listen with genuine interest.)*

LINDNER: Yes—that's the way we feel out in Clybourne Park. And that's why I was elected to come here this afternoon and talk to you people. Friendly like, you know, the way people should talk to each other and see if we couldn't find some way to work this thing out. As I say, the whole business is a matter of *caring* about the other fellow. Anybody can see that you are a nice family of folks, hard working and honest I'm sure.

(BENEATHA *frowns slightly, quizzically, her head tilted regarding him.)*

Today everybody knows what it means to be on the outside of *something.* And of course, there is always somebody who is out to take the advantage of people who don't always understand.

WALTER: What do you mean?

LINDNER: Well—you see our community is made up of people who've worked hard as the dickens for years to build up that little community. They're not rich and fancy people; just hard-working, honest people who don't really have much but those little homes and a dream of the kind of community they want to raise their children in. Now, I don't say we are perfect and there is a lot wrong in some of the things they want. But you've got to admit that a man, right or wrong, has the right to want to have the neighborhood he lives in a certain kind of way. And at the moment the overwhelming majority of our people out there feel that people get along better, take more of a common interest in the life of the community, when they share a common background. I want you to believe me when I tell you that race prejudice simply doesn't enter into it. It is a matter of the people of Clybourne Park believing, rightly or wrongly, as I say, that for the happiness of all concerned that our Negro families are happier when they live in their *own* communities.

BENEATHA: *(With a grand and bitter gesture.)* This, friends, is the Welcoming Committee!

WALTER: *(Dumbfounded, looking at* LINDNER.) Is this what you came marching all the way over here to tell us?

LINDNER: Well, now we've been having a fine conversation. I hope you'll hear me all the way through.

WALTER: *(Tightly.)* Go ahead, man.

LINDNER: You see—in the face of all things I have said, we are prepared to make your family a very generous offer. . . .

BENEATHA: Thirty pieces and not a coin less!

WALTER: Yeah?

LINDNER: *(Putting on his glasses and drawing a form out of the briefcase.)* Our association is prepared, through the collective effort of our people, to buy the house from you at a financial gain to your family.

RUTH: Lord have mercy, ain't this the living gall!

WALTER: All right, you through?

LINDNER: Well, I want to give you the exact terms of the financial arrangement—

WALTER: We don't want to hear no exact terms of no arrangements. I want to know if you got any more to tell us 'bout getting together?

LINDNER: *(Taking off his glasses.)* Well—I don't suppose that you feel . . .

WALTER: Never mind how I feel—you got any more to say 'bout how people ought to sit down and talk to each other? . . . Get out of my house, man. *(He turns his back and walks to the door.)*

LINDNER: *(Looking around at the hostile faces and reaching and assembling his hat and briefcase.)* Well—I don't understand why you people are reacting this way. What do you think you are going to gain by moving into a neighborhood where you just aren't wanted and where some elements—well—people can get awful worked up when they feel that their whole way of life and everything they've ever worked for is threatened.

WALTER: Get out.

LINDNER: *(At the door, holding a small card.)* Well—I'm sorry it went like this.

WALTER: Get out.

LINDNER: (*Almost sadly regarding* WALTER.) You just can't force people to change their hearts, son. (*He turns and puts his card on the table and exits.*)

(WALTER *pushes the door to with stinging hatred, and stands looking at it.* RUTH *just sits and* BENEATHA *just stands. They say nothing.* MAMA *and* TRAVIS *enter.*)

MAMA: Well—this all the packing got done since I left out of here this morning. I testify before God that my children got all the energy of the dead. What time the moving men due?

BENEATHA: Four o'clock. You had a caller, Mama. (*She is smiling, teasingly.*)

MAMA: Sure enough—who?

BENEATHA: (*Her arms folded saucily.*) The Welcoming Committee.

(WALTER *and* RUTH *giggle.*)

MAMA: (*Innocently.*) Who?

BENEATHA: The Welcoming Committee. They said they're sure going to be glad to see you when you get there.

WALTER: (*Devilishly.*) Yeah, they said they can't hardly wait to see your face.

(*Laughter.*)

MAMA: (*Sensing their facetiousness.*) What's the matter with you all?

WALTER: Ain't nothing the matter with us. We just telling you 'bout the gentleman who came to see you this afternoon. From the Clybourne Park Improvement Association.

MAMA: What he want?

RUTH: (*In the same mood as* BENEATHA *and* WALTER.) To welcome you, honey.

WALTER: He said they can't hardly wait. He said the one thing they don't have, that they just *dying* to have out there is a fine family of colored people! (*To* RUTH *and* BENEATHA.) Ain't that right!

RUTH *and* BENEATHA: (*Mockingly.*) Yeah! He left his card in case—

(*They indicate the card, and* MAMA *picks it up and throws it on the floor—understanding and looking off as she draws her chair up to the table on which she has put her plant and some sticks and some cord.*)

MAMA: Father, give us strength. (*Knowingly—and without fun.*) Did he threaten us?

BENEATHA: Oh—Mama—they don't do it like that anymore. He talked Brotherhood. He said everybody ought to learn how to sit down and hate each other with good Christian fellowship.

(*She and* WALTER *shake hands to ridicule the remark.*)

MAMA: (*Sadly.*) Lord, protect us. . . .

RUTH: You should hear the money those folks raised to buy the house from us. All we paid and then some.

BENEATHA: What they think we going to do—eat 'em?

RUTH: No, honey, marry 'em.

MAMA: (*Shaking her head.*) Lord, Lord, Lord . . .

RUTH: Well—that's the way the crackers crumble. Joke.

BENEATHA: (*Laughingly noticing what her mother is doing.*) Mama, what are you doing?

MAMA: Fixing my plant so it won't get hurt none on the way. . . .

BENEATHA: Mama, are you going to take *that* to the new house?

MAMA: Un-huh—

BENEATHA: That raggedy-looking old things?

MAMA: (*Stopping and looking to her.*) It expresses *me.*

RUTH: (*With delight, to* BENEATHA.) So there, Miss Thing!

(WALTER *comes to* MAMA *suddenly and bends down behind her and squeezes her in his arms with all his strength. She is overwhelmed by the suddenness of it and, though delighted, her manner is like that of* RUTH *with* TRAVIS.)

MAMA: Look out now, boy! You make me mess up my thing here!

WALTER: (*His face lit, he slips down his knees besides her, his arms still about her.*) Mama . . . you know what it means to climb up in the chariot?

MAMA: (*Gruffly, very happy.*) Get on away from me now. . . .

RUTH: (*Near the gift-wrapped package, trying to catch* WALTER's *eye.*) Psst—

WALTER: What the old song say, Mama . . .

RUTH: Walter—now? (*She is pointing at the package.*)

WALTER: (*Speaking the lines, sweetly, playfully, in his mother's face.*)

I got wings . . . you got wings . . .
All God's Children got wings . . .

MAMA: Boy—get out of my face and do some work. . . .

WALTER:

When I get to heaven gonna put on my wings,
Gonna fly all over God's heaven . . .

BENEATHA: (*Teasingly, from across the room.*) Everybody talking 'bout heaven ain't going there!

WALTER: (*To* RUTH, *who is carrying the box across to them.*) I don't know, you think we ought to give her that. . . . Seems to me she ain't been very appreciative around here.

MAMA: (*Eyeing the box, which is obviously a gift.*) What is that?

WALTER: (*Taking it from* RUTH *and planting it on the table in front of* MAMA.) Well—what you all think? Should we give it to her?

RUTH: Oh—she was pretty good today.

MAMA: I'll good you—(*She turns her eyes to the box again.*)

BENEATHA: Open it, Mama.

(She stands up, looks at it, turns and looks at all of them, and then presses her hands together and does not open the package.)

WALTER: *(Sweetly.)* Open it, Mama, It's for you.

(MAMA looks in his eyes. It is the first present in her life without its being Christmas. Slowly she opens her package and lifts out, one by one, a brand-new sparkling set of gardening tools.)

(WALTER continues, prodding.) Ruth made up the note—read it. . . .

MAMA: *(Picking up the card and adjusting her glasses.)* "To our own Mrs. Miniver—Love from Brother, Ruth and Beneatha." Ain't that lovely. . . .

TRAVIS: *(Tugging at his father's sleeve.)* Daddy, can I give her mine now?

WALTER: All right, son.

(TRAVIS flies to get his gift.)

Travis didn't want to go in with the rest of us, Mama. He got his own. *(Somewhat amused.)* We don't know what it is. . . .

TRAVIS: *(Racing back in the room with a large hatbox and putting it in front of his grandmother.)* Here!

MAMA: Lord have mercy, baby. You done gone and bought your grandmother a hat?

TRAVIS: *(Very proud.)* Open it!

(She does and lifts out an elaborate, but very elaborate, wide gardening hat, and all the adults break up at the sight of it.)

RUTH: Travis, honey, what is that?

TRAVIS: *(Who thinks it is beautiful and appropriate.)* It's a gardening hat! Like the ladies always have on in the magazines when they work in their gardens.

BENEATHA: *(Giggling fiercely.)* Travis—we were trying to make Mama Mrs. Miniver—not Scarlett O'Hara!

MAMA: *(Indignantly.)* What's the matter with you all! This here is a beautiful hat! *(Absurdly.)* I always wanted me one just like it! *(She pops it on her head to prove it to her grandson, and the hat is ludicrous and considerably oversized.)*

RUTH: Hot dog! Go, Mama!

WALTER: *(Doubled over with laughter.)* I'm sorry, Mama—but you look like you ready to go out and chop you some cotton sure enough!

(They all laugh except MAMA, out of deference to TRAVIS' feelings.)

MAMA: *(Gathering the boy up to her.)* Bless your heart—this is the prettiest hat I ever owned . . .

(WALTER, RUTH and BENEATHA chime in—noisily, festively and insincerely congratulating TRAVIS on his gift.)

What are we all standing around here for? We ain't finished packin' yet. Bennie, you ain't packed one book.

(The BELL rings.)

BENEATHA: That couldn't be the movers . . . it's not hardly two good yet—

(BENEATHA goes into her room.)

(MAMA starts for door.)

WALTER: *(Turning, stiffening.)* Wait—wait—I'll get it. *(He stands and looks at the door.)*

MAMA: You expecting company, son?

WALTER: *(Just looking at the door.)* Yeah—yeah . . .

(MAMA looks at RUTH, and they exchange innocent and unfrightened glances.)

MAMA: *(Not understanding.)* Well, let them in, son.

BENEATHA: *(From her room.)* We need some more string.

MAMA: Travis—you run to the hardware and get me some string cord.

(MAMA goes out and WALTER turns and looks at RUTH. TRAVIS goes to a dish for money.)

RUTH: Why don't you answer the door, man?

WALTER: *(Suddenly bounding across the floor to her.)* 'Cause sometimes it hard to let the future begin! *(Stooping down in her face.)*

I got wings! you got wings!
All God's children got wings!

(He crosses to the door and throws it open. Standing there is a very slight little MAN in a not too prosperous business suit and with haunted frightened eyes and a hat pulled down tightly, brim up, around his forehead. TRAVIS passes between the men and exits.)

(WALTER leans deep in the man's face, still in his jubilance.)

When I get to heaven gonna put on my wings,
Gonna fly all over God's heaven . . .

(The little MAN stares at him.)

Heaven—

(Suddenly he stops and looks past the little man into the empty hallway.) Where's Willy, Man?

BOBO: He ain't with me.

WALTER: *(Not disturbed.)* Oh—come on in. You know my wife.

BOBO: *(Dumbly, taking off his hat.)* Yes—h'you, Miss Ruth.

RUTH: *(Quietly, a mood apart from her husband already, seeing BOBO.)* Hello, Bobo.

WALTER: You right on time today . . . Right on time. That's the way! *(He slaps BOBO on his back.)* Sit down . . . lemme hear.

(RUTH stands stiffly and quietly in back of them, as though somehow she senses death, her eyes fixed on her husband.)

BOBO: *(His frightened eyes on the floor, his hat in his hands.)* Could I please get a drink of water, before I tell you about it, Walter Lee?

(WALTER *does not take his eyes off the man.* RUTH *goes blindly to the tap and gets a glass of water and brings it to* BOBO.)

WALTER: There ain't nothing wrong, is there?

BOBO: Lemme tell you—

WALTER: Man—didn't nothing go wrong?

BOBO: Lemme tell you—Walter Lee. (*Looking at* RUTH *and talking to her more than to* WALTER.) You know how it was. I got to tell you how it was. I mean first I got to tell you how it was all the way . . . I mean about the money put in, Walter Lee. . . .

WALTER: (*With taut agitation now.*) What about the money you put in?

BOBO: Well—it wasn't much as we told you—me and Willy—(*He stops.*)—I'm sorry, Walter. I got a bad feeling about it. I got a real bad feeling about it. . . .

WALTER: Man, what you telling me about all this for? . . . Tell me what happened in Springfield. . . .

BOBO: Springfield.

RUTH: (*Like a dead woman.*) What was supposed to happen in Springfield?

BOBO: (*To her.*) This deal that me and Walter went into with Willy—me and Willy was going to go down to Springfield and spread some money 'round so's we wouldn't have to wait so long for the liquor license . . . that's what we were going to do. Everybody said that was the way you had to do, you understand, Miss Ruth?

WALTER: Man—what happened down there?

BOBO: (*A pitiful man, near tears.*) I'm trying to tell you, Walter.

WALTER: (*Screaming at him suddenly.*) THEN TELL ME, GODDAMMIT . . . WHAT'S THE MATTER WITH YOU?

BOBO: Man . . . I didn't go to no Springfield, yesterday.

WALTER: (*Halted, life hanging in the moment.*) Why not?

BOBO: (*The long way, the hard way to tell.*) 'Cause I didn't have no reasons to. . . .

WALTER: Man, what are you talking about!

BOBO: I'm talking about the fact that when I got to the train station yesterday morning—eight o'clock like we planned . . . man—*Willy didn't never show up.*

WALTER: Why . . . where was he . . . where is he?

BOBO: That's what I'm trying to tell you . . . I don't know . . . I waited six hours . . . I called his house . . . and I waited . . . six hours . . . I waited in that train station six hours. . . . (*Breaking into tears.*) That was all the extra money I had in the world. . . . (*Looking up at* WALTER *with the tears running down his face.*) Man, *Willy is gone.*

WALTER: Gone, what you mean Willy is gone? Gone where? You mean he went by himself. You mean he went off to Springfield by himself—to take care of—getting the license—(*Turns and looks anxiously at* RUTH.) You mean maybe he didn't want too many people in on the business

down there? (*Looks to* RUTH *again, as before.*) You know Willy got his own ways. (*Looks back to* BOBO.) Maybe you was late yesterday and he just went on down there without you. Maybe—maybe—he's been callin' you at home tryin' to tell you what happened or something. Maybe—maybe—he just got sick. He's somewhere—he's got to be somewhere. We just got to find him—me and you got to find him. (*Grabs* BOBO *senselessly by the collar and starts to shake him.*) We got to!

BOBO: (*In sudden angry, frightened agony.*) What's the matter with you, Walter! WHEN A CAT TAKE OFF WITH YOUR MONEY HE DON'T LEAVE YOU NO MAPS!

WALTER: (*Turning madly, as though he is looking for* WILLY *in the very room.*) Willy! . . . Willy . . . don't do it . . . please don't do it . . . man, not with that money . . . man, please, not with that money . . . oh, God . . . don't let it be true. . . . (*He is wandering around, crying out for* WILLY *and looking for him or perhaps for help from God.*) Man . . . I trusted you . . . man, I put my life in your hands. . . . (*He starts to crumple down on the floor as* RUTH *just covers her face in horror.*)

(MAMA *opens the door and comes into the room, with* BENEATHA *behind her.*)

Man . . . (*He starts to pound the floor with his fists, sobbing wildly.*) THAT MONEY IS MADE OUT OF MY FATHER'S FLESH. . . .

BOBO: (*Standing over him helplessly.*) I'm sorry, Walter . . .

(*Only* WALTER's *sobs reply.*)

(BOBO *puts on his hat.*) I had my life staked on this deal, too. . . . (*He exits.*)

MAMA: (*To* WALTER.) Son—(*She goes to him, bends down to him, talks to his bent head.*)—son . . . is it—gone? Son, I gave you sixty-five hundred dollars. Is it gone? All of it? Beneatha's money too!

WALTER: (*Lifting his head slowly.*) Mama . . . I never . . . went to the bank at all. . . .

MAMA: (*Not wanting to believe him.*) You mean . . . your sister's school money . . . you used that too . . . Walter? . . .

WALTER: Yessss! All of it . . . It's all gone . . .

(*There is total silence.* RUTH *stands with her face covered with her hands;* BENEATHA *leans forlornly against a wall, fingering a piece of red ribbon from the mother's gift.* MAMA *stops and looks at her son without recognition and then, quite without thinking about it, starts to beat him senselessly in the face.* BENEATHA *goes to them and stops it.*)

BENEATHA: Mama!

(MAMA *stops and looks at both of her children and rises slowly and wanders vaguely, aimlessly away from them.*)

MAMA: I seen . . . him . . . night after night . . . come in . . . and look at that rug . . . and then look at me . . . the red showing in his eyes . . . the veins moving in his head . . . I seen him grow thin and old before he was forty . . . working and working and working like somebody's old horse . . . killing himself . . . and you—you give it all away in a day. . . .

BENEATHA: Mama—

MAMA: Oh, God . . . *(She looks up to Him.)* Look down here—and show me the stength.

BENEATHA: Mama—

MAMA: *(Folding over.)* Strength . . .

BENEATHA: *(Plaintively.)* Mama . . .

MAMA: Strength!

CURTAIN

ACT 3

An hour later.

At Curtain there is sullen light of gloom in the living room, gray light not unlike that which began the first scene of Act 1. At Left we can see WALTER *within his room, alone with himself. He is stretched out on the bed, his shirt out and open, his arms under his head. He does not smoke, he does not cry out, he merely lies there, looking up at the ceiling, much as if he were alone in the world.*

In the living room BENEATHA *sits at the table, still surrounded by the now almost ominous packing crates. She sits looking off. We feel that this is a mood struck perhaps an hour before, and it lingers now, full of the empty sound of profound disappointment. We see on a line from her brother's bedroom the sameness of their attitudes. Presently the* BELL *rings and* BENEATHA *rises without ambition or interest in answering. It is* ASAGAI, *smiling broadly, striding into the room with energy and happy expectation and conversation.*

ASAGAI: I came over . . . I had some free time. I thought I might help with the packing. Ah, I like the look of packing crates! A household in preparation for a journey! It depresses some people . . . but for me . . . it is another feeling. Something full of the flow of life, do you understand? Movement, progress . . . it makes me think of Africa.

BENEATHA: Africa!

ASAGAI: What kind of mood is this? Have I told you how deeply you move me?

BENEATHA: He gave away the money, Asagai . . .

ASAGAI: Who gave away what money?

BENEATHA: The insurance money. My brother gave it away.

ASAGAI: Gave it away?

BENEATHA: He made an investment! With a man even Travis wouldn't have trusted.

ASAGAI: And it's gone?

BENEATHA: Gone!

ASAGAI: I'm very sorry . . . And you, now?

BENEATHA: Me? . . . Me? . . . Me I'm nothing . . . me. When I was very small . . . we used to take our sleds out in the wintertime and the only hills we had were the ice-covered stone steps of some houses down the street. And we used to fill them in with snow and make them smooth and slide down them all day . . . and it was very dangerous you know . . . far too steep . . . and sure enough one day a kid named Rufus came down too fast and hit the sidewalk . . . and we saw his face just split open right there in front of us . . . and I remember standing there looking at his bloody open face thinking that was the end of Rufus. But the ambulance came and they took him to the hospital and they fixed the broken bones and they sewed it all up . . . and the next time I saw Rufus he just had a little line down the middle of his face . . . I never got over that. . . .

(WALTER sits up, listening on the bed. Throughout this scene it is important that we feel his reaction at all times, that he visibly respond to the words of his sister and ASAGAI.*)*

ASAGAI: What?

BENEATHA: That that was what one person could do for another, fix him up—sew up the problem, make him all right again. That was the most marvelous thing in the world . . . I wanted to do that. I always thought it was the one concrete thing in the world that a human being could do. Fix up the sick, you know—and make them whole again. This was truly being God. . . .

ASAGAI: You wanted to be God?

BENEATHA: No—I wanted to cure. It used to be so important to me. I wanted to cure. It used to matter. I used to care. I mean about people and how their bodies hurt. . . .

ASAGAI: And you've stopped caring?

BENEATHA: Yes—I think so.

ASAGAI: Why?

(WALTER rises, goes to the door of his room and is about to open it, then stops and stands listening, leaning on the door jamb.)

BENEATHA: Because it doesn't seem deep enough, close enough to what ails mankind—I means this thing of sewing up bodies or administering drugs. Don't you understand? It was a child's reaction to the world. I thought that doctors had the secret to all the hurts. . . . That's the way a child sees things— or an idealist.

ASAGAI: Children see things very well sometimes— and idealists ever better.

BENEATHA: I know that's what you think. Because you are still where I left off—you still care. This is what you see for the world, for Africa. You with the dreams of the future will patch up all Africa—you are going to cure the Great Sore of colonialism with Independence—

ASAGAI: Yes!

BENEATHA: Yes—and you think that one word is the penicillin of the human spirit. "Independence!" But then what?

ASAGAI: That will be the problem for another time. First we must get there.

BENEATHA: And where does it end?

ASAGAI: End? Who even spoke of an end? To life? To living?

BENEATHA: An end to misery!

ASAGAI: (*Smiling.*) You sound like a French intellectual.

BENEATHA: No! I sound like a human being who just had her future taken right out of her hands! While I was sleeping in my bed in there, things were happening in this world that directly concerned me—and nobody asked me, consulted me—they just went out and did things—and changed my life. Don't you see there isn't any real progress, Asagai, there is only one large circle that we march in, around and around, each of us with our own little picture—in front of us—our own little mirage that we think is the future.

ASAGAI: That is the mistake.

BENEATHA: What?

ASAGAI: What you just said—about the circle. It isn't a circle—it is simply a long line—as in geometry, you know, one that reaches into infinity. And because we cannot see the end—we also cannot see how it changes. And it is very odd but those who see the changes are called "idealists"—and those who cannot, or refuse to think, they are the "realists." It is very strange, and amusing too, I think.

BENEATHA: You—you are almost religious.

ASAGAI: Yes . . . I think I have the religion of doing what is necessary in the world—and of worshipping man—because he is so marvelous, you see.

BENEATHA: Man is foul! And the human race deserves its misery!

ASAGAI: You see; *you* have become the religious one in the old sense. Already, and after such a small defeat, you are worshipping despair.

BENEATHA: From now on, I worship the truth—and the truth is that people are puny, small and selfish. . . .

ASAGAI: Truth? Why is it that you despairing ones always think that only you have the truth? I never thought to see *you* like that. You! Your brother made a stupid, childish mistake—and you are grateful to him. So that now you can give up the ailing human race on account of it. You talk about what good is struggle; what good is anything? Where are we all going? And why are we bothering?

BENEATHA: AND YOU CANNOT ANSWER IT! All your talk and dreams about Africa and Independence. Independence and then what? What about all the crooks and petty thieves and just plain idiots who will come into power to steal and plunder the same as before—only now they will be black and do it in the name of the new Independence—You cannot answer that.

ASAGAI: (*Shouting over her.*) I LIVE THE ANSWER! (*Pause.*) In my village at home it is the exceptional man who can even read a newspaper . . . or who ever *sees* a book at all. I will go home and much of what I will have to say will seem strange to the people of my village. . . . But I will teach and work and things will happen, slowly and swiftly. At times it will seem that nothing changes at all . . . and then again . . . the sudden dramatic events which make history leap into the future. And then quiet again. Retrogression even. Guns, murder, revolution. And I even will have moments when I wonder if the quiet was not better than all that death and hatred. But I will look about my village at the illiteracy and disease and ignorance and I will not wonder long. And perhaps . . . perhaps I will be a great man . . . I mean perhaps I will hold on to the substance of truth and find my way always with the right course . . . and perhaps for it I will be butchered in my bed some night by the servants of empire. . . .

BENEATHA: THE MARTYR!

ASAGAI: Or perhaps I shall live to be a very old man, respected and esteemed in my new nation . . . and perhaps I shall hold office and this is what I'm trying to tell you, Alaiyo; perhaps the things I believe now for my country will be wrong and outmoded, and I will not understand and do terrible things to have things my way or merely to keep my power. Don't you see that there will be young men and women, not British soldiers then, but my own black countrymen . . . to step out of the shadows some evening and slit my then useless throat? Don't you see they have always been there . . . that they always will be. And that such a thing as my own death will be an advance? They who might kill me even . . . actually replenish me!

BENEATHA: Oh, Asagai, I know all that.

ASAGAI: Good! Then stop moaning and groaning and tell me what you plan to do.

BENEATHA: Do?

ASAGAI: I have a bit of a suggestion.

BENEATHA: What?

ASAGAI: (*Rather quietly for him.*) That when it is all over—that you come home with me—

BENEATHA: (*Slapping herself on the forehead with exasperation born of misunderstanding.*) Oh—Asagai—at this moment you decide to be romantic!

ASAGAI: (*Quickly understanding the misunderstanding.*) My dear, young creature of the New World—I do not mean across the city—I mean across ocean; home—to Africa.

BENEATHA: (*Slowly understanding and turning to him with murmured amazement.*) To—to Nigeria?

ASAGAI: Yes! . . . (*Smiling and lifting his arms playfully.*) Three hundred years later the African Prince rose up out of the seas and swept the maiden back across the middle passage over which her ancestors had come—

BENEATHA: *(Unable to play.)* Nigeria?

ASAGAI: Nigeria. Home. *(Coming to her with genuine romantic flippancy.)* I will show you our mountains and our stars; and give you cool drinks from gourds and teach you the old songs and the ways of our people—and, in time, we will pretend that—*(Very softly.)*—you have only been away for a day—

(She turns her back to him, thinking. He swings her around and takes her full in his arms in a long embrace which proceeds to passion.)

BENEATHA: *(Pulling away.)* You're getting me all mixed up—

ASAGAI: Why?

BENEATHA: Too many things—too many things have happened today. I must sit down and think. I don't know what I feel about anything right this minute. *(She promptly sits down and props her chin on her fist.)*

ASAGAI: *(Charmed.)* All right, I shall leave you. No—don't get up. *(Touching her, gently, sweetly.)* Just sit awhile and think . . . never be afraid to sit awhile and think. *(He goes to door and looks at her.)* How often I have looked at you and said, "Ah—so this is what the New World hath finally wrought . . ."*(He exits.)*

*(*BENEATHA *sits on alone. Presently* WALTER *enters from his room and start to rummage through things, feverishly looking for something. She looks up and turns in her seat.)*

BENEATHA: *(Hissingly.)* Yes—just look at what the New World hath wrought! . . . Just look! *(She gestures with bitter disgust.)* There he is! *Monsieur le petit bourgeois noir*—himself! There he is! Symbol of a Rising Class! Entrepreneur! Titan of the system!

*(*WALTER *ignores her completely and continues frantically and destructively looking for something and hurling things to floor and tearing things out of their place in his search.)*

*(*BENEATHA *ignores the eccentricity of his actions and goes on with the monologue of insult.)* Did you dream of yachts on Lake Michigan, Brother? Did you see yourself on that Great Day sitting down at the Conference Table, surrounded by all the mighty bald-headed men in America? All halted, waiting, breathless, waiting for your pronouncements on industry? Waiting for you—Chairman of the Board?

*(*WALTER *finds what he is looking for—a small piece of white paper—and pushes it in his pocket and puts on his coat and rushes out without ever having looked at her.)*

(She shouts after him.) I look at you and I see the final triumph of stupidity in the world!

(The door slams and she returns to just sitting again. RUTH *comes quickly out of* MAMA*'s room.)*

RUTH: Who was that?

BENEATHA: Your husband.

RUTH: Where did he go?

BENEATHA: Who knows—maybe he has an appointment at U.S. Steel.

RUTH: *(Anxiously, with frightened eyes.)* You didn't say nothing bad to him, did you?

BENEATHA: Bad? Say anything bad to him? No—I told him he was a sweet boy and full of dreams and everything is strictly peachy keen, as the ofay kids say!

*(*MAMA *enters from her bedroom. She is lost, vague, trying to catch hold, to make some sense of her former command of the world, but it still eludes her. A sense of waste overwhelms her gait; a measure of apology rides on her shoulders. She goes to her plant, which has remained on the table, looks at it, picks it up and takes it to the window sill and sits it outside, and she stands and looks at it a long moment. Then she closes the window, straightens her body with effort and turns around to her children.)*

MAMA: Well—ain't it a mess in here, though? *(A false cheerfulness, a beginning of something.)* I guess we all better stop moping around and get some work done. All this unpacking and everything we got to do.

*(*RUTH *raises her head slowly in response to the sense of the line; and* BENEATHA *in similar manner turns very slowly to look at her mother.)*

One of you all better call the moving people and tell 'em not to come.

RUTH: Tell 'em not to come?

MAMA: Of course, baby. Ain't no need in 'em coming all the way here and having to go back. They charges for that too. *(She sits down, fingers to her brow, thinking.)* Lord, ever since I was a little girl, I always remembers people saying, "Lena—Lena Eggleston, you aims too high all the time. You needs to slow down and see life a little more like it is. Just slow down some." That's what they always used to say down home—"Lord, that Lena Eggleston is a high-minded thing. She'll get her due one day!"

RUTH: No, Lena . . .

MAMA: Me and Big Walter just didn't never learn right.

RUTH: Lena, no! We gotta go. Bennie—tell her—*(She rises and crosses to* BENEATHA *with her arms outstretched.)*

*(*BENEATHA *doesn't respond.)*

—tell her we can still move . . . the notes ain't but a hundred and twenty-five a month. We got four grown people in this house—we can work. . . .

MAMA: *(To herself.)* Just aimed too high all the time—

RUTH: *(Turning and going to* MAMA *fast—the words pouring out with urgency and desperation.)* Lena—I'll work . . . I'll work twenty hours a day in all the kitchens in Chicago . . . I'll strap my baby on my back if I have to and scrub all the floors in America and wash all the sheets in America if I have to—but we got to move . . . We got to get of here. . . .

*(*MAMA *reaches out absently and pats* RUTH*'s hand.)*

MAMA: No—I sees things differently now. Been thinking 'bout some of the things we could do to fix this place up some. I seen a second-hand bureau over on Maxwell Street just the other day that could fit right there. (She points to where the new furniture might go.)

(RUTH wanders away from her.)

Would need some new handles on it and then a little varnish and then it look like something brand-new. And—we can put up them new curtains in the kitchen . . . why this place be looking fine. Cheer us all up so that we forget trouble ever came. . . . (To RUTH.) And you could get some nice screens to put up in your room round the baby's bassinet. . . . (She looks at both of them, pleadingly.) Sometimes you just got to know when to give up some things . . . and hold on to what you got.

(WALTER enters from the outside, looking spent and leaning against the door, his coat hanging from him.)

MAMA: Where you been, son?

WALTER: (Breathing hard.) Made a call.

MAMA: To who, Son?

WALTER: To The Man.

MAMA: What man, baby?

WALTER: The Man, Mama. Don't you know who The Man is?

RUTH: Walter Lee?

WALTER: The Man. Like the guys in the streets say—The Man. Captain Boss—Mistuh Charley . . . Old Captain Please Mr. Bossman . . .

BENEATHA: (Suddenly.) Lindner!

WALTER: That's right! That's good. I told him to come right over.

BENEATHA: (Fiercely, understanding.) For what? What do you want to see him for?

WALTER: (Looking at his sister.) We going to do business with him.

MAMA: What you talking 'bout, son?

WALTER: Talking 'bout life, Mama. You all always telling me to see life like it is. Well—I laid in there on my back today . . . and I figured it out. Life just like it is. Who gets and who don't get. (He sits down with his coat on and laughs.) Mama, you know it's all divided up. Life is. Sure enough. Between the takers and the "tooken." (He laughs.) I've figured it out finally. (He looks around at them.) Yeah. Some of us always getting "tooken." (He laughs.) People like Willy Harris, they don't never get "tooken." And you know why the rest of us do? 'Cause we all mixed up. Mixed up bad. We get to looking 'round for the right and the wrong; and we worry about it and cry about it and stay up nights trying to figure out 'bout the wrong and the right of things all the time . . . and all the time, man, them takers is out there operating, just taking and taking. Willy Harris? Shoot—Willy Harris

don't even count. He don't even count in the big scheme of things. But I'll say one thing for old Willy Harris . . . he's taught me something. He's taught me to keep my eye on what counts in this world. Yeah—(Shouting out a little.)—thanks, Willy!

RUTH: What did you call that man for, Walter Lee?

WALTER: Called him to tell him to come on over to the show. Gonna put on a show for the man. Just what he wants to see. You see, Mama, the man came here today and he told us that them people out there where you want us to move—well they so upset they willing to pay us not to move out there. (He laughs again.) And—and oh, Mama—you would of been proud of the way me and Ruth and Bennie acted. We told him to get out. . . . Lord have mercy! We told the man to get out. Oh, we was some proud folks this afternoon, yeah. (He lights a cigarette.) We were still full of that old-time stuff. . . .

RUTH: (Coming toward him slowly.) You talking 'bout taking them people's money to keep us from moving in that house?

WALTER: I ain't just talking 'bout it, baby—I'm telling you that's what's going to happen.

BENEATHA: Oh, God! Where is the bottom! Where is the real honest-to-God bottom so he can't go any farther!

WALTER: See—that's the old stuff. You and that boy that was here today. You all want everybody to carry a flag and a spear and sing some marching songs, huh? You wanna spend your life looking into things and trying to find the right and the wrong part, huh? Yeah. You know what's going to happen to that boy someday—he'll find himself sitting in a dungeon, locked in forever—and the takers will have the key! Forget it, baby! There ain't no causes—there ain't nothing but taking in this world, and he who takes most is smartest—and it don't make a damn bit of difference how.

MAMA: You making something inside me cry, son. Some awful pain inside me.

WALTER: Don't cry, Mama. Understand. That white man is going to walk in that door able to write checks for more money than we ever had. It's important to him and I'm going to help him . . . I'm going to put on the show, Mama.

MAMA: Son—I come from five generations of people who was slaves and sharecroppers—but ain't nobody in my family never let nobody pay 'em no money that was a way of telling us we wasn't fit to walk the earth. We ain't never been that poor. (Raising her eyes and looking at him.) We ain't never been that dead inside.

BENEATHA: Well—we are dead now. All the talk about dreams and sunlight that goes on in this house. All dead.

WALTER: What's the matter with you all! I didn't make this world! It was give to me this way! Hell, yes, I want me some yachts someday! Yes, I want to hang some real pearls 'round my wife's neck. Ain't she supposed to wear no pearls? Somebody tell me—tell me, who decides which women is suppose to wear pearls in this world. I tell you I am a *man*—and I think my wife should wear some pearls in this world!

(This last line hangs a good while and WALTER *begins to move about the room. The word "Man" has penetrated his consciousness, he mumbles it to himself repeatedly between strange agitated pauses as he moves about.)*

MAMA: Baby, how you going to feel on the inside?

WALTER: Fine! . . . Going to feel fine . . . a man . . .

MAMA: You won't have nothing left then, Walter Lee.

WALTER: *(Coming to her.)* I'm going to feel fine, Mama. I'm going to look that son-of-a-bitch in the eyes and say—*(He falters.)*—and say, "All right, Mr. Lindner—*(He falters even more.)*—that's your neighborhood out there. You got the right to keep it like you want. You got the right to have it like you want. Just write the check and—the house is yours." And, and I am going to say—*(His voice almost breaks.)*—and you—you people just put the money in my hand and you won't have to live next to this bunch of stinking niggers! . . . *(He straightens up and moves away from his mother, walking around the room.)* Maybe—maybe I'll just get down on my black knees . . . *(He does so.)*

(RUTH and BENNIE and MAMA watch him in frozen horror.)

Captain, Mistuh, Bossman. *(He starts crying.)* A-hee-hee-hee! *(Wringing his hands in profoundly anguished imitation.)* Yassssssuh! Great White Father, just gi' ussen de money, fo' God's sake, and we's ain't gwine come out deh and dirty up yo' white folks neighborhood. . . . *(He breaks down completely, then gets up and goes into the bedroom.)*

BENEATHA: This is not a man. That is nothing but a toothless rat.

MAMA: Yes—death done come in this here house. *(She is nodding, slowly, reflectively.)* Done come walking in my house. On the lips of my children. You what supposed to be my beginning again. You—what supposed to be my harvest. *(To* BENEATHA.*)* You—you mourning your brother?

BENEATHA: He's no brother of mine.

MAMA: What you say?

BENEATHA: I said that that individual in that room is no brother of mine.

MAMA: That's what I thought you said. You feeling like you better than he is today?

(BENEATHA does not answer.)

Yes? What you tell him a minute ago? That he wasn't a man? Yes? You give him up for me? You done wrote his epitaph too—like the rest of the world? Well, who give you the privilege?

BENEATHA: Be on my side for once! You saw what he just did, Mama! You saw him—down on his knees. Wasn't it you who taught me—to despise any man who would do that. Do what he's going to do.

MAMA: Yes—I taught you that. Me and your daddy. But I thought I taught you something else too . . . I thought I taught you to love him.

BENEATHA: Love him? There is nothing left to love.

MAMA: There is always something left to love. And if you ain't learned that, you ain't learned nothing. *(Looking at her.)* Have you cried for that boy today? I don't mean for yourself and for the family 'cause we lost the money. I mean for him; what he been through and what it done to him. Child, when do you think is the time to love somebody the most; when they done good and made things easy for everybody? Well then, you ain't through learning—because that ain't the time at all. It's when he's at his lowest and can't believe in hisself 'cause the world done whipped him so. When you starts measuring somebody, measure him right, child, measure him right. Make sure you done taken into account what hills and valleys he come through before he got to wherever he is.

(TRAVIS bursts into the room at the end of the speech, leaving the door open.)

TRAVIS: Grandmama—the moving men are downstairs! The truck just pulled up.

MAMA: *(Turning and looking at him.)* Are they, baby? They downstairs? *(She sighs and sits.)*

(LINDNER appears in the doorway. He peers in and knocks lightly, to gain attention, and comes in. All turn to look at him.)

LINDNER: *(Hat and briefcase in hand.)* Uh-hello. . . .

(RUTH crosses mechanically to the bedroom door and opens it and lets it swing open freely and slowly as the lights come up on WALTER within, still in his coat, sitting at the far corner of the room. He looks up and out through the room to LINDNER.)

RUTH: He's here.

(A long minute passes and WALTER slowly gets up.)

LINDNER: *(Coming to the table with efficiency, putting his briefcase on the table and starting to unfold papers and unscrew fountain pens.)* Well, I certainly was glad to hear from you people.

(WALTER has begun the trek out of the room, slowly and awkwardly, rather like a small boy, passing the back of his sleeve across his mouth from time to time.)

Life can really be so much simpler than people let it be most of the time. Well—with whom do I negotiate? You, Mrs. Younger, or your son here?

(MAMA sits with her hands folded on her lap and her eyes closed as WALTER advances. TRAVIS gets closer to LINDNER and looks at the papers curiously.)

Just some official papers, sonny.

RUTH: Travis, you go downstairs.

MAMA: (*Opening her eyes and looking into* WALTER*'s.*) No. Travis, you stay right here. And you make him understand what you doing, Walter Lee. You teach him good. Like Willy Harris taught you. You show where our five generations done come to. Go ahead, son—

WALTER: (*Looks down into his son's eyes.*)

(TRAVIS *grins at him merrily and* WALTER *draws him beside him with his arm lightly around his shoulders.*)

Well, Mr. Lindner.

(BENEATHA *turns away.*)

We called you—(*There is a profound, simple groping quality in his speech.*)—because, well, me and my family—(*He looks around and shifts from one foot to the other.*)—well—we are very plain people. . . .

LINDNER: Yes—

WALTER: I mean—I have worked as a chauffeur most of my life—and my wife here, she does domestic work in people's kitchens. So does my mother. I mean—we are plain people. . . .

LINDNER: Yes, Mr. Younger—

WALTER: (*Really like a small boy, looking down at his shoes and then up at the man.*) And—uh—well, my father, well, he was a laborer most of his life.

LINDNER: (*Absolutely confused.*) Uh, yes—

WALTER: (*Looking down at his toes once again.*) My father almost beat a man to death once because this man called him a bad name or something, you know what I mean?

LINDNER: No, I'm afraid I don't.

WALTER: (*Finally straightening up.*) Well, what I mean is that we come from people who had a lot of pride. I mean—we are very proud people. And that's my sister over there and she's going to be a doctor—and we are very proud—

LINDNER: Well—I am sure that is very nice, but—

WALTER: (*Starting to cry and facing the man eye to eye.*) What I am telling you is that we called you over here to tell you that we are very proud and that this is—this is my son, who makes the sixth generation of our family in this country, and that we have all thought about your offer and we have decided to move into our house because my father—my father—he earned it.

(MAMA *has her eyes closed and is rocking back and forth as though she were in church, with her head nodding the amen yes.*)

We don't want to make no trouble for nobody or fight no causes—but we will try to be good neighbors. That's all we got to say. (*He looks the man absolutely in the eyes.*) We don't want your money. (*He turns and walks away from the man.*)

LINDNER: (*Looking around at all of them.*) I take it then that you have decided to occupy.

BENEATHA: That's what the man said.

LINDNER: (*To* MAMA *in her reverie.*) Then I would like to appeal to you, Mrs. Younger. You are older and wiser and understand things better I am sure . . .

MAMA: (*Rising.*) I am afraid you don't understand. My son said we was going to move and there ain't nothing left for me to say. (*Shaking her head with double meaning.*) You know how these young folks is nowadays, mister. Can't do a thing with 'em. Good-bye.

LINDNER: (*Folding up his materials.*) Well—if you are that final about it . . . there is nothing left for me to say. (*He finishes. He is almost ignored by the family, who are concentrating on* WALTER LEE. *At the door* LINDNER *halts and looks around.*) I sure hope you people know what you're doing. (*He shakes his head and exits.*)

RUTH: (*Looking around and coming to life.*) Well, for God's sake—if the moving men are here—LET'S GET THE HELL OUT OF HERE!

MAMA: (*Into action.*) Ain't it the truth! Look at all this here mess. Ruth, put Travis' good jacket on him . . . Walter Lee, fix your tie and tuck your shirt in, you look just like somebody's hoodlum. Lord have mercy, where is my plant? (*She flies to get it amid the general bustling of the family, who are deliberately trying to ignore the nobility of the past moment.*) You all start on down . . . Travis child, don't go empty-handed . . . Ruth, where did I put that box with my skillets in it? I want to be in charge of it myself . . . I'm going to make us the biggest dinner we ever ate tonight . . . Beneatha, what's the matter with them stockings? Pull them things up, girl. . . .

(*The family starts to file out as* TWO MOVING MEN *appear and begin to carry out the heavier pieces of furniture, bumping into the family as they move about.*)

BENEATHA: Mama, Asagai asked me to marry him today and go to Africa—

MAMA: (*In the middle of her getting-ready activity.*) He did? You ain't old enough to marry nobody—(*Seeing the moving men lifting one of her chairs precariously.*)—darling, that ain't no bale of cotton, please handle it so we can sit in it again. I had that chair twenty-five years. . . .

(*The* MOVERS *sigh with exasperation and go on with their work.*)

BENEATHA: (*Girlishly and unreasonably trying to pursure the conversation.*) To go to Africa, Mama—be a doctor in Africa. . . .

MAMA: (*Distracted.*) Yes, baby—

WALTER: Africa! What he want you to go to Africa for?

BENEATHA: To practice there. . . .

WALTER: Girl, if you don't get all them silly ideas out your head! You better marry yourself a man with some loot. . . .

BENEATHA: (*Angrily, precisely as in the first scene of the play.*) What have you got to do with who I marry!

WALTER: Plenty. Now I think George Murchison—

(HE *and* BENEATHA *go out yelling at each other vigorously;* BENEATHA *is heard saying that she would not marry* GEORGE MURCHISON *if he were Adam and she were Eve, etc. The anger is loud and real till their voices diminish.* RUTH *stands at the door and turns to* MAMA *and smiles knowingly.*)

MAMA: *(Fixing her hat at last.)* Yeah—they something all right, my children. . . .

RUTH: Yeah—they're something. Let's go, Lena.

MAMA: *(Stalling, starting to look around at the house.)* Yes—I'm coming, Ruth—

RUTH: Yes?

MAMA: *(Quietly, woman to woman.)* He finally come into his manhood today, didn't he? Kind of like a rainbow after the rain. . . .

RUTH: *(Biting her lip lest her own pride explode in front of* MAMA.*)* Yes, Lena.

(WALTER's *voice calls for them raucously.*)

MAMA: *(Waving* RUTH *out vaguely.)* All right, honey—go on down. I be down directly.

(RUTH *hesitates, then exits,* MAMA *stands, at last alone in the living room, her plant on the table before her as the* LIGHTS *start to come down. She looks around at all the walls and ceilings and suddenly, despite herself, while the children call below, a great heaving thing rises in her and she puts her fist to her mouth, takes a final desperate look, pulls her coat about her, pats her hat and goes out. The* LIGHTS *dim down. The door opens and she comes back in, grabs her plant, and goes out for the last time.*)

Alice Childress (1920–1994)

At the age of five, Alice Childress left her Charleston, South Carolina, home to live with her grandmother in Harlem. In the 1940s, she began her writing career, a career that also included acting and directing plays. An active member of the American Negro Theater, she wrote plays that were controversial for her times. *Trouble in Mind* (1955), which won an Obie Award, deals with lynching. *Like One of the Family* (1956) originally was serialized in black newspapers. The book's conversations between Mildred and her friend, Marge, use humor to show the interior lives of black women domestic workers and their astute analyses of racial and sexual politics in America. The televised version of her play *Wedding Band* (1966), a story about an interracial love affair, caused a stir with several stations refusing to show it. In 1969, *Wine in the Wilderness* sparked controversy because of its discussion of riots. Besides writing a number of provocative plays, Childress wrote children's books. Some school systems banned *A Hero Ain't Nothin' But a Sandwich* (1973), a story about a young boy fighting a drug addiction.

From *Like One of the Family: Conversations from a Domestic's Life*

Like One of the Family

Hi Marge! I have had me one hectic day. . . . Well, I had to take out my crystal ball and give Mrs. C . . . a thorough reading. She's the woman that I took over from Naomi after Naomi got married. . . . Well, she's a pretty nice woman as they go and I have never had too much trouble with her, but from time to time she really gripes me with her ways.

When she has company, for example, she'll holler out to me from the living room to the kitchen: "Mildred dear! Be sure and eat *both* of those lamb chops for your lunch!" Now you know she wasn't doing a thing but tryin' to prove to the company how "good" and "kind" she was to the servant, because she had told me *already* to eat those chops.

Today she had a girl friend of hers over to lunch and I was real busy afterwards clearing the things away and she called me over and introduced me to the woman. . . . Oh no, Marge! I didn't object to that at all. I greeted the lady and then went back to my work. . . . And then it started! I could hear her talkin' just as loud . . . and she says to her friend, "We *just* love her! She's *like* one of the family and she *just adores* our little Carol! We don't know *what* we'd do without her! We don't think of her as a servant!" And on and on she

went . . . and every time I came in to move a plate off the table both of them would grin at me like chessy cats.

After I couldn't stand it any more, I went in and took the platter off the table and gave 'em both a look that would have frizzled a egg. . . . Well, you might have heard a pin drop and then they started talkin' about something else.

When the guest leaves, I go in the living room and says, "Mrs. C . . ., I want to have a talk with you."

"By all means," she says.

I drew up a chair and read her thusly: "Mrs. C . . ., you are a pretty nice person to work for, but I wish you would please stop talkin' about me like I was a *cocker spaniel* or a *poll parrot* or a *kitten*. . . . Now you just sit there and hear me out.

"In the first place, you do not *love* me; you may be fond of me, but that is all. . . . In the second place, I am *not* just like one of the family at all! The family eats in the dining room and I eat in the kitchen. Your mama borrows your lace table-cloth for her company and your son entertains his friends in your parlor, your daughter takes her afternoon nap on the living room couch and the puppy sleeps on your satin spread . . . and whenever your husband gets tired of something you are talkin' about he says, 'Oh, for Pete's sake, forget it. . . .' So you can see I am not *just* like one of the family.

"Now for another thing, I do not *just* adore your little Carol. I think she is a likable child, but she is also fresh and sassy. I know you call it 'uninhibited' and that is the way you want your child to be, but *luckily* my mother taught me some inhibitions or else I would smack little Carol once in a while when she's talkin' to you like you're a dog, but as it is I just laugh it off the way you do because she is *your* child and I am *not* like one of the family.

From *Like One of the Family: Conversations from a Domestic's Life* (1956), Beacon Press.

"Now when you say, 'We don't know *what* we'd do without her' this is a polite lie . . . because I know that if I dropped dead or had a stroke, you would get somebody to replace me.

"You think it is a compliment when you say, 'We don't think of her as a servant. . . .' but after I have worked myself into a sweat cleaning the bathroom and the kitchen . . . making the beds . . . cooking the lunch . . . washing the dishes and ironing Carol's pinafores . . . I do not feel like no weekend house guest. I feel like a servant, and in the face of that I have been meaning to ask you for a slight raise which will make me feel much better toward everyone here and make me know my work is appreciated.

"Now I hope you will stop talkin' about me in my presence and that we will get along like a good employer and employee should."

Marge! She was almost speechless but she *apologized* and said she'd talk to her husband about the raise. . . . I knew things were progressing because this evening Carol came in the kitchen and she did not say, "I want some bread and jam!" but she did say, "*Please*, Mildred, will you fix me a slice of bread and jam."

I'm going upstairs, Marge. Just look . . . you done messed up that buttonhole!

Ridin' the Bus

I sure am glad we got a seat near the window, I'm that tired. . . . What do you mean by you thought I'd never stop walkin'? I like to sit in the back of the bus. . . . I certainly do, for many good reasons. . . . Well, the back is always less crowded, the air is better, it is also nearer to the exit door. . . . Why do I sound strange to you? . . . Marge, there is no way that you can compare ridin' in the back because you want to with ridin' there because you have to! . . . No indeed, I'll argue you down on that! . . . I've ridden both ways a whole lot so I can tell you the difference.

Well, for one thing when I walked to the back of this bus nobody was freezin' me up with stares. Have you forgotten what it feels like? All of them eyes that always have to follow you to your seat lookin' at you real mockin' like. Well, nobody pays us any mind and we didn't have to die little on the inside because there was nothin' to this except findin' a seat. The next difference was the fact that when we took this seat it simply showed which one we had picked out and not which one was picked for us. Why don't you look around you and see who else is sittin' back here? . . . That's right, there's plenty

of white folks too. Now, if they are from the South, it's probably the first time in their lives that *they* have had the opportunity to sit where *they* want!

. . . Why sure, they *can't* sit in the back down home and it seems that a lot of 'em think that's the best place to be. . . . No, I don't think of it in that way. Good, better or best, it is only the individual that can say which they like. Another thing, I get annoyed ridin' Jim Crow because you get a little more than just *separate seatin'*. You get rudeness, meanness and less for your money in every other way. There's been many a time when I was down home when the driver wouldn't stop when I pulled the cord, that is if I was the only one who wanted to get off, or if it was any other colored for that matter. I'd be so mad when he wouldn't let me off 'til we was four or five blocks past my stop. There's been many a time I've been left standin' with my hand held up to stop the bus and the driver would go whizzin' right on past. There's been other times when them drivers would go out of the way to splash a mud puddle on you. . . . Well, you know they was bein' upheld in everything they did! But the most miserable thing of all was when the back of the bus was full and the front almost empty. Yes, you'd just stand there and get madder and madder, especially when you'd be standin' by a colored mother holdin' her baby in her arms and look toward the front and see four or five white men and women ridin' along with about twenty seats between. I can tell you that although we knew it was the law, it didn't make anybody feel good to notice how the folks sittin' in the front would just go on readin' their newspapers and never even look up or feel least bit self-conscious about us. . . . Oh, yes, there are some places down South where the passengers are supposed to fill up from the front and the back as they come in, but I never liked that too much because if there were more colored we'd have to move back when the whites came on, and of course that was worse than bein' in the back in the first place.

. . . You are right, Marge, some people still think we want to sit with white people when they hear us talkin' about that Jim Crow ridin' and what they seem to forget is that there was never nothin' *equal* about those *separate* seats even though they were all on the same bus.

Watch where this white man sits when he gets back here. Well now, did you see that? He sat next to a colored man. . . . No, I don't think he especially wanted to or didn't want to. See how he's busy readin' his magazine? It is good to note also that the colored man never noticed him sitting beside him and went right on lookin' for his street. That's the way things *should* be—nice and easy like with no fuss or bother one way or the other. Sure, and when I feel like bein' exclusive, I take a *cab*!

All About My Job

Marge, I sure am glad that you are my friend. . . . No, I do not want to borrow anything or ask any favors and I wish you'd stop bein' suspicious everytime somebody pays you a compliment. It's a sure sign of a distrustful nature.

I'm glad that you are my friend because everybody needs a friend but I guess I need one more than most people. . . . Well, in the first place I'm colored and in the second place I do housework for a livin' and so you can see that I don't need a third place because the first two ought to be enough reason for anybody to need a friend.

You are not only a good friend but you are also a convenient friend and fill the bill in every other way. . . . Well, we are both thirty-two years old; both live in the same building; we each have a three room apartment for which we pay too devilish much, but at the same time we got better sense than to try and live together. And there are other things, too. We both come from the South and we also do the same kinda work: *housework*.

Of course, you have been married, and I have not yet taken the vows, but I guess that's the only difference unless you want to count the fact that you are heavier than I am and wear a size eighteen while I wear a sixteen. . . . Marge, you know that you are larger, that's a fact! Oh, well, let's not get upset about it! The important thing is that I'm your friend, and you're mine and I'm glad about it!

Why, I do believe I'd lose my mind if I had to come home after a day of hard work, rasslin' 'round in other folks' kitchens if I did not have a friend to talk to when I got here. . . . Girl, don't you move 'cause it would be terrible if I couldn't run down a flight of steps and come in here to chew the fat in the evenin'. But if you ever get tired of me, always remember that all you have to do is say, "Mildred, go home," and I'll be on my way! . . . I did not get mad the last time you told me that! Girl, you ought to be ashamed of yourself! . . . No, I'm not callin' you a liar but I'm sayin' you just can't remember the truth.

Anyhow, I'm glad that we're friends! I got a story to tell you about what happened today. . . . No, not where I work although it was *about* where I work.

The church bazaar was open tonight and I went down to help out on one of the booths and, oh, my nerves! you never saw so many la-de-da fancy folks in all your life! And such introducin' that was goin' on. You shoulda *heard* 'em. "Do meet Mrs. So-and-so who has just returned from *Europe*," and "Do meet Miss This-and-that who has just finished her new *book*" and "Do meet Miss This-that-and-the-other who is on the Board of Directors of everything that is worthwhile!"

Honey, it was a dog! . . . Oh, yes, it was a real snazzy affair, and the booths was all fixed up so pretty, and they had these fine photographs pinned up on the wall. The photographs showed people doin' all manner of work. Yes, the idea of the pictures was to show how we are improvin' ourselves by leaps and bounds through the kinda work that we're doin'.

Well, that was a great old deal with me except that if they was talkin' 'bout people doin' work, it seemed to me that I was the only one around there that had took a lick at a snake in years! . . . No, it wasn't a drag at all because I was really enjoyin' the thing just like you'd go for a carnival or a penny-arcade once in a while.

My booth was the "Knick-Knack" corner and my counter was full of chipped-china doo-dads and ash trays and penny banks and stuff like that, and I was really sellin' it, too. There was a little quiet lady helpin' me out and for the life of me I couldn't figure why she was so scared-like and timid lookin'.

I was enjoyin' myself to no end, and there was so many big-wigs floatin' around the joint 'til I didn't know what to expect next! . . . Yes, girl, any second I thought some sultan or king or somebody like that was gonna fall in the door! Honey, I was how-do-you-doin' left and right! Well, all the excitement keeps up 'til one group of grand folks stopped at our booth and begun to chat with us and after the recitation 'bout what they all did, one lady turned to my timid friend and says, "What do *you* do?"

Marge, Miss Timid started sputterin' and stammerin' and finally she outs with, "Nothin' much." That was a new one on me 'cause I had never heard 'bout nobody who spent their time doin' "nothin' much," Then Miss Grand-lady turns to me and says, "And what do *you* do?" . . . Of course I told her! "I do housework," I said. "Oh," says she, "you are a housewife." "Oh, no," says I, "I do housework, and I do it every day because that is the way I make my livin' and if you look around at these pictures on the wall you will see that people do all kinds of work, I do housework."

Marge, they looked kinda funny for a minute but the next thing you know we were all laughin' and talkin' 'bout everything in general and nothin' in particular. I mean all of us was chattin' except Miss Timid.

When the folks drifted away, Miss Timid turns to me and says, "I do housework too but I don't always feel like tellin'. People look down on you so".

Well, I can tell you that I moved on in after that remark and straightened her out! . . . Now, wait a minute, Marge! I know people do make nasty cracks about houseworkers. Sure, they will say things like "pot-slingers" or "the Thursday-night-off" crowd, but nobody gets away with that stuff around me, and I will sound off in a second about how I feel about my work.

Marge, people who do this kinda work got a lot of different ideas about their jobs, I mean some folks are ashamed of it and some are proud of it, but I don't feel either way. You see, on accounta many reasons I find that I got to do it and while I don't think that housework is the grandest job I ever hope to get, it makes me *mad* for any fools to come lookin' down their nose at me!

If I had a child, I would want that child to do something that paid better and had some opportunity to it, but on the other hand it would distress me no end to see that child get some arrogant attitude toward me because I do domestic work. Domestic workers have done a awful lot of good things in this country besides clean up peoples' houses. We've taken care of our brothers and fathers and husbands when the factory gates and office desks and pretty near everything else was closed to them; we've helped many a neighbor, doin' everything from helpin' to clothe their children to buryin' the dead.

. . . Yes, mam, and I'll help you to tell it! We built that church that the bazaar was held in! And it's a rare thing for anybody to find a colored family in this land that can't trace a domestic worker somewhere in their history. . . . How 'bout that, girl! . . . Yes, there's many a doctor, many a lawyer, many a teacher, many a minister that got where they are 'cause somebody worked in the kitchen to put 'em there, and there's also a lot of 'em that worked in kitchens themselves in order to climb up a little higher!

Of course, lot of people think it's *smart* not to talk about *slavery* anymore, but after freedom came, it was domestics that kept us from perishin' by the wayside. . . . Who you tellin'? I know it was our dollars and pennies that built many a school! . . .

Yes, I know I said I wasn't particular proud about bein' a domestic worker, but I guess I am. What I really meant to say was that I had plans to be somethin' else, but time and trouble stopped me from doin' it. So I told this little Miss Meek, "Dear, throw back your shoulders and pop your fingers at the *world* because the way I see it there's nobody with common sense that can look down on the domestic worker!"

Mrs. James

Well Marge, you haven't heard anything! You should hear the woman I work for . . . she's really something. Calls herself "Mrs. James!" All the time she says "Mrs. James."

The first day I was there she come into the kitchen and says, "Mildred, Mrs. James would like you to clean the pantry." Well I looked 'round to see if she meant her mother-in-law or somebody and then she adds, "If anyone calls, Mrs. James is out shopping." And with that she sashays out the door.

Now she keeps on talking that way all the time, the whole time I'm there. That woman wouldn't say "I" or "me"

for nothing in the world. The way I look at it . . . I guess she thought it would be too personal.

Now Marge, you know I don't work Saturdays for nobody! Well sir! Last Friday she breezed in the kitchen and fussed around a little . . . movin' first the salt and then the pepper, I could feel something brewin' in the air. Next thing you know she speaks up. "Mildred," she says, "Mrs. James will need you this Saturday." I was polishin' silver at the time but I turned around and looked her dead in the eye and said, "Mildred does not work on Saturdays."

Well, for the rest of the day things went along kind of quiet-like but just before time for me to go home she drifted by the linen closet to check the ruffle on a guest towel and threw in her two cents more. "Mildred," she says, "a depression might do this country some good, then some people might work eight days a week and be glad for the chance to do it."

I didn't bat an eyelash, but about 15 minutes later when I was headin' for home, I stopped off at the living room and called to her, "That's very true, but on the other hand some folks might be doin' their own housework . . . don'tcha know." With that and a cool "goodnight" I gently went out the front door. . . .

Oh, but we get along fine now. . . . Just fine!

I Hate Half-Days Off

Girl, people have got some crust! Some folks' notion of what's *fair* is all out of whack, and it takes your friend Mildred to tell it! You know, Marge, I told you how I was sick and tired of runnin' from hither to yon in order to make a bare livin'? . . . That's right, days work can carry you all over town, workin' first for this one and then the other. There's some mornin's that it takes me a good five minutes to remember just where I'm goin' to work. So I decided to try steady time once more and look me up a permanent place to work. . . . Yes, I got it out the newspaper and telephoned the lady before the print was dry.

Honey, you never heard such a interview as she put me through. You shoulda heard her! "Now, Mildred, why do you want this job?" Don't laugh, I know you want to but try and listen. Did you ever hear such a simple question? I could of told her the truth and make mention of that nasty word *money*, but I knew that would make her sad, so I said very prettily. "Because I'd like a nice steady job with a good family."

Hot dog! I struck pay-dirt, her smile was the sunshine of a May afternoon. Sure she asked me some more things. I had to give her references, the name of my minister and my doctor, how long I worked in my last three places and how come this and why not that until we was both fair worn out with talk and more talk. Finally she seems all satisfied and made the summin' up, "I think you'll do just fine, and I hope we can make some satisfactory arrangement that'll make us both happy." Marge, before I can get in a word about what'll make me happy she takes a sheet of paper out of her desk and starts readin' off how things will go. "Mildred," she says, "on Monday you will report at eight o'clock in the mornin' and after the breakfast dishes you will do the washin'. Of course we have a machine." "Naturally," I says, then she starts runnin' her finger down this devilish list: "After the washin' you will take care of the children's lunch, prepare dinner, clean the baby's room *thoroughly* and leave after the supper dishes, that's Monday." "So much for Monday," I says, "and how about Tuesday?" "Well," she says, "you don't come in until noon on Tuesday, then you fix the children's lunch, iron, give the kitchen a thorough cleaning, prepare dinner and leave after the supper dishes." "Well," I says, "here we are at Wednesday already." "Yes," she says, "on Wednesday you come in at eight in the mornin' and do all the floors, fix the children's lunch, do the mendin', give the foyer and the baths a thorough cleanin', prepare the dinner . . ." ". . . and leave after the supper dishes," I says. "That's right," she says, "and the schedule remains pretty much the same for the rest of the week; on Thursday you thoroughly clean the bedrooms, on Friday the livin' room, on Saturday the pantry shelves, silver, and clothes closets and on Sunday you fix early dinner and leave after one-thirty."

Marge, I must have looked pure bewildered because she adds, "Do you have any comment?" "A little," I says, "when is my off-time?" "Oh, that," she says. "Yes mam," I says, and

then she begins to run her finder down the list again. "Well, you have one half-day off every Tuesday and one half-day off every Sunday and every other Thursday you get a full day off, which makes it a five and a half day week."

How 'bout that Marge! I was never too good at arithmetic, but I really had to tip my hat to her. Even somebody as smart as Einstein couldn't have figured nothin' as neat as that. Before I could get a word in on what I considered the deal of the year, she played her trump card, "I will pay you two weeks pay on the first and fifteenth of each month." "But that way," I says, "I lose a week's pay every time the month has five weeks." Well, she repeats herself, "I pay on the first and fifteenth."

No, Marge, you know I wasn't comin' on that! In the first place I could see me workin' myself into such a lather that there wouldn't be nothin' to do but crawl into the doctor's office on the first and fifteenth and give every blessed nickel I had in order that he could try and straighten me out in time to meet the second and the sixteenth. In the second place . . . oh, well, what's the use? You get the picture! I backed out of there so fast 'til I bet she's not sure that I was ever there.

But it set me to thinkin'. How come all of them bigshots in Washington that can't balance the budget or make the taxes cover all our expenses, how *come* they don't send for that woman to help straighten them out? Why, in two or three weeks she'd not only get everything on a payin' basis, but she'd have enough money left over to buy every citizen a free ice cream cone for the Fourth of July, not countin' all the loot we'd have left over to bury at Fort Knox! Genius like that just pure takes your breath away. It's almost beautiful in a disgustin' sort of way, ain't it?

Naomi Long Madgett (b. 1923)

Born in Norfolk, Virginia, to a Baptist minister and a schoolteacher, Naomi Long Madgett moved with her family to New Jersey when she was two years old. When she was fourteen, her family moved to St. Louis, an area she found rich in African American culture and history. After high school, she attended Virginia State and upon graduation spent a semester doing graduate work at New York University. Madgett writes about African American heritage and identity.

The Old Women

They are young.
They do not understand
what the old women are saying.

They see the gnarled hands raised
and think they are praying.
They cannot see the weapons hung

between their fingers. When the mouths
gape and the rasping noises
crunch like dead leaves,

they laugh at the voices
they think are trying to sing.
They are young

and have not learned
the many faces of endurance, the furtive
triumphs earned through suffering.

Attitude at Seventy-Five

In this recurring dream I am Tina Turner
flinging my wild wig at the world,
strut-stomping across the stage

on miniskirted gams ageless and untamed,
completely in command and belting out my song,
What's Time Got to Do With It!

Gray Strands

1   Badge of trial
    and triumph:
    it is mine, I have
    earned it.
    I wear it proudly

2   There is nothing
    more lovely
    than silver framing
    a face
    of old ebony.

Maya Angelou (b.1928)

Long before Maya Angelou delivered the Inaugural poem, "On the Pulse of Morning," for President Clinton in 1993, many thought of her as an unofficial poet laureate. Such poems as "Still I Rise" and "Phenomenal Woman" capture the resiliency and regality of black womanhood. Her autobiography, *I Know Why the Caged Bird Sings* (1969), describes the story of a young black girl who is raped and silent for years thereafter, but who retrieves her voice—a voice that writes, sings, and performs. Born Marguerite Johnson in St. Louis, Angelou attended public schools in Stamps, Arkansas, where she and her brother, Bailey, lived with their grandmother. While visiting her mother in St. Louis when she was seven years old, Angelou experienced a trauma that changed her life. Her mother's boyfriend, Mr. Freeman, raped Angelou. The trial and the subsequent killing of Freeman made Angelou feel guilty; she spent the next five years not speaking to anyone. Angelou chronicles her life story in her serial autobiographies: *Gather Together in My Name* (1974); *Singin' and Swingin' and Getting' Merry Like Christmas* (1976); *The Heart of a Woman* (1981), and *All God's Children Need Traveling Shoes* (1986). Angelou holds the Reynolds Professor of American Studies chair at Wake Forest University.

Still I Rise

You may write me down in history
With your bitter, twisted lies,
You may trod me in the very dirt
But still, like dust, I'll rise.

Does my sassiness upset you?
Why are you beset with gloom?
'Cause I walk like I've got oil wells
Pumping in my living room.

Just like moons and like suns,
with the certainly of tides,
Just like hopes springing high,
Still I'll rise.

Did you want to see me broken?
Bowed head and lowered eyes?
Shoulders falling down like teardrops,
Weakened by my soulful cries.

Does my haughtiness offend you?
Don't you take it awful hard
'Cause I laugh like I've got gold mines
Diggin' in my own back yard.

You may shoot me with your words,
You may cut me with your eyes,
You may kill me with your hatefulness,
But still, like air, I'll rise.

Does my sexiness upset you?
Does it come as a surprise
That I dance like I've got diamonds
At the meeting of my thighs?

Out of the huts of history's shame
I rise
Up from a past that's rooted in pain
I rise
I'm a black ocean, leaping and wide,
Welling and swelling I bear in the tide.

Leaving behind nights of terror and fear
I rise
Into a daybreak that's wondrously clear
I rise
Bringing the gifts that my ancestors gave,
I am the dream and the hope of the slave.
I rise
I rise
I rise.

Paule Marshall (b. 1929)

Paule Marshall's writings build a bridge between the Caribbean and the Americas. Whether writing about Brooklyn, Brazil, British Guiana, or Barbados, Marshall crafts narratives about the maturation processes of black girls and women. Growing up in Brooklyn, she listened to the West Indian stories of her parents and their friends who were immigrants struggling to carve a new space in Brooklyn without losing the memories and traditions of their homeland, Barbados. Born Valenza Pauline Burke to Samuel and Ada Clement Burke, Marshall graduated Phi Beta Kappa from Brooklyn College. During the course of her writing career she has received a number of prestigious awards including a Guggenheim fellowship (1960), the American Book Award (1984), and the MacArthur Award (1992).

Marshall has written four novels and several novellas, short stories, and essays. *Brown Girl, Brownstones* (1959) is the story of a young girl growing up in Brooklyn to West Indian parents. *Soul Clap Hands and Sing* (1961) is a collection of short stories set in aforementioned locales that depicts the relationships between young women and aging men. *The Chosen Place, the Timeless People* (1969) illuminates postcolonial issues in the Caribbean. *Praisesong for the Widow* (1983) is the story of widow Avey Johnson's diasporic journey. *Daughters* (1991) chronicles the career of a young black professional as she negotiates life in New York and the Caribbean. Marshall credits the everyday voices of domestic women, "poets in the kitchen," as literary and expressive cultural influences.

From *Soul Clap Hands and Sing*

Brooklyn

A summer wind, soaring just before it died, blew the dusk and the first scattered lights of downtown Brooklyn against the shut windows of the classroom, but Professor Max Berman—B.A., 1919., M.A., 1921, New York; Docteur de l'Université, 1930, Paris—alone in the room, did not bother to open the windows to the cooling wind. The heat and airlessness of the room, the perspiration inching its way like an ant around his starched collar were discomforts he enjoyed; they obscured his larger discomfort: the anxiety which chafed his heart and tugged his left eyelid so that he seemed to be winking, roguishly, behind his glasses.

To steady his eye and ease his heart, to fill the time until his students arrived and his first class in years began, he reached for his cigarettes. As always he delayed lighting the cigarette so that his need for it would be greater and, thus, the relief and pleasure it would bring, fuller. For some time he fondled it, his fingers shaping soft, voluptuous gestures,

his warped old man's hands looking strangely abandoned on the bare desk and limp as if the bones had been crushed, and so white—except for the tobacco burn on the index and third fingers—it seemed his blood no longer traveled that far.

He lit the cigarette finally and as the smoke swelled his lungs, his eyelid stilled and his lined face lifted, the plume of white hair wafting above his narrow brow; his body—short, blunt, the shoulders slightly bent as if in deference to his sixty-three years—settled back in the chair. Delicately Max Berman crossed his legs and, looking down, examined his shoes for dust. (The shoes were of a very soft, fawn-colored leather and somewhat foppishly pointed at the toe. They had been custom made in France and were his one last indulgence. He wore them in memory of his first wife, a French Jewess from Alsace-Lorraine whom he had met in Paris while lingering over his doctorate and married to avoid returning home. She had been gay, mindless and very excitable—but at night, she had also been capable of a profound stillness as she lay in bed waiting for him to turn to her, and this had always awed and delighted him. She had been a gift—and her death in a car accident had been a judgment on him for never having loved her, for never, indeed, having even allowed her to matter.) Fastidiously Max Berman unbuttoned his jacket and straightened his vest, which had a stain two decades old on the pocket. Through the smoke his veined eyes contemplated other, more pleasurable scenes. With his neatly shod foot swinging and his cigarette at a rakish tilt, he might have been an old *boulevardier* taking the sun and an absinthe before the afternoon's assignation.

A young face, the forehead shiny with earnestness, hung at the half-opened door. "Is this French Lit, fifty-four? Camus and Sartre?"

Max Berman winced at the rawness of the voice and the flat "a" in Sartre and said formally, "This is Modern French Literature, number fifty-four, yes, but there is some question as to whether we will take up Messieurs Camus and Sartre this session. They might prove hot work for a summer-evening course. We will probably do Gide and Mauriac, who are considerably more temperate. But come in nonetheless. . . ."

He was the gallant, half rising to bow her to a seat. He knew that she would select the one in the front row directly opposite his desk. At the bell her pen would quiver above her blank notebook, ready to commit his first word—indeed, the clearing of his throat—to paper, and her thin buttocks would begin sidling toward the edge of her chair.

His eyelid twitched with solicitude. He wished that he could have drawn the lids over her fitful eyes and pressed a cool hand to her forehead. She reminded him of what he had been several lifetimes ago: a boy with a pale, plump face and harried eyes, running from the occasional taunts at his yamilke along the shrill streets of Brownsville in Brooklyn, impeded by the heavy satchel of books which he always carried as proof of his scholarship. He had been proud of his brilliance at school and the Yeshiva, but at the same time he had been secretly troubled by it and resentful, for he could never believe that he had come by it naturally or that it belonged to him alone. Rather, it was like a heavy medal his father had hung around his neck—the chain bruising his flesh—and constantly exhorted him to wear proudly and use well.

The girl gave him an eager and ingratiating smile and he looked away. During his thirty years of teaching, a face similar to hers had crowded his vision whenever he had looked up from a desk. Perhaps it was fitting, he thought, and lighted another cigarette from the first, that she should be present as he tried again at life, unaware that behind his rimless glasses and within his ancient suit, he had been gutted.

He thought of those who had taken the last of his substance—and smiled tolerantly. "The boys of summer," he called them, his inquisitors, who had flailed him with a single question: "Are you now or have you ever been a member of the Communist party?" Max Berman had never taken their question seriously—perhaps because he had never taken his membership in the party seriously—and he had refused to answer. What had disturbed him, though, even when the investigation was over, was the feeling that he had really been under investigation for some other offense which did matter and of

which he was guilty; that behind their accusations and charges had lurked another which had not been political but personal. For had he been disloyal to the government? His denial was a short, hawking laugh. Simply, he had never ceased being religious. When his father's God had become useless and even a little embarrassing, he had sought others: his work for a time, then the party. But he had been middle-aged when he joined and his faith, which had been so full as a boy, had grown thin. He had come, by then, to distrust all pieties, so that when the purges in Russia during the thirties confirmed his distrust, he had withdrawn into a modest cynicism.

But he had been made to answer for that error. Ten years later his inquisitors had flushed him out from the small community college in upstate New York where he had taught his classes from the same neat pack of notes each semester and had led him bound by subpoena to New York and bandied his name at the hearings until he had been dismissed from his job.

He remembered looking back at the pyres of burning autumn leaves on the campus his last day and feeling that another lifetime had ended—for he had always thought of his life as divided into many small lives, each with its own beginning and end. Like a hired mute, he had been present at each dying and kept the wake and wept professionally as the bier was lowered into the ground. Because of this feeling, he told himself that his final death would be anticlimactic.

After his dismissal he had continued living in the small house he had built near the college, alone except for an occasional visit from a colleague, idle but for some tutoring in French, content with the income he received from the property his parents had left him in Brooklyn—until the visits and tutoring had tapered off and a silence had begun to choke the house, like weeds springing up around a deserted place. He had begun to wonder then if he were still alive. He would wake at night from the recurrent dream of the hearings, where he was being accused of an unstated crime, to listen for his heart, his hand fumbling among the bedclothes to press the place. During the day he would pass repeatedly in front of the mirror with the pretext that he might have forgotten to shave that morning or that something had blown into his eye. Above all, he had begun to think of his inquisitors with affection and to long for the sound of their voices. They, at least, had assured him of being alive.

As if seeking them out, he had returned to Brooklyn and to the house in Brownsville where he had lived as a boy and had boldly applied for a teaching post without mentioning the investigation. He had finally been offered the class which would begin in five minutes. It wasn't much: a six-week course in the summer evening session of a college without a rating, where classes were held in a converted factory building, a college whose campus took in the bargain department stores, the five-and-dime emporiums and neon-spangled movie houses of downtown Brooklyn.

Through the smoke from his cigarette, Max Berman's eyes—a waning blue that never seemed to focus on any one thing—drifted over the students who had gathered meanwhile. Imbuing them with his own disinterest, he believed that even before the class began, most of them were longing for its end and already anticipating the soft drinks at the soda fountain downstairs and the synthetic dramas at the nearby movie.

They made him sad. He would have liked to lead them like a Pied Piper back to the safety of their childhoods—all of them: the loud girl with the formidable calves of an athlete who reminded him, uncomfortably, of his second wife (a party member who was always shouting political heresy from some picket line and who had promptly divorced him upon discovering his irreverence); the two sallow-faced young men leaning out the window as if searching for the wind that had died; the slender young woman with crimped black hair who sat very still and apart from the others, her face turned toward the night sky as if to a friend.

Her loneliness interested him. He sensed its depth and his eye paused. He saw then that she was a Negro, a very pale mulatto with skin the color of clear, polished amber and a thin, mild face. She was somewhat older than the others in the room—a schoolteacher from the South, probably, who came north each summer to take courses toward a graduate degree. He felt a fleeting discomfort and irritation: discomfort at the thought that although he had been sinned against as a Jew he still shared in the sin against her and suffered from the same vague guilt, irritation that she recalled his own humiliations: the large ones, such as the fact that despite his brilliance he had been unable to get into a medical school as a young man because of the quota on Jews (not that he had wanted to be a doctor; that had been his father's wish) and had changed his studies from medicine to French; the small ones which had worn him thin: an eye widening imperceptibly as he gave his name, the savage glance which sought the Jewishness in his nose, his chin, in the set of his shoulders, the jokes snuffed into silence at his appearance. . . .

Tired suddenly, his eyelid pulsing, he turned and stared out the window at the gaudy constellation of neon lights. He longed for a drink, a quiet place and then sleep. And to bear him gently into sleep, to stay the terror which bound his heart then reminding him of those oleographs of Christ with the thorns binding his exposed heart—fat drops of blood from one so bloodless—to usher him into sleep, some pleasantly erotic image: a nude in a boudoir scattered with her frilled garments and warmed by her frivolous laugh, with the sun like a voyeur at the half-closed shutters. But this time instead of the usual Rubens nude with things like twin portals

and a belly like a huge alabaster bowl into which he poured himself, he chose Gauguin's Aita Parari, her languorous form in the straight-back chair, her dark, sloping breasts, her eyes like the sun under shadow.

With the image still on his inner eye, he turned to the Negro girl and appraised her through a blind of cigarette smoke. She was still gazing out at the night sky and something about her fixed stare, her hands stiffly arranged in her lap, the nerve fluttering within the curve of her throat, betrayed a vein of tension within the rock of her calm. It was as if she had fled long ago to a remote region within herself, taking with her all that was most valuable and most vulnerable about herself.

She stirred finally, her slight breasts lifting beneath her flowered summer dress as she breathed deeply—and Max Berman thought again of Gauguin's girl with the dark, sloping breasts. What would this girl with the amber-colored skin be like on a couch in a sunlit room, nude in a straight back chair? And as the question echoed along each nerve and stilled his breathing, it seemed suddenly that life, which had scorned him for so long, held out her hand again—but still a little beyond his reach. Only the girl, he sensed, could bring him close enough to touch it. She alone was the bridge. So that even while he repeated to himself that he was being presumptuous (for she would surely refuse him) and ridiculous (for even if she did not, what could he do—his performance would be a mere scramble and twitch), he vowed at the same time to have her. The challenge eased the tightness around his heart suddenly; it soothed the damaged muscle of his eye and as the bell rang he rose and said briskly, "Ladies and gentlemen, may I have your attention, please. My name is Max Berman. The course is Modern French Literature, number fifty-four. May I suggest that you check your program cards to see whether you are in the right place at the right time."

Her essay on Gide's *The Immoralist* lay on his desk and the note from the administration informing him, first, that his past political activities had been brought to their attention and then dismissing him at the end of the session weighed the inside pocket of his jacket. The two, her paper and the note, were linked in his mind. Her paper reminded him that the vow he had taken was still an empty one, for the term was half over and he had never once spoken to her (as if she understood his intention she was always late and disappeared as soon as the closing bell rang, leaving him trapped in a clamorous circle of students around his desk), while the note which wrecked his small attempt to start anew suddenly made that vow more urgent. It gave him the edge of desperation he needed to act finally. So that as soon as the bell rang, he returned all the papers but hers, announced that all questions would have to wait until their next meeting and, waving off the students from his desk, called above their protests,

"Miss Williams, if you have a moment, I'd like to speak with you briefly about your paper."

She approached his desk like a child who has been cautioned not to talk to strangers, her fingers touching the backs of the chair as if for support, her gaze following the departing students as though she longed to accompany them.

Her slight apprehensiveness pleased him. It suggested a submissiveness which gave him, as he rose uncertainly, a feeling of certainty and command. Her hesitancy was somehow in keeping with the color of her skin. She seemed to bring not only herself but the host of black women whose bodies had been despoiled to make her. He would not only possess her but them also, he thought (not really thought, for he scarcely allowed these thoughts to form before he snuffed them out). Through their collective suffering, which she contained, his own personal suffering would be eased; he would be pardoned for whatever sin it was he had committed against life.

"I hope you weren't unduly alarmed when I didn't return your paper along with the others," he said, and had to look up as she reached the desk. She was taller close up and her eyes, which he had thought were black, were a strong, flecked brown with very small pupils which seemed to shrink now from the sight of him. "But I found it so interesting I wanted to give it to you privately."

"I didn't know what to think," she said, and her voice— he heard it for the first time for she never recited or answered in class—was low, cautious, Southern.

"It was, to say the least, refreshing. It not only showed some original and mature thinking on your part, but it also proved that you've been listening in class—and after twenty-five years and more of teaching it's encouraging to find that some students do listen. If you have a little time I'd like to tell you, more specifically, what I liked about it. . . ."

Talking easily, reassuring her with his professional tone and a deft gesture with his cigarette, he led her from the room as the next class filed in, his hand cupped at her elbow but not touching it, his manner urbane, courtly, kind. They paused on the landing at the end of the long corridor with the stairs piled in steel tiers above and plunging below them. An intimate silence swept up the stairwell in a warm gust and Max Berman said, "I'm curious. Why did you choose *The Immoralist?*"

She started suspiciously, afraid, it seemed, that her answer might expose and endanger the self she guarded so closely within.

"Well," she said finally, her glance reaching down the stairs to the door marked EXIT at the bottom, "when you said we could use anything by Gide I decided on *The Immoralist*, since it was the first book I read in the original French when I was in undergraduate school. I didn't understand it then because my French was so weak, I guess, but I always thought

about if afterward for some odd reason. I was shocked by what I did understand, of course, but something else about it appealed to me, so when you made the assignment I thought I'd try reading it again. I understood it a little better this time. At least I think so. . . ."

"Your paper proves you did."

She smiled absently, intent on some other thought. Then she said cautiously, but with unexpected force, "You see, to me, the book seems to say that the only way you begin to know what you are and how much you are capable of is by daring to try something, by doing something which tests you. . . ."

"Something bold," he said.

"Yes."

"Even sinful."

She paused, questioning this, and then said reluctantly, "Yes, perhaps even sinful."

"The salutary effects of sin, you might say." He gave the little bow.

But she had not heard this; her mind had already leaped ahead. "The only trouble, at least with the character in Gide's book, is that what he finds out about himself is so terrible. He is so unhappy. . . ."

"But at least he knows, poor sinner." And his playful tone went unnoticed.

"Yes," she said with the same startling forcefulness. "And another thing, in finding out what he is, he destroys his wife. It was as if she had to die in order for him to live and know himself. Perhaps in order for a person to live and know himself somebody else must die. Maybe there's always a balancing out. . . . In a way"—and he had to lean close now to hear her—"I believe this."

Max Berman edged back as he glimpsed something move within her abstracted gaze. It was like a strong and restless seed that had taken root in the darkness there and was straining now toward the light. He had not expected so subtle and complex a force beneath her mild exterior and he found it disturbing and dangerous, but fascinating.

"Well, it's a most interesting interpretation," he said. "I don't know if M. Gide would have agreed, but then he's not around to give his opinion. Tell me, where did you do your undergraduate work?"

"At Howard University."

"And you majored in French?"

"Yes."

"Why, if I may ask?" he said gently.

"Well, my mother was from New Orleans and could still speak a little Creole and I got interested in learning how to speak French through her, I guess. I teach it now at a junior high school in Richmond. Only the beginner courses because I don't have my master's. You know, *je vais, tu vas, il va* and *Frère Jacques*. It's not very inspiring."

"You should do something about that then, my dear Miss Williams. Perhaps it's time for you, like our friend in Gide, to try something new and bold."

"I know," she said, and her pale hand sketched a vague, despairing gesture. "I thought maybe if I got my master's . . . that's why I decided to come north this summer and start taking some courses. . . ."

Max Berman quickly lighted a cigarette to still the flurry inside him, for the moment he had been awaiting had come. He flicked her paper, which he still held. "Well, you've got the makings of a master's thesis right here. If you like I will suggest some ways for you to expand it sometime. A few pointers from an old pro might help."

He had to turn from her astonished and grateful smile—it was like a child's. He said carefully, "The only problem will be to find a place where we can talk quietly. Regrettably, I don't rate an office. . . ."

"Perhaps we could use one of the empty classrooms," she said.

"That would be much too dismal a setting for a pleasant discussion."

He watched the disappointment wilt her smile and when he spoke he made certain that the same disappointment weighed his voice. "Another difficulty is that the term's half over, which gives us little or no time. But let's not give up. Perhaps we can arrange to meet and talk over a weekend. The only hitch there is that I spend weekends at my place in the country. Of course you're perfectly welcome to come up there. It's only about seventy miles from New York, in the heart of what's very appropriately called the Borsch Circuit, even though, thank God, my place is a good distance away from the borsch. That is, it's very quiet and there's never anybody around except with my permission."

She did not move, yet she seemed to start; she made no sound, yet he thought he heard a bewildered cry. And then she did a strange thing, standing there with the breath sucked into the hollow of her throat and her smile, that had opened to him with such trust, drying—her eyes, her hands faltering up begged him to declare himself.

"There's a lake near the house," he said, "so that when you get tired of talking—or better, listening to me talk—you can take a swim, if you like. I would very much enjoy that sight." And as the nerve tugged at his eyelid, he seemed to wink behind his rimless glasses.

Her sudden, blind step back was like a man groping his away through a strange room in the dark, and instinctively Max Berman reached out to break her fall. Her arms, bare to the shoulder because of the heat (he knew the feel of her skin without even touching it—it would be like a rich, fine-textured cloth which would soothe and hide him in its amber warmth), struck out once to drive him off and then fell limp at her side, and her eyes became vivid and convulsive in her numbed face. She strained toward the stairs and the exit door at the bottom, but she could not move. Nor could she speak. She did not even cry. Her eyes remained dry and dull with disbelief. Only her shoulders trembled as though she was silently weeping inside.

It was as though she had never learned the forms and expressions of anger. The outrage of a lifetime, of her history, was trapped inside her. And she stared at Max Berman with this mute, paralyzing rage. Not really at him but to his side, as if she caught sight of others behind him. And remembering how he had imagined a column of dark women trailing her to his desk, he sensed that she glimpsed a legion of old men with sere flesh and lonely eyes flanking him: "old lechers with a love on every wind . . ."

"I'm sorry, Miss Williams," he said, and would have welcomed her insults, for he would have been able, at least, to distill from them some passion and a kind of intimacy. It would have been, in a way, like touching her. "It was only that you are a very attractive young woman and although I'm no longer young"—and he gave the tragic little laugh which sought to dismiss that fact—"I can still appreciate and even desire an attractive woman. But I was wrong. . . ." His self-disgust, overwhelming him finally, choked off his voice. "And so very crude. Forgive me. I can offer no excuse for my behavior other than my approaching senility."

He could not even manage the little marionette bow this time. Quickly he shoved the paper on Gide into her lifeless hand, but it fell, the pages separating, and as he hurried past her downstairs and out the door, he heard the pages scattering like dead leaves on the steps.

She remained away until the night of the final examination, which was also the last meeting of the class. By that time Max Berman, believing that she would not return, had almost succeeded in forgetting her. He was no longer even certain of how she looked, for her face had been absorbed into the single, blurred, featureless face of all the women who had ever refused him. So that she startled him as much as a stranger would have when he entered the room that night and found her alone amid a maze of empty chairs, her face turned toward the window as on the first night and her hands serene in her lap. She turned at his footstep and it was as if she had also forgotten all that had passed between them. She waited until he said, "I'm glad you decided to take the examination. I'm sure you won't have any difficulty with it"; then she gave him a nod that was somehow reminiscent of his little bow and turned again to the window.

He was relieved yet puzzled by her composure. It was as if during her three-week absence she had waged and won a decisive contest with herself and was ready not to act. He was wary suddenly and all during the examination he tried to discover what lay behind her strange calm, studying her bent head amid the shifting heads of the other students, her slim hand guiding the pen across the page, her legs—the long bone visible, it seemed, beneath the flesh. Desire flared and quickly died.

"Excuse me, Professor Berman, will you take up Camus and Sartre next semester, maybe?" The girl who sat in front of his desk was standing over him with her earnest smile and finished examination folder.

"That might prove somewhat difficult, since I won't be here."

"No more?"

"No."

"I mean, not even next summer?"

"I doubt it."

"Gee, I'm sorry. I mean, I enjoyed the course and everything."

He bowed his thanks and held his head down until she left. Her compliment, so piteous somehow, brought on the despair he had forced to the dim rear of his mind. He could no longer flee the thought of the exile awaiting him when the class tonight ended. He could either remain in the house in Brooklyn, where the memory of his father's face above the radiance of the Sabbath candles haunted him from the shadows, reminding him of the certainty he had lost and never found again, where the mirrors in his father's room were still shrouded with sheets, as on the day he lay dying and moaning into his beard that his only son was a bad Jew; or he could return to the house in the country, to the silence shrill with loneliness.

The cigarette he was smoking burned his fingers, rousing him, and he saw over the pile of examination folders on his desk that the room was empty except for the Negro girl. She had finished—her pen lay aslant the closed folder on her desk—but she had remained in her seat and she was smiling across the room at him—a set, artificial smile that was both cold and threatening. It utterly denuded him and he was wildly angry suddenly that she had seen him give way to despair; he wanted to remind her (he could not stay the thought; it attacked him like an assailant from a dark turn in his mind) that she was only black after all. . . . His head dropped and he almost wept with shame.

The girl stiffened as if she had seen the thought and then the tiny muscles around her mouth quickly arranged the bland smile. She came up to his desk, placed her folder on top of the others and said pleasantly, her eyes like dark, shattered glass that spared Max Berman his reflection, "I've changed my mind. I think I'd like to spend a day at your place in the country if your invitation still holds."

He thought of refusing her, for her voice held neither promise nor passion, but he could not. Her presence, even if it was only for a day, would make his return easier. And there was still the possibility of passion despite her cold manner and the deliberate smile. He thought of how long it had been since he had had someone, of how badly he needed the sleep which followed love and of awakening certain, for the first time in years, of his existence.

"Of course the invitation still holds. I'm driving up tonight."

"I won't be able to come until Sunday," she said firmly. "Is there a train then?"

"Yes, in the morning," he said, and gave her the schedule. "You'll meet me at the station?"

"Of course. You can't miss my car. It's a very shabby but venerable Chevy."

She smiled stiffly and left, her heels awakening the silence of the empty corridor, the sound reaching back to tap like a warning finger on Max Berman's temple.

The pale sunlight slanting through the windshield lay like a cat on his knees, and the motor of his old Chevy, turning softly under him could have been the humming of its heart. A little distance from the car a log-cabin station house—the logs blackened by the seasons—stood alone against the hills, and the hills, in turn, lifted softly, still green although the summer was ending, into the vague autumn sky.

The morning mist and pale sun, the green that was still somehow new, made it seem that the season was stirring into life even as it died, and this contradiction pained Max Berman at the same time that it pleased him. For it was his own contradiction after all: his desires which remained those of a young man even as he was dying.

He had been parked for some time in the deserted station, yet his hands were still tensed on the steering wheel and his foot hovered near the accelerator. As soon as he had arrived in the station he had wanted to leave. But like the girl that night on the landing, he was too stiff with tension to move. He could only wait, his eyelid twitching with foreboding, regret, curiosity and hope.

Finally and with no warning the train charged through the fiery green, setting off a tremor underground. Max Berman imagined the girl seated at a window in the train, her hands arranged quietly in her lap and her gaze scanning the hills that were so familiar to him, and yet he could not believe that she was really there. Perhaps her plan had been to disappoint him. She might be in New York or on her way back to Richmond now, laughing at the trick she had played on him. He was convinced of this suddenly, so that even when he saw her walking toward him through the blown steam from under the train, he told himself that she was a mirage created by the steam. Only when she sat beside him in the car, bringing with her, it seemed, an essence she had distilled from the morning air and rubbed into her skin, was he certain of her reality.

"I brought my bathing suit but it's much too cold to swim," she said and gave him the deliberate smile.

He did not see it; he only heard her voice, its warm Southern lilt in the chill, its intimacy in the closed car—and an excitement swept him, cold first and then hot, as if the sun had burst in his blood.

"It's the morning air," he said. "By noon it should be like summer again."

"Is that a promise?"

"Yes."

By noon the cold morning mist had lifted above the hills and below, in the lake valley, the sunlight was a sheer gold net spread out on the grass as if to dry, draped on the trees and flung, glinting, over the lake. Max Berman felt it brush his shoulders gently as he sat by the lake waiting for the girl, who had gone up to the house to change into her swimsuit.

He had spent the morning showing her the fields and small wood near his house. During the long walk he had been careful to keep a little apart from her. He would extend a hand as they climbed a rise or when she stepped uncertainly over a rock, but he would not really touch her. He was afraid that at his touch, no matter how slight and casual, her scream would spiral into the morning calm, or worse, his touch would unleash the threatening thing he sensed behind her even smile.

He had talked of her paper and she had listened politely and occasionally even asked a question or made a comment. But all the while detached, distant, drawn within herself as she had been that first night in the classroom. And then halfway down a slope she had paused and, pointing to the canvas tops of her white sneakers, which had become wet and dark from the dew secreted in the grass, she had laughed. The sound, coming so abruptly in the midst of her tense quiet, joined her, it seemed, to the wood and wide fields, to the hills; she shared their simplicity and held within her the same strong current of life. Max Berman had felt privileged suddenly, and humble. He had stopped questioning her smile. He had told himself then that it would not matter even if she stopped and picking up a rock bludgeoned him from behind.

"There's a lake near my home, but it's not like this," the girl said, coming up behind him. "Yours is so dark and serious-looking."

He nodded and followed her gaze out to the lake, where the ripples were long, smooth welts raised by the wind, and across to the other bank, where a group of birches stepped delicately down to the lake and bending over touched the water with their branches as if testing it before they plunged.

The girl came and stood beside him now—and she was like a pale-gold naiad, the spirit of the lake, her eyes reflecting its somber autumnal tone and her body as supple as the birches. She walked slowly into the water, unaware, it seemed, of the sudden passion in his gaze, or perhaps uncaring; and as she walked she held out her arms in what seemed a gesture of invocation (and Max Berman remembered his father with the fringed shawl draped on his outstretched arms as he invoked their God each Sabbath with the same gesture); her head was bent as if she listened for a voice beneath the water's murmurous surface. When the ground gave way she still seemed to be walking and listening, her arms outstretched. The water reached her waist, her small breasts, her shoulders. She lifted her head once, breathed deeply and disappeared.

She stayed down for a long time and when her white cap finally broke the water some distance out, Max Berman felt strangely stranded and deprived. He understood suddenly the profound cleavage between them and the absurdity of his hope. The water between them became the years which separated them. Her white cap was the sign of her purity, while the silt darkening the lake was the flotsam of his failures. Above all, their color—her arms a pale, flashing gold in the sunlit water and his bled white and flaccid with the veins like angry blue penciling—marked the final barrier.

He was sad as they climbed toward the house late that afternoon and troubled. A crow cawed derisively in the bracken, heralding the dusk which would not only end their strange day but would also, he felt, unveil her smile, so that he would learn the reason for her coming. And because he was sad, he said wryly, "I think I should tell you that you've been spending the day with something of an outcast."

"Oh," she said and waited.

He told her of the dismissal, punctuating his words with the little hoarse, deprecating laugh and waving aside the pain with his cigarette. She listened, polite but neutral, and because she remained unmoved, he wanted to confess all the more. So that during dinner and afterward when they sat outside on the porch, he told her of the investigation.

"It was very funny once you saw it from the proper perspective, which I did, of course," he said. "I mean here they were accusing me of crimes I couldn't remember committing and asking me for the names of people with whom I had never associated. It was pure farce. But I made a mistake. I should have done something dramatic or something just as farcical. Bared my breast in the public market place or written a tome on my apostasy, naming names. It would have been a far different story then. Instead of my present ignominy I would have been offered a chairmanship at Yale. . . . No? Well, Brandeis then. I would have been draped in honorary degrees. . . ."

"Well, why didn't you confess?" she said impatiently.

"I've often asked myself the same interesting question, but I haven't come up with a satisfactory answer yet. I suspect, though, that I said nothing because none of it really mattered that much."

"What did matter?" she asked sharply.

He sat back, waiting for the witty answer, but none came, because just then the frame upon which his organs were strung seemed to snap and he felt his heart, his lungs, his vital parts fall in a heap within him. Her question had dealt the severing blow, for it was the same question he understood suddenly that the vague forms in his dream asked repeatedly. It had been the plaintive undercurrent to his father's dying moan, the real accusation behind the charges of his inquisitors at the hearing.

For what had mattered? He gazed through his sudden shock at the night squatting on the porch steps, at the hills asleep like gentle beasts in the darkness, at the black screen of the sky where the events of his life passed in a mute, accusing review—and he saw nothing there to which he had given himself or in which he had truly believed since the belief and dedication of his boyhood.

"Did you hear my question?" she asked, and he was glad that he sat within the shadows clinging to the porch screen and could not be seen.

"Yes, I did," he said faintly, and his eyelid twitched. "But I'm afraid it's another one of those I can't answer satisfactorily." And then he struggled for the old flippancy. "You make an excellent examiner, you know. Far better than my inquisitors."

"What will you do now?" Her voice and cold smile did not spare him.

He shrugged and the motion, a slow, eloquent lifting of the shoulders, brought with it suddenly the weight and memory of his boyhood. It was the familiar gesture of the women hawkers in Belmont Market, of the men standing outside the temple on Saturday mornings, each of them reflecting his image of God in their forbidding black coats and with the black, tumbling beards in which he had always imagined he could hide as in a forest. All this had mattered, he called loudly to himself, and said aloud to the girl, "Let me see if I can answer this one at least. What *will* I do?" He paused and swung his leg so that his foot in the fastidious French shoe caught the light from the house. "Grow flowers and write my memoirs. How's that? That would be the proper way for a gentleman and scholar to retire. Or hire one of those hefty housekeepers who will bully me and when I die in my sleep draw the sheet over my face and call my lawyer. That's somewhat European, but how's that?"

When she nothing for a long time, he added soberly, "But that's not a fair question for me any more. I leave all such considerations to the young. To you, for that matter. What will you do, my dear Miss Williams?"

It was as if she had been expecting the question and had been readying her answer all the time that he had been talking.

She leaned forward eagerly and with her face and part of her body full in the light, she said, "I will do something. I don't know what yet, but something."

Max Berman started back a little. The answer was so unlike her vague, resigned "I know" on the landing that night when he had admonished her to try something new.

He edged back into the darkness and she leaned further into the light, her eyes overwhelming her face and her mouth set in a thin, determined line. "I will do something," she said, bearing down on each word, "because for the first time in my life I feel almost brave."

He glimpsed this new bravery behind her hard gaze and sensed something vital and purposeful, precious, which she had found and guarded like a prize within her center. He wanted it. He would have liked to snatch it and run like a thief. He no longer desired her but it, and starting forward with a sudden envious cry, he caught her arm and drew her close, seeking it.

But he could not get to it. Although she did not pull away her arm, although she made no protest as his face wavered close to hers, he did not really touch her. She held herself and her prize out of his desperate reach and her smile was a knife she pressed to his throat. He saw himself for what he was in her clear, cold gaze: an old man with skin the color and texture of dough that had been kneaded by the years into tragic folds, with faded eyes adrift behind a pair of rimless glasses and the roughened flesh at his throat like a bird's wattles. And as the disgust which he read in her eyes swept him, his hand dropped from her arm. He started to murmur, "Forgive me . . ." when suddenly she caught hold of his wrist, pulling him close again, and he felt the strength which had borne her swiftly through the water earlier hold him now as she said quietly and without passion, "And do you know why, Dr. Berman, I feel almost brave today? Because ever since I can remember my parents were always telling me, 'Stay away from white folks. Just leave them alone. You mind your business and they'll mind theirs. Don't go near them.' And they made sure I didn't. My father, who was the principal of a colored grade school in Richmond, used to drive me to and from school every day. When I needed something from downtown my mother would take me and if the white saleslady asked me anything she would answer. . . ."

"And my parents were also always telling me, 'Stay away from niggers,' and that meant anybody darker than we were." She held out her arm in the light and Max Berman saw the skin almost as white as his but for the subtle amber shading. Staring at the arm she said tragically, "I was so confused I never really went near anybody. Even when I went away to college I kept to myself. I didn't marry the man I wanted to because he was dark and I knew my parents would disapprove. . . ." She paused, her wistful gaze searching the darkness for the face of the man she had refused, it seemed, and not finding it she went on sadly, "So after graduation I returned home and started teaching and I was just as confused and frightened and ashamed as always. When my parents died I went on the same way. And I would have gone on like that the rest of my life if it hadn't been for you, Dr. Berman"—and the sarcasm leaped behind her cold smile. "In a way you did me a favor. You let me know how you—and most of the people like you—see me."

"My dear Miss Williams, I assure you I was not attracted to you because you were colored. . . ." And he broke off, remembering just how acutely aware of her color he had been.

"I'm not interested in your reasons!" she said brutally. "What matters is what it meant to me. I thought about this these last three weeks and about my parents—how wrong they had been, how frightened, and the terrible thing they had done to me . . . And I wasn't confused any longer." Her head lifted, tremulous with her new assurance. "I can do something now! I can begin," she said with her head poised. "Look how I came all the way up here to tell you this to your face. Because how could you harm me? You're so old you're like a cup I could break in my hand." And her hand tightened on his wrist, wrenching the last of his frail life from him, it seemed. Through the quick pain he remembered her saying on the landing that night: "Maybe in order for a person to live someone else must die" and her quiet "I believe this" then. Now her sudden laugh, an infinitely cruel sound in the warm night, confirmed her belief.

Suddenly she was the one who seemed old, indeed ageless. Her touch became mortal and Max Berman saw the darkness that would end his life gathered in her eyes. But even as he sprang back, jerking his arm away, a part of him rushed forward to embrace that darkness, and his cry, wounding the night, held both ecstasy and terror.

"That's all I came for," she said, rising. "You can drive me to the station now."

They drove to the station in silence. Then, just as the girl started from the car, she turned with an ironic, pitiless smile and said, "You know, it's been a nice day, all things considered. It really turned summer again as you said it would. And even though your lake isn't anything like the one near my home, it's almost as nice."

Max Berman bowed to her for the last time, accepting with that gesture his responsibility for her rage, which went deeper than his, and for her anger, which would spur her finally to live. And not only for her, but for all those at last whom he had wronged through his indifference: his father lying in the room of shrouded mirrors, the wives he had never loved, his work which he had never believed in enough and, lastly (even though he knew it was too late and he would not be spared), himself.

Too weary to move, he watched the girl cross to the train which would bear her south, her head lifted as though she carried life as lightly there as if it were a hat made of tulle. When the train departed his numbed eyes followed it until its rear light was like a single firefly in the immense night or the last flickering of his life. Then he drove back through the darkness.

Kristin Hunter (b. 1931)

Kristin Hunter writes for both adults and young adults. In 1964, she published the popular *God Bless the Child.* Her young adult book, *The Soul Brothers and Sister Lou* (1968), sold over a million copies and won the Council on Interracial Book Children's Award. *Guests in the Promised Land* won the Christopher Award in 1975 and was a National Book Award finalist. Hunter was born in Philadelphia and while still young did a column and some feature writing for *The Pittsburgh Courier.* Both of her parents were teachers, and her father pressured her into teaching. After receiving a B.S. in education from the University of Pennsylvania, she took a job as a third-grade teacher but quit mid-year because she wanted to become a writer. Winning the CBS television documentary competition for *Minority of One* in 1955 helped to place her in the public's eye.

From *Guests in the Promised Land*

Mom Luby and the Social Worker

Puddin' and I been livin' with Mom Luby three years, ever since our mother died. We like it fine. But when Mom Luby took us down to the Welfare, we thought our happy days were over and our troubles about to begin.

"Chirren," she said that day, "I got to get some of this State Aid so I can give you everything you need. Shoes for you, Elijah, and dresses for Puddin' now she's startin' school. And lunch money and carfare and stuff like that. But the only way I can get it is to say I'm your mother. So don't mess up my lie."

Mom Luby is old as Santa Claus, maybe older, with hair like white cotton and false teeth that hurt so much she takes them out and gums her food. But she's strong as a young woman and twice as proud. Much too proud to say she's our grandmother, which is something the Welfare people might believe.

So we went down there scared that morning, Puddin' holding tight onto both our hands. But we was lucky. The lady behind the desk didn't even look at us, and we got out of that gloomy old State Building safe and free. Man! Was I glad to get back to Division Street where people don't ask questions about your business.

When we got home, a whole bunch of people was waiting for Mom to let them in the speakeasy she runs in the back room. Jake was there, and Sissiemae, and Bobo and Walter and Lucas and Mose and Zerline. They are regular customers who come every evening to drink the corn liquor Mom gets from down South and eat the food she fixes, gumbo and chicken wings and ribs and potato salad and greens.

Bobo picked Puddin' up to see how much she weighed (a lot), until she hollered to be let down. Jake gave me a quarter to take his shoes down to Gumby's Fantastic Shoe Shine Parlor and get them shined and keep the change. We let the people in the front door and through the red curtain that divides the front room from the back. Soon they were settled around the big old round table with a half-gallon jar of corn. Then Sissiemae and Lucas wanted chicken wings, and I had to collect the money while Mom heated them up on the stove. There was so much to do, I didn't pay no attention to the tapping on the front door.

But then it came again, louder, like a woodpecker working on a tree.

"Elijah," Mom says, "run see who it is trying to chip a hole in that door. If it be the police, tell them I'll see them Saturday,"

But it wasn't the cops, who come around every Saturday night to get their money and drink some of Mom's corn and put their big black shoes up on the table. It was a little brownskin lady with straightened hair and glasses and black high-top shoes. She carried a big leather envelope and was dressed all in dark blue.

"Good afternoon," she says. "I am Miss Rushmore of the Department of Child Welfare, Bureau of Family Assistance. Is Mrs. Luby at home?"

"I am she," says Mom. "Never been nobody else. Come in, honey, and set yourself down. Take off them shoes, they do look like real corn-crushers to me."

"No thank you," says Miss Rushmore. She sits on the edge of one of Mom's chairs and starts pulling papers out of the envelope. "This must be Elijah."

"Yes ma'am," I say.

"And where is Arlethia?"

"Taking her nap," says Mom, with a swat of the broom at the middle of the curtain, which Puddin' was peeking through. She's five and fat, and she loves to hang around grownups. Especially when they eating.

Mom hit the curtain with the broom again, and Puddin' ran off. The lady didn't even notice. She was too busy peeking under the lids of the pots on the stove.

"Salt pork and lima beans," she says. "Hardly a proper diet for growing children."

"Well," says Mom, "when I get me some of this State Aid, maybe I can afford to get them canned vegetables and box cereal. Meanwhile you welcome to what we have."

The lady acted like she didn't hear that. She just wrinkled up her nose like she smelled something bad.

"First," she says, "we must have a little talk about your budget. Do you understand the importance of financial planning?"

"Man arranges and God changes," says Mom. "When I got it, I spends it, when I don't I do without."

"That," says the lady, "is precisely the attitude I am here to correct." She pulls out a big yellow sheet of paper. "Now this is our Family Budget Work Sheet. What is your rent?"

"I ain't paid it in so long I forgot," Mom says. Which set me in a fit because everybody but this dumb lady knows Mom owns the house. Behind her back Mom gave me a whack that stopped my giggles.

The lady sighed. "We'll get to the budget later," she says. "First, there are some questions you left blank today. How old were you when Elijah was born?"

"Thirty-two," says Mom.

"And he is now thirteen, which would make you forty-five," says the lady.

"Thirty-eight," says Mom without batting an eye.

"I'll put down forty-five," says the lady, giving Mom a funny look. "No doubt your hard life has aged you beyond your years. Now, who is the father, and where is he?"

"Lemme see," says Mom, twisting a piece of her hair. "I ain't seen Mr. Luby since 1942. He was a railroad man, you see, and one time he just took a train out of here and never rode back."

"1942," Miss Rushmore wrote on the paper. And then said, "But that's impossible!"

"The dear Lord do teach us," says Mom, "that nothing in life is impossible if we just believe enough."

"Hey, Mom, we're out of corn!" cries Lucas from the back room.

Miss Rushmore looked very upset. "Why," she says, "you've got a man in there."

"Sure do sound like it, don't it?" Mom says. "Sure do. You got one too, honey?"

"That's my business," says the lady.

"I was just trying to be sociable," says Mom pleasantly. "You sure do seem interested in mine."

I ran back there and fetched another mason jar of corn from the shed kitchen. I told Lucas and Bobo and them to be quiet. Which wasn't going to be easy, cause them folks get good and loud when they get in a card game. I also dragged Puddin' away from the potato salad bowl, where she had stuck both her hands, and brought her in the front room with me. She was bawling. The lady gave her a weak smile.

"Now," Mom says. "About these shoes and school clothes."

"I am not sure," Miss Rushmore says, "that you can get them. There is something wrong in this house that I have not yet put my finger on. But this is what you do. First you fill out Form 905, which you get at the Bureau of Family Assistance, room 1203. Then you call the Division of Child Welfare and make an appointment with Mr. Jenkins. He will give you Form 202 to fill out. Then you go to the fifth floor, third corridor on the left, turn right, go in the second door. You stand at the first desk and fill out Form 23-B, Requisition for Clothing Allowance. You take *that* to Building Three, room 508, third floor, second door, fourth desk and then—"

"Lord," Mom says, "By the time we get clothes for these chirren, they will have done outgrowed them."

"I don't make the rules," the lady says.

"Well, honey," says Mom, "I ain't got time to do all that, not right now. Tonight I got to go deliver a baby. Then I got to visit a sick old lady and work on her with some herbs. Then I got to go down to the courthouse and get a young man out of jail. He's not a bad boy, he's just been keepin' bad company. *Then* I got to preach a funeral."

The lady looked at Mom like she was seeing a spirit risen from the dead. "But you can't do those things!" she says.

But I happen to know Mom Luby *can*. She's a midwife and a herb doctor and an ordained minister of the Gospel, besides running a place to eat and drink after hours. And she wouldn't need Welfare for us if people would only pay her sometimes.

Mom says, "Honey, just come along and watch me." She picked up her old shopping bag full of herbs and stuff. Miss Rushmore picked up her case and followed like somebody in a trance. Mom has that effect on people sometimes.

They were gone about two hours, and me and Puddin' had a good time eating and joking and looking into everybody's card hands.

I was surprised to see Mom bring Miss Rushmore straight into the back room when they got back. She sat her down at the table and poured her a drink of corn. To tell the truth, that lady looked like she needed it. Her glasses was crooked, and her shoes were untied, and her hair had come loose from its pins. She looked kind of pretty, but lost.

"Mrs. Luby," she said after a swallow of corn, "you don't need my help."

"Ain't it the truth," says Mom.

"I came here to help you solve your problems. But now I don't know where to begin."

"What problems?" Mom asks.

"You are raising these children in an unhealthy atmosphere. I am not even sure they are yours. And you are practicing law, medicine, and the ministry without a license. I simply can't understand it."

"Can't understand what, honey?"

The lady sighed. "How you got more done in two hours than I ever get done in two years."

"You folks oughta put me on the payroll," says Mom with a chuckle.

"We can't," says Miss Rushmore. "You're not qualified."

Lucas started laughing, and Bobo joined in, and then we all laughed, Mose and Zerline and Jake and Sissiemae and Puddin' and me. We laughed so hard we rocked the room and shook the house and laughed that social worker right out the door.

"She got a point though," Mom says after we finished laughing. "You need an education to fill out forty pieces of paper for one pair of shoes. Never you mind, chirren. We'll make out fine, like we always done. Cut the cards, Bobo. Walter, deal."

Sonia Sanchez (b. 1934)

Known for their energizing, performative styles, poets of the Black Arts Movement won the hearts of many people. One such poet whose popularity has continued is Sonia Sanchez. A strong voice for freedom, Sanchez has written many volumes of poetry. Her titles reflect the odyssey of a black woman responding to her community during a time of revolution and struggle: *Homecoming* (1969), *We a Baddddd People* (1970), *It's a New Day: Poems for Young Brothas and Sisthus* (1971), *Love Poems* (1973), *A Blues Book for Blue Black Magical Women* (1973), *I've Been a Woman* (1978), *homegirls & handgrenades* (1984), and *Under a Soprano Sky* (1987). More recently, she has published *Does Your House Have Lions?*—a tribute to her brother who died of AIDS—and *like the singing coming off the drums*—a volume about the many forms that love takes.

Holder of the Laura Carnell Professor of English and Women's Studies at Temple University, Sanchez was born in Birmingham, Alabama, and in 1955 received a B.A. degree from Hunter College. In the mid 1960s, she was very active in the movement to add black studies to the curriculum at San Francisco State College. Since those days, she has continued her interest in curriculum building, teaching at various colleges. She has also been committed to writing for children, as demonstrated by several collections, including *The Adventures of Small Head, Square Head and Fathead* (1973).

Homecoming

i have been a
way so long
once after college
i returned tourist
style to watch all
the niggers killing
themselves with
3 for oners
with
needles
that
cd
not support
their
stutters.
       now woman
i have returned
leaving behind me
all those hide and
seek faces peeling
with freudian dreams.

this is for real.
             black
      niggers
               my beauty.
baby.
i have learned it
ain't like they say
in the newspapers.

Poem at Thirty

it is midnight
no magical bewitching
hour for me
i know only that
i am here waiting
remembering that
once as a child
i walked two
miles in my sleep.
did i know
then where i
was going?
traveling. i'm
always traveling.
i want to tell

you about me
about nights on a
brown couch when
i wrapped my
bones in lint and
refused to move.
no one touches
me anymore.
father do not
send me out
among strangers.
you you black man
stretching scraping
the mold from your body.
here is my hand.
i am not afraid
of the night.

The Final Solution/

the leaders speak

america.
            land of free/
                        dom
land of im/mi/grant
                        wh/ites
            and slave/
                        blacks. there is
no real problem here.
                        we the
lead/ers of free
                        a/mer/ica
say. gives us your
            hungry/
                        illiterates/
                                    criminals/
                                                dropouts/
            (in other words)
                        your blacks
                                    and we will
let them fight
            in vietnam
                        defending america's honor.
we will make responsible
            citi/
                        zens out of them or
                                    kill them trying.

america
            land of free/dom
            free/
                        enter/
                                    prise and   de/mo/
                                                                        cracy.
bring us your problems.
                                    we your lead/ers
always find a solution.
                                    after all
what else are
            we get/
                        ting pd for?

For Our Lady

yeh.
            billie.   if someone
had loved u like u
shud have been loved
ain't no tellin what
kinds of songs
                        u wud have swung
gainst this country's wite mind.
or what kinds of lyrics
                        wud have pushed us from
our blue / nites.
                        yeh.   billie.
if some blk / man
                        had reallee
made u feel
            permanentlee warm.
ain't no tellen
                        where the jazz of yo / songs.
                        wud have led us.

Summer Words of
a Sistuh Addict

the first day i shot dope
was on a sunday.
                        i had just come
home from church
                        got mad at my motha

cuz she got mad at me. u dig?
                went out. shot up
behind a feelen against her.
                   it felt good.
gooder than dooing it. yeah.
                 it was nice.
i did it. uh huh. i did it.   uh. huh.
i want to do it again. it felt so gooooood.
          and as the sistuh
          sits in her silent /
          remembered / high
          someone leans for

ward gently asks her:
      sistuh.
      did u
      finally
      learn how to hold yo / mother?
and the music of the day
               drifts in the room
to mingle with the sistuh's young tears.
     and we all sing.

June Jordan (1936–2002)

Like Paule Marshall, June Jordan grew up in a brownstone in Brooklyn to immigrant West Indian parents. The only child of Granville Ivanhoe and Mildred Maud Jordan, she attended a predominately white girls' preparatory school before entering Barnard College in 1953. Jordan taught at a number of colleges, including City University of New York, Connecticut College, Sarah Lawrence, State University of New York, and Berkeley. She also directed the Search for Education, Elevation, and Knowledge (SEEK) program. Jordan wrote in a number of genres, including poetry volumes such as *Some Changes* (1971), *Living Room* (1985), *Naming our Destiny* (1989); children's literature, such as *His Own Where* (1971), *New Room: New Life* (1975); plays; and essay collections. In *Civil Wars* (1981), Jordan recounts the time of her life when interracial marriage was still a felony in forty-three states—a time when she had a white husband and a two-year-old child. The book is a commentary on the years 1964 to 1980 when Jordan states that her goal was to "be free to be who I am, Black and female, without fear, without pain, without humiliation."

Independence Day in the U.S.A.

I wanted to tell you about July 4th
in northamerica and the lights computerized
shrapnel in white
or red or fast-fuse blue
to celebrate the only revolution
that was legitimate
in human history

I wanted to tell you about the baby
screaming this afternoon where the park
and the music of thousands who eat
food and stay hungry or homicidal
on the subways or the windowsills of the city
came together loud
like the original cannon shots
from that only legitimate revolution
in human history

I wanted to tell you about my Spanish
how it starts like a word aggravating the beat
of my heart then rushes up to my head
where my eyes dream Carribean
flowers and my mouth waters
around black beans
or coffee that lets me forget
the hours before morning

But I am living inside the outcome
of the only legitimate revolution
in human history
and the operator will not place my call to Cuba
the mailman will not carry my letters to Managua
the State Department will not okay my visa
for a short-wave conversation
and you do not speak English

and I can dig it

Song of the Law Abiding Citizen

so hot so hot so hot so what
so hot so what so hot so hot

They made a mistake
I got more than I usually take
I got food stamps food stamps I got
so many stamps in the mail
I thought maybe I should put them on sale
How lucky I am
I got food stamps: Hot damn!
I made up my mind
to be decent and kind
to let my upright character shine

I sent 10,000 food stamps
back to the President (and his beautiful wife)
and I can't pay the rent
but I sent 10,000 food stamps
back to the President (and his beautiful wife)
how lucky I am
hot damn
They made a mistake
for Chrissake
And I gave it away to the President
I thought that was legal I thought that was kind
and I can't pay the rent
but I sent 10,000 food stamps
back back back to the President
so hot so hot so hot so what
so hot so what so hot so hot

Trucks cruisin' down the avenue
carrying nuclear garbage right next to you
and it's legal
it's radioaction ridin' like a regal
load of jewels
past the bars the cruel
school house and the church and if
the trucks wipeout or crash
or even lurch too hard around a corner
we will just be goners
and it's legal
it's radioaction ridin' regal
through the skittery city street
and don't be jittery
because it's legal
radioaction ridin' the road

Avenue A Avenue B Avenue C Avenue D
Avenue of the Americas

so hot so hot so hot so what
so hot so what so hot so hot
so hot so hot so hot so what

Poem about My Rights

Even tonight and I need to take a walk and clear
my head about this poem about why I can't

go out without changing my clothes my shoes
my body posture my gender identity my age
my status as a woman alone in the evening/
alone on the streets/alone not being the point/
the point being that I can't do what I want
to do with my own body because I am the wrong
sex the wrong age the wrong skin and
suppose it was not here in the city but down on the beach/
or far into the woods and I wanted to go
there by myself thinking about God/or thinking
about children or thinking about the world/all of it
disclosed by the stars and the silence:
I could not go and I could not think and I could not
stay there
alone
as I need to be
alone because I can't do what I want to do with my own
body and
who in the hell set things up
like this
and in France they say if the guy penetrates
but does not ejaculate then he did not rape me
and if after stabbing him if after screams if
after begging the bastard and if even after smashing
a hammer to his head if even after that if he
and his buddies fuck me after that
then I consented and there was
no rape because finally you understand finally
they fucked me over because I was wrong I was
wrong again to be me being me where I was/wrong
to be who I am
which is exactly like South Africa
penetrating into Namibia penetrating into
Angola and does that mean I mean how do you know if
Pretoria ejaculates what will the evidence look like the
proof of the monster jackboot ejaculation on Blackland
and if
after Namibia and if after Angola and if after Zimbabwe
and if after all of my kinsmen and women resist even to
self-immolation of the villages and if after that
we lose nevertheless what will the big boys say will they
claim my consent:
Do You Follow Me: We are the wrong people of
the wrong skin on the wrong continent and what
in the hell is everybody being reasonable about
and according to the *Times* this week
back in 1966 the C.I.A. decided that they had this
   problem
and the problem was a man named Nkrumah so they
killed him and before that it was Patrice Lumumba
and before that it was my father on the campus

of my Ivy League school and my father afraid
to walk into the cafeteria because he said he
was wrong the wrong age the wrong skin the wrong
gender identity and he was paying my tuition and
before that
it was my father saying I was wrong saying that
I should have been a boy because he wanted one/a
boy and that I should have been lighter skinned and
that I should have had straighter hair and that
I should not be so boy crazy but instead I should
just be one/a boy and before that
it was my mother pleading plastic surgery for
my nose and braces for my teeth and telling me
to let the books loose to let them loose in other
words
I am very familiar with the problems of the C.I.A.
and the problems of South Africa and the problems
of Exxon Corporation and the problems of white
America in general and the problems of the teachers
and the preachers and the F.B.I. and the social
workers and my particular Mom and Dad/I am very
familiar with the problems because the problems
turn out to be
me
I am the history of rape
I am the history of the rejection of who I am
I am the history of the terrorized incarceration of
my self
I am the history of battery assault and limitless
armies against whatever I want to do with my mind
and my body and my soul and
whether it's about walking out at night
or whether it's about the love that I feel or
whether it's about the sanctity of my vagina or
the sanctity of my national boundaries
or the sanctity of my leaders or the sanctity
of each and every desire
that I know from my personal and idiosyncratic
and indisputably single and singular heart
I have been raped
be-
cause I have been wrong the wrong sex the wrong age
the wrong skin the wrong nose the wrong hair the
wrong need the wrong dream the wrong geographic
the wrong sartorial I
I have been the meaning of rape
I have been the problem everyone seeks to
eliminate by forced
penetration with or without the evidence of slime and/
but let this be unmistakable this poem
is not consent I do not consent

to my mother to my father to the teachers to
the F.B.I. to South Africa to Bedford-Stuy
to Park Avenue to American Airlines to the hardon
idlers on the corners to the sneaky creeps in
cars
I am not wrong: Wrong is not my name
My name is my own my own my own
and I can't tell you who the hell set things up like this
but I can tell you that from now on my resistance
my simple and daily and nightly self-determination
may very well cost you your life

Poem for Guatemala

Dedicated to Rigoberto Manchú
(With thanks to *Journey to the Depths*, the testimony of Rigoberto Manchú
translated into English by Patricia Goedicke, October, 1982)

No matter how loudly I call you the sound of your name
makes the day soft
Nothing about it sticks to my throat
Guatemala
syllables that lilt into twilight and lust
Guatemala
syllables to melt bullets

They call you Indian
They called me West Indian
You learned to speak Spanish when I did
We were thirteen
I wore shoes
I ate rice and peas
The beans and the rice in your pot
brought the soldiers
to hack off your arms

"Walk like that into the kitchen!
Walk like that into the clearing!
Girl with no arms!"

I had been playing the piano

Because of the beans and the rice in your pot
the soldiers arrived with an axe
to claim you guerilla
girl with no arms

An Indian is not supposed to own a pot of food
An Indian is too crude

An Indian covers herself with dirt so the cold
times will not hurt her

Cover yourself with no arms!

They buried my mother in New Jersey.
Black cars carried her there.
She wore flowers and a long dress.

Soldiers pushed into your mother
and tore out her tongue
and whipped her under a tree
and planted a fly in the bleeding
places so that worms
spread through the flesh
then the dogs
then the buzzards
then the soldiers laughing
at the family of the girl
with no arms
guerilla girl
with no arms
You go with no arms
among the jungle treacheries
You go with no arms
into the mountains hunting
revenge

I watch you
walk like that
into the kitchen
walk like that
into the clearing
girl with no arms

I am learning new syllables
of revolution

Guatemala
Guatemala
Girl with no arms

The Female and the Silence
of a Man

(c.f. W.B. Yeats' "Leda and the Swan")

And now she knows: The big fist shattering her face.
Above, the sky conceals the sadness of the moon.

And windows light, doors close, against all trace
of her: She falls into the violence of a woman's ruin.

How should she rise against the plunging of his lust?
She vomits out her teeth. He tears the slender legs apart.
The hairy torso of his rage destroys the soft last bastion
        of her trust.
He lacerates her breasts. He claws and squeezes out her
   heart.

She sinks into a meadow pond of lilies and a swan.
She floats above an afternoon of music from the trees.
She vanishes like blood that people walk upon.
She reappears: A mad *bitch* dog that reason cannot seize;
A fever withering the river and the crops:
A lovely girl protected by her cruel/incandescent energies.

Intifada

In detention
in concentration camps
we trade stories
we take turns sharing the straw mat
or a pencil
we watch what crawls in and out
of the sand

As-Salāmm 'Alaykum

The guards do not allow the blue
woolen blanket
my family travelled far
to bring
to this crepuscular and gelid cell
where my still breathing infant son
and I
defy the purgatory implications
of a state-created hell

Wa 'Alaikum As-Salām

The village trembles from the heavy
tanks that try
to terrify the children:
Everyday
my little brother runs behind the rubble
practising the tactics of the stones
against the rock

In January soldiers broke his fingers
one by one. Time has healed
his hands but not the fury that controls
what used to be
his heart.

Insha Ā'llāh

Close the villages
Close the clinics
Close the school
Close the house
Close the windows of the house
Kill the vegetables languishing under the sun
Kill the milk of the cows left to the swelling of pain
Cut the electricity
Cut the telephones
Confine the people to the people

Do Not Despair of the Mercy of Allah

Fig trees will grow and oranges
erupt from desert
holdings on which plastic
bullets (70% zinc, 20% glass, and 10%
plastic) will prove blood
soluble and fertilize the earth
where sheep will graze
and women no longer grieve and beat
their breasts
They will beat clean
fine-woven rugs outside a house
smelling of cinnamon
and nutmeg

Ahamdullilah

So says *Iman*
the teacher of peace
the shepherd on the mountain of the lamb
the teacher of peace
who will subdue the howling of the lion
so that we may kneel
as we must
five times beginning just after dawn
and ending just before dusk
in the *Ibādah*
of prayer

Allāhu Akbar

Allāhu Akbar

Allāhu Akbar

Glossary:

As-Salāmm 'Alaykum: peace be unto you
Wa 'Alaikum As-Salām: and peace be unto you
Insha Ā'llāh: as/if Allah wills it
"Do Not Despair of the Mercy of Allah": verse from *The Qur'ān*
Ahamdullilah: praise be to Allah
Iman: faith
Ibādah: worship in a ritual sense
Allāhu Akbar: Allah is the Greatest

Nikki Giovanni (b. 1943)

Long hailed as the princess of black poetry, a title she earned during the Black Arts Movement, Nikki Giovanni wrote what was considered militant poetry—poetry that protested white America's injustices and celebrated black America's achievements. These collections include *Black Judgment* (1968) and *Black Feeling, Black Talk* (1970). Additionally, she has several collections that deal with black womanhood, including *My House* (1972), *The Women and the Men* (1975), and *Cotton Candy on a Rainy Day* (1978). Her later collections, such as *Those Who Ride the Night Winds* (1983), take on a range of social and political issues. As with so many other third world women writers, Giovanni has written volumes for children: *Spin a Soft Black Song: Poems for Children* (1971), *Ego Tripping and Other Poems for Young Readers* (1973), and *Vacation Time: Poems for Children* (1980). She has also written an autobiography and several essay collections, including *Racism 101* (1994), heralded as a survival guide for black students on predominately white campuses.

Giovanni was born in Knoxville, Tennessee, to Jones 'Gus' and Yolande Cornelia Giovanni and graduated from Fisk University. She also attended the School of Social Work at the University of Pennsylvania and the School of Fine Arts at Columbia University. She has held academic appointments at a number of universities, and her activist voice remains popular on the college lecture circuit. Currently, Giovanni lives in Cincinnati where she has spent most of her life.

For Saundra

i wanted to write
a poem
that rhymes
but revolution doesn't lend
itself to be-bopping

then my neighbor
who thinks i hate
asked—do you ever write
tree poems—i like trees
so i thought
i'll write a beautiful green tree poem
peeked from my window
to check the image
noticed the school yard was covered
with asphalt
no green—no trees grow
in manhattan

then, well, i thought the sky
i'll do a big blue sky poem

but all the clouds have winged
low since no-Dick was elected

so i thought again
and it occurred to me
maybe i shouldn't write
at all
but clean my gun
and check my kerosene supply

perhaps these are not poetic
times
at all

Nikki-Rosa

childhood remembrances are always a drag
if you're Black
you always remember things like living in Woodlawn
with no inside toilet
and if you become famous or something
they never talk about how happy you were to have
your mother

all to yourself and
how good the water felt when you got your bath
from one of those
big tubs that folk in chicago barbecue in
and somehow when you talk about home
it never gets across how much you
understood their feelings
as the whole family attended meetings about Hollydale
and even though you remember
your biographers never understand
your father's pain as he sells his stock
and another dream goes
And though you're poor it isn't poverty that
concerns you

and though they fought a lot
it isn't your father's drinking that makes any difference
but only that everybody is together and you
and your sister have happy birthdays and very good
Christmasses
and I really hope no white person ever has cause
to write about me
because they never understand
Black love is Black wealth and they'll
probably talk about my hard childhood
and never understand that
all the while I was quite happy

Carolyn M. Rodgers (b. 1945)

Born in Chicago, Carolyn Rodgers was one of the founders of the Third World Press. She received her B.A. degree from Roosevelt University. Her poetry collections include *Paper Soul* (1968), *Songs of a Black Bird* (1969), *how I got ovah* (1975), and *The Heart as Ever Green* (1978) and reflect her negotiation of a Christian background with black nationalist issues. Like other writers of the Black Arts Movement, she was a member of the Organization of Black American Culture, a literary group where such writers as one of Rodgers' mentors, Gwendolyn Brooks, offered workshops. Rodgers' poems demonstrate an ear for vernacular idioms and a penchant for the plight and pride of black women.

It Is Deep

(don't never forget the bridge that you crossed over on)

Having tried to use the
witch cord
that erases the stretch of
thirty-three blocks
and tuning in the voice which
   woodenly stated that the
   talk box was "disconnected"

My mother, religiously girdled in
her god, slipped on some love, and
laid on my bell like a truck,
blew through my door warm wind from the south
concern making her gruff and tight-lipped
     and scared
that her "baby" was starving.
she, having learned, that disconnection results from
         non-payment of bill (s).

She did not
recognize the poster of the
grand le-roi (al) cat on the wall
had never even seen the books of
Black poems that I have written
thinks that I am under the influence of
     communists
when I talk about Black as anything
other than something ugly to kill it befo it grows
   in any impression she would not be

considered "relevant" or "Black"
              but
there she was, standing in my room
not loudly condemning that day and
not remembering that I grew hearing her
curse the factory where she "cut uh slave"
and the cheap j-boss wouldn't allow a union,
not remembering that I heard the tears when
they told her a high school diploma was not enough,
and here now, not able to understand, what she had
been forced to deny, still—

she pushed into my kitchen so
she could open my refrigerator to see
what I had to eat, and pressed fifty
bills in my hand saying "pay the talk bill and buy
some food; you got folks who care about you. . . ."

My mother, religious-negro, proud of
having waded through a storm, is very obviously,
a sturdy Black bridge that I
crossed over, on.

How I Got Ovah

i can tell you
about them
i have shaken rivers
out of my eyes
i have waded eyelash deep
have crossed rivers

have shaken the water weed out
of my lungs
have swam for strength
pulled by strength
through waterfalls with electric beats
i have bore the shocks
of water deep deep
waterlogs are my bones
i have shaken the water free of my hair
have kneeled on the banks
and kissed my ancestors of the dirt
whose rich dark root fingers rose up reached out
grabbed and pulled me rocked me cupped me

gentle strong and firm
carried me
made me swim for strength
cross rivers
though i shivered
was wet was cold
and wanted to sink down
and float as water, yea—
i can tell you.
i have shaken rivers
out of my eyes.

Literature of the Second Renaissance:
The 1970s and 1980s

Toni Morrison (b. 1931)

One of the most talented American writers of all time, Toni Morrison has a treasure chest of densely written, award-winning novels, culminating in a Pulitzer Prize for fiction in 1988 and a Nobel Prize for Literature in 1993. Her first novel, *The Bluest Eye* (1969) tells the story of Pecola Breedlove, a young black girl with no self-esteem who madly desires blue eyes. In 1973, Morrison published *Sula*, which received a National Book Award nomination. *Sula* is the story of two black girls, Nel and Sula, who grow into womanhood ever aware that ". . . they were neither white nor male . . ." After *Sula*, Morrison published *Song of Solomon*, which won the National Book Critics Circle Award and the American Academy and Institute of Arts and Letters Award. *Song of Solomon* is the story of Milkman Dead who goes on a journey to find gold but ends up finding out something that his African ancestors always knew—"If you surrendered to the air, you could *ride* it." In 1981, Morrison, elected to the American Academy and Institute of Arts and Letters, published *Tar Baby*, a story about what happens when one "loses her ancient properties"—her connections to her community and past. With *Beloved* (1987), Morrison forever changed the narrative of slavery. With a tree on her back from whippings and a "haint"/ghost in her house from having killed her baby girl, Sethe gives us a portrait of slavery that fills in all the gaps and opens all the wounds of the "unspeakable." Morrison's sixth novel, *Jazz* (1992), is a story of love and murder that takes place in Harlem during the 1920s. Morrison's novel *Paradise* (1998) begins after the Civil War and goes through the 1970s, describing the interactions between the men of a small all-black town and the women in a nearby convent. The setting of her most recent novel, *Love* (2003), changes to a hotel and ocean resort, where generations of a community confront their interlocking past and present.

All of Morrison's novels are about a community—its formation, its scapegoats, its destruction. She tightly weaves mythologies, folk stories, and historical incidents in a tapestry that confronts the past and present of America through the lens of what she calls in *Playing in the Dark: Whiteness and the Literary Imagination* (1992) an "Africanist Presence." Never one to form a binary between art and protest, Morrison argues that "a novel should be unquestionably political and irrevocably beautiful." Given her interest in community and nationhood, it is not surprising that she has edited works on the Anita Hill/Clarence Thomas hearing and the O. J. Simpson trial, as well as written a play, "Dreaming Emmett" (1986), about the 1955 murder of 14-year-old Emmett Till. Her short story, "Recitatif" (1995), foregrounds and erases race as an issue.

Born Chloe Anthony Wofford, Morrison grew up in Lorain, Ohio. Currently, she holds the Robert F. Goheen Professorship at Princeton University.

Recitatif

My mother danced all night and Roberta's was sick. That's why we were taken to St. Bonny's. People want to put their arms around you when you tell them you were in a shelter, but it really wasn't bad. No big long room with one hundred beds like Bellevue. There were four to a room, and when Roberta

and me came, there was a shortage of state kids, so we were the only ones assigned to 406 and could go from bed to bed if we wanted to. And we wanted to, too. We changed beds every night and for the whole four months we were there we never picked one out as our own permanent bed.

It didn't start out that way. The minute I walked in and the Big Bozo introduced us, I got sick to my stomach. It was one thing to be taken out of your own bed early in the morning—it was something else to be stuck in a strange place with a girl from a whole other race. And Mary, that's my mother, she was right. Every now and then she would stop dancing long enough to tell me something important and one of the things

From *Skin Deep: Black Women and White Women Write About Race* by Marita Golden, Susan Shreve, and Susan Richards Shreve. © 1995. Reprinted by permission of International Creative Management, Inc., copyright © 2004 by Toni Morrison.

she said was that they never washed their hair and they smelled funny. Roberta sure did. Smell funny, I mean. So when the Big Bozo (nobody ever called her Mrs. Itkin, just like nobody ever said St. Bonaventure)—when she said, "Twyla, this is Roberta. Roberta, this is Twyla. Make each other welcome," I said, "My mother won't like you putting me in here."

"Good," said Bozo. "Maybe then she'll come and take you home."

How's that for mean? If Roberta had laughed I would have killed her, but she didn't. She just walked over to the window and stood with her back to us.

"Turn around," said the Bozo. "Don't be rude. Now Twyla. Roberta. When you hear a loud buzzer, that's the call for dinner. Come down to the first floor. Any fights and no movie." And then, just to make sure we knew what we would be missing, "*The Wizard of Oz.*"

Roberta must have thought I meant that my mother would be mad about my being put in the shelter. Not about rooming with her, because as soon as Bozo left she came over to me and said, "Is your mother sick too?"

"No," I said. "She just likes to dance all night."

"Oh." She nodded her head and I liked the way she understood things so fast. So for the moment it didn't matter that we looked like salt and pepper standing there and that's what the other kids called us sometimes. We were eight years old and got F's all the time. Me because I couldn't remember what I read or what the teacher said. And Roberta because she couldn't read at all and didn't even listen to the teacher. She wasn't good at anything except jacks, at which she was a killer: pow scoop pow scoop pow scoop.

We didn't like each other all that much at first, but nobody else wanted to play with us because we weren't real orphans with beautiful dead parents in the sky. We were dumped. Even the New York City Puerto Ricans and the up-state Indians ignored us. All kinds of kids were in there, black ones, white ones, even two Koreans. The food was good, though. At least I thought so. Roberta hated it and left whole pieces of things on her plate: Spam, Salisbury steak—even Jell-O with fruit cocktail in it, and she didn't care if I ate what she wouldn't. Mary's idea of supper was popcorn and a can of Yoo-Hoo. Hot mashed potatoes and two weenies was like Thanksgiving for me.

It really wasn't bad, St. Bonny's. The big girls on the second floor pushed us around now and then. But that was all. They wore lipstick and eyebrow pencil and wobbled their knees while they watched TV. Fifteen, sixteen, even, some of them were. They were put-out girls, scared runaways most of them. Poor little girls who fought their uncles off but looked tough to us, and mean. God, did they look mean. The staff tried to keep them separate from the younger children, but sometimes they caught us watching them in the orchard where they played radios and danced with each other. They'd light out after us and pull our hair or twist our arms. We were scared of them, Roberta and me, but neither of us wanted the other one to know it. So we got a good list of dirty names we could shout back when we ran from them through the orchard. I used to dream a lot and almost always the orchard was there. Two acres, four maybe, of these little apple trees. Hundreds of them. Empty and crooked like beggar women when I first came to St. Bonny's but fat with flowers when I left. I don't know why I dreamed about that orchard so much. Nothing really happened there. Nothing all that important, I mean. Just the big girls dancing and playing the radio. Roberta and me watching. Maggie fell down there once. The kitchen woman with legs like parentheses. And the big girls laughed at her. We should have helped her up, I know, but we were scared of those girls with lipstick and eyebrow pencil. Maggie couldn't talk. The kids said she had her tongue cut out, but I think she was just born that way: mute. She was old and sandy-colored and she worked in the kitchen. I don't know if she was nice or not. I just remember her legs like parentheses and how she rocked when she walked. She worked from early in the morning till two o'clock, and if she was late, if she had too much cleaning and didn't get out till two-fifteen or so, she'd cut through the orchard so she wouldn't miss her bus and have to wait another hour. She wore this really stupid little hat—a kid's hat with ear flaps—and she wasn't much taller than we were. A really awful little hat. Even for a mute, it was dumb—dressing like a kid and never saying anything at all.

"But what about if somebody tries to kill her?" I used to wonder about that. "Or what if she wants to cry? Can she cry?"

"Sure," Roberta said. "But just tears. No sounds come out."

"She can't scream?"

"Nope. Nothing."

"Can she hear?"

"I guess."

"Let's call her," I said. And we did.

"Dummy! Dummy!" She never turned her head.

"Bow legs! Bow legs!" Nothing. She just rocked on, the chin straps of her baby-boy hat swaying from side to side. I think we were wrong. I think she could hear and didn't let on. And it shames me even now to think there was somebody in there after all who heard us call her those names and couldn't tell on us.

We got along all right, Roberta and me. Changed beds every night, got F's in civics and communication skills and gym. The Bozo was disappointed in us, she said. Out of 130 of us state cases, 90 were under twelve. Almost all were real orphans with beautiful dead parents in the sky. We were the only ones dumped and the only ones with F's in three classes including gym. So we got along—what with her leaving whole pieces of things on her plate and being nice about not asking questions.

I think it was the day before Maggie fell down that we found out our mothers were coming to visit us on the same Sunday. We had been at the shelter twenty-eight days (Roberta twenty-eight and a half) and this was their first visit with us. Our mothers would come at ten o'clock in time for chapel, then lunch with us in the teachers' lounge. I thought if my dancing mother met her sick mother it might be good for her. And Roberta thought her sick mother would get a big bang out of a dancing one. We got excited about it and curled each other's hair. After breakfast we sat on the bed watching the road from the window. Roberta's socks were still wet. She washed them the night before and put them on the radiator to dry. They hadn't, but she put them on anyway because their tops were so pretty—scalloped in pink. Each of us had a purple construction-paper basket that we had made in craft class. Mine had a yellow crayon rabbit on it. Roberta's had eggs with wiggly lines of color. Inside were cellophane grass and just the jelly beans because I'd eaten the two marshmallow eggs they gave us. The Big Bozo came herself to get us. Smiling, she told us we looked very nice and to come downstairs. We were so surprised by the smile we'd never seen before, neither of us moved.

"Don't you want to see your mommies?"

I stood up first and spilled the jelly beans all over the floor. Bozo's smile disappeared while we scrambled to get the candy up off the floor and put it back in the grass.

She escorted us downstairs to the first floor, where the other girls were lining up to file into the chapel. A bunch of grown-ups stood to one side. Viewers mostly. The old biddies who wanted servants and the fags who wanted company looking for children they might want to adopt. Once in a while a grandmother. Almost never anybody young or anybody whose face wouldn't scare you in the night. Because if any of the real orphans had young relatives they wouldn't be real orphans. I saw Mary right away. She had on those green slacks I hated and hated even more now because didn't she know we were going to chapel? And that fur jacket with the pocket linings so ripped she had to pull to get her hands out of them. But her face was pretty—like always—and she smiled and waved like she was the little girl looking for her mother, not me.

I walked slowly, trying not to drop the jelly beans and hoping the paper handle would hold. I had to use my last Chiclet because by the time I finished cutting everything out, all the Elmer's was gone. I am left-handed and the scissors never worked for me. It didn't matter, though; I might just as well have chewed the gum. Mary dropped to her knees and grabbed me, mashing the basket, the jelly beans, and the grass into her ratty fur jacket.

"Twyla, baby. Twyla, baby!"

I could have killed her. Already I heard the big girls in the orchard the next time saying, "Twyyyyyla, baby!" But I couldn't stay mad at Mary while she was smiling and hugging me and smelling of Lady Esther dusting powder. I wanted to stay buried in her fur all day.

To tell the truth I forgot about Roberta. Mary and I got in line for the traipse into chapel and I was feeling proud because she looked so beautiful even in those ugly green slacks that made her behind stick out. A pretty mother on earth is better than a beautiful dead one in the sky even if she did leave you all alone to go dancing.

I felt a tap on my shoulder, turned, and saw Roberta smiling. I smiled back, but not too much lest somebody think this visit was the biggest thing that ever happened in my life. Then Roberta said, "Mother, I want you to meet my roommate, Twyla. And that's Twyla's mother."

I looked up it seemed for miles. She was big. Bigger than any man and on her chest was the biggest cross I'd ever seen. I swear it was six inches long each way. And in the crook of her arm was the biggest Bible ever made.

Mary, simpleminded as ever, grinned and tried to yank her hand out of the pocket with the raggedy lining—to shake hands, I guess. Roberta's mother looked down at me and then looked down at Mary too. She didn't say anything, just grabbed Roberta with her Bible-free hand and stepped out of line, walking quickly to the rear of it. Mary was still grinning because she's not too swift when it comes to what's really going on. Then this light bulb goes off in her head and she says, "That bitch!" really loud and us almost in the chapel now. Organ music whining, the Bonny Angels singing sweetly. Everybody in the world turned around to look. And Mary would have kept it up—kept calling names if I hadn't squeezed her hands as hard as I could. That helped a little, but she still twitched and crossed and uncrossed her legs all through service. Even groaned a couple of times. Why did I think she would come there and act right? Slacks. No hat like the grandmothers and viewers, and groaning all the while. When we stood for hymns she kept her mouth shut. Wouldn't even look at the words on the page. She actually reached in her purse for a mirror to check her lipstick. All I could think of was that she really needed to be killed. The sermon lasted a year, and I knew the real orphans were looking smug again.

We were supposed to have lunch in the teachers' lounge, but Mary didn't bring anything, so we picked fur and cellophane grass off the mashed jelly beans and ate them. I could have killed her. I sneaked a look at Roberta. Her mother had brought chicken legs and ham sandwiches and oranges and a whole box of chocolate-covered grahams. Roberta drank milk from a thermos while her mother read the Bible to her.

Things are not right. The wrong food is always with the wrong people. Maybe that's why I got into waitress work later—to match up the right people with the right food. Roberta just let those chicken legs sit there, but she did bring a stack of grahams up to me later when the visit was over. I think she was sorry that her mother would not shake my mother's hand. And I liked that and I liked the fact that she didn't say a word about Mary groaning all the way through the service and not bringing any lunch.

Roberta left in May when the apple trees were heavy and white. On her last day we went to the orchard to watch the big girls smoke and dance by the radio. It didn't matter that they said, "Twyyyyyla, baby." We sat on the ground and breathed. Lady Esther. Apple blossoms. I still go soft when I smell one or the other. Roberta was going home. The big cross and the big Bible was coming to get her and she seemed sort of glad and sort of not. I thought I would die in that room of four beds without her and I knew Bozo had plans to move some other dumped kid in there with me. Roberta promised to write every day, which was really sweet of her because she couldn't read a lick so how could she write anybody? I would have drawn pictures and sent them to her but she never gave me her address. Little by little she faded. Her wet socks with the pink scalloped tops and her big serious-looking eyes—that's all I could catch when I tried to bring her to mind.

I was working behind the counter at the Howard Johnson's on the Thruway just before the Kingston exit. Not a bad job. Kind of a long ride from Newburgh, but okay once I got there. Mine was the second night shift, eleven to seven. Very light until a Greyhound checked in for breakfast around six-thirty. At that hour the sun was all the way clear of the hills behind the restaurant. The place looked better at night—more like shelter—but I loved it when the sun broke in, even if it did show all the cracks in the vinyl and the speckled floor looked dirty no matter what the mop boy did.

It was August and a bus crowd was just unloading. They would stand around a long while: going to the john, and looking at gifts and junk-for-sale machines, reluctant to sit down so soon. Even to eat. I was trying to fill the coffeepots and get them all situated on the electric burners when I saw her. She was sitting in a booth smoking a cigarette with two guys smothered in head and facial hair. Her own hair was so big and wild I could hardly see her face. But the eyes. I would know them anywhere. She had on a powder-blue halter and shorts outfit and earrings the size of bracelets. Talk about lipstick and eyebrow pencil. She made the big girls look like nuns. I couldn't get off the counter until seven o'clock, but I

kept watching the booth in case they got up to leave before that. My replacement was on time for a change, so I counted and stacked my receipts as fast as I could and signed off. I walked over to the booth, smiling and wondering if she would remember me. Or even if she wanted to remember me. Maybe she didn't want to be reminded of St. Bonny's or to have anybody know she was ever there. I know I never talked about it to anybody.

I put my hands in my apron pockets and leaned against the back of the booth facing them.

"Roberta? Roberta Fisk?"

She looked up. "Yeah?"

"Twyla."

She squinted for a second and then said, "Wow."

"Remember me?"

"Sure. Hey. Wow."

"It's been a while," I said, and gave a smile to the two hairy guys.

"Yeah. Wow. You work here?"

"Yeah," I said. "I live in Newburgh."

"Newburgh? No kidding?" She laughed then, a private laugh that included the guys but only the guys, and they laughed with her. What could I do but laugh too and wonder why I was standing there with my knees showing out from under that uniform. Without looking I could see the blue-and-white triangle on my head, my hair shapeless in a net, my ankles thick in white oxfords. Nothing could have been less sheer than my stockings. There was this silence that came down right after I laughed. A silence it was her turn to fill up. With introductions, maybe, to her boyfriends or an invitation to sit down and have a Coke. Instead she lit a cigarette off the one she'd just finished and said, "We're on our way to the Coast. He's got an appointment with Hendrix." She gestured casually toward the boy next to her.

"Hendrix? Fantastic," I said. "Really fantastic. What's she doing now?"

Roberta coughed on her cigarette and the two guys rolled their eyes up at the ceiling.

"Hendrix. Jimi Hendrix, asshole. He's only the biggest— Oh, wow. Forget it."

I was dismissed without anyone saying good-bye, so I thought I would do it for her.

"How's your mother?" I asked. Her grin cracked her whole face. She swallowed. "Fine," she said. "How's yours?"

"Pretty as a picture," I said and turned away. The backs of my knees were damp. Howard Johnson's really was a dump in the sunlight.

James is as comfortable as a house slipper. He liked my cooking and I liked his big loud family. They have lived in Newburgh all of their lives and talk about it the way people do who have always known a home. His grandmother has a porch swing older than his father and when they talk about streets and avenues and buildings they call them names they no longer have. They still call the A&P Rico's because it stands on property once a mom-and-pop store owned by Mr. Rico. And they call the new community college Town Hall because it once was. My mother-in-law puts up jelly and cucumbers and buys butter wrapped in cloth from a dairy. James and his father talk about fishing and baseball and I can see them all together on the Hudson in a raggedy skiff. Half the population of Newburgh is on welfare now, but to my husband's family it was still some upstate paradise of a time long past. A time of ice houses and vegetable wagons, coal furnaces and children weeding gardens. When our son was born my mother-in-law gave me the crib blanket that had been hers.

But the town they remembered had changed. Something quick was in the air. Magnificent old houses, so ruined they had become shelter for squatters and rent risks, were bought and renovated. Smart IBM people moved out of their suburbs back into the city and put shutters up and herb gardens in their backyards. A brochure came in the mail announcing the opening of a Food Emporium. Gourmet food, it said—and listed items the rich IBM crowd would want. It was located in a new mall at the edge of town and I drove out to shop there one day—just to see. It was late in June. After the tulips were gone and the Queen Elizabeth roses were open everywhere. I trailed my cart along the aisle, tossing in smoked oysters and Robert's sauce and things I knew would sit in my cupboard for years. Only when I found some Klondike ice cream bars did I feel less guilty about spending James's fireman's salary so foolishly. My father-in-law ate them with the same gusto little Joseph did.

Waiting in the checkout line I heard a voice say, "Twyla!"

The classical music piped over the aisles had affected me and the woman leaning toward me was dressed to kill. Diamonds on her hand, a smart white summer dress. "I'm Mrs. Benson," I said.

"Ho. Ho. The Big Bozo," she sang.

For a split second I didn't know what she was talking about. She had a bunch of asparagus and two cartons of fancy water.

"Roberta!"

"Right."

"For heaven's sake. Roberta."

"You look great," she said.

"So do you. Where are you? Here? In Newburgh?"

"Yes. Over in Annandale."

I was opening my mouth to say more when the cashier called my attention to her empty counter.

"Meet you outside." Roberta pointed her finger and went into the express line.

I placed the groceries and kept myself from glancing around to check Roberta's progress. I remembered Howard Johnson's and looking for a chance to speak only to be greeted with a stingy "wow." But she was waiting for me and her huge hair was sleek now, smooth around a small, nicely shaped head. Shoes, dress, everything lovely and summery and rich. I was dying to know what happened to her, how she got from Jimi Hendrix to Annandale, a neighborhood full of doctors and IBM executives. Easy, I thought. Everything is so easy for them. They think they own the world.

"How long," I asked her. "How long have you been here?"

"A year. I got married to a man who lives here. And you, you're married too, right? Benson, you said."

"Yeah. James Benson."

"And is he nice?"

"Oh, is he nice?"

"Well, is he?" Roberta's eyes were steady as though she really meant the question and wanted an answer.

"He's wonderful, Roberta. Wonderful."

"So you're happy."

"Very."

"That's good," she said and nodded her head. "I always hoped you'd be happy. Any kids? I know you have kids."

"One. A boy. How about you?"

"Four."

"Four?"

She laughed. "Step kids. He's a widower."

"Oh."

"Got a minute? Let's have a coffee."

I thought about the Klondikes melting and the inconvenience of going all the way to my car and putting the bags in the trunk. Served me right for buying all that stuff I didn't need. Roberta was ahead of me.

"Put them in my car. It's right here."

And then I saw the dark blue limousine.

"You married a Chinaman?"

"No." She laughed. "He's the driver."

"Oh, my. If the Big Bozo could see you now."

We both giggled. Really giggled. Suddenly, in just a pulse beat, twenty years disappeared and all of it came rushing back. The big girls (whom we called gar girls—Roberta's misheard word for the evil stone faces described in a civics class) there dancing in the orchard, the ploppy mashed potatoes, the double weenies, the Spam with pineapple. We went into the coffee shop holding on to one another and I tried to think why we were glad to see each other this time and not before. Once, twelve years ago, we passed like strangers. A black girl and a white girl meeting in a Howard Johnson's on the road and having nothing to say. One in a blue-and-white-triangle waitress hat, the other on her way to see Hendrix. Now we were behaving like sisters separated for much too long. Those four short months were nothing in time. Maybe it was the thing itself. Just being there, together. Two little girls who knew what nobody else in the world knew—how not to ask questions. How to believe what had to be believed. There was politeness in that reluctance and generosity as well. Is your mother sick too? No, she dances all night. Oh—and an understanding nod.

We sat in a booth by the window and fell into recollection like veterans.

"Did you ever learn to read?"

"Watch." She picked up the menu. "Special of the day. Cream of corn soup. Entrées. Two dots and a wriggly line. Quiche. Chef salad, scallops. . . ."

I was laughing and applauding when the waitress came up.

"Remember the Easter baskets?"

"And how we tried to *introduce* them?"

"Your mother with that cross like two telephone poles."

"And yours with those tight slacks."

We laughed so loudly heads turned and made the laughter hard to suppress.

"What happened to the Jimi Hendrix date?"

Roberta made a blow-out sound with her lips.

"When he died I thought about you."

"Oh, you heard about him finally?"

"Finally. Come on, I was a small-town country waitress."

"And I was a small-town country dropout. God, were we wild. I still don't know how I got out of there alive."

"But you did."

"I did. I really did. Now I'm Mrs. Kenneth Norton."

"Sounds like a mouthful."

"It is."

"Servants and all?"

Roberta held up two fingers.

"Ow! What does he do?"

"Computers and stuff. What do I know?"

"I don't remember a hell of a lot from those days, but Lord, St. Bonny's is as clear as daylight. Remember Maggie? The day she fell down and those gar girls laughed at her?"

Roberta looked up from her salad and stared at me. "Maggie didn't fall," she said.

"Yes, she did. You remember."

"No, Twyla. They knocked her down. Those girls pushed her down and tore her clothes. In the orchard."

"I don't—that's not what happened."

"Sure it is. In the orchard. Remember how scared we were?"

"Wait a minute. I don't remember any of that."

"And Bozo was fired."

"You're crazy. She was there when I left. You left before me."

"I went back. You weren't there when they fired Bozo."

"What?"

"Twice. Once for a year when I was about ten, another for two months when I was fourteen. That's when I ran away."

"You ran away from St. Bonny's?"

"I had to. What do you want? Me dancing in that orchard?"

"Are you sure about Maggie?"

"Of course I'm sure. You've blocked it, Twyla. It happened. Those girls had behavior problems, you know."

"Didn't they, though. But why can't I remember the Maggie thing?"

"Believe me. It happened. And we were there."

"Who did you room with when you went back?" I asked her as if I would know her. The Maggie thing was troubling me.

"Creeps. They tickled themselves in the night."

My ears were itching and I wanted to go home suddenly. This was all very well but she couldn't just comb her hair, wash her face, and pretend everything was hunky-dory. After the Howard Johnson's snub. And no apology. Nothing.

"Were you on dope or what that time at Howard Johnson's?" I tried to make my voice sound friendlier than I felt.

"Maybe, a little. I never did drugs much. Why?"

"I don't know, you acted sort of like you didn't want to know me then."

"Oh, Twyla, you know how it was in those days: black—white. You know how everything was."

But I didn't know. I thought it was just the opposite. Busloads of blacks and whites came into Howard Johnson's together. They roamed together then: students, musicians, lovers, protesters. You got to see everything at Howard Johnson's, and blacks were very friendly with whites in those days. But sitting there with nothing on my plate but two hard tomato wedges wondering about the melting Klondikes it seemed childish remembering the slight. We went to her car and, with the help of the driver, got my stuff into my station wagon.

"We'll keep in touch this time," she said.

"Sure," I said. "Sure. Give me a call."

"I will," she said, and then, just as I was sliding behind the wheel, she leaned into the window. "By the way. Your mother. Did she ever stop dancing?"

I shook my head. "No. Never."

Roberta nodded.

"And yours? Did she ever get well?"

She smiled a tiny sad smile. "No. She never did. Look, call me, okay?"

"Okay," I said, but I knew I wouldn't. Roberta had messed up my past somehow with that business about Maggie. I wouldn't forget a thing like that. Would I?

Strife came to us that fall. At least that's what the paper called it. Strife. Racial strife. The word made me think of a bird—a big shrieking bird out of 1,000,000,000 B.C. Flapping its wings and cawing. Its eye with no lid always bearing down on you. All day it screeched and at night it slept on the rooftops. It woke you in the morning, and from the "Today" show to the eleven o'clock news it kept you an awful company. I couldn't figure it out from one day to the next. I knew I was supposed to feel something strong, but I didn't know what, and James wasn't any help. Joseph was on the list of kids to be transferred from the junior high school to another one at some far-out-of-the-way place and I thought it was a good thing until I heard it was a bad thing. I mean I didn't know. All the schools seemed dumps to me, and the fact that one was nicer looking didn't hold much weight. But the papers were full of it and then the kids began to get jumpy. In August, mind you. Schools weren't even open yet. I thought Joseph might be frightened to go over there, but he didn't seem scared so I forgot about it, until I found myself driving along Hudson Street out there by the school they were trying to integrate and saw a line of women marching. And who do you suppose was in line, big as life, holding a sign in front of her bigger than her mother's cross? MOTHERS HAVE RIGHTS TOO! it said.

I drove on and then changed my mind. I circled the block, slowed down, and honked my horn.

Roberta looked over and when she saw me she waved. I didn't wave back, but I didn't move either. She handed her sign to another woman and came over to where I was parked.

"Hi."

"What are you doing?"

"Picketing. What's it look like?"

"What for?"

"What do you mean, 'What for?' They want to take my kids and send them out of the neighborhood. They don't want to go."

"So what if they go to another school? My boy's being bussed too, and I don't mind. Why should you?"

"It's not about us, Twyla. Me and you. It's about our kids."

"What's more us than that?"

"Well, it is a free country."

"Not yet, but it will be."

"What the hell does that mean? I'm not doing anything to you."

"You really think that?"

"I know it."

"I wonder what made me think you were different."

"I wonder what made me think you were different."

"Look at them," I said. "Just look. Who do you think they are? Swarming all over the place like they own it. And now they think they can decide where my child goes to school. Look at them, Roberta. They're Bozos."

Roberta turned around and looked at the women. Almost all of them were standing still now, waiting. Some were even

edging toward us. Roberta looked at me out of some refrigerator behind her eyes. "No, they're not. They're just mothers."

"And what am I? Swiss cheese?"

"I used to curl your hair."

"I hated your hands in my hair."

The women were moving. Our faces looked mean to them of course and they looked as though they could not wait to throw themselves in front of a police car or, better yet, into my car and drag me away by my ankles. Now they surrounded my car and gently, gently began to rock it. I swayed back and forth like a sideways yo-yo. Automatically I reached for Roberta, like the old days in the orchard when they saw us watching them and we had to get out of there, and if one of us fell the other pulled her up and if one of us was caught the other stayed to kick and scratch, and neither would leave the other behind. My arm shot out of the car window but no receiving hand was there. Roberta was looking at me sway from side to side in the car and her face was still. My purse slid from the car seat down under the dashboard. The four policemen who had been drinking Tab in their car finally got the message and strolled over, forcing their way through the women. Quietly, firmly they spoke. "Okay, ladies. Back in line or off the streets."

Some of them went away willingly; others had to be urged away from the car doors and the hood. Roberta didn't move. She was looking steadily at me. I was fumbling to turn on the ignition, which wouldn't catch because the gearshift was still in drive. The seats of the car were a mess because the swaying had thrown my grocery coupons all over and my purse was sprawled on the floor.

"Maybe I am different now, Twyla. But you're not. You're the same little state kid who kicked a poor old black lady when she was down on the ground. You kicked a black lady and you have the nerve to call me a bigot."

The coupons were everywhere and the guts of my purse were bunched under the dashboard. What was she saying? Black? Maggie wasn't black.

"She wasn't black," I said.

"Like hell she wasn't, and you kicked her. We both did. You kicked a black lady who couldn't even scream."

"Liar!"

"You're the liar! Why don't you just go on home and leave us alone, huh?"

She turned away and I skidded away from the curb.

The next morning I went into the garage and cut the side out of the carton our portable TV had come in. It wasn't nearly big enough, but after a while I had a decent sign: red spray-painted letters on a white background— AND SO DO CHILDREN****. I meant just to go down to the school and tack it up somewhere so those cows on the picket line across the street could see it, but when I got there, some ten or so others had already assembled—protesting the cows across the street. Police permits and everything. I got in line and we strutted in time on our side while Roberta's group strutted on theirs. That first day we were all dignified, pretending the other side didn't exist. The second day there was name calling and finger gestures. But that was about all. People changed signs from time to time, but Roberta never did and neither did I. Actually my sign didn't make sense without Roberta's. "And so do children what?" one of the women on my side asked me. Have rights, I said, as though it was obvious.

Roberta didn't acknowledge my presence in any way, and I got to thinking maybe she didn't know I was there. I began to pace myself in the line, jostling people one minute and lagging behind the next, so Roberta and I could reach the end of our respective lines at the same time and there would be a moment in our turn when we would face each other. Still, I couldn't tell whether she saw me and knew my sign was for her. The next day I went early before we were scheduled to assemble. I waited until she got there before I exposed my new creation. As soon as she hoisted her MOTHERS HAVE RIGHTS TOO I began to wave my new one, which said, HOW WOULD YOU KNOW? I know she saw that one, but I had gotten addicted now. My signs got crazier each day, and the women on my side decided that I was a kook. They couldn't make heads or tails out of my brilliant screaming posters.

I brought a painted sign in queenly red with huge black letters that said, IS YOUR MOTHER WELL? Roberta took her lunch break and didn't come back for the rest of the day or any day after. Two days later I stopped going too and couldn't have been missed because nobody understood my signs anyway.

It was a nasty six weeks. Classes were suspended and Joseph didn't go to anybody's school until October. The children—everybody's children—soon got bored with that extended vacation they thought was going to be so great. They looked at TV until their eyes flattened. I spent a couple of mornings tutoring my son, as the other mothers said we should. Twice I opened a text from last year that he had never turned in. Twice he yawned in my face. Other mothers organized living room sessions so the kids would keep up. None of the kids could concentrate, so they drifted back to "The Price Is Right" and "The Brady Bunch." When the school finally opened there were fights once or twice and some sirens roared through the streets every once in a while. There were a lot of photographers from Albany. And just when ABC was about to send up a news crew, the kids settled down like nothing in the world had happened. Joseph hung my HOW WOULD YOU KNOW? sign in his bedroom. I don't know what became of AND SO DO CHILDREN****. I think my father-in-law cleaned some fish on it. He was always puttering around in our garage. Each of his five children lived in Newburgh, and he acted as though he had five extra homes.

I couldn't help looking for Roberta when Joseph graduated from high school, but I didn't see her. It didn't trouble me much what she had said to me in the car. I mean the kicking part. I know I didn't do that, I couldn't do that. But I was puzzled by her telling me Maggie was black. When I thought about it I actually couldn't be certain. She wasn't pitch-black, I knew, or I would have remembered that. What I remember was the kiddie hat and the semicircle legs. I tried to reassure myself about the race thing for a long time until it dawned on me that the truth was already there, and Roberta knew it. I didn't kick her; I didn't join in with the gar girls and kick that lady, but I sure did want to. We watched and never tried to help her and never called for help. Maggie was my dancing mother. Deaf, I thought, and dumb. Nobody inside. Nobody who would hear you if you cried in the night. Nobody who could tell you anything important that you could use. Rocking, dancing, swaying as she walked. And when the gar girls pushed her down and started roughhousing, I knew she wouldn't scream, couldn't—just like me—and I was glad about that.

We decided not to have a tree, because Christmas would be at my mother-in-law's house, so why have a tree at both places? Joseph was at SUNY New Paltz and we had to economize, we said. But at the last minute, I changed my mind. Nothing could be that bad. So I rushed around town looking for a tree, something small but wide. By the time I found a place, it was snowing and very late. I dawdled like it was the most important purchase in the world and the tree man was fed up with me. Finally I chose one and had it tied onto the trunk of the car. I drove away slowly because the sand trucks were not out yet and the streets could be murder at the beginning of a snowfall. Downtown the streets were wide and rather empty except for a cluster of people coming out of the Newburgh Hotel. The one hotel in town that wasn't built out of cardboard and Plexiglas. A party, probably. The men huddled in the snow were dressed in tails and the women had on furs. Shiny things glittered from underneath their coats. It made me tired to look at them. Tired, tired, tired. On the next corner was a small diner with loops and loops of paper bells in the window. I stopped the car and went in. Just for a cup of coffee and twenty minutes of peace before I went home and tried to finish everything before Christmas Eve.

"Twyla?"

There she was. In a silvery evening gown and dark fur coat. A man and another woman were with her, the man fumbling for change to put in the cigarette machine. The woman was humming and tapping on the counter with her fingernails. They all looked a little bit drunk.

"Well. It's you."

"How are you?"

I shrugged. "Pretty good. Frazzled. Christmas and all."

"Regular?" called the woman from the counter.

"Fine," Roberta called back and then, "Wait for me in the car."

She slipped into the booth beside me. "I have to tell you something, Twyla. I made up my mind if I ever saw you again, I'd tell you."

"I'd just as soon not hear anything, Roberta. It doesn't matter now, anyway."

"No," she said. "Not about that."

"Don't be long," said the woman. She carried two regulars to go and the man peeled his cigarette pack as they left.

"It's about St. Bonny's and Maggie."

"Oh, please."

"Listen to me. I really did think she was black. I didn't make that up. I really thought so. But now I can't be sure. I just remember her as old, so old. And because she couldn't talk—well, you know, I thought she was crazy. She'd been brought up in an institution like my mother was and like I thought I would be too. And you were right. We didn't kick her. It was the gar girls. Only them. But, well, I wanted to. I really wanted them to hurt her. I said we did it, too. You and me, but that's not true. And I don't want you to carry that around. It was just that I wanted to do it so bad that day— wanting to is doing it."

Her eyes were watery from the drinks she'd had, I guess. I know it's that way with me. One glass of wine and I start bawling over the littlest thing.

"We were kids, Roberta."

"Yeah. Yeah. I know, just kids."

"Eight."

"Eight."

"And lonely."

"Scared, too."

She wiped her cheeks with the heel of her hand and smiled. "Well, that's all I wanted to say."

I nodded and couldn't think of any way to fill the silence that went from the diner past the paper bells on out into the snow. It was heavy now. I thought I'd better wait for the sand trucks before starting home.

"Thanks, Roberta."

"Sure."

"Did I tell you? My mother, she never did stop dancing."

"Yes. You told me. And mine, she never got well." Roberta lifted her hands from the tabletop and covered her face with her palms. When she took them away she really was crying. "Oh, shit, Twyla. Shit, shit, shit. What the hell happened to Maggie?"

Adrienne Kennedy (b. 1931)

Adrienne Kennedy is probably one of the most experimental of African American women playwrights. Her plays are eclectic and elastic in form. She uses composite and fragmented characters and masks to stage the surreal. Born in Pittsburgh to Etra Haugebook Hawkins, a teacher, and Cornell Wallace Hawkins, the executive secretary of the YMCA, Kennedy graduated from The Ohio State University in 1953. Shortly after graduation, she married Joseph C. Kennedy who went off to war in Korea. When he returned, Joseph, Adrienne, and Joseph Jr. moved to New York where both parents attended Columbia University, with Kennedy focusing on creative writing. The Kennedys then began a series of treks to Africa and Europe, and Kennedy's plays reflect the breadth of these travels. She wrote *Funnyhouse of a Negro* (1962) while living in Africa and Italy.

Throughout her career, Kennedy has received many fellowships, including a Guggenheim, Rockefeller, and National Endowment and has taught creative writing at a number of schools, including Yale, Princeton, Brown, Berkeley, and Harvard. In addition to *Funnyhouse*, which Edward Albee produced Off-Broadway, Kennedy has written a long list of plays, including *The Owl Answers* (1965), *A Beast Story* (1966), *A Rat's Mass* (1966), *A Lesson in a Dead Language* (1968), *Boats* (1969), *Sun: A Poem for Malcolm X Inspired by His Murder* (1970), *A Movie Star Has to Star in Black and White* (1976), and *Orestes and Electra* (1980). In 1992, Kennedy published *The Alexander Plays: She Talks to Beethoven, The Ohio State Murders, The Film Club: A Monologue,* and *The Dramatic Circle.* Kennedy has also written a children's musical and a novel.

Motherhood 2000

Motherhood 2000 was produced and commissioned by the McCarter Theater in Princeton, New Jersey, for Winter's Tales '94, January 12 through January 23, 1994. The staged reading was directed by Michael Kahn.

CAST

MOTHER/WRITER,	Lynne Thigpen
RICHARD FOX,	Karl Light
PASSION PLAY ACTOR,	James Morrison
PASSION PLAY ACTOR,	Stephen Lee
PASSION PLAY ACTOR,	Brendan McClain

PRODUCTION

ASSISTANT DIRECTOR,	David Herskovits
TECHNICAL DIRECTOR,	Colin Hodgson
SOUND OPERATOR,	John Collins

Bonnie Marranca, ed. *Plays for the End of the Century,* pp. 1–8. © 1996. Reprinted with permission of The Johns Hopkins University Press.

MOTHER/WRITER: I finally found the policeman who beat my son that January night in 1991. He ran a theater on the steps of the Soldiers and Sailors monument on Riverside Drive at 89th Street.

Homeless people who had lived in the park under the 89th Street overlook now lived on 89th Street on the sidewalks, in the hallways of apartment buildings 311 and 145 Riverside Drive, as well as in the apartments with the legal tenants.

This policeman who had haunted me for nine years performed a play nightly: it was an ancient miracle play.

How amazing that this man should appear on the very street where I lived.

Evenings I could hear the actors, from the roof of my brownstone where I went to rest. The "Soldiers" spoke to "Christ."

(Quoting actors)

"And I have gone for gear good speed. Both hammers and nails large and long, then maybe boldly do this deed."

I walked to the edge of the roof and listened.

This man who I had thought of constantly since 1991 was playing Christ.

The soldiers spoke again to him.
(Quoting actors)

"The foulest death of all shall he die for his deeds. That means cross him we shall."

It was quite by accident that I had found him. I had come out of my brownstone one morning when I saw a band of disheveled men walking up Riverside Drive in the rain. They stopped when they came to the Soldiers and Sailors monument. One stepped forward and climbed the steps to the doorway of the statue. I recognized him immediately.

I had seen Richard Fox only on videotape. The night of the beating my sister hid in the doorway of her house and photographed him: he handcuffed my son and kicked him again and again in the stomach.

I had wanted to find him. I wanted to find his house somewhere in the suburbs of Virginia, but the lawyers concealed any information about Fox from me.

"You're behaving like a mother," the lawyer said. "You could hurt your son's case. Don't interfere. We have a detective looking into this policeman's history. Anyway, we've heard he will no longer be with the force. He's going to work for the Secret Service at the White House. Mrs. Alexander, please go back to your classes. Don't interfere. You will hurt your son's case."

Now nine years later I sat on the grass at the monument and watched Fox: acting the role of the Savior. The name of the troupe was The Oliviers.

I recognized the other actors. They were the former district attorney, the country manager, the police chief, and two policemen who had been involved in my son's case. They had been at the hearing.

At that time I wrote to them as well as to the governor, congress-men, the NAACP, and friends.

"I am writing to you again. On Friday night, January 11, my son was knocked to the ground and beaten in the head and face, kicked in the chest and stomach and dragged in the mud by a policeman.

My son was stopped because he had a tail light out . . . "

I wrote again and again:

Congressmen

The Black Caucus

The County Manager

NAACP

Chief of Police

My beloved son was also a Rhodes Scholar and traveled the country giving speeches for the causes of Blacks.

Nine years had passed. It was 2000.

The sun and the ships on the Hudson were still wonderful. But I hadn't been to Broadway for more than a year. It was impossible to make my way through the men on the sidewalks fighting among themselves. Shootings occurred daily.

I remembered the lovely street fairs when I strolled and bought faded voile dresses and sweet oils in green bottles. The children and David and I gorged on ice cream and crimson ices and bought paperback books on trees and gardens: trees and shrubs, trees for shade and shelter on the lawn.

"Mom," the children said, "We want another ice."

Now I was often hungry. Food was at the market on Broadway and 91st, but unexpected shootings on the street kept me fearful. I saved sacks of potatoes so that in case of shootings I would always have something to eat.

It was then I daydreamed of old movies, *The Sound of Music*, Fellini's *Amarcord*. The old movie theaters, the Thalia, New Yorker, the Symphony, had closed long ago.

Refugees from New Jersey arrived every morning at the 79th Street Boat Basin where armies of people lived.

Riverside Park between 86th Street and 116th was dangerous: inhabited only by gangs.

I remembered when my baby sons and I had walked in the snow deep into this park down to the highway, across to the shore of the Hudson. The Circle Line cruise ship sailed past. We waved, then walked to 116th Street and Broadway and stopped at Prexy's for chocolate. I dreamed of the beauty of Columbia University Mall where civil unrest and chaos now never ceased.

Members of The Oliviers were all white. They seemed protected by the soldier costumes they wore. My neighbor, a casting director, Judy, said she thought The Oliviers were one of the groups who traveled from national monument to monument trying to find asylum.

Judy still delivered tapes of her clients to an agency on 47th and Sixth and said things in that area were sometimes pretty much as they had been in the past.

She said the most popular movie downtown was called *Suicide Mission*, about a group of unhappy housewives from Davis, California. Sometimes she still went shopping at Saks and once bought me a straw hat. I wore it when I sat on the roof to read. Sometimes she had to stay downtown for the night. You never knew when bombings would occur. Still she was younger than I was and less afraid.

Often people who made it across the Hudson lived in the Path Station for weeks. Civil strife had destroyed a great deal of New Jersey. Yet some suburbs remained intact.

In the brownstone I lived in it was impossible to tell friends from enemies: the five floors were occupied by Bosnians, Californians, Haitians, Neo-Nazis: all were split into subgroups and each group had their own agenda, wars, and language.

My sons were somewhere in Washington but I didn't know where.

I lived on money from the royalties of my plays, a very small but sufficient amount.

City officials were constantly drowned near the Statue of Liberty.

Nights I continued to watch the ancient miracle play from the roof.

One night I came into the park just as a scene began. The soldiers spoke.

Although my asthma was very bad due to the conditions of the dirty streets, I tried to speak along with the actors.

And I never took my eyes off Richard Fox. His costume was very shabby; soldiers closed in upon him. I realized how agonized I still was by him.

I decided to join their company. I told them I had once been a playwright and had taught at Harvard. I was relieved to see they did not remember my name from my son's case.

I became their only Black member. They said I could rewrite a section of the play.

That night as I sat on the roof writing I remembered my son screaming when the policemen kicked him in the stomach, my son who as a child laughed at his turtle and ate pop tarts and watched *Rawhide* with his cowboy hat on.

The next night I arrived at the monument early.

On that night The Oliviers allowed me to perform with them. I was to be one of the soldiers.

The play began.

(The play appears before her. Three SOLDIERS *and Jesus—* RICHARD FOX— *stand directly opposite her.)*

SOLDIER: We have them here even at our hand.
SOLDIER: Give me this wedge; I shall it in drive.
SOLDIER: Here is another yet ordand.
SOLDIER: Do take it me hither belive.
SOLDIER: Lay on them fast.
SOLDIER: Yes, I warrant
 I thring them sam, so mote I thrive.
 Now will this cross full stably stand;
 All if he rave, they will not rive.

SOLDIER: *(to Christ)* Say, sir, how likes you now
 This work that we have wrought?
SOLDIER: We pray you say us how
 Ye feel, or faint ye aught.
*(*WRITER *speaks with them.)*
SOLDIER: We! Hark! he jangles like a jay.
SOLDIER: Methink he patters like a pie.
SOLDIER: He has been doing so all day,
 And made great moving of mercy.
SOLDIER: Is this the same that gan us say
 That he was God's Son almighty?
SOLDIER: Therefore he feels full fell affray,
 And deemed this day for to die.
SOLDIER: Vah! qui destruis templum . . .
SOLDIER: His saws were so, certain.
SOLDIER: And, sirs, he said to some
 He might raise it again.
SOLDIER: To muster that he had no might,
 For all the cautels that he could cast;
 As Pilate deemed, is done and dight;
 Therefore I rede that we go rest.
SOLDIER: This race mun be rehearsed right,
 Through the world both east and west.
SOLDIER: Yea, let him hang there still,
 And make mows on the moon.
SOLDIER: Then may we wend at will.
SOLDIER: Nay, good sirs, not so soon.
 For certes us needs another note:
 This kirtle would I of you crave.
SOLDIER: Nay, nay, sir, we will look by lot
 Which of us four falls it to have.
SOLDIER: I rede we draw cut for this coat—
 Lo, see how soon—all sides to save.
SOLDIER: The short cut shall win, that well yet wot,
 Whether it fall to knight or knave.
SOLDIER: Fellows, ye thar not flite,
 For this mantle is mine.
SOLDIER: Go we then hence tite;
 This travail here we tine.
WRITER: I spoke my lines coughing, wheezing . . . then found
 my place directly before Fox and struck him in the head
 with a hammer.
(She does.)
(He falls.)

Audre Lorde (1934–1992)

When Audre Lorde died at 58 years old in St. Croix, feminists worldwide and American, European, and Caribbean newspapers paid tribute to her. The most prominent black lesbian feminist, Lorde wrote poetry, a distinctive autobiography, and essays. Through all of these genres, she announced and developed her interlocking identities as woman, black, feminist, lesbian, activist, poet, and essayist.

Lorde was born in Harlem to parents from Grenada, West Indies. She had limited speech skills throughout her childhood and teens. In 1954, she attended the National University of Mexico and began to speak in full sentences. Lorde continued her education at Hunter College where she graduated in 1959. Throughout her career, she was concerned with language and speaking, admonishing her readers that "your silences will not protect you." In 1960, Lorde received a Masters of Library Science from Columbia University and was head librarian of the City University of New York before accepting a post as poet-in-residence at Tougaloo College in Mississippi where she published her first collection of poems, *The First Cities* (1968). Several collections followed: *Cables of Rage* (1970), *From a Land Where Other People Live* (1973), *The New York Head Shop and Museum* (1974), *Coal* (1976), *Between Ourselves* (1976), *The Black Unicorn* (1978), *Our Dead Behind Us* (1986), and *Undersong: Chosen Poems Old and New* (1992).

In addition to the poetry collections, Lorde wrote *Zami: A New Spelling of My Name* (1982), which she termed a biomythography—a combination of fiction, myth, and poetry. In feminist theory, Lorde is best known for her essays, especially those in *Sister Outside: Essays and Speeches.* The titles of two of these essays capture Lorde's preoccupations: "The Master's Tools Will Never Dismantle the Master's House" and "Age, Race, Class and Sex: Women Redefining Difference." Early in her career, Lorde shared with her readers her battle with breast cancer. Long before the general public was aware of environment and dietary influences on breast cancer, Lorde was concerned about the toll that the disease would take on women. In *The Cancer Journals* (1980) she describes herself as a black, lesbian activist—a warrior.

A Litany for Survival

For those of us who live at the shoreline
standing upon the constant edges of decision
crucial and alone
for those of us who cannot indulge
the passing dreams of choice
who love in doorways coming and going
in the hours between dawns
looking inward and outward
at once before and after
seeking a now that can breed
futures
like bread in our children's mouths

so their dreams will not reflect
the death of ours;

For those of us
who were imprinted with fear
like a faint line in the center of our foreheads
learning to be afraid with our mother's milk
for by this weapon
this illusion of some safety to be found
the heavy-footed hoped to silence us
For all of us
this instant and this triumph
We were never meant to survive.

And when the sun rises we are afraid
it might not remain
when the sun sets we are afraid

it might not rise in the morning
when our stomachs are full we are afraid
of indigestion
when our stomachs are empty we are afraid
we may never eat again
when we are loved we are afraid
love will vanish
when we are alone we are afraid
love will never return
and when we speak we are afraid

our words will not be heard
nor welcomed
but when we are silent
we are still afraid.

So it is better to speak
remembering
we were never meant to survive.

Lucille Clifton (b. 1936)

A past Poet Laureate for the state of Maryland, Lucille Clifton is known for her extraordinary poems about the ordinary. Whether writing about daughters or sons, hips or hair, love or lore, black heroes or biblical patriarchs, she does so with simplicity and precision. Clifton was born Thelma Lucille Sayles in Depew, New York, to Thelma Moore Sayles, who worked in a laundry, and Samuel L. Sayles, Sr., who worked in the steel mills. She attended Howard University and Fredonia State Teachers College in New York. After marrying Fred Clifton in 1958, she held various jobs. In 1969, at thirty-three years old and with six children, she published her first book of poetry, *Good Times*. In quick succession, she published *Good News about the Earth* (1972), *An Ordinary Woman* (1974), and several children's books, including the popular Everett Anderson series. The 1980s and 1990s were also prolific for Clifton: *Two-Headed Woman* (1980), *Good Woman: Poems and a Memoir* (1987), *Next: New Poems* (1987), *Quilting: Poems 1987–1990* (1991), and *Book of Light* (1993). In *Generations: A Memoir* (1976), Clifton writes about her great-great-grandmother, Caroline Donald, who was captured in West Africa, and walked from New Orleans to Virginia when she was eight years old. Clifton's great-grandmother and namesake, Lucille, was the first black woman legally hanged in Virginia. She killed the white father of her only son.

Homage to My Hips

these hips are big hips
they need space to
move around in.
they don't fit into little
petty places. these hips
are free hips.
they don't like to be held back.
these hips have never been enslaved,
they go where they want to go
they do what they want to do.
these hips are mighty hips.
these hips are magic hips.
I have known them
to put a spell on a man and
spin him like a top!

Homage to My Hair

when i feel her jump up and dance
i hear the music! my God
i'm talking about my nappy hair!
she is a challenge to your hand
Black man,
she is as tasty on your tongue as good greens
Black man,
she can touch your mind
with her electric fingers and
the grayer she do get, good God,
the Blacker she do be!

Jayne Cortez (b. 1936)

Born on a military base in Fort Huachuca, Arizona, Jayne Cortez began her writing career in Los Angeles, cofounding the Watts Repertory Theatre in 1964. She also founded her own publishing company, Bola Press. "Bola" is Yoruba for successful. Her poetry collections include *Pisstained Stairs and the Monkey Man's Wares* (1969) and *Festivals and Funerals* (1971). Known for the performative nature of her poetry, Cortez is interested in the merging of poetical and musical traditions, especially the fusion of jazz and language. She writes of John Coltrane, Charlie "Bird" Parker, and Billie Holiday. Like Ntozake Shange, she has also written about rape. Cortez's awards include the Before Columbus Foundation American Book Award for excellence in literature.

Rape

What was Inez supposed to do for
the man who declared war on her body
the man who carved a combat zone between her
breasts
Was she supposed to lick crabs from his hairy ass
kiss every pimple on his butt
blow hot breath on his big toe
draw back the corners of her vagina and
hee haw like a California burrow

This being war time for Inez
she stood facing the knife
the insults and
her own smell drying on the penis of
the man who raped her

She stood with a rifle in her hand
doing what a defense department will do in times of
war
And when the man started grunting and panting and
wobbling forward like
a giant log
She pumped lead into his three hundred pounds of
shaking flesh
Send it flying to the Virgin of Guadalupe
then celebrated day of the dead rapist punk
and just what the fuck else was she supposed to do?

And what was Joanne supposed to do for
the man who declared war on her life
Was she supposed to tongue his encrusted
toilet stool lips
suck the numbers off of his tin badge
choke on his clap trap balls
squeeze on his nub of rotten maggots and
sing god bless America thank you for fucking my life
away

This being war time for Joanne
she did what a defense department will do in times of
war
and when the piss drinking shit sniffing guard said
I'm gonna make you wish you were dead black bitch
come here
Joanne came down with an ice pick in
the swat freak motherfucker's chest
yes in the fat neck of that racist policeman
Joanne did the dance of the ice picks once again
from coast to coast
house to house
we celebrated day of the dead rapist punk
and just what the fuck else were we supposed to do

Toni Cade Bambara (1939–1995)

Toni Cade Bambara's humor, ear for dialogue, and keen sense of intergenerational issues infuse the stories in *Gorilla, My Love* (1972). The collection contains most of her short stories written between 1959 and 1970. In 1970, she edited a pioneering text: *The Black Woman: An Anthology.* Her collection of short stories, *The Sea Birds Are Still Alive* (1972) is about passengers on a refugee ship from a war-torn Asian nation. *The Salt Eaters* (1980) is a novel about healing the body, the mind, and the community. Both narratives eschew linear development, opting for the more improvisational, multilayered approach of jazz.

Born in New York City to Helen Brent Henderson Cade, Bambara adopted her last name from a signature she found in her great-grandmother's trunk. She received her B.A. from Queens College and a graduate degree from City College of New York. In addition to teaching in the SEEK program (Search for Education, Elevation, and Knowledge), she held teaching appointments at a number of colleges and universities including Livingston, Spelman, Rutgers, and Duke. Bambara's second novel was published just before her death in December 1995. That novel, *Those Bones Are Not My Child* (1999), is set during the Atlanta child murders, and narrated through the eyes of a mother of three children.

From Gorilla, My Love

The Lesson

Back in the days when everyone was old and stupid or young and foolish and me and Sugar were the only ones just right, this lady moved on our block with nappy hair and proper speech and no makeup. And quite naturally we laughed at her, laughed the way we did at the junk man who went about his business like he was some big-time president and his sorry-ass horse his secretary. And we kinda hated her too, hated the way we did the winos who cluttered up our parks and pissed on our handball walls and stank up our hallways and stairs so you couldn't halfway play hide-and-seek without a goddamn gas mask. Miss Moore was her name. The only woman on the block with no first name. And she was black as hell, cept for her feet, which were fish-white and spooky. And she was always planning these boring-ass things for us to do, us being my cousin, mostly, who lived on the block cause we all moved North the same time and to the same apartment then spread out gradual to breathe. And our parents would yank our heads into some kinda shape and crisp up our clothes so we'd be presentable for travel with Miss Moore, who always looked like she was going to church, though she never did. Which is just one of the things the grownups talked about when they talked behind her back like a dog. But when she came calling with some sachet she'd sewed up or some gingerbread she'd made or some book, why then they'd all be too embarrassed to turn her down and we'd get handed over all spruced up. She'd been to college and said it was only right that she should take responsibility for the young ones' education, and she not even related by marriage or blood. So they'd go for it. Specially Aunt Gretchen. She was the main gofer in the family. You got some ole dumb shit foolishness you want somebody to go for, you send for Aunt Gretchen. She been screwed into the go-along for so long, it's a blood-deep natural thing with her. Which is how she got saddled with me and Sugar and Junior in the first place while our mothers were in a la-de-da apartment up the block having a good ole time.

So this one day Miss Moore rounds us all up at the mailbox and it's purdee hot and she's knockin herself out about arithmetic. And school suppose to let up in summer I heard, but she don't never let up. And the starch in my pinafore scratching the shit outta me and I'm really hating this nappy-head bitch and her god-damn college degree. I'd much rather go to the pool or to the show where it's cool. So me and Sugar leaning on the mailbox being surly, which is a Miss

Moore word. And Flyboy checking out what everybody brought for lunch. And Fat Butt already wasting his peanut-butter-and-jelly sandwich like the pig he is. And Junebug punchin on Q.T.'s arm for potato chips. And Rosie Giraffe shifting from one hip to the other waiting for somebody to step on her foot or ask her if she from Georgia so she can kick ass, preferably Mercedes'. And Miss Moore asking us do we know what money is, like we a bunch of retards. I mean real money, she say, like it's only poker chips or monopoly papers we lay on the grocer. So right away I'm tired of this and say so. And would much rather snatch Sugar and go to the Sunset and terrorize the West Indian kids and take their hair ribbons and their money too. And Miss Moore files that remark away for next week's lesson on brotherhood, I can tell. And finally I say we oughta get to the subway cause it's cooler and besides we might meet some cute boys. Sugar done swiped her mama's lipstick, so we ready.

So we heading down the street and she's boring us silly about what things cost and what our parents make and how much goes for rent and how money ain't divided up right in this country. And then she gets to the part about we all poor and live in the slums, which I don't feature. And I'm ready to speak on that, but she steps out in the street and hails two cabs just like that. Then she hustles half the crew in with her and hands me a five-dollar bill and tells me to calculate 10 percent tip for the driver. And we're off. Me and Sugar and Junebug and Flyboy hangin out the window and hollering to everybody, putting lipstick on each other cause Flyboy a faggot anyway, and making farts with our sweaty armpits. But I'm mostly trying to figure how to spend this money. But they all fascinated with the meter ticking and Junebug starts laying bets as to how much it'll read when Flyboy can't hold his breath no more. Then Sugar lays bets as to how much it'll be when we get there. So I'm stuck. Don't nobody want to go for my plan, which is to jump out at the next light and run off to the first bar-b-que we can find. Then the driver tells us to get the hell out cause we there already. And the meter reads eighty-five cents. And I'm stalling to figure out the tip and Sugar say give him a dime. And I decide he don't need it bad as I do, so later for him. But then he tries to take off with Junebug foot still in the door so we talk about his mama something ferocious. Then we check out that we on Fifth Avenue and everybody dressed up in stockings. One lady in a fur coat, hot as it is. White folks crazy.

"This is the place," Miss Moore say, presenting it to us in the voice she uses at the museum. "Let's look in the windows before we go in."

"Can we steal?" Sugar asks very serious like she's getting the ground rules squared away before she plays. "I beg your pardon," say Miss Moore, and we fall out. So she leads us around the windows of the toy store and me and Sugar

screamin, "This is mine, that's mine, I gotta have that, that was made for me, I was born for that," till Big Butt drowns us out.

"Hey, I'm goin to buy that there."

"That there? You don't even know what it is, stupid."

"I do so," he say punchin on Rosie Giraffe. "It's a microscope."

"Whatcha gonna do with a microscope, fool?"

"Look at things."

"Like what, Ronald?" ask Miss Moore. And Big Butt ain't got the first notion. So here go Miss Moore gabbing about the thousands of bacteria in a drop of water and the somethinorother in a speck of blood and the million and one living things in the air around us is invisible to the naked eye. And what she say that for? Junebug go to town on that "naked" and we rolling. Then Miss Moore ask what it cost. So we all jam into the window smudgin it up and the price tag say $300. So then she ask how long'd take for Big Butt and Junebug to save up their allowances. "Too long," I said. "Yeh," adds Sugar, "outgrown it by that time." And Miss Moore say no, you never outgrow learning instruments. "Why, even medical students and interns and," blah, blah, blah. And we ready to choke Big Butt for bringing it up in the first damn place.

"This here costs four hundred eighty dollars," say Rosie Giraffe. So we pile up all over her to see what she pointin out. My eyes tell me it's a chunk of glass cracked with something heavy and different-color inks dripped into the splits, then the whole thing put into a oven or something. But for $480 it don't make sense.

"That's a paperweight made of semi-precious stones fused together under tremendous pressure," she explains slowly, with her hands doing the mining and all the factory work.

"So what's a paperweight?" asks Rosie Giraffe.

"To weigh paper with, dumbbell," say Flyboy, the wise man from the East.

"Not exactly," say Miss Moore, which is what she say when you warm or way off too. "It's to weigh paper down so it won't scatter and make your desk untidy." So right away me and Sugar curtsy to each other and then to Mercedes who is more the tidy type.

"We don't keep paper on top of the desk in my class," say Junebug, figuring Miss Moore crazy or lyin one.

"At home, then," she say. "Don't you have a calendar and a pencil case and a blotter and a letter-opener on your desk at home where you do your homework?" And she know damn well what our homes look like cause she nosys around in them every chance she gets.

"I don't even have a desk," say Junebug. "Do we?"

"No. And I don't get no homework neither," say Big Butt.

"And I don't even have a home," say Flyboy like he do at school to keep the white folks off his back and sorry for him. Send this poor kid to camp posters is his specialty.

"I do," say Mercedes. "I have a box of stationery on my desk and a picture of my cat. My godmother bought the stationery and the desk. There's a big rose on each sheet and the envelopes smell like roses."

"Who wants to know about your smelly-ass stationery," say Rosie Giraffe fore I can get my two cents in.

"It's important to have a work area all your own so that . . . "

"Will you look at this sailboat, please," say Flyboy, cuttin her off and pointin to the thing like it was his. So once again we tumble all over each other to gaze at this magnificent thing in the toy store which is just big enough to maybe sail two kittens across the pond if you strap them to the posts tight. We all start reciting the price tag like we in assembly. "Handcrafted sailboat of fiberglass at one thousand one hundred ninety-five dollars."

"Unbelievable," I hear myself say and am really stunned. I read it again for myself just in case the group recitation put me in a trance. Same thing. For some reason this pisses me off. We look at Miss Moore and she lookin at us, waiting for I dunno what.

Who'd pay all that when you can buy a sailboat set for a quarter at Pop's, a tube of glue for a dime, and a ball of string for eight cents? "It must have a motor and a whole lot else besides," I say. "My sailboat cost me about fifty cents."

"But will it take water?" say Mercedes with her smart ass.

"Took mine to Alley Pond Park once," say Flyboy. "String broke. Lost it. Pity."

"Sailed mine in Central Park and it keeled over and sank. Had to ask my father for another dollar."

"And you got the strap," laugh Big Butt. "The jerk didn't even have a string on it. My old man wailed on his behind."

Little Q.T. was staring hard at the sailboat and you could see he wanted it bad. But he too little and somebody'd just take it from him. So what the hell. "This boat for kids, Miss Moore?"

"Parents silly to buy something like that just to get all broke up," say Rosie Giraffe.

"That much money it should last forever," I figure.

"My father'd buy it for me if I wanted it."

"Your father, my ass," say Rosie Giraffe getting a chance to finally push Mercedes.

"Must be rich people shop here," say Q.T.

"You are a very bright boy," say Flyboy. "What was your first clue?" And he rap him on the head with the back of his knuckles, since Q.T. the only one he could get away with. Though Q.T. liable to come up behind you years later and get his licks in when you half expect it.

"What I want to know is," I say to Miss Moore though I never talk to her, I wouldn't give the bitch that satisfaction, "is how much a real boat costs? I figure a thousand'd get you a yacht any day."

"Why don't you check that out," she say, "and report back to the group?" Which really pains my ass. If you gonna mess up a perfectly good swim day least you could do is have some answers. "Let's go in," she say like she got something up her sleeve. Only she don't lead the way. So me and Sugar turn the corner to where the entrance is, but when we get there I kinda hang back. Not that I'm scared, what's there to be afraid of, just a toy store. But I feel funny, shame. But what I got to be shamed about? Got as much right to go in as anybody. But somehow I can't seem to get hold of the door, so I step away for Sugar to lead. But she hangs back too. And I look at her and she looks at me and this is ridiculous. I mean, damn, I have never ever been shy about doing nothing or going nowhere. But then Mercedes steps up and then Rosie Giraffe and Big Butt crowd in behind and shove, and next thing we all stuffed into the doorway with only Mercedes squeezing past us, smoothing out her jumper and walking right down the aisle. Then the rest of us tumble in like a glued-together jigsaw done all wrong. And people lookin at us. And it's like the time me and Sugar crashed into the Catholic church on a dare. But once we got in there and everything so hushed and holy and the candles and the bowin and the handkerchiefs on all the drooping heads, I just couldn't go through with the plan. Which was for me to run up to the altar and do a tap dance while Sugar played the nose flute and messed around in the holy water. And Sugar kept givin me the elbow. Then later teased me so bad I tied her up in the shower and turned it on and locked her in. And she'd be there till this day if Aunt Gretchen hadn't finally figured I was lyin about the boarder takin a shower.

Same thing in the store. We all walkin on tiptoe and hardly touchin the games and puzzles and things. And I watched Miss Moore who is steady watchin us like she waitin for a sign. Like Mama Drewery watches the sky and sniffs the air and takes note of just how much slant is in the bird formation. Then me and Sugar bump smack into each other, so busy gazing at the toys, specially the sailboat. But we don't laugh and go into our fat-lady bump-stomach routine. We just stare at that price tag. Then Sugar run a finger over the whole boat. And I'm jealous and want to hit her. Maybe not her, but I sure want to punch somebody in the mouth.

"Watcha bring us here for, Miss Moore?"

"You sound angry, Sylvia. Are you mad about something?" Givin me one of them grins like she tellin a grown-up joke that never turns out to be funny. And she's lookin very closely at me like maybe she plannin to do my portrait from memory. I'm mad, but I won't give her that satisfaction. So I slouch around the store being very bored and say, "Let's go."

Me and Sugar at the back of the train watchin the tracks whizzin by large then small then gettin gobbled up in the dark. I'm thinkin about this tricky toy I saw in the store.

A clown that somersaults on a bar then does chin-ups just cause you yank lightly at his leg. Cost $35. I could see me askin my mother for a $35 birthday clown. "You wanna who that costs what?" she'd say, cocking her head to the side to get a better view of the hole in my head. Thirty-five dollars could buy new bunk beds for Junior and Gretchen's boy. Thirty-five dollars and the whole household could go visit Granddaddy Nelson in the country. Thirty-five dollars would pay for the rent and the piano bill too. Who are these people that spend that much for performing clowns and $1,000 for toy sailboats? What kinda work they do and how they live and how come we ain't in on it? Where we are is who we are, Miss Moore always pointin out. But it don't necessarily have to be that way, she always adds then waits for somebody to say that poor people have to wake up and demand their share of the pie and don't none of us know what kind of pie she talkin about in the first damn place. But she ain't so smart cause I still got her four dollars from the taxi and she sure ain't gettin it. Messin up my day with this shit. Sugar nudges me in my pocket and winks.

Miss Moore lines us up in front of the mailbox where we started from, seem like years ago, and I got a headache for thinkin so hard. And we lean all over each other so we can hold up under the draggy-ass lecture she always finishes us off with at the end before we thank her for borin us to tears. But she just looks at us like she readin tea leaves. Finally she say, "Well, what did you think of F.A.O. Schwarz?"

Rosie Giraffe mumbles, "White folks crazy."

"I'd like to go there again when I get my birthday money," says Mercedes, and we shove her out the pack so she has to lean on the mailbox by herself.

"I'd like a shower. Tiring day," said Flyboy.

Then Sugar surprises me by sayin, "You know, Miss Moore, I don't think all of us here put together eat in a year what that sailboat costs." And Miss Moore lights up like somebody goosed her. "And?" she say, urging Sugar on. Only I'm standin on her foot so she don't continue.

"Imagine for a minute what kind of society it is in which some people can spend on a toy what it would cost to feed a family of six or seven. What do you think?"

"I think," say Sugar pushing me off her feet like she never done before, cause I whip her ass in a minute, "that this is not much of a democracy if you ask me. Equal chance to pursue happiness means an equal crack at the dough, don't it?" Miss Moore is besides herself and I am disgusted with Sugar's treachery. So I stand on her foot one more time to see if she'll shove me. She shuts up, and Miss Moore looks at me, sorrowfully I'm thinkin. And somethin weird is goin on, I can feel it in my chest.

"Anybody else learn anything today?" lookin dead at me. I walk away and Sugar has to run to catch up and don't even seem to notice when I shrug her arm off my shoulder.

"Well, we got four dollars anyway," she said.

"Uh hunh."

"We could go to Hascombs and get half a chocolate layer and then go to the Sunset and still have plenty money for potato chips and ice-cream sodas."

"Uh hunh."

"Race you to Hascombs," she say.

We start down the block and she gets ahead which is O.K. by me cause I'm goin to the West End and then over to the Drive to think this day through. She can run if she want to and even run faster. But ain't nobody gonna beat me at nuthin.

My Man Bovanne

Blind people got a hummin jones if you notice. Which is understandable completely once you been around one and notice what no eyes will force you into to see people, and you get past the first time, which seems to come out of nowhere, and it's like you in church again with fat-chest ladies and old gents gruntin a hum low in the throat to whatever the preacher be saying. Shakey Bee bottom lip all swole up with Sweet Peach and me explainin how come the sweet-potato bread was a dollar-quarter this time stead of dollar regular and he say uh huh he understand, then he break into this *thizzin* kind of hum which is quiet, but fiercesome just the same, if you ain't ready for it. Which I wasn't. But I got used to it and the onliest time I had to say somethin bout it was when he was playin checkers on the stoop one time and he commenst to hummin quite churchy seem to me. So I says, "Look here Shakey Bee, I can't beat you and Jesus too." He stop.

So that's how come I asked My Man Bovanne to dance. He ain't my man mind you, just a nice ole gent from the block that we all know cause he fixes things and the kids like him. Or used to fore Black Power got hold their minds and mess em around till they can't be civil to ole folks. So we at this benefit for my niece's cousin who's runnin for somethin with this Black party somethin or other behind her. And I press up close to dance with Bovanne who blind and I'm hummin and he hummin, chest to chest like talkin. Not jammin my breasts into the man. Wasn't bout tits. Was bout vibrations. And he dug it and asked me what color dress I had on and how my hair was fixed and how I was doin without a man, not nosy but nice-like, and who was at this affair and was the canapés dainty-stingy or healthy enough to get hold of proper. Comfy and cheery is what I'm tryin to get across. Touch talkin like the heel of the hand on the tambourine or on a drum.

But right away Joe Lee come up on us and frown for dancin so close to the man. My own son who knows what kind of warm I am about; and don't grown men call me long distance and in the middle of the night for a little Mama comfort? But he frown. Which ain't right since Bovanne can't see and defend himself. Just a nice old man who fixes toasters and busted irons and bicycles and things and changes the lock on my door when my men friends get messy. Nice man. Which is not why they invited him. Grass roots you see. Me and Sister Taylor and the woman who does heads at Mamies and the man from the barber shop, we all there on account of we grass roots. And I ain't never been souther than Brooklyn Battery and no more country than the window box on my fire escape. And just yesterday my kids tellin me to take them countrified rags off my head and be cool. And now can't get Black enough to suit em. So everybody passin sayin My Man Bovanne. Big deal, keep steppin and don't even stop a minute to get the man a drink or one of them cute sandwiches or tell him what's goin on. And him standin there with a smile ready case someone do speak he want to be ready. So that's how come I pull him on the dance floor and we dance squeezin past the tables and chairs and all them coats and people standin round up in each other face talkin bout this and that but got no use for this blind man who mostly fixed skates and skooters for all these folks when they was just kids. So I'm pressed up close and we touch talkin with the hum. And here come my daughter cuttin her eye at me like she do when she tell me about my "apolitical" self like I got hoof and mouf disease and there ain't no hope at all. And I don't pay her no mind and just look up in Bovanne shadow face and tell him his stomach like a drum and he laugh. Laugh real loud. And here come my youngest, Task, with a tap on my elbow like he the third-grade monitor and I'm cuttin up on the line to assembly.

"I was just talkin on the drums," I explained when they hauled me into the kitchen. I figured drums was my best defense. They can get ready for drums what with all this heritage business. And Bovanne stomach just like that drum Task give me when he come back from Africa. You just touch it and it hum thizzm, thizzm. So I stuck to the drum story. "Just drummin that's all."

"Mama, what are you talkin about?"

"She had too much to drink," say Elo to Task cause she don't hardly say nuthin to me direct no more since that ugly argument about my wigs.

"Look here Mama," say Task, the gentle one. "We just trying to pull your coat. You were makin a spectacle of yourself out there dancing like that."

"Dancin like what?"

Task run a hand over his left ear like his father for the world and his father before that.

"Like a bitch in heat," say Elo.

"Well uhh, I was goin to say like one of them sex-starved ladies gettin on in years and not too discriminating. Know what I mean?"

I don't answer cause I'll cry. Terrible thing when your own children talk to you like that. Pullin me out the party and hustlin me into some stranger's kitchen in the back of a bar just like the damn police. And ain't like I'm old old. I can still wear me some sleeveless dresses without the meat hangin off my arm. And I keep up with some things through my kids. Who ain't kids no more. To hear them tell it. So I don't say nuthin.

"Dancin with that tom," say Elo to Joe Lee, who leanin on the folks' freezer. "His feet can smell a cracker a mile away and go into their shuffle number post haste. And them eyes. He could be a little considerate and put on some shades. Who wants to look into them blown-out fuses that—"

"Is this what they call the generation gap?" I say.

"Generation gap," spits Elo, like I suggested castor oil and fricassee possum in the milk-shakes or somethin. "That's a white concept for a white phenomenon. There's no generation gap among Black people. We are a col—"

"Yeh, well never mind," says Joe Lee. "The point is Mama . . . well, it's pride. You embarrass yourself and us too dancin like that."

"I wasn't shame." Then nobody say nuthin. Them standin there in they pretty clothes with drinks in they hands and gangin up on me, and me in the third-degree chair and nary a olive to my name. Felt just like the police got hold to me.

"First of all," Task say, holding up his hand and tickin off the offenses, "the dress. Now that dress is too short, Mama, and too low-cut for a woman your age. And Tamu's going to make a speech tonight to kick off the campaign and will be introducin you and expecting you to organize the council of elders—"

"Me? Didn nobody ask me nuthin. You mean Nisi? She change her name?"

"Well, Norton was supposed to tell you about it. Nisi wants to introduce you and then encourage the older folks ass. And people'll say, 'Ain't that the horny bitch that was to form a Council of the Elders to act as an advisory—"

"And you going to be standing there with your boobs out and that wig on your head and that hem up to your ass. And people'll say, 'Ain't that the horny bitch that was grindin with the blind dude?'"

"Elo, be cool a minute," say Task, gettin to the next finger. "And then there's the drinkin. Mama, you know you can't drink cause next thing you know you be laughin loud and carryin on," and he grab another finger for the loudness. "And then there's the dancin. You been tattooed on the man for four records straight and slow draggin even on the fast numbers. How you think that look for a woman your age?"

"What's my age?"

"What?"

"I'm axin you all a simple question. You keep talkin bout what's proper for a woman my age. How old am I anyhow?" And Joe Lee slams his eyes shut and squinches up his face to figure. And Task run a hand over his ear and stare into his glass like the ice cubes goin calculate for him. And Elo just starin at the top of my head like she goin rip the wig off any minute now.

"Is your hair braided up under that thing? If so, why don't you take it off? You always did do a neat cornroll."

"Uh huh," cause I'm thinkin how she couldn't undo her hair fast enough talking bout cornroll so countrified. None of which was the subject. "How old, I say?"

"Sixtee-one or—"

"You a damn lie Joe Lee Peoples."

"And that's another thing," say Task on the fingers.

"You know what you all can kiss," I said, gettin up and brushin the wrinkles out my lap.

"Oh, Mama," Elo say, puttin a hand on my shoulder like she hasn't done since she left home and the hand landin light and not sure it supposed to be there. Which hurt me to my heart. Cause this was the child in our happiness fore Mr. Peoples die. And I carried that child strapped to my chest till she was nearly two. We was close is what I'm tryin to tell you. Cause it was more me in the child than the others. And even after Task it was the girlchild I covered in the night and wept over for no reason at all less it was she was a chub-chub like me and not very pretty, but a warm child. And how did things get to this, that she can't put a sure hand on me and say Mama we love you and care about you and you entitled to enjoy yourself cause you a good woman?

"And then there's Reverend Trent," say Task, glancin from left to right like they hatchin a plot and just now lettin me in on it. "You were suppose to be talking with him tonight, Mama, about giving us his basement for campaign headquarters and—"

"Didn nobody tell me nuthin. If grass roots mean you kept in the dark I can't use it. I really can't. And Reven Trent a fool anyway the way he tore into the widow man up there on Edgecomb cause he wouldn't take in three of them foster children and the woman not even comfy in the ground yet and the man's mind messed up and—"

"Look here," say Task. "What we need is a family conference so we can get all this stuff cleared up and laid out on the table. In the meantime I think we better get back into the other room and tend to business. And in the meantime, Mama, see if you can't get to Reverend Trent and—"

"You want me to belly rub with the Reven, that it?"

"Oh damn," Elo say and go through the swingin door.

"We'll talk about all this at dinner. How's tomorrow night, Joe Lee?" While Joe Lee being self-important I'm wonderin who's doin the cookin and how come no body ax me if I'm free and do I get a corsage and things like that. Then Joe nod that it's O.K. and he go through the swingin door and just a little hubbub come through from the other room. Then Task smile his smile, lookin just like his daddy, and he leave. And it just me in this stranger's kitchen, which was a mess I wouldn't never let my kitchen look like. Poison you just to look at the pots. Then the door swing the other way and it's My Man Bovanne standin there sayin Miss Hazel but lookin at the deep fry and then at the steam table, and most surprised when I come up on him from the other direction and take him on out of there. Pass the folks pushin up towards the stage where Nisi and some other people settin and ready to talk, and folks gettin to the last of the sandwiches and the booze fore they settle down in one spot and listen serious. And I'm thinkin bout tellin Bovanne what a lovely long dress Nisi got on and the earrings and her hair piled up in a cone and the people bout to hear how we all gettin screwed and gotta form our own party and everybody there listenin and lookin. But instead I just haul the man on out of there, and Joe Lee and his wife look at me like I'm terrible, but they ain't said boo to the man yet. Cause he blind and old and don't nobody there need him since they grown up and don't need they skates fixed no more.

"Where we goin, Miss Hazel?" Him knowin all the time.

"First we gonna buy you some dark sunglasses. Then you comin with me to the supermarket so I can pick up tomorrow's dinner, which is goin to be a grand thing proper and you invited. Then we goin to my house."

"That be fine. I surely would like to rest my feet." Bein cute, but you got to let men play out they little show, blind or not. So he chat on bout how tired he is and how he appreciate me takin him in hand this way. And I'm thinkin I'll have him change the lock on my door first thing. Then I'll give the man a nice warm bath with jasmine leaves in the water and a little Epsom salt on the sponge to do his back. And then a good rubdown with rose water and olive oil. Then a cup of lemon tea with a taste in it. And a little talcum, some of that fancy stuff Nisi mother sent over last Christmas. And then a massage, a good face massage round the forehead which is the worryin part. Cause you gots to take care of the older folks. And let them know they still needed to run the mimeo machine and keep the spark plugs clean and fix the mailboxes for folks who might help us get the breakfast program goin, and the school for the little kids and the campaign and all. Cause old folks is the nation. That what Nisi was sayin and I mean to do my part.

"I imagine you are a very pretty woman, Miss Hazel."

"I surely am," I say just like the hussy my daughter always say I was.

J. California Cooper (b. 1940?)

Playwright, short story writer, and novelist, J. California Cooper is known for writing affirmative stories that deal with vice and virtue, good and evil. Her first-person narrators tell simple stories of their struggles and triumphs. *A Piece of Mine* (1984) was the first book to be published by Wild Tree Press, started by Alice Walker and Robert Allen. In her foreword to the collection, Walker comments on the "strong folk flavor" of Cooper's work. *Homemade Love* (1986), winner of an American Book Award, is a collection of thirteen stories about what Cooper calls "love that is not bought, not wrapped in fancy packaging with glib lines that often lie." *Some Soul to Keep* (1987) consists of five stories about friendships, betrayal, racism, and virtue. Cooper published three novels in quick succession: *Family* (1991), about a slave woman who tries to kill herself and her children; the children live, but she dies. Her death, however, does not stop her from continuing to narrate her story, a story about how all races share the same blood. *In Search of Satisfaction* (1994) is a morality story that takes place in the postslavery era. In 1998, she published *Wake of the Wind*, another post-slavery saga of a resilient black family. Cooper has also written seventeen plays and three other fiction collections: *The Matter Is Life* (1991), *Some Love, Some Pain, Sometime* (1995), and *The Future Has a Past* (2000). Born in Berkeley, California, Cooper attended various colleges and in 1978 was named Black Playwright of the Year. In addition to the American Book Award, she received the James Baldwin Writing Award (1988) and the Literary Lion Award from the American Library Association (1988).

From *A Piece of Mine*

A Jewel for a Friend

I have my son bring me down here to this homegrown graveyard two or three times a week so I can clean it and sweep it and sit here among my friends in my rocking chair under this Sycamore tree, where I will be buried one day, soon now, I hope. I'm 90 years old and I am tired . . . and I miss all my friends too. I come back to visit them because ain't nobody left in town but a few old doddering fools I didn't bother with when I was younger so why go bothern now just cause we all hangin on? Its peaceful here. The wind is soft, the sun is gentle even in the deep summer. Maybe it's the cold that comes from under the ground that keeps it cool. I don't know. I only know that I like to rest here in my final restin place and know how its gonna be a thousand years after I am put here under that stone I have bought and paid for long ago . . . long ago.

After I eat my lunch and rest a bit, I gets down to my real work here in this graveyard! I pack a hammer and chisel

in my bags and when I's alone, I take them and go over to Tommy Jones' beautiful tombstone his fancy daughter bought for him and chip, grind and break away little pieces of it! Been doin it for eleven years now and its most half gone. I ain't gonna die til its all gone! Then I be at peace! I ain't got to tell a wise one that I hate Tommy Jones, you must know that yourself now! . . . If I am killin his tombstone! I hate him. See, his wife, my friend, Pearl, used to lay next to him, but I had her moved, kinda secret like, least without tellin anyone. I hired two mens to dig her coffin up and move her over here next to where I'm going to be and they didn't know nobody and ain't told nobody. It don't matter none noway cause who gon pay somebody to dig her up again? And put her back? Who cares bout her? . . . and where she lay for eternity? Nobody! But me . . . I do.

See, we growed up together. I am Ruby and she is Pearl and we was jewels. We use to always say that. We use to act out how these jewels would act. I was always strong, deep red and solid deep. She was brown but she was all lightness and frail and innocent, smooth and weak and later on I realized, made out of pain.

I grew up in a big sprawling family and my sons take after them, while Pearl grew up in a little puny one. Her mama kissed her daddy's ass til he kicked her's on way from

---

From *A Piece of Mine*, copyright © 1984 by Joan Cooper. Used by permission of Doubleday, a division of Random House, Inc.

here! That's her grave way over there . . . Way, way over there in the corner. That's his with that cement marker, from when he died two years later from six bullets in his face by another woman what didn't take that kickin stuff! Well, they say what goes around . . . But "they" says all kinda things . . . can't be sure bout nothin "they" says. Just watch your Bible . . . that's the best thing I ever seen and I'm 90! Now!

Anyway, Pearl and me grew up round here, went to school and all. A two room school with a hall down the middle. Pearl nice and everybody should of liked her, but they didn't. Them girls was always pickin on her, til I get in it. See I was not so nice and everybody did like me! Just loved me sometime! I pertected her. I wouldn't let nobody hurt her! Some of em got mad at me, but what could they do? I rather fight than eat! Use to eat a'plenty too! I was a big strong, long-armed and long-legged girl. Big head, short hair. I loved my eyes tho! Oh, they was pretty. They still strong! And I had pretty hands, even with all that field work, they still was pretty! My great grandchildren takes care of em for me now . . . rubs em and all. So I can get out here two or three times a week and hammer Tommy Jones' gravestone. Its almost half gone now . . . so am I.

When we got to marryin time . . . everybody got to that, some in love and some just tryin to get away from a home what was full of house work and field work and baby sister and brother work. I don't know how we was all too dumb to know, even when we got married and in a place of our own, it was all headin down to the same road we thought we was gettin away from! Well, I went after Gee Cee! He was the biggest boy out there and suited me just fine! I use to run that man with rocks and sticks and beat him up even. He wouldn't hurt me, you know, just play. But I finally got him to thinkin he loved me and one night, over there by the creek behind the church, way behind the church, I gave him somethin he musta not forgot . . . and we was soon gettin married. I didn't forget it . . . I named it George, Jr. That was my first son.

In the meantime the boys all seem to like Pearl and she grinned at all of em! She seem to be kinda extra stuck on that skinny rail, Tommy Jones, with the bare spot on the side of his head! He liked everybody! A girl couldn't pass by him without his hand on em, quick and fast and gone. I didn't like him! Too shifty for me . . . a liar! I can't stand a liar! His family had a little money and he always looked nice but he still wasn't nothin but a nice lookin liar what was shifty! Still and all, when I had done pushed Pearl around a few times tryin to make her not like him, he began to press on her and every way she turned, he was there! He just wouldn't let up when he saw I didn't like him for her! He gave her little trinkets and little cakes, flowers, home picked. Finally she let him in her deepest life and soon she was pregnant and then he got mad cause he had to marry her! I fought against that and

when he found out it made him grin all the way through the little ceremony. I was her best lady or whatever you call it, cause I was her best friend.

Then everything was over and we was all married and havin children and life got a roll on and we had to roll with it and that took all our energies to survive and soon we was back in the same picture we had run away from cept the faces had changed. Stead of mama's faces, they was ours. And daddy's was the men we had married. Lots of times the stove and sink was the same and the plow was the same. In time, the mules changed.

Well, in time, everything happened. I had three sons and two daughters, big ones! Liked to kill me even gettin here! Pearl had one son and one daughter. Son was just like his daddy and daughter was frail and sickly. I think love makes you healthy and I think that child was sickly cause wasn't much love in that house of Pearl's, not much laughter. Tommy Jones, after the second child, never made love to Pearl again regular, maybe a year or two or three apart. She stayed faithful, but hell, faithful to what? He had done inherited some money and was burnin these roads up! He'd be a hundred miles away for a week or two, whole lotta times. Pearl worked, takin them children with her when I could'n keep em. But I had to rest sometimes, hell! I had five of my own and I had done told her bout that Tommy Jones anyway! But I still looked out for her and fed em when she couldn't. Yet and still, when he came home he just fall in the bed and sleep and sleep til time to get up and bathe and dress in the clothes he bought hisself and leave them again! If she cry and complain he just laugh and leave. I guess that's what you call leavin them laughin or somethin!

One day he slapped her and when he saw she wasn't gonna do nothin but just cry and take it, that came to be a regular thing! For years, I mean years, I never went over her house to take food when she didn't have some beatin up marks on her! I mean it! That's when she started comin over to the cemetery to clean it up and find her place. She also began savin a nickle here and a dime there to pay for her gravestone. That's what she dreamed about! Can you imagine that?!! A young, sposed to be healthy woman daydreamin bout dyin!!? Well, she did! And carried that money faithfully to the white man sells them things and paid on a neat little ruby colored stone, what he was puttin her name on, just leavin the dates out! Now!

My sons was gettin married, havin babies, strong like they mama and papa, when her son got killed, trying to be like his daddy! He had done screwed the wrong man's daughter! They put what was left of him in that grave over there, behind that bush of roses Pearl planted years ago to remember him by. Well, what can I say? I'm a mother, she was a mother, you love them no matter what! The daughter had strengthened up and was goin on to school somewhere with the help of her father's people. And you know, she didn't give her mother no concern, no respect? Treated her like the house dog in a manger. I just don't believe you can have any luck like that! It takes time, sometime, to get the payback, but time is always rollin on and one day, it will roll over you! Anyway even when the daughter had made it up to a young lady and was schoolin with the sons and daughters of black business people, she almost forgot her daddy too! She was gonna marry a man with SOMETHIN and she didn't want them at the weddin! Now! And tole em! Her daddy went anyway, so she dressed him cause he was broke now, and after the weddin, got his drunk ass out of town quick as lightnin cross the sky and he came home and taunted Pearl that her own daughter didn't love her! Now!

Well, time went on, I had troubles with such a big family, grandchildren comin and all. Love, love, love everywhere, cause I didn't low nothin else! Pretty faces, pretty smiles, round, fat stomachs, and pigtails flying everywhere and pretty nappy-headed boys growin up to be president someday, even if they never were . . . they was my presidents and congressmen! I could chew em up and swollow em sometimes, even today, grown as they are! We could take care of our problems, they was just livin problems . . . everyday kinds.

Pearl just seem to get quiet way back in her mind and heart. She went on, but she was workin harder to pay for that tombstone. The name was complete, only the last date was open and finally it was paid for. With blood, sweat and tears for true . . . seem like that's too much to pay for dyin!

One night I had bathed and smelled myself up for that old hard head of mine, Gee Cee, when a neighbor of Pearl's came runnin over screamin that Tommy Jones was really beatin up on Pearl. I threw my clothes on fast as I could and ran all the way and I was comin into some age then, runnin was not what I planned to do much of! When I got there, he had done seen me comin and he was gone, long gone, on them long, narrow, quick to run to mischief feet of his! I had got there in time to keep him from accidently killin her, but she was pretty well beat! He had wanted her rent and food money, she said, but she would not give it to him, so he beat her. She cried and held on to me, she was so frail, so little, but she was still pretty to me, little grey hairs and all. She thanked me as I washed her and changed the bed and combed her hair and fed her some warm soup and milk. She cried a little as she was tellin me all she ever wanted was a little love like I had. I cried too and told her that's all anybody wants.

When I was through fixin her and she was restin nice and easy, I sat by the bed and pulled the covers up and she said, "Hold my hand, I'm so cold." Well I grabbed her hand and held, then I rubbed her arms tryin to keep her warm and alive. Then, I don't know, life just kept rollin and I began to rub her whole little beautiful sore body . . . all over . . . and when I got to them bruised places I kissed them and licked them too and placed my body beside her body in her bed and the love for her just flowed and flowed. One minute I loved her like a child, the next like a mother, then she was the mother, then I was the child, then as a woman friend, then as a man. Ohhhhh, I loved her. I didn't know exactly what to do but my body did it for me and I did everything I could to make her feel loved and make her feel like Gee Cee makes me feel, so I did everything I could that he had ever done to me to make me feel good, but I forgot Gee Cee . . . and I cried. Not sad crying, happy cryin, and my tears and my love were all over her and she was holding me. She was holding me . . . so close, so close. Then we slept and when I wakened up, I went home . . . and I felt good, not bad. I know you don't need nothin "forever," just so you get close to love sometime.

Well Pearl got better. When we saw each other, we weren't embarrassed or shamed. She hit me on my shoulder and I thumped her on her head as we had done all our lives anyway. We never did it again, we didn't have to!

Pearl wasn't made, I guess, for the kind of life she had somehow chosen, so a few years later she died and Tommy Jones picked her plot, right over there where she used to be, and put her there and the tombstone man put that old-brand-new ruby colored gravestone on her grave. The preacher said a few words cause there wasn't much to pay him with and we all went home to our own lifes, of course.

Soon, I commence to comin over here and sweepin and cleanin up and plantin plants around and this ole Sycamore tree, Pearl had planted at her house, was moved over here before Tommy Jones got put out for not payin rent. I planted it right here over where Gee Cee, me and Pearl gonna be. I likes shade. Anyway I was out here so much that's how I was able to notice the day Pearl's tombstone disappeared. Well, I like to died! I knew what that tombstone had gone through to get there! Right away I had my sons get out and find out what had happened and they found out that Tommy Jones was livin mighty hard and was mighty broke and had stole that tombstone and took it way off and sold if for a few dollars! You can chisel the name off, you know? But I can't understand what anyone would want a used tombstone for! I mean, for God's sake, get your own!! At least die first-class even if you couldn't live that way! Well, we couldn't find how to get it back so that's when I started payin on another one for her, and yes, for me and Gee Cee too. They's paid for now.

In the meantime, liquor and hard livin and a knife put Tommy Jones to rest, and imagine this, that daughter of theirs came down here and bought ONE gravestone for her DADDY!!! To hold up her name I guess, but that's all she did, then she left! Ain't been back!

Well, life goes on, don't it! Whew!

Now I come here over the years and chip away and chisel and hammer away cause he don't deserve no stone since he stole Pearl's. He never give her nothin but them two babies what was just like him and then he stole the last most important thing she wanted! So me, I'm gonna see that he don't have one either! When it's through, I'm gonna be through, then the gravestone man can bring them two stones over here, they bought and paid for! And he can place them here beside each other, for the rest of thousands of years. I'm in the middle, between Gee Cee and Pearl, like I'm sposed to be. They don't say much, but Ruby and the dates and Pearl's on hers, and the dates. Then my husband's name and the children on mine and her children's on hers. And that's all. I mean, how much can a gravestone say anyway?

Afterword

After Ruby died at 91 years of age, Gee Cee was still living at 90 years of age and he had a marker laid across the two graves saying, "Friends, all the way to the End." It's still there.

BarbaraNeely (b. 1941)

When BarbaraNeely published *Blanche on the Lam* (1992), she won three awards for best first mystery novel: the Agatha, the Anthony, and the Macavity Awards. Like Alice Childress's domestic worker, Mildred, Blanche is a working-class domestic who is able to explode and theorize the lives of her employers. Rather than being doubly white as her name would imply, Blanche White is a dark-skinned black woman with the smarts necessary to solve any crime. Neely followed her first novel with *Blanche among the Talented Tenth* (1994), *Blanche Cleans Up* (1998), and *Blanche Passes Go* (2000), thus claiming the mystery novel as territory for African American women writers, as Walter Mosley has done for African American male writers. Neely grew up in Lebanon, Pennsylvania. She earned a Master's degree in urban and regional planning from the University of Pittsburgh in 1971.

Spilled Salt

"I'm home, Ma."

Myrna pressed down hard on the doorknob and stared blankly up into Kenny's large brown eyes and freckled face so much like her own he was nearly her twin. But he was taller than she remembered. Denser.

He'd written to say he was getting out. She hadn't answered his letter, hoping her lack of response would keep him away.

"You're here." She stepped back from the door, pretending not to see him reach out and try to touch her.

But a part of her had leaped to life at the sight of him. No matter what, she was glad he hadn't been maimed or murdered in prison. He at least looked whole and healthy of body. She hoped it was a sign that he was all right inside, too.

She tried to think of something to say as they stood staring at each other in the middle of the living room. A fly buzzed against the window screen in a desperate attempt to get out.

"Well, Ma, how've you—"

"I'll fix you something to eat," Myrna interrupted. "I know you must be starved for decent cooking." She rushed from the room as though a meal were already in the process of burning.

For a moment she was lost in her own kitchen. The table, with its dented metal legs, the green-and-white cotton curtains, and the badly battered coffeepot were all familiar-looking strangers. She took a deep breath and leaned against the back of a chair.

In the beginning she'd flinched from the very word. She couldn't even think it, let alone say it. Assault, attack, molest, anything but rape. Anyone but her son, her bright and funny boy, her high school graduate.

At the time, she'd been sure it was a frame-up on the part of the police. They did things like that. It was in the newspapers every day. Or the girl was trying to get revenge because he hadn't shown any interest in her. Kenny's confession put paid to all those speculations.

She'd have liked to believe that remorse had made him confess. But she knew better. He'd simply told the wrong lie. If he'd said he'd been with the girl but it hadn't been rape, he might have built a case that someone would have believed—although she didn't know how he could have explained away the wound on her neck where he'd held his knife against her throat to keep her docile. Instead, he'd claimed not to have offered her a ride home from the bar where she worked, never to have had her in his car. He'd convinced Myrna. So thoroughly convinced her that she'd fainted dead away when confronted with the semen, fiber, and hair evidence the police quickly collected from his car, and the word of the woman who reluctantly came forth to say she'd seen Kenny ushering Crystal Roberts into his car on the night Crystal was raped.

Only then had Kenny confessed. He'd said he'd been doing the girl a favor by offering her a ride home. In return, she'd teased and then refused him, he'd said. "I lost my head," he'd said.

"I can't sleep. I'm afraid to sleep." The girl had spoken in barely a whisper. The whole courtroom had seemed to tilt as everyone leaned toward her. "Every night he's there in my mind, making me go through it all over again, and again, and again."

Was she free now that Kenny had done his time? Or was she flinching from hands with short, square fingers, and crying when the first of September came near? Myrna moved around the kitchen like an old, old woman with bad feet.

After Kenny had confessed, Myrna spent days that ran into weeks rifling through memories of the past she shared with him, searching for some incident, some trait or series of events that would explain why he'd done such a thing. She'd tried to rationalize his actions with circumstances: Kenny had seen his father beat her. They'd been poorer than dirt. And when Kenny had just turned six, she'd finally found the courage to leave Buddy to raise their son alone. What had she really known about raising a child? What harm might she have done out of ignorance, out of impatience and concentration on warding off the pains of her own life?

Still, she kept stumbling over the knowledge of other boys, from far worse circumstances, with mothers too tired and worried to do more than strike out at them. Yet those boys had managed to grow up and not do the kind of harm Kenny had done. The phrases "I lost my head," and "doing the girl a favor," reverberated through her brain, mocking her, making her groan out loud and startle people around her.

Myrna dragged herself around the room, turning eggs, bacon, milk, and margarine into a meal. In the beginning the why of Kenny's crime was like a tapeworm in her belly, consuming all her strength and sustenance, all her attention. In the first few months of his imprisonment she'd religiously paid a neighbor to drive her the long distance to the prison each visiting day. The visits were as much for her benefit as for his.

"But why?" she'd kept asking him, just as she'd asked him practically every day since he'd confessed.

He would only say that he knew he'd done wrong. As the weeks passed, silence became his only response—a silence that had remained intact despite questions like: "Would you have left that girl alone if I'd bought a shotgun and blown your daddy's brains out after the first time he hit me in front of you?" and, "Is there a special thrill you feel when you make a woman ashamed of her sex?" and, "Was this the first time? The second? The last?"

Perhaps silence was best, now, after so long. Anything could happen if she let those five-year-old questions come rolling out of her mouth. Kenny might begin to question her, might ask her what there was about her mothering that made him want to treat a woman like a piece of toilet paper. And what would she say to that?

It was illness that had finally put an end to her visits with him. She'd written the first letter—a note really—to say she was laid up with the flu. A hacking cough had lingered. She hadn't gotten her strength back for nearly two months. By that time their correspondence was established. Letters full of: How are you? I'm fine. . . . The weather is . . . The print shop is . . . The dress I made for Mrs. Rothstein was . . . were so much more manageable than those silence-laden visits. And she didn't have to worry about making eye contact with Kenny in a letter.

Now Myrna stood staring out the kitchen window while Kenny ate his bacon and eggs. The crisp everydayness of clothes flapping on the line surprised her. A leaf floated into her small cemented yard and landed on a potted pansy. Outside, nothing had changed; the world was still in spring.

"I can't go through this again," she mouthed soundlessly to the breeze.

"Come talk to me, Ma," her son called softly around a mouthful of food.

Myrna turned to look at him. He smiled an egg-flecked smile she couln't return. She wanted to ask him what he would do now, whether he had a job lined up, whether he planned to stay long. But she was afraid of his answers, afraid of how she might respond if he said he had no job, no plans, no place to stay except with her and that he hadn't changed in any important way.

"I'm always gonna live with you, Mommy," he'd told her when he was a child, "Always." At the time, she'd wished it was true, that they could always be together, she and her sweet, chubby boy. Now the thought frightened her.

"Be right back," she mumbled, and scurried down the hall to the bathroom. She eased the lock over so that it made barely a sound.

"He's my son!" she hissed at the drawn woman in the mirror. Perspiration dotted her upper lip and glistened around her hair line.

"My son!" she repeated pleadingly. But the words were not as powerful as the memory of Crystal Roberts sitting in the courtroom, her shoulders hunched and her head hung down, as though she were the one who ought to be ashamed. Myrna wished him never born, before she flushed the toilet and unlocked the door.

In the kitchen Kenny had moved to take her place by the window. His dishes littered the table. He'd spilled the salt, and there were crumbs on the floor.

"It sure is good to look out the window and see something besides guard towers and cons." Kenny stretched, rubbed his belly, and turned to face her.

"It's good to see you, Ma." His eyes were soft and shiny.

Oh, Lord! Myrna moaned to herself. She turned her back to him and began carrying his dirty dishes to the sink: first the plate, then the cup, the knife, fork, and spoon, drawing out the chore.

"This place ain't got as much room as the old place," she told him while she made dishwater in the sink.

"It's fine, Ma, just fine."

Oh, Lord, Myrna prayed.

Kenny came to lean against the stove to her right. She dropped a knife and made the dishwater too cold.

"Seen Dad?"

"Where and why would I see *him?*" She tried to put ice in her voice. It trembled.

"Just thought you might know where he is." Kenny moved back to the window.

Myrna remembered the crippling shock of Buddy's fist in her groin and scoured Kenny's plate and cup with a piece of steel wool before rinsing them in scalding water.

"Maybe I'll hop a bus over to the old neighborhood. See some of the guys, how things have changed."

He paced the floor behind her. Myrna sensed his uneasiness and was startled by a wave of pleasure at his discomfort.

After he'd gone, she fixed herself a large gin and orange juice and carried it into the living room. She flicked on the TV and sat down to stare at it. After two minutes of frenetic, over-bright commercials, she got up and turned it off again. Outside, children screamed each other to the finish line of a footrace. She remembered that Kenny had always liked to run. So had she. But he'd had more childhood than she'd had. She'd been hired out as a mother's helper by the time she was twelve, and pregnant and married at sixteen. She didn't begrudge him his childhood fun. It just seemed so wasted now.

Tears slid down her face and salted her drink. Tears for the young Myrna who hadn't understood that she was raising a boy who needed special handling to keep him from becoming a man she didn't care to know. Tears for Kenny who was so twisted around inside that he could rape a woman. Myrna drained her gin, left Kenny a note reminding him to leave her door key on the kitchen table, and went to bed.

Of course, she was still awake when he came in. He bumped into the coffee table, ran water in the bathroom sink for a long time, then quiet. Myrna lay awake in the dark blue-gray night listening to the groan of the refrigerator, the hiss of the hot-water heater, and the rumble of large trucks on a distant street. *He* made no sound where he lay on the opened-out sofa, surrounded by her sewing machine, dress dummy, marking tape, and pins.

When sleep finally came, it brought dreams of walking down brilliantly lit streets, hand in hand with a boy about twelve who looked, acted, and talked like Kenny but who she knew with certainty was not her son, at the same time she also knew he could be no one else.

She woke to a cacophony of church bells. It was late. Too late to make it to church service. She turned her head to look at the crucifix hanging by her bed and tried to pray, to summon up that feeling of near weightlessness that came over her in those moments when she was able to free her mind of all else and give herself over to prayer. Now nothing came but a dull ache in the back of her throat.

She had begun attending church regularly after she stopped visiting Kenny. His refusal to respond to her questions made it clear she'd have to seek answers elsewhere. She'd decided to talk to Father Giles. He'd been at St. Mark's, in their old neighborhood, before she and Kenny had moved there. He'd seen Kenny growing up. Perhaps he'd noticed something, understood something about the boy, about her, that would explain what she could not understand.

"It's God's will, my child—put it in His hands," he'd urged, awkwardly patting her arm and averting his eyes.

Myrna took his advice wholeheartedly. She became quite adept at quieting the questions boiling in her belly with, "His will," or "My cross to bear." Many nights she'd "Our Fathered" herself to sleep. Acceptance of Kenny's inexplicable act became a test God had given her. One she passed by visiting the sick, along with other women from the church, working on the neighborhood cleanup committee; avoiding all social contact with men. With sex. She put "widowed" on job applications and never mentioned a son to new people she met. Once she'd moved away from the silent accusation of their old apartment, prayer and good works became a protective shield separating her from the past.

Kenny's tap on her door startled her back to the present. She cleared her throat and straightened the covers before calling to him to come in.

A rich, aromatic steam rose from the coffee he'd brought her. The toast was just the right shade of brown, and she was sure that when she cracked the poached egg it would be cooked exactly to her liking. Not only was everything perfectly prepared, it was the first time she'd had breakfast in bed since he'd been arrested. Myrna couldn't hold back the tears or the flood of memories of many mornings, just so: him bending over her with a breakfast tray.

"You wait on people in the restaurant all day and sit up all night making other people's clothes. You need some waiting on, too."

Had he actually said that, this man as a boy? Could this man have been such a boy? Myrna nearly tilted the tray in her confusion.

"I need to brush my teeth." She averted her face and reached for her bathrobe.

But she couldn't avoid her eyes in the medicine cabinet mirror, eyes that reminded her that despite what Kenny had done, she hadn't stopped loving him. But her love didn't need his company. It thrived only on memories of him that were more than four years old. It was as much a love remembered as a living thing. But it was love, nonetheless. Myrna pressed her clenched fist against her lips and wondered if love was enough. She stayed in the bathroom until she heard him leave her bedroom and turn on the TV in the living room.

When he came back for the tray, she told him she had a sick headache and had decided to stay in bed. He was immediately sympathetic, fetching aspirin and a cool compress for her forehead, offering to massage her neck and temples, to lower the blinds and block out the bright morning sun. Myrna told him she wanted only to rest.

All afternoon she lay on her unmade bed, her eyes on the ceiling or idly roaming the room, her mind moving across the surface of her life, poking at old wounds, so amazingly raw after all these years. First there'd been Buddy. He'd laughed at her country ways and punched her around until he'd driven her and their child into the streets. But at least she was rid of him. Then there was his son. Her baby. He'd tricked a young woman into getting into his car where he proceeded to ruin a great portion of her life. Now he'd come back to spill salt in her kitchen.

I'm home, Ma, homema, homema. His words echoed in her inner ear and made her heart flutter. Her neighbors would want to know where he'd been all this time and why. Fear and disgust would creep into their faces and voices. Her nights would be full of listening. Waiting.

And she would have to live with the unblanketed reality that whatever anger and meanness her son held toward the world, he had chosen a woman to take it out on.

A woman.

Someone like me, she thought, like Great Aunt Faye, or Valerie, her eight-year-old niece, like Lucille, her oldest friend, or Dr. Ramsey, her dentist. A woman like all the women who'd helped feed, clothe, and care for Kenny; who'd tried their damnedest to protect him from as much of the ugly and awful in life as they could; who'd taught him to ride a bike and cross the street. All women. From the day she'd left Buddy, not one man had done a damned thing for Kenny. Not one.

And he might do it again, she thought. The idea sent Myrna rolling back and forth across the bed as though she could actually escape her thoughts. She'd allowed herself to believe she was done with such thoughts. Once she accepted Kenny's crime as the will of God, she immediately saw that it wouldn't have made any difference how she'd raised him if this was God's unfathomable plan for him. It was a comforting idea, one that answered her question of why and how her much-loved son could be a rapist. One that answered the question of the degree of her responsibility for Kenny's crime

by clearing her of all possible blame. One that allowed her to forgive him. Or so she'd thought.

Now she realized all her prayers, all her studied efforts to accept and forgive were like blankets thrown on a forest fire. All it took was the small breeze created by her opening the door to her only child to burn those blankets to cinders and release her rage—as wild and fierce as the day he'd confessed.

She closed her eyes and saw her outraged self dash wildly into the living room to scream imprecations in his face until her voice failed. Specks of froth gathered at the corners of her mouth. Her flying spit peppered his face. He cringed before her, his eyes full of shame as he tore at his own face and chest in self-loathing.

Yet, even as she fantasized, she knew Kenny could no more be screamed into contrition than Crystal or any woman could be bullied into willing sex. And what, in fact, was there for him to say or do that would satisfy her? The response she really wanted from him was not available: there was no way he could become the boy he'd been before that night four years ago.

No more than I can treat him as if he were that boy, she thought.

And the thought stilled her. She lay motionless, considering.

When she rose from her bed, she dragged her old green Samsonite suitcase out from the back of the closet. She moved with the easy, effortless grace of someone who knows what she is doing and feels good about it. Without even wiping off the dust, she plopped the suitcase on the bed. When she lifted the lid, the smell of leaving and goodbye flooded the room and quickened her pulse. For the first time in two days, her mouth moved in the direction of a smile.

She hurried from dresser drawer to closet, choosing her favorites: the black two-piece silk knit dress she'd bought on sale, her comfortable gray shoes, the lavender sweater she'd knitted as a birthday present to herself but had never worn, both her blue and her black slacks, the red crepe blouse she'd made to go with them, and the best of her underwear. She packed in a rush, as though her bus or train were even now pulling out of the station.

When she'd packed her clothes, Myrna looked around the room for other necessary items. She gathered up her comb and brush and the picture of her mother from the top of her bureau, then walked to the wall on the left side of her bed and lifted down the shiny metal and wooden crucifix that hung there. She ran her finger down the slim, muscular body. The Aryan plaster-of-Paris Christ seemed to writhe in bittersweet agony. Myrna stared at the crucifix for a few moments, then gently hung it back on the wall.

When she'd finished dressing, she sat down in the hard, straight-backed chair near the window to think through her plan. Kenny tapped at her door a number of times until she was able to convince him that she was best left alone and would be fine in the morning. When dark came, she waited for the silence of sleep, then quietly left her room. She set her suitcase by the front door, tiptoed by Kenny, where he slept on the sofa, and went into the kitchen. By the glow from the back alley streetlight, she wrote him a note and propped it against the sugar bowl:

Dear Kenny,

I'm sorry. I just can't be your mother right now. I will be back in one week. Please be gone. Much love,
Myrna.

Kenny flinched and frowned in his sleep as the front door clicked shut.

Alice Walker (b. 1944)

With the writing of *The Color Purple* (1982), Alice Walker received national attention, garnering the first Pulitzer Prize for a novel written by an African American woman. The novel also won the National Book Award and the American Book Award. Celie's letters to God and her sister became a testament to the physical and psychic survival of a black woman who declares, "I'm pore, I'm black, I may be ugly and can't cook. . . . But I'm here." Although *The Color Purple* was a turning point in her career, Walker's canon before this popular novel was full of promise. At age twenty-four she published *Once: Poems.* In 1970, she published her first novel, *The Third Life of Grange Copeland*, which centered on the entrapped lives of women. In 1973, she received the Lillian Smith Award for her poems *Revolutionary Petunias* and the National Institute of Arts and Letters award for *In Love and Trouble*, a collection of stories about women living their lives during the changing times of the civil rights movement. One of the best novels to come out of the civil rights movement is Walker's *Meridian* (1976), a work that questions what revolutionary and struggle mean. A few years later, Walker received a Guggenheim Fellowship and published the poetry collection, *Good Night, Willie Lee, I'll See You in the Morning.*

In recent years, Walker's career has been just as rich with poetry collections, *Horses Make the Landscape Look More Beautiful* (1984); short story collections, *You Can't Keep a Good Woman Down* (1981); and several novels that foreground sociopolitical issues: *The Temple of My Familiar* (1989), *Possessing the Secret of Joy* (1992), and *By the Light of My Father's Smile* (1998). Additionally, Walker has authored children's books and several important essay collections, including *In Search of Our Mothers' Gardens* (1983), where she describes her experience in finding and marking Zora Neale Hurston's grave and where she defines "womanist," a term describing feminism as practiced by women of color. "Womanist" is grounded in the traditions and legacies of all those foremothers who spoke of "womanish" ways.

Born one of eight children to Willie Lee Walker and Minnie Lou Grant, sharecroppers in Eatonton, Georgia, Walker attended Spelman and Sarah Lawrence colleges. In 1967 she married Jewish civil rights activist, Melvyn Leventhal. They divorced in 1977, and their daughter, Rebecca, is now one of the prominent voices of third wave feminism. Walker writes about her marriage, daughter, and friendships in *The Way Forward Is with a Broken Heart* (2000).

Roselily

Dearly Beloved,

She dreams; dragging herself across the world. A small girl in her mother's white robe and veil, knee raised waist high through a bowl of quicksand soup. The man who stands beside her is against this standing on the front porch of her house, being married to the sound of cars whizzing by on highway 61.

---

we are gathered here

Like cotton to be weighed. Her fingers at the last minute busily removing dry leaves and twigs. Aware it is a superficial sweep. She knows he blames Mississippi for the respectful way the men turn their heads up in the yard, the women stand waiting and knowledgeable, their children held from mischief by teachings from the wrong God. He glares beyond them to the occupants of the cars, white faces glued to promises beyond a country wedding, noses thrust forward like dogs on a track. For him they usurp the wedding.

in the sight of God

Yes, open house. That is what country black folks like. She dreams she does not already have three children. A squeeze around the flowers in her hands chokes off three and four and five years of breath. Instantly she is ashamed and frightened in her superstition. She looks for the first time at the preacher, forces humility into her eyes, as if she believes he is, in fact, a man of God. She can imagine God, a small black boy, timidly pulling the preacher's coattail.

to join this man and this woman

She thinks of ropes, chains, handcuffs, his religion. His place of worship. Where she will be required to sit apart with covered head. In Chicago, a word she hears when thinking of smoke, from his description of what a cinder was, which they never had in Panther Burn. She sees hovering over the heads of the clean neighbors in her front yard black specks falling, clinging, from the sky. But in Chicago. Respect, a chance to build. Her children at last from underneath the detrimental wheel. A chance to be on top. What a relief, she thinks. What a vision, a view, from up so high.

in holy matrimony.

Her fourth child she gave away to the child's father who had some money. Certainly a good job. Had gone to Harvard. Was a good man but weak because good language meant so much to him he could not live with Roselily. Could not abide TV in the living room, five beds in three rooms, no Bach except from four to six on Sunday afternoons. No chess at all. She does not forget to worry about her son among his father's people. She wonders if the New England climate will agree with him. If he will ever come down to Mississippi, as his father did, to try to right the country's wrongs. She wonders if he will be stronger than his father. His father cried off and on throughout her pregnancy. Went to skin and bones. Suffered nightmares, retching and falling out of bed. Tried to kill himself. Later told his wife he found the right baby through friends. Vouched for, the sterling qualities that would make up his character.

It is not her nature to blame. Still, she is not entirely thankful. She supposes New England, the North, to be quite different from what she knows. It seems right somehow to her that people who move there to live return home completely changed. She thinks of the air, the smoke, the cinders. Imagines cinders big as hailstones; heavy, weighing on the people. Wonders how this pressure finds its way into the veins, roping the springs of laughter.

If there's anybody here that knows a reason why

But of course they know no reason why beyond what they daily have come to know. She thinks of the man who will be her husband, feels shut away from him because of the stiff severity of his plain black suit. His religion. A lifetime of black and white. Of veils. Covered head. It is as if her children are already gone from her. Not dead, but exalted on a pedestal, a stalk that has no roots. She wonders how to make new roots. It is beyond her. She wonders what one does with memories in a brand-new life. This had seemed easy, until she thought of it. "The reasons why . . . the people who" . . . she thinks, and does not wonder where the thought is from.

these two should not be joined

She thinks of her mother, who is dead. Dead, but still her mother. Joined. This is confusing. Of her father. A gray old man who sold wild mink, rabbit, fox skins to Sears, Roebuck. He stands in the yard, like a man waiting for a train. Her young sisters stand behind her in smooth green dresses, with flowers in their hands and hair. They giggle, she feels, at the absurdity of the wedding. They are ready for something new. She thinks the man beside her should marry one of them. She feels old. Yoked. An arm seems to reach out from behind her and snatch her backward. She thinks of cemeteries and the long sleep of grandparents mingling in the dirt. She believes that she believes in ghosts. In the soil giving back what it takes.

together,

In the city. He sees her in a new way. This she knows, and is grateful. But is it new enough? She cannot always be a bride and virgin, wearing robes and veil. Even now her body itches to be free of satin and voile, organdy and lily of the valley. Memories crash against her. Memories of being bare to the sun. She wonders what it will be like. Not to have to got to a job. Not to work in a sewing plant. Not to worry about learning to sew straight seams in workingmen's overalls, jeans, and dress pants. Her place will be in the home, he has said, repeatedly, promising her rest she had prayed for. But now she wonders. When she is rested, what will she do? They will make babies—she thinks practically about her fine brown body, his strong black one. They will be inevitable. Her hands will be full. Full of what? Babies. She is not comforted.

let him speak

She wishes she had asked him to explain more of what he meant. But she was impatient. Impatient to be done with sewing. With doing everything for three children, alone. Impatient to leave the girls she had known since childhood, their children growing up, their husbands hanging around her, already old, seedy. Nothing about them that she wanted, or needed. The fathers of her children driving by, waving, not waving; reminders of times she would just as soon forget. Impatient to see the South Side, where they would live and build and be respectable and respected and free. Her husband would free her. A romantic hush. Proposal. Promises. A new life! Respectable, reclaimed, renewed. Free! In robe and veil.

or forever hold

She does not even know if she loves him. She loves his sobriety. His refusal to sing just because he knows the tune. She loves his pride. His blackness and his gray car. She loves his understanding of her *condition*. She thinks she loves the effort he will make to redo her into what he truly wants. His love of her makes her completely conscious of how unloved she was before. This is something; though it makes her unbearably sad Melancholy. She blinks her eyes. Remembers she is finally being married, like other girls. Like other girls, women? Something strains upward behind her eyes. She thinks of the something as a rat trapped, cornered, scurrying to and fro in her head, peering through the windows of her eyes. She wants to live for once. But doesn't know quite what that means. Wonders if she has ever done it. If she ever will. The preacher is odious to her. She wants to strike him out of the way, out of her light, with the back of her hand. It seems to her he has always been standing in front of her, barring her way.

his peace.

The rest she does not hear. She feels a kiss, passionate, rousing, within the general pandemonium. Cars drive up blowing their horns. Firecrackers go off. Dogs come from under the house and begin to yelp and bark. Her husband's hand is like the clasp of an iron gate. People congratulate. Her children press against her. They look with awe and distaste mixed with hope at their new father. He stands curiously apart, in spite of the people crowding about to grasp his free hand. He smiles at them all but his eyes are as if turned inward. He knows they cannot understand that he is not a Christian. He will not explain himself. He feels different, he looks it. The old women thought he was like one of their sons except that he had somehow got away from them. Still a son, not a son. Changed.

She thinks how it will be later in the night in the silvery gray car. How they will spin through the darkness of Mississippi and in the morning be in Chicago, Illinois. She thinks of Lincoln, the president. That is all she knows about the place. She feels ignorant, *wrong*, backward. She presses her worried fingers into his palm. He is standing in front of her. In the crush of well-wishing people, he does not look back.

Pat Parker (1944–1989)

Poet and gay and lesbian rights activist, Pat Parker wrote poems and speeches that critiqued the health care system and homophobia. One such collection is *Jonestown and Other Madness* (1985). Other collections include *Child of Myself* (1971), *Pit Stop* (1974), *Womanslaughter* (1978), and *Movement in Black* (1990). Well known for her grassroots work in the Oakland and San Francisco areas, Parker had a loyal following. She died of breast cancer at the height of her career.

For the White Person Who Wants To Know How to Be My Friend

The first thing you do is to forget that i'm Black.
Second, you must never forget that i'm Black.

You should be able to dig Aretha,
but don't play her every time i come over.
And if you decide to play Beethoven—don't tell me
his life story. They made us take music appreciation too.

Eat soul food if you like it, but don't expect me
to locate your restaurants
or cook it for you.

And if some Black person insults you,
mugs you, rapes your sister, rapes you,
rips your house or is just being an ass—
please, do not apologize to me
for wanting to do them bodily harm.
It makes me wonder if you're foolish.

And even if you really believe Blacks are better lovers than
whites—don't tell me. I start thinking of charging stud fees.

In other words—if you really want to be my friend—*don't*
make a labor of it. I'm lazy. Remember.

Sherley Anne Williams (1944–1999)

Poet, critic, and novelist, Sherley Anne Williams was born in Bakersfield, California, to parents who worked in the fruit and cotton fields. She earned her B.A. in history from California State University, Fresno, and did graduate work at Howard University, eventually earning a Master's degree from Brown University in 1972. Her first published short story, "Tell Martha Not to Moan" appeared in the Massachusetts Review in 1967 and in *The Black Woman*, 1970, edited by Toni Cade Bambara. Her first work of literary criticism was *Give Birth to Brightness: A Thematic Study in Neo-Black Literature*. Her first poetry collection, *The Peacock Poems* (1975) was nominated for the National Book Award. In 1982, she published another poetry/blues collection, *Some One Sweet Angel Chile*.

Her novel, *Dessa Rose* (1986), tells the story of Dessa, who leads a slave rebellion while pregnant. Based on a true incident, *Dessa Rose* is a novel about claiming one's name and one's history. When Dessa is captured, a white historian, Adam Neherniah, wants to write her story for his own purposes. The story he writes conflicts with the story that is written/whipped on Dessa's body. With the help of the black community, Dessa escapes her cell and takes refuge with some other runaway slaves at the home of Ruth/Rufel, a white woman whose husband has left her. The unlikely cohort concocts a plan that frees all of them from their various enslavements. The novel ends with an epilogue wherein Dessa reflects on her life.

Any Woman's Blues

Every Woman is a Victim
of the Feel Blues, too

Soft lamp shinin
    and me alone in the night.
Soft lamp is shinin
    and me alone in the night.
Can't take no one beside me
    need mo'n jest some man to set me right.

I left many peoples and places
    tryin not to be alone.
Left many a person and places
    I lived my life alone.
I need to get myself together.
    Yes, I need to make myself to home.

What's gone can be a window
    a circle in the eye of the sun.

What's gone can be a window
    a circle, well, in the eye of the sun.
Take the circle from the world, girl,
    you find the light have gone.

These is old blues
    and I sing em like any woman do.
These the old blues
    and I sing em, sing em, sing em. Just like any woman do.
My life ain't done yet.
    Naw. My song ain't through.

I Want Aretha to Set
This to Music:

I surprise girlhood
in your face; I know
my own, have been a

prisoner of my own
dark skin and fleshy
lips, walked that same high
butty strut despite
all this; rejected
the mask my mother
wore so stolidly
through womanhood and
wear it now myself.

I see the mask, sense
the girl and the woman
you became, wonder
if mask and woman
are one, if pain is
the sum of all your
knowing, victim the
only game you learned.

Old and in pain and
bearing up bearing up
and hurt and age These
are the signs of our
womanhood but I'll
make book Bessie did
more than just endure.
hear it?

                                    hear it?

Oh I'm lonesome now
            but I won't be lonesome long
Say I'm lonely now
            but I don't need to be lonesome long

You know it take a man wid some style and passion
            to make a single woman sing these lonely songs

                        one-sided bed Blues

Never had a man talk to me
            to say the things he say
Never had a man talk like this, honey,
            say the things you say.

Man talk so strong
            till I can't tell Night from Day.

His voice be low words come slow
            and he be movin all the while
His voice be low words come slow
            and he be movin, Lawd! all the while.
I'm his radio and he sho
            know how to tune my dial.

My bed one-sided from me
            sleepin alone all the time
My bed *wop*-sided from me
            sleepin alone so much of the time
And the fact that it empty
            show how this man is messin wid my mind.

what's out there knockin
      Is what the world
      don't get enough of

Marilyn Nelson Waniek (b. 1946)

Like Jayne Cortez, Marilyn Nelson Waniek lived on military bases. Born in Cleveland, Ohio, to Melvin Nelson, who served in the Air Force, and Jonnie Mitchell Nelson, a teacher, Waniek moved from military base to military base. The military background laid a foundation for writing about the Tuskegee Airmen, America's various landscapes, and a wide range of ethnic groups. Waniek earned her B.A. in 1968 from the University of California, her M.A. in 1970 from the University of Pennsylvania, and her Ph.D. in 1979 from the University of Minnesota. Her early collections include *For the Body* (1978) and *Mama's Promises* (1985). Her later collections of poetry won many awards: *The Homeplace* (1990) won the 1992 Annisfield-Wolf Award and was a finalist for the 1991 National Book Award, and *The Fields of Praise: New and Selected Poems* (1997) was a finalist for the 1997 National Book Award, the Lenore Marshall Poetry Award, and the PEN Winship Award. Other collections include *Magnificat* (1994) and a collection of verse for children, *The Cat Walked through the Casserole and Other Poems for Children* (with Pamela Espeland, 1984). A professor of English at the University of Connecticut, Waniek previously taught at such universities as Louisiana State University, St. Olaf College, and Reed College.

The Writer's Wife

She watched him take his books away
into the bedroom,
where he stayed for hours on end.
She counted pencils whittled down
to nubs, their shiny leads
licked and rounded.
After suppers, as she drew
the dishes toward her
on the table, scraping bits
of fat and cold potato onto
her plate for the cat,
she bit her lip, watching him
rise to the newspaper.
She wanted a child.
Night after night, she lay
curled like a dog around her
womb, while he pecked away
at the typewriter in the other room.

When he published, she smiled
for the camera, licked
her thin lips
and turned away.

The Lost Daughter

One morning just before Christmas
When I was four or five years old
I followed Mama's muskrat coat
and her burgundy cloche
from counter to counter in The May Co.
as she tested powders and colognes,
smoothed silk scarves and woolen vests,
and disappeared down the aisle
into the life she lived before I was born.

The mirrors rendered nothing more
at my eye level than a small brown blur;
I understood why the salesclerks didn't see
a little girl in a chesterfield coat,
plaid bows on her five skimpy braids,
or stop me as I wept my way

toward the outside doors
and was spun through their transparency
out into the snow.

On the sidewalk Santa rang a shiny bell
and shifted from his right boot to his left
as the fingers in my mittens froze
and fell off, one by one.
My skin, then my bones turned to stone
that parted the hurrying crowd,
until at last I drifted, thinned as the smoke
from an occasional pipe or cigarette,
through the thick white words people spoke.
Sometimes a taxi squealed its brakes
or beeped to pierce the solid, steady roar
of voices, wheels, and motors.
The same blue as the sky by now,

I rose like a float in the parade
I'd seen not long before:
a mouse tall as a department store
that nodded hugely as it moved
above our wonder down the avenue.

When Mama spat out my name
in fury and relief, I felt my face
fly back into focus. I formed again
instantaneously under her glaring eyes.
In the plate glass window I recognized
the shape Mama shook and embraced—
the runny nose, the eyes' frightened gleam,
the berer askew on hair gone wild—
and knew myself made whole again, her child.

Michelle Cliff (b. 1946)

Like Paule Marshall and Audre Lorde, Michelle Cliff bridges the Caribbean and the United States. Born in Kingston, Jamaica, Cliff came to New York when she was three years old. At ten years old, she returned to Jamaica to attend a private school for girls. She received her B.A. from Wagner College (1969) and later her Ph.D in comparative literature from London's Warburg Institute. Cliff writes about migrations, identities, histories, and colonialism. Race, caste, and sexuality permeate her major themes. Her books include *Abeng* (1984), *Claiming an Identity They Taught Me to Despise* (1980), *The Land of Look Behind* (1985), *No Telephone to Heaven* (1987), *Bodies of Water* (1990), and *Free Enterprise* (1993).

From *Abeng*

From Chapter Two: [Nanny, the Sorceress]

In 1733, Nanny, the sorceress, the *obeah*-woman, was killed by a *quashee*—a slave faithful to the white planters—at the height of the War of the Maroons.

Nanny, who could catch a bullet between her buttocks and render the bullet harmless, was from the empire of the Ashanti, and carried the secrets of her magic into slavery. She prepared amulets and oaths for her armies. Her Nanny Town, hidden in the crevices of the Blue Mountains, was the headquarters of the Windward Maroons—who held out against the forces of the white men longer than any rebel troops. They waged war from 1655–1740. Nanny was the magician of this revolution—she used her skill to unite her people and to consecrate their battles.

There is absolutely no doubt that she actually existed. And the ruins of her Nanny Town remain difficult to reach.

The Tabernacle was alive with voices and movement.

"Um-hmm."

"Oh, yes, Lord. Oh, yes."

"Amen, Brother."

These words were being spoken in ones or twos—together or distinct—as Brother Emmanuel got into the substance of his sermon. It was the usual message he gave his congregation every week. Brother Emmanuel was not a man of any rare gifts of imagination—he just plied his trade as a man of God, Sunday after Sunday, striving to be a respected somebody on his own account, as well as trying to save the souls of his flock from damnation. He was not inspired in his delivery of the word—for instance, no one could remember him telling a joke to illustrate one of his sermons. Perhaps preachers were not meant to tell jokes. He had said something funny once, but the joke was not meant to be. Brother Emmanuel had begun a sentence with "brethren," then glanced across the congregation and his eyes met with those of Sisters Icilda and Girlie. His mind reckoned with the presence of so many women in his congregation, and he matched brethren with "sistern"—which the congregation of course heard as "cistern." Some smiled—Brother Emmanuel coughed, then continued.

Now, he was in full swing—

"No dancing, children . . . No dancing, no movies . . . No dancing, children, no movies, and no liquor. These t'ings are the work of the devil. These t'ings serve us not, except to weaken us—in spirit *and* in body."

"Yes, Brother. Yes. Lord."

"We mus' not smoke the weed, mus' not smoke tobacco, nor ganja, my children. For with these t'ings, we become as lotos eaters, and we accomplish no-t'ing in our days."

"Mm-hmm. Yes, Brother. Wunna speak true."

"And let there be no carousing among my flock, no contention between mother and child, husband and wife, sister and brother, woman and man. Contention will mek us weak. Contention will tun us 'gainst one another. Contention will tun us from the Lord Almighty, the maker of heaven and of earth, in whom all t'ings are possible."

"Yes, Brother. Yes, Lord."

"We mus' bide our time. We mus' be patient. We will wait on the Lord. This is the way, children. This is the way to the life everlasting. In which we will all meet over yonder. In the sweet by-and-by. When the trumpet of the Lord shall sound, and the world shall be no more. When the saints of earth have gathered over on the other shore, and the roll is called up yonder I'll be there. When the roll, when the roll is called up yonder, I'll be there."

With that, Sister Shirley pumped the organ and the congregation rose.

In front of the Tabernacle, next to the grocery store which carried dried saltfish and soft drinks and cooking oil and rice and sundries, was a rum shop, where men with crisscrossed red eyeballs swung in and out all hours of the day and all days of the year. Down the road was a moviehouse, the Rialto, which showed triple features of American gangster movies and B-grade westerns and jungle serials starring Johnny Sheffield. There was a shop next to the moviehouse which sold raffle tickets. And another close by which was an offtrack betting parlor, selling wagers on the Epsom Derby and the Grand National at Aintree, as well as the races at home. Number one South Windward Road was known to be a badhouse, where women, gambling, rum, ganja, and all manner of *sint'ing* could be had.

The men who were in the Tabernacle were being sorely tempted. As were their brothers outside. And there was little that Brother Emmanuel could do to alleviate the temptation. To relieve them. The space the temptation entered could not be filled by hymn-singing or sermons, no matter how terrifying. The space had been carved so long ago, carried so long within, it was a historic fact. "Every dog have him day, every puss their four o'clock," was something people said—but saying this was not enough.

The white Jesus, with his chestnut hair, brown eyes, and soft mustache, was handsomer than the white queen, and seemed kinder, but the danger to these men was beyond him. The men—when they worked—were servants to light-skinned or white families; waiters at South Camp, Myrtle Bank, or Courtleigh Manor; porters at Palisadoes Airport. They pumped gas at Texaco or Esso stations. They swept sidewalks. They carried garbage. They cut grass and trimmed hedges. Killed rats. Fed dogs. They balanced trays of Red Stripe beer or Appleton Estate rum on their upturned palms. They were paid with a small brown envelope of cash. They lived from week to week.

The women in the Tabernacle had their spaces of need also—but for most of them, the space had been reduced over time, so that the filling of it became a matter for family. Their anguish in this life became for them identifiable in the faces of the people they were part of. Their pain was unto themselves. As the men's relief was unto themselves. But to the women fell the responsibility for kin—sisters, mothers, children.

The women also served. Cleaned. Mopped. Cooked. Cared for babies lighter than their own. Did other people's laundry. Bought other people's goods in the markets at Cross-roads and Constant Spring. They too received some cash each week. To their mothers and sisters and their aunts they gave some toward the care of their children. They saw these children perhaps once a week, if the children were kept in town. Less often if they were not. Many of these women had never been married, but they kept their children and gave them names and supervised their rearing as best they could. Some had been married, but their husbands had left them for America to pick fruit. Or for the north of England to work in factories. Others had husbands employed in households or hotels in different parts of Kingston—these men lived-in, as did their wives—and over the years these people lost touch. So much was ranged against the upkeep of these connections. At times they felt the cause of their losses lay in themselves—their people's *wuthlessness*.

"Like one of the family" was a reality they lived with—taking Christmas with their employers and saving Boxing Day for their own. "Like one of the family" meant staying in a small room with one light and a table and a bed—listening to a sound system which piped in Radio Jamaica. They waited for tea-time and prepared lap trays dressed with starched and ironed linen cloths. They asked missis for the key to the larder so they could remove caddies of Earl Grey or Lapsang Souchong leaves, tins of sardines, English biscuits, Cross and Blackwell or Tiptree preserves—gooseberry or greengage plum.

Sometimes this other family became more familiar to them than the people they were closest to. The people they were part of.

* * * *

An hour a week with Jesus and Brother Emmanuel, backed up by Sisters Icilda and Girlie and the choir, Sister Shirley and her pump organ, eased them somewhat. It was a steady easing—they too lived from week to week. They could count on the ease and there was no one who could take it away from them. They were "washed in the blood of the Lamb."

In the beginning there had been two sisters—Nanny and Sekesu. Nanny fled slavery. Sekesu remained a slave. Some said this was the difference between the sisters.

It was believed that all island children were descended from one or the other. All island people were first cousins.

Chapter Three

Do-fe-do mek guinea nigger come a Jamaica.*
                                                    —PROVERB

---

*Translation: Fighting among themselves brought West African slaves to Jamaica.

The people in the Tabernacle could trace their bloodlines back to a past of slavery. But this was not something they talked about much, or knew much about. In school they were told that their ancestors had been pagan. That there had been slaves in Africa, where Black people had put each other in chains. They were given the impression that the whites who brought them here from the Gold Coast and the Slave Coast were only copying a West African custom. As though the whites had not named the Slave Coast themselves.

The congregation did not know that African slaves in Africa had been primarily household servants. They were not seasoned. They were not worked in canefields. The system of labor was not industrialized. There was in fact no comparison between the two states of servitude: that practiced by the tribal societies of West Africa and that organized by the Royal African Company of London, chartered by the Crown. These people did not know that one of the reasons the English Parliament and the Crown finally put an end to the slave trade was that because of the Victorian mania for cleanliness, manufacturers needed West African palm oil to make soap—soon the trade in palm oil became more profitable than the trade in men and women and the merchants shifted their investments.

No one had told the people in the Tabernacle that of all the slave societies in the New World, Jamaica was considered among the most brutal. They did not know that the death rate of Africans in Jamaica under slavery exceeded the rate of birth, and that the growth of the slave population from 1,500 in 1655 to 311,070 in 1834, the year of freedom, was due *only* to the importation of more people, more slaves. They did not know that some slaves worked with their faces locked in masks of tin, so they would not eat the sugar cane as they cut. Or that there were few white women on the island during slavery, and so the grandmothers of these people sitting in a church on a Sunday evening during mango season, had been violated again and again by the very men who whipped them. The rape of Black women would have existed with or without the presence of white women, of course, but in Jamaica there was no pretense of civility—all was in the open.

* * * *

Now her head is tied. Now braided. Strung with beads and cowrie shells. Now she is disguised as a *chasseur*. Now wrapped in a cloth shot through with gold. Now she stalks the Red Coats as they march toward her cave, where she spins her Akan chants into spells which stun her enemies. Calls on the goddesses of the Ashanti forests. Remembers the battle formations of the Dahomey Amazons. She turns her attention to the hunt. To the cultivation of cassava and yam and plantain—hiding the places for use in case of flight.

The forests of the island are wild and remind her of Africa. In places the mountains are no more than cliff-faces.

The precipices of these mountains often hold caves she can use for headquarters or to conceal the weapons of her army. She mixes dyes from roots and teaches others to cast images on the walls. She collects bark from the trunk and limbs of the birch gum to touch to the skin of her enemies while they sweat—and instructs her followers in the natural ways of death. She moves on her elbows and knees across narrow rock ledges. Through corridors created by stone.

The entryways are covered in some places with vines—in others with cascades of water. She teaches her troops to be sure-footed and to guard the points of access. They hunt with bow and arrow. Spears. Warclubs. They fill the muskets stolen from plantations with pebbles, buttons, coins. She teaches them to become bulletproof. To catch a bullet in their left hand and fire it back at their attackers. Only she can catch a bullet between her buttocks—that is a secret she keeps for herself.

She teaches them if they are caught to commit suicide by eating dirt.

* * * *

The capture of the island from the Spanish had been an afterthought. The British fleet, under the command of Penn and Venables, following the orders of the Lord Protector Oliver Cromwell, was unable to take Santo Domingo, and so moved on Jamaica. This took place in 1655. Over the course of the next 180 years, until freedom was obtained in 1834, there was armed, sustained guerrilla warfare against the forces of enslavement. A complex intelligence system between the rebels and the plantation slaves. A network of towns and farms and camps independent from the white planters. An army of thousands—literally thousands—called the Maroons. And this army had moved over the mountains now shadowed at the back of the Tabernacle.

Their name came from *cimarrón*: unruly, runaway. A word first given to cattle which had taken to the hills. Beyond its exact meaning, the word connoted fierce, wild, unbroken.

* * * *

Through the open louvers came the light from the rumshop and the voices of drinkers staggering home. The smell of the sea and the smell of mangoes mixed with each other.

The people in the Tabernacle did not know that their ancestors had been paid to inform on one another: given their freedom for becoming the *blackshots* of the white man. The *blackshot* troops were the most skilled at searching out and destroying the rebels—but they also had a high desertion rate and had been know to turn against their white commanders in battle.

The people in the Tabernacle did not know that Kishee, one of Nanny's commanders, had been killed by Scipio, a

Black slave—but of course they did not know who Kishee had been.

They did not know about the Kingdom of the Ashanti or the Kingdom of Dahomey, where most of their ancestors had come from. They did not imagine that Black Africans had commanded thousands of warriors. Built universities. Created systems of law. Devised language. Wrote history. Poetry. Were traders. Artists. Diplomats.

They did not know that their name for papaya— *pawpaw*—was the name of one of the languages of Dahomey. Or that the *cotta*, the circle of cloth women wound tightly to make a cushion to balance baskets on their heads, was an African device, an African word. That Brer Anancy, the spider who inspired tricks and tales, was a West African invention. Or that Cuffee was the name of a Maroon commander—the word had come down to them as *cuffy*, and meant upstart, social climber.

Some of them were called Nanny, because they cared for the children of other women, but they did not know who Nanny had been.

• • • •

When the English troops advanced on Nanny Town the second time, she decided to move her army across the Blue Mountains—so when the Red Coats arrived the village would be abandoned and the enemy would be confused. At night she and her army set out to find Cudjoe, the leader of the Maroons across the island, and to join with him in a final attack to defeat the whites and take control of the island for the Africans. Her warriors marched in front and behind. In the center of the single file were the women and children, the old people, the young men and women who carried provisions. They had planted all along the route, and Nanny had marked the places where they could take shelter for a day and a night, while the warriors hunted for wild pig, and the others built fires to roast the meat. They marched in this way for over a hundred miles, and finally reached Accompong Town, where Cudjoe and his men were.

A settlement in the Cockpit Country, the land of endless funnels in the earth, the land of look behind. At the heart of the limestone plateau which forms the center of the island. A place of seemingly purposeless crevasses—created when the island sank during the Pliocene Period and the limestone layers dissolved in places—the dissolution stopping where the limestone met with insoluble rock. Swallow-holes. Cockpits. Places to hide. Difficult to reach. Not barren but deep and magnificent indentations populated by bush and growth and wild orchids—collectors of water—natural goblets.

Nanny moved forward to the small dark man with the hump on his back. Cudjoe wore knee-length breeches, an old ragged coat, and a hat with no brim. On his right side he carried a cow's horn of gunpowder and a bag of shots for his musket. From his left shoulder a sheathed cutlass dangled from a strap. His Black skin was reddened from the bauxite in the earth. His followers—those who now surrounded him—were also reddened men. His eyes met with those of Nanny—the small and old Black woman whose only decoration was a necklace fashioned from the teeth of white men. She did not speak, but instructed Kishee to begin the negotiations with Cudjoe. Kishee told him of their plan to join with Cudjoe and his men—the Leeward Maroons—against the Red Coats. He told Cudjoe about the band of Miskito Indians brought to the island to fight against them. The Miskitos—almost every one—had come over to the Maroon side. Through the Miskitos the Windward Maroons had contacted the Spanish on Cuba; and the Spanish governor agreed to respect the freedom of all the Africans on the island, if the rebels won the colony back for Spain.

Cudjoe refused this offer of alliance. He only gave the Windwards temporary refuge before their journey home. They stayed a short time in his camp, then walked back across the plateau and the mountains, through the rainforests, to their own territory.

Not long after, Nanny was murdered, and Cudjoe signed a separate peace with the British governor, in which he was permitted freedom and promised to hunt down other rebels for the Crown. He and his followers became known as the King's Negroes.

Some said he had tired of fighting. Others that he wanted to consolidate his power.

• • • •

The service was over and the congregation was wishing a "good evening" to Brother Emmanuel. The Savages left with the others and drove home through the by-now-cool night, in which the scent of ripe mangoes was present and heavy. As Mr. Savage drove along the Halfway Tree Road his headlights flashed on the side of Holy Cross—CASTRO SÍ, BATISTA NO. In black paint. In large letters against the cathedral.

Octavia Butler (b. 1947)

One of the most prominent women writers of the genre of science fiction, Octavia Butler was born in Pasadena, California, the only child of a maid and a shoeshine man. Her father died shortly after her birth, and her mother and grandmother raised her. She graduated from Pasadena City College and attended California State University in Los Angeles. Butler's fiction tackles a genre that has not been associated with black women writers. Rather than using the term "science fiction," Butler has called such works as *Kindred* (1979) a "grim fantasy." She reshapes the genre to accommodate her stories that are heavily infused with issues of gender and race. Her works have attracted popular, academic, and cult followers. Her "Patternist series," *Patternmaster* (1976), *Mind of My Mind* (1977), *Survivor* (1978), *Wild Seed* (1980), and *Clay's Ark* (1984), tells the story of a four-thousand-year-old immortal, Doro, who can appropriate whatever body he wants, regardless of race or gender and whose descendants all follow the same pattern. *Dawn* (1987), *Adulthood Rites* (1988), and *Imago* (1989) are part of her Xenogenesis trilogy—a series where humans and extraterrestrials compete for power. *Parable of the Sower* (1993) takes place in California in 2025 and is a coming-of-age novel about a black woman who suffers from a hereditary trait whereby she feels others' pain as well as her own. Butler's short story "Speech Sounds" won the 1984 Hugo Award and "Bloodchild" won the 1984 Nebula Award and a 1985 Hugo Award.

Bloodchild

My last night of childhood began with a visit home. T'Gatoi's sister had given us two sterile eggs. T'Gatoi gave one to my mother, brother, and sisters. She insisted that I eat the other one alone. It didn't matter. There was still enough to leave everyone feeling good. Almost everyone. My mother wouldn't take any. She sat, watching everyone drifting and dreaming without her. Most of the time she watched me.

I lay against T'Gatoi's long, velvet underside, sipping from my egg now and then, wondering why my mother denied herself such a harmless pleasure. Less of her hair would be gray if she indulged now and then. The eggs prolonged life, prolonged vigor. My father, who had never refused one in his life, had lived more than twice as long as he should have. And toward the end of his life, when he should have been slowing down, he had married my mother and fathered four children.

But my mother seemed content to age before she had to. I saw her turn away as several of T'Gatoi's limbs secured me closer. T'Gatoi liked our body heat and took advantage of it whenever she could. When I was little and at home more, my mother used to try to tell me how to behave with T'Gatoi—how to be respectful and always obedient because T'Gatoi was the Tlic government official in charge of the Preserve, and thus the most important of her kind to deal directly with Terrans. It was an honor, my mother said, that such a person had chosen to come into the family. My mother was at her most formal and severe when she was lying.

I had no idea why she was lying, or even what she was lying about. It *was* an honor to have T'Gatoi in the family, but it was hardly a novelty. T'Gatoi and my mother had been friends all my mother's life, and T'Gatoi was not interested in being honored in the house she considered her second home. She simply came in, climbed onto one of her special couches, and called me over to keep her warm. It was impossible to be formal with her while lying against her and hearing her complain as usual that I was too skinny.

"You're better," she said this time, probing me with six or seven of her limbs. "You're gaining weight finally. Thinness is dangerous." The probing changed subtly, became a series of caresses.

"He's still too thin," my mother said sharply.

T'Gatoi lifted her head and perhaps a meter of her body off the couch as though she were sitting up. She looked at my mother, and my mother, her face lined and old looking, turned away.

"Lien, I would like you to have what's left of Gan's egg."

"The eggs are for the children," my mother said.

"They are for the family. Please take it."

Unwillingly obedient, my mother took it from me and put it to her mouth. There were only a few drops left in the now-shrunken, elastic shell, but she squeezed them out, swallowed them, and after a few moments some of the lines of tension began to smooth from her face.

"It's good," she whispered. "Sometimes I forget how good it is."

"You should take more," T'Gatoi said. "Why are you in such a hurry to be old?"

My mother said nothing.

"I like being able to come here," T'Gatoi said. "This place is a refuge because of you, yet you won't take care of yourself."

T'Gatoi was hounded on the outside. Her people wanted more of us made available. Only she and her political faction stood between us and the hordes who did not understand why there was a Preserve—why any Terran could not be courted, paid, drafted, in some way made available to them. Or they did understand, but in their desperation, they did not care. She parceled us out to the desperate and sold us to the rich and powerful for their political support. Thus, we were necessities, status symbols, and an independent people. She oversaw the joining of families, putting an end to the final remnants of the earlier system of breaking up Terran families to suit impatient Tlic. I had lived outside with her. I had seen the desperate eagerness in the way some people looked at me. It was a little frightening to know that only she stood between us and that desperation that could so easily swallow us. My mother would look at her sometimes and say to me, "Take care of her." And I would remember that she too had been outside, had seen.

Now T'Gatoi used four of her limbs to push me away from her onto the floor. "Go on, Gan," she said. "Sit down there with your sisters and enjoy not being sober. You had most of the egg. Lien, come warm me."

My mother hesitated for no reason that I could see. One of my earliest memories is of my mother stretched alongside T'Gatoi, talking about things I could not understand, picking me up from the floor and laughing as she sat me on one of T'Gatoi's segments. She ate her share of eggs then. I wondered when she had stopped, and why.

She lay down now against T'Gatoi, and the whole left row of T'Gatoi's limbs closed around her, holding her loosely, but securely. I had always found it comfortable to lie that way, but except for my older sister, no one else in the family liked it. They said it made them feel caged.

T'Gatoi meant to cage my mother. Once she had, she moved her tail slightly, then spoke. "Not enough egg, Lien. You should have taken it when it was passed to you. You need it badly now."

T'Gatoi's tail moved once more, its whip motion so swift I wouldn't have seen it if I hadn't been watching for it. Her sting drew only a single drop of blood from my mother's bare leg.

My mother cried out—probably in surprise. Being stung doesn't hurt. Then she sighed and I could see her body relax. She moved languidly into a more comfortable position within the cage of T'Gatoi's limbs. "Why did you do that?" she asked, sounding half asleep.

"I could not watch you sitting and suffering any longer."

My mother managed to move her shoulders in a small shrug. "Tomorrow," she said.

"Yes. Tomorrow you will resume your suffering—if you must. But just now, just for now, lie here and warm me and let me ease your way a little."

"He's still mine, you know," my mother said suddenly. "Nothing can buy him from me." Sober, she would not have permitted herself to refer to such things.

"Nothing," T'Gatoi agreed, humoring her.

"Did you think I would sell him for eggs? For long life? My son?"

"Not for anything," T'Gatoi said, stroking my mother's shoulders, toying with her long, graying hair.

I would like to have touched my mother, shared that moment with her. She would take my hand if I touched her now. Freed by the egg and the sting, she would smile and perhaps say things long held in. But tomorrow, she would remember all this as a humiliation. I did not want to be part of a remembered humiliation. Best just be still and know she loved me under all the duty and pride and pain.

"Xuan Hoa, take off her shoes," T'Gatoi said. "In a little while I'll sting her again and she can sleep."

My older sister obeyed, swaying drunkenly as she stood up. When she had finished, she sat down beside me and took my hand. We had always been a unit, she and I.

My mother put the back of her head against T'Gatoi's underside and tried from that impossible angle to look up into the broad, round face. "You're going to sting me again?"

"Yes, Lien."

"I'll sleep until tomorrow noon."

"Good. You need it. When did you sleep last?"

My mother made a wordless sound of annoyance. "I should have stepped on you when you were small enough," she muttered.

It was an old joke between them. They had grown up together, sort of, though T'Gatoi had not, in my mother's lifetime, been small enough for any Terran to step on. She was nearly three times my mother's present age, yet would still be young when my mother died of age. But T'Gatoi and my mother had met as T'Gatoi was coming into a period of rapid development—a kind of Tlic adolescence. My mother was only a child, but for a while they developed at the same rate and had no better friends than each other.

T'Gatoi had even introduced my mother to the man who became my father. My parents, pleased with each other in spite of their different ages, married as T'Gatoi was going into her family's business—politics. She and my mother saw each other less. But sometime before my older sister was born, my mother promised T'Gatoi one of her children. She would have to give one of us to someone, and she preferred T'Gatoi to some stranger.

Years passed. T'Gatoi traveled and increased her influence. The Preserve was hers by the time she came back to my mother to collect what she probably saw as her just reward for her hard work. My older sister took an instant liking to her and wanted to be chosen, but my mother was just coming to term with me and T'Gatoi liked the idea of choosing an infant and watching and taking part in all the phases of development. I'm told I was first caged within T'Gatoi's many limbs only three minutes after my birth. A few days later, I was given my first taste of egg. I tell Terrans that when they ask whether I was ever afraid of her. And I tell it to Tlic when T'Gatoi suggests a young Terran child for them and they, anxious and ignorant, demand an adolescent. Even my brother who had somehow grown up to fear and distrust the Tlic could probably have gone smoothly into one of their families if he had been adopted early enough. Sometimes, I think for his sake he should have been. I looked at him, stretched out on the floor across the room, his eyes open, but glazed as he dreamed his egg dream. No matter what he felt toward the Tlic, he always demanded his share of egg.

"Lien, can you stand up?" T'Gatoi asked suddenly.

"Stand?" my mother said. "I thought I was going to sleep."

"Later. Something sounds wrong outside." The cage was abruptly gone.

"What?"

"Up, Lien!"

My mother recognized her tone and got up just in time to avoid being dumped on the floor. T'Gatoi whipped her three meters of body off her couch, toward the door, and out at full speed. She had bones—ribs, a long spine, a skull, four sets of limb bones per segment. But when she moved that way, twisting, hurling herself into controlled falls, landing running, she seemed not only boneless, but aquatic—something swimming through the air as though it were water. I loved watching her move.

I left my sister and started to follow her out the door, though I wasn't very steady on my own feet. It would have been better to sit and dream, better yet to find a girl and share a waking dream with her. Back when the Tlic saw us as not much more than convenient, big, warm-blooded animals, they would pen several of us together, male and female, and

feed us only eggs. That way they could be sure of getting another generation of us no matter how we tried to hold out. We were lucky that didn't go on long. A few generations of it and we would have *been* little more than convenient, big animals.

"Hold the door open, Gan," T'Gatoi said. "And tell the family to stay back."

"What is it?" I asked.

"N'Tlic."

I shrank back against the door. "Here? Alone?"

"He was trying to reach a call box, I suppose." She carried the man past me, unconscious, folded like a coat over some of her limbs. He looked young—my brother's age perhaps—and he was thinner than he should have been. What T'Gatoi would have called dangerously thin.

"Gan, go to the call box," she said. She put the man on the floor and began stripping off his clothing.

I did not move.

After a moment, she looked up at me, her sudden stillness a sign of deep impatience.

"Send Qui," I told her. "I'll stay here. Maybe I can help."

She let her limbs begin to move again, lifting the man and pulling his shirt over his head. "You don't want to see this," she said. "It will be hard. I can't help this man the way his Tlic could."

"I know. But send Qui. He won't want to be of any help here. I'm at least willing to try."

She looked at my brother—older, bigger, stronger, certainly more able to help her here. He was sitting up now, braced against the wall, staring at the man on the floor with undisguised fear and revulsion. Even she could see that he would be useless.

"Qui, go!" she said.

He didn't argue. He stood up, swayed briefly, then steadied, frightened sober.

"This man's name is Bram Lomas," she told him, reading from the man's armband. I fingered my own armband in sympathy. "He needs T'Khotgif Teh. Do you hear?"

"Bram Lomas, T'Khotgif Teh," my brother said. "I'm going." He edged around Lomas and ran out the door.

Lomas began to regain consciousness. He only moaned at first and clutched spasmodically at a pair of T'Gatoi's limbs. My younger sister, finally awake from her egg dream, came close to look at him, until my mother pulled her back.

T'Gatoi removed the man's shoes, then his pants, all the while leaving him two of her limbs to grip. Except for the final few, all her limbs were equally dexterous. "I want no argument from you this time, Gan," she said.

I straightened. "What shall I do?"

"Go out and slaughter an animal that is at least half your size."

"Slaughter? But I've never—"

She knocked me across the room. Her tail was an efficient weapon whether she exposed the sting or not.

I got up, feeling stupid for having ignored her warning, and went into the kitchen. Maybe I could kill something with a knife or an ax. My mother raised a few Terran animals for the table and several thousand local ones for their fur. T'Gatoi would probably prefer something local. An achti, perhaps. Some of those were the right size, though they had about three times as many teeth as I did and a real love of using them. My mother, Hoa, and Qui could kill them with knives. I had never killed one at all, had never slaughtered any animal. I had spent most of my time with T'Gatoi while my brother and sisters were learning the family business. T'Gatoi had been right. I should have been the one to go to the call box. At least I could do that.

I went to the corner cabinet where my mother kept her large house and garden tools. At the back of the cabinet there was a pipe that carried off waste water from the kitchen—except that it didn't anymore. My father had rerouted the waste water below before I was born. Now the pipe could be turned so that one half slid around the other and a rifle could be stored inside. This wasn't our only gun, but it was our most easily accessible one. I would have to use it to shoot one of the biggest of the achti. Then T'Gatoi would probably confiscate it. Firearms were illegal in the Preserve. There had been incidents right after the Preserve was established—Terrans shooting Tlic, shooting N'Tlic. This was before the joining of families began, before everyone had a personal stake in keeping the peace. No one had shot a Tlic in my lifetime or my mother's, but the law still stood—for our protection, we were told. There were stories of whole Terran families wiped out in reprisal back during the assassinations.

I went out to the cages and shot the biggest achti I could find. It was a handsome breeding male, and my mother would not be pleased to see me bring it in. But it was the right size, and I was in a hurry.

I put the achti's long, warm body over my shoulder—glad that some of the weight I'd gained was muscle—and took it to the kitchen. There, I put the gun back in its hiding place. If T'Gatoi noticed the achti's wounds and demanded the gun, I would give it to her. Otherwise, let it stay where my father wanted it.

I turned to take the achti to her, then hesitated. For several seconds, I stood in front of the closed door wondering why I was suddenly afraid. I knew what was going to happen. I hadn't seen it before but T'Gatoi had shown me diagrams and drawings. She had made sure I knew the truth as soon as I was old enough to understand it.

Yet I did not want to go into that room. I wasted a little time choosing a knife from the carved, wooden box in which my mother kept them. T'Gatoi might want one, I told myself, for the tough, heavily furred hide of the achti.

"Gan!" T'Gatoi called, her voice harsh with urgency.

I swallowed. I had not imagined a single moving of the feet could be so difficult. I realized I was trembling and that shamed me. Shame impelled me through the door.

I put the achti down near T'Gatoi and saw that Lomas was unconscious again. She, Lomas, and I were alone in the room—my mother and sisters probably sent out so they would not have to watch. I envied them.

But my mother came back into the room as T'Gatoi seized the achti. Ignoring the knife I offered her, she extended claws from several of her limbs and slit the achti from throat to anus. She looked at me, her yellow eyes intent. "Hold this man's shoulders, Gan."

I stared at Lomas in panic, realizing that I did not want to touch him, let alone hold him. This would not be like shooting an animal. Not as quick, not as merciful, and, I hoped, not as final, but there was nothing I wanted less than to be part of it.

My mother came forward. "Gan, you hold his right side," she said. "I'll hold his left." And if he came to, he would throw her off without realizing he had done it. She was a tiny woman. She often wondered aloud how she had produced, as she said, such "huge" children.

"Never mind," I told her, taking the man's shoulders. "I'll do it." She hovered nearby.

"Don't worry," I said. "I won't shame you. You don't have to stay and watch."

She looked at me uncertainly, then touched my face in a rare caress. Finally, she went back to her bedroom.

T'Gatoi lowered her head in relief. "Thank you, Gan," she said with courtesy more Terran than Tlic. "That one . . . she is always finding new ways for me to make her suffer."

Lomas began to groan and make choked sounds. I had hoped he would stay unconscious. T'Gatoi put her face near his so that he focused on her.

"I've stung you as much as I dare for now," she told him. "When this is over, I'll sting you to sleep and you won't hurt anymore."

"Please," the man begged. "Wait . . ."

"There's no more time, Bram. I'll sting you as soon as it's over. When T'Khotgif arrives she'll give you eggs to help you heal. It will be over soon."

"T'Khotgif!" the man shouted, straining against my hands.

"Soon, Bram." T'Gatoi glanced at me, then placed a claw against his abdomen slightly to the right of the middle, just below the left rib. There was movement on the right side—tiny, seemingly random pulsations moving his brown flesh, creating a concavity here, a convexity there, over and over until I could see the rhythm of it and knew where the next pulse would be.

Lomas's entire body stiffened under T'Gatoi's claw, though she merely rested it against him as she wound the rear section of her body around his legs. He might break my grip, but he would not break hers. He wept helplessly as she used his pants to tie his hands, then pushed his hands above his head so that I could kneel on the cloth between them and pin them in place. She rolled up his shirt and gave it to him to bite down on.

And she opened him.

His body convulsed with the first cut. He almost tore himself away from me. The sound he made . . . I had never heard such sounds come from anything human. T'Gatoi seemed to pay no attention as she lengthened and deepened the cut, now and then pausing to lick away blood. His blood vessels contracted, reacting to the chemistry of her saliva, and the bleeding slowed.

I felt as though I were helping her torture him, helping her consume him. I knew I would vomit soon, didn't know why I hadn't already. I couldn't possibly last until she was finished.

She found the first grub. It was fat and deep red with his blood—both inside and out. It had already eaten its own egg case but apparently had not yet begun to eat its host. At this stage, it would eat any flesh except its mother's. Let alone, it would have gone on excreting the poisons that had both sickened and alerted Lomas. Eventually it would have begun to eat. By the time it ate its way out of Lomas's flesh, Lomas would be dead or dying—and unable to take revenge on the thing that was killing him. There was always a grace period between the time the host sickened and the time the grubs began to eat him.

T'Gatoi picked up the writhing grub carefully and looked at it, somehow ignoring the terrible groans of the man.

Abruptly, the man lost consciousness.

"Good," T'Gatoi looked down at him. "I wish you Terrans could do that at will." She felt nothing. And the thing she held . . .

It was limbless and boneless at this stage, perhaps fifteen centimeters long and two thick, blind and slimy with blood. It was like a large worm. T'Gatoi put it into the belly of the achti, and it began at once to burrow. It would stay there and eat as long as there was anything to eat.

Probing through Lomas's flesh, she found two more, one of them smaller and more vigorous. "A male!" she said happily. He would be dead before I would. He would be through his metamorphosis and screwing everything that would hold still before his sisters even had limbs. He was the only one to make a serious effort to bite T'Gatoi as she placed him in the achti.

Paler worms oozed to visibility in Lomas's flesh. I closed my eyes. It was worse than finding something dead, rotting, and filled with tiny animal grubs. And it was far worse than any drawing or diagram.

"Ah, there are more," T'Gatoi said, plucking out two long, thick grubs. You may have to kill another animal, Gan. Everything lives inside you Terrans."

I had been told all my life that this was a good and necessary thing Tlic and Terran did together—a kind of birth. I had believed it until now. I knew birth was painful and bloody, no matter what. But this was something else, something worse. And I wasn't ready to see it. Maybe I never would be. Yet I couldn't not see it. Closing my eyes didn't help.

T'Gatoi found a grub still eating its egg case. The remains of the case were still wired into a blood vessel by their own little tube or hook or whatever. That was the way the grubs were anchored and the way they fed. They took only blood until they were ready to emerge. Then they ate their stretched, elastic egg cases. Then they ate their hosts.

T'Gatoi bit away the egg case, licked away the blood. Did she like the taste? Did childhood habits die hard—or not die at all?

The whole procedure was wrong, alien. I wouldn't have thought anything about her could seem alien to me.

"One more, I think," she said. "Perhaps two. A good family. In a host animal these days, we would be happy to find one or two alive." She glanced at me. "Go outside, Gan, and empty your stomach. Go now while the man is unconscious."

I staggered out, barely made it. Beneath the tree just beyond the front door, I vomited until there was nothing left to bring up. Finally, I stood shaking, tears streaming down my face. I did not know why I was crying, but I could not stop. I went further from the house to avoid being seen. Every time I closed my eyes I saw red worms crawling over redder human flesh.

There was a car coming toward the house. Since Terrans were forbidden motorized vehicles except for certain farm equipment, I knew this must be Lomas's Tlic with Qui and perhaps a Terran doctor. I wiped my face on my shirt, struggled for control.

"Gan," Qui called as the car stopped. "What happened?" He crawled out of the low, round, Tlic-convenient car door. Another Terran crawled out the other side and went into the house without speaking to me. The doctor. With his help and a few eggs, Lomas might make it.

"T'Khotgif Teh?" I said.

The Tlic driver surged out of her car, reared up half her length before me. She was paler and smaller than T'Gatoi—probably born from the body of an animal. Tlic from Terran bodies were always larger as well as more numerous.

"Six young," I told her. "Maybe seven, all alive. At least one male."

"Lomas?" she said harshly. I liked her for the question and the concern in her voice when she asked it. The last coherent thing he had said was her name.

"He's alive," I said.

She surged away to the house without another word.

"She's been sick," my brother said, watching her go.

"When I called, I could hear people telling her she wasn't well enough to go out even for this."

I said nothing. I had extended courtesy to the Tlic. Now I didn't want to talk to anyone. I hoped he would go in—out of curiosity if nothing else.

"Finally found out more than you wanted to know, eh?"

I looked at him.

"Don't give me one of her looks," he said. "You're not her. You're just her property."

One of her looks. Had I picked up even an ability to imitate her expressions?

"What'd you do, puke?" He sniffed the air. "So now you know what you're in for."

I walked away from him. He and I had been close when we were kids. He would let me follow him around when I was home, and sometimes T'Gatoi would let me bring him along when she took me into the city. But something had happened when he reached adolescence. I never knew what. He began keeping out of T'Gatoi's way. Then he began running away—until he realized there was no "away." Not in the Preserve. Certainly not outside. After that he concentrated on getting his share of every egg that came into the house and on looking out for me in a way that made me all but hate him—a way that clearly said, as long as I was all right, he was safe from the Tlic.

"How was it, really?" he demanded, following me.

"I killed an achti. The young ate it."

"You didn't run out of the house and puke because they ate an achti."

"I had . . . never seen a person cut open before." That was true, and enough for him to know. I couldn't talk about the other. Not with him.

"Oh," he said. He glanced at me as though he wanted to say more, but he kept quiet.

We walked, not really headed anywhere. Toward the back, toward the cages, toward the fields.

"Did he say anything?" Qui asked. "Lomas, I mean."

Who else would he mean? "He said 'T'Khotgif.'"

Qui shuddered. "If she had done that to me, she'd be the last person I'd call for."

"You'd call for her. Her sting would ease your pain without killing the grubs in you."

"You think I'd care if they died?"

No. Of course he wouldn't. Would I?

"Shit!" He drew a deep breath. "I've seen what they do. You think this thing with Lomas was bad? It was nothing."

I didn't argue. He didn't know what he was talking about.

"I saw them eat a man," he said.

I turned to face him. "You're lying!"

"I saw them eat a man." He paused. "It was when I was little. I had been to the Hartmund house and I was on my way home. Halfway here, I saw a man and a Tlic and the man was N'Tlic. The ground was hilly. I was able to hide from them and watch. The Tlic wouldn't open the man because she had nothing to feed the grubs. The man couldn't go any further and there were no houses around. He was in so much pain, he told her to kill him. He begged her to kill him. Finally, she did. She cut his throat. One swipe of one claw. I saw the grubs eat their way out, then burrow in again, still eating."

His words made me see Lomas's flesh again, parasitized, crawling. "Why didn't you tell me that?" I whispered.

He looked startled as though he'd forgotten I was listening. "I don't know."

"You started to run away not long after that, didn't you?"

"Yeah. Stupid. Running inside the Preserve. Running in a cage."

I shook my head, said what I should have said to him long ago. "She wouldn't take you, Qui. You don't have to worry."

"She would . . . if anything happened to you."

"No. She'd take Xuan Hoa. Hoa . . . wants it." She wouldn't if she had stayed to watch Lomas.

"They don't take women," he said with contempt.

"They do sometimes." I glanced at him. "Actually, they prefer women. You should be around them when they talk among themselves. They say women have more body fat to protect the grubs. But they usually take men to leave the women free to bear their own young."

"To provide the next generation of host animals," he said, switching from contempt to bitterness.

"It's more than that!" I countered. Was it?

"If it were going to happen to me, I'd want to believe it was more, too."

"It is more!" I felt like a kid. Stupid argument.

"Did you think so while T'Gatoi was picking worms out of that guy's guts?"

"It's not supposed to happen that way."

"Sure it is. You weren't supposed to see it, that's all. And his Tlic was supposed to do it. She could sting him unconscious and the operation wouldn't have been as painful. But she'd still open him, pick out the grubs, and if she missed even one, it would poison him and eat him from the inside out."

There was actually a time when my mother told me to show respect for Qui because he was my older brother. I walked away, hating him. In his way, he was gloating. He was safe and I wasn't. I could have hit him, but I didn't think I would be able to stand it when he refused to hit back, when he looked at me with contempt and pity.

He wouldn't let me get away. Longer legged, he swung ahead of me and made me feel as though I were following him.

"I'm sorry," he said.

I strode on, sick and furious.

"Look, it probably won't be that bad with you. T'Gatoi likes you. She'll be careful."

I turned back toward the house, almost running from him.

"Has she done it to you yet?" he asked, keeping up easily. "I mean, you're about the right age for implantation. Has she—"

I hit him. I didn't know I was going to do it, but I think I meant to kill him. If he hadn't been bigger and stronger, I think I would have.

He tried to hold me off, but in the end, had to defend himself. He only hit me a couple of times. That was plenty. I don't remember going down, but when I came to, he was gone. It was worth the pain to be rid of him.

I got up and walked slowly toward the house. The back was dark. No one was in the kitchen. My mother and sisters were sleeping in their bedrooms—or pretending to.

Once I was in the kitchen, I could hear voices—Tlic and Terran from the next room. I couldn't make out what they were saying—didn't want to make it out.

I sat down at my mother's table, waiting for quiet. The table was smooth and worn, heavy and well crafted. My father had made it for her just before he died. I remembered hanging around underfoot when he built it. He didn't mind. Now I sat leaning on it, missing him. I could have talked to him. He had done it three times in his long life. Three clutches of eggs, three times being opened up and sewed up. How had he done it? How did anyone do it?

I got up, took the rifle from its hiding place, and sat down again with it. It needed cleaning, oiling.

All I did was load it.

"Gan?"

She made a lot of little clicking sounds when she walked on bare floor, each limb clicking in succession as it touched down. Waves of little clicks.

She came to the table, raised the front half of her body above it, and surged onto it. Sometimes she moved so smoothly she seemed to flow like water itself. She coiled herself into a small hill in the middle of the table and looked at me.

"That was bad," she said softly. "You should not have seen it. It need not be that way."

"I know."

"T'Khotgif—Ch'Khotgif now—she will die of her disease. She will not live to raise her children. But her sister will provide for them, and for Bram Lomas." Sterile sister. One fertile female in every lot. One to keep the family going. That sister owed Lomas more than she could ever repay.

"He'll live then?"

"Yes."

"I wonder if he would do it again."

"No one would ask him to do that again."

I looked into the yellow eyes, wondering how much I saw and understood there, and how much I only imagined. "No one ever asks us," I said. "You never asked me."

She moved her head slightly. "What's the matter with your face?"

"Nothing. Nothing important." Human eyes probably wouldn't have noticed the swelling in the darkness. The only light was from one of the moons, shining through a window across the room.

"Did you use the rifle to shoot the achti?"

"Yes."

"And do you mean to use it to shoot me?"

I stared at her, outlined in the moonlight—coiled, graceful body. "What does Terran blood taste like to you?"

She said nothing.

"What are you?" I whispered. "What are we to you?"

She lay still, rested her head on her topmost coil. "You know me as no other does," she said softly. "You must decide."

"That's what happened to my face," I told her.

"What?"

"Qui goaded me into deciding to do something. It didn't turn out very well." I moved the gun slightly, brought the barrel up diagonally under my own chin. "At least it was a decision I made."

"As this will be."

"Ask me, Gatoi."

"For my children's lives?"

She would say something like that. She knew how to manipulate people, Terran and Tlic. But not this time.

"I don't want to be a host animal," I said. "Not even yours."

It took her a long time to answer. "We use almost no host animals these days," she said. "You know that."

"You use us."

"We do. We wait long years for you and teach you and join our families to yours." She moved restlessly. "You know you aren't animals to us."

I stared at her, saying nothing.

"The animals we once used began killing most of our eggs after implantation long before your ancestors arrived," she said softly. "You know these things, Gan. Because your people arrived, we are relearning what it means to be a healthy, thriving people. And your ancestors, fleeing from their homeworld, from their own kind who would have killed or enslaved them—they survived because of us. We saw them as people and gave them the Preserve when they still tried to kill us as worms."

At the word "worms," I jumped. I couldn't help it, and she couldn't help noticing it.

"I see," she said quietly. "Would you really rather die than bear my young, Gan?"

I didn't answer.

"Shall I go to Xuan Hoa?"

"Yes!" Hoa wanted it. Let her have it. She hadn't had to watch Lomas. She'd be proud. . . . Not terrified.

T'Gatoi flowed off the table onto the floor, startling me almost too much.

"I'll sleep in Hoa's room tonight," she said. "And sometime tonight or in the morning, I'll tell her."

This was going too fast. My sister Hoa had had almost as much to do with raising me as my mother. I was still close to her—not like Qui. She could want T'Gatoi and still love me.

"Wait! Gatoi!"

She looked back, then raised nearly half her length off the floor and turned to face me. "These are adult things, Gan. This is my life, my family!"

"But she's . . . my sister."

"I have done what you demanded. I have asked you!"

"But—"

"It will be easier for Hoa. She has always expected to carry other lives inside her."

Human lives. Human young who should someday drink at her breasts, not at her veins.

I shook my head. "Don't do it to her, Gatoi." I was not Qui. It seemed I could become him, though, with no effort at all. I could make Xuan Hoa my shield. Would it be easier to know that red worms were growing in her flesh instead of mine?

"Don't do it to Hoa," I repeated.

She stared at me, utterly still.

I looked away, then back at her. "Do it to me."

I lowered the gun from my throat and she leaned forward to take it.

"No," I told her.

"It's the law," she said.

"Leave it for the family. One of them might use it to save my life someday."

She grasped the rifle barrel, but I wouldn't let go. I was pulled into a standing position over her.

"Leave it here!" I repeated. "If we're not your animals, if these are adult things, accept the risk. There is risk, Gatoi, in dealing with a partner."

It was clearly hard for her to let go of the rifle. A shudder went through her and she made a hissing sound of distress. It occurred to me that she was afraid. She was old enough to have seen what guns could do to people. Now her young and this gun would be together in the same house. She did not know about the other guns. In this dispute, they did not matter.

"I will implant the first egg tonight," she said as I put the gun away. "Do you hear, Gan?"

Why else had I been given a whole egg to eat while the rest of the family was left to share one? Why else had my mother kept looking at me as though I were going away from her, going where she could not follow? Did T'Gatoi imagine I hadn't known?

"I hear."

"Now!" I let her push me out of the kitchen, then walked ahead of her toward my bedroom. The sudden urgency in her voice sounded real. "You would have done it to Hoa tonight!" I accused.

"I must do it to someone tonight."

I stopped in spite of her urgency and stood in her way. "Don't you care who?"

She flowed around me and into my bedroom. I found her waiting on the couch we shared. There was nothing in Hoa's room that she could have used. She would have done it to Hoa on the floor. The thought of her doing it to Hoa at all disturbed me in a different way now, and I was suddenly angry.

Yet I undressed and lay down beside her. I knew what to do, what to expect. I had been told all my life. I felt the familiar sting, narcotic, mildly pleasant. Then the blind probing of her ovipositor. The puncture was painless, easy. So easy going in. She undulated slowly against me, her muscles forcing the egg from her body into mine. I held on to a pair of her limbs until I remembered Lomas holding her that way. Then I let go, moved inadvertently, and hurt her. She gave a low cry of pain and I expected to be caged at once within her limbs. When I wasn't, I held on to her again, feeling oddly ashamed.

"I'm sorry," I whispered.

She rubbed my shoulders with four of her limbs.

"Do you care?" I asked. "Do you care that it's me?"

She did not answer for some time. Finally, "You were the one making the choices tonight, Gan. I made mine long ago."

"Would you have gone to Hoa?"

"Yes. How could I put my children into the care of one who hates them?"

"It wasn't . . . hate."

"I know what it was."

"I was afraid."

Silence.

"I still am." I could admit it to her here, now.

"But you came to me . . . to save Hoa."

"Yes." I leaned my forehead against her. She was cool velvet, deceptively soft. "And to keep you for myself," I said. It was so. I didn't understand it, but it was so.

She made a soft hum of contentment. "I couldn't believe I had made such a mistake with you," she said. "I chose you. I believed you had grown to choose me."

"I had, but . . ."

"Lomas."

"Yes."

"I had never known a Terran to see a birth and take it well. Qui has seen one, hasn't he?"

"Yes."

"Terrans should be protected from seeing."

I didn't like the sound of that—and I doubted that it was possible. "Not protected," I said. "Shown. Shown when we're young kids, and shown more than once. Gatoi, no Terran ever sees a birth that goes right. All we see is N'Tlic—pain and terror and maybe death."

She looked down at me. "It is a private thing. It has always been a private thing."

Her tone kept me from insisting—that and the knowledge that if she changed her mind, I might be the first public example. But I had planted the thought in her mind. Chances were it would grow, and eventually she would experiment.

"You won't see it again," she said. "I don't want you thinking any more about shooting me."

The small amount of fluid that came into me with her egg relaxed me as completely as a sterile egg would have, so that I could remember the rifle in my hands and my feelings of fear and revulsion, anger and despair. I could remember the feelings without reviving them. I could talk about them.

"I wouldn't have shot you," I said. "Not you." She had been taken from my father's flesh when he was my age.

"You could have," she insisted.

"Not you." She stood between us and her own people, protecting, interweaving.

"Would you have destroyed yourself?"

I moved carefully, uncomfortable. "I could have done that. I nearly did. That's Qui's 'away.' I wonder if he knows."

"What?"

I did not answer.

"You will live now."

"Yes." *Take care of her*, my mother used to say. Yes.

"I'm healthy and young," she said. "I won't leave you as Lomas was left—alone, N'Tlic. I'll take care of you."

Ntozake Shange (b. 1948)

Ntozake ("She who comes with her own things") and Shange ("She who walks like a lion") are fitting names for the woman who wrote the award-winning *for colored girls who have considered suicide when the rainbow is enuf* (1977), the first play to be performed on Broadway by an African American woman since Lorraine Hansberry's *A Raisin in the Sun*. Shange calls her mixture of poetry, music, and dance a choreopoem. Born Paulette Williams in Trenton, New Jersey, to Paul Williams, a surgeon, and Eloise Williams, a psychiatric social worker, Shange writes about growing up middle-class in her novel, *Betsey Brown* (1985). In 1966 she graduated from Barnard College and during her graduate years at UCLA changed and selected her Zulu name. All of Shange's work shows her deep awareness of herself as a racialized and gendered being. Her other prominent works include *Nappy Edges* (1978), *Sassafrass, Cypress, & Indigo* (1982), and *Ridin' the Moon in Texas: Word Paintings* (1987).

From *for colored girls who have considered suicide when the rainbow is enuf*

Latent Rapists

lady in blue
a friend is hard to press charges against

lady in red
if you know him
you must have wanted it

lady in purple
a misunderstanding

lady in red
you know
these things happen

lady in blue
are you sure
you didnt suggest

lady in purple
had you been drinkin

lady in red
a rapist is always to be a stranger
to be legitimate
someone you never saw
a man wit obvious problems

lady in purple
pin-ups attached to the insides of his lapels

lady in blue
ticket stubs from porno flicks in his pocket

lady in purple
a lil dick

lady in red
or a strong mother

lady in blue
or just a brutal virgin

lady in red
but if you've been seen in public wit him
danced one dance
kissed him good-bye lightly

lady in purple
wit closed mouth

lady in blue
pressin charges will be as hard
as keepin yr legs closed
while five fools try to run a train on you

lady in red
these men friends of ours
who smile nice
stay employed
and take us out to dinner

lady in purple
lock the door behind you

lady in blue
wit fist in face
to fuck

lady in red
who make elaborate mediterranean dinners
& let the art ensemble carry all ethical burdens
while they invite a coupla friends over to have you
are sufferin from latent rapist bravado
& we are left wit the scars

lady in blue
bein betrayed by men who know us

lady in purple
& expect
like the stranger
we always thot waz comin

lady in blue
that we will submit

lady in purple
we must have known

lady in red
women relinquish all personal rights
in the presence of a man
who apparently cd be considered a rapist

lady in purple
especially if he has been considered a friend

lady in blue
& is no less worthy of bein beat witin an inch of his life
bein publicly ridiculed
havin two fists shoved up his ass

lady in red
than the stranger
we always thot it wd be

lady in blue
who never showed up

lady in red
cuz it turns out the nature of rape has changed

lady in blue
we can now meet them in circles we frequent for
companionship

lady in purple
we see them at the coffeehouse

lady in blue
wit someone else we know

lady in red
we cd even have em over for dinner
& get raped in our own houses
by invitation
a friend

From *Nappy Edges*

With No Immediate Cause

every 3 minutes a woman is beaten
every five minutes a
woman is raped/ every ten minutes
a lil girl is molested
yet i rode the subway today
i sat next to an old man who
may have beaten his old wife
3 minutes ago or 3 days/ 30 years ago
he might have sodomized his
daughter but i sat there
cuz the young men on the train
might beat some young women
later in the day or tomorrow
i might not shut my door fast
enuf/ push hard enuf
every 3 minutes it happens
some woman's innocence
rushes to her cheeks/ pours from her mouth
like the betsy wetsy dolls have been torn
apart/ their mouths
mensis red & split/ every
three minutes a shoulder
is jammed through plaster & the oven door/
chairs push thru the rib cage/ hot water or
boiling sperm decorate her body
i rode the subway today
& bought a paper from a
man who might

have held his old lady onto
a hot pressing iron/ i dont know
maybe he catches lil girls in the
park & rips open their behinds
with steel rods/ i cdnt decide
what he might have done i only
know every 3 minutes
every 5 minutes every 10 minutes/ so
i bought the paper
looking for the announcement
there has to be an announcement
of the women's bodies found
yesterday/ the missing little girl
i sat in a restaurant with my
paper looking for the announcement
a yng man served me coffee
i wondered did he pour the boiling
coffee/ on the woman cuz she waz stupid/
did he put the infant girl/ in
the coffee pot/ with the boiling coffee/ cuz she cried too much
what exactly did he do with hot coffee
i looked for the announcement
the discovery/ of the dismembered
woman's body/ the
victims have not all been
identified/ today they are
naked & dead/ refuse to
testify/ one girl out of 10's not
coherent/ i took the coffee
& spit it up/ i found an
announcement/ not the woman's
bloated body in the river/ floating
not the child bleeding in the
59th street corridor/ not the baby

broken on the floor/
    "there is some concern
    that alleged battered women
    might start to murder their
    husbands & lovers with no
    immediate cause"
i spit up   i vomit   i am screaming
we all have immediate cause
every 3 minutes
every 5 minutes
every 10 minutes
every day
women's bodies are found
in alleys & bedrooms/ at the top of the stairs
before i ride the subway/ buy a paper/ drink
coffee/ i must know/
have you hurt a woman today
did you beat a woman today
throw a child cross a room
    are the lil girl's panties
    in yr pocket
did you hurt a woman today

i have to ask these obscene questions
the authorities require me to
establish
immediate cause

every three minutes
every five minutes
every ten minutes
every day

Jewelle Gomez (b. 1948)

Author and social activist, Jewelle Gomez was born in Boston. For the first twenty-two years of her life, she lived with her great-grandmother who was born on an Indian reservation in Iowa. In her writings, Gomez blends African American and Native American traditions. Her novel, *The Gilda Stories* (1991) tells the story of Gilda, a vampire/healer, who begins her life as a runaway slave in Louisiana around 1850, and ends up living among Native American and African American vampire lesbians. Rather than a horror story, *Gilda* is about recovering and healing the psyche and the power to create one's own notion of family. *Gilda* won Lambda Literary awards in the fiction and science fiction categories. The Urban Bush Women Company have performed an adaptation of *Gilda* for the stage, "Bones & Ash: A Gilda Story." Gomez has also written poetry, *The Lipstick Papers* (1980) and *Flamingoes and Bears* (1986), as well as collections of essays, such as *Don't Explain* (1998). Gomez earned her B.A. in 1971 from Northeastern University and her M.S. in 1973 from Columbia University. She is well known for her work as founding board member of Gay and Lesbian Alliance Against Defamation (GLAAD). She has given lectures and/or taught at a number of universities.

A Swimming Lesson

At nine years old I didn't realize that my grandmother, Lydia, and I were doing an extraordinary thing by packing a picnic and riding the elevated train from Roxbury to Revere Beach. It seemed part of the natural rhythm of summer to me. I didn't notice until much later how the subway cars slowly emptied most of their Black passengers as the train left Boston's urban center and made its way into the Italian and Irish suburban neighborhoods to the north. It didn't seem odd that all of the Black families sorted themselves out in one section of the beach and never ventured onto the boardwalk to the concession stands or the rides, except in groups.

I do remember Black women perched cautiously on their blankets, tugging desperately at bathing suits rising too high in the rear and complaining about their hair "going back." Not my grandmother, though. She glowed with unembarrassed athleticism as she waded out, just inside the reach of the waves, and moved along the riptide parallel to the shore. Once submerged, she would load me onto her back and begin her tireless, long strokes. With the waves partially covering us, I followed her rhythm, my short, chubby arms taking my cue from the power in her back muscles. We did this over and over until I'd fall off, then she'd catch me and set me upright in the strong New England surf. I was thrilled by the wildness of the sea and my grandmother's fearless relationship to it. I loved that she didn't continually consult her mirror but looked as if she had been born to the shore, a kind of aquatic heiress.

None of the larger social issues had a chance of catching my attention in 1957. All that existed was my grandmother rising from the surf like a Dahomean queen, shaking her head free of the torturous, useless rubber cap, beaming down on me when I, at long last, took the first swim strokes on my own. She towered over me in the sun with a confidence that made simply dwelling in her presence a reward in itself. Under her gaze I felt like part of a long line of royalty. I was certain that everyone around us—Black and white—felt and respected her magnificence.

Although I intuited her power, I didn't know the real significance of our summer together as Black females in a white part of town. Unlike winter when we're protected by the concealment of coats, boots, and hats, the summer is a vulnerable time. I am left exposed, at odds with all the expectations handed down from the mainstream culture and its media: narrow hips, straight hair, flat stomach, small feet. But Lydia never seemed to notice. Her long, chorus-girl legs ended in size-nine shoes. She seemed unafraid to make herself even bigger, stretching the broad back of a woman with a purpose: teaching her granddaughter how to swim against the tide of prevailing opinion and propriety. It may have looked like a superfluous skill to those watching our lessons. After all, it was obvious I wouldn't be doing the backstroke on the Riviera or in the pool

---

"A Swimming Lesson" appeared in *Whatever It Takes*, by Jewelle Gomez; "Don't Explain" appeared in *Don't Explain*, by Jewelle Gomez. Used by permission of the author.

of a penthouse spa. Certainly nothing in the popular media had made the great outdoors seem a hospitable place for Blacks or women. It was a place in which, at best, we were meant to feel uncomfortable, and at worst—hunted. But the potential prospects for actually utilizing the skill were irrelevant to me; it was simply the skill itself that mattered. When I finally got it right I felt I held an invaluable life secret.

It wasn't until college that the specifics of slavery and the Middle Passage were made available to me. The magnitude of that "peculiar institution" was almost beyond my comprehension. It wasn't like anything else I'd learned in school about Black people in this country. It was impossibly contradictory trying to make my own connection to the descendants of slaves—myself, others I knew—and at the same time see slaves not exactly as Americans I might know but as Africans set adrift from their own, very different land. My initial reaction was, *Why didn't the slaves simply jump from the ships while still close to shore and swim home?* The child in me who'd been taught how to survive in water was crushed to learn my ancestors had not necessarily shared this skill. Years later, when I visited West Africa and found out about the poisonous, spiny fish inhabiting much of the inhospitable coastline, rocky and turbulent, I understood why swimming was not a local sport there as it is in New England. I often remember that innocent inquiry, and now every time I visit a beach I think of those ancestors and of Lydia.

The sea has been a fearful place for us. It swallowed us whole when there was no other escape from the holds of slave ships, and did so again more recently with the flimsy refugee flotillas from Haiti. To me, for whom the dark recesses of a tenement hallway were the most unknowable thing encountered in my first nine years, the ocean was a mystery of terrifying proportions. In teaching me to swim Lydia took away that fear. I understood something outside my self—the sea—and consequently something about myself as well. I was no longer simply a fat little girl. My body became a sea vessel—sturdy, enduring, graceful.

Before she died in the summer of 1988 I discovered that she herself didn't really swim that well. All that time I was splashing desperately, trying to learn the right rhythm—*face down, eyes closed, air out, face up, eyes open, air in, reach*—Lydia would be brushing the sandy bottom under the water to keep us both afloat. As she told me this it didn't seem such a big deal to her, but I was shocked. I reached back in my memory trying to put this new information together with the Olympic vision of her I'd always kept inside my head. At first I felt disappointed, tricked. Like I used to feel when I learned that my favorite movie stars were only five feet tall. But I later realized that it was an incredible act of bravery and intelligence for her to pass on to me a skill she herself had not quite mastered—a skill she knew would always bring me a sense of pride in accomplishment.

And it's not just the swimming, or the ability to stand on any beach anywhere and be proud of my large body, my African hair. It's being unafraid of the strong muscles in my own back, accepting control over my own life. Now when the weather turns cold and I don the layers of wool and down that protect me from the eastern winter, from those who think a Black woman can't do her job, from those who think I'm simply sexual prey, I remember the power of my grandmother's broad back and I imagine I'm wearing my swimsuit.

Face up, eyes open, air in, reach.

Don't Explain

Boston 1959

Letty deposited the hot platters on the table effortlessly. She slid one deep-fried chicken, a club steak with boiled potatoes, and a fried porgy plate down her arm as if removing beaded bracelets. Each one landed with a solid clink on the shiny Formica in its appropriate place. The last barely settled before Letty turned back to the kitchen to get Savannah and Skip their lemonade and extra biscuits. Then to put her feet up. Out of the corner of her eye she saw Tip come in the lounge. His huge shoulders, draped in sharkskin, narrowly cleared the doorframe.

Damn! He's early tonight! she thought, but kept going. Tip was known for his extravagance; that's how he'd gotten his nickname. He always sat at Letty's station because they were both from Virginia, although neither had been back in years.

Letty had come up to Boston in 1946 and been waiting tables in the 411 Lounge since '52. She liked the casual community formed around it. The pimps were not big thinkers but good for a laugh; the musicians who played the small clubs around Boston often ate at the 411, providing some glamour—and now and then a jam session. The "business" girls were usually generous and always willing to embroider a wild story. After Letty's mother died there'd been no family to go back to down in Burkeville.

Letty took her newspaper from the locker behind the kitchen and filled a tall glass with the tart grape juice punch for which the cook, Henrietta, was famous.

"I'm going on break, Henrietta. Delia's takin' my station."

She sat in the back booth nearest the kitchen, beside the large blackboard which displayed the menu. When Delia came out of the bathroom, Letty hissed to get her attention. The reddish-brown of Delia's face was shiny with a country freshness that always made Letty feel a little shy.

"What's up, Miss Letty?" Her voice was soft and saucy.

"Take my tables for twenty minutes. Tip just came in."

The girl's already bright smile widened as she started to thank Letty.

"Go 'head, go 'head. He don't like to wait. You can thank me if he don't run you back and forth fifty times."

Delia hurried away as Letty sank into the coolness of the overstuffed booth and removed her shoes. After a few sips of her punch she rested her head on the back of the seat with her eyes closed. The sounds around her were as familiar as her own breathing: squeaking Red Cross shoes as Delia and Vinnie passed, the click of high heels around the bar, the clatter of dishes in the kitchen, and ice cascading into glasses. The din of conversation rose, leveled, and rose again over the jukebox. Letty had not played her record in days, but the words spun around in her head as if they were on a turntable:

> Right or wrong don't matter
> When you're with me sweet
> Hush now, don't explain
> You're my joy and pain.

Letty sipped her cool drink; sweat ran down her spine, soaking into the nylon uniform. July weather promised to give no breaks, and fans were working overtime like everybody else.

She saw Delia cross to Tip's table again. In spite of the dyed red hair, no matter how you looked at her. Delia was still a country girl. Long, self-conscious, shy—she was bold only because she didn't know any better. She'd moved up from Anniston with her cousin a year before and landed the job at the 411 immediately. She was full of fun, but that didn't get in the way of her working hard. Sometimes she and Letty shared a cab going uptown after work, when Delia's cousin didn't pick them up in her green Pontiac.

Letty caught Tip eyeing Delia as she strode on tight-muscled legs back to the kitchen. That lounge lizard! Letty thought to herself. Letty had trained Delia how to balance plates, how to make tips, and how to keep the customer's hands on the table. She was certain Delia would have no problem putting Tip in his place. In the year she'd been working at the 411, Delia hadn't gone out with any of the bar flies, though plenty had asked. Letty figured that Delia and her cousin must run with a different crowd. They talked to each other sporadically in the kitchen or during their break, but Letty never felt that wire across her chest like Delia was going to ask her something she couldn't answer.

She closed her eyes again for the few remaining minutes. The song was back in her head, and Letty had to squeeze her

lips together to keep from humming aloud. She pushed her thoughts onto something else. But when she did she always stumbled upon Maxine. Letty opened her eyes. When she'd quit working at Salmagundi's and come to the 411 she'd promised herself never to think about any woman like that again. She didn't know why missing Billie so much brought it all back to her.

She heard the bartender, Duke, shout a greeting from behind the bar to the owner as he walked in. Aristotle's glance skimmed his dimly lit domain before he made his way to his stool, the only one at the bar with a back. That was Letty's signal. No matter that it was her break: she knew white people didn't like to see their employees sitting down, especially with their shoes off. By the time he was settled near the door, Letty was up, her glass in hand, and on her way through the kitchen's noisy swinging door.

"You finished your break already?" Delia asked.

"Ari just come in."

"Uh oh, let me git this steak out there. Boy, he sure is nosy!"

"Who, Tip?"

"Yeah. He ask me where I live, who I live with, where I come from, like he supposed to know me!"

"Well, just don't take nothing he say to heart and you'll be fine. And don't take no rides from him!"

"Yeah. He asked if he could take me home after I get off. I told him me and you had something to do." Letty was silent as she sliced the fresh bread and stacked it on plates for the next orders.

"My cousin's coming by, so it ain't a lie, really. She can ride us."

"Yeah," Letty said as Delia giggled and turned away with her platter.

Vinnie burst through the door like she always did, breathless and bossy. "Ari up there, girl! You better get back on station."

Letty drained her glass with deliberation, wiped her hands on her thickly starched white apron, and walked casually past Vinnie as if she'd never spoken. She heard Henrietta's soft chuckle float behind her. She went over to Tip, who was digging into the steak like his life depended on devouring it before the plate got dirty.

"Everything all right tonight?" Letty asked, her ample brown body towering over the table.

"Yeah, baby, it's all right. You ain't working this side no more?"

"I was on break. My feet can't wait for your stomach, you know."

Tip laughed, "*Break*. What you need a break for, big and healthy as you is!"

"We all get old, Tip. But the feet get old first, let me tell you that!"

"Not in my business, baby. Why you don't come on and work for me and you ain't got to worry 'bout your feet."

Letty sucked her teeth loudly, the exaggeration a part of the game they'd played over the years. "Man, I'm too old for that mess!"

"You ain't too old for me."

"Ain't nobody too old for *you*. Or too young, neither, looks like."

"Where you and that gal goin' tonight?"

"To a funeral," Letty responded dryly.

"Aw, woman, get on away from my food!" The gold cap on his front tooth gleamed from behind his greasy lips when he laughed. Letty was pleased. Besides giving away money, Tip liked to hurt people. It was better when he laughed.

The kitchen closed at 11:00. Delia and Letty slipped off their uniforms in the tiny bathroom and were on their way out the door by 11:15. Delia looked even younger in her knife-pleated skirt and white cotton blouse. Letty felt old in her slacks and long-sleeved shirt as she stood on Columbus Avenue in front of the neon 411 sign. The movement of car headlights played across her face, which was set in exhaustion. The dark green car pulled up and they got in quietly, both anticipating Sunday, the last night of their work week.

Delia's cousin was a stocky woman who looked about thirty-five, Letty's age. She never spoke much. Not that she wasn't friendly. She always greeted Letty with a smile and laughed at Delia's stories about the customers. Just close to the chest like me, that's all, Letty often thought. As they pulled up to the corner of Cunard Street, Letty opened the rear door. Delia turned to her and said, "I'm sorry you don't play your record on break no more, Miss Letty. I know you don't want to, but I'm sorry just the same."

Delia's cousin looked back at them with a puzzled expression but said nothing. Letty said goodnight, shut the car door, and turned to climb the short flight of stairs to her apartment. Cunard Street was quiet outside her window, and for once the guy upstairs wasn't blasting his record player. After her bath, Letty lay awake and restless in her bed. The electric fan was pointed at the ceiling, bouncing warm air over her, rustling her sheer nightgown.

Inevitably the strains of Billie Holiday's songs brushed against her, much like the breeze that moved around her. She felt silly when she thought about it, but the melody gripped her like a solid presence. It was more than the music. Billie was her hero. Letty saw Billie as big, like herself, with big hungers and a hard secret she couldn't tell anyone. Two weeks before, when Letty had heard that Lady was dead, sorrow had enveloped her. A door had closed that she could not consciously identify to herself or to anyone. It embarrassed her to think about. Like it did when she remembered how she'd felt about Maxine.

Letty had met Billie soon after she started working at the 411 when the singer had stopped in the club with several musicians on their way back from the Jazz Festival. There the audience, curious to see what a real, live junkie looked like, had sat back waiting for Billie to fall on her face. Instead she'd killed them dead with her liquid voice and rough urgency. Still, in the bar, the young, thin horn player had continued to reassure her: "Billie, you were the show, the whole show!"

Soon the cloud of insecurity receded from her face and it lit up with a center-stage smile. Once convinced, Billie became the show again, loud and commanding. She demanded her food be served up front, at the bar, and sent Henrietta, who insisted on waiting on her personally, back to the kitchen fifteen times. Billie laughed at jokes that Letty could barely hear as she bustled back and forth between the abandoned kitchen and her own tables. The sound of that laugh from the bar penetrated her bones. She'd watched and listened, certain she saw something no one else did. Vulnerability was held at bay, and behind that, a hunger even bigger than the one for food or heroin. Letty found reasons to walk up to the front—to use the telephone, to order a drink she paid for and left in the kitchen—just to catch the scent of her, the scent of sweat and silk emanating from her.

"Hey, baby," Billie said when Letty reached past her to pick up her drink from Duke.

"Henny sure can cook, can't she," Letty responded, hoping to see into Billie's eyes.

"Cook? She in these pots, sister!" the horn player shouted from down the bar, sitting behind his own heaping plateful of food.

Billie laughed, holding a big white napkin in front of her mouth, her eyes watering. Letty enjoyed the sound even though she still sensed something deeper, unreachable.

When Billie finished eating and gathered her entourage to get back on the road, she left a tip, not just for Henrietta but for each of the waitresses and the bartender. Generous just like the "business" girls, Letty was happy to note. She still had the two one-dollar bills in an envelope at the back of her lingerie drawer.

After that, Letty felt even closer to Billie. She played one of the few Lady Day records on the jukebox every night during her break. Everyone at the 411 had learned not to bother her when her song came on. Letty realized, as she lay waiting for sleep, that she'd always felt if she had been able to say or do something that night to make friends with Billie, it might all have been different. The faces of Billie, her former lover Maxine, and Delia blended in her mind in half-sleep. Letty slid her hand along the soft nylon of her gown to rest it between her full thighs. She pressed firmly, as if holding desire inside herself. Letty could have loved her enough to make it better.

Sunday nights at the 411 were generally quiet. Even the pimps and prostitutes used it as a day of rest. Letty came in early to have a drink at the bar and talk with Duke before going to the back to change into her uniform. She saw Delia through the window as the younger woman stepped out of the green Pontiac, looking as if she'd just come from Concord Baptist Church. "Satin Doll" played on the jukebox, wrapping the bar in mellow nostalgia for the Sunday dinners they'd serve.

Aristotle let Henrietta close the kitchen early on Sunday, and Letty looked forward to getting done by 9:30 or 10:00 and maybe enjoying some of the evening. When her break time came, she started for the jukebox automatically. She hadn't played anything by Billie in two weeks. Now, looking down at the inviting glare, she knew she still couldn't do it. She punched the buttons that would bring up Jackie Wilson's "Lonely Teardrops" and went to the back booth.

She'd almost dropped off to sleep when she heard Delia whisper her name. Letty opened her eyes and looked up into the girl's smiling face. Her head was haloed in tight, shiny curls.

"Miss Letty, won't you come home with me tonight?"

"What?"

"I'm sorry to bother you, but your break time almost up. I wanted to ask if you'd come over to the house tonight . . . after work. My cousin'll bring you back home after."

Letty didn't speak. Her puzzled look prompted Delia to start again.

"Sometime on Sunday my cousin's friends from work come over to play cards, listen to music, you know. Nothin' special, just some of the girls from the office building down on Winter Street where she work, cleaning. She, I mean we, thought you might want to come over tonight. Have a drink, play some cards—"

"I don't play cards much."

"Well, not everybody play cards . . . just talk . . . sitting around talking. My cousin said you might like to for a change."

Letty wasn't sure she liked the last part—*for a change*—as if they had to entertain an old aunt.

"I really want you to come, Letty. They always her friends, but none of them is my own friends. They all right, I don't mean nothin' against them, but it would be fun to have my own personal friend there, you know?"

Delia was a good girl. Perfect words to describe her, Letty thought, smiling. "Sure, honey. I'd just as soon spend my time with you as lose my money with some fools."

By ten o'clock the kitchen was clean. Once they'd changed out of their uniforms and were out on the street Delia apologized that they had to take a cab uptown. She explained that her cousin and her friends didn't work on Sunday so they were already at home. Letty almost declined, tempted to go home. But she didn't. She stepped into the street and waved down a

Red and White cab with brisk, urban efficiency. All the way uptown Delia explained that the evening wasn't a big deal and cautioned Letty not to expect much. "Just a few friends, hanging around, drinking and talking." She was jumpy, and Letty tried to put her at ease. She had not expected her visit would make Delia so anxious.

The apartment was located halfway up Blue Hill Avenue in an area where a few blacks had recently been permitted to rent. They entered a long, carpeted hallway and heard the sounds of laughter and music ringing from the rooms at the far end.

Inside, with the door closed, Delia shed her nervousness. This was clearly her home turf, and Letty couldn't believe she ever really needed an ally to back her up. Delia stepped out of her shoes at the door and walked to the back with her same long-legged gait. They passed a closed door, which Letty assumed to be one of the bedrooms, then came to a kitchen ablaze with light. Food and bottles were strewn across the blue-flecked table top. A counter opened from the kitchen into the dining room, which was the center of activity. Around a large mahogany table sat five women in smoke-filled concentration, playing poker.

Delia's cousin looked up from her cards with the same slight smile she displayed when she picked them up at work. Here it seemed welcoming, not guarded as it did in those brief moments in her car. She wore brown slacks and a matching sweater. The pink, starched points of her shirt collar peeked out at the neck.

Delia crossed to her and kissed her cheek lightly. Letty looked around the table to see if she recognized anyone. The women all seemed familar in the way that city neighbors can, but Letty was sure she hadn't met any of them before. Delia introduced them, and each acknowledged Letty without diverting her attention from her cards; Karen, a short, round woman with West Indian bangles almost up to her elbow; Betty, who stared intently at her cards through thick eyeglasses encased in blue cat's-eye frames; Irene, a big, dark woman with long black hair and a gold tooth in front. Beside her sat Myrtle, who was wearing army fatigues and a gold Masonic ring on her pinkie finger. She said hello in the softest voice Letty had every heard. Hovering over her was Clara, a large redbone woman whose hair was bound tightly in a bun at the nape of her neck. She spoke with a delectable Southern accent that drawled her "How're you doin'" into a full paragraph draped around an inquisitive smile.

Letty felt Delia tense again. Then she pulled Letty by the arm toward the French doors behind the players. There was a small den with a desk, some books, and a television set. Through the second set of glass doors was a living room. At the record player was an extremely tall, brown-skinned woman. She bent over the wooden cabinet searching for the next selection, oblivious to the rest of the gathering. Two women sat on the divan in deep conversation punctuated with constrained laughter.

"Maryalice, Sheila, Dolores . . . this is Letty. She work with me at the 411."

They looked up at her quickly, smiled, then went back to their preoccupations. Two of them resumed their whispered conversation; the other returned to the record collection. Delia directed Letty back toward the foyer and the kitchen.

"Come on, let me get you a drink. You know, I don't even know what you drink!"

"Delia?" Her cousin's voice reached them over the counter, just as they stepped into the kitchen. "Bring a couple of beers back when you come, okay?"

"Sure, babe." Delia went to the refrigerator and pulled out two bottles. "Let me just take these in. I'll be right back."

"Go 'head, I can take care of myself in this department, girl." Letty surveyed the array of bottles on the table. Delia went to the dining room and Letty mixed a Scotch and soda. She poured slowly as the reality settled on her. These women were friends, perhaps lovers, like she and Maxine had been. The name she'd heard for women like these burst inside her head: *bulldagger*. Letty flinched, angry she had let it in, angry that it frightened her. "Ptuh!" She blew through her teeth as if spitting the word back at the air.

She did know these women, Letty thought, as she stood at the counter looking out at the poker game. They were oblivious to her, except for Terry. Letty finally remembered that that was Delia's cousin's name.

As Letty took her first sip, Terry called over to her, "We gonna be finished with this hand in a minute, Letty, then we can talk." This time her face was filled by a large grin.

"Take your time," Letty said. She went out through the foyer door and around to the living room. She walked slowly on the carpet and adjusted her eyes to the light, which was a bit softer. The tall woman, Maryalice, had just put a record on the turntable and sat down on a love seat across from the other two women. Letty stood in the doorway a moment before the tune began:

Hush now, don't explain
Just say you'll return
I'm glad you're back
Don't explain . . .

Letty was stunned. She realized the song sounded different among these women: Billie sang just to them. Letty watched Maryalice sitting with her long legs stretched out tensely in front of her. She was wrapped in her own thoughts, her eyes closed. She appeared curiously disconnected after what had clearly been a long search for this record. Letty watched her face as she swallowed several times. Then Letty sat beside her. They listened to the music while the other two women spoke in low voices.

Maryalice didn't move when the song was over.

"I met her once," Letty said.

"I beg your pardon?"

"Kinda met her. At the 411 Lounge where me and Delia work."

"Naw!" Maryalice said as she sat up.

"She was just coming back from a gig."

"Honestly?" Maryalice's voice caught with excitement.

"She just had dinner—smothered chicken, potato salad, green beans, side of stewed tomatoes, and an extra side of cornbread."

"Big eater."

"Child, everybody is when Henrietta's cooking. Billie was . . . ," Letty searched for the words, "she was sort of stubborn."

Maryalice laughed. "You know, that's kinda how I pictured her."

"I figure she had to be stubborn to keep going," Letty said. "And not stingy, either!"

"Yeah," Maryalice said, enjoying the confirmation of her image of Billie.

Letty rose from the sofa and went to the record player. Delia stood tentatively watching from the doorway of the living room. Letty picked up the arm of the phonograph and replaced it at the beginning of the record. Letty noticed the drops of moisture on Maryalice's lashes, but she relaxed as Letty settled onto the seat beside her. They listened to Billie together, for the first time.

Alexis De Veaux (b. 1948)

Alexis De Veaux writes narratives and plays for juvenile and adult audiences. Born in New York City, she received her B.A. from Empire State College of the State University of New York in 1976. She has taught for the Urban League and other community initiatives. Her best known juvenile books are *Na-Ni* (1973), which won the Art Books for Children Award from the Brooklyn Museum, and *An Enchanted Hair Tale* (1987), a story about Sudan, who must learn to see his strange hair as enchanted. De Veaux has also written several prose poems, including *Don't Explain: A Song of Billie Holiday* (1980). Her short fiction deals with life in Harlem and coming-of-age stories. Her one-act plays and full-length drama, as well as her poetry, all attest to artistic versatility. One poem, "Sister Love," pleads for an understanding of the struggles of black lesbian love. De Veaux has spoken of the difficulty that she has had placing her lesbian pieces in black publications.

The Woman Who Lives in the Botanical Gardens

is a man. who. sleeping on a hill and a bench among the Chinese maple trees lives there. sleeping in her petticoats of ackee leaf and banana leaf though neither grows in this city: O see: how tall she is the tallest lean: O see: the delicate spread of her branch a thickly muscled arm. how it sways there (quiet) how it dreams of plaintain and rice and the Black Star Line:

O Jah

and the hairless face/the primitive hollow of cheeks taut: with rebellion. black with the dust of upturned earth and the plantings of memory.

O Jah see
O Jah

see: the barest of back/like an island and the hair the long: dangling mats of hair under armpits; the perfumed hair laden with anarchy: hangs from the pit of the arm dangling over the bench.

THE WOMAN WHO LIVES IN THE BOTANICAL GARDENS wears underneath her banana ackee leaf petticoat the pants of three generations: her grandfather's her father's: her own. THE WOMAN WHO never comes outside the gates never comes outside the rags around her pine bark hair; the reams of rage: O see, O Jah:

THE WOMAN WHO LIVES IN THE BOTANICAL GARDENS/ THE WOMAN WHO LIVES IN THE BOTANICAL GARDENS: is named South Africa. See there how she holds the m-16: how she holds the Gardens hostage. and the bullets in her earlobes: bullets at her breasts: the red green and gold rage. And the necklace of fallopian tube and the egg of children and the bits of blood of hair in the tumors of the homeland: O Jah: O Jah: see her how she: stalks the gates. O Jah/ THE WOMAN WHO THE WOMAN WHO LIVES: on the squirrels and stray cats of the Garden LIVES. like a guard dog. gums bared. teeth pointed: she snap at the gate:

THERE WILL BE NO VISITORS
AT THE GARDEN TODAY
OR TOMORROW NEITHER
IN FACT
DON'T COME NO CLOSER:
I REALLY DO MEAN TO SHOOT UP THE MUSEUM
I REALLY DO MEAN TO SHOOT UP THE PARKWAY
I REALLY DO MEAN TO SHOOT UP THE HELICOPTER
SO: DON'T COME NO CLOSER.

WHO IS ME??
THIS IS SOUTH AFRICA SPEAKING
BLACK SOUTH AFRICA BLACK
SOUTH AFRICA
AND I AM TAKING OVAH THIS SHIT
I AM TAKING OVAH.

Published in "Confirmation," New York, NY: Quill, 1983, ed. Amiri Baraka (Leroi Jones).

Gloria Naylor (b. 1950)

Winner of the 1983 American Book Award, *The Women of Brewster Place* (1982) brought Gloria Naylor to the attention of large numbers of readers. A novel told in seven stories, *Brewster Place* recounts the lives of various black women, who "each in her own time and with her own season had a story." Their stories unveil their problems with their children, their parents, and their lovers. Whereas most of the women in *Brewster Place* are poor, *Linden Hills* (1985) is about middle-class African American life—its materialism, its caste system, its sexism. *Mama Day* (1988) takes place in Willow Springs in the Sea Islands off the coast of South Carolina and Georgia. It is in Willow Springs that Miranda Day (Mama Day) works her magic. In *Bailey's Café* (1992), like *The Women of Brewster Place*, Naylor writes of a place where people who are in pain come for comfort and relief. The café is a place where society's misfits reexamine their lives. Throughout her fiction, Naylor is known for what she does with landscape and geography and the way in which she draws upon European literature, even as she creates distinctively African American novels. Whether building upon Shakespeare's *A Midsummer Night's Dream*, *King Lear*, or *The Tempest*, or Dante's *Inferno*, Naylor writes stories that resonate with early canonical texts, but are distinctively African American.

Naylor was born in New York, the daughter of Roosevelt Naylor, a transit worker, and Alberta McAlpin Naylor, a telephone operator. For a number of years she worked as a missionary for Jehovah's Witnesses and as a hotel telephone operator. After earning her B.A. in English from Brooklyn College, she earned an M.A. in Afro-American Studies from Yale. In addition to the American Book Award for Best First Novel, she has received a National Endowment for the Arts Fellowship, a Guggenheim Fellowship, and the Lillian Smith Award.

From *The Women of Brewster Place*

Kiswana Browne

From the window of her sixth-floor studio apartment, Kiswana could see over the wall at the end of the street to the busy avenue that lay just north of Brewster Place. The late-afternoon shoppers looked like brightly clad marionettes as they moved between the congested traffic, clutching their packages against their bodies to guard them from sudden bursts of the cold autumn wind. A portly mailman had abandoned his cart and was bumping into indignant window shoppers as he puffed behind the cap that the wind had snatched from his head. Kiswana leaned over to see if he was going to be successful, but the edge of the building cut him off from her view.

A pigeon swept across her window, and she marveled at its liquid movements in the air waves. She placed her dreams on the back of the bird and fantasized that it would glide forever in transparent silver circles until it ascended to the center of the universe and was swallowed up. But the wind died down, and she watched with a sigh as the bird beat its wings in awkward, frantic movements to land on the corroded top of a fire escape on the opposite building. This brought her back to earth.

Humph, it's probably sitting over there crapping on those folks' fire escape, she thought. Now, that's a safety hazard . . . And her mind was busy again, creating flames and smoke and frustrated tenants whose escape was being hindered because they were slipping and sliding in pigeon shit. She watched their cussing, haphazard descent on the fire escapes until they had all reached the bottom. They were milling around, oblivious to their burning apartments, angrily planning to march on the mayor's office about the pigeons. She materialized placards and banners for them, and they had just reached the corner, boldly sidestepping fire hoses and broken glass, when they all vanished.

A tall copper-skinned woman had met this phantom parade at the corner, and they had dissolved in front of her long, confident strides. She plowed through the remains of their faded mists, unconscious of the lingering wisps of their presence on her leather bag and black fur-trimmed coat. It took a few seconds for this transfer from one realm to another to reach Kiswana, but then suddenly she recognized the woman.

"Oh, God, it's Mama!" She looked down guiltily at the forgotten newspaper in her lap and hurriedly circled random job advertisements.

By this time Mrs. Browne had reached the front of Kiswana's building and was checking the house number against a piece of paper in her hand. Before she went into the building she stood at the bottom of the stoop and carefully inspected the condition of the street and the adjoining property. Kiswana watched this meticulous inventory with growing annoyance but she involuntarily followed her mother's slowly rotating head, forcing herself to see her new neighborhood through the older woman's eyes. The brightness of the unclouded sky seemed to join forces with her mother as it highlighted every broken stoop railing and missing brick. The afternoon sun glittered and cascaded across even the tiniest fragments of broken bottle, and at that very moment the wind chose to rise up again, sending unswept grime flying into the air, as a stray tin can left by careless garbage collectors went rolling noisily down the center of the street.

Kiswana noticed with relief that at least Ben wasn't sitting in his usual place on the old garbage can pushed against the far wall. He was just a harmless old wino, but Kiswana knew her mother only needed one wino or one teenager with a reefer within a twenty-block radius to decide that her daughter was living in a building seething with dope factories and hangouts for derelicts. If she had seen Ben, nothing would have made her believe that practically every apartment contained a family, a Bible, and a dream that one day enough could be scraped from those meager Friday night paychecks to make Brewster Place a distant memory.

As she watched her mother's head disappear into the building, Kiswana gave silent thanks that the elevator was broken. That would give her at least five minutes' grace to straighten up the apartment. She rushed to the sofa bed and hastily closed it without smoothing the rumpled sheets and blanket or removing her nightgown. She felt that somehow the tangled bedcovers would give away the fact that she had not slept alone last night. She silently apologized to Abshu's memory as she heartlessly crushed his spirit between the steel springs of the couch. Lord, that man was sweet. Her toes curled involuntarily at the passing thought of his full lips moving slowly over her instep. Abshu was a foot man, and he always started his lovemaking from the bottom up. For that reason Kiswana changed the color of the polish on her toenails every week. During the course of their relationship she had gone from shades of red to brown and was now into the purples. I'm gonna have to start mixing them soon, she

thought aloud as she turned from the couch and raced into the bathroom to remove any traces of Abshu from there. She took up his shaving cream and razor and threw them into the bottom drawer of her dresser beside her diaphragm. Mama wouldn't dare pry into my drawers right in front of me, she thought, as she slammed the drawer shut. Well, at least not the *bottom* drawer. She may come up with some sham excuse for opening the top drawer, but never the bottom one.

When she heard the first two short raps on the door, her eyes took a final flight over the small apartment, desperately seeking out any slight misdemeanor that might have to be defended. Well, there was nothing she could do about the crack in the wall over that table. She had been after the landlord to fix it for two months now. And there had been no time to sweep the rug, and everyone knew that off-gray always looked dirtier than it really was. And it was just too damn bad about the kitchen. How was she expected to be out job-hunting every day and still have time to keep a kitchen that looked like her mother's, who didn't even work and still had someone come in twice a month for general cleaning. And besides—

Her imaginary argument was abruptly interrupted by a second series of knocks, accompanied by a penetrating, "Melanie, Melanie, are you there?"

Kiswana strode toward the door. She's starting before she even gets in here. She knows that's not my name anymore.

She swung the door open to face her slightly flushed mother. "Oh, hi, Mama. You know, I thought I heard a knock, but I figured it was for the people next door, since no one hardly ever calls me Melanie." Score one for me, she thought.

"Well, it's awfully strange you can forget a name you answered to for twenty-three years," Mrs. Browne said, as she moved past Kiswana into the apartment. "My, that was a long climb. How long has your elevator been out? Honey, how do you manage with your laundry and groceries up all those steps? But I guess you're young, and it wouldn't bother you as much as it does me."

This long string of questions told Kiswana that her mother had no intentions of beginning her visit with another argument about her new African name.

"You know I would have called before I came, but you don't have a phone yet. I didn't want you to feel that I was snooping. As a matter of fact, I didn't expect to find you home at all. I thought you'd be out looking for a job." Mrs. Browne had mentally covered the entire apartment while she was talking and taking off her coat.

"Well, I got up late this morning. I thought I'd buy the afternoon paper and start early tomorrow."

"That sounds like a good idea." Her mother moved toward the window and picked up the discarded paper and glanced over the hurriedly circled ads. "Since when do you have experience as a fork-lift operator?"

Kiswana caught her breath and silently cursed herself for her stupidity. "Oh, my hand slipped—I meant to circle file clerk." She quickly took the paper before her mother could see that she had also marked cutlery salesman and chauffeur.

"You're sure you weren't sitting here moping and day-dreaming again?" Amber specks of laughter flashed in the corner of Mrs. Browne's eyes.

Kiswana threw her shoulders back and unsuccessfully tried to disguise her embarrassment with indignation.

"Oh, God, Mama! I haven't done that in years—it's for kids. When are you going to realize that I'm a woman now?"

She sought desperately for some womanly thing to do and settled for throwing herself on the couch and crossing her legs in what she hoped looked like a nonchalant arc.

"Please, have a seat," she said, attempting the same tones and gestures she'd seen Bette Davis use on the late movies.

Mrs. Browne, lowering her eyes to hide her amusement, accepted the invitation and sat at the window, also crossing her legs. Kiswana saw immediately how it should have been done. Her celluloid poise clashed loudly against her mother's quiet dignity, and she quickly uncrossed her legs. Mrs. Browne turned her head toward the window and pretended not to notice.

"At least you have a halfway decent view from here. I was wondering what lay beyond that dreadful wall—it's the boulevard. Honey, did you know that you can see the trees in Linden Hills from here?"

Kiswana knew that very well, because there were many lonely days that she would sit in her gray apartment and stare at those trees and think of home, but she would rather have choked than admit that to her mother.

"Oh, really? I never noticed. So how is Daddy and things at home?"

"Just fine. We're thinking of redoing one of the extra bedrooms since you children have moved out, but Wilson insists that he can manage all that work alone. I told him that he doesn't really have the proper time or energy for all that. As it is, when he gets home from the office, he's so tired he can hardly move. But you know you can't tell your father anything. Whenever he starts complaining about how stubborn you are, I tell him the child came by it honestly. Oh, and your brother was by yesterday," she added, as if it had just occurred to her.

So that's it, thought Kiswana. That's why she's here.

Kiswana's brother, Wilson, had been to visit her two days ago, and she had borrowed twenty dollars from him to get her winter coat out of layaway. That son-of-a-bitch probably ran straight to Mama—and after he swore he wouldn't say anything. I should have known, he was always a snotty-nosed sneak, she thought.

"Was he?" she said aloud. "He came by to see me, too, earlier this week. And I borrowed some money from him because

my unemployment checks hadn't cleared in the bank, but now they have and everything's just fine." There, I'll beat you to that one.

"Oh, I didn't know that," Mrs. Browne lied. "He never mentioned you. He had just heard that Beverly was expecting again, and he rushed over to tell us."

Damn. Kiswana could have strangled herself.

"So she's knocked up again, huh?" she said irritably.

Her mother started. "Why do you always have to be so crude?"

"Personally, I don't see how she can sleep with Willie. He's such a dishrag."

Kiswana still resented the stance her brother had taken in college. When everyone at school was discovering their blackness and protesting on campus, Wilson never took part; he had even refused to wear an Afro. This had outraged Kiswana because, unlike her, he was dark-skinned and had the type of hair that was thick and kinky enough for a good "Fro." Kiswana had still insisted on cutting her own hair, but it was so thin and fine-textured, it refused to thicken even after she washed it. So she had to brush it up and spray it with lacquer to keep it from lying flat. She never forgave Wilson for telling her that she didn't look African, she looked like an electrocuted chicken.

"Now that's some way to talk. I don't know why you have an attitude against your brother. He never gave me a restless night's sleep, and now he's settled with a family and a good job."

"He's an assistant to an assistant junior partner in a law firm. What's the big deal about that?"

"The job has a future, Melanie. And at least he finished school and went on for his law degree."

"In other words, not like me, huh?"

"Don't put words into my mouth, young lady. I'm perfectly capable of saying what I mean."

Amen, thought Kiswana.

"And I don't know why you've been trying to start up with me from the moment I walked in. I didn't come here to fight with you. This is your first place away from home, and I just wanted to see how you were living and if you're doing all right. And I must say, you've fixed this apartment up very nicely."

"Really, Mama?" She found herself softening in the light of her mother's approval.

"Well, considering what you had to work with." This time she scanned the apartment openly.

"Look, I know it's not Linden Hills, but a lot can be done with it. As soon as they come and paint, I'm going to hang my Ashanti print over the couch. And I thought a big Boston fern would go well in that corner, what do you think?"

"That would be fine, baby. You always had a good eye for balance."

Kiswana was beginning to relax. There was little she did that attracted her mother's approval. It was like a rare bird, and she had to tread carefully around it lest it fly away.

"Are you going to leave that statue out like that?"

"Why, what's wrong with it? Would it look better somewhere else?"

There was a small wooden reproduction of a Yoruba goddess with large protruding breasts on the coffee table.

"Well"—Mrs. Browne was beginning to blush—"it's just that it's a bit suggestive, don't you think? Since you live alone now, and I know you'll be having male friends stop by, you wouldn't want to be giving them any ideas. I mean, uh, you know, there's no point in putting yourself in any unpleasant situations because they may get the wrong impression and uh, you know, I mean, well . . ." Mrs. Browne stammered on miserably.

Kiswana loved it when her mother tried to talk about sex. It was the only time she was at a loss for words.

"Don't worry, Mama." Kiswana smiled. "That wouldn't bother the type of men I date. Now maybe if it had big feet—"And she got hysterical, thinking of Abshu.

Her mother looked at her sharply. "What sort of gibberish is that about feet? I'm being serious, Melanie."

"I'm sorry, Mama." She sobered up. "I'll put it away in the closet," she said, knowing that she wouldn't.

"Good," Mrs. Browne said, knowing that she wouldn't either. "I guess you think I'm too picky, but we worry about you over here. And you refuse to put in a phone so we can call and see about you."

"I haven't refused, Mama. They want seventy-five dollars for a deposit, and I can't swing that right now."

"Melanie, I can give you the money."

"I don't want you to be giving me money—I've told you that before. Please, let me make it by myself."

"Well, let me lend it to you, then."

"No!"

"Oh, so you can borrow money from your brother, but not from me."

Kiswana turned her head from the hurt in her mother's eyes. "Mama, when I borrow from Willie, he makes me pay him back. You never let me pay you back," she said into her hands.

"I don't care. I still think it's downright selfish of you to be sitting over here with no phone, and sometimes we don't hear from you in two weeks—anything could happen—especially living among these people."

Kiswana snapped her head up. "What do you mean, *these people*? They're my people and yours, too, Mama—we're all black. But maybe you've forgotten that over in Linden Hills."

"That's not what I'm talking about, and you know it. These streets—this building—it's so shabby and rundown. Honey, you don't have to live like this."

"Well, this is how poor people live."

"Melanie, you're not poor."

"No, Mama, *you're* not poor. And what you have and I have are two totally different things. I don't have a husband in real estate with a five-figure income and a home in Linden Hills—*you* do. What I have is a weekly unemployment check and an overdrawn checking account at United Federal. So this studio on Brewster is all I can afford."

"Well, you could afford a lot better," Mrs. Browne snapped, "if you hadn't dropped out of college and had to resort to these dead-end clerical jobs."

"Uh-huh, I knew you'd get around to that before long." Kiswana could feel the rings of anger begin to tighten around her lower backbone, and they sent her forward onto the couch. "You'll never understand, will you? Those bourgie schools were counterrevolutionary. My place was in the streets with my people, fighting for equality and a better community."

"Counterrevolutionary!" Mrs. Browne was raising her voice. "Where's your revolution now, Melanie? Where are all those black revolutionaries who were shouting and demonstrating and kicking up a lot of dust with you on that campus? Huh? They're sitting in wood-paneled offices with their degrees in mahogany frames, and they won't even drive their cars past this street because the city doesn't fix potholes in this part of town."

"Mama," she said, shaking her head slowly in disbelief, "how can you—a black woman—sit there and tell me that what we fought for during the Movement wasn't important just because some people sold out?"

"Melanie, I'm not saying it wasn't important. It was damned important to stand up and say that you were proud of what you were and to get the vote and other social opportunities for every person in this country who had it due. But you kids thought you were going to turn the world upside down, and it just wasn't so. When all the smoke had cleared, you found yourself with a fistful of new federal laws and a country still full of obstacles for black people to fight their way over—just because they're black. There was no revolution, Melanie, and there will be no revolution."

"So what am I supposed to do, huh? Just throw up my hands and not care about what happens to my people? I'm not supposed to keep fighting to make things better?"

"Of course you can. But you're going to have to fight within the system, because it and these so-called 'bourgie' schools are going to be here for a long time. And that means that you get smart like a lot of your old friends and get an important job where you can have some influence. You don't have to sell out, as you say, and work for some corporation, but you could become an assembly-woman or a civil liberties lawyer or open a freedom school in this very neighborhood. That way you could really help the community. But what help are you going to be to these people on Brewster while you're living hand-to-mouth on file-clerk jobs waiting for a revolution? You're wasting your talents, child."

"Well, I don't think they're being wasted. At least I'm here in day-to-day contact with the problems of my people. What good would I be after four or five years of a lot of white brainwashing in some phony prestige institution, huh? I'd be like you and Daddy and those other educated blacks sitting over there in Linden Hills with a terminal case of middle-class amnesia."

"You don't have to live in a slum to be concerned about social conditions, Melanie. Your father and I have been charter members of the NAACP for the last twenty-five years."

"Oh, God!" Kiswana threw her head back in exaggerated disgust. "That's being concerned? That middle-of-the-road Uncle Tom dumping ground for black Republicans!"

"You can sneer all you want, young lady, but that organization has been working for black people since the turn of the century, and it's still working for them. Where are all those radical groups of yours that were going to put a Cadillac in every garage and Dick Gregory in the White House? I'll tell you where."

I knew you would, Kiswana thought angrily.

"They burned themselves out because they wanted too much too fast. Their goals weren't grounded in reality. And that's always been your problem."

"What do you mean, my problem? I know exactly what I'm about."

"No, you don't. You constantly live in a fantasy world—always going to extremes—turning butterflies into eagles, and life isn't about that. It's accepting what is and working from that. Lord, I remember how worried you had me, putting all that lacquered hair spray on your head. I thought you were going to get lung cancer—trying to be what you're not."

Kiswana jumped up from the couch. "Oh, God, I can't take this anymore. Trying to be something I'm not—trying to be something I'm not, Mama? Trying to be proud of my heritage and the fact that I was of African descent. If that's being what I'm not, then I say fine. But I'd rather be dead than be like you—a white man's nigger who's ashamed of being black!"

Kiswana saw streaks of gold and ebony light follow her mother's flying body out of the chair. She was swung around by the shoulders and made to face the deadly stillness in the angry woman's eyes. She was too stunned to cry out from the pain of the long fingernails that dug into her shoulders, and she was brought so close to her mother's face that she saw her reflection, distorted and wavering, in the tears that stood in the older woman's eyes. And she listened in that stillness to a story she had heard as a child.

"My grandmother," Mrs. Browne began slowly in a whisper, "was a full-blooded Iroquois, and my grandfather a free black from a long line of journeymen who had lived in Connecticut since the establishment of the colonies. And my father was a Bajan who came to this country as a cabin boy on a merchant mariner."

"I know all that," Kiswana said, trying to keep her lips from trembling.

"Then know this." And the nails dug deeper into her flesh. "I am alive because of the blood of proud people who never scraped or begged or apologized for what they were. They lived asking only one thing of this world—to be allowed to be. And I learned through the blood of these people that black isn't beautiful and it isn't ugly—black is! It's not kinky hair and it's not straight hair—it just is."

"It broke my heart when you changed your name. I gave you my grandmother's name, a woman who bore nine children and educated them all, who held off six white men with a shotgun when they tried to drag one of her sons to jail for 'not knowing his place.' Yet you needed to reach into an African dictionary to find a name to make you proud."

"When I brought my babies home from the hospital, my ebony son and my golden daughter, I swore before whatever gods would listen—those of my mother's people or those of my father's people—that I would use everything I had and could ever get to see that my children were prepared to meet this world on its own terms, so that no one could sell them short and make them ashamed of what they were or how they looked—whatever they were or however they looked. And Melanie, that's not being white or red or black—that's being a mother."

Kiswana followed her reflection in the two single tears that moved down her mother's cheeks until it blended with them into the woman's copper skin. There was nothing and then so much that she wanted to say, but her throat kept closing up every time she tried to speak. She kept her head down and her eyes closed, and thought, Oh, God, just let me die. How can I face her now?

Mrs. Browne lifted Kiswana's chin gently. "And the one lesson I wanted you to learn is not to be afraid to face anyone, not even a crafty old lady like me who can outtalk you." And she smiled and winked.

"Oh, Mama, I . . ." and she hugged the woman tightly.

"Yeah, baby." Mrs. Browne patted her back. "I know." She kissed Kiswana on the forehead and cleared her throat. "Well, now, I better be moving on. It's getting late, there's dinner to be made, and I have to get off my feet—these new shoes are killing me."

Kiswana looked down at the beige leather pumps. "Those are really classy. They're English, aren't they?"

"Yes, but, Lord, do they cut me right across the instep." She removed the shoe and sat on the couch to massage her foot.

Bright red nail polish glared at Kiswana through the stockings. "Since when do you polish your toenails?" she gasped. "You never did that before."

"Well"—Mrs. Browne shrugged her shoulders—"your father sort of talked me into it, and, uh, you know, he likes it and all, so I thought, uh, you know, why not, so . . ." And she gave Kiswana an embarrassed smile.

I'll be damned, the young woman thought, feeling her whole face tingle. Daddy's into feet! And she looked at the blushing woman on her couch and suddenly realized that her mother had trod through the same universe that she herself was now traveling. Kiswana was breaking no new trails and would eventually end up just two feet away on that couch. She stared at the woman she had been and was to become.

"But I'll never be a Republican," she caught herself saying aloud.

"What are you mumbling about, Melanie?" Mrs. Browne slipped on her shoe and got up from the couch.

She went to get her mother's coat. "Nothing, Mama. It's really nice of you to come by. You should do it more often."

"Well, since it's not Sunday, I guess you're allowed at least one lie."

They both laughed.

After Kiswana had closed the door and turned around, she spotted an envelope sticking between the cushions of her couch. She went over and opened it up; there was seventy-five dollars in it.

"Oh, Mama, darn it!" She rushed to the window and started to call to the woman, who had just emerged from the building, but she suddenly changed her mind and sat down in the chair with a long sigh that caught in the upward draft of the autumn wind and disappeared over the top of the building.

From *Mama Day*

[Willow Springs]

Willow Springs. Everybody knows but nobody talks about the legend of Sapphira Wade. A true conjure woman: satin black, biscuit cream, red as Georgia clay: depending upon which of us takes a mind to her. She could walk through a lightning storm without being touched; grab a bolt of lightning in the palm of her hand; use the heat of lightning to start the kindling going under her medicine pot: depending upon which of us takes a mind to her. She turned the moon into salve, the stars into a swaddling cloth, and healed the wounds of every

creature walking up on two or down on four. It ain't about right or wrong, truth or lies; it's about a slave woman who brought a whole new meaning to both them words, soon as you cross over here from beyond the bridge. And somehow, some way, it happened in 1823: she smothered Bascombe Wade in his very bed and lived to tell the story for a thousand days. 1823: married Bascombe Wade, bore him seven sons in just a thousand days, to put a dagger through his kidney and escape the hangman's noose, laughing in a burst of flames. 1823: persuaded Bascombe Wade in a thousand days to deed all his slaves every inch of land in Willow Springs, poisoned him for his trouble, to go on and bear seven sons—by person or persons unknown. Mixing it all together and keeping everything that done shifted down through the holes of time, you end up with the death of Bascombe Wade (there's his tombstone right out by Chevy's Pass), the deeds to our land (all marked back to the very year), and seven sons (ain't Miss Abigail and Mama Day the granddaughters of that seventh boy?). The wild card in all this is the thousand days, and we guess if we put our heads together we'd come up with something—which ain't possible since Sapphira Wade don't live in the part of our memory we can use to form words.

But ain't a soul in Willow Springs don't know that little dark girls, hair all braided up with colored twine, got their "18 & 23's coming down" when they lean too long over them back yard fences, laughing at the antics of little dark boys who got the nerve to be "breathing 18 & 23" with mother's milk still on their tongues. And if she leans there just a mite too long or grins a bit too wide, it's gonna bring a holler straight through the dusty screen door. "Get your bow-legged self 'way from my fence, Johnny Blue. Won't be no 'early 18 & 23's' coming here for me to rock. I'm still raising her." Yes, the *name* Sapphira Wade is never breathed out of a single mouth in Willow Springs. But who don't know that old twisted-lip manager at the Sheraton Hotel beyond the bridge, offering Winky Browne only twelve dollars for his whole boatload of crawdaddies—"tried to 18 & 23 him," if he tried to do a thing? We all sitting here, a hop, skip, and one Christmas left before the year 2000, and ain't nobody told him niggers can read now? Like the menus in his restaurant don't say a handful of crawdaddies sprinkled over a little bowl of crushed ice is almost twelve dollars? Call it shrimp cocktail, or whatever he want—we can count, too. And the price of everything that swims, crawls, or lays at the bottom of The Sound went up in 1985, during the season we had that "18 & 23 summer" and the bridge blew down. Folks didn't take their lives in their hands out there in that treacherous water just to be doing it— ain't that much 18 & 23 in the world.

But that old hotel manager don't make no never mind. He's the least of what we done had to deal with here in Willow Springs. Malaria. Union soldiers. Sandy soil. Two big depressions. Hurricanes. Not to mention these new real estate developers who think we gonna sell our shore land just because we ain't fool enough to live there. Started coming over here in the early '90s, talking "vacation paradise," talking "pic-ture-ess." Like Winky said, we'd have to pick their ass out the bottom of the marsh first hurricane blow through here again. See, they just thinking about building where they ain't got no state taxes—never been and never will be, 'cause Willow Springs ain't in no state. Georgia and South Carolina done tried, though—been trying since right after the Civil War to prove that Willow Springs belong to one or the other of them. Look on any of them old maps they hurried and drew up soon as the Union soldiers pulled out and you can see that the only thing connects us to the mainland is a bridge—and even that gotta be rebuilt after every big storm. (They was talking about steel and concrete way back, but since Georgia and South Carolina couldn't claim the taxes, nobody wanted to shell out for the work. So we rebuild it ourselves when need be, and build it how we need it—strong enough to last till the next big wind. Only need a steel and concrete bridge once every seventy years or so. Wood and pitch is a tenth of the cost and serves us a good sixty-nine years—matter of simple arithmetic.) But anyways, all forty-nine square miles curves like a bow, stretching toward Georgia on the south end and South Carolina on the north, and right smack in the middle where each foot of our bridge sits is the dividing line between them two states.

So who it belong to? It belongs to us—clean and simple. And it belonged to our daddies, and our daddies before them, and them too—who at one time all belonged to Bascombe Wade. And when they tried to trace him and how he got it, found out he wasn't even American. Was Norway-born or something, and the land had been sitting in his family over there in Europe since it got explored and claimed by the Vikings—imagine that. So thanks to the conjuring of Sapphira Wade we got it from Norway or theres about, and if taxes owed, it's owed to them. But ain't no Vikings or anybody else from over in Europe come to us with the foolishness that them folks out of Columbia and Atlanta come with—we was being un-American. And the way we saw it, America ain't entered the question at all when it come to our land: Sapphira was African-born, Bascombe Wade was from Norway, and it was the 18 & 23'ing that went down between them two put deeds in our hands. And we wasn't even Americans when we got it—was slaves. And the laws about slaves not owning nothing in Georgia and South Carolina don't apply, 'cause the land wasn't then—and isn't now—in either of them places. When there was lots of cotton here, and we baled it up and sold it beyond the bridge, we paid our taxes to the U.S. of A. And we keeps account of all the fishing that's done and sold beyond the bridge, all the little truck farming. And

later when we had to go over there to work or our children went, we paid taxes out of them earnings. We pays taxes on the telephone lines and electrical wires run over The Sound. Ain't nobody here about breaking the law. But Georgia and South Carolina ain't seeing the shine off a penny for our land, our homes, our roads, or our bridge. Well, they fought each other up to the Supreme Court about the whole matter, and it came to a draw. We guess they got so tired out from that, they decided to leave us be—until them developers started swarming over here like sand flies at a Sunday picnic.

Sure, we coulda used the money and weren't using the land. But like Mama Day told 'em (we knew to send 'em straight over there to her and Miss Abigail), they didn't come huffing and sweating all this way in them dark gaberdine suits if they didn't think our land could make them a bundle of money, and the way we saw it, there was enough land—shoreline, that is—to make us all pretty comfortable. And calculating on the basis of all them fancy plans they had in mind, a million an acre wasn't asking too much. Flap, flap, flap—Lord, didn't them jaws and silk ties move in the wind. The land wouldn't be worth that if they couldn't *build* on it. Yes, suh, she told 'em, and they couldn't build on it unless we *sold* it. So we get ours now, and they get theirs later. You shoulda seen them coattails flapping back across The Sound with all their lies about "community uplift" and "better jobs." 'Cause it weren't about no them now and us later—was them now and us never. Hadn't we seen it happen back in the '80s on St. Helena, Daufuskie, and St. John's? And before that in the '60s on Hilton Head? Got them folks' land, built fences around it first thing, and then brought in all the builders and high-paid managers from mainside—ain't nobody on them islands benefited. And the only dark faces you see now in them "vacation paradises" is the ones cleaning the toilets and cutting the grass. On their own land, mind you, their own land. Weren't gonna happen in Willow Springs. 'Cause if Mama Day say no, everybody say no. There's 18 & 23, and there's 18 & 23—and nobody was gonna trifle with Mama Day's, 'cause she know how to use it—her being a direct descendant of Sapphira Wade, piled on the fact of springing from the seventh son of a seventh son—uh, uh. Mama Day say no, everybody say no. No point in making a pile of money to be guaranteed the new moon will see you scratching at fleas you don't have, or rolling in the marsh like a mud turtle. And if some was waiting for her to die, they had a long wait. She says she ain't gonna. And when you think about it, to show up in one century, make it all the way through the next, and have a toe inching over into the one approaching *is* about as close to eternity anybody can come.

Well, them developers upped the price and changed the plans, changed the plans and upped the price, till it got to be a game with us. Winky bought a motorboat with what they offered him back in 1987, turned it in for a cabin cruiser two years later, and says he expects to be able to afford a yacht with the news that's waiting in the mail this year. Parris went from a new shingle roof to a split-level ranch and is making his way toward adding a swimming pool and greenhouse. But when all the laughing's done, it's the principle that remains. And we done learned that anything coming from beyond the bridge gotta be viewed real, real careful. Look what happened when Reema's boy—the one with the pear-shaped head—came hauling himself back from one of those fancy colleges mainside, dragging his notebooks and tape recorder and a funny way of curling up his lip and clicking his teeth, all excited and determined to put Willow Springs on the map.

We was polite enough—Reema always was a little addle-brained—so you couldn't blame the boy for not remembering that part of Willow Springs's problems was that it got put on some maps right after the War Between the States. And then when he went around asking us about 18 & 23, there weren't nothing to do but take pity on him as he rattled on about "ethnography," "unique speech patterns," "cultural preservation," and whatever else he seemed to be getting so much pleasure out of while talking into his little gray machine. He was all over the place—What 18 & 23 mean? What 18 & 23 mean? And we all told him the God-honest truth: it was just our way of saying something. Winky was awful, though, he even spit tobacco juice for him. Sat on his porch all day, chewing up the boy's Red Devil premium and spitting so the machine could pick it up. There was enough fun in that to take us through the fall and winter when he had hauled himself back over The Sound to wherever he was getting what was supposed to be passing for an education. And he sent everybody he'd talked to copies of the book he wrote, bound all nice with our name and his signed on the first page. We couldn't hold Reema down, she was so proud. It's good thing she didn't read it. None of us made it much through the introduction, but that said it all: you see, he had come to the conclusion after "extensive field work" (ain't never picked a boll of cotton or head of lettuce in his life—Reema spoiled him silly), but he done still made it to the conclusion that 18 & 23 wasn't 18 & 23 at all—was really 81 & 32, which just so happened to be the lines of longitude and latitude marking off where Willow Springs sits on the map. And we were just so damned dumb that we turned the whole thing around.

Not that he called it being dumb, mind you, called it "asserting our cultural identity," "inverting hostile social and political parameters." 'Cause, see, being we was brought here as slaves, we had no choice but to look at everything upside-down. And then being that we was isolated off here on this island, everybody else in the country went on learning good English and calling things what they really was—in the dictionary and all that—while we kept on calling things ass-backwards. And he

thought that was just so wonderful and marvelous, etcetera, etcetera . . . Well, after that crate of books came here, if anybody had any doubts about what them developers was up to, if there was just a tinge of seriousness behind them jokes about the motorboats and swimming pools that could be gotten from selling a piece of land, them books squashed it. The people who ran the type of schools that could turn our children into raving lunatics—and then put his picture on the back of the book so we couldn't even deny it was him—didn't mean us a speck of good.

If the boy wanted to know what 18 & 23 meant, why didn't he just ask? When he was running around sticking that machine in everybody's face, we was sitting right here—every one of us—and him being one of Reema's we woulda obliged him. He coulda asked Cloris about the curve in her spine that came from the planting season when their mule broke its leg, and she took up the reins and kept pulling the plow with her own back. Winky woulda told him about the hot tar that took out the corner of his right eye the summer we had only seven days to rebuild the bridge so the few crops we had left after the storm could be gotten over before rot sat in. Anybody woulda carried him through the fields we had to stop farming back in the '80s to take outside jobs—washing cars, carrying groceries, cleaning house—anything—'cause it was leave the land or lose it during the Silent Depression. Had more folks sleeping in city streets and banks foreclosing on farms than in the Great Depression before that.

Naw, he didn't really want to know what 18 & 23 meant, or he woulda asked. He woulda asked right off where Miss Abigail Day was staying, so we coulda sent him down the main road to that little yellow house where she used to live. And she woulda given him a tall glass of ice water or some cinnamon tea as he heard about Peace dying young, then Hope and Peace again. But there was the child of Grace—the grandchild, a girl who went mainside, like him, and did real well. Was living outside of Charleston now with her husband and two boys. So she visits a lot more often than she did when she was up in New York. And she probably woulda pulled out that old photo album, so he coulda seen some pictures or her grandchild, Cocoa, and the Cocoa's mama, Grace. And Miss Abigail flips right through to the beautiful one of Grace resting in her satin-lined coffin. And as she walks him back out to the front porch and points him across the road to a silver trailer where her sister, Miranda, lives, she tells him to grab up and chew a few sprigs of mint growing at the foot of the steps—it'll help kill his thirst in the hot sun. And if he'd known enough to do just that, thirsty or not, he'd know when he got to that silver trailer to stand back a distance calling *Mama, Mama Day*, to wait for her to come out and beckon him near.

He'da told her he been sent by Miss Abigail and so, more likely than not, she lets him in. And he hears again about the child of Grace, her grandniece, who went mainside, like him, and did real well. Was living outside of Charleston now with her husband and two boys. So she visits a lot more often than she did when she was up in New York. Cocoa is like her very own, Mama Day tells him, since she never had no children.

And with him carrying that whiff of mint on his breath, she surely woulda walked him out to the side yard, facing that patch of dogwood, to say she has to end the visit a little short 'cause she has some gardening to do in the other place. And if he'd had the sense to offer to follow her just a bit of the way—then and only then—he hears about that summer fourteen years ago when Cocoa came visiting from New York with her first husband. Yes, she tells him, there was a first husband—a stone city boy. How his name was George. But how Cocoa left, and he stayed. How it was the year of the last big storm that blew her pecan trees down and even caved in the roof of the other place. And she woulda stopped him from walking just by a patch of oak: she reaches up, takes a bit of moss for him to put in them closed leather shoes—they're probably sweating his feet something terrible, she tells him. And he's to sit on the ground, right there, to untie his shoes and stick in the moss. And then he'd see through the low bush that old graveyard just down the slope. And when he looks back up, she woulda disappeared through the trees; but he's to keep pushing the moss in them shoes and go on down to that graveyard where he'll find buried Grace, Hope, Peace, and Peace again. Then a little ways off a grouping of seven old graves, and a little ways off seven older again. All circled by them live oaks and hanging moss, over a rise from the tip of The Sound.

Everything he needed to know coulda been heard from that yellow house to that silver trailer to that graveyard. Be too late for him to go that route now, since Miss Abigail's been dead for over nine years. Still, there's an easier way. He could just watch Cocoa any one of these times she comes in from Charleston. She goes straight to Miss Abigail's to air out the rooms and unpack her bags, then she's across the road to call out at Mama Day, who's gonna come to the door of the trailer and wave as Cocoa heads on through the patch of dogwoods to that oak grove. She stops and puts a bit of moss in her open-toe sandals, then goes on past those graves to a spot just down the rise toward The Sound, a little bit south of that circle of oaks. And if he was patient and stayed off a little ways, he'd realize she was there to meet up with her first husband so they could talk about that summer fourteen years ago when she left, but he stayed. And as her and George are there together for a good two hours or so—neither one saying a word—Reema's boy coulda heard from them everything there was to tell about 18 & 23.

But on second thought, someone who didn't know how to ask wouldn't know how to listen. And he coulda listened to them the way you been listening to us right now. Think about it: ain't nobody really talking to you. We're sitting here in Willow Springs, and you're God-knows-where. It's August 1999—ain't but a slim chance it's the same season where you are. Uh, huh, listen. Really listen this time: the only voice is your own. But you done just heard about the legend of Sapphira Wade, though nobody here breathes her name. You done heard it the way we know it, sitting on our porches and shelling June peas, quieting the midnight cough of a baby, taking apart the engine of a car—you done heard it without a single living soul really saying a word. Pity, though, Reema's boy couldn't listen, like you, to Cocoa and George down by them oaks—or he woulda left here with quite a story.

Marita Golden (b. 1950)

Marita Golden earned her B.A. from American University and her M.A. from Columbia University. *Migrations of the Heart* (1983) details her experience of growing up in Washington, D.C., marrying a Nigerian architect that she met while at Columbia, and returning with him to Nigeria only to learn that cross-cultural marriages can be turbulent. Her first novel, *A Woman's Place* (1986) deals with the friendships of three black women, Faith, Serena, and Crystal, who meet at a New England College during the late 1960s. *Long Distance Life* (1989) presents a sweeping coverage of African American history as it follows the life of Naomi Johnson, who leaves a poverty-stricken life in the South to go to Washington, D.C., in the 1920s. Her daughter, Esther, grows up during the wake of the civil rights movement, and Esther's sons, Logan and Nathaniel, live very divergent lives during the 1970s and 1980s. In *And Do Remember Me* (1992), which takes place during Freedom Summer in 1963, Golden once again chronicles the lives and friendships of African American women during a pivotal point in African American history.

From *Long Distance Life*

Chapter 3: Naomi

When I saw Washington, D.C., for the first time in 1926, I thought I'd never seen a prettier place. Down where I come from, Spring Hope, North Carolina, there wasn't nothing, not a single thing, to compare with what I saw here. The big government office buildings, the White House, the Washington Monument . . . and this is where I saw my first streetcar. And the way some colored folks lived! Had colored professors at Howard University and colored folks had houses sometimes just as good as white folks. Some people called it "up South," but it was far enough away from where I come to be North to me.

I'd come to join my cousin Cora, who'd come up the year before to keep house for the son of the family she'd worked for in Raleigh. Their boy had just got a big job as a judge and they let Cora go to come up here and work for him and his family. Cora didn't have husband nor child and she'd lost her mama and daddy back in 1918 when that influenza killed so many people. So when her white folks said they'd buy her ticket North and see to it that their son paid her a few more dollars a month, she just up and went.

Soon as Cora got up here, I started getting letters all about what a good time she was having going to the Howard

Theater, how she'd joined a penny-savers' club, and one night on U Street had seen Bessie Smith, who she said was prettier in person than in any of her pictures. And how there was a whole bunch of folks from North Carolina in Washington, how it seemed like damn near every colored person in North Carolina was living in Washington, D.C. She stayed with that judge for a little while, but got sick of "living in," couldn't have no freedom or do what she wanted when she wanted, only had one day off. She wrote in one letter, "Sure they pay me a few dollars more and I got my own room, but the running never stops and they act like I don't never get tired. And his wife like to almost have a stroke if she sees me sitting down. You s'posed to be grateful for the chance to wait on them from six in the morning to whenever at night. They think I come North to work for them. I come North to be free." Then, sooner than you could say Jack Johnson, Cora wrote me saying she had quit her white folks and was working two jobs—at Bergmann's laundry and doing day's work. "I'd be working a third job if I hadn't met me a real nice man from Richmond who I spends my Saturday nights with and who takes me to church on Sunday morning," she said.

Sometimes young people ask why we all left down there. Well, I think folks just got tired. Tired of saying *Yessuh* and being ground down into nothing by crackers or hard work and sometimes both at the same time. And in those days the whites'd lynch you as soon as look at you. It's a shame young folks today don't know nothing about how we were treated then. It's too bad we were so ashamed, we figured it was best to forget and our children not to know. I had a cousin lynched in Florida, a boy—just fourteen years old. He'd been playing with some little po' white trash children and one of the girls said he touched her in her private parts. The white men got together, just rode up to Jimmy's folks' cabin and took him away while his daddy was out in the fields. They lynched Jimmy that night. And his daddy had to cut him down from that tree the next day and bury him. The daddy just went crazy little bit by little bit after that and rode into town one day a coupla months later, walked into the general store and shot the man who'd lynched his boy, then shot himself before they could grab him. Oh, and if you worked hard and made something of yourself, got a little store or some land, the white folks seem like they couldn't sleep nor rest easy till they took that away from you. Maybe they'd burn your store down or run you out of town. Colored folks just got tired. That don't sound like much of a reason, but it's the best one I can think of.

Now my folks, Beatrice and Jameson Reeves, were sharecroppers. We lived in one of them shotgun houses, 'bout one room wide and three or four rooms deep. To tell the truth, it wasn't no house at all, it was a shack, but it was the first home I ever knew. We raised tobacco, 'bacca's what we called it then. All I ever saw my daddy do was work and I might have heard him speak ten words a month to us kids and my mama combined. He worked hard. But not never seeing nothing for all his labor kinda took something out of him. There was many a year my daddy never saw a dollar to hold in his hand. By the time old man Cartwright, who Daddy rented the land from, charged us for all them molasses, grits, fatback and syrup'd been sold on credit, the sale of the 'bacca almost wasn't worth it. And 'cause Daddy couldn't read or figger, Cartwright's word was law. I think my daddy was so beat down by the life he had he didn't even know *what* to say. And I watched my daddy get old before he should've.

Now my mama, you couldn't shut her up! No matter what she was doing—stripping 'bacca, cooking, washing clothes, you'd find her either talking to the Lord or singing some song or talking with herself. My daddy didn't as a rule say much, but he did say he didn't want Mama working in no white folks' homes. It was funny, they always wanted to get the colored woman up in their kitchen, or cleaning up the house, but scared to let the colored man within a mile, 'less he crawled all the way. No, Mama wasn't allowed to work in no white folks' house. So she did wash for the white families and helped on the farm.

Washing clothes meant boilin' them over a fire. Washing clothes meant using lye soap that eat up your hands like acid. Sometimes, at the end of the day, my mama would look at her hands and just sit there and cry. And she'd say, "I used to have such pretty hands, such pretty hands." And Daddy would start hollerin', "You worried 'bout your hands, I'm worried 'bout getting food for y'all to eat." And Mama'd tell

him, "A woman wants to be proud of something she came in the world with, wants to think some part of her is beautiful. Even a colored woman wants that." And Daddy'd look all ashamed and confused and suck harder on his pipe and get up and go on the front porch. My mama was like all the women I ever saw down there—they worked and worked like dogs, with no thought that there was no other way to live. And we *all* worked, every one of us. There was Jackson, my older brother, then me and after me come my sister Ruby that died of TB and my youngest brother Jesse. By the time I was three I'd been trained up to bring wood for the stove, stack logs, even carry small buckets of water. When I was nine I was washing, ironing, cooking. And there wasn't no such thing as free time. Every one of your spare minutes you were finishing up that day's work or getting ready for the next day's. Humph, many's the time I walked a half a mile to a neighbor's farm to milk their cow so we could have milk. By the time I was thirteen, I was a woman.

And don't even talk about 'bacca. You never got through with it. The whole year long you were either getting ready to plant it, harvest it or cure it. My daddy was just a "hanging on" farmer with five acres and two mules. All of us helped with the 'bacca. No matter how small we was, there was something we could do. You'd start planting the seedlings in the wintertime and while the seeds were growing you'd be cutting the wood to use for curing in July and August. Whole families'd get together and cut enough wood for all of us— oak, sweetgum, poplar. In the spring Daddy'd pull out our two mules, Nat Turner and Frederick Douglass—my mama named them that 'cause they were so strong—and he'd start breaking the ground. Then you had to transplant the 'bacca. We'd use spoons to put them little baby plants in the ground. Then once it start growing you had to top it, sucker it and prime it and cure it.

With 'bacca you worked from can't see till can't see. Mama'd get up at four o'clock to fix the dinner we was gonna eat at noontime. Dew'd still be on the 'bacca when you'd go out to the fields. And if you were priming, picking off the ripe leaves, well, you could be in the fields all morning.

One time one of our barns caught on fire when Daddy was curing. All it took was one old leaf that fell into the flute, caught fire and burnt up that whole crop. Daddy liked to had a fit. When the fire was finally out, he went to town and was gone a week, come back so full of whiskey we could smell him coming home a mile away.

We were poor, but it was the kind of poor where the Lord provides just enough and surprises you now and then with some extra. Mama washed those white folks' clothes so good, the women were all the time giving her old clothes and castoff things they didn't want no more just 'cause they wasn't new. We got a pair of shoes once a year and had to make them last, and they were mostly for Sundays. Mama dragged us to church every Sunday and we stayed all day. But there were times it seemed like the Lord forgot all about us. We was poor and so I know how it feels to be hungry. *Real* hungry. I've gone days just eating a thin slice of fatback and a hunk of bread and was so grateful that I just went on working at whatever I was doing and just put the hunger pains outta my mind.

I got me a little schooling now and then when we could spare time from the farm, so I didn't learn regular like. My daddy couldn't read at all. But Mama could and she was all the time tutoring us and teaching the ABC's and such. I wasn't never interested in no books, I'll tell you that right now. But that didn't mean I didn't have no imagination. One time I heard a carnival show was coming to town. Mama said the show was bad, had fancy women, dangerous men and city slickers. She complained so long and hard about how awful the carnival was, I knew I had to go see it. Didn't have a penny to my name, but I sneaked off from the fields one day and went on to town.

Now, we didn't usually go to town but two or three times a year. And when I got there I saw all the posters advertising the carnival. Since I didn't have no money, I stood out in front of the tent and set to wailing and crying for my life. Just boo-hooed something awful. Pretty soon a old white man come along and asked me what I was crying for. I told him I'd lost the money my daddy give me for the carnival. You know that old man reached in his pocket and gimme a dime! Tapped me on the behind and told me to get along. Well, once I got in that tent, I saw more things than I knew God had ever made—a fat lady, must've weighed three hundred pounds, a dwarf couple, a man eating fire. Even had brought a tiger and I almost fell over when the man put his head in that tiger's mouth. And looking at all those amazing things gave me a powerful appetite. I'd spent a nickel on cotton candy and needed money for some soda pop and ice cream. Don't you know I used that crying number two more times and got folks to feeling so sorry for me I had money left over.

Well, naturally, I paid for my fun. Got home that night and got beat from sundown to sunup. Mama and Daddy were so mad they took turns beating me. I couldn't sit down too good for a coupla days, but every night for a long time I sure had some powerful interesting dreams. And I entertained Jackson and Jesse and Ruby a mighty long time with stories about what I'd seen. I wouldn't have missed that carnival for nothing.

Mama and Daddy were always telling me I thought I was grown, thought I was big and how I was headed for trouble if I didn't watch out. I think they thought that would scare me, but it just made me get excited about what kind of trouble they meant and what it would be like. And I didn't

see nothing wrong with wanting to be big. Hell, Spring Hope, North Carolina, was so small it didn't take much to get bigger than that.

I got married the first time when I was seventeen. And I'm gonna tell you the truth, I got married mostly to get away from home. His name was Isaiah Matthews and he was a real nice boy. His daddy was a real farmer, not a sharecropper like mine, and he had twenty-five acres of land. He grew a little bit of everything—'bacca, corn—and he even had other colored folks working for him.

Isaiah was tall and skinny and he was one of those boys that everybody's mama likes—the kind that's all *Yes, ma'ams* and *Please* and *Thank you* and tipping his hat and opening doors. To this day, I swear I don't really know what Isaiah saw in me. Mama'd tease me about my big eyes, said with eyes as big as mine I'd always find what I was looking for. We'd have these church socials in the spring and summer and he was always asking me to dance and wanting to take me for a walk. I went along with it 'cause I didn't see no reason not to and he seemed like a nice enough fella. Now, I can talk up a storm most of the time, but Isaiah couldn't get a word outta me the first times we danced or walked by ourselves. Then he commenced to coming by our place. And Mama and Daddy were always so glad to see him, I felt like I had to say something. Isaiah'd talk to me about what he knew best—his daddy's farm—and I couldn't stand hearing that, but didn't want to tell him. And the more I listened to Isaiah talk about that farm and the work he and his daddy and their hands did on it, and not just about how much they made on their crops, but the smell and feel of the soil and what having land meant, the more I got to know him. The land he and his daddy had was theirs and they was doing good enough so that it gave them a good life. So Isaiah could tell me things about farming I'd never seen or felt—what it feels like to look at land and know it's yours, how it feels to harvest your crop and know *you* can set *your* price, about how it feels to be master of the land instead of slave to it. The land never gave me and my family no real bounty, so I never saw its beauty. But Isaiah made me think about things different.

We courted for a while and then got married in the same church we'd both been christened in and met each other. We moved into a little house Isaiah had built with his daddy for us, and Isaiah started farming his own acreage. I helped out around the farm, but 'cause Isaiah had field hands, there wasn't much for me to do. Pretty soon I got tired of talking about crops and I wanted to talk about something else, but I didn't know what. Then I started wishing I'd paid attention in school 'cause at least I'd have been able to read some books better than I could. At night Isaiah'd come to bed, the smell of soil and fertilizer still on him, despite a bath, and he'd reach for me with those big old hands and get on top of me like he was mounting a horse. And Oh Lord! I'd cry all the way through it, but silent, like, so he wouldn't hear. And not never nary a kiss. That hurt more than anything, I think. I got more affection from the little boys I'd played house with in the fields. But he was happy. His daddy'd come by in the evenings sometimes, just pop in on us, and Isaiah'd hold me and slap me on my butt, playful like, and squeeze me and go on and on about what a lucky man he was.

I used to ride over to talk to Mama. She'd be in the back-yard standing over a big tub of clothes, humming "Precious Lord" or some other hymn, when I'd come up on her and she'd act surprised to see me, like, now that I had my own home, I couldn't never come back to my first. And one day I went back home in this new dress Isaiah'd bought me, he'd ordered it from the Sears catalogue, and, not saying a word, I just commenced to washing clothes with Mama, stuck my hands in that water and stood there with her, rubbing and scrubbing and wringing till my wrists felt like they were gonna fall off.

When we got through, I just plopped down on top of a upturned basket and said, "Mama, I just don't feel a thing." Mama touched my cheek with her hands, those old wrinkled-up raw hands that made her cry, and said, "Honey, go on back to your house and your husband. People do the best they can. Remember that. People can't be nothin' that ain't in 'em, or do what they think is impossible. You'd be surprised how a little love can go a long way."

I stood up and she hugged me and then told me to go on home. I figured then, maybe if I had a baby, I'd be happy. But six months after the baby was born, we woke up one morning and she was dead. Just lay there in the crib Isaiah's father had gone all the way to Charlotte for, her little face turned almost gray, no breathing, no life. These days they got a name for what killed my baby—sudden infant death—but back then, we didn't know what had happened or why. And I could tell Isaiah thought somehow I'd failed Martha, been a bad mother, neglected her somehow. He never said nothing, not direct like, but I could feel what he was thinking, and that's all I needed to know. And I was hurting and grieving and just tore up inside and whenever I'd mention Martha's name he'd just walk away.

And that's when Cora started writing me. And the more letters I got, the more I knew I had to go North. But Isaiah didn't want to hear nothing about going North. "What I'm a go up there for?" he'd ask me. "They ain't got no land for no niggers up there. I got family been up there and come back, say there's no room, no space, the crackers got you penned in, just as tight up there as down here. What I'm a go work in a factory for when I got my own land?"

But the more letters I got from Cora, the more I realized I wanted to go North, but mostly I wanted to get away from

seeing my daddy sharecropping with a mule and a hoe and my sister laying on the bed on the back porch, little bit by lit-tle bit dying of tuberculosis. And I wanted to leave the mem-ory of my dead baby. Got so me and Isaiah didn't have hardly nothing to say no more. Martha's ghost was still in the house with us. And since we couldn't talk about her, seemed like nothing else made no sense.

Then one night Isaiah told me I could leave. Said I could go on North, since North meant more to me than him. I didn't say a word. But that night he come to bed and held me real tight, but real gentle like, and we made love like I'd given up hoping we ever would. And he kissed me all over my body that night. But when we finished, he lay next to me and said, "Naomi, you can go North, but if you do, don't look back 'cause there won't be nothin' here no more that belongs to you."

Cora had wrote me in one of her letters that soon as she got on the train to leave North Carolina she felt free. Said she felt like she was being born all over again. Sure she was sitting in the Jim Crow section, up front where all the coal, smoke and dust rose up, got in the windows and ruined your clothes. But she said the chugging of that train couldn't hardly keep up with her heart, she was so excited. I wish it'd been like that for me when I left. Pretty soon I left Isaiah and moved back home. Daddy stopped speaking to me altogether when he found out I was going North. And Mama took me out in the yard one day and we stooped down on our knees underneath of a big old juniper tree we had and she commenced to dig-ging. Next thing I knew, she was pulling a cigar box out the ground. She rubbed the dirt off the top of it and opened the lid and inside I saw a pile of coins and paper money.

"This here is the little extra I been making over the years, setting aside for the worst times and the special times," she said. I don't think there coulda been more than thirty dollars in that box. But Mama reached in that box and gave me everything in it. She wrapped the money in a small rag and stuffed it down the front of my dress. And before I could say a word, she said, "Now, when you get settled up there, maybe Jackson can come up too. Your daddy don't want him to go, but you and Jackson's the strongest ones the Lord give us. You got to get away from here."

A few days later Mama and Jackson and Jesse rode over to the train station with me. And before I got on the train, Mama said, "Girl, you better write us every two weeks." "Mama, you know I ain't one for sitting still that long, or puttin' that many words on paper." "Well, now's the time to learn," she says. She hugged me and I thought how I'd never seen her look so pretty and sad at the same time. She had on her Sunday dress, you'd have thought she was going instead of me—she was so excited. Jackson hugged me and while I was holding on to him, I looked over his shoulder and I saw Daddy standing way off near the ticket booth, looking like he'd just come out the fields.

He just stood there and held up his hand like he was waving at me, but not really waving goodbye.

Cora was living in a rooming house on Ninth and O streets. Room wasn't no bigger than a minute, but it seemed like a palace to me. She had a Victrola and had cut out pictures of Josephine Baker, Ma Rainey and Louis Armstrong and put them all over her mirror and the walls. Cora was what we used to call a good-time girl. Even down home, she was always the one knew where the fun was and if there was no fun happening she could make some.

First thing I wanted to do was get a job so I could start sending money back home. But Cora wouldn't even let me talk about a job that first week. And all we did was party. The woman that run the rooming house was a big old Black woman named Blue. All you had to do was look at her and you'd know how she got that name. And seemed like the downstairs where Blue lived was always filled with folks coming in all hours of the day and night. And it was always liquor flowing and cardplaying.

We'd go over to the O Street Market and you could get pigs' feet and chitlins and fresh geens as good as down home. And Cora seemed to never run outta money. I figured that had to do with her never running outta men.

We were having a good time, then one night when we were getting ready to go to a party, I noticed Cora putting this cream all over herself. I asked her what it was and she showed it to me. It was bleaching cream. Now, Cora's about the color of half-done toast, so I was confused. "What you using this stuff for?" I asked.

"Everybody uses it, men and women," she told me, snapping her stocking tops into her garter. "Girl, there ain't no such thing as a brown beauty in this here town. You either yellow or you ain't mellow." Cora was just rubbing the cream in her skin, all over her face and arms, as she told me this, like she was trying to get it down into her bones.

"Well, I'm gonna take my chances," I told her. "I sure ain't gonna use no mess like this. Besides ain't you heard 'the blacker the berry, the sweeter the juice'?"

But Cora had to have the last word, saying "Naomi, I ain't heard *nobody* say that since I come up here and I'll bet money you won't neither."

Finally I started working. I lived in with a Jewish family for a while, but living in didn't suit my style. The madam worried me to death, all day long talking and complaining 'bout her husband, scared he didn't love her, scared he was running around with somebody else, scared she was getting old. That was 'bout the loneliest woman I ever knew. I could hardly do my work for her bending my ear. But the worst thing was I couldn't go when and where I wanted. Nighttime I'd be so tired, all I wanted to do was go to bed. And so then I started doing day's work, had three or four families I cleaned

up for and I got my own room in Blue's house and started sending money home regular like.

Now, day's work wasn't no celebration either. And I had every kinda woman for a madam you could think of—the kind that went behind you checking corners for dust and dirt, the kind that run her fingers over the furniture you just got through dusting, the kind that just got a thrill outta giving orders, the kind that asked more questions 'bout my personal business than anybody got a right to, the kind that tried to cheat me outta some of my pay. But in those days there wasn't much else a colored woman could do. Hell, even some of the college girls—the dinkty, saditty ones—cleaned up for white folks in the summertime.

For the longest time I just worked and saved and worked and saved. Then one evening I come in and Blue was sitting in the dining room. For a change, she was by herself. Seemed like Blue wasn't happy unless there was a crowd of people around her. But this night she was by herself. I'd been having this same dream over and over about somebody named Macon and I figured I might bet a few pennies on the dream's number. So I asked her to look up Macon in her dream book. She looked it up and said the number was 301. "I think I'll put fifteen cents on it," I told her, reaching into my pocketbook. I thought Blue was gonna laugh me right outta that room. "Fifteen cents?" she hollered. "Fifteen cents?" And she commenced to laughing so hard she was shaking all over and tears came into her eyes and start to rolling down her fat old Black cheeks. She wiped her face with a handkerchief and says, "Girl, what you waiting for? I been watching you going out here day after day, cleaning up the white folks' houses. That all you want to do with yourself?"

Now nobody'd ever asked that—what I wanted to do—the whole time I'd been North. Cora was so busy partying and I was so busy struggling I hadn't had time to think further than the day I was in. So I didn't quite know what to say at first. "Well," Blue said, folding her arms in front of her, looking at me like the schoolmarm in that one-room schoolhouse I went to did, when she knew I wasn't ready to give the right answer. And that look in Blue's eyes and her laughing at me made me pull up something I'd been carrying around since I moved in her house. And I just said it all of a sudden. "I want what you got. I want a house. And I want plenty money." And just saying it like that set me trembling so hard I dropped my pocketbook on the floor and my feet kicked over the bag of clothes one of my madams had give me that day instead of my regular pay.

"Well, tell me how you aim to get it? Lessen you got some book education or your folks gonna *leave* you some money, there ain't no legal way for you to get either one. You gonna have to start gambling with everything you got."

"But I ain't got nothing," I cried.

"You got more than you think. You got dreams, like the one you come to me with just now, and, honey, they worth more than you think. They sho 'nuff worth more than fifteen cents. You got sense and deep-down feelings. Listen to 'em. They'll tell you what to do. You think the Rockefellers got to be Rockefellers playing it straight? And if all you gonna put on 301 is fifteen cents, I won't even write it up."

I put a quarter on 301 and it come out the next day. I give Blue a cut and that was how it started.

I got to playing the numbers pretty regular then and soon I was playing every day. To be honest about the thing, though, most folks never won nothing. But seemed like I had some kinda gift. Numbers were about the only thing I paid attention to in that one-room schoolhouse in Spring Hope. That first year I hit two times for small change. Then I played a number that come to me the night one of my madams accused me of stealing. I played that number and hit for enough to start me on the way to saving for a house.

My first house was over on R Street. I rented out the top two floors to decent folks, respectable people who'd come up from the South like me. But where Blue'd let anybody live in her house, I'd only let families or married couples or single folks I thought wouldn't give me no trouble live in my place. Folks who went to church on Sunday and went to bed at night 'cause they had to work the next day. Now, that don't mean I was a saint, but I sure didn't want to live amongst a whole buncha sinners.

I found out I couldn't live in a whole house like I lived in one room. Cora took me downtown and bought me the kinda clothes that said I was a lady and just putting those clothes on made me feel different, made me feel *big* like Mama and Daddy'd always said I wanted to be. Then Cora told me I couldn't have a house without a car and her and her boyfriend took me to this place where I bought a big black Chevrolet.

When I got settled good in the house, I sent for Mama and Daddy and Jackson and Jesse to come up and spend some time with me. Mama had a time getting Daddy to come, even after I sent them all train fare. But finally they came. And seeing that house through Mama's eyes was like seeing it for the first time. I'd planted a Carolina garden out in the backyard of squash, tomatoes and peas, just like I'd have done back home and Mama sat on the back porch when she saw it, shaking her head and smiling. I'd put a big mirror with gilt framing over the fireplace and seemed like every time I looked up Mama was staring at herself in that mirror, almost like she'd never seen herself before. She took off her shoes in the house and walked barefoot on the carpeting I'd put all on the first floor. And she had me take a bunch of pictures of her sitting in my car. And the big bathtub with running hot water, humph, I thought Mama was gonna live in it, she found a excuse to take a bath three times a day.

But Daddy, seemed like the house just made him mad. Mama was all the time pointing something out to him and he'd just go on out on my porch like he did on the porch back home, and sit there sucking on his pipe and not saying a thing. Daddy and one of my roomers, Mr. Chavis, would sit out there talking about down home. He talked to Mr. Chavis more than he talked to me. And so one night I just went outside and butt into their conversation, told Mr. Chavis I wanted to talk to my daddy. "Now, you ain't said hardly nothin' to me since y'all got here," I told him. "Not even *Congratulations* or *Good job*. I worked hard for what I got, Daddy, and I want you to be proud."

He took the pipe outta his mouth and said, "I am proud of you, Naomi. Real proud. But you got to understand. I've worked another man's land for over twenty years and just barely kept my family from starvin'. My daughter comes North and gets so much it puts me to shame. Tell me how I'm s'posed to feel about me. Sure I'm proud of you. So proud I'm damn near ready to bust. But I look at all you done and feel like all my life's been a waste. You a landlord. I'm your daddy and I'm still a tenant."

"Why don't y'all just stay on up here? You don't have to go back."

"I got to go back 'cause of the land. That farm, little as it is, is all I know. I ain't got much longer. I'm too old to learn a new way of living. 'Sides, they can't run us all out. That land's got more of our blood in it than theirs. Not all us s'posed to leave. Some of us got to stay, so y'all have a place to come back to."

Well, ended up Jackson stayed on and I gave him a room in the house and he got a job as janitor at the post office.

Now, in all this, I hadn't really had me no romancing. There'd been one or two men, but if they'd been worth remembering, I woulda told you about them. And most times I was working so hard to get something, make some money, I didn't have time to be courtin' nobody. The truth is, I didn't make no time. So when Mama and Daddy went back home, I went with them and filed my papers and got my divorce from Isaiah.

Well, with Cora's help, I finally found me a sweetheart. It was 1929. Now, whenever you say 1929 to folks, first thing they think of is the Depression. Well, I think white folks were hurt most by those bad times. Colored folks were born in a Depression, everything just about that they knowed was Depression. Yeah, times got tough. But then, they'd always been tough for us, weren't no big thing, so we knew how to get through it.

Folks down home were hit real hard. I was sending home not just money but clothes and food. And going down three or four times a year just to check for good measure. But lots of folks just gave up and that made it easier for folks like me who wanted to get going!

I was renting out my second house by then, over on P Street, and Cora was living in it, collecting rents for me. One night we had a fish fry. I was hitting numbers pretty good and was even a bag lady now and then, what they call a courier, taking folks' numbers and their money and delivering it to a old Italian guy downtown. The coloreds was the front men, but it was the whites that really controlled the numbers game. I was figuring to get outta that end of things 'cause that old Italian couldn't take the money without putting his hands on me, no matter what I said.

So we had this fish fry and the house was packed. I can't remember now the exact reason we had that party, but in those days didn't always *need* a reason. That night me and Cora was frying up the fish when her boyfriend Harold walked in with the handsomest man I'd ever seen. Now, I don't mean handsome in the way he looked so much, but the way he stood and carried himself. It was just something king-like about him. He stood up so tall and straight and looked at you like you'd be a fool not to like him. And when him and Harold come in the kitchen out there in the living room somebody had put a Alberta Hunter record on. The song was "Gimme All the Love You Got."

I was standing at the table, my hands covered in corn-meal, dipping porgies in batter, and Rayford Johnson looked at me like he didn't plan to never look nowhere else. He was half bald and the top of his head was real shiny. And he had a mustache and the Lord knows I'm a fool for a man with hair on his face.

Harold introduced Rayford to me and Cora and since I couldn't shake his hand I gave Rayford Johnson the biggest, brightest smile I could muster. Then him and Harold went on into the parlor, where folks were dancing and laughing and Alberta was singing, "I want all your loving 'cause I can stand a lot." Dipping some fish in a frying pan of oil, Cora says, "Harold told me Rayford's a teacher over at Dunbar."

"Well, I wouldn't mind studying with him sometimes." I laughed.

Well, all the while we were cooking those fish, Rayford was hanging around near the kitchen, peeking in now and then, like what we were doing was the most interesting thing. I had a houseful of liquor, music, fast and pretty women and he wanted to watch us cook fish, so I told him to come on in and pull up a chair. He had a bottle of beer, looked like he hadn't took a single sip from it. Soon as he got settled in a chair, though, Cora took off her apron and said, "I'm going to dance."

He watched Cora leave us alone, like he was glad to see her gone, and I went on frying the fish, just like he wasn't even there. "So all this belongs to you?" he asked me.

"What you mean?"

"This house."

"Yessir, I guess it does," I said, kinda cold and suspicious-like, wondering if he was after my money.

"You should be proud of what you've achieved."

"I am."

"I can look at you and if you don't mind my saying, I can tell you believe in dreams *and* hard work."

I didn't know what to say. Hadn't too many folks been able to read me so fast and especially not saying it like he did.

"Our race needs women like you if we're ever to progress. Our men do too."

I had gone to the sink and was washing my hands and his words just felt like a warm welcome cloak all around me. I'd gone to the sink 'cause he was looking at me so open like and yet so friendly and trusting I could hardly stand it.

"Miss Naomi, I can look at you and tell you're a good woman, somebody I'd like to know."

And you know, all those words didn't sound like jive to me. He had the sincerest way of saying things. Rayford made you feel like he wasn't the kind of man who'd lie to you.

So with all that noise going on in the living room and fish frying on the stove, Rayford Johnson acted like he didn't care about neither. And I sat down at the table with a plate of porgies in front of me and I asked him, "You sound like one of those race men."

"And proud to be," he said, real serious. He kept looking at me like he was trying to figure me out. He looked just like a schoolteacher. But I knew I could make him crack a smile if I wanted to. He took a big swiggle from his beer and then he says, "What do you think the Negro's got to do to progress in this country?"

Now, I'll tell you, I wasn't expecting no question like that right then. I was thinking he'd tell me how good I looked or ask me to go out and dance. Politics and all that—well, the folks I run with, we didn't get too concerned about all that. But after I got over being surprised I felt kind of special. He must've thought I could answer the question or he wouldn't have asked it. So I said, clearing my throat real good before I started to speak, "Well, I think the colored, I mean the Negro, has got to depend on himself and develop something of his own before anybody will respect him."

"You're a very astute observer," he said, smiling at me like I was one of his students who'd done him proud.

"Well, I don't know about all that," I said, getting up to turn over the fish. "But I do know we won't make no progress unless we all make it together."

"So you don't subscribe to Du Bois's Talented Tenth theory?"

Now, I hadn't heard nothing about this man Du Bois or his theory, but I asked Rayford, just guessing, "What happens to the other ninety percent?" And don't you know he smiled and then laughed and I could see the part of him he tried to hide. He took a swig of his beer and just said, "Miss Naomi, you got real good sense, real good."

When I sat down I asked him, "You don't sound like you from the South, where you from original?"

"Oklahoma. An all-Negro town called Langston. My folks were some of the first Negroes to go to the West in the 1880s. They left Tennessee, looking for land and a better life than they had in the South."

"Did they find it?"

"Took them some time, but they did. My daddy's a undertaker and my mother teaches music."

Now, with all that behind him, coming from those kinda folks, I'd have figured Rayford to be stuck on himself, but all he was telling me didn't seem to phase him one bit.

"How come you left Oklahoma?"

"Well, I'd been teaching school and then I heard about Marcus Garvey."

"You mean that little old Black man from the West Indies? The one always talking about Black this and Black that?"

"Well, I wouldn't describe him quite that way. He was and is a prophet. A man ahead of his times."

"Ain't he in jail now?"

"Unfortunately, yes. But that's where most prophets end up at some point in their career. He was a Moses, a *Black* Moses for his people."

"What did you do with him?"

"I was business manager of the *Negro World*, the paper of the Universal Negro Improvement Association. Worked for him three years. That was the best time of my life."

"Why you say that?"

"The man's vision, his accomplishments. And for a period of my life I was part of it all, helping to make a difference in the lot of the Negro." Rayford got real sad when he said that, like he was remembering something so special he didn't know how to put a value on it. "I mean, do you know what the man and the organization did?" he asked me. "The UNIA set up grocery stores, had a chain of laundries in cities all over the country, a publishing company. We had members in the Caribbean and Africa. And, of course, the Black Star Line."

"I heard that ship almost sunk," I said, sucking in my jaws.

"The white men that sold it to us took advantage of our inexperience, sold us a piece of junk, a ship that wasn't seaworthy. But had there ever been a shipping line owned by the Black man in America before?"

I felt ashamed for saying what I did. Then Rayford reached in his pocket and pulled out his wallet and in a little side compartment he pulled out a cigar ring and shows it to me and it's got Garvey's picture on it. As he handed the paper ring to me he says, "The best years of my life, bar none."

Well, by the time Rayford got through talking about Garvey, I didn't feel like eating no fish. But me and Cora set everything out. I didn't feel like dancing neither. I just felt like sitting there, looking at Rayford Johnson.

We sat in the kitchen till two o'clock in the morning, just telling each other stories about what we'd done. Until I met Rayford, I didn't think I had much to tell that anybody'd be interested in. When I told him about my parents sharecropping, he talked about all the poor Black folks down South, when I told him how bad I felt for my daddy and what he'd said about my house, Rayford talked about all Negro men, and when I told him how Jackson had settled into his job cleaning over at the post office, he wondered if the North was really gonna be much better. When Rayford Johnson left my house that night, I knew I had found me a sweetheart.

Now, imagine that, me, who hated the thought of the inside of a schoolhouse, courting a teacher!

Well, me and Rayford became a pretty hot item. And 'cause of the kind of man he was, I kinda cut back on so much partying and almost turned into a homebody. In the summertime, we'd go over to Griffith Stadium and see one of the Negro League teams play and one time Rayford took me to the Jungle Inn to see Jelly Roll Morton. But Rayford could turn a evening just having dinner and listening to the radio into something special. But he was the seriousest man I ever met. He was renting a room and all in the corners and under the bed he had stacks and stacks of those "race" magazines, *The Crisis* and *Opportunity*. It was 'cause of Rayford that I started reading more than the comics and the obituaries in the paper. I had to keep up with him so I started reading the news too.

One day I went over to Dunbar and watched Rayford teach a class. He had those kids eating out of the palm of his hand. He lectured them about everybody from Hannibal to Herbert Hoover and Mrs. Bethune. The thing I liked was, he talked about folks living right then and showed the kids how they were making history. I'd grown up thinking education was studying folks that were dead. Rayford let me know education was just about everything you did or thought, no matter when it happened.

I felt pretty good. Had a sweetheart and no more empty bed blues. And serious as he was, Rayford Johnson knew how to please a woman. Some mornings I'd get outta bed when we'd been together and feel like I could tear up the house and put it back together again. He wasn't making no whole lotta money as a teacher but he never asked me for a dime. He had a old Ford somebody gave him and when we went out we went in his car, not mine. He had pride and I think that's what won my heart more than anything else.

Well, we'd been going together almost a year and I knew what I wanted. So one night he came to see me. I'd fixed pork chops, rice, gravy, collard greens and biscuits. He coulda took one look at that meal and knew I meant business. We listened to some Louis Armstrong records he'd brought over and then we got in the bed. Oh, he fixed me real good that night! And afterwards, we're laying there, him smoking them Chesterfield cigarettes he'd been smoking, he told me once, since he was sixteen, and I'm feeling all soft and warm and happy and I just asked him, just like that, to marry me. I hadn't never seen a man blush before, but Rayford laid there, looking like what I'd said had made his day.

When he got himself composed, he says, "You don't leave nothing to chance, do you, *Miss* Naomi Reeves?"

And I told him, "Only way I'm gonna get what I want is to ask for it. I always figure on hearing yes. And no don't scare me 'cause I heard no all my life and it ain't never stopped me yet. But smart as you are, I knew you'd have sense enough to say yes."

Now, once I become Mrs. Rayford Johnson, I was happy as a fox in a henhouse. I turned over the running of my two houses to Rayford, let him collect all the rents, cut him in on everything. I've heard women talk about *Never let the left hand know what the right hand is doing* and you know who the left hand is. But you can't keep secrets in a marriage. Not a real marriage anyway. And I'd waited too long to share my blessings with a man to play hide-and-seek once I got him.

I was twenty-four when me and Rayford got married. And I felt like I had already lived a lifetime. In those days wasn't no such thing as waiting till you grew up, life just come along and dragged you into it. Yeah, I was young, but had already had one husband, lost a child, been divorced, been dirt-poor, left home, worked like a dog, cleaned up other folks' homes, played the numbers, got a house and decided I could have the kind of life I wanted. I was young, but only in age. And where I had come from, age didn't mean nothing no way.

When I got pregnant, then I had everything I'd always wanted. I went back home to Spring Hope to have my baby. Back then, no matter where you lived—in New York, Chicago, Philadelphia, wherever—*home* was where you come from, and it was just natural to go home to do something as important as having your child.

Mama and Daddy was still inching along on the farm, but the money I was sending made a difference. They'd bought some new furniture and Daddy'd bought a car, but it sat in the yard half the time, 'cause he ran out of money for tags or repairs. I went home in April to have Esther and maybe 'cause I was gonna give birth, or 'cause I was so happy—whatever—seemed like home was the most beautiful place. I just took it easy till my time come, sitting on the porch in the day, doing little chores around the house, going for a walk with Mama sometimes in the afternoon, staring at the stars at night. No place else smells like the South in springtime—the azaleas, the flowering dogwood just bust out and you can't hardly smell nothing else. And waiting for Esther to come, I realized that it was the beauty and the feel of the South that I missed, living in the North.

Well, Esther start coming about two o'clock one morning. They say a child that comes early in the morning won't have trouble finding their way through life. Mama told Daddy to go on over and get the midwife, Aunt Gin, but when he went out to start that old car, the engine was dead. So Jesse got on the old mule, Nat Turner, to ride the two miles to Aunt Gin's. Daddy's out in the yard in his long johns, cussing at the car and kicking it. And my water's broke and the pains are coming so fast I can't hardly breathe. Well, don't you know, Mama's just holding my hand and praying real hard, trying to drown out Daddy's cussing and telling me to push, to push real hard, and I'm moaning and screaming for God and Rayford and by the time Aunt Gin gets there Esther's come on out.

About the only thing Aunt Gin was good for by the time she got there was to give me some of that special root tea they give to women after they give birth. I'd lost one baby in Spring Hope and now I had come home and had another one and I'd decided that this child was gonna live.

About a week after Esther was born, I'm still taking it easy and waiting for Rayford to come and drive us back to Washington and Mama comes in the bedroom while I'm nursing Esther and tells me Isaiah had come to see me. Now, you know how it is when somebody is on your mind and you just can't shake them and next thing you know, there they are, well, there was Isaiah.

I finished nursing Esther and put her down to sleep and I combed my hair and put on a pretty dress Rayford had bought me and then Isaiah comes in the room.

"Howdy, Naomi," he says, fumbling with his hat. He's dressed in a suit and I could smell he'd just shaved before he come.

"Howdy, Isaiah." He'd filled out some and looked like a man, not the boy I married. He sits down in a chair beside the bed and says, "I see the North's been good to you."

"You could say that."

"That's a pretty little baby you got there. What you name her?"

"Esther."

"I got two boys, Gregory and William," he says. Then he takes out a picture of them and shows me. And they look just like him.

"Mama told me you and Vera Robinson had got married. She's a good woman," I said.

"Sure is. Don't take a lot to satisfy her."

"You satisfied me, Isaiah, as far as you could. I was just s'posed to leave, that's all."

"And I was s'posed to stay."

We sat there talking a pretty good time, about crops and the land, some of the things we used to talk about and about some new things. I told him about Rayford and then he told me all about Vera. Just felt like I was talking to a friend, not somebody who I'd hurt real bad one time. Then Mama comes in and invites Isaiah to stay to dinner, but he says no, he's late getting home already. And then he tells me to bring Rayford to the house when he comes and not to be a stranger. And I feel real good when he leaves 'cause I know Isaiah just like I'd never left him and I know he meant every word he said.

Being a daddy don't change Rayford much, except he spoiled Esther and got even more serious than ever, worried about the world and the Negro's place in it. Then those nine boys down in Scottsboro got accused of raping two white women on a train and the white folks tried them in lickety-split time and wanted to send them to the electric chair. I felt pretty bad about those boys. All you had to do was read the story and know the women made the whole thing up. And one of the boys wasn't but twelve years old, still a child. Rayford got involved with a bunch of folks raising money for their defense. Although he didn't cotton much to the NAACP, he attended their rallies and even wrote a couple of articles for the *Chicago Defender* about the case. Then in '33, he took me and Esther down to a big protest in front of the White House to try to get Roosevelt to get the Scottsboro boys out of jail. Now, I've never been one for raising Cain in the streets and I'll tell you I didn't want to go, but Rayford said I had to bear witness, had to put myself on the line. Said if all those white folks, the Communists and the socialists, if they could come from all over and march for nine Negro men, why couldn't I? Well, I did and carried Esther too, although Mama woulda had a fit if she had known that. Roosevelt not in office a good three months and us knocking on his door about the Scottsboro Boys.

That demonstration didn't set them free, but I did feel good being part of it. And to this day, one of my favorite pictures is one Rayford took of me standing in front of the White House gate, holding Esther, and she's got a sign in her hand that reads:

Roosevelt Enforce Full Rights For Negroes

When it come to Esther, Rayford told her everything he knew, and I give her everything I never had. She had her daddy's walk, come into a room just like a queen coming into a court, and she had my spirit. I wanted her to have everything I never did, so I gave her tap dance and piano lessons. And Esther had the prettiest room in the house. But she was my daughter so I couldn't raise her to be useless. I trained her to help me around the house and in the summertime she'd go to Spring Hope for a few weeks and help Mama and Daddy on the farm, same way I did.

Rayford was all the time reading to her. He didn't believe in fairy tales and such and at bedtime he'd tell Esther stories about folks like Harriet Tubman and Sojourner Truth. I asked him once why he was always pounding all that stuff in Esther's head all the time, why he couldn't just let her be a little girl. "She'll find out she's a Negro soon enough," I told him. And he just said, "But we got to let her know what it means."

Those were good years. Roosevelt had set up a whole bunch of agencies—the NRA, the "ABC" and the this-that-and-the-other—to turn the Depression around and we were doing OK. I felt like my life was set—you know how it is when you finally get everything in place, just the way you want it and everything you touch, near 'bout, turns to gold. Well, we had a coupla years like that. Then, the same year that fool Hitler got the white folks to killing themselves in every country they lived in, my world turned upside down too.

Rayford had been feeling poorly for some time, had been coughing a lot and having trouble breathing. Finally he got to feeling so bad he went to the doctor. Turned out he had a cancer of the lungs. Now, back then, if you had cancer they just wrote you off and started digging your grave. Folks didn't even like to say the word in public, that's how much it scared them. The doctor gave Rayford six months to live, but he held on for two years.

Rayford fought that cancer the way he fought everything, like he couldn't think of not winning. Mostly, he just decided not to give up, and he threw away those Chesterfields and never smoked another one. We found a doctor that put him on a special diet and we thought we had it licked, but it come back and come back strong. He started losing weight and got so sick he had to be put in Freedmen's Hospital. The doctors there said it'd be a waste of time to operate. Well, I just about moved in the hospital with him. Slept on the floor beside him every night and I'd hear him wheezing and rasping and his breath coming so hard and slow it sounded like every breath was his last one. He couldn't breathe good and he couldn't sleep. He was too proud to let them shoot him full of morphine, so the pain was always there. He'd lost so much weight he was down to damn near nothing, cheeks all sunk, and his hair had got gray.

And I'd get up from the pallet on the floor and let him know I was there for him. Help him struggle to get a sip of water and just hold his hand. And he'd whisper sometimes, when he could muster a breath, "Tell me a story, Naomi. Tell me a story." And I'd tell him about Spring Hope or the time I ran away to the carnival or how Blue shamed me into playing the numbers. I'd tell him, real slow like, to make the time last and it wouldn't be until I was finished with the story that I'd feel the tears on my face.

One night Rayford opened his eyes while I was talking to him and he saw me crying and he says, "Dying is the most frightening thing I ever had to do and, Naomi, I'm so scared." And then we both started crying and somehow us crying together like that gave me strength.

Rayford died in his sleep one night with my laying there on the floor beside his bed. I woke up the next morning and loved Rayford Johnson so much I was glad his misery was finally over. Then I saw a piece of paper on the bedstand next to his medicine. He'd scribbled on the paper in a handwriting that looked like something Esther would write: "I had all the time that belonged to me and I found you."

Esther didn't speak a word for a year after Rayford died. And I wore black so long my friends had to talk me out of it. I wish'd I'd been a child so I could've just shut out everybody and closed in on myself. I birthed Esther, so I knew she hadn't gone crazy or got retarded like folks was saying, telling me to take her to the doctors. Hell, my baby missed her daddy and she just didn't have the words to say how bad she felt. And when she did start talking, the first thing Esther says over dinner one night is, "Mama, he's coming back. He told me." And I said to her, "Baby, he didn't go nowhere. I got him right here in my heart."

Rita Dove (b. 1952)

Thirty-six years after Gwendolyn Brooks won a Pulitzer Prize for Poetry, Rita Dove became the second African American to do so with the publication of *Thomas and Beulah* (1986). Based on the lives of her grandparents, *Thomas and Beulah* is a collection of crisp, graceful poems that chronicles the drama around the everyday events of Thomas and Beulah: their exodus from Tennessee to Akron, the loss of Thomas's friend, life in Akron's factories, memories of their courtship, the birth of their children, the buying of a car, the keeping of secrets, the moment of death—a rich history of the particular.

Dove's first collection, *The Yellow House on the Corner* (1980) was well received because of its "broad sense of history" and its "directness and dramatic intensity." In *Museum* (1983), Dove deals with material more distant in time and place: a tomb that Tou Wan constructs for her dead husband, Liu Sheng; a German Writers' conference in Munich; a Tel Aviv-Haifa Freeway; a sailor in Africa. Dove followed *Thomas and Beulah* with *Grace Notes* (1989), another technically exquisite collection about "the melody of daily life." Other popular collections include *Mother Love* (1995), a collection of mostly sonnets retelling the Demeter/Persephone, mother/daughter story. Talented in many genres, Dove has also written a volume of short stories, *Fifth Sunday* (1985), a novel, *Through the Ivory Gate* (1992), and a classical play in blank verse, *The Darker Face of the Earth* (1994), based on the story of Oedipus, but set on a plantation in antebellum South Carolina.

Born in Akron, Ohio, Dove graduated *summa cum laude* from Miami University in Oxford, Ohio, in 1973 and received her M.F.A. from the University of Iowa in 1977. The recipient of a Guggenheim and a Fulbright-Hays Fellowship, Dove also has the honor of being the first African American to hold the title of Poet Laureate of the United States, a title she held from 1993 to 1995.

Thomas and Beulah

These poems tell two sides of a story
and are meant to be read in sequence.

I

Mandolin

Black Boy, O Black Boy,
is the port worth the cruise?
—Melvin B. Tolson,
Harlem Gallery

The Event

Ever since they'd left the Tennessee ridge
with nothing to boast of
but good looks and a mandolin,

the two Negroes leaning
on the rail of a riverboat
were inseparable: Lem plucked

to Thomas' silver falsetto.
But the night was hot and they were drunk.
They spat where the wheel

churned mud and moonlight,
they called to the tarantulas
down among the bananas

to come out and dance.
*You're so fine and mighty; let's see
what you can do*, said Thomas, pointing

to a tree-capped island.
Lem stripped, spoke easy: *Them's chestnuts,*
I believe. Dove

quick as a gasp. Thomas, dry
on deck, saw the green crown shake
as the island slipped
under, dissolved
in the thickening stream.
At his feet

a stinking circle of rags,
the half-shell mandolin.
Where the wheel turned the water

gently shirred.

Variation on Pain

Two strings, one pierced cry.
So many ways to imitate
The ringing in his ears.

He lay on the bunk, mandolin
In his arms. Two strings
For each note and seventeen
Frets; ridged sound
Humming beneath calloused
Fingertips.

There was a needle
In his head but nothing
Fit through it. Sound quivered
Like a rope stretched clear
To land, tensed and brimming,
A man gurgling air.

Two greased strings
For each pierced lobe:
So is the past forgiven.

Motherhood

She dreams the baby's so small she keeps
misplacing it—it rolls from the hutch
and the mouse carries it home, it disappears
with his shirt in the wash.
Then she drops it and it explodes
like a watermelon, eyes spitting.

Finally they get to the countryside;
Thomas has it in a sling.
He's strewing rice along the road
while the trees chitter with tiny birds.
In the meadow to their right three men
are playing rough with a white wolf. She calls

warning but the wolf breaks free
and she runs, the rattle
rolls into the gully, then she's
there and tossing the baby behind her,
listening for its cry as she straddles
the wolf and circles its throat, counting
until her thumbs push through to the earth.
White fur seeps red. She is hardly breathing.
The small wild eyes
go opaque with confusion and shame, like a child's.

Daystar

She wanted a little room for thinking;
but she saw diapers steaming on the line,
a doll slumped behind the door.

So she lugged a chair behind the garage
to sit out the children's naps.

Sometimes there were things to watch—
the pinched armor of a vanished cricket,
a floating maple leaf. Other days
she stared until she was assured
when she closed her eyes
she'd see only her own vivid blood.

She had an hour, at best, before Liza appeared
pouting from the top of the stairs.
And just *what* was mother doing
out back with the field mice? Why,

building a palace. Later
that night when Thomas rolled over and
lurched into her, she would open her eyes
and think of the place that was hers
for an hour—where
she was nothing,
pure nothing, in the middle of the day.

Jewell Parker Rhodes (b. 1954)

Jewell Parker Rhodes is professor of Creative Writing and American Literature and former Director of the M.F.A. Creative Writing Program at Arizona State University. She earned her Ph.D. from Carnegie Mellon University. Her first novel, *Voodoo Dreams* (1993) is based on the story of Marie Laveau, the infamous 19th-century Louisiana voodoo woman. In 1997, she published a second novel, *Magic City*, a story about a black man falsely accused of raping a white woman during the era of the Tulsa Riots of 1921. Rhodes is also known for her short stories, which have been well anthologized. The recipient of many honors, including a Yaddo Creative Writing Fellowship and a National Endowment of the Arts Fellowship, she has also been nominated twice for the Pushcart Prize. Rhodes lives in Phoenix, Arizona.

A Personal Past

Long Distances

Nate couldn't remember the moment when it had happened, let alone why. Was it in the supermarket buying kidney beans or touring through Allegheny Park with its man-made pond when he knew just from looking at her, he would have to go to California? Knew from fixed stares, drooping mouth, her restlessness.

Knew he'd have to leave his humid and river-choked valley with its steel-mill-sooted hills to drive across Plains, Rockies and desert until sand gave way to heaving ocean. And for what? Her dreaming?

Three thousand miles. A man could get lost.

Della showed him a postcard picture book of California. Flat-topped roofs and pastel stucco. Palm trees bent by breezes. He'd be trapped by distance. Sunshine.

"We'll be pioneers," Della said.

He wondered if he'd miss shoveling snow, crushing ice while sprinkling salt? If he'd miss the ugliness of brick homes with rain slicking off slant roofs into mud-packed gutters? He'd never see the three rivers overflow.

Would he miss driving over cobblestones getting his wheels caught by streetcar tracks the city was too cheap to dig up? Or parking on hills with the clutch in, the tires turned toward the curb?

He'd miss his mother.

For what? Della's dreaming? Or his fear she'd go with or without him? No matter.

Nate had traded in his muscle Chevy for a dreamboat Chrysler. A 300 with a red interior that wasn't as bright as the red metal outside and never would be. The skinny-ass man who sold him the car said it would get him around the world if that's where he wanted to go. He said he didn't. But Della had been sold with that line. And here he was driving on a stretch of highway about ready to cross into INDIANA WELCOME. A truck was coming out of Indiana, flicking its headlights to low. It started to rain. He turned on his windshield wipers, his high beams. Night driving was dangerous. But Della couldn't wait another day. Had to leave at midnight to make better time. Now she and the kids were sleeping.

He looked at the trip odometer: 270 miles. At least two more days and nights of driving. 800, 1,000 miles a day. No unnecessary stops. No motels. Della needed to get to Los Angeles fast, to make it big. Somehow. He'd drive until his mind warped and then maybe he'd forget his guilt. Forget his momma's unnatural quiet, forget her solemn shuffling about the house. Forget her leaning over a porch railing, watching them pack up as if she couldn't believe it. Forget her refusing to say or wave goodbye. Nate wished he had a drink. He'd promised to call his momma from Wheeling. But it'd seemed like too soon. He plain forgot to call at Dayton.

He looked in the side mirror and saw the Ford his father-in-law, Ben Williams, was driving. Ben was no comfort. For weeks, Ben told folks at the *Pier Point Bar*, "No way I'd allow my baby girl travel from Pittsburgh to L.A. alone."

"What you mean *alone*, Ben? Nate's going. He's her husband, ain't he?"

Then Ben Williams would puff his chest, suck his gut, and glare until the person nervously admitted, "Ain't right to let a woman travel alone. Not with two kids."

A dozen slicks and low-lifes had told Nate that Ben was drinking bourbon and calling him a faggot. But what was he supposed to do? Beat up on an old man? Have his wife holler? Nate gripped the steering wheel.

Since the first time he called on Della, the old man kept one-upping him. Nate remembered being seventeen, squirming on a plastic-covered sofa, his hands itching with sweat. Ben Williams, an ex-cop, had a bit of money. He had a bit if Irish too. He was a freckle-faced Negro and proud of it. Nate was just poor and black.

Ben Williams slipped in questions like artillery fire: "Where you been, boy?"

"Home." He remembered how his plain, brown-faced momma could make a run-down house seem like the world. Make you never want to leave. He promised he'd never leave.

"Where you going, boy?"

"Uh, work, sir. I be wanting my own butcher shop." He liked the feel of a cleaver ripping away flesh from bone and the soft whishing sound of bloodied sawdust beneath his feet.

"What do you want with my girl?"

That one he couldn't answer.

Looking at Della with her head leaning up against the window and slightly cocked back, breathing through her nose in a slight snore—he still didn't know. Now she didn't look so pretty and when she was angry, she seemed less so. Maybe it was the old man that made him want her. Him with his attitude that his baby girl was so special and Nate was just another no-good hood from the streets.

Nate sighed, pressing the aching small of his back into the vinyl seat. He was twenty-eight. Still poor and black with a wife longing for the "opportunities" of California. She used to long for him.

At fifteen, Della was eager to do it anywhere. He remembered her hitching up her dress, begging him in the laundromat. Together they moaned; he had a kid. Responsibilities. Della was smart—she finished school. He dropped out to cut beef full-time. God, how his momma screamed. Wasn't a man supposed to support his family? What choice did he have?

Another pretty baby. Della was less eager to do it. She started spreading her legs again when she started talking California. When he'd admitted he was scared that if the family couldn't make it in Pittsburgh, they couldn't make it anywhere, she pressed him down upon her breasts, reminding him while he suckled that he'd promised California. He rubbed himself between her thighs until the world and regrets faded.

Momma never liked Della. "She attracts men like bugs to flypaper. Her uppity dad is a yellow fool. Her momma is just as bad." Then she would grin, smack her hips, before uttering her final condemnation. "Spoiled."

The smell and sound of stale heat passing through vents sickened Nate. He felt like rolling down the window, but the cool wind would cut right back to the children. His two daughters, Carrie and Jackie, almost smothered beneath blankets,

were two squirrelly balls in the back. He wondered when his momma would see her grandkids again? No more dressing them in white and carrying them to church to sing, shout and Praise the Lord. Who would she rock and sing lullabies to? It was his fault they were leaving. Dammit, why couldn't he say "no" to Della? He should've called his momma from Dayton.

A yellow sign with a vertical ripple told him the road up ahead was curved. Nate took one hand away from the wheel. His right hand adjusting the turn of the wheel was all he really needed. He loved the feel of cars. Even this one. And as the green fluorescent speedometer showed his increase in speed, the better he felt, 70, 75, 80. Without looking in the mirror, he knew the old man would be straining his car to keep up with him. He could just about hear Ben Williams cursing. Ben needed to be with his daughter more than he needed to breathe. What do I need? Nate thought.

As the asphalt turnpike straightened itself out, Nate lowered the speed. He didn't understand his feelings, but it didn't much matter. If he understood everything, he'd still hurt. Understanding didn't ease pain.

He was eight when his momma told him matter-of-factly his dad and Sondra were gone. They were at the kitchen table eating collard greens and rice. Even at eight, he'd understood the attraction of the neighbor woman with her flowery dresses and jasmine perfume. Him and his dad both laughed and smiled at her jokes. He understood his momma was too fat, awkward, and glum around Miss Sondra. Nonetheless he'd kicked the wall and tried to hide his crying. That night he slept on his daddy's side of the bed. Curled in the crook of his mother's arms, touching her round face, he promised he'd never leave. She didn't ask him to say it. But he was eight and thought words had power. For many nights thereafter, before uncoiling his wiry body against hers, he'd whisper, "I'll be here." And when he married, it was simple enough to live in the same house, two floors up, across the hall. Della hadn't threatened to take the kids. He couldn't even use that excuse.

The car was pulling him farther away from his mother.

At the point where the skyline met the road in his vision, Nate was sure he could see her. Her breasts sagging, her eyes dim. Was there a difference between what the two of them were feeling? His mother, flat in bed, hearing the sound of no one breathing; him, maneuvering through rain, hearing the car and bodies exhaling the same heated air. Who would care for his mother? He wished he could turn on the radio. There were buttons to push rather than knobs to turn. Too much noise though. Besides, he'd probably only get country.

Nate wanted to piss and buy some coffee. A red neon sign blinked, Food, Gas, 5 miles, Terre Haute. He would call his mother and tell her he loved her. He would get change. A hundred quarters. Call her every stop from a pay phone.

First, Terre Haute. Then, St. Louis. Topeka. Denver. Would she weep?

He wanted to hit something. Wanted to run the car off the road. A twist to the right, and into the embankment. Kill them all. Metal, concrete, blood. The car would pleat like an accordion. He wished he could see Ben Williams's face then. Yeah. What would Ben say seeing his daughter smashed up? Her toes meeting her elbows; her head twisted off. What would Ben do?

Nate missed the exit. A dairy truck hauling cows rumbled past. The rain was easing. He looked at his watch: 4:28 A.M. His momma was probably asleep now. He should wait till morning. After he crossed the Mississippi, Columbia, Missouri, then. He'd call her there. Veins popped up like worms along his hands. What if she refused to talk to him? He stumbled a bent Kool out of his right pocket. He lit the cigarette, dragged deep, and smoke filled his lungs like a caress. He exhaled. Smoke blanketed the dash. He stubbed the cigarette out.

"Della," he whispered plaintively. "Della."

Her eyes opened. Disoriented, she registered the night, the bold headlights whizzing by, Route 70 heading across the Wabash River and into Illinois.

She turned her head to the left and looked at Nate. "What is it?"

He grit his teeth and stared straight ahead at the road.

"Would you have gone without me?" His voice was barely a whisper. The heater's fan kicked in again.

"Yes," she said.

He felt like the time a line drive hit him in the gut. Wind went right out of him. Driving was easy. Automatic. He concentrated on feeling the murmurs of the engine.

The sky was clear. He switched off the wipers and rear window defrost. Della was sleeping.

Kansas City. Maybe he'd call his mother then. She'd be up. 10:00 A.M. Monday was laundry day. She'd be gathering clothes, stuffing them into her basket to carry them down the first flight of steps. She needn't worry anymore about shaking out sawdust, starching his collars, or lifting bloodstains from his shirts. He'd probably miss her if he called. When the phone would ring, she'd already be racketing her way down the basement steps. He'd call her that evening. After dinner. In Wichita.

Maybe Colorado Springs? Yeah. She'd have more time to adjust to him being gone. Another 1,000 miles, he'd be in Los Angeles. His family needed him. Nate pressed his foot hard on the gas. Los Angeles. He'd call his mother there and tell her he loved her nonetheless.

"Pop?" It was Jackie.

"Sssh. You'll wake your momma and sister up."

"Carrie keeps kicking me."

"In her sleep, she don't mean it."

Nate watched his daughter scowl in the mirror. She was resting her chin on top of the front seat, next to his shoulder—her fuzzy blue blanket covering her head like a nun's cloth.

"Can I help drive?"

"Come on, but be careful."

Jackie lifted her tennis shoe foot over and onto the front seat. Nate, with his right hand, grabbed her by her collar and pulled her down between him and Della. Jackie shifted herself onto his lap. He relaxed, feeling her small hands gripping his two hands on the wheel.

"Wow. I ain't never drove on the turnpike before."

"You just keep your eyes on the road so none of us don't get killed."

Jackie tightly clutched her father's hands. "Can I turn on the radio?"

"No."

"Aw, Pop."

Nate nudged her head with the side of his jaw.

Together, they watched the road. A clear, straight line to the horizon. Him looking over the arch of the wheel, Jackie right beneath it. It felt good to have company. He needed the distraction.

"Look, there's a dog, Pop. Running across the road."

Nate didn't see anything but he pumped the brakes anyway so Jackie could be satisfied they wouldn't hit the animal.

"And there. It's a raccoon. See it? Scootin' across the road."

"Nothing's there."

"It *is*."

Nate pumped the brakes. He felt his heart lighten at his daughter's silliness. He slowed for deer, a wily old fox. Ben Williams must be thinking he's driving crazy. Nate didn't care. Jackie was the child most like himself. Carrie took after Della, feminine and sweet when she wanted something, Jackie was the one who should've been a boy.

Feeling her shoes bang his knees, her spine curling into his chest, and a stumpy braid tickling his chin, Nate felt more her father than any other time he could remember. They were alone in the car, driving to California. The sun was coming up.

"Angels are digging out the sun to wake up the world," said an awed Jackie. "Digging it right out of the earth."

"The sun doesn't come out of the earth."

"Does so," she said, fiercely whispering, staring at him through the mirror. "Right now, it's half in and half out."

"Who told you that?"

"Grandma."

Nate felt shaken. He remembered his momma telling him such things too. Telling him that stars were God's words in light. The moon, His mirror. Rainbows were the fluttering glow of angels' wings. The horizon was the blue gust of God's breath. All of a sudden his mother's presence was real.

"If Grandma said it, it must be true," Nate whispered.

Jackie tried burying her face in his shoulder. "I didn't want to leave," she said.

"I didn't want to go." Nate hugged his daughter closer, and hearing, feeling her soft shuddering sigh, he had a clear sense of what a damn fool he'd been.

"You think she'll forget me?" asked Jackie.

"Naw," he said. "Your grandma loves you."

"She wouldn't let me kiss her goodbye."

"She was just hurt."

Nate stared straight ahead at the gray roadway. He didn't want to look up and see Jackie's reflection in the overhead mirror. He didn't want to look up and see her looking at him. "There's a cat." he said, pumping the brakes, trying to stop his headlong drive. In his mind, he lost the image of a road map. He couldn't see a red-marked line named 70 winding its way to California. He saw him and his daughter marooned in a car, whispering secrets.

When the sun was halfway up in sky, Jackie fell asleep. Her hands slipped off his hands and he could feel her fingers lightly touching the hair on his arms. "Jackie?" All the women in the car were sleeping.

In the side mirror, Nate looked yearningly at Ben William's car. He wished the old Ford would catch up with him. They could drive side by side past cornfields and wheat, at least until the Rockies.

Sunlight was baking him. He couldn't slip off his jacket without disturbing Jackie. He cursed under his breath. In the grease-slicked patches on the road, he saw shreds of rainbows. The sun loomed. He knew angels were moving it.

If Grandma said it, it must be true.

Literature from the New Millennium: The 1990s to the 21st Century

Tina McElroy Ansa (b. 1949)

Born in Macon, Georgia, Tina McElroy Ansa attended Spelman College. Previously a free-lance journalist for the *Atlanta Constitution* and the *Charlotte Observer*, she has taught writing at Brunswick College, Emory University, and Spelman. Her four novels include *Baby of the Family* (1989), *Ugly Ways* (1993), *The Hand I Fan With* (1996), and *You Know Better* (2002). Ansa's novels take place in the fictional small town of Mulberry, Georgia. Mulberry is a place where babies born with cauls have special powers and laying a dead mother's body to rest is not easy. It is also a place where a one-hundred-year-old ghost can become an eligible bachelor and wayward daughters disappear.

Willie Bea and Jaybird

When Willie Bea first saw Jaybird in The Place, she couldn't help herself. She wanted him so bad she sucked in her bottom lip, cracked with the cold, then she ran her tongue so slowly over her top lip that she could taste the red Maybelline lipstick she had put on hours before. He looked like something that would be good to eat, like peach cobbler or a hot piece of buttered cornbread.

She had just entered the bar clutching her black purse under her arm and smiling to try to make herself look attractive among the 6 o'clock crowd of drinkers and dancers and socializers, every one of them glad to be done with work for the day. He was there at the end of the bar in his golden Schlitz uniform sharing a quart of Miller High Life beer with a buddy. Willie Bea noticed right away how he leaned his long frame clear across the bar, bent at the waist, his elbows resting easily on the Formica counter. There didn't seem to be a tense bone in his lean efficient body.

"He look like he could go anywhere in the world," Willie Bea thought as she followed her big-butt friend Patricia as she weaved her way to a nearby table already jammed with four of her friends, two men and two women. "If somebody put him in a white jacket and a flower in his buttonhole, he could pass for an actor in a Technicolor movie."

As the jukebox started up again, playing a driving Sam and Dave number, he looked around the bar, picked up his glass of beer and headed toward her table with his chin held high over the other patrons. When he smoothly pulled up a chair to her table and straddled it backwards, Willie Bea crossed her stick legs and pinched her friend Pat's thigh under the table to give her some Sen-Sen for her breath.

"Hey, Little Mama, you got time for a tired working man?"

She had to remember to wipe the uncomfortable moisture from the corners of her mouth with her fingertips before she could respond to him.

She still felt that way, four years after they had started going together, when she looked at him.

Nothing gave her more pleasure than to be asked her marital status with Jaybird around.

"Willie Bea, girl, where you been keeping yourself?" some big-mouthed woman would shout at her over the din of the jukebox at The Place. "I ain't seen you in a month of Sundays. You still living with your aunt, ain't you?" This last expectantly with pity.

Willie Bea would roll her shoulders and dip her ears from side to side a couple of times in feigned modesty.

"Naw, girl, I *been* moved out of my aunt's," Willie Bea would answer. "I'm married now. I live with my . . . *husband*."

The old horse's big mouth would fall open, then close, then open as if she were having trouble chewing this information.

"Husband? Married??!!"

"Uh-huh. That's my *husband* over there by the jukebox. Naw, not him. My Jay is the tall light-skinned one, the one with the head full of curly hair."

Willie Bea never even bothered to look at her inquisitor when she pointed out Jay. She could hear the effect the weight of the revelation had had on the woman. And Willie Bea only glanced smugly at the old cow as she raced around the bar nearly knocking over a chair to ask her friends and companions why no one told her that skinny little shiny-faced Willie Bea had a man.

"I thought she was sitting there mighty sassy looking."

Even Willie Bea would have admitted it: Most days, she did feel sassy, and it was Jaybird who made her so. He burst

Tina McElroy Ansa. "Willie Bea and Jaybird." *Callaloo* 13:2 (1990), 307–312. © Charles H. Rowell. Reprinted with permission of The Johns Hopkins University Press.

into the bathroom while she was in the bathtub and pretended to take pictures of her with an imaginary camera. He teased her about flirting with Mr. Maurice who owned the store on the corner near their boardinghouse when the merchant sliced her baloney especially thin, the way she liked it.

Now, she really thought she was cute, with her little square monkey face and eager-to-please grin, a cheap jet black Prince Valiant wig set on the top of her head like a wool cap with her short hair plaited underneath and a pair of black eyeglasses so thick that her eyes looked as if they were in fish bowls.

Jaybird had done that to her. He even called her "fine," an appellation that actually brought tears to her eyes made huge and outlandish by the Coke-bottle-thick glasses.

"Fine." It was the one thing in life Willie Bea longed to be. She had no shape to speak of. She was just five feet tall and weighed about 90 pounds. But she did her best to throw that thing even though she had very little to throw.

"If I had me a big old butt like you, Pat," she would say to her friend, "ya'll couldn't stand me."

The pitiful little knot of an ass that she had was her sorrow, especially after noticing from Jaybird's gaze that he appreciated a full ass. His favorite seemed to be the big heart-shaped ones that started real low and hung and swayed like a bustle when the woman walked. Many mornings, Jay lay in bed watching Bea move around the room getting dressed and thought, "Her behind ain't to bigger than my fist." But he didn't dare say anything, even as a joke. He knew it would break her heart.

But since she knew she didn't have a big ass, she did what she had done since she was a child when someone told her what she was lacking: She pretended she did and acted as if her ass was the prize one in town. The one men in jukejoints talked about.

Wherever she went—to the market, to work cleaning houses, to The Place, downtown to shop—she dressed as if she had that ass to show off.

She wore tight little straight skirts that she made herself on her landlady's sewing machine. Skirts of cotton or wool or taffeta no wider than 12 inches across. Not that wide, really, because she wanted the skirt to "cup," if possible, under the pones of her behind and to wrinkle across her crotch in front. Using less than a yard of material and a Simplicity quickie pattern she had bought years before and worked away to tatters, she took no more than an hour to produce one of her miniature skirts.

On Sundays, when the house was empty of other boarders or quiet from their sleep, Willie Bea used her landlady's sewing machine that she kept in the parlor. The steady growl of the old foot-pedal-run Singer disturbed no one. In fact, on those Sundays she and Jaybird went out and she did no sewing, the other tenants of the large white wooden house felt an unidentified longing and found themselves on the verge of complaining about the silence.

Willie Bea looked on the ancient sewing machine, kept in mint condition by the genial landlady who always wore plaid housedresses and her thin crimpy red hair in six skinny braids, as a blessing. She didn't mind that the machine was a foot-propelled model rather than an electric one. It never occurred to her to expect anything as extravagant as that. For her, the old machine was a step up from the tedious hand-sewing that she had learned and relied on as a child. With the waist bands neatly attached and the short zippers eased into place by machine, her skirts had a finished look that would have taken her all night to accomplish by hand.

Many times, she felt herself rocking gently to the rhythm she set with her bare feet on the cold iron treadle to ease a crick in her stiff back before she realized that she had been at the job non-stop all afternoon. Just using the machine made her happy, made her think of men watching her at the bus stops in her new tight skirt and later, maybe, these same men letting some sly comment drop in front of Jaybird about her shore looking good.

She imagined Jaybird jumping in the men's faces, half-angry, half-proud, to let them know that was his *wife* they were talking about. Just thinking of Jaybird saying, "my wife" made her almost as happy as her being able to say "my husband."

She loved to go over in her head how it had come to pass, their marriage. They had been living together in one room of the boardinghouse at the top of Pleasant Hill for nearly three years, with him seeming to take for granted that they would be together for eternity and with her hardly daring to believe that he really wanted her, afraid to ask him why he picked her to love.

As with most of his decisions, movements, he surprised her.

One evening in August, he walked into their room and said, "Let's get married." As if the idea had just come to him, his and original. She responded in kind.

"Married? Married, Jay?" she said, pretending to roll the idea around in her head a while. Then, "Okay, if you want."

It was her heart's desire, the play-pretty of her dreams, being this man's wife.

She bought stiff white lace from Newberry's department store to make a loose cropped sleeveless overblouse and a yard of white polished cotton and sewed a tight straight skirt for the ceremony at the courthouse.

When they returned to their room for the honeymoon, Willie Bea thought as she watched him take off his wedding suit that no other man could be so handsome, so charming, so full of self-assured cockiness . . . and still love her.

He was tall and slender in that way that made her know that he would be lean all his life, never going sway-backed and to fat around his middle like a pregnant woman. He was lithe and strong from lifting cases and kegs of Schlitz beer all day long, graceful from leaping on and off the running board of the moving delivery truck as it made its rounds of bars and stores.

Once when he had not seen her, Willie Bea had spied him hanging fearlessly off the back of the beer truck like a prince, face directly into the wind, his eyes blinking back the wind tears, a vacant look on his face. His head full of curly hair quivering in the wind. The setting sunlight gleamed off the chrome and steel of the truck, giving a golden-orange color to the aura that Willie Bea felt surrounded him all the time.

Overcome by the sight, Willie Bea had had to turn away into an empty doorway to silently weep over the beauty of her Jaybird.

Jaybird even made love the way she knew this man would—sweet and demanding. When her friend Pat complained about her own man's harsh unfeeling fucking, Willie Bea joined in and talked about men like dogs. But first, in her own mind, she placed Jaybird outside the dog pack.

"Girl, just thank your lucky stars that you ain't hooked up with a man like Henry," Pat told her. "Although God knows they all alike. You may as well put 'em all in a crocker sack and pick one out. They all the same. One just as good as the other. Just take your pick."

"Uh-huh, girl, you know you telling the truth," Willie Bea would answer.

"Why, that old dog of mine will just wake any time of the night and go to grabbing me and sticking his hand up my nightdress. He don't say nothing, just grunt. He just goes and do his business. I could be anything, a sack of flour, that chair you sitting on."

"What you be doing?" Willie Bea asked in her soft singsong voice even though she already knew because Pat always complained about the same thing. But she asked because she and Pat had grown up together, she had been Pat's friend longer than anyone outside of her family. And Willie Bea knew what a friend was for.

"Shoot, sometimes I just lay there like I *am* a sack of flour. I thought that would make him see I wasn't getting nothing out of his humping. Then, I saw it didn't make no difference to him whether I was having a good time or not. So, now, sometimes I push him off me just before he come. That makes him real mad. Or I tell him I got my period.

"Some nights, we just lay there jostling each other like little children jostling over a ball. I won't turn over or open up my legs and he won't stop tugging on me."

"Girl, both of ya'll crazy. That way, don't neither of you get a piece. That's too hard," Willie Bea said sincerely.

"Shoot, girl, some nights we tussle all night." Pat gave a hot dry laugh. "Henry thinks too much of hisself to fight me for it, really hit me up side my head or yell and scream 'cause with those little paper sheer walls, everybody next door would know your business. So while we fighting, it's real quiet except for some grunts and the bed squeaking."

Then, she laughed again.

"I guess that's all you'd be hearing anyway."

Willie Bea tried to laugh in acknowledgement. Once Pat told her, "Shoot, girl, I've gotten to liking the scuffling we do in bed better than I ever liked the screwing."

That made Willie Bea feel cold all over.

"It's like it make it more important," Pat continued. "Something worth fighting for. Some nights when he just reach for me like that, it's like he calling me out my name. And I turn over ready to fight.

"I would get somebody else, but they all the same, you may as well pick one from the sack as another. But look at you, Bea. You just agreeing to be nice. You don't believe that, do you?"

"I didn't say nothing," Willie Bea would rush to say. "I believe what you say about you and Henry. I believe you."

"That ain't what I mean and you know it. I'm talking about mens period."

"I know what you saying about men."

"Yeah, but you don't think they all alike, do you?" Pat asked.

Willie Bea would start dipping her head from side to side and grinning her sheepish closed-mouth grin.

"Go on and admit it, girl," Pat would prod.

After a moment, Willie Bea would admit it. "I don't know why he love me so good."

Then, Pat would sigh and urge her friend to tell her how sweet Jay was to her . . . in bed, at the table, after work. Especially in bed.

Willie Bea balked at first, each time the subject came up. But she always gave in, too. She was just dying to talk about Jaybird.

Most women she knew held the same beliefs that Pat did about men. They sure as hell didn't want to hear about her and the bliss her man brought her. She had found they may want to hear about you "can't do with him and can't do without him" or how bad he treat you and you still can't let him go. All of that. But don't be coming around them with those thick window pane eyes of hers all bright and enlarged with stories of happiness and fulfillment. Those stories cut her other girlfriends and their lives to the quick.

But her friend Pat, big-butt Pat, urged Bea to share her stories with her. Sometimes, these reminiscences made Pat smile and glow as if she were there in Willie Bea's place. But sometimes, they left her morose.

Willie Bea, noticing this at first, began leaving out details that she thought made Pat's love pale in comparison. But Pat, alert to nuances in the tales, caught on an insisted that Willie Bea never leave stuff out again if she was going to tell it.

And Willie Bea, eager to tell it all, felt as if she were pleasing her friend as much as herself. So, she continued telling stories of love and dipping her ear down toward her shoulder in a gay little shy gesture.

"When Jaybird and me doing it, he has this little gruff-like voice he uses when he talks to me."

"Talk to you? What ya'll be doing, screwing or talking?" Pat would interrupt, but not seriously.

"He says things like, 'Is that all? That ain't all. I want it all. Uh-huh.' "

At first, Willie Bea was embarrassed disclosing these secrets of her and Jaybird's passionate and tender lovemaking. But Pat seemed so enthralled by her stories that Willie Bea finally stopped fighting it and gave herself over to the joy of recounting how Jaybird loved her.

Pat never told Willie Bea that many of the woman at The Place talked under their breaths when Jaybird and Willie Bea came in together.

"He may sleep in the same bed with her, but I heard he put an ironing board between 'em first," some said.

"He can't really want that little old black gal. He just like her worshipping the ground he walk on," another would add.

Pat knew Willie Bea would have tried to kill whoever said such things. But even Pat found it hard to believe sometimes that her little friend had attracted Jaybird.

Mornings, Pat watched Willie Bea step off the city bus they both took to their jobs, her too-pale dimestore stockings shining in the early light, her narrow shoulders rotating like bicycle pedals in the direction opposite the one she sent her snake hips inside her straight skirt and thought how changed her friend was by the love of Jaybird. Now, that walk is something new, Pat thought as the bus pulled away from the curb.

Willie Bea, who lived two blocks above Pat, got on the bus first, then alit first when she got near the white woman's house she cleaned five days a week. Pat stayed on until the bus reached downtown near the box factory where she worked. They rode to and from work together nearly every day.

So, one evening when Pat wasn't on the bus when she got on returning home, Willie Bea began to worry about her. All that one of Pat's co-workers on the bus said when Willie Bea asked was, "She left work early."

"I wonder if she's sick," Willie Bea thought.

She was still thinking about her friend when the bus began making its climb up Pleasant Hill. "I better stop and see 'bout her," Willie Bea thought.

She was still standing with her hand near the signal wire when the bus slowed to a stop in front of the cinder block duplex where Pat lived, and Willie Bea saw the gold of a Schiltz beer uniform slip back inside the dusty screen door of her friend's house.

The bus driver paused a good while with the bus door open waiting for Willie Bea to leave. Then, he finally, hollered toward the back of the bus, "You getting off or not?"

Willie Bea turned around to the driver's back and tried to smile as she took her regular seat again. When she reached her boardinghouse, she was anxious to see Jaybird and ask him who the new man was working on the beer truck. But he wasn't home.

She sat up alone on the bed in the boardinghouse room long after it grew dark.

Willie Bea didn't know how long she had been asleep when she heard the rusty door knob turn and felt a sliver of light from the hall fall across her face. Jaybird almost never stayed out late without her or telling her beforehand.

"You okay, Jay?" she asked sleepily.

He only grunted and rubbed her back softly. "Go back to sleep, Bea," he said. "I'm coming to bed now."

Willie Bea lay waiting for Jaybird to say something more, to say where he had been, to say he saw her friend Pat that day. But he said nothing.

And when he did finally slip into bed, it felt as if an ironing board was between them.

Bebe Moore Campbell (b. 1950)

Bebe Moore Campbell was born in 1950 in Philadelphia. She attended the University of Pittsburgh and worked as a public school teacher for six years after graduating from college. In addition to her early work as a freelance journalist, she has written an autobiography, *Sweet Summer: Growing Up With and Without My Dad* (1989), and four novels: *Your Blues Ain't Like Mine* (1992), *Brothers and Sisters* (1994), *Singing in the Comeback Choir* (1998), and *What You Owe Me* (2001). *Your Blues Ain't Like Mine* tells the story of fourteen-year-old Armstrong Todd, who like Emmett Till, is killed in 1954 for speaking to a white woman. In Campbell's story, the killing happens at the beginning of the novel, allowing the story to focus on the effects of the event on a cast of characters: Lily, the offended white woman, and her daughter, Doreen; Delotha and Wydell, Armstrong's mother and father; Ida, a single African American mother; and other white and black people in the southern town. Like *Your Blues, Brothers and Sisters* takes place during a volatile moment in racial relations—Los Angeles during the aftermath of the Rodney King incident. Campbell's most recent novel, *What You Owe Me* (2001), is the story of the friendship, betrayal, and healing of a relationship between a Holocaust survivor and an African American woman and their daughters.

From *Your Blues Ain't Like Mine*

Chapter 5 ["Two Small Pretty Women Staring Down an Empty Train Track"]

From the front porch, the women watched as Lester, John Earl, and Floyd drove off in the truck. Lily wanted to call after them and say, "Ain't nothing happened with that boy," but one look at Mamie's stern, intractable face, at Louetta's accusing eyes, and she shut her mouth. If Floyd and them were going to do something crazy and ruinous, she couldn't stop them. Going to Memphis suddenly felt like a receding dream.

Louetta turned to Lily, her round face bobbing forward, her eyes streaked with alert meanness. "Well, seems like things done got stirred up," she said. "What you think they gonna do, Miss Mamie?"

The older woman's words sizzled. "Whatever they does in menfolks' business. Us women ain't got nary to do with it." She gazed at Lily, whose shoulders jerked and shook under her mother-in-law's hard stare. "You. Miss Magnolia Queen. What'd you do to get that nigger's eyes on you?"

Lily watched Floydjunior playing with an empty box of Argo cornstarch in the middle of the porch. "I ain't done nothing," she said, bolting from her chair. She scooped up her little boy and fled across the yard. "C'mon, Floydjunior. Let's you and me take us a walk."

As she trudged down the road, Floydjunior on her hip, Lily tried not to think about Floyd, Lester, and John Earl and what they might be doing together that night. She had felt happy and exhilarated sneaking into the pool hall, like a child stealing cookies that were cooling on the porch, but now she felt guilty, and frightened for the boy and herself. She knew that Floyd's father had done terrible things to more than one colored man in Hopewell. And she knew that Floyd would go along with anything he and John Earl suggested.

She didn't stop walking until she reached the train station. Behind it, the Yabalusha shimmered in the twilight. The ancient depot was located at the edge of town, and at eight o'clock every evening the Illinois Central passed through Hopewell. The train was already in the station, and Lily sat down on a bench marked "For Whites Only," holding Floydjunior on her lap. "Look at the choo-choo," she said softly to the boy. "One day you're gonna ride away on the train, and when you come back you'll be somebody important, Floydjunior." She nuzzled the boy's neck. She was the only person on the white side; the colored side was always full. She peered into the sad clump of people at the other end of the small station. *I wonder if she came tonight,* Lily thought as she watched the colored people waving goodbye to each other, their faces solemn. She searched through the crowd of brown faces. And then she saw her, a small, almost white-looking colored woman, with braids like thick ropes trailing down her back. A small boy was clutching her hand.

The two women had met at the depot nearly five years earlier, not long after Lily quit school and married Floyd, which was when she began going to the train station. They had seen each other many times before, on the road that led from the Quarters to the poor-white section. They had even spoken to each other. But not until she became a regular at the depot did she become aware of the colored girl around her age who, like Lily, appeared to be at the station simply as an observer. Finally one night, after the women had eyed each other for nearly a month, Lily said to her, "What do the colored do up in Chicago?"

"Ma'am?"

"I said, what do all them colored do up in Chicago?"

"They work," the girl said.

Lily snorted, "They's plenty of work for 'em right here."

The girl spoke gently, as though trying to rouse a sleeping child. "Ma'am, don't nobody want to be in the fields. That's why people be leaving."

The discovery that colored people had dreams of a better life was the most profound and shocking of Lily's life, and so frightening that every time she saw the girl afterwards she felt a fear and anger she couldn't explain or control, and at the same time she was overcome with confusion and helplessness. She always wanted to shout to her, "I ain't done nothing to you."

She didn't speak to the girl again for almost two years. Then one Friday night Lily sat on the hard wooden bench after the train had been gone for a good ten minutes; she was still straining to hear its echoes. Two days earlier, Floyd had hit her for the first time, and she stared at the bluish bruise above her right elbow as though the mark were a map that led somewhere. She glanced up, and the girl was down near the other end of the track. They were the only ones there, two small pretty women staring down an empty train track. "Sure do wish I was on that train," the colored girl called to her.

Lily stood up and looked around, then moved closer to her. "I'd tell that conductor, 'Mister, take me straight to Memphis,'" Lily said.

"Take me to Chicago. What I care if it's cold." The girl walked toward Lily; there were flames in her eyes.

Lily stepped back. Something in the girl's tone told her that she was unafraid, that she could hop a train to Chicago, alone or with a baby, and be strong enough to survive. *She don't hafta have no husband telling her what to do*, thought Lily. The idea, audacious and unspeakable, sparkled before her as bright as a Christmas ornament. She almost put her hands on the girl, almost asked her how she got to be like

that, to think like that, but she stopped herself when she realized that she was standing there envying a colored person. She remembered Louetta telling her that colored women were like men, that their private parts were different from white women's. What if Floyd found out that she talked with the girl? She thought: *He ain't never gon' find out.*

The colored woman's name was Ida Long. Together they dreamed of escape.

This night, after the train left and all the colored people had gone, Lily walked down to the other end of the tracks and stood next to Ida. "Hey," said.

"Hey yourself. What's wrong, Miss Lily?"

"Nothing."

"Something is wrong with you."

Lily took a deep breath. The air was thick and hot, waterlogged. She could still smell the rain. Floyd hadn't fixed the roof, she thought. If it rains again . . .

"What is it?"

"Nothing." She looked down at Ida's little boy, who had grabbed Floydjunior's hand. "It's just that sometimes I wish I wasn't married. Like you."

Their eyes met. "Yeah, well, I wanted to marry Sweetbabe's daddy," Ida said, "but he run off to Detroit when he found out about the baby."

"That boy probably wasn't no good," Lily said quickly. "You deserve somebody good."

"I wanted my child to know his daddy." She paused for several moments. "I don't know mine."

"I thought you lived with your daddy," Lily said.

"William been like a daddy to me, but he ain't my real father. My real father is . . ." She looked at Lily, who was staring at her.

"Is what?"

"Is a white man."

"Oh," Lily said.

"Only I don't know who he is, and William keeps saying he don't know either. I want to know." She stared at Lily, who seemed to be studying her every feature. "Did I shock you, Miss Lily?"

"No. You ain't shocked me. My uncle Charlie had him a baby by a colored woman. A little boy, dark little chocolate, with blue eyes, like my uncle Charlie." She lowered her voice. "My uncle Charlie wasn't no good." She spread her small hands in front of her and began picking at the chipped polish on her fingernails.

"Because he got a baby off a colored woman?"

"That wasn't nothing." Lily gave Ida a hard look. "If I tell you something . . ."

"Ain't nobody for me to tell."

"He used to touch me, when I wasn't nothing but a little-bitty girl. He'd sit me on his lap and feel me and afterwards he'd give me candy. He made me promise not to tell, but I told anyway."

"What happened?" Ida said. She had her hand on Lily's shoulder.

Her tears started falling before she could speak. "I told Mama. She whipped me for lying. I wasn't but six years old. Why would I lie about that?" She began crying harder, so that her shoulders shook and her face turned red. Ida quickly brushed away the tears that had begun falling from her own eyes and patted her friend's shoulder. Lily put her arms around the black woman. "Ida," she said, leaning against her friend, "I gotta tell you something. Somebody told my husband that this colored boy was—uh, said something fresh to me today. But he didn't. I told my husband that. And everything's all right now. It's just I been a little upset, that's all."

Ida stepped back a little and grabbed her son's hand. "Be still, Sweetbabe," she told him. When she turned to Lily, all the color had drained from her face; she was almost as pale as Lily. "What was the boy's name?"

"I don't know his name."

"What did the look like?"

"I can't remember."

"How old was he?"

"Maybe about sixteen or seventeen."

"Was he tall?"

"Yes."

"Was he dark-skinned or light-skinned?"

"Darker than you. He had freckles. Never seen a nig—a colored person with freckles before. Everything is all right. I told my husband, 'That boy didn't say not one bad thing.' Everything is all right now. I'm just a little upset, that's all. Ida! Ida, where you going?"

Freckles, That simple Armstrong, Ida thought, as she ran through the Quarters, Sweetbabe bobbing on her hip. The fool was all the time smart-mouthing, and now he'd gone and opened his mouth to the wrong person. How many times had Odessa told him, had she herself told him, that he couldn't say anything he felt like saying to these crazy crackers living in Hopewell. For the first time since she'd met Lily, Ida felt nagging doubts as she raced home. Her friend—she wasn't sure she could call a white woman that—was married to a Cox, and everyone in the Quarters knew those rednecks were mean as snakes eating hot sauce. How could everything be all right? "Mama told me never to trust crackers," she said aloud. Sweetbabe looked up at her with bright sparkling eyes.

With her two braids bouncing against her sweaty back, Ida ran up the steps to Odessa's house, which was near her own. The houses in the Quarter were all in shouting distance of one another, built closer together than in the area where the poor whites lived. The shacks had a transient quality.

A close look revealed that what should have been nailed was merely propped up. What should have been stored was merely put aside.

There were, of course, other settlements of colored around Hopewell. A small number of dicty high yellows, including the owner of the funeral parlor and his family, the principal and some of the teachers at Booker T. Washington School, and several well-to-do landowners, all lived near the south gin and worshiped at Bright Star AME, where, according to folks in the Quarters, the only requirement for membership was to be bright as a star.

Not that the Quarters didn't claim people of all complexions; the multicolored offspring of every conceivable race's union with blacks could be found there: Fair-skinned children of white men. Lemon- and cinnamon-shaded people with high cheekbones and hawk noses, and ebony-hued folks with straight black hair, all claiming the blood of Choctaws. Even progeny of colored women and Chinese men, who'd been enticed to pick cotton when colored workers first began fleeing north, could be seen, with their flattish faces, almond eyes, and kinky hair. These rainbow-hued children were absolute testimony that if colored women hadn't been honored, they'd certainly been desired. Although in practical terms that meant only that they and their children had been abandoned by men of every race.

Ida found Odessa on the porch, shelling peas.

"Hey there, gal," Odessa called cheerfully to her. "What's your hurry?"

Ida walked over to where she was sitting. "How you doing, Miss 'Dessa?"

"Fair to middling. Waiting on that boy to pack his clothes. How's your good-looking daddy? He come to his senses yet? I'm a whole lotta woman going to waste and ruin." She chuckled.

Odessa had been one of the women her father courted after her mother died. Because William was a carpenter and had built his own home, he was considered quite a catch. But William didn't want to remarry, and he and Odessa had broken up when she began to pressure him. "Where's Armstrong?" Ida asked.

"He in the house, getting ready for school. Mr. Hayes is driving him to Flower City tomorrow. Then I'll have me some peace around here." She grinned.

Suddenly Ida wasn't so sure of what to do. Odessa had been like a mother to her. And now she seemed so happy. She'd hate to upset her over nothing. *Miss Lily said that everything was all right*, she thought. *Besides, what could happen between the evening and the morning?* "Now, Miss Odessa, you know you gon' miss Armstrong, when he go," Ida said with a little laugh.

Odessa just grunted.

Armstrong was sitting on the porch when Odessa came outside. "Boy, you finish packing?" she asked.

"Yes."

"Yes, what?" Odessa snapped.

Armstrong sighed. "Yes, ma'am." He'd be glad when he could get away from all the yes-sir and yes-ma'am shit. "Grandma, you heard from my mother? Did she say when I could go back to Chicago?"

"Your mama's working hard, trying to be somebody. That takes time. Now you just go on up to that school tomorrow and get your lessons. You ought to be glad you can stay with your cousins in Flower City. If you had to go school around here, you wouldn't go until after the cotton was in. These white folks in Hopewell don't want black youngins fit for nothin' but the fields," Odessa muttered. "Don't worry about getting back to Chicago. Chicago ain't going nowhere."

"But every year I stay here, she's always saying this will be the year when I move back," Armstrong said dejectedly. "Then she changes her mind."

"Well, your mama's doing all she can do. If your daddy was any good, he'd help your mama with you. That Wydell's just as trifling as the day is long. Drinking liquor, that's his job. He ain't sent your mama a quarter to help keep you."

Armstrong began chewing his bottom lip. Why did she always have to talk about his old man? Why couldn't she just shut up about him? Every time he thought about his father, it was like being punched in the stomach. Now he felt that same hurt, helpless feeling engulfing him, and he hated his grandmother for causing it. He had been about to tell her what happened at the pool hall, but now he wasn't going to say a damn thing. He hated her.

"I'm going up to see Ida and them. You want to come?" she asked.

"No."

"No, what?"

He sighed. "No, ma'am."

Oblivious to the mosquitoes that were swarming as night fell, Armstrong sat on the porch, thinking about the money he'd made from playing pool and what Mr. Pinochet had given him. He could double the twenty dollars by selling sandwiches at the school. Maybe triple the money. His ruminations were jarred by the sudden barking of his neighbor's dogs.

He looked up when he heard the truck. Stood up when he heard the motor stop. The headlights revealed three men, one sort of short, the other two tall and strong-looking, their expressions fixed and hard. For a moment he sat in dazed uncertainty. Then fear, as primal as the first scream, flooded his body. "Turn them damn lights out!" he heard one of the men say. They're coming for me, he thought. He didn't realize that

he'd bitten his tongue until he tasted blood in his mouth as he called, "Mama."

Without thinking, he ran. Into the yard. Toward the outhouse. In the direction of the chicken coop. His movements were wild, scattered. The faster he ran, the louder the barking became.

"Watchu running fer, nigger?" he heard one of them say. Then: "Go get him. He's yourn." It was what his grandmother's friend said when they went hunting.

"Nigger, you better make it easy on yourself," another voice said.

The three men finally caught him near the edge of Odessa's yard. In the moonlight he saw that the old one didn't have teeth. The tallest one had a cut across his cheek. The short one was Floyd Cox. What made terror slam into Armstrong like a lash across his back was the fear he saw in Floyd's eyes.

The tall younger man hit him, a heavy, open-palm slap that struck against his head. Armstrong fell down in a daze. "What did I do?" he asked. He tried to get up, but his legs seemed to lock and then buckle. When he finally regained his balance and was able to stand, the man knocked him down again and began kicking him in his stomach, his chest, his head.

Nobody said anything. Armstrong repeated, "What did I do?" He began to cry, but the yelping dogs, their barking growing louder and more frenzied, drowned out his sobbing. He curled up like a baby, trying to avoid the blows, but then the old man yanked Armstrong's arms back so that his son could get to him. Each time the tall one kicked him, Armstrong screamed, "Please stop," but the beating only got worse. Armstrong looked down and saw that his shirt was wet with blood. "What . . . did . . . I . . . do?" he kept repeating, gasping for breath between each word.

He watched as the white men looked at one another, each waiting for someone to articulate Armstrong's crime. His head was throbbing, and blood seeped from his nose, but he ached so badly he didn't have the strength to reach up and wipe it. Finally Floyd said, "You was talking crazy talk to my wife. That's what."

In spite of his pain, Armstrong remembered his grandmother's tutelage; her admonishments came to him in one long hope-filled wave. He would act polite and stupid. Wasn't that what white people wanted? "No, sir," he said respectfully. "No, sir. I wasn't talking to your wife, sir. I was talking to my friend, and when I turned around, she was looking at me." Armstrong managed to smile a little and even tried to nod as he had seen Jake do.

The tall one turned violently red and started hitting him again, as Floyd watched helplessly. "Looking at you, was she?" he screamed. Armstrong realized his mistake too late to call back his words. He saw the old man observing Floyd as though he wanted to beat him into the ground. "You gon' fight your own battles, or is your brother gon' hafta do it all? She's your wife. Yourn," he yelled at his younger son.

What could he do to make them stop? What did they want of him? Armstrong remembered bullies in the Chicago schoolyard where he had attended grammar school and thought of the bloodless scuffles over lunch money. And then he remembered the two ten-dollar bills in his pocket. "I have some money," he said weakly.

Floyd inched toward him as the tall one stepped aside, and Armstrong could see the rage pouring from his eyes. "You got money, nigger? You think that makes you good as me?" Floyd said.

Armstrong tried to say no, to mouth the word, but his lips were so sore and swollen he couldn't move them. They were going to kick his ass, and there wasn't anything he could do about it. One, two, three . . . By the time I count to a hundred, he thought, they'll be gone and Grandma will be here and she'll fix me up. Four, five, six . . . The moonlight revealed something shiny in Floyd's hand. A gun. I'm seeing things, he told himself.

The air around him was completely silent; the dogs, the crickets, the wind, were all still. He couldn't hear himself breathing; his tears seemed suspended, as though his sobs were dammed up in his chest, roiling around like furious ocean waves. "Please, mister," he managed to whisper. When he looked in Floyd's eyes he saw pain, rage, and loathing, but no mercy. "Mama," he cried.

"Get on your knees, nigger," Floyd said. He swaggered around Armstrong, waving the gun in the air, stealing glances at his father and brother, who said nothing.

Armstrong attempted to obey, but his legs wouldn't co-operate. He heard a trickling sound that seemed to come from a great distance.

"Nigger's peeing his pants," the tall one said. The terse laughter that surrounded Armstrong was as brutal as brass knuckles against his skull.

"You just gon' stand there?" the old one said.

Through half-closed eyes, Armstrong could barely see Floyd's face, the fear and loathing and monstrous rage coagulating around the set of his mouth, the cruelty in his stare. Where did all that hatred come from?

"I hate niggers," Floyd screamed, his mouth contorted. He faced his father and brother as he yelled.

Armstrong heard the click of the trigger, and he took a deep breath. He felt his bowels ripping through him, then a soft, warm mushiness in his pants. He heard an explosion; fire seared the inside of his chest. His head slammed into the dirt. Nearby, a tired dog began panting, its ragged breathing engulfing him. If only he could find the hound, he could maybe lean against its soft, warm fur, raise himself up a little, But he couldn't see anything. He pictured his father then, as

the moans of pain dribbled from his lips: his father, tall and strong, coming toward him bathed in white light, his arms like steel bands stretched out for the boy to grab. As he heard the retreating footsteps in the air around him. he thought: *My daddy could whip all of you.*

John Earl took the wheel and drove out of Odessa's yard. The men's faces were stern and composed, their lips drawn together in three tight, satisfied lines. The cab of the truck was cramped, and their shoulders pressed together as they settled back in their seats. John Earl fiddled with the radio dial. There was nothing but static until he found the Greenwood station and then they heard Hank William's voice, full force and pure.

"That Hank, now, he's a singer," said Lester. He opened a pack of Marlboros and passed it to Floyd and then to John Earl, and each one took a cigarette, lit it, and flicked the ashes on the floor of the battered truck. "I'm so lonesome I could cry," Lester sang, in a voice that was low and off key but contained such a thrumming heartiness that it was infectious, and Floyd and John Earl began singing too. When the song was over, Lester said, "Well, you might can't fix everything that needs fixing, but damned if you can't make some things right."

Later, when Floyd would try to forget everything else about this night, he would still recall the ride back home, the smoky air of the congested cab, the three of them pressed in close together, singing and laughing as their shoulders touched. What warmed him more than anything was the sure, true knowing that his father, at last, was satisfied with him.

From Brothers and Sisters

From Chapter 15 [LaKeesha's Job Interview]

Esther stared at the scrolling figures on her computer screen. It was hard to comprehend that people could be so careless about their finances that they forgot they had money in the bank, but as she reviewed the dormant accounts, a task she undertook every few months, the evidence was indisputable. In the downtown branch alone, there was nearly three million dollars in accounts that hadn't been active in months, sometimes years. Two million, nine hundred thousand and seventy-eight dollars, to be exact. She logged in the amount. Of course, some of the holders of the accounts were deceased, but in those cases, she would have thought that relatives would come and claim the cash. All that money going to waste. She shook her head.

Esther heard a soft knock at the door. She looked at her watch: nine-thirty. She had completely forgotten about her appointment. Well, the interview wouldn't take long. She'd already decided that she was going to hire David Weaver. "Come in," she called.

The door opened slowly, and a young, dark-brown-skinned woman stood in front of Esther's desk. Their eyes met, and Esther could read in them the girl's uncensored surprise. Esther realized immediately the reason for the startled look in the young woman's eyes: she hadn't expected another black person to be interviewing her.

Two months earlier, Angel City had formed a partnership with the city's social service agency. The bank was obligated to interview a certain number of welfare recipients who were involved in a job training program, although they weren't obligated to hire them. Today's interviewee was Esther's first from the program. Office scuttlebutt said the candidates were pretty poorly qualified.

Esther found the girl's astonishment amusing. Why, the child couldn't even speak. "Were you expecting someone else?" Esther said.

"Oh, no. Well, I—" The girl stopped, and they both laughed. "I'm glad it's you," she said, and they chuckled again. "No, I mean, like, it makes me feel good to know that one of us is the boss. You know what I mean?"

"Yes, I know what you mean," Esther said. The girl seemed a little awkward. This was probably her first job interview. Esther felt a twinge of guilt, knowing that her mind was already made up. Thinking, she probably needs a job worse than old Alex Keaton, Esther extended her hand. When the girl shook it, Esther could feel her fingers trembling like a frightened kitten; then she felt something hard and sharp cutting into her palm. She looked down. Good God! Long. Curved. Bright Red with a capital R. And rhinestones were embedded in the pinkie nails. Genuine Hootchy Mama fingernails. "I'm Esther Jackson. Thank you for coming. Sit down, La . . . La . . ."

"LaKeesha. LaKeesha Jones." She talks so proper, LaKeesha thought. Just like a white woman.

LaKeesha sat down in the chair near the desk. Esther gave her a quick once-over. The dress was too tight and too short, but not awful. The girl's face was pleasant, even thought she wore too much makeup. The braids, well, they weren't the proper hairstyle for a black woman who wanted to get ahead in business. "Tell me a little about yourself, LaKeesha," Esther said. "Have you had any teller experience?"

LaKeesha took a breath, trying not be nervous in spite of the way Esther was looking at her. Her eyes were like fingers lifting her collar to check for dirt. LaKeesha attempted to concentrate. She'd been through a number of practice interviews. She paused, remembering what Mrs. Clark had told her: Look the person straight in her eyes; smile a lot; speak clearly; sell yourself; don't be nervous. But Esther's language, each word so precisely enunciated, was erecting a brick wall between them. There was nothing to be nervous about, LaKeesha told herself. She smiled at Esther. "I just, like, finished the South-Central Alternative Education Center's bank teller program. I was, like, you know, number one in my class. . . ."

An around-the-way girl if ever I saw one, Esther said to herself as she listened to LaKeesha describe her course work and a month-long internship at one of the city's banks. "The manager wanted to hire me, but they didn't have no openings at the time."

Esther flinched at the double negative. "Well," she said, getting a word in, "it certainly appears that you've been well trained. Tell me about the school you attended."

"See, I dropped out of high school after I had my baby. Then I met this lady named Mrs. Clark; her and her husband run the school, and so she talked me into going there to get my GED. She has a contract with the city to train people, so after I got my GED, I decided that I wanted to take the bank teller course, because, well, I'm on the county and I want to get off." LaKeesha sat back in her chair. She hadn't meant to talk so much, to get so personal. Mrs. Clark told her to be professional. Maybe she shouldn't have mentioned being on the county. She looked at Esther's black suit, the shiny low heels, and all that gold jewelry she wore, not the kind that screamed at you but a nice quiet gold. And words came out her mouth so sharp they could draw blood. She probably thought she was white, sitting up in her own office, being everybody's boss. She shouldn't have said anything about being on the county.

A baby, Esther thought. She could just hear the phone calls, the excuses: the baby is sick; the baby-sitter can't make it. Hiring a single mother with a baby—because of course she wasn't married—was asking for trouble. She looked at LaKeesha, who was staring at her uneasily. "Do you know TIPS?"

LaKeesha grinned. "That's what we was trained in."

Esther scratched the back of her neck. The child wasn't ready for prime time, and the bad thing about it was that she probably had no idea just how deficient she was. Esther thought fleetingly of what that asshole Fred Gaskins would say if he were listening to her conversation with LaKeesha. He'd say that LaKeesha was another product of a *substandard high school in South-Central*. She could just see the operations manager, his fat little lightbulb head bobbing back and forth, his bantam chest heaving in and out. Fred Gaskins can go to hell, she thought to herself. She glanced at her watch; ten o'clock. "Come with me, LaKeesha. I'd like to see what you can do."

Leading the young woman out the door to the operations area, Esther guided her past the customer reps' desks, around to the back of the tellers' cage. There were five people on duty. Hector Bonilla smiled in his usual polite manner as soon as he saw the two women approaching him. "Hector, I'd like you to meet LaKeesha Jones. Hector, LaKeesha and I have been chatting about the possibility of her becoming a teller here. I'd like for you two to work together for an hour or so, and then I'll come back for you, LaKeesha. Hector, may I see you for a second?"

Esther walked the young man a few feet away from his station. "Listen, I want you to really pay attention to how LaKeesha works. Look at the way she deals with customers, how she handles money, and how well she knows TIPS. I'll talk with you later, all right?"

"Yes, Esther," Hector said, nodding his head so vigorously that his straight black hair rippled over his forehead. In the eighteen months that he had been with the bank, Hector and proved himself to be a good worker, stable and serious. He always came early and stayed late. Esther knew she could depend upon him for a fair assessment. She might not hire LaKeesha this time, but if the girl had decent skills, she might consider her when there was another opening.

One hour later, Esther stepped outside her office, caught Hector's eye, and motioned him over. In a few moments, he appeared at her door, and she ushered him to a seat inside. "How did she do?" Esther asked.

"She is very good worker," Hector said solemnly, his dark, serious eyes looking straight into hers. "She is polite to customers. She is accurate with money. She knows the computer system too. I didn't have to tell her very much at all." His smile was as earnest and diffident as he was.

"Thank you, Hector. Would you tell LaKeesha to come to my office, please."

"Well, Hector told me you did very well," Esther said after LaKeesha settled herself into her chair. The young woman beamed. Esther asked her a few questions about the transactions she'd just made. Finally, she stood up and extended her hand. "I've enjoyed chatting with you, and I'll be in touch."

LaKeesha stood up. "My grandmother, she lives with me and she keeps my baby, even if he's sick, so you don't have to worry about that."

Esther nodded her head. "Well," she said, opening the door just a little wider, "that's just fine."

She felt the girl's eyes on her. "Just fine," Esther repeated, waiting for LaKeesha to leave.

The young woman stepped toward her. "I know I can do a good job for you. I'll come on time. I know how to be a good worker. I can smile at the customers and be polite and hand them their money. I want to work." She knew she was talking too much, that she should just leave, but the words seemed to be bubbling up from some spring. "My whole family's been on the county for as long as I can remember. I didn't tell none of

them where I was going, because I didn't want to get their hopes up. I want to be a good example for my younger sisters. They need to see somebody working," She paused and stood up straighter. "If I don't get this job, would you just please call me and, like, tell me what I did wrong, so I won't make the same mistake on the next interview? Because if I don't get this job, I'm gonna get me a job from somebody."

Esther hesitated a moment, then closed the door. "Sit down," she told LaKeesha.

"First of all, get rid of those fingernails. This is a place of business, not a nightclub. Second, your dress is too tight and too short, and your heels are too high. Third, you're wearing too much makeup. Fourth, your grammar is poor. It's 'I didn't tell *any* of them, not '*none* of them.' And don't say 'like' so much. And another thing: get rid of the braids. I think they're beautiful, but when you're working for white folks you want to fit in, not stand out." Seeing the distraught look on LaKeesha's face, Esther spoke a little more gently. "Now, everything I'm telling you can be corrected. It's up to you."

"If I change all those things, will you give me a job?" LaKeesha's expression was eager, hungry.

"I can't promise you that," Esther said quickly, "but I believe that if you make those adjustments, somebody will hire you. And don't think in terms of a job. You have to think about a career."

LaKeesha's eyes, which seemed to grow larger and more hopeful every minute, didn't leave Esther's face.

"You need to think: I'll start as a teller, then I'll become an operation assistant, then I'll get in the operations training program, and then I'll become an operations manager. That's the kind of mind-set employers want to see in an employee."

LaKeesha's face brightened, and she stood up. Before she realized what she was doing, she was hugging Esther and mumbling in her ear: "Thank you, sister."

Esther felt the word even more than she heard it. There was obligation in that word. And she didn't want any part of that.

She pulled away. "Don't ever call me that here," she said quickly. Esther watched as LaKeesha passed through the bank and out the door. Even after she left, the musky odor of TLC oil sheen spray clung to the air in the room. Esther knew the odor well; it was her scent too.

Esther closed her eyes. She could see herself making those fast deals. Lending millions just on her say-so. If she played her cards right, maybe she could be the one who'd transcend the glass ceiling. Every once in a while, they let somebody black slip through. Why shouldn't she be the one?

Esther walked around her desk with her hands clasped together in front of her and then behind her. She pictured LaKeesha's face, the yearning in her eyes. No, no, no! She wouldn't sacrifice her career in the name of racial solidarity. Forget it. She was going to pick up the phone and hire an acceptable white boy, with acceptable grammar and short fingernails, because that was the right move to make. The smart move.

Sister.

That and a dollar won't even get you a ride on the bus.

Esther picked up the telephone.

From *What You Owe Me*

Chapter 2 [The Braddock Hotel]

The Braddock Hotel was the rich old uncle of downtown Los Angeles. I'd never seen anything as grand in Inez, where the largest hotel was only three stories high and always needed a new coat of paint. Braddock was nearly fifty years old and took up half a city block; the entire front was beige marble, and the entrance was two huge glass doors. Inside there were fifteen floors and a gigantic ballroom. The lobby was grand, with two huge crystal chandeliers, exactly like the one that was in the ballroom. The walls were the color of cream and the carpet was a swirl of soft rose and green. Plush sofas, comfortable armchairs, and carved tables sitting on a soft rug—it was like a magazine picture. The guest rooms were spacious and furnished even more luxuriously than the lobby. Mostly businessmen came to Braddock, and the place got its share of conventions, too.

It was not far from the Hollywood Freeway. I was used to one-lane highways and dirt roads, but LA had the Hollywood and the Pasadena freeways, and more were being built every day, connecting different parts of the city and even the suburbs, which I'd only heard about. From the upper floors in Braddock I could look out the windows and watch cars that seemed to fly along the asphalt ribbon that was divided into three lanes. I'd never seen so many automobiles in my life, and the sight of them, the thrumming sound they made, excited me and made me imagine going places far away from brooms and mops.

By the time she'd been working at Braddock for a year, we all were used to Gilda's quiet ways. Mr. Weinstock put Gilda and me on the same shift. Some days we worked from five o'clock in the morning until two or three in the afternoon. Early morning was the time we washed the linens and towels and folded everything. We mopped the grand hotel lobby, polished all the marble and glass. Sometimes when I was giving her the ammonia our hands would touch. She had soft hands, and I wondered how long they would stay nice.

Thanksgiving rolled around again. The maids weren't looking forward to the holidays, at least not *working* them. There were always lots of parties and formal affairs at Braddock during this time. People would get plenty liquored up, and drunk people are not the most fastidious. This was the time of year we had to wipe up vomit and urine that didn't make it to the toilet bowl. And then, too, even though Los Angeles didn't have a real winter like the ones in Texas that could turn your skin the kind of gray colored folks call ashy, people still caught colds. A lot of the maids would stay out sick, and then Mr. Weinstock would put us on double shift. By Christmas we'd be too worn out to enjoy our own festivities. But what else was new?

The first weekend in December, Gilda and I both got put on midday and late shift, which meant we had to come in at one and we didn't go home until after midnight. You wouldn't think that there would be that much to do late at night but that's when Mr. Weinstock wanted us to wash windows, clean the mezzanine bathrooms, and change the big Chinese vases of flowers that were always in the lobby. It took two people to carry those vases. And he liked to have some maids on hand when there were big parties in the hotel. People would stay in bed all day and then go out at night, and when they came back they expected clean rooms.

That Saturday night around ten o'clock, Mr. Weinstock told us to go up to the sixth floor. Guests had just left, and two rooms needed to be made up. When we got there, the floor seemed deserted, except for Brewster, who did repairs. He was carrying his toolbox, standing in front of the service elevator when we got off. He smiled politely when he saw us, especially at Gilda. "How are you girls doing tonight?"

"Fine," we both said.

We chatted with him for a few minutes before we made our way down the hall.

I worked on one room and Gilda cleaned the other. They were only about three doors apart. Maybe because I trained Gilda, she and I had similar timing, and we'd end up at the carts together. That's where we were when the man came in holding the boy by the hand.

We both smelled evil at the same moment. The first thing that hit me was that the man was white and the boy, who must have been about seven or eight, was Mexican. He was a scrawny little kid, not dressed for the chilly weather. He was wearing shorts and an undershirt, and he had on sandals. His little legs and arms were dirty. The man was drunk, and the boy looked scared, the kind of scared that means he has to go along with the show because of the money that's waiting when the curtain comes down. I'd seen that fear before at Braddock, in the eyes of young hookers with old johns who stumbled down the hall beside them. I'd never seen that expression on a child's face, and to tell you the truth, I didn't want to look.

They went into the room between the ones we'd just made up. When the door closed, my eyes met Gilda's. She whispered, "He is a bad man." When she said the words her body started shaking, and she had to wipe away the moisture that started popping out on her forehead.

I knew he was a bad man but he was a bad *white* man, and he was a guest. I thought about calling Mr. Weinstock, but Ole Sweat and Farts wouldn't do anything to help a Mexican street kid if it meant offending a paying customer. I considered contacting the police, but then I'd have to give my name, take them to the room, and by that time the damage would be done. And if Mr. Weinstock found out, I could forget about my job, and my candy store.

Gilda walked right to the room. We could hear the boy crying, soft, pitiful sounds. I knocked on the door and said, "Is everything all right in there?" I tried to sound stern, like a teacher, which is what I would have been if my daddy had had money for college.

Before he could answer, Gilda had pulled out her key and opened the door. "Girrrrrrl," I said, and put my hand on her shoulder to hold her back. But she shook it off and walked in, and I followed her.

The room smelled like sour milk. The little boy was naked, lying on the bed facedown. The man was on top of him with his pants and shorts around his ankles. He jumped up. His penis was hard and red. His cheeks looked slapped. "What the hell are you doing in here?" he said. "Get out, the both of you."

"You stop hurting that boy," Gilda said.

"Get the hell outta here." He turned back to the child.

Gilda pulled something shiny out of her sweater pocket. When I saw it was a knife, I opened my mouth and couldn't close it, but not a sound came out. The next thing I knew she was stabbing the man in his ass.

He jumped up and grabbed himself, wiping off the blood and staring at Gilda as though he couldn't believe what he was seeing. Truth be told, I was looking at her the same way.

"Get out! Get out! Get out!" She was screaming, waving the knife. He started coming toward Gilda. I grabbed the table lamp and held it like I was going to bash his head in. He stopped when he saw me do that, then he started backing up toward the door, pulling up his pants. Crazy Gilda kept coming toward him, waving the knife so close to him that I was afraid he was going to take it away from her and I would have to hit him upside his head. But he kept backing up. She got right up on him and then her voice went down real low. She said, "You go tell. See what happens to you tonight. I have the key."

"Fucking bitch," he said, and with his next breath he turned to me. "Nigger." Then he fled out the door.

After he left, Gilda went over to the little boy. He was still crying and whimpering something in Spanish. We took

him in the bathroom, gave him a bath and washed his hair. Gilda dried him off and took a small bottle from her sweater pocket, poured something white and creamy in her palms, and started rubbing him all over with it. Then we helped him get dressed. He didn't say anything, but he wasn't crying anymore.

We took him down the back stairwell that led to the street. Outside the air was biting. Gilda took off her sweater and put it on the child, and we each gave him a dollar. Then we watched as he walked back to wherever he came from.

"Damn, girl," I said when we were riding up on the service elevator. I kept looking at her, trying to see what I couldn't see.

We were back in Our Room when I noticed the numbers on Gilda's arm, little blue tattooed numbers, a brand. Then I figured things out, but not all of it. Even on this side of the fence, there are some things I'll never understand.

We were sitting on the broken-down sofa. There was some church music playing in the background. Gilda started talking. Gilda loved gospel music and all kinds of hymns. The first time I played the Five Blind Boys for her, she started crying. On this night, The Mighty Clouds of Joy were singing a real slow song. I can't remember the name of it but the lyrics seemed to meld into her story. She told me how the Germans rounded up her family and put them in the death camps and how everybody she loved—her mother, father, brother, aunts, uncles, grandparents—had been killed. Her father's brother had settled in America before the war. When she was liberated she came to Los Angeles, because he and his wife lived here with their children. Four people were her only remaining relatives. It was her uncle who got her the job. Mr. Weinstock's brother owned the apartment building where they lived.

Her crying started as a tiny, weak noise, like a newborn might make. Came from way down inside her somewhere and then kept rising and getting deeper. I pulled her into my chest and held her, rubbed her back a little, told her not to be afraid, that everything was all right now. I spoke the words as soon as they came to my mind. "You need to take those numbers off your arm."

She sat up, looked at me, then cried a little bit more. She said, "I have no one, no one, no one," the words an echo that kept turning on itself.

"You do have someone," I said. "You have *you*. And you have what's *in* you. That's how you survived, girl."

Gilda didn't say anything for a long time. Then she looked at me and said, "Will you take me to get it done?"

I took her to the dentist first. The way I figured, the sooner she started smiling, the better for her. I asked her if she knew of any dentists in her neighborhood but she looked troubled and told me that we couldn't go there. So, one day after work, I took her to a colored dentist over on Central Avenue. He seemed surprised to see the two of us together, but that was just in his eyes. He didn't say anything. She had to go back a couple of times but he cleaned her teeth, got all the brown off, and when she smiled that first time, she looked pretty, not like Lana Turner or Liz Taylor, or any of the movie stars or models. She had her own special kind of frizzy-haired beauty, which wasn't even American, at least not yet.

We went to a tattoo parlor not too far from the dentist and the owner examined the numbers under a magnifying glass, and then patted her arm the same kind of way my daddy used to when I fell down or was crying. He told her that whatever he could do for her would leave a scar. Gilda hesitated, then she said, "Go head." I guess she figured that the numbers were the worst scar. He used needles and some kind of acid. Gilda was moaning a little bit the entire time he was working on her. She grabbed my hand while he was doing it, and she liked to squeezed me to death.

Riding the bus on our way back from the tattoo place, I told her about Inez. Gilda said it was another kind of death camp, that the poison gas came out in spurts, not enough to kill the body, just the soul. She had a lot of questions for me. She wanted to know why colored people couldn't go certain places, why our hair wasn't as long as white people's, why our voices sounded different from theirs. I didn't have all the answers but I did my best.

"They are envious of you," she told me.

"Who?"

"The white people."

"Why?"

"Because you have the most beautiful skin. White people sit in the sun to try to get your color. Your features, your lips

and nose, are warm. You make wonderful music. And your spirit is powerful. They try to crush your spirit, but they can't."

We never heard from the man Gilda stabbed, and she and I never mentioned him. I found myself looking whenever I saw a group of Mexicans, but I didn't see the little boy again either. Gilda and I seemed to be together a lot more after what happened. When we had lunch at the same time, we ate side by side. Sometimes at the end of our break, she'd pull out a book and start reading. She still studied from the English manual, but she read other things as well. Her books were about history and science, and she liked novels, too. Often she'd read a portion to me and get me so interested in the story that when she finished, I'd pick it up. A couple of times, Fern would ask me what I was reading, and I'd share it with her.

Gilda told me that she had been attending college when the war broke out. "I studied literature," she said, and there was sadness in her voice.

I hadn't ever had enough time to read just for the pure pleasure of it, but that's one hobby I acquired from Gilda. As I read, I became aware of mistakes that I was making when I spoke, and I began to improve, little by little. In a way, I started sounding like Thomasine, who Tuney had broken up with, thank God.

The other maids noticed the new way I was speaking. One time when I finished saying something, Winnie said, "La-di-da," and looked toward Hattie, who was muttering under her breath that I was trying to be white. She knew better than to say it to my face. But those "la-di-das" put an alley between the other women and me. Gilda and I were walking down the main boulevard together.

Terry McMillan (b. 1951)

When Terry McMillan published *Waiting to Exhale* (1992), she became a household name and started a publishing bonanza of texts by African American women writers. Made into a very popular film of the same name, *Waiting to Exhale* is the story of four women who are trying to make sense of their love lives. While looking for more meaningful relationships, they hold deep breaths, "waiting to exhale." McMillan's first novel, *Mama* (1987), is a humorous, down-to-earth story of a woman who keeps her five children together, even as the men in her life come and go. Begun as a short story, *Mama* evolved into a novel during McMillan's stints at the MacDowell and Yaddo artist colonies. In *Disappearing Acts* (1989), two characters, Zora and Franklin, tell their love story. The novel deals with a situation that has become a common issue—the problems and rewards of an educated woman dating a high school dropout. McMillan's next novel, *How Stella Got Her Groove Back* (1996) was also adapted into a very popular film. Stella, a forty-two-year-old woman, goes to Jamaica and forms a love relationship with a twenty-year-old man, who returns home with her. *A Day Late and A Dollar Short* (2001) uses six voices to tell a story about a family facing a range of problems. Known for writing characters that everyone seems to know, McMillan has become one of the more popular authors in African American literature. She has edited the acclaimed anthology, *Breaking Ice: An Anthology of Contemporary African-American Fiction* (1990). McMillan was born in Port Huron, Michigan, and earned her B.S. from Berkeley and her M.F.A. from Columbia University.

Ma'Dear

(For Estelle Ragsdale)

Last year the cost of living crunched me and I got tired of begging from Peter to pay Paul, so I took in three roomers. Two of 'em is live-in nurses and only come around here on weekends. Even then they don't talk to me much, except when they hand me their money orders. One is from Trinidad and the other is from Jamaica. Every winter they quit their jobs, fill up two and three barrels with I don't know what, ship 'em home, and follow behind on an airplane. They come back in the spring and start all over. Then there's the little college girl, Juanita, who claims she's going for architecture. Seem like to me that was always men's work, but I don't say nothing. She grown.

I'm seventy-two. Been a widow for the past thirty-two years. Weren't like I asked for all this solitude: just that couldn't nobody else take Jessie's place is all. He knew it. And I knew it. He fell and hit his head real bad on the tracks going to fetch us some fresh picked corn and okra for me to make us some succotash, and never come to. I couldn't picture myself with no other man, even though I looked after a few years

of being alone in this big old house, walking from room to room with nobody to talk to, cook or clean for, and not much company either.

I missed him for the longest time and thought I could find a man just like him, sincerely like him, but I couldn't. Went out for a spell with Esther Davis's ex-husband, Whimpy, but he was crazy. Drank too much bootleg and then started memorizing on World War I and how hard he fought and didn't get no respect and not a ounce of recognition for his heroic deeds. The only war Whimpy been in is with me for not keeping him around. He bragged something fearless about how he coulda been the heavyweight champion of he world. Didn't weigh but 160 pounds and shorter than me.

Chester Rutledge almost worked 'ceptin' he was boring, never had nothing on his mind worth talking about; claimed he didn't think about nothing besides me. Said his mind was always clear and visible. He just moved around like a zombie and worked hard at the cement foundry. Insisted on giving me his paychecks, which I kindly took for a while, but when I didn't want to be bothered no more, I stopped taking his money. He got on my nerves too bad, so I had to tell him I'd rather have a man with no money and a busy mind, least I'd know he's active somewheres. His feelings was hurt bad and he cussed me out, but we still friends to this very day. He in the home, you know, and I visits him regular. Takes him

From *Callaloo*, © 1990, The Johns Hopkins University Press.

366

magazines and cuts out his horoscope and the comic strips from the newspaper and lets him read 'em in correct order.

Big Bill Ronsonville tried to convince me that I shoulda married him instead of Jessie, but he couldn't make me a believer of it. All he wanted to do was put his big rusty hands all on me without asking and smile at me with that big gold tooth sparkling and glittering in my face and tell me how lavish I was, lavish being a new word he just learnt. He kept wanting to take me for night rides way out in the country, out there by Smith Creek where ain't nothing but deep black ditches, giant mosquitoes, loud crickets, lightning bugs, and loose pigs, and turn off his motor. His breath stank like whiskey though he claimed and swore on the Bible he didn't drank no liquor. Aside from that his hands were way too heavy and hard, hurt me, sometimes left red marks on me like I been sucked on. I told him finally that I was too light for him, that I needed a smaller, more gentle man, and he said he knew exactly what I meant.

If you want to know the truth, after him I didn't think much about men the way I used too. Lost track of the ones who upped and died or the ones who couldn't do nothing if they was alive nohow. So, since nobody else seemed to be able to wear Jessie's shoes, I just stuck to myself all these years.

My life ain't so bad now 'cause I'm used to being alone and takes good care of myself. Occasionally I still has a good time. I goes to the park and sits for hours in good weather, watch folks move and listen in on confidential conversations. I add up numbers on license plates to keep my mind alert unless they pass too fast. This gives me a clear idea of how many folks is visiting from out of town. I can about guess the color of every state now, too. Once or twice a month I go to the matinee on Wednesdays, providing ain't no long line of senior citizens 'cause they can be so slow; miss half the picture show waiting for them to count their change and get their popcorn.

Sometimes, when I'm sitting in the park, I feed the pigeons old cornbread crumbs, and I wonders what it'll be like not looking at the snow falling from the sky, not seeing the leaves form on the trees, not hearing no car engines, no sirens, no babies crying, not brushing my hair at night, drinking my Lipton tea, and not being able to go to bed early.

But right now, to tell you the truth, it don't bother me all *that* much. What is bothering me is my case worker. She supposed to pay me a visit tomorrow because my nosy neighbor, Clarabelle, saw two big trucks outside, one come right after the other, and she wondered what I was getting so new and so big that I needed trucks. My mama used to tell me that sometimes you can't see for looking. Clarabelle's had it out to do me in ever since last spring when I had the siding put on the house. I used the last of Jessie's insurance money 'cause the roof had been leaking so bad and the wood rotted

and the paint chipped so much that it looked like a wicked old witch lived here. The house looked brand-new, and she couldn't stand to see an old woman's house looking better than hers. She know I been had roomers, and now all of a sudden my case worker claim she just want to visit to see how I'm doing, when really what she want to know is what I'm up to. Clarabelle work in her office.

The truth is my boiler broke and they was here to put in a new one. We liked to froze to death in here for two days. Yeah, I had a little chump change in the bank, but when they told me it was gonna cost $2,000 to get some heat, I cried. I had $862 in the bank; $300 of it I had just spent on this couch I got on sale; it was in the other truck. After twenty years the springs finally broke, and I figured it was time to buy a new one 'cause I ain't one for living in poverty, even at my age. I figured $200 was for my church's cross-country bus trip this summer.

Jessie's sister, Willamae, took out a loan for me to get the boiler, and I don't know how long it's gonna take me to pay her back. She only charge me fifteen or twenty dollars a month, depending. I probably be dead by the time it get down to zero.

My bank wouldn't give me the loan for the boiler, but then they keep sending me letters almost every week trying to get me to refinance my house. They must think I'm senile or something. On they best stationery, they write me. They say I'm up in age and wouldn't I like to take that trip I've been putting off because of no extra money. What trip? They tell me if I refinance my house for more than what I owe, which is about $3,000, that I could have enough money left over to go anywhere. Why would I want to refinance my house at fourteen and a half percent when I'm paying four and a half now? I ain't that stupid. They say dream about clear blue water, palm trees, and orange suns. Last night I dreamt I was doing a backstroke between big blue waves and tipped my straw hat down over my forehead and fell asleep under an umbrella. They made me think about it. And they asked me what would I do if I was to die today? They're what got me to thinking about all this dying mess in the first place. It never would've layed in my mind so heavy if they hadn't kept reminding me of it. Who would pay off your house? Wouldn't I feel bad leaving this kind of a burden on my family? What family they talking about? I don't even know where my people is no more.

I ain't gonna lie. It ain't easy being old. But I ain't complaining neither, 'cause I learned how to stretch my social security check. My roomers pay the house note and I pay the taxes. Oil is sky-high. Medicaid pays my doctor bills. I got a letter what told me to apply for food stamps. That case worker come here and checked to see if I had a real kitchen. When she saw I had a stove and sink and refrigerator, she didn't like the idea that my house was almost paid for, and just knew I was lying about having roomers. "Are you certain that you reside here alone?" she asked me. "I'm certain," I said. She searched every inch of my cabinets to make sure I didn't have two of the same kinds of food, which would've been a dead giveaway. I hid it all in the basement inside the washing machine and dryer. Luckily, both of the nurses was in the islands at the time, and Juanita was visiting some boy what live in D.C.

After she come here and caused me so much eruptions, I had to make trip after trip down to that office. They had me filling out all kinds of forms and still held up my stamps. I got tired of answering the same questions over and over and finally told 'em to keep their old food stamps. I ain't got to beg nobody to eat. I know how to keep myself comfortable and clean and well fed. I manage to buy my staples and toiletries and once in a while a few extras, like potato chips, ice cream, and maybe a pork chop.

My mama taught me when I was young that, no matter how poor you are, always eat nourishing food and your body will last. Learn to conserve, she said. So I keeps all my empty margarine containers and stores white rice, peas and carrots (my favorites), or my turnips from the garden in there. I can manage a garden when my arthritis ain't acting up. And water is the key. I drinks plenty of it like the doctor told me, and I cheats, eats Oreo cookies and saltines. They fills me right up, too. And when I feels like it, rolls, homemade biscuits, eats them with Alga syrup if I can find it at the store, and that sticks with me most of the day.

Long time ago, used to be I'd worry like crazy about gaining weight and my face breaking out from too many sweets, and about cellulite forming all over my hips and thighs. Of course, I was trying to catch Jessie then, though I didn't know it at the time. I was really just being cute, flirting, trying to see if I could get attention. Just so happens I lucked up and got all of his. Caught him like he was a spider and I was the web.

Lord, I'd be trying to look all sassy and prim. Have my hair all did, it be curled tight in rows that I wouldn't comb out for hours till they cooled off after Connie Curtis did it for a dollar and a Budweiser. Would take that dollar out my special savings, which I kept hid under the record player in the front room. My hair used to be fine, too: long and thick and black, past my shoulders, and mens used to say, "Girl, you sure got a head of hair on them shoulders there, don't it make your neck sweat?" But I didn't never bother answering, just blushed and smiled and kept on walking, trying hard not to switch 'cause mama told me my behind was too big for my age and to watch out or I'd be luring grown mens toward me. Humph! I loved it, though, made me feel pretty, special, like I had attraction.

Ain't quite the same no more, though. I looks in the mirror at myself and I sees wrinkles, lots of them, and my skin look like it all be trying to run down toward my toes but then it changed its mind and just stayed there, sagging and laugging, laying limp against my thick bones. Shoot, mens used to say how sexy I was with these high cheeks, tell me I looked swollen, like I was pregnant, but it was just me, being all healthy and everything. My teeth was even bright white and straight in a row then. They ain't so bad now, 'cause ain't none of 'em mine. But I only been to the dentist twice in my whole life and that was 'cause on Easter Sunday I was in so much pain he didn't have time to take no X-ray and yanked it right out 'cause my mama told him to do anything he had to shut me up. Second time was the last time, and that was 'cause the whole top row and the fat ones way in the back on the bottom ached me so bad the dentist yanked 'em all out so I wouldn't have to be bothered no more.

Don't get me wrong, I don't miss being young. I did everything I wanted to do and then some. I loved hard. But you take Jessie's niece, Thelma. She pitiful. Only twenty-six, don't think she made it past the tenth grade, got three children by different men, no husband and on welfare. Let her tell it, ain't nothing out here but dogs. I know some of these men out here ain't worth a pot to piss in, but all of 'em ain't dogs. There's gotta be some young Jessies floating somewhere in this world. My mama always told me you gotta have something to give if you want to get something in return. Thelma got long fingernails.

Me, myself, I didn't have no kids. Not 'cause I didn't want none or couldn't have none, just that Jessie wasn't full and couldn't give me the juices I needed to make no babies. I accepted it 'cause I really wanted him all to myself, even if he couldn't give me no new bloodlines. He was satisfying enough for me, quite satisfying if you don't mind me repeating myself.

I don't understand Thelma, like a lot of these young peoples. I be watching 'em on the streets and on TV. I be hearing things they be doing to themselves when I'm under the dryer at the beauty shop. (I go to the beauty shop once a month 'cause it make me feel like thangs ain't over yet. She give me a henna so the silver have a gold tint to it.) I can't afford it, but there ain't too many luxuries I can. I let her put makeup on me, too, if it's a Saturday and I feel like doing some window shopping. I still know how to flirt and sometimes I get stares, too. It feel good to be looked at and admired at my age. I try hard to keep myself up. Every weekday morning at five-thirty I do exercises with the TV set, when it don't hurt to stretch.

But like I was saying, Thelma and these young people don't look healthy, and they spirits is always so low. I watch 'em on the streets, on the train, when I'm going to the doctor. I looks in their eyes and they be red or brown where they supposed to be milky white and got bags deeper and heavier than mine, and I been through some thangs. I hear they be using these drugs of variety, and I can't understand why they need to use all these thangs to get from day to day. From what I do hear, it's supposed to give 'em much pleasure and make their minds disappear or make 'em not feel the thangs they supposed to be feeling anyway.

Heck, when I was young, we drank sarsaparilla and couldn't even buy no no wine or any kind of liquor in no store. These youngsters ain't but eighteen and twenty and buys anything with a bite to it. I've seen 'em sit in front of the store and drank a whole bottle in one sitting. Girls, too.

We didn't have no dreams of carrying on like that, and specially on no corner. We was young ladies and young men with respect for ourselfs. And we didn't smoke none of them funny cigarettes all twisted up with no filters that smell like burning dirt. I ask myself, I say Ma'Dear, what's wrong with these kids? They can read and write and do arithmetic, finish high school, go to college and get letters behind their names, but every day I hear the neighbors complain that one of they youngsters done dropped out.

Lord, what I wouldn'ta done to finish high school and been able to write a full sentence or even went to college. I reckon I'da been a room decorator. I know they calls it by that fancy name now, interior designer, but it boil down to the same thing. I guess it's 'cause I loves so to make my surroundings pleasant, even right pretty, so I feels like a invited guest in my own house. And I always did have a flair for color. Folks used to say, "Hazel, for somebody as poor as a church mouse, you got better taste in thangs than them Rockefellers!" Used to sew up a storm, too. Covered my mama's raggedy duffold and chairs. Made her a bedspread with matching pillowcases. Didn't mix more than two different patterns either. Make you dizzy.

Wouldn't that be just fine, being an interior designer? Learning the proper names of thangs and recognizing labels in catalogs, giving peoples my business cards and wearing a two-piece with white gloves. "Yes, I decorated the Hartley's and Cunninghams' home. It was such a pleasant experience. And they're such lovely people, simply lovely," I'da said. Coulda told those rich folks just what they needed in their bedrooms, front rooms, and specially in the kitchen. So many of 'em still don't know what to do in there.

But like I was saying before I got all off the track, some of these young people don't appreciate what they got. And they don't know thangs like we used to. We knew about eating fresh vegetables from the garden, growing and picking 'em ourselves. What going to church was, being honest and faithful. Trusting each other. Leaving our front door open. We knew what it was like to starve and get cheated yearly when our crops didn't add up the way we figured. We suffered together, not separately. These youngsters don't know about suffering for any stretch of time. I hear 'em on the train complaining 'cause they can't afford no Club Med, no new record playing albums, cowboy boots, or those Brooke Shields—Calvin Klein blue jeans I see on TV. They be complaining about nonsense. Do they ever read books since they been taught is what I want to know? Do they be learning things and trying to figure out what to do with it?

And these young girls with all this thick makeup caked on their faces, wearing these high heels they can't hardly walk in. Trying to be cute. I used to wear high heels, mind you, with silk stockings, but at least I could walk in 'em. Jessie had a car then. Would pick me up, and I'd walk real careful down the front steps like I just won the Miss America pageant, one step at a time, and slide into his shiny black Ford. All the neighbors peeked through the curtains 'cause I was sure enough riding in a real automobile with my legitimate boyfriend.

If Jessie was here now I'd have somebody to talk to. Somebody to touch my skin. He'd probably take his fingers and run 'em through my hair like he used to; kiss me on my nose and tickle me where it made me laugh. I just loved it when he kissed me. My mind be so light, and I felt tickled and precious. Have to sit down sometime just to get hold of myself.

If he was here, I probably woulda beat him in three games of checkers by now and he'd be trying to get even. But since today is Thursday, I'd be standing in that window over there waiting for him to get home from work, and when I got tired or the sun be in my eyes, I'd hear the taps on his wing tips coming up the front porch. Sometime, even now, I watch for him, but I know he ain't coming back. Not that he wouldn't if he could, mind you, 'cause he always told me I made him feel lightning lighting up his heart.

Don't get me wrong, I got friends, though a heap of 'em is dead or got tubes coming out of their noses or going all through their bodies every which-a-way. Some in the old folks' home. I thank the Lord I ain't stuck in one of them places. I ain't never gonna get that old. They might as well just bury me standing up if I do. I don't want to be no nuisance to nobody, and I can't stand being around a lot of sick people for too long.

I visits Gunther and Chester when I can, and Vivian who I grew up with, but no soon as I walk through them long hallways, I get depressed. They lay there all limp and helpless, staring at the ceiling like they're really looking at something, or sitting stiff in their rocking chairs, pitiful, watching TV and don't be knowing what they watching half the time. They laugh when ain't nothing funny. They wait for it to get dark so they know it's time to go to sleep. They relatives don't hardly come visit 'em, just folks like me. Whimpy don't understand a word I say, and it makes me grateful I ain't lost no more than I have.

Sometime we sits on the sun porch rocking like fools; don't say one word to each other for hours. But last time

Gunther told me about his grandson what got accepted to Stanford University, and another one at a university in Michigan. I asked him where was Stanford and he said he didn't know. "What difference do it make?" he asked. "It's one of those uppity schools for rich smart white people," he said. "The important thang is that my black grandson won a scholarship there, which mean he don't have to pay a dime to go." I told him I know what a scholarship is. I ain't stupid. Gunther said he was gonna be there for at least four years or so, and by that time he would be a professional. "Professional what?" I asked. "Who cares, Ma'Dear, he gonna be a professional at whatever it is he learnt." Vivian started mumbling when she heard us talking, 'cause she still like to be the center of attention. When she was nineteen she was Miss Springfield Gardens. Now she can't stand the thought that she old and wrinkled. She started yakking about all the places she'd been to, even described the landscape like she was looking at a photograph. She ain't been but twenty-two miles north of here in her entire life, and that's right there in that home.

Like I said, and this is the last time I'm gonna mention it. I don't mind being old, it's just that sometime I don't need all this solitude. You can't do everything by yourself and expect to have as much fun if somebody was there doing it with you. That's why when I'm feeling jittery or melancholy for long stretches, I read the Bible, and it soothes me. I water my morning glories and amaryllis. I baby-sit for Thelma every now and then, 'cause she don't trust me with the kids for too long. She mainly call on holidays and my birthday. And she the only one who don't forget my birthday: August 19th. She tell me I'm a Leo, that I got fire in my blood. She may be right, 'cause once in a while I gets a churning desire to be smothered in Jessie's arms again.

Anyway, it's getting late, but I ain't tired. I feel pretty good. That old case worker think she gonna get the truth out of me. She don't scare me. It ain't none of her business that I got money coming in here besides my social security check. How they 'spect a human being to live off $369 a month in this day and age is what I wanna know. Every time I walk out my front door it cost me at least two dollars. I bet she making thousands and got credit cards galore. Probably got a summer house on the Island and goes to Florida every January. If she found out how much I was getting from my roomers, the government make me pay back a dollar for every two I made. I best to get my tail on upstairs and clear everything off their bureaus. I can hide all the nurse's stuff in the attic; they won't be back till next month. Juanita been living out of trunks since she got here, so if the woman ask what's in 'em, I'll tell her, old sheets and pillowcases and memories.

On second thought, I think I'm gonna take me a bubble bath first, and dust my chest with talcum powder, then I'll make myself a hot cup of Lipton's and paint my fingernails clear 'cause my hands feel pretty steady. I can get up at five and do all that other mess; case worker is always late anyway. After she leave, if it ain't snowing too bad, I'll go to the museum and look at the new paintings in the left wing. By the time she get here, I'ma make out like I'm a lonely old widow stuck in a big old house just sitting here waiting to die.

Julie Dash (b. 1952)

Julie Dash's film, *Daughters of the Dust* (1992), won Best Cinematography at the Sundance Film Festival. Dash has won many awards including the Oscar Micheaux, Black Filmmakers Hall of Fame, Best Independent Producer, Maya Deren, and the American Film Institute award. She grew up in a housing project in Long Island City, New York, and studied film at New York University, the American Film Institute, and the University of California. *Daughters of the Dust*, independently produced, was the first commercial feature-length film produced by a black woman. Set in the Sea Island off the Georgia–South Carolina coast, the film chronicles the life of the Peazant family, whose daily lives confront their Ibo heritage and the impending exodus of many of the family members to mainland USA. Following the film, Dash published the screenplay and in 1997, the novel adaptation. Her other short films include *Four Women* (1975), *Diary of an African Nun* (1977), and *Illusions* (1983). Dash is also screenwriter, producer, and director of documentaries and music videos performed by Peabo Bryson, Sweet Honey in the Rock, Tracy Chapman, and others.

From *Daughters of the Dust*

The Story of Ibo Landing

As told by Ben Peazant

When I was a lil boy, dere was an ol man live on de beach. Him name Paymore. Him one of de elders, good friend wit Nana. Folks say de elders use to sit in Nana yard an talk bout de ol days, use some of dem ol words, have a good time wit each other. You know, I never see Nana. Her pass on fore I come. But I know she. Everybody come from she, know she.

Paymore, him come over on one of de las ships bring de captives cross de big water. Him a funny ol man. Him got heself a lil shack on de beach and live dere all de days. Big storm come and knock down dat shack plenty times, him build it right back. Daddy say to he, "Paymore, why don you build dat house back in de woods where you got some cover from de big storm?" Him laugh, say, "Dat my place, right dere! I know my fambly right cross de water!" And him go right on, build dat house in de same spot. Daddy shake he head an jus keep on helpin he build dat house in de same spot.

What I member was dat him can read. Wasnt none of dem elders could read. Dint need to. But Paymore can read. All day long him walk roun carryin de book him have from when him come over. I remember dere was some pictures in

it. Him have a fair han at picture makin. Sometime him make picture in de sand for we; tree, strange houses, big boats, plenty women. Him tell we to run through dem real fast fore de waves wash dem away. Course we like dat!

Often times him stop by de house, him stand at de edge of de yard an watch all we chilren runnin roun, screamin an playin, raisin all kinds of noise. Him laugh jus to see us play. Mama always bring he a plate of food, an him always say something make she blush.

You know how bold Lucy is. One day him standin dere, laughing at we, an she go over to he an say, "Why you always laughing at we?" Mama mad cause Lucy so bold! But ol Paymore, him dont mind none. Him jus laugh an say, "I see de faces of Africa! When I see yall runnin roun like dat, I see all de faces of Africa!" Course Lucy took a whippin behin dat.

I dint know what him mean when him say dat. It wasnt till I come up on my time an Daddy sen me to Paymore to learn de ways of bein a man dat I see what him mean. For long time, ever boy-child get send to Paymore to learn de ol ways, de secret ways been passed down from one to de next. Paymore, him know all de ways. Like I say, him come straight from dere to here. So him de one teach we. Now dat him gone, I don know who gonna teach de ol ways. Dont nobody know all of it like Paymore. Gal, I aint tellin dem secrets! Him tell de secrets, struck dead in de middle of de night!

Well, him build a big fire on de beach, an us all sit roun an listen to what him got to say. Him point at we and say, "Fida, Ewe, Kisse, Mende, Gola, Ibo . . . All de faces of Africa right here cross de Big Water! Fida known for de cunning; Akan de fightin spirit; Ewe de hard worker, can grow jus bout everting; Kisse comely, sweet-nature women, learn fast, good in de house; Gola tall, strong, dark like de bark of de walla tree, not run off, not sickly like de po sad Ibo. Ibo, lil, de color of dark honey, melancholy run all through de Ibo." Him know we, him know where us ol people come from back in Africa. Him look at de face, an him can tell where de family stolen from. I ask he how him come to know all dis, an for de first time him not smile, "I put dem on de boats."

Paymore come from long line of captives. Dey been captives from de beginning. It all him people know. De work of de gatherin de captives dey pass on from one to de other. Him learn when him a lil one running in he daddy footsteps. Him say dey live in de place where many captives come to be put on de boats dat cross de big water. It a big place, bigger dan Charleston, him say, get big off de money come from gatherin de captives. Him know how to look at de turn of de head, de bend in de back, de flash in de eye, an him could tell whether a body is good for de field or de house. Him know how dey is, which one gonna run, which one gonna fight, which one gonna steal he soul back. Men come through offer plenty money for Paymore, but him master say, "No!"

Paymore plenty proud of de work him do. Now, he master, him no trust de captain on de boat. Him sen Paymore an him own son on de boat to see to he business. An you know, de master right! Paymore say dat boat get out on de big water, an de captain kill de son an throw Paymore down dere wit de other captives. It like to drove Paymore out of he min! In de ol land, him a captive, but long as him do de good work for he master, him almos free. Could come an go like him please. Him eat de same food as he master. Him take de same lesson as he master children when dey lil. Dat how he learn to read an cipher like him do. Now him down in de hole, praying to be God to save he!

Him say it a terrible ting. Caint nobody magine de sickness of it, treat like dey aint got no souls whatsoever! De captain make Paymore an de others take out de ones who pass over an throw dem in de big water. Paymore say de big shark follow de boat all de way cross, jus waitin on dem bodies to fall. Sometime dey not pass over an dey jump in de big water, trying to get back to dey family, dey home, to Africa! It misery all over! Paymore never know de misery til he in it heself.

De boat finally land in de place him call Brazil. Paymore say dey many captives dere. Seem like every tongue heard dere! Plenty Akan dere, too! De Akan always takin off to de woods, an de buckra caint find dem. One day Paymore workin in de fiel, an dis woman come up on him. Her carryin de water. Her look at he an den throw dat water an come after he. Her try to fight he! Rain curses down on he an he family cause he de one put she an she baby on de boat! Baby die. Woman fix it so her can have no more chilren be sold to de buckra. Paymore, he shame. Him see what all he work come to.

Den de sickness come. Folks fallin sick an dyin like flies. Buckra an captives. Now, you know what him say? Him say de captives call up an old conjure man from Africa. Dat ol man take the water from de sores from the sickness, an him scratch folks an put dat water on dem, an dose folks dont get de sickness. Dat what him say!

Paymore catch de sickness, an him glad. Him ready to pass over cause dis worl too bad for he. Him send de conjure man away. Him lay dere too weak to eat, caint hardly draw breath, feelin he spirit bout to fly. But who come dere but dat woman. Her say he aint goin no place so easy. Her gonna see dat him live wit de misery him cause.

Oh, yea, her brought he back. Him almos gone, but her pull he back. You got to know wasnt a lick of kindness in what her do for Paymore. It hate drive she to it.

De next ting him know dey back on de boat. Seem dat de captain hear dey more money to be made up dis way, so him head on out. Sick as dey still was, it dint make no difference to de captain. Him bring dem up to Charleston. Take dem off at night. Put dem in de pens out back so folks not see how bad dey is.

Dey fill dem with flour water to make dem not look so poorly. It one of de worse tings dey can do, dey die all the quicker. De captain man he mad cause he not gonna get de money he want from dem. Paymore watch he dicker wit de man in de money house. Paymore laugh when he tell dis part. It a funny laugh like he hurt in de body. De captain sell dem for lil or nuttin, and Paymore say him shame cause him know dey worth more dan de captain get. Den him shame cause him still tinkin de way like did fore him cross de big water.

Dey brung dem out here. Paymore say him never see place where de lan float on de water like dis an de water everywhere. De place him come from dry as de bone, wind blow all de time. De water come everyday, him tink dey gonna float back over de big water. But him say it remin him of home cause him dont hardly see no buckra out here. Aint nothin but captives live out here. Caint hardly no buckra cept maybe de Boss Man live out here cause de sickness in de water run dem out. Only de captive can stan de sickness out here. He see captive from everywhere living out here, Fida, Ewe, Kisse, Mende, Gola, and Mandingo! Dey out dere turnin de land, build de house, drain de field for de rice. Everting dey learn back in dey own place, dey do here. Fida known for raising de rice, dey raise de rice. Gola make de basket. Kisse build de boat, make de net, an fish de waters, can catch anyting! Paymore shame cause all him know to gather an sell de captive, an aint nobody out dere got use for dat. It a shame him carry all he days.

Him work de fields, clear de land. It hard work, but dat all right wit he. Him too tired to tink bout how he come to dis. But one day him come in from de field, an dey new captives dere, just come in. He look at dem an see dey Ibo. He shake he head. De Ibo, dont nobody who know bout sellin de captive want de Ibo. Dey lil people, hard to make to work, given to de sickness of de min. Him never see an Ibo laugh, only cry an wail, lookin back over de water to dey place. Soon as dey snatch away from dey place, de Ibo sen dey spirit to go home. Him look in dey eyes an see dey spirit done gone back home.

Dey put de Ibo men to work in de fields, but it no good. Dey lay down an not get up even when dey beat half to death. It like dey want to die, an dey help demselves to it. Dey put dem to all kinds of work, but dey no good for nuttin. Dey set de Ibo women to work in de yard, an it not much better. De other captives mad wit dem cause when de Boss Man mad wit dey, it bad for everybody. Paymore him tell de Boss Man dey fair builders, an de Boss Man put dem to work carryin de wood for de new landing. De ol landing blow way wit de big storm. Even Paymore hisself surprise at how dey help wit de landing. Him say dey want to work through de night, but de Boss Man stop dem. It not long dat dey hear de Ibo say dey buildin de landing to take dem back home. It gonna go cross de big water an everbody gonna be back home. Paymore know it foolishness, but it aint in he heart to say no different. If dat what dey need to keep dey minds strong, him not say nuttin.

When de Boss Man say dey finished, de Ibo start wailin an carryin on. Cryin so dat de birds in de trees stop de callin, de animals in de woods run for cover, all de work stop cause de cryin hurt so bad. De Ibo women come from de garden an walk on de landing to be wit de men. When dey start de wailin, even de Boss Man scared, de cryin so fierce. Him tell dem to get off de landing, but dey dont hear he! Him call to de other captives to get de Ibo off de landing, but dey too scared cause dey hear another sound, bigger dan de one de Ibo makin. Paymore swear it come from cross de big water! It coming for de Ibo! It cuttin through de other captives like an evil spirit, take dey strength away, weak dey minds. Dey know it carry de hex from all de Ibo! De Boss Man havin a fit cause nobody want to mess wit de Ibo!

Dey stop dey crying all de sudden. Everting stay quiet! All de Ibo start to walk to down de landing headed to dey home. De Boss Man try to stop dey, but dey walk right through he! Das what Paymore say! Dey go through he like dey a summer breeze. Him holler for de others to come help he, but de other captives can see de Ibo walk right in he front an come out he back. Dey aint messin wit dat! Oh, no! Dey step off de landing an start to walk cross de water, head for home. De other captives run to see the Ibo walk de water. Dey walkin all right! Caint nobody say dey aint walkin de water. De Boss Man hair turn white as cotton when him see dem walk de water. Now dey get aways out, an de other captives dey run to follow dem, but when dey step off de landin dey fall in de water. Dey pull some of de captives from de water, but some just gone like dat! Everbody watch dem Ibos cross de water til dey couldnt see dem no more.

Folks look to where the Ibo go an see the sky turn black an start to boil like a stew pot. It seem like de sky an de water come together an is comin for dem! Dey run to dey house an hide from de madness to come! De Boss Man hide wit dey, an Paymore say he worse dan a lil one cryin to he Lord to save he! De madness tear de roof off de house an reach down to snatch de weak ones! De water wash all de way back to de creek an take everting back to de water. De madness las seem like one two days. Folks wet, cold, dont have no food or fresh water. Dey wish dey dead, an den . . . de madness go way!

When dey come out, dey see everting tore up. A lil boy come runnin up an say come see de landin. Well, de landin still standin dere like the madness never come! Strong jus like de Ibo build it. Den it start to break up, bit by bit, like somebody takin it apart. Dey watch as de wooden planks lift in de air an fall in de water. De nails fly out, lan on de beach. It sway an make a noise like sick ol man, den it tremble an fall into de water cept for de poles holding it up. Dat what Paymore clare to be absolute truth! Dat why it call Ibo Landin.

Harryette Mullen (b. 1953)

Poet and scholar, Harryette Mullen was born in Florence, Alabama and grew up in Fort Worth, Texas. She received her undergraduate degree from the University of Texas at Austin and her M.A. and Ph.D. degrees from the University of California, Santa Cruz. Mullen has taught at Cornell University and currently is Professor of English at the University of California, Los Angeles. She has written several books of poetry, including *Muse & Drudge* (1995), *S*PeRM**K*T* (1992), *Trimmings* (1991), *Tree Tall Woman* (1981), and *Blues Baby: Early Poems* (2002). Her poetry collection, *Sleeping with the Dictionary* (2002), was a finalist for the National Book Award, the Los Angeles Times Book Prize, and the National Book Critics Circle Award. The titles of the fifty-seven poems in *Sleeping with the Dictionary* range from A to Z, from "All She Wrote" to "Zombie Hat." Mullen's love for language and wordplay permeates throughout the collection.

Denigration

Did we surprise our teachers who had niggling doubts about the picayune brains of small black children who reminded them of clean pickaninnies on a box of laundry soap? How muddy is the Mississippi compared to the third-longest river of the darkest continent? In the land of the Ibo, the Hausa, and the Yoruba, what is the price per barrel of nigrescence? Though slaves, who were wealth, survived on niggardly provisions, should inheritors of wealth fault the poor enigma for lacking a dictionary? Does the mayor demand a recount of every bullet or does city hall simply neglect the black alderman's district? If I disagree with your beliefs, do you chalk it up to my negligible powers of discrimination, supposing I'm just trifling and not worth considering? Does my niggling concern with trivial matters negate my ability to negotiate in good faith? Though Maroons, who were unruly Africans, not loose horses or lazy sailors, were called renegades in Spanish, will I turn any blacker if I renege on this deal?

Exploring the Dark Content

This dream is not a map.
A poem is not the territory.

The dreamer reclines in a barbershop
carpeted with Afro turf.
In the dark some soul yells.

It hurts to walk barefoot
on cowrie shells.

Souvenir from Anywhere

People of color untie-dyed. Got nothing to lose but your CPT-shirts. You're all just a box of crayons. The whole ball of wax would make a lovely decorator candle on a Day of the Dead Santeria Petro Vodou altar. Or how about these yin-yang earrings to balance your energy? This rainbow crystal necklace, so good for unblocking your chi and opening the charkras? Hey, you broke it, you bought it! No checks accepted. Unattended children will be sold as slaves.

Itabari Njeri (b. 1954)

Winner of the 1990 American Book Award, Itabari Njeri's *Every Good-Bye Ain't Gone: Family Portraits and Personal Escapades* is a memoir that the *San Francisco Chronicle* rightly describes as "part detective story, part history lesson." Whether describing her journey to find the bigots who killed her grandfather, or her grandmother who threw bedpans at her nurses, or her father, a Marxist historian/philosopher who never received the critical acclaim that he sought, Njeri writes stories that resonate with the lives of all those who try to make sense of their family legacies, lies, and lore. Born Jill Stacey Moreland in Brooklyn, New York, to historian, Marc Marion Moreland, and hospital administrator, Yvonne Delcinia Lord Moreland Williams, Njeri earned a B.S. from Boston University and her M.S. from Columbia University Graduate School of Journalism. She has worked as a journalist, as well as a professional singer and actress. Njeri also has written two collections of essays, *Sushi & Grits: The Challenge of Diversity* (1993) and *The Last Plantation: Color, Conflict, and Identity: Reflections of a New World Black* (1997).

From *Every Good-Bye Ain't Gone*

Ruby

My grandmother must be feeling a lot of holiday goodwill. She hasn't thrown a bedpan at a nurse or told a doctor to kiss her derriere since Thanksgiving, and it's almost Christmas. She seems to be adjusting to life in a New York City nursing home at just the time of year I'd expect her to be most recalcitrant. I am worried. She is even speaking kindly of Earl Lord.

"I saw him," she said. In the early morning darkness she looked toward the foot of her bed and there he was.

My uncle, Alex Lord, the spit of Earl, cocked his head, pulled back his chin so it doubled, then squinted at her with one open, disbelieving eye.

"Daddy? Here?"

"Oh yes, right here," she said, patting the bottom right corner of the bed.

"Mama, you got loving on your mind?" he teased, then bit into the sandwich she had failed to eat for lunch.

I sat in a chair opposite them, watching my uncle devour Grandma's food while she stared into space, her back to the wall of windows that framed the East River outside Doctor's Hospital. A medical emergency—a blockage in her intestines—had brought her here from the nursing home ten days earlier. The growth was nonmalignant and, despite the blockage, better

left alone given her age, the doctors said. As she sat upright on the edge of the bed, the windows behind her held a gray, midday sky. A light snow fell steadily, gently pocking the river's surface then vanishing, lost in the poisoned waters. She sat captured in the cityscape, but her mind wandered beyond its dimensions. As it did, her countenance seemed all-knowing, her spoken, splintered thoughts seemed to say the past had been retrieved and made intelligible—to her. She tossed a fragment at no one in particular, "My mother . . . If only I had known . . ." My uncle eyed her; his arms were across his chest. He'd polished off the sandwich. ". . . And he called my name," my grandmother said, her eyes tightly closed.

"Who did?" my uncle goaded.

"Your father," she said firmly.

"You sure, Mama?"

She puffed up defiantly. "Yes," she said, as if it were the answer to all questions for all time. Her head started to move slowly from side to side as she recalled Earl Lord's voice in the twilight. "'Ruby, Ruby, Ruby.'" Her head began to move like the heaviest frond of a tall palm, bending . . . yielding to a breeze only she perceived. Perhaps it was the warm breath of my grandfather . . . close to her face . . . one night . . . long ago. "'Ruby.'"

He had hurt her; he had loved her and hurt her. But he *had* loved her, she said, and came to her that morning seeking forgiveness.

I'd never seen my grandmother so . . . so . . . sensuously mellow. Though she was eighty-nine and physically deteriorating, she was mentally razor-sharp and had never done anything that indicated she was out of touch with reality. Perhaps it was the place. She liked it here. Doctor's Hospital was her style. She could look out the window and see Gracie Mansion. Here she was treated like the privileged women she still thought herself to be. In this congenial atmosphere of quiet corridors, attentive nurses and a friendly roommate, my grandmother seemed relaxed and open to myriad impulses from her subconscious.

In her East Side nursing home, she usually sat in a chair scowling at the wall in front of her, while her two roommates lay on either side of her dying. Her hatred for that warehouse of decaying flesh was evident from the bedpans she hurled at the nurses and her shouts of "Kiss my ass" to the doctor. But during my periodic phone calls to her from Miami, where I then lived, I had detected a certain registration. My mother had confirmed this latest change in attitude. But to hear her speak with such obvious longing for my grandfather was most disconcerting. I'd always thought his name was spelled B-A-S-T-A-R-D in her dictionary. He had been long dead and they had been long divorced before that. Between their marriage and his death, there had been a series of adulterous affairs—one of which produced a child who could be my mother's twin, I've been told—followed by his marriage to my grandma Madelyn, a woman nearly fifteen years younger than Ruby and so much lighter she could pass for white (a significant factor to extremely color-conscious West Indians). Maybe the doctors had drugged Ruby and this was the afterglow. I don't know. But I could feel the heat of her memories that day as surely as I'd felt the sting of the wind off the river as I walked toward the hospital to see her.

She spoke to me now but I only half heard. My uncle's teasing had finally broken her reverie and she was issuing instructions for her funeral. It was a constant topic of hers and by now a family joke. "Four flower cars. . . . And no, absolutely no, in-laws in the first car. . . ." I ignored the familiar litany. I hadn't seen her in more than a year and I studied her face now. It sagged. But her light brown skin was still soft as a baby's and wrinkleless. Her nose, with its African fullness and East Indian prominence in profile, was finally "Roman," my uncle Alex used to declare, "'cause it roamed all over the place." Her wide, brown eyes were still expressive, registering all she saw, but their color now was a milky brown. I looked at her thin lips and remembered the words that rushed past them on late fall days such as these when I was growing up. Her sound broke our sleep long before the dawn.

"Tide and time wait for no man," she'd bellow, rousing the house like a Jamaican drill sergeant if we weren't ready for breakfast by 7:00 A.M. She'd been raucously rattling cake pans in the kitchen since 5:00 A.M. If she was up, you should be up. She wanted that kitchen clear for baking. She had fruitcake orders to fill.

What a pain she was on a Saturday morning. But what a voice to rise to: the island lilt of it, the royal imperiousness of its tone. The sun and the Queen were in every word.

By the time I'd hit the kitchen she was in high gear: burning sugar, dicing currants, pouring out the extra-proof rum—sipping the extra-proof rum. Be aware: The cake my grandmother made bore no resemblance to the pale, dry, maraschino cherry–pocked fruitcakes most Americans know. This was a traditional West Indian fruitcake and an exquisite variation of it at that.

As a little girl and since, I've been to more than a few West Indian celebrations where the host served a dry, crumbling, impotent confection and dared to call it fruitcake. Only good manners prevented me from going *spittooey* on the floor, like some animated cartoon character. Instead, the members of any family would take a bite, control themselves, then exchange smug glances: Nothing like Ruby's, we'd agree telepathically.

What Ruby Hyacinth Duncombe Lord created was the culmination of a months-long ritual. The raisins, the prunes, the currants and the citron were soaked in a half gallon of port wine and a pint of rum for three months in a cool, dark place. Even after the cake was baked, liquor was poured on it regularly to preserve it and keep it moist for months. When you finally bit into a piece, the raisins spat back rum.

On the special occasions the cake was served—holidays, birthdays, weddings—I was often outfitted in some party frock my mother, or one of the West Indian seamstresses on the block, had made. Sometimes a bit of hem or a snap required last-minute adjustments. My grandmother would run for the sewing tin and make the alterations with me still in the dress. Her mending done, the needle and thread poised in her upheld hand, she grabbed my wrist.

"Grandmaaaaaah," I squealed extravagantly. She sucked her teeth at my absurd resistance.

"Stop that noise before I knock you into oblivion. Are you insane? Do you actually wish to walk around in your burial shroud?" she asked incredulously. And then she pricked the inside of my wrist, breaking the spell of death that fell when cloth was sewn on a living soul.

I do not know the origins of the practice. Perhaps it was African, as were many things, I later learned, we did and said without realizing it. But such things were not unsual in that place, at that time.

I lived in a country one Brooklyn block long. It was an insular world of mostly West Indians who dwelled in both stately and sagging brownstones, and the occasional wood house that dotted the street.

Scattered among them were Afro-American immigrants from the South. Most mornings, the elder members of these extended families could be seen sweeping and hosing down the sidewalk in front of their row or wood-frame homes. Many of them had come north during the first great migration of blacks from the South around World War I. They were escaping the neoslavery of the post-Reconstruction period. At the same time, my maternal grandparents were sailing from the Caribbean to the United States, fleeing the social prison of British colonialism.

Many of these early Afro-British and Afro-American migrants had saved enough money to buy homes in this Clinton Hill enclave and the surrounding Fort Greene neighborhood in the 1940s when the area opened up to blacks.

Our landlady, and hairdresser, too—she operated a discreet salon on the ground floor of her 1860 Italianate row house—was from Barbados. For years, beginning with my mother, she rented the tree-shaded second floor of her home to members of my family before they bought houses of their own.

The block's most recent arrivals seemed to live in the one tenement I recall on our street, a sturdy, pre–World War II structure whose communal corridors were as tidy as the foyers in the block's private homes.

Like most immigrants, those on our street seemed to possess a drive, tenacity and pride that often set them apart from their countrymen. The social ravages of northern, urban life had yet to engulf the citizens of St. James Place. And the American century, a little past its midpoint, had not fully become what it is—vulgar and dangerous without respite.

As I prepared to leave this country each morning, boarding the bus to the Adelphi Academy nursery school, the old man hosing down the street would wave to me and say, "Be good now." I do not remember his name, if I ever knew it. The people outside of my immediate family and their intimate circle of friends were of fleeting significance to me then. My first seven years on earth were dominated by island voices, resounding in narrow brownstone parlors where all that was wood was perfumed by lemon oil, and parquet floors glowed with the reflected light of chandeliers. It was here, in this world, that we cut the fruitcake.

"Love doll, come give Mariella a kiss," my brother's godmother called to me at one of these house parties, extending her arms and jiggling her bosom. She lived across the street and ran a boardinghouse with a crew of mostly male students from Africa, the Middle East and the Caribbean. She was a good friend to my mother and a second grandmother to me. Ruby took her latter status as a personal insult, an offense compounded by Mariella's looks (pretty), size (petite), manner (flirtatious), and age (ten to fifteen years off my grandmother's).

Among her other sins, Mariella was from St. Croix, and her musical accent and speech tended to be as informal and coquettish as Ruby's were imperial and bellicose.

"Y'know," said Mariella, pointing to me, "I raise her since she was this high." She bent down and measured about a foot off the floor. I was five and looked at her strangely. Even then I could figure out she'd probably had too much rum.

Ruby sucked her teeth disgustedly at Mariella's familial claims, and my mother shot her a don't-start-anything glance. Later, I'd hear my grandmother mutter, "Old gypsy pussy," and label anything Mariella said "Anansi story anyway."

"Gypsy pussy" went right over my head at the time, and it took years of repeated hearings—my grandmother sticking the label on any woman she considered flighty—before its meaning dawned on me.

As for "Anansi story," I always thought she was talking about Nancy, some lady I'd never met. I didn't know Anansi was the famed character of West African folklore, the spider who spun tales, his stories still told by the descendants of Africans who'd been brought to Jamaica.

With my two grandmothers in the room—the monarch and the gypsy—someone offered a toast. All raised their glasses but no one drank before a bit of liquor had been flicked with fingers to the floor. Ruby had already sprinkled spirits over the threshold when my mother moved into the apartment. Both gestures were a blessing and an ancestral offering.

While I did spend a lot of time with Mariella, who had two grandchildren my age, it was Ruby who was waiting for me after a hard half day at nursery school, then kindergarten, then the first and second grades. I'd tarry with my friends at the candy store before coming home, stocking up on red licorice, candy lipsticks and peppermint sticks. But Ruby and the whole block knew when I was approaching home; my voice came around corners before I did. I knew the Hit Parade by heart, a fact that did not always please my grandmother.

"You too forward," she'd call down to me, her voice floating from our kitchen window above the limestone stairs where I'd planted myself with my bag of candy. Elbows on the stoop, legs dangling the length of three stone steps, I ignored my grandmother and kept singing.

"*Oh the wayward wind is a restless wind, a restless wind that yearns to wander, and I was born—*"

"What you know about a wayward wind, child? Come upstairs." I loved the regal lilt of my grandmother's accent, her tickled tone, despite the firmness of her call. But I pretended not to hear.

"*Sixteen tons and whadiya get, another day older and deeper in—*"

"Jill Stacey!" she bellowed, as I began "Blueberry Hill."

Still stretched along the steps, I bent my long neck back, looked toward the sky and saw my grandmother's head sticking out the kitchen window. "Grandma, you want me?" I asked, my scuffed saddle shoes still beating time against the pavement. "*I found my thrill . . .*"

"Eh-eh," Ruby uttered quickly, then sucked her teeth. "Yes, it's you that I want. Come and don't try me. Ya know I old and fricasseed."

"What's fricasseed?"

"It's what you do to a tough old bird like me. Now come," she shouted, pulled her head in, then shut the window.

Most afternoons, after I climbed the stairs, we listened to *Our Gal Sunday* and *Helen Trent* during the waning days of radio melodramas. And when my mother bought a television set, we became equally avid fans of *As the World Turns*. As we stared at the tube, I rubbed my grandmother's thickly callused feet with a pumice stone. It was the ritual that accompanied our afternoon entertainment.

Grandma would put down her washboard, wipe her hands on the skirt of her white apron, then sit with her feet in the basin of hot water I had prepared. These were no longer the feet of a pampered, Creole, island princess. And from my spot on the floor, I could smell the Clorox on her hands.

As I tended her crusty feet, I had only the faintest notion then of what life had been like for her in Jamaica. The details of her past came in fragments over the years—a long snatch from her every now and then, a snippet from my mother, a revelation from a cousin or an aunt.

I'd seen only one picture of her back in Jamaica. It was taken in Kingston, where she was born in 1897, shortly before she came to America, circa 1917. The photograph captured her standing regally erect, her buxom, hourglass figure wrapped in an ankle-length white dress. Her cotton-soft hair was pulled tightly into a bun, stretching her taupish-brown skin taut across her cheekbones.

I've often entertained the idea of putting that picture on a round, ruby-red tin that held my grandmother's fruitcake and selling it. The label would read:

DUNCOMBE-LORD

"The World's Finest Traditional West Indian Fruitcake"

You'd have to order it through Bloomingdale's or Neiman-Marcus. Grandma would like that. But the recipe would have to be kept a secret.

When my grandmother came to the United States, she promised her brother, James Vincent Duncombe, that she would never give the coveted formula to anyone outside the family. He was a lawyer and probably realized a mint could be made from these cakes if Ruby ever had the capital and opportunity to go into business. In fact, wealthy Americans for whom she had worked as a housekeeper and cook tried to buy it from her so they could sell it commercially. "Never," she told them. But it wasn't just the pact with her brother. The measure and the manner of her culinary alchemy was one of the few family treasures she still possessed in America. Her middle-class, multiracial background meant next to nothing

here. And given the reality of colonial Jamaica, her place of privilege there was severely circumscribed by an odious color-caste system. The island's lighter-hued, mixed-race population may have isolated itself from the black majority, but its members remained second-class citizens under British colonial rule.

There was a gate in front of my grandmother's house in Kingston, she once told me. She was forbidden to go beyond it to play with certain children.

"Why?" I asked her when I was an adult.

Her response was vague but firm. "We just could not."

"What reason did your mother give?"

She looked at me as if I were stupid, then sucked her teeth. "We did not question our parents."

I suspected her lack of candor came from embarrassment. She did not want to admit that color and class differences were the probable reasons she was forbidden to play with the children. In America, she had become a follower of Marcus Garvey. His wife, Amy, had been one of her childhood friends.

Nonetheless, I've always suspected my grandmother of being an ambivalent black nationalist, drawn to the Garveyites because there was no caste to insulate her from the rawness of American racism.

But I can't be certain; she never offered any clear ideological argument for her "Back to Africa" sympathies.

On the one hand, to this day, if she could she would stand for the Queen of England if Elizabeth appeared on TV and the British national anthem were played. She did so when I was growing up. But if you asked her if she wanted to go back to Jamaica, she'd ask you emphatically, "For what? There's nothing in Jamaica I want to go back to."

Otherwise, she did display a certain nationalist consistency. She proudly quoted the King James Bible: "Princes shall come out of Egypt; and Ethiopia shall soon stretch out her hands unto God." She would always say it dramatically, her arms reaching out to me, ending the quote with a booming "*Yes!*"

She joined the African Orthodox Church, too, renouncing her family's Catholicism in the 1930s because the Pope, she said, had blessed the ammunition the Italians used to kill the Ethiopians.

And she made it plain that her father was a Haitian, proudly declaring his complexion "black, black, black," to make a clear distinction between him and the European father of her half sister, Marie.

More about her father I couldn't say. On this matter, Ruby was also curiously vague. In her day, she insisted again, children didn't press their parents about such matters as paternity.

But I do know something about her mother, Alice Dacre Duncombe. My oldest first cousin, Karen, saw a picture of her and described her as a pretty woman with pale, nearly white skin and long dark hair that she wore in two braids, each one draped over a shoulder. Exactly how my great-grandmother

Alice managed to own so much property and run her own business, a dry goods store, in the late nineteenth century is a mystery to me. Shopkeeping had long been a common occupation for free men and women of color in Jamaica. But whether she inherited her property from her well-to-do mixed-race and European relatives, or from her husbands, remains a puzzle.

Though I've heard the stories of the servants and the grand house the Duncombes had in Jamaica and have seen some of the exquisite jewelry and silverware they owned, I suspect Ruby was at best shakily middle-class in Kingston. If not, why did her brother, my uncle Vin, have to come to Detroit and work in Henry Ford's factory to make enough money to finish law school? And he chose to stay in the States after receiving his degree, maintaining a marginal law practice under American apartheid in the 1930s, 1940s and 1950s. (His grandchildren did much better. One granddaughter, Beth Duncombe, is part of a flourishing law practice in Detroit. Her sister, Trudy Duncombe Archer, was assistant dean of the Detroit College of Law, where her grandfather got his degree, and is now a district court judge in Michigan. Her husband, Dennis Archer, is Michigan's second black supreme court justice.)

But in early twentieth-century Jamaica, the Duncombe family's position was precarious. They were mixed-race but dominantly African, and the real nonwhite, middle-class power brokers in colonial Jamaica were the East Indians and Chinese.

There couldn't have been many available men in my grandmother's class to choose from. My aunt Rae, confirming this one day, laughed and said, "You think Mama would have come here if they had any prospects for her in Jamaica?"

Fresh from Ellis Island, Ruby joined her brother, my uncle Vin, in Detroit. In the motor city, she met my granddaddy, and pinned her hopes on this soon-to-be physician from Guyana.

Earl Lord defined arrogance. He truly was tall, dark and handsome, the product of a New World mixture of African, English, East Indian and Amer-Indian. The black Lords of the New World were the descendants of a notorious pirate named Sam Lord. He was my great-great-great-grandfather, and you can spend a few nights in his castle if you go to Barbados. The Marriott hotel chain has turned the place into a popular resort hotel.

This pirate, so they story goes (his life was fictionalized in a 1980 novel called *A Regency Rascal* by W. P. Drury), was actually a landlubbing one. With the aid of slaves from his plantation, he lured ships to a nearby reef by hanging lanterns in the coconut trees. Mariners seeing them thought they were the lights of ships anchored in a safe harbor. When the ships ran aground on the shoals, Lord took possession of the cargo, dispatching the sailors who had not drowned.

The castle he had built in Barbados in 1820 was constructed entirely by slave labor. And though he and his wife had only one child that lived, Samuel Lord had twenty children by four enslaved African women. I wish my family knew as much about those anonymous women, one of whom was my great-great-great-grandmother, as they do about this bandit who allegedly stole money entrusted to him by his nieces and nephews and regularly threw his wife into the dungeon till she fled back to England. He returned to England, too, eventually, and died there in 1845.

The black branch of the Lord clan migrated to Guyana toward the end of the last century, and the men, true to the Lord tradition, were tyrannical patriarchs and womanizers. Though my grandfather didn't deviate from that pattern in his youth, he had mellowed considerably, my mother said, by the time I was born.

To this day, I don't know for certain how many children he had, but there were nine "legitimate" ones, as well as my mother's "twin," at last count. Just as Granddaddy was ending years of financial struggle and starting his medical practice, he left the first four of those children and my grandmother to marry Madelyn Parsons. It was the middle of the Depression, and my grandmother was ill prepared to support a family alone—being a foreign dignitary without portfolio here.

But it seems that Earl Lord was not an irresponsible father, just a dictatorial one. He attempted to bring his children to the South, where he'd established his medical practice. But by that time, his first set of offspring were in their teens, and they apparently didn't want to cross the Mason-Dixon line.

Uncle Alex had to drop out of school to support the family. Always a hard worker, he was never without a job. But there are few good jobs any man, especially a black man, can get without a high school diploma.

My aunt Rae, thought to have the brains of the bunch and destined for law school, married too young and spent her working life in dead-end clerical jobs.

Aunt Glo, the youngest, had theatrical aspirations. She decided to be "hep" till she dropped. Her fast life finally made a few newspapers, I understand, the shame of which compelled my mother to move to Brooklyn after college instead of Harlem, where Aunt Glo was the moll of a well-known gangster. Like Thomas Wolfe, I guess my mom thought only the dead knew Brooklyn.

Vivien, my mother, was the only one who escaped the destructive economic and social consequences of my grandfather's absence. She was beautiful, the oldest, very practical and sickly. She went south for the warm weather and lived with Granddaddy while she was in high school. She wanted to be a social worker. Granddaddy wanted her to be a nurse and he made it clear that if he was paying her college tuition, she was going to be a nurse.

Meanwhile, my grandmother was not entirely without resources of her own. She had a good education and spoke with a refined, Afro-British accent. The former was of no particular value in America. But the latter, combined with her color and talent in the kitchen, qualified her as an exotic variation of the colored housekeeper/cook. After moving from Detroit to Washington, D.C., where Granddaddy was enrolled at Howard University, Ruby moved to New York to be with other members of her family. In Greenwich Village, she was welcomed into the homes of doctors and lawyers for a while as head cook and bottle washer. But rich people fall on hard times, too. Grandma was out of work. She and her children went on the relief rolls. To make extra money, she sold her fruitcakes for wedding and holidays.

I never saw my grandmother in a place of her own. Perhaps she could have done more with her life despite the profound and pervasive racism that defined America most of her eighty-nine years. Some of her children seemed to think so. "Spoiled" and "lazy" were words family members often used to describe Ruby. "A con artist," too. As an adult, I have seen my grandmother play both ends against the middle, with cash as the reward. But as a child, I thought she could do no wrong.

When the Oxydol commercial ended the half-hour television drama we'd been watching, I dried her feet and smoothed on the almond-scented lotion we both loved. These concluding actions overlapped seamlessly each day and were ceremoniously sealed by the *clang-clang* of the junk man's belled cart and the *clip-clop* of his horse down St. James Place.

If I recall this time and this place too idyllically, do not blame it on a child's naive rendering of reality, or an adult's wistful longing alone. St. James Place, now part of a landmark district because of its unique architecture and social history, was a haven. My mother sought a more genteel existence and found it there. My recollections are testimony to her determination to insulate me from the certain cruelty that lay just beyond the borders of the block. For contrary to what I felt, the world was a dangerous place for black people.

As I sat tending my grandmother's feet that afternoon in 1957, another year would have to pass before the NAACP could report, for the first time in its history, that there had been *no* lynchings in America. Just an avenue away, my mother couldn't rent an apartment because "No Negroes" were allowed. And I know the block I loved was not held together by culture and class alone. Segregation was the glue, too. It was, after all, just a genteel ghetto.

The junk man's clanging bell became faint music as he rolled south toward Fulton Street. Her feet soothed, my grandmother dozed in the parlor, her elbow propped on the arm of the chair, her chin and jowls resting in the palm of her hand. I crept toward the TV to turn it off. She stirred. "What you doing?" she asked, her voice phlegm-filled and hoarse. "Leave that set alone," she said, squinting at me. "Every shut eye ain't sleep. Every goodbye ain't gone." Indeed the earth has ears. The night has eyes. "And put *that* in your pipe and smoke it," she instructed.

Several years later, circumstances would compel us to leave St. James Place and I would eventually cease to think of myself as a West Indian first and foremost.

We would buy fifteen-cent tokens, take the A train north of there to 125th, and move into the apartment my father had rented since the waning days of the Harlem renaissance. There, I would discover a new kind of beauty, a new kind of brilliance, a new kind of pain.

"I have to go, Grandma." I rose to leave her hospital room. She had given me the deed to her burial plot and the handwritten instructions for her funeral. As I put on my coat, she became quite formal, as she was wont to do.

"Thank you so much for coming," she said, then nodded as Queen Victoria might have, indicating she was through with me, and that I might take my leave.

Thylias Moss (b. 1954)

Born in Cleveland, Ohio, Thylias Moss earned her B.A. from Oberlin in 1981 and her M.F.A. from the University of New Hampshire. She has taught at Phillips Academy in Andover and at Brandeis University. Currently, she teaches at the University of Michigan. She has won many honors: the Dewar's Profiles Performance Artist Award, the Witter Bynner Prize from the American Academy and Institute of Arts and Letters, a Guggenheim fellowship, and a MacArthur fellowship. Among her collections are *Hosiery Seams on a Bowlegged Woman* (1983), *Pyramid of Bone* (1988), *Rainbow Remnants in Rock Bottom Ghetto Sky* (1991), *Small Congregations: New and Selected Poems* (1993), and *Last Chance for the Tarzan Holler* (1998).

The Warmth of Hot Chocolate

Somebody told me I didn't exist even though he was
looking dead at me. He said that since I defied logic,
I wasn't real for reality is one of logic's definitions.
He said I was a contradiction in terms, that one side
of me cancelled out the other side leaving nothing.
His shaking knees were like polite maracas in the small
clicking they made. His moustache seemed a misplaced
smile. My compliments did not deter him from insisting
he conversed with an empty space since there was no
such thing as an angel who doesn't believe in God.
I showed him where my wings had been recently trimmed.
Everybody thinks they grow out of the back, some people
even assume shoulder blades are all that man has left
of past glory, but my wings actually grow from my scalp,
a heavy hair that stiffens for flight by the release
of chemical secretions activated whenever I jump off a
bridge. Many angels are discovered when people trying
to commit suicide ride and tame the air. I was just
such an accident. We're simply a different species,
not intrinsically holy, just intrinsically airborne.
Demons have practical reasons for not flying; it's too
hot in their home base to endure all the hair; besides,
the heat makes the chemicals boil away so demons plummet
when they jump and keep falling. Their home base isn't
solid. Demons fall perpetually, deeper and deeper into
evil until they reach a level where even to ascend is
to fall.

I think God covets my wings. He forgot to create some
for himself when he was forging himself out of pure thoughts
rambling through the universe on the backs of neutrons.
Pure thoughts were the original cowboys. I suggested
to God that he jump off a bridge to activate the wings
he was sure to have, you never forget yourself when you
divvy up the booty, but he didn't have enough faith that
his fall wouldn't be endless. I suggested that he did
in fact create wings for himself but had forgotten; his
first godly act had been performed a long time ago, afterall.

I don't believe in him; he's just a comfortable
acquaintance, a close associate with whom I can
be myself. To believe in him would place him in
the center of the universe when he's more secure
in the fringes, the farthest corner so that he
doesn't have to look over his shoulder to nab the
backstabbers who want promotions but are tired of
waiting for him to die and set in motion the natural
evolution. God doesn't want to evolve. Has been
against evolution from its creation. He doesn't
figure many possibilities are open to him. I think
he's wise to bide his time although he pales in the
moonlight to just a glow, just the warmth of hot
chocolate spreading through the body like a subcu-
taneous halo. But to trust him implicitly would
be a mistake for he then would not have to maintain
his worthiness to be God. Even the thinnest,
flyweight modicum of doubt gives God the necessity
to prove he's worthy of the implicit trust I can
never give because I protect him from corruption,
from the complacence that rises within him sometimes,
a shadowy ever-descending brother.

Remembering Kitchens

In the kitchen we compensate for missiles
in the world by fluting edges of crust
to bake rugged, primping rosettes and peaks
on cakes that are round tables with white
butter cloths swirled on, portable
Communion altars.

On the Sundays, ham toasted itself
with lipid melts, the honey veneer
waxed pork conceit to unnameable luster
and humps of rump poked
through the center of pineapple slices
so as to form tonsured clerical heads,
the Sundays being exceptional.

The waiting for the bread
helped us learn, when it arrived steaming
like kicked-up chariot dust then died down
quickly to the staid attitude of its brown dress,
the lovely practical.
In the center of the table
we let it loaf. When that was through
we sliced it into a file to rival the keeping
of the Judgment notes. So we kept our own,

a second set, and judged the judges, toasting
with cranberry water in Libbey glasses
that came from deep in the Duz. All this
in moon's skim light.

Somehow the heat of the stove,
flames shooting up tall and blue, good looking
in the uniform, had me pulling down the door,
the seat of the Tappan's pants, having the heat push
against me, melting off my pancake makeup, nearly
a chrysalis moment, my face registering then
at least four hundred degrees, and rising
in knowledge, the heat rising too, touching
off the sensors for the absolute mantra
of the ringing, the heat sizzling through cornices
and shingles, until the house is a warm alternative
to heavenly and hellish extremes,
and I remove Mama's sweet potato pie, one made
—as are her best—in her sleep when she can't
interfere, when she's dreaming at the countertop
that turns silk beside her elegant leaning, I slice it
and put the whipped cream on quick, while the pie
is hot so the peaks of cream will froth; these
are the Sundays my family suckles grace.

From *Small Congregation,* © 1993 by Thylias Moss; used by permission of Ecco press.

Jessica Care Moore (b. 1972)

If you can make it at Harlem's Apollo Theater, you can make it anywhere. During Amateur Night competitions, Jessica Care Moore won a stunning five weeks in a row by delivering her bullet-shooting poems—poems that "attack with deliberate grace." She published her collection, *The Words Don't Fit in My Mouth* (1997), on her own press, Moore Black Press. She has been featured in many documentaries and also in the feature film, *Slam*, which won the 1998 Sundance Film Festival. Born and raised in Detroit, Moore teaches poetry workshops to high school students.

princess

Cement &
blood
& dairy queen ice cream licks melt
like butter and fold into my batter
I am whipped into resistance with switches and cords
I cannot recognize love, can't spell lord

They named me princess
I live in the projects
My castle has 25 floors
400 families
One day I will be the queen

on monday, I'll get to wear my favorite jeans
on tuesday, I'll start a revolution
no one will notice, but it will be happening
bombs/ firecrackers/exploding glass
water ballons, rubber bands and bottle rockets
drop
ping
from my

roof.

Thousands of little girls like me, in riot gear
jump from my chin, climb down my arms,
reach for breathable air then let go
suddenly, without any warning.

In the middle of an average weekday
I will fly to my early death
Hanging from brown fingertips
Still sweaty from my birth
"Mama, no!"
We would scream.
Watching as others escaped
Ran for freedom, went to college
gave birth
to families

I would become a child martyr
A product of welfare cycles
And poison grape-flavored water
With round thin foil tops
I grab for my sisters small hands
And we fly like mystery angels

25 floors before hitting the ground

We are beautiful night owls
And momma won't have to watch us starve no more
We have won the war on drugs
And we became destiny's daughters

danced with clouds
drank from the retrograde of mercury
We gonna be black stars momma
We're gonna be on tv!!

an appalling scene here in Harlem.
a black woman apparently jumps to her death
her three small children in her arms.
news at eleven.

I remember how surprised they seemed.
guess it caught them off
guard deciding our own fate
they didn't get a chance to finish their crack
baby experiment their faces are red
they're angry cause they didn't get to push us
or pick which tree
this time

How could a mother of three kill her own children?
When she could've left them with the system
That doesn't provide adequate health care
Or any access to education

Why do you think they love Oprah, but hated Beloved?
Blacks folks ain't allowed to be magic.

They look taken back, ma.
Cause you took us back from them
Your womb an underground railroad
We died like royalty.
Wearing wings shaped by
old wire coat hangers

You named me princess
I live in America
My castle has 25 floors
400 families
and one day
I will be

queen.

The poem we have to write before thirty, because people will ask or I don't have a five year plan!

I don't have a five year plan
I didn't plan the first 29
I know I have poems & I'm gonna eat them when I'm
hungry
Feed them to my children.
Paint them all over my body, when I am too broke for
clothes
I'm gonna make love to them after he leaves
I'm gonna call on them when I'm lonely

Maybe I'll become a smoothie queen
Or take tickets at the roller rink
Maybe I'll titty dance at Magic City, but just on
Fridays

Just on Fridays

Maybe I'll end up working for CNN
Maybe I'll perm my hair
Finally take those African dance classes
Cartwheel while others walk.
Make love in the snow again
I don't know how to predict the next book
The next lover, the next meal, the next gig
But I know your next line.

I love your work.

you love me on the page.
you love me where tragedy doesn't bleed
you love me where gun shots blow up rainbows
you love me inside my magic
you love me as your antagonist

you really just love you.
you love that you can see yourself in me
you want to break our mirror
you love to watch me dance
you've never bought me shoes

maybe I'll spend my entire life
committing myself to a men
and they all end up hating and resenting me for it
maybe all men should be committed
maybe I'll learn to love being functional
that's so sexy
like a dishwasher or toaster
maybe I'll be a holly hobby easy bake oven
maybe I'll find a way to come off weak
inside my independence
maybe I'll stay modest so he can shine
maybe I'll be a failure to feed his ego
maybe I'll write the next American classic
maybe I'll sweat and play ball on Sundays
maybe I'll win the Pulitzer
maybe I'll begin a polyandry movement
maybe I will stress myself into thinking
I will die on the first of the month
But the first of the month tricks me
& comes
& somehow
I am left breathing!

Maybe I'll stop writing poems
& begin waiting tables at Steak & Ale
I think I made more money that way.
Maybe I'll just shop on Melrose for the rest of my
life
And give away all my clothes to the Salvation Army
every two months
Maybe I'll move to an Island off the tip of everywhere
And do NOTHING the rest of my life

I've lived so many lifetimes already.

I don't know what my plans are
For the next five years.
I know I have poems & I will eat them when I'm hungry
Make love to them when I'm lonely
Incite a riot with them when I'm bored
Maybe I'll start a publishing house/market a literacy
campaign/raise a son/be a wife/start a rock band/bury
my daddy twice/put up three plays/travel the world/run
a performance space/keep my toes polished/clean greens
and bake macaroni, well/start a scholarship fund/be
forced to do accounting after avoiding all those math
classes/read books/make love/be a woman/edit an
anthology/translate my poems into Japanese, German and
French/learn Arabic/keep my faith when It's not
blackwomanpoetry history month/teach in my
hometown/learn to swim/ buy a house/average four hours
of sleep/make salaat in a muslim country/horseback
ride through the ghetto/fight to be called a writer &
not a spoken word artist while being marketed as a
spoken word artist/be a freakin' Apollo legend/stay
grounded/ do it all before five o'clock/& laugh when
the shit don't seem funny.

But, Just on Fridays

Just on Fridays!

What about you?

That's what he told me quite boldly
The whole thing was scary
He didn't think I'd relate to the
Blacker the Berry
His skin was like mine
I guess he wanted us to bond
Like a weaves hair glue
Fool
I started to talking to the brotha in Haiku
He still didn't understand
Putting down my sistas was not the way
To win my hand
Me down mentality
Brotha so white-washed
He couldn't see his own dirty laundry
And he didn't want to come clean
So, I started taking him to school
I said, don't be ashamed cause Melanin is cool
Still, he insisted on enlightening me
Frightening me
I was out of luck
Light-skinned brotha was color struck
Run-a-muck
Silly punk
Wanted to place my sistas face
Next to a brown paper bag
Now, Isn't that the job of the so-called "man"
Brown, Copper, Coal, Sand or Tan
We should all be the same to you
Black
Man
Gotta understand why my darker sistas are mad
Now you think she's pretty cause Afro-centric
Is your fad
Kente Cloth and Cowry shells
Oh, unconscious brotha you wear it well
Around your neck, hangs a gold cow bell
That rings out the words
"House nigga for sale."

No, I don't want your number!

Colorstruck!

*excerpt from my play, The Revolutions in the Ladies Room . . . Performed
at The Nuyorican Poets Cafe in 1996.

Hey Baby, can I have your phone number?
I really prefer your light skin

Pearl Cleage (b.1948)

Pearl Cleage is a playwright, poet, novelist, and a contributing editor to *Essence* magazine. Her works include *Mad at Miles: A Black Woman's Guide to Truth, Deals with the Devil and Other Reasons to Riot*, and *What Looks Like Crazy on an Ordinary Day*, an Oprah's Book Club selection and a *New York Times* bestseller. Her latest book, *I Wish I Had a Red Dress* (2001), tells the story of Joyce Mitchell, who is trying to help provide social services to young women and start her life anew after losing her husband. Known for her humor and remarkable characters, Cleage was born in Springfield, Massachusetts, grew up in Detroit, and currently lives in Atlanta.

From *I Wish I Had a Red Dress*

Black Ice

They crossed the line! You know that line you have to be real clear about in your own head so that when people step over it, you can be ready to bring their inappropriate behavior to their attention by whatever means necessary? Well, Senator Busbee and his buddies definitely crossed it and I definitely brought it to their attention, but whether or not the end justified the means remains to be seen.

I merged into the traffic leaving Lansing and flipped on the radio, trying to calm down. Aretha Franklin's voice came pouring out like somebody had cued her.

"All I'm askin' is for a little respect!"

And the backup sisters wailing "Just a little bit! Just a little bit!"

Sing it, Ree! I thought, but I was still too agitated to sing along. Politicians don't know anything about respect! I should have known this was not a good place for me to be when I walked into the meeting room this morning and saw the guys on the committee all sitting up on a raised platform behind a gigantic oak table with one tiny chair out front for the humble citizen who's coming to ask for their stamp of approval. That big old table and that little bitty chair are supposed to

make you feel *small*, like Dorothy and the Scarecrow coming in to see the Wizard of Oz. The wizard didn't really have to *be* powerful. He just had to *look* like he was.

I think all negotiations should take place at a round table and everybody should have to rotate counterclockwise once an hour so that even the perception of head of the table, or foot, are ritually obliterated. It's not good to sit still longer than an hour in meetings anyway. Pools the blood and encourages the territorial spreading of notes, expensive pens, leather-bound legal pads and a variety of electronic devices aimed at keeping in constant touch with the world outside of the room in which the meeting has been convened.

Politicians are especially good at this. I don't know whether they believe that an overcrowded desk is just the thing to impress a constituent or what, but I've been in meetings with these guys where they spread out so much stuff in front of them that it terminally clutters your brain if you even glance down at it. Sort of like being turned to stone for sneaking a glance at Medusa.

"Re, re, re, re, re, re, re, re—spect!"

The car skidded suddenly on a patch of black ice and I realized I was driving too fast. I turned off the radio and took a deep breath. The sun was already on its way down and all the snow that turned to slush during the day would be frozen solid in a few more hours. This was not the time to be careless. This was the time to review the events of the day and figure out *what went wrong?*

I thought the proposal was perfect. Visionary without being mystical. Specific without being exclusionary. Optimistic yet firmly grounded in reality. Practical and passionate, it was, *if I do say so myself*, a fine example of the best kind of sixties rhetoric grafted onto the new millennium's require-ment that we "cut to the chase."

Maybe I should have taken better notes in that grant writing class. I can't believe I actually took a *class* in saying what you don't really mean so you can get money they don't really want you to have. The instructors kept telling me the key to raising money was to maintain a "businesslike tone," like I'm supposed to be ashamed of the fact that I tend to get excited when I'm talking about things that are important to me. As a true sixties *voodoo child*, I know I am *required* to bring passion to the table just like this generation is required to bring technology and rap music.

That's my legacy, but when I protested all this focus on what I regarded as style over substance, they gently suggested that I adopt a more civil *tone* when voicing my objections. At that point, I informed them on my way out the door that toning down is of zero importance to me. I would instead simply commit to the passionate telling of the complete, un-varnished truth.

Seems like a simple statement, right? But it gets tricky. First of all, there's the problem of presuming that everybody thinks it's always a good idea to tell the truth when there's re-ally nothing to suggest that we all agree on that. In fact, there's overwhelming evidence that we don't, including the fact that as soon as most of us read a statement advocating universal truth-telling as a goal worthy of pursuit, we start thinking of exceptions immediately.

Sure, we think, *truth is great*, except when:

- it's your boss;
- it's your lover/mate/partner/spouse or kid;
- it's scary;
- you might lose money/power/love/your job;
- you might get killed for it.

The thing is, once you start allowing for exceptions, everything becomes relative and people start talking about absurd notions like "everybody's got a right to their own truth," as if there can be more than one real truth, and the next thing you know, they're putting up fences and assem-bling armies and we're right back to where we started.

But it couldn't be my *tone*. The chairman even com-plimented me on the quality of our application and told me we'd have no problem being approved. At the appro-priate time, they allowed me to make a three-minute state-ment and I used my time to stress the importance of self-sufficiency, since I know politicians are big on self-sufficiency and I am too. I worked in phrases like "breaking the cycle of poverty" and "taking personal responsibility for correcting societal ills."

I even handed out copies of our basic Circus credo, which I wrote at my kitchen table when we were brand new:

Ten Things Every Free Woman Should Know

1. How to grow food and flowers
2. How to prepare food nutritiously
3. Self-defense
4. Basic first aid/sex education and midwifery
5. Child care (prenatal/early childhood development)
6. Basic literacy/basic math/basic computer skills
7. Defensive driving/map reading/basic auto and home repairs
8. Household budget/money management
9. Spiritual practice
10. Physical fitness/health/hygiene

The professional grant-writing people told me it was a pretty radical statement for general distribution so I agreed to leave it out, but at the last minute, I made enough copies to hand out anyway. I wanted to give these guys a feeling for how seriously we're trying to impact the totality of these young women's lives.

Secure in my delusion, I chattered on for my allocated three minutes, then thanked them for their time and offered to respond to any questions they might have for me. At that point, I thought I was doing pretty good. Nobody had yawned or excused himself to go to the bathroom and then the Honorable Ezra Busbee cleared his throat and cocked his head in my direction.

Congressman Busbee is a tall, thin, intense-looking man whose jacket sleeves and pant legs are always a little too short, which makes him bear more than a passing resemblance to Ichabod Crane. In spite of this unfortunate image problem and his total lack of support outside of his own small district, he's been around long enough to sit on a number of powerful committees, including this one.

"I've got a question for you, *Joyce*," he said with a tight little smile like we had a first-name relationship going. "May I call you Joyce?"

I wanted to say, *Of course, if I can call you Ezra*, but I didn't. I needed his vote.

"Certainly," I said, with my own small smile.

"Well, *Joyce*." He held up his copy of the "Ten Things." "This is a very interesting document."

Was "interesting" good or bad?

"Thank you," I said.

"Can you do all these things?"

"Almost all," I said.

"Then would you call yourself a *free woman*?"

"Yes," I said. "I would."

"And that's what you're raising over there in . . . Idlewild, is it? *Free women?*"

He made it sound like I was running an illegal mink ranch.

"Well, I wouldn't say *we're raising them*," I said. "Most of our core constituency is eighteen to twenty-two."

"And they already have babies?"

I kept my voice as neutral as possible. "Not all, but many of them do have children, yes."

He nodded and peered through his glasses at the list, reading through it again quickly. "And what's your definition of a free woman again?"

I think that for some men, using the word "free" and "woman" so close together seems such an obvious oxymoron that they assume it must be the setup for a funny story. Ezra struck me as that kind of guy.

"A free woman," I said, reminding myself to keep smiling too, "is one who can fully conceive and consciously execute all the moments of her life."

I could tell he had no idea what I was talking about.

"Look out, Ezra," chuckled the committee chairman, a jovial grandfather from a tiny town as far into northern Michigan as you can go without falling into Lake Superior. "I have it on good authority that Mrs. Mitchell here is something of a *women's libber*."

What century were they living in? The other members of the committee chuckled, but Ezra was not impressed. He waved the "Ten Things" in my face a bit more aggressively.

"Well, I don't know much about women's lib," he said, "but I can't see much point in spending people's hard-earned money giving sex education to unwed mothers. Isn't that a little like closin' the door after the cow's already out of the barn?"

Several members of the committee laughed. That's what I get for saying he could call me *Joyce*. Give these guys an inch and they'll take a mile.

"That's just a small part of what we do," I said.

"But you do it, right?"

"Yes."

The laughter had awakened the dozing reporter for *The Capital Daily* and her note taking inspired Ezra to pursue the question.

"And you think that's the role of government, do you Joyce?"

Truth, I reminded myself. *Just tell him the truth.*

"Yes, I do," I said. "I think the role of government is to support and nurture a strong, self-reliant population, regardless of gender. Don't you?"

He looked at me and frowned. "I think I'm asking the questions here, Ms. Mitchell, not you. That's what I think."

I felt my face flush. "Excuse me?"

"In fact," he said, turning to the chairman. "I have a number of questions that I would like to ask Joyce about her training ground for so-called *free women* before we vote."

"I object to that characterization of our program!" I said.

"It is not your place to object," Ezra interrupted me.

"*My place?*"

"I move to table this application until we have time to study it more carefully and determine the full scope of Joyce's program goals. I'm tired of the taxpayers' money being wasted when all these girls need is for somebody to teach 'em how to keep their dresses down and just say *no!*"

"Mr. Chairman, I have a right to respond!" I said.

"If you're not a member of this committee, you have no rights in this room!" Ezra snapped.

Enough was enough. I stood up. "Then I don't belong here," I said, reaching for my coat.

"There is a motion to table on the floor!" The chairman was tapping his gavel for order. The reporter was scribbling enthusiastically now, happy for any kind of story at the end of a long, dull day.

"I second it," boomed a freshman legislator from Grand Rapids who had a pretty young female constituent watching his lackluster performance admiringly.

Before I could object any further, they had delayed action on our proposal pending my satisfactory answers to a list of questions that Ezra handed to the committee chairman, who accepted them, took another fast vote and adjourned the meeting for the day.

For a minute, I was too stunned to move as they all began to file out of the small room. I caught up with the chairman in the hallway, scurrying back to his office.

"Bob," I said, too frustrated for formalities. "You know it will take months for us to get back on the agenda if we get turned back now! What happened?"

He patted my shoulder without slowing down and handed me Ezra's list. "Don't take it personal, Joyce," he said and winked. "It's an election year, remember?"

Then I understood. Ezra wanted to use his opposition to us as a way of getting a little free campaign publicity. I looked at the list. The first question was "How many illegitimate babies have your followers brought into the world for somebody else to take care of?"

There were six or seven more, but that was enough for me. I crumpled the paper in my hand and just stood there for a minute. What now? I closed my eyes and took a deep breath. I had said I was a free woman, so what would a free woman do?

I walked over to the chairman, who had stopped to have a word with Ezra.

"Excuse me," I said, tossing the balled-up paper in his direction so he had to fumble to catch it. "I won't be needing those. I withdraw our application."

He looked at me, too surprised to say anything, which was fine with me. I turned to Ezra.

"Two things," I said to him. "There are no *illegitimate* babies; and from now on, *you can call me Ms. Mitchell.*"

When I passed a big trash can in the parking lot, I slowed down long enough to take out my last copy of that carefully crafted proposal and tossed it in. Whatever happens next, The Sewing Circus is going to stand or fall on our own reality. What's the point of fighting for the truth if you're not allowed to tell it?

Tayari Jones (b. 1970)

The Atlanta child murders of 1979–80 serve as the point of departure for James Baldwin's *Evidence of Things Not Seen* (1985), Toni Cade Bambara's *These Bones Are Not My Children* (1999), and more recently, Tayari Jones's *Leaving Atlanta* (2002). Jones tells her story from the perspective of three Atlanta fifth-graders, Tasha, Rodney, and Octavia, whose lives are affected when their classmates disappear. *Leaving Atlanta* won the 2000 Zora Neale Hurston/Richard Wright Foundation Award, an Arizona Artist Fellowship Award, and the Martindale Foundation Award. Jones is an "urban southerner," growing up in Atlanta where she spent most of her early life, except for 1982–83 when her family moved to Nigeria so that her father could accept a Fulbright Fellowship. Jones graduated from Spelman College in 1991 with a B.A. in English. She completed her M.A. in English at the University of Iowa and in 2002 finished her M.F.A. at Arizona State University.

From *Leaving Atlanta*

The Direction Opposite of Home

Morning begins the moment Father swings his cracked feet over the side of the bed and stands. With the grace of the blind, he dresses in the dark of his and Mother's bedroom. You hear a crisp sound like pages turning as he pulls his starched coveralls around himself and fastens the zipper.

You are tense between your Snoopy sheets as he heads to the kitchen. When he pauses before your room, his body blocks the yellow light that arches underneath your door. Is he standing there recalling some criticism he forgot to deliver yesterday? You imagine him making a mental note to berate you tonight, over dinner. He continues down the hallway as you study the ceiling over your bed, wondering who arranged the tiny stalagmites in such an intricate pattern, and wondering why your father hates you.

Father's small A.M. radio belches out WAOK. The shrieking teakettle cannot muffle Ron Sailor's funereal report from the newsroom. One of your classmates, Jashante Hamilton, has been missing for two weeks. You do not miss Jashante; he had terrorized you for most of your elementary-school career. But you do not want to know that he has been found murdered, for whoever could kill Jashante, could destroy you effortlessly.

As you chant nursery rhymes to distract yourself from the news report, Father stacks his breakfast dishes in the sink and shuts off the radio. Father rattles the back burglar door, assuring himself that it is as locked now as it was last night

when he turned the key and checked it twice. Exiting through the front door, he turns the double dead bolt behind him with a responsible clunk. You close your eyes and stop humming. He's gone to work. You can dream again.

At daybreak, Mother whisks into your room in a long satin robe, waking you with a contrived coloratura, "Good morning, Rodney." Ignoring her salutation, you do not stir. "Wake up," she sings, shaking you with hands that smell faintly of glue. You emit a grunting surrender to discourage her from tickling you or covering your face with cold-creamed kisses. Satisfied that you are awake, she leaves you alone. Her blue robe swishes with inappropriate elegance as she moves to Sister's room.

As you pull on your favorite pair of Toughskins, you notice the morning air is not heavy with too-crispy bacon and scorched eggs. A long assessing breath detects rubber cement. You take another guilty inhalation, savoring the smell in the same way that you enjoy damp ditto sheets held briefly to your face at school. But intoxicating or not, this is no breakfast smell. You make your way to the kitchen, picking up the odor of paint as well.

Mother frets over a sequined shoe box in the center of the sturdy oak kitchen table. It is a diorama, Sister's fall project. Mr. Harrell ordered you fifth-graders to create festive posters illustrating the theme, "Reaching as we climb." The purple mimeographed sheet with the instructions is crumpled in the sticky bottom of your book bag.

Sister's pretty little brow is creased as she carefully prints her name on the pencil line beside the word *by*. "Right here, honey," Mother says. Sister is six years old and very obedient.

"Your poster is in the living room," Mother tells you as she carefully encloses the diorama in bubble wrap.

You are surprised, but you shouldn't be. This is hardly the first time that your mother's industry has thwarted your strides toward underachievement. But what else has she found rifling through your bag? Has she seen the candy wrappers? Maybe, but that doesn't prove anything. Furthermore, Mother is not predisposed to think ill of either of her children by virtue of love liberally mingled with instability. You walk to the living room and retrieve the poster without comment.

"I'm hungry," says Sister, not unpleasantly.

The kitchen is covered with putty, spangles, twine, and toxic solvents. Mother glances at the daisy-shaped clock over the stove. "I have a hair appointment at eight. You'll have to get breakfast at school."

"What?" you sputter although you hadn't intended to say anything. Since your words are almost invariably misinterpreted, you avoid speech in general and abstain entirely from rhetorical questions.

"We're going to eat at school!" Sister is happy, partly because she is a naturally effervescent little girl, but also because the cafeteria ladies love her and give her extra cartons of chocolate milk. You have not made such a good impression on the heavy women whose round faces are framed by hair nets. They actually *dislike* you, demonstrating this antipathy by a subtle twist of the wrist, ensuring that your serving of casserole never has cheese on top.

And besides, school breakfast is eaten nearly exclusively by kids whose families are so poor that they don't have anything to eat at home. They carry meal cards, given out at the first of the week, marked FREE so they receive their trays without paying. You'd rather not be associated with this group, but you don't mention this to your mother. She would accuse you of pretension. Never mind that the shoe box she chose to make your sister's diorama conspicuously bears the label of her only Italian pumps.

Arriving at school, you head toward the cafeteria, but pause in the hallway in front of a huge cardboard tree. Dangling from the branches are construction-paper apples bearing the names of the Students of the Month. No apple reads RODNEY GREEN. Mother once demanded a conference with the principal to discuss this oversight. She arrived for the meeting smartly dressed, clutching a copy of your standardized test scores in a gloved hand.

"We tend to reward achievement rather than aptitude," the principal explained, ushering her out.

You are starving. Why not push the cafeteria doors, walk in casually, and get yourself a tray? Every student is allowed to eat. Hadn't Mother said that you should be the *most* welcome because your family pays the taxes that make the breakfast possible? But sponsoring the meal does not erase the stigma of actually eating it, so you stay hungrily in the hall.

When the project kids file out of the cafeteria, you offer them the courtesy of not looking into their faces. For some reason, they hesitate a moment when they see you. Are they looking at your clothes? Can they tell that your socks, though similar, are not an exact match? Or is it your howling stomach that attracts such attention? Finally, you realize that in the hallway's fluorescent light, your poster—Mother's masterpiece—is magnificently luminous like the pulsing lights of a parking lot carnival.

You ignore the spectacle in your hands, and look at the toes of your shoes. They still look new although you have walked countless laps around your living room to rid them of that Stride Rite shine. As you meditate on the condition of your penny loafers, one of the breakfast eaters says, "Hi, Rodney." You are so startled that you swallow whole a double wad of bubble gum, still cinnamon sweet.

It is Octavia, who has always occupied the desk in front of yours. (Teachers are certain that alphabetic seating accelerates the learning process.) You are not surprised to discover that she is a breakfast eater. Having sat behind her for five going on six years of education, you know that her lunch card is stamped REDUCED so that she pays for her meal with a dime while you pay forty cents. She sometimes comes to school very early, even before breakfast; Mrs. Willingham or one of the other teachers gives her soap to wash with. Since you are one of the nicer boys in class, you never speak to her.

"Hey, Octavia," you mumble, noticing that she is also carrying a decorated posterboard.

It is not as ornate as yours because she made it herself. Her smile fades a little bit as she sees that your design is carefully shaded to create an illusion of depth.

"You'll probably win a prize," she says.

You feel that you should say something nice about her creation. Reciprocity is the cornerstone of good manners. But fifth-grade social institutions discourage mingling freely. Poor Octavia is drowning in a sea of untouchability and you don't want to be submerged as she thrashes.

Leon Simmons is about twenty feet from you; his new shoes look much less new than yours. He cracks his knuckles expressively as you speak to Octavia. His face is turned up on one side. A snicker? Smirk? You doubt he is just admiring your mother's handiwork. You want to turn all the way around so that your view of Leon is not obstructed by the handle of your glasses. But to look closely is the very same thing as admission, so you continue to examine your shoe.

You report to your classroom, pausing a moment at the door. Mr. Harrell is writing on the chalkboard. You hate him. In an unusual moment of candor you told this to your mother and were scolded.

"Hate is a strong word," she said, as if you didn't know this already.

Your distaste for this narrow man began the moment you laid eyes on him. You had been expecting pretty Miss Maddox, whom you met last year when you were sent out into the hallway for some inconsequential social transgression. She walked by with a dainty clattering of high heels and said, "I know that a handsome boy like you hasn't been causing trouble." And from that moment, you looked forward to starting fifth grade. But when you walked into your classroom on the first day, bearing several sharpened number-two pencils to impress her, you found out that lovely Miss Maddox had gotten married and moved to Arizona.

In her place is Mr. Harrell, who insists on addressing the students by Mr. and Miss. You missed your turn the first time he called roll because you are accustomed to being called by your first name.

"Did you say Rodney Green?" you asked, realizing that you had been passed. "I'm here."

"Tardy," Mr. Harrell pronounced, with a malevolent stroke of his red pen.

"But I've been here since before the first bell."

"In body maybe. But apparently, your mind has just arrived."

You slumped in your chair mumbling truncated obscenities. Mr. Harrell tapped the corner of your desk with his ruler. "Do you have something to say to me, Mr. Green?"

"No sir," you said, over Forsythia Collier's wind-chime laughter.

Mr. Harrell turns from the blackboard as you enter. Your eyes travel downward in what looks like humility but is not. His shoes, buffed to a high gloss, are identical to your own.

"For me?" he says, reaching for the poster as if it were a gift. "Very nice, Mr. Green. I am glad to see that you have decided to take your schoolwork more seriously."

It is hard to tell if he is being sarcastic or just stupid, so you say nothing.

He reaches behind you to Octavia, who is holding her project, with the decorated side toward the floor. Mr. Harrell examines it without enthusiasm. "Not bad, Miss Fuller."

You have made it to your seat and are covertly studying Octavia's hair when Mr. Harrell bangs his ruler on his desk. The gesture is dramatic, but not unusual, so you do not move your eyes from Octavia's mesmerizing braids, which travel an intricate winding path along her scalp. He brings the ruler down hard again. You reluctantly leave your scopophilic trance.

"Our guest today is Officer Brown from the Atlanta Police Department." Mr. Harrell sounds like Bob Barker. "He is going to talk to us about personal safety."

Cautious excitement spreads through the class. No child in this room has felt safe since Jashante disappeared.

Officer Brown is softer and rounder than you imagine a police officer should be. His wide toothy smile is naggingly familiar. Was he the man inside the clown suit at your sister's party last year?

"Hi, kids," he says. "Let's talk about safety. I have a feeling that this might be a topic on your mind lately. Am I right?"

The class stares at him. He looks at Mr. Harrell, who then glares at all of you.

"Not everyone at once," the officer says, with a stiff laugh much like a snort. "Okay." He claps his hands together. "How about you tell me what you already know."

No one speaks. What all of you already know is too terrible to trust to unreliable words. Officer Brown tries again. "I am sure that you guys watch the news with your parents. What have you seen that has to do with kids and safety?" He points at Angelite Armstrong; her long braids always attract attention. "I don't know," she whispers.

"Well, who knows?" He aims his finger at Cinque Freeman. "You look like a sharp young man."

Cinque is not flattered, but he condescends to reply. "Everybody knows somebody is killing black kids."

Officer Brown looks suddenly taken aback as if he only now notices that he is white. You wonder how long it will be before he realizes that he is fat. He looks quickly at Mr. Harrell but gets no reaction. Officer Brown presses his smile, displaying bluish teeth set in pink gums. He looks away from Cinque. "Yes, little lady, you have something to say?"

LaTasha Baxter says, "It's too late to talk to us. Somebody from this class is already—" She bites on her lip and looks at the ceiling as if the word for the unknowable is spelled out in the fluorescent lights. She shakes her head at the officer.

"Jashante," Cinque says. "My cousin."

"He got killed," someone shouted.

This is the first time since Jashante was added to the list of Missing and Murdered Children that he is mentioned at school. Now the syllables of his name are everywhere. Octavia's lips are moving privately, as if in prayer. You hear thirty-two-part harmony.

Officer Brown extends his hands in front of him as if he were saying, playfully, *Don't shoot*. Mr. Harrell bangs his gavel and the class comes to order.

"I am familiar with the Hamilton case," says Officer Brown. "But to my knowledge, Jashante is only missing. Lots of missing children are found each day and returned to their parents."

Not around here. Not this year. You now know, as undeniably as if you had read it in the World Book Encyclopedia, that Officer Brown has nothing useful to share. As a matter of fact, you are more fearful than ever to know that this man is all that stands between your generation and an early death.

"My daddy say it's the police that's doing it," Cinque shouts from the back of the room.

The class is instantly silenced. Of course, you have long since concluded that the police are ineffective at best. After all, twelve children have been abducted. But could the police actually be responsible?

"How else a white man going to get a kid to get in a car with him?"

A good point. The class turns its head toward Officer Brown like spectators at a tennis match. The pudgy man does not respond.

Mr. Harrell intervenes. "Mr. Freeman, out in the hall."

"Man," Cinque complains, slamming his desk shut. "He *my* cousin. I'm just trying to tell y'all what I know."

Officer Brown composes himself. "Wait, young man. Sit back down."

The eyes swing to the teacher. Is he going to allow this rotund white man to reverse his command? And what about Cinque? Will he be broken by the iron will of the law?

"No," says Cinque. "Man done put me out and I'm gone."

Heads turn again to Mr. Harrell. "Take your seat, Mr. Freeman."

Cinque obeys, but not without complaint. "Folks need to make up they mind."

Officer Brown clears his throat and speaks. "Listen, kids. Don't rule anyone out. If we don't know who *is* responsible, then we don't know who's *not*." Now his tone becomes deliberately authoritative, not unlike the voice that omnisciently declares that four out of five dentists surveyed recommend sugarless gum for their patients who chew gum. "But we *do* know that each Atlanta police officer has taken a sacred oath to protect the public, not harm it." He pauses dramatically and looks toward the American flag flaccid in its perch on top of the file cabinet.

"There may be some individuals *impersonating* officers of the law. But the impostor will not have this!" He dips into his pocket and triumphantly produces a glossy piece of metal. "This," he announces, displaying his shield between his thumb and forefinger, "is the official badge of the Atlanta P.D." He gives it to Angelite and indicates that she should pass it around. "Take a good look. Run your hands across it and feel the raised letters. I've seen a lot of fakes, and not one of them has had the letters raised up so high that you can read it with your fingers."

This man is clearly delusional, so you do not point out that a criminal who could steal an official police *uniform* certainly would not neglect to take an official police *badge*. Furthermore, it is nearly time for recess.

• • • •

Sister is in an especially good mood after school today. She grabs your hand and swings it as you walk the quarter mile to the bus stop.

"Know why it's not raining no more?" she says.

You shake your head no, as you try to disentangle your fingers from hers.

"Cause we got our report cards!" she sings, holding tight to your sticky hand.

You've received your report card too. It is sealed like a state secret in an envelope squashed in the bottom of your book bag.

"What's the matter, Brother?" she asks you, over the hiss of the opening bus door.

"Nothing," you say, sitting aboard the bus, heading in the direction of home. Sister, you know, believes that a progress report is merely an occasion for gift-giving. Last term, she was given a doll that wept. You, on the other hand, understand that the Cs written in Mr. Harrell's careful hand will only remind Father why he hates you.

You could do better. Some of your classmates, whom standardized testing deem to be barely above average, take home exemplary grades. But you, despite your ability, do not memorize multiplication tables or spelling words, although the rote drills are all that stand between you and a student-of-the-month award. They could protect you from Father's belt.

"We're here." Sister tugs your hand. You follow her to the front of the bus. When she exits the city bus, drivers of cars in both directions are pleased to stop although the law does not require this. Sister walks quickly; the plastic barrettes on the ends of her ten or so neat braids click charmingly as she makes her way.

When you come in the house, Sister has already hung her red-and-white jumper dress in her closet and is sitting at the table in her slip polishing an apple with a napkin. In the center of the table is a white envelope. You see it, sigh, and take a similar one from your own backpack. It is gummed with residue of purple candy, but you put it on the table next to hers. The contrast is almost humiliating.

"I hope that's good news!" Mother is cheerful as she eyes the tattered envelope.

She knows full well that it is not, but you say nothing. *It's alright* is what you said last time, but lately you have become bored with the ritualistic lies.

"Your sister is going to do some reading before dinner. Don't you want to read for a few minutes before your father gets home?" Mother has read somewhere that children who read at least an hour a day are somehow better than those who don't. Sister absently chews a green apple as she looks at her kids' book with big letters. You read too, but you are not an exhibitionist.

Three hours later, Father arrives, reeking of hard work. "Did you clean your room like I told you?"

You shake your head. "Homework." Luckily you have an open book on your lap to appease Mother.

Father exhales. He is disappointed that he has nothing better for a son. A boy who is not only too short but *trifling, lazy, sloven, and spoiled.*

"Little overdue for a haircut, boy," he says, as if it is a moral defect. You say nothing because you are sure that eventually it will dawn upon him that you are too young to drive and that he is the person ultimately responsible for your upkeep in all matters male. "My daddy told me never to trust a man without a decent edge up," he says emphatically. You hunch your shoulders to hide the two nappy trails of hair running down your neck.

When dinner is served you are full of stolen candy. Mother, a terrible cook, is unaware of her culinary limitations and misprepares complex dishes without remorse. Sister asks for another serving of vichyssoise. Father wipes his mouth with a blue paper napkin and reaches for the envelopes in the center of the table. He takes the clean one first. Sister smiles down at her plate as he rips through the adhesive with his square fingernail.

"Look at this, Beverly," he says. "Almost all Es. And look here. A note on the bottom. It says her report was excellent." Mother now looks down at *her* plate shyly. You know that it is because she did most of the work on that particular project. All Sister did was hand her the glue or the construction paper.

Father opens the second envelope. He looks at it quickly and hands it to your mother. He wants to know what your problem is. You shrug but offer no response.

"He's not challenged," Mother says in your defense.

"Challenged?" Spittle flies from his lips. "This boy's problem is he never had to pick cotton. When you pick cotton you don't sit out there and see if you can be *challenged* by the cotton. You don't bring your bag in empty at the end of the day and tell that white man that the cotton didn't *challenge* you. You just pick the goddamn cotton!"

"Daddy!" Sister says. "You said a bad word."

He apologizes, kissing the top of her lovely head. You stare at your plate, plot murder, say nothing.

Father will beat you tonight. The tiny column of letters defacing your report card mandates that he pull his belt from its loops and swing it hard. His pants will fall below his waist revealing clean white undershorts as he swings at your shins, forcing you to dance a humiliating jig. There is a boy in the special ed class whose legs are immobilized by braces of reinforced metal. Father's belt coils around your left thigh, the buckle collides with your knee. You wish you were a special boy whose legs could not move and could not dance to the rhythm of the licks.

"You have to learn to get your lesson," he says.

You cry despite your resolve to be impassive.

"Never going to amount to nothing." Each word is accentuated by a whack.

You recall Octavia hurling rocks at Leon's head. What would she do if she were in your place? Then, you remember that people say that she has no father. The envy leaves a taste in your mouth that is as bitter as blood.

Father is exhausted now. He takes his air in gulps as he fastens his belt around his trousers. Both of your faces shine with saltwater.

"Let's not let this happen again," he says, opening your bedroom door.

Mother is in the hallway. "Did you hurt him?"

"No," Father assures her. "I hurt his feelings, that's all."

• • • •

On Wednesday morning, your full bladder forces you out of bed. You open your bedroom door and dart across the hall to the bathroom. In the clean and bright room, you use the toilet, being careful not to splash the green tile. Mother has complained to Father about your bad aim. "Get a little closer next time," he told you, as you rubbed the floor with a soapy sponge. "It's not as long as you think it is."

You are on your way back to bed when your parents' door opens. Father is ready for breakfast.

"Well, looka here," he says. "What you doing up?"

You point at the bathroom door and stare longingly at your bedroom.

"Come on in the kitchen and talk to me while I get me some breakfast."

You stand in the hallway barefoot and vulnerable in your Snoopy pajamas. He smiles as if he hadn't hit you with his belt just hours earlier. Will he swing it again if you refuse his invitation?

"Okay," you say.

Father is cheerful as he turns on the radio and shuts it off again. "Don't need that since I got my boy to talk to this morning."

The teakettle shrieks and Father turns brown pebbles into coffee. "Kids don't like coffee, right?"

You don't.

"What it is y'all drink? Hot chocolate? Tea?"

"Hot chocolate is okay."

He rummages in the cabinet. "I don't see none. How about a Coke?"

You shrug. You have not brushed your teeth yet; whatever you drink will taste terrible.

You watch Father's broad back as he breaks three eggs into a little bowl and beats them with a fork. He slurps coffee while dotting slices of white bread with golden margarine. He doesn't turn around before he starts to speak.

"My daddy worked in the sawmill. He couldn't read. He would turn over in his grave if he could hear me because he worked so hard to keep people from knowing. Daddy could write his name as good as a schoolteacher. But that was all." Now Father turns to look at you. "I hate that he died before you could get to know him."

"Yes sir," you say.

"The reason I know that he couldn't read, is that he used to bring me books when I was a boy. I don't even want to think about where he must've gotten them from." Father stirs the eggs in the little black skillet, shaking his head gently from side to side. He takes a big gulp from his mug. "But the reason I know he couldn't read those books is that some of them were straight pornography." He turns and grins at you before lifting perfect slices of toast from the oven. Yellow splotches make the bread look like dice. He hands you two slices on a white saucer trimmed in silver.

"Jelly?" he asks.

"No sir."

"I thought kids were supposed to like sweet stuff." Sitting at the table, he chases his eggs around the plate with the perfect toast. There are crumbs in his mustache.

"Now Daddy was a religious man—we spent all *day* Sunday in church. I know that if he had even a little piece of an idea what was in them books, he never would have let me have them." He laughs and looks at you, expecting a smile. You show your teeth and he continues. "He wanted me to have things a little better. He didn't want me to end up at the sawmill, you see?"

You nod. But you are confused. Father has never given you a book.

"He always made sure I got my lesson, you see."

Your throat tightens and you cannot swallow your toast. You calm yourself by noting that he does not wear a belt with his coveralls.

"Daddy used to beat my tail good if he even *thought* that I wasn't doing my homework." He smiles at his near-empty plate, savoring the memory of pain. "I used to be mad because he would beat me all out in the yard. My friends who probably had did the same thing would be out laughing at me. They had daddies who didn't care enough to take a switch to them when they needed it." He wipes his plate with the last scrap of toast. "Today, somebody would call the police on Daddy and have him taken away for *child abuse*." He smiles at you. Soft bread is lodged between his teeth.

You try to drink some Coke but your throat is shut. You hold the stinging bubbles in your mouth.

"But now, I thank him for it. Some of the fellas I grew up with ain't got half of what I got. Or even look at Joe. Daddy was too old when he was coming up to give him a good whipping when he needed it. What's Joe doing now? Picking up the garbage. If his boss decides to cut his wages, there ain't much that Joe can do. But me, I'm my own boss."

Father scoots back a little from the table, inviting you to take a long admiring look at him. "Your mama don't even have to work." He smiles. "You see what I mean?" Father leaves the kitchen. You go to the bathroom and vomit buttered toast and soda.

You're at school early again this morning. Wednesday is Mother's day to help prepare meals at church for the shut-ins. You are hungry as you wind through the corner store before the bell, but Mrs. Lewis's candies do not tempt you this morning. You tuck a pair of red lollipops in your pocket but they will not do for breakfast. Cherry candy, always improbably bright, never evokes the dark July sweetness of real fruit.

Turning the candy over in your pocket, you watch the breakfast kids through the narrow slit between the cafeteria doors. They eat with hungry appreciation but not with the starving abandon that you have envisioned. Octavia sits alone at an oval table absently eating eggs and cheese while reading a hardcover book. A chunk of egg falls on the page and she looks around her with darting eyes before wiping the book with her napkin. Leon tips a bowl of cereal to his mouth. Puffed corn and milk travel down his throat in waves.

You put your hand to the double doors and give a tentative shove. They yield easily and you walk inside. The room is much cleaner and quieter than it will be at twelve-twenty, lunchtime for fifth-graders. You make your way toward the serving line as a bell rings. A cafeteria lady is wiping down the counter with a stained rag.

"Can I help you?" She is eyeing your penny loafers suspiciously.

"I wanted to get some breakfast."

"Come again?" She plants her hands on her hips to brace herself against any foolishness of yours.

"I wanted to have some breakfast." You clear your throat and add, "Ma'am."

"Breakfast's over."

"Already?" There is a small lake of steaming water where vats of grits, eggs, and bacon had been warmed.

"Your mama didn't fix you nothing before you left the house?" Her eyes soften slightly.

You should be loyal to your mother and explain that you refused the meal she offered you. But to explain this rejection requires that you betray Father. You shrug.

"We got some toast left." She puts two slices on a plate.

You do not reach for it.

"What? Ain't nothing wrong with that toast." She's looking at your loafers again.

You cry. Hard, shoulder-shaking sobs bring her from behind the serving bar. She kneels before you. Her uniform smells of fried food and fabric softener.

"What's wrong, baby?" She lifts your chin and dabs your face with a clean corner of apron. "What you crying for? You sick? You need to call your mama?"

You shake your head vigorously from side to side.

"It's alright," she says. "We don't have to call her." She hugs you, and you allow yourself to sink into the space between her arms. This is a guilty pleasure you have not enjoyed since before Sister was born. The cafeteria lady's body is as firm and comfortable as a good mattress. She rubs your hair in wide spirals. "Shh." Her kiss on the top of your head is as gentle as music.

Finally, you struggle in her embrace. You should tell her that you will be late for class. Embarrassment tangles your words like twine and you cannot speak.

"Better?" she asks, as if she has just adjusted the brakes on your bicycle.

You nod, glad to avoid words.

"Hold on," she says, disappearing momentarily behind a metal door. She returns and presses a banana into your hand. "You can't go all day without something on your stomach."

• • • •

At recess you sit under the sliding board and carefully pull back the yellow peel. The banana inside is the clean color of eggshells and soft as a kiss. You hug your knees to warm yourself after you eat. The slanted metal above you blocks the wind. You pretend to be in a cozy attic room and fall asleep.

You are shaken awake by a seventh-grader, Lumumba Jones. His sister is in your class.

"You alright?" he asks.

You nod.

"He's okay," Lumumba says to Delvis Watson, another older boy. "You in the fifth, right?"

Another nod.

"Man, you must have stayed up late last night to be sleep all this time out here on the cold ground." He pulls you up. "You got dirt all over your pants."

Delvis starts to laugh. "His name need to be Black Van Winkle."

"Leave him alone," Lumumba says; he turns his head to one side. "You sure you okay? You want us to take you to the nurse?"

"Where's my class?" you croak.

"They just getting out of lunch. If you hurry up, you might get to class before they notice you cut."

You thank him and run toward the building. You hear Lumumba say to Delvis, "Little man sho do run flickted."

You are able to fall in with the rest of your class as they leave the cafeteria. You file into the classroom and slide into your desk. "Mr. Green," says Mr. Harrell. "Please step outside."

What does he want? Is he angry that you missed lunch? You stand before his desk, waiting for him to rise and follow you beyond the trailer door.

"You have a question, Mr. Green?"

You shake your head no and leave the trailer alone.

Father stands on the covered walkway. His filthy coveralls stink of oil and anger.

"Sir?" You draw your cold hands up into the sleeves of your sweater.

He looks at you for a long appraising moment and then glances around as if searching for someplace to spit. "Virginia Lewis called me on my job today."

Your heart falls hard in your stomach like a missed pop fly tumbling past your glove to the ground.

"I don't know what your problem is." Father shakes his head in what seems to be genuine bewilderment.

"Did you hear one word I said to you this morning?" The outdoor air coaxes a thin transparent trickle from his nostril. "Do you think I take the time to tell you things just because I want to exercise my face?"

"No sir." But you have no idea why he says what he does.

"Virginia told me you been hanging with the wrong crowd. Coming in her store and stealing candy." He pauses.

"I didn't," you begin.

"Don't lie to me, boy. I didn't come way out here to listen to you lie. I came out here for you to listen." He takes a breath. "Then I call up to the school and they tell me you ain't where you supposed to be. I come running up here and then you seem to have found your way back." His voice rises in the damp air.

"But—"

"You can hang out with your friends when you supposed to be in school. You can hang out with the crowd and steal from Virginia. But let me tell you this, the crowd ain't going to be there for you when it matters. When you have to make something of yourself, you stand alone. You hear me?" His stained index finger grazes your nose.

"Yes sir." But you have never been part of a crowd. It is even difficult for you to recall being in the presence of more than one kid at a time. "Can I—"

"What I just tell you?" Father says. "I didn't come here to hear you lie. I came here to show you that *I* am your father and you do what *I* say do. Not what your friends want you to do."

Now you notice the belt rolled tight and stashed in his palm.

"We going to go in that classroom and I am going to beat your behind. And you'll see that the crowd can't do nothing to help you."

You are required to stand before Mr. Harrell's desk, which he has cleared to accommodate the impending ritual of humiliation. The room is silent as death when you lean over the oak desk and grip its opposite edge with your quivering fingers. You are not the first child to be humiliated before his peers. Twice already this year, mothers on lunch breaks have snatched unsuspecting youngsters from their chairs, flogged them briefly, apologized to Mr. Harrell for disrupting math lessons, and dashed off to work again while the children sobbed and sucked snot.

But there had been no preamble to the other beatings. No agonizing suspense. The mothers were not their own bosses and would hardly waste hired minutes announcing what would soon be apparent anyway. But Father has plenty of time.

"I'm sorry, sir, for disrupting your class," he says to Mr. Harrell. "But Rodney has got to learn not to go running off without no one knowing where's he's at. These days are too dangerous for that."

The class behind you emits a sudden murmur of comprehension. The tension in the room snaps in two like a pencil as the full import of Father's words settles. Everyone understands that he is punishing you for putting yourself in harm's way. You know this is a lie. You release the edge of the desk and fill your lungs to scream, "I stole!" but Father has begun swinging his belt.

The licks are not as hard as the ones last night, but the leather against your behind smarts. You open your mouth wide to shout above the whisk of the belt and Father's grunts, "I STOLE!"

"I," you say as loud as you have ever said anything.

Father interprets this utterance as a cry of pain or an admission of defeat. He stops whipping you.

"Stole," you finish, but Father speaks louder than you and the word is lost.

"Mr. Harrell, I hope this takes care of the problem. If there is any more trouble, just call me."

You walk back to your chair on legs as unsteady as spaghetti. Your classmates look at you with faces splashed with horror. "What he do?" someone asked. "He went off by hisself and almost got snatched." There were no clucks of sympathy. No one said, "He didn't have to whip him like that, all in front of everybody," like they had when the tired mothers invaded the classroom with their violence and fury.

You put your head on your desk and wrap your face with your bony forearms.

"Mr. Green, do you need to excuse yourself to the lavatory?"

You don't answer.

"He said no," Octavia says. "I heard him."

You are grateful but do not lift your head. With closed eyes you try to trace memory to its origin, to the instant you were born. And then maybe you could take your recollections back a single moment earlier to the place before. To the time when you weren't even thought about.

You are awakened by the final bell.

"Wake up, Rodney." Octavia pats your arms with hands that smell like lemons. "You alright?"

You open your eyes. Her face is dark as pencil lead and shiny as a new penny.

"I stole."

"You told?" she says. "Told what to who?"

"Never mind." You reach into your pockets and give her the two cherry lollipops.

• • • •

You are cold without your tweed coat. You should return to the classroom and retrieve it from the coat rack. No one will be there. All the kids are gone. Sister will be ready to walk home now. You must turn back. Nothing you know is in the direction you're heading. Home is the other way. You keep moving, ignoring the blistering rub of your sock, which is twisted inside your loafer. There is the sting of rain in the air that beats you around the ears. You would be much warmer wearing your good tweed coat.

At Martin Luther King Drive, you dart across four lanes of traffic against the blinking warning of the cross signal. Car horns scream, but the drivers accelerate when you find yourself alive and disappointed on the north side of the road. Carillon bells sing from the college campus nearby and you walk toward downtown. Home is the other way.

A blue sedan pulls up beside you.

"Excuse me," says the driver, lowering the passenger-side window. "I'm a police officer. There has been a bank robbery in this area. We need to get all the civilians off the street." A tree-shaped air freshener swings back and forth from his mirror.

"You're not a real policeman."

"What did I just say? Hurry up, kid, and get in the car. I don't have all day." He produces a U-shaped piece of metal. You run your finger across the metal. It is as smooth as chocolate and fake as a glass eye.

The car burps sour exhaust onto the November day. You inhale deeply, tasting the gray poison. "Which way are you going?"

He points toward downtown. Against the overcast sky, you make out the lights rimming the Peachtree Plaza Hotel. When you enter the car, you press your eyelids against your eyes until you see only dancing spots the color of marigolds. The door shuts and the sedan vaults away in the direction opposite of home.

Black Feminist Criticism
and Womanist Theories

Barbara Christian

Barbara Christian received her Ph.D. from Columbia University and was professor of English and African American Studies at the University of California, Berkeley until her death in 2000. Her publications include *Black Women Novelists: The Development of a Tradition, 1892–1976* (1980) and *Black Feminist Criticism: Perspective on Black Women Writers* (1985).

The Race for Theory

I have seized this occasion to break the silence among those of us, critics, as we are now called, who have been intimidated, devalued by what I call the race for theory. I have become convinced that there has been a takeover in the literary world by Western philosophers from the old literary elite, the neutral humanists. Philosophers have been able to effect such a takeover because so much of the literature of the West has become pallid, laden with despair, self-indulgent, and disconnected. The New Philosophers, eager to understand a world that is today fast escaping their political control, have redefined literature so that the distinctions implied by that term, that is, the distinctions between everything written and those things written to evoke feeling as well as to express thought, have been blurred. They have changed literary critical language to suit their own purposes as philosophers, and they have reinvented the meaning of theory.

My first response to this realization was to ignore it. Perhaps, in spite of the egocentrism of this trend, some good might come of it. I had, I felt, more pressing and interesting things to do, such as reading and studying the history and literature of black women, a history that had been totally ignored, a contemporary literature bursting with originality, passion, insight, and beauty. But, unfortunately, it is difficult to ignore this new takeover, because theory has become a commodity that helps determine whether we are hired or promoted in academic institutions—worse, whether we are heard at all. Due to this new orientation works (a word that evokes labor) have become texts. Critics are no longer concerned with literature but with other critics' texts, for the critic yearning for attention has displaced the writer and has conceived of herself or himself as the center. Interestingly, in the first part of this century, at least in England and America, the critic was usually also a writer of poetry, plays, or novels. But today, as a new generation of professionals develops, she or he is increasingly an academic. Activities such as teaching or writing one's response to specific works of literature have, among this group, become subordinated to one primary thrust—that moment when one creates a theory, thus fixing a constellation of ideas for a time at least, a fixing which no doubt will be replaced in another month or so by somebody else's competing theory as the race accelerates. Perhaps because those who have effected the takeover have the power (although they deny it) first of all to be published, and thereby to determine the ideas that are deemed valuable, some of our most daring and potentially radical critics (and by *our* I mean black, women, Third World) have been influenced, even co-opted into speaking a language and defining their discussion in terms alien to and opposed to our needs and orientation. At least so far, the creative writers I study have resisted this language.

For people of color have always theorized—but in forms quite different from the Western form of abstract logic. And I am inclined to say that our theorizing (and I intentionally use the verb rather than the noun) is often in narrative forms, in the stories we create, in riddles and proverbs, in the play with language, because *dynamic* rather than fixed ideas seem more to our liking. How else have we managed to survive with such spiritedness the assault on our bodies, social institutions, countries, our very humanity? And "women," at least the women I grew up around, continuously speculated about the nature of life through pithy language that unmasked the power relations of their world. It is this language, and the grace and pleasure with which they played with it, that I find celebrated, refined, critiqued in the works of writers like Toni Morrison and Alice Walker. My folk, in other words, have always been a race for theory—though more in the form of the hieroglyph, a written figure that is both sensual and abstract, both beautiful and communicative. In my own work I try to illuminate and explain these hieroglyphs, which is, I think, an activity quite different from the creating of the hieroglyphs themselves. As the Buddhists would say, the finger pointing at the moon is not the moon.

From *Cultural Critique* 6 (Spring 1987) published by the University of Minnesota Press.

In this discussion, however, I am more concerned with the issue raised by my first use of the term, the race for theory, in relation to its academic hegemony, and possibly of its inappropriateness to the energetic emerging literatures in the world today. The pervasiveness of this academic hegemony is an issue continually spoken about—but usually in hidden groups, lest we, who are disturbed by it, appear ignorant to the reigning academic elite. Among the folk who speak in muted tones are people of color, feminists, radical critics, creative writers, who have struggled for much longer than a decade to make their voices, their various voices heard, and for whom literature is not an occasion for discourse among critics but is necessary nourishment for their people and one way by which they come to understand their lives better. Clichéd though this may be, it bears, I think, repeating here.

The race for theory—with its linguistic jargon; its emphasis on quoting its prophets; its tendency toward "biblical" exegesis; its refusal even to mention specific works of creative writers, far less contemporary ones; its preoccupations with mechanical analyses of language; graphs; algebraic equations; its gross generalizations about culture—has silenced many of us to the extent that some of us feel we can no longer discuss our own literature, and others have developed intense writing blocks and are puzzled by the incomprehensibility of the language set adrift in literary circles. There have been, in the last year, any number of occasions on which I had to convince literary critics who have pioneered entire new areas of critical inquiry that they did have something to say. Some of us are continually harassed to invent wholesale theories regardless of the complexity of the literature we study. I, for one, am tired of being asked to produce a black feminist literary theory as if I were a mechanical man. For I believe such theory is prescriptive—it ought to have some relationship to practice. Because I can count on one hand the number of people attempting to be black feminist literary critics in the world today, I consider it presumptuous of me to invent a theory of how we ought to read. Instead, I think we need to read the works of our writers in our various ways and remain open to the intricacies of the intersection of language, class, race and gender in the literature. And it would help if we share our process, that is, our practice, as much as possible because, finally, our work is a collective endeavor.

The insidious quality of this race for theory is symbolized for me by a term like "minority discourse," a label that is borrowed from the reigning theory of the day but which is untrue to the literatures being produced by our writers, for many of our literatures (certainly Afro-American literature) are central, not minor. I have used the passive voice in my last sentence construction, contrary to the rules of black English, which like all languages has a particular value system, because I have not placed responsibility on any particular person or group. But that is precisely because this new ideology has become so prevalent among us that it behaves like so many of the other ideologies with which we have had to contend. It appears to have neither head nor center. At the least, though, we can say that the terms "minority" and "discourse" are located firmly in a Western dualistic or "binary" frame which sees the rest of the world as minor and tries to convince the rest of the world that it is major, usually through force and then through language, even as it claims many of the ideas that we, its "historical" other, have known and spoken about for so long. For many of us have never conceived of ourselves only as somebody's other.

Let me not give the impression that by objecting to the race for theory I ally myself with or agree with the neutral humanists who see literature as pure expression and will not admit to the obvious control of its production, value, and distribution by those who have power, who deny, in other words, that literature is, of necessity, political. I am studying an entire body of literature that has been denigrated for centuries by such terms as *political*. For an entire century Afro-American writers, from Charles Chesnutt in the nineteenth century through Richard Wright in the 1930s, Imamu Baraka in the 1960s, Alice Walker in the 1970s, have protested the literary hierarchy of dominance, which declares when literature is literature, when literature is great, depending on what it thinks is to its advantage. The black arts movement of the 1960s, out of which black studies, the feminist literary movement of the 1970s, and women's studies grew, articulated precisely those issues, which came *not* from the declarations of the New Western Philosophers but from these groups' reflections on their own lives. That Western scholars have long believed their ideas to be universal has been strongly opposed by many such groups. Some of my colleagues do not see black critical writers of previous decades as eloquent enough. Clearly they have not read Richard Wright's "Blueprint for Negro Writing," Ralph Ellison's *Shadow and Act*, Charles Chesnutt's resignation from being a writer, or Alice for this general ignorance of what our writer-critics have said. One is that black writing has been generally ignored in this country. Because we, as Toni Morrison has put it, are seen as a discredited people, it is no surprise, then, that our creations are also discredited. But this is also due to the fact that, until recently, dominant critics in the Western world have also been creative writers who have had access to the upper-middle-class institutions of education, and, until recently, our writers have decidedly been excluded from these institutions and in fact have often been opposed to them. Because of the academic world's general ignorance about the literature of black people, and of women, whose work too has been discredited, it is not surprising that so many of our critics think that the position arguing that literature is political begins with these New Philosophers. Unfortunately, many of our young critics do not investigate the reasons *why* that statement—literature is political—is now acceptable when before it was not; nor do we look to our own antecedents for the sophisticated arguments upon which we can build in order to change the tendency of any established Western idea to become hegemonic.

For I feel that the new emphasis on literary critical theory is as hegemonic as the world it attacks. I see the language it creates as one that mystifies rather than clarifies our condition, making it possible for a few people who know that particular language to control the critical scene. That language surfaced, interestingly enough, just when the literature of peoples of color, black women, Latin Americans, and Africans began to move to "the center." Such words as *center* and *periphery* are themselves instructive. *Discourse, canon, texts*, words as Latinate as the tradition from which they come, are quite familiar to me. Because I went to a Catholic mission school in the West Indies I must confess that I cannot hear the word "canon" without smelling incense, that the word "text" immediately brings back agonizing memories of biblical exegesis, that "discourse" reeks for me of metaphysics forced down my throat in those courses that traced *world* philosophy from Aristotle through Aquinus to Heidegger. "Periphery" too is a word I heard throughout my childhood, for if anything was seen as being at the periphery, it was those small Caribbean islands that had neither land mass nor military power. Still I noted how intensely important this periphery was, for U.S. troops were continually invading one island or another if any change in political control even seemed to be occurring. As I lived among folk for whom language was an absolutely necessary way of validating our existence, I was told that the minds of the world lived only in the small continent of Europe. The metaphysical language of the New Philosophy, then, I must admit, is repulsive to me and is one reason why I raced from philosophy to literature, because the latter seemed to me to have the possibilities of rendering the world as large and as complicated as I experienced it, as sensual as I knew it was. In literature I sensed the possibility of the integration of feeling/knowledge, rather than the split between the abstract and the emotional in which Western philosophy inevitably indulged.

Now I am being told that philosophers are the ones who write literature; that authors are dead, irrelevant, mere vessels through which their narratives ooze; that they do not work nor have they the faintest idea what they are doing—rather, they produce texts as disembodied as the angels. I am frankly astonished that scholars who call themselves Marxists or post-Marxists could seriously use such metaphysical language even as they attempt to deconstruct the philosophical tradition from which their language comes. And as a student of literature,

I am appalled by the sheer ugliness of the language, its lack of clarity, its unnecessarily complicated sentence constructions, its lack of pleasurableness, its alienating quality. It is the kind of writing for which composition teachers would give a first-year student a resounding F.

Because I am a curious person, however, I postponed readings of black women writers I was working on and read some of the prophets of this new literary orientation. These writers did announce their dissatisfaction with some of the cornerstone ideas of their own tradition, a dissatisfaction with which I was born. But in their attempt to change the orientation of Western scholarship, they, as usual, concentrated on themselves and were not in the slightest interested in the worlds they had ignored or controlled. Again I was supposed to know them, while they were not at all interested in knowing me. Instead, they sought to "deconstruct" the tradition to which they belonged even as they used the same forms, style, and language of that tradition, forms that necessarily embody its values. And increasingly as I read them and saw their substitution of their philosophical writings for literary ones, I began to have the uneasy feeling that their folk were not producing any literature worth mentioning. For they always harkened back to the masterpieces of the past, again reifying the very texts they said they were deconstructing. Increasingly, as their way, their terms, their approaches remained central and became the means by which one defined literary critics, many of my own peers who had previously been concentrating on dealing with the other side of the equation—the reclamation and discussion of past and present Third World literatures—were diverted into continually discussing the new literary theory.

From my point of view as a critic of contemporary Afro-American women's writing, this orientation is extremely problematic. In attempting to find the deep structures in the literary tradition, a major preoccupation of the new New Criticism, many of us have become obsessed with the nature of reading itself to the extent that we have stopped writing about literature being written today. Since I am slightly paranoid, it has begun to occur to me that the literature being produced *is* precisely one of the reasons why this new philosophical-literary-critical theory of relativity is so prominent. In other words, the literature of blacks, women of South America and Africa, and so forth, as overtly "political" literature was being preempted by a new Western concept which proclaimed that reality does not exist, that everything is relative, and that every text is silent about something—which indeed it must necessarily be.

There is, of course, much to be learned from exploring how we know what we know, how we read what we read, an exploration which, of necessity, can have no end. But there also has to be a "what," and that "what," when it is even mentioned by the New Philosophers, are texts of the past, primarily Western male texts, whose norms are again being transferred onto Third World and female texts as theories of reading proliferate. Inevitably a hierarchy has now developed between what is called theoretical criticism and practical criticism, as mind is deemed superior to matter. I have no quarrel with those who wish to philosophize about how we know what we know. But I do resent the fact that this particular orientation is so privileged, and has diverted so many of us from doing the first readings of the literature being written today as well as of past works about which nothing has been written. I note, for example, that there is little work done on Gloria Naylor, that most of Alice Walker's works have not been commented on—despite the rage around *The Color Purple*—that there has yet to be an in-depth study of Frances Harper, the nineteenth-century abolitionist poet and novelist. If our emphasis on theoretical criticism continues, critics of the future may have to reclaim the writers we are now ignoring, that is, if they are even aware these artists exist.

I am particularly perturbed by the movement to exalt theory, as well, because of my own adult history. I was an active member of the black arts movement of the sixties and know how dangerous theory can become. Many today may not be aware of this, but the black arts movement tried to create black literary theory and in doing so became prescriptive. My fear is that when theory is not rooted in practice, it becomes prescriptive, exclusive, elitish.

An example of this prescriptiveness is the approach the black arts movement took toward language. For it, blackness resided in the use of black talk which they defined as hip urban language. So that when Nikki Giovanni reviewed Paule Marshall's *Chosen Place, Timeless People*, she criticized the novel on the grounds that it was not black, for the language was too elegant, too white. Blacks, she said, did not speak that way. Having come from the West Indies where we do, some of the time, speak that way, I was amazed by the narrowness of her vision. The emphasis on one way to be black resulted in the works of Southern writers being seen as nonblack because the black talk of Georgia does not sound like the black talk of Philadelphia. Because the ideologues, like Baraka, came from the urban centers, they tended to privilege their way of speaking, thinking, writing, and to condemn other kinds of writing as not being black enough. Whole areas of the canon were assessed according to the dictum of the black arts nationalist point of view, as in Addison Gayle's *The Way of the New World*, and other works were ignored because they did not fit the scheme of cultural nationalism. Older writers like Ralph Ellison and James Baldwin were condemned because they saw that the intersection of Western and African influences resulted in a new Afro-American cul-

ture, a position with which many of the black nationalist ideologues disagreed. Writers were told that writing love poems was not being black. Further examples abound.

It is true that the Black Arts Movements resulted in a necessary and important critique both of previous Afro-American literature and of the white-established literary world. But in attempting to take over power, it, as Ishmael Reed satirizes so well in *Mumbo Jumbo*, became much like its opponent, monolithic and downright repressive.

It is this tendency toward the monolithic, monotheistic, and so on, that worries me about the race for theory. Constructs like the *center* and the *periphery* reveal that tendency to want to make the world less complex by organizing it according to one principle, to fix it through an idea which is really an ideal. Many of us are particularly sensitive to monolithism because one major element of ideologies of dominance, such as sexism and racism, is to dehumanize people by stereotyping them, by denying them their variousness and complexity. Inevitably, monolithism becomes a metasystem, in which there is a controlling ideal, especially in relation to pleasure. Language as one form of pleasure is immediately restricted and becomes heavy, abstract, prescriptive, monotonous.

Variety, multiplicity, eroticism are difficult to control. And it may very well be that these are the reasons why writers are often seen as persona non grata by political states, whatever form they take, because writers/artists have a tendency to refuse to give up their way of seeing the world and of playing with possibilities; in fact, their very expression relies on that insistence. Perhaps that is why creative literature, even when written by politically reactionary people, can be so freeing, for in having to embody ideas and recreate the world, writers cannot merely produce "one way."

The characteristics of the black arts movement are, I am afraid, being repeated again today, certainly in the other area to which I am especially tuned. In the race for theory, feminists, eager to enter the halls of power, have attempted their own prescriptions. So often I have read books on feminist literary theory that restrict the definition of what *feminist* means and overgeneralize about so much of the world that most women as well as men are excluded. And seldom do feminist theorists take into account the complexity of life—that women are of many races and ethnic backgrounds with different histories and cultures and that as a rule women belong to different classes that have different concerns. Seldom do they note these distinctions, because if they did they could not articulate a theory. Often as a way of clearing themselves they do acknowledge that women of color, for example, do exist, then go on to do what they were going to do anyway, which is to invent a theory that has little relevance for us.

That tendency toward monolithism is precisely how I see the means to creating a female language, because language, they say, is male and necessarily conceives of woman as other. Clearly many of them have been irritated by the theories of Lacan for whom language is phallic. But suppose there are peoples in the world whose language was invented primarily in relation to women, who after all are the ones who relate to children and teach language. Some native American languages, for example, use female pronouns when speaking about non-gender-specific activity. Who knows who, according to gender, created languages? Further, by positing the body as the source of everything, French feminists return to the old myth that biology determines everything and ignore the fact that gender is a social rather than a biological construct.

I could go on critiquing the positions of French feminists who are themselves more various in their points of view than the label used to describe them, but that is not my point. What I am concerned about is the authority this school now has in feminist scholarship—the way it has become authoritative discourse, monologic, which occurs precisely because it does have access to the means of promulgating its ideas. The black arts movement was able to do this for a time because of the political movements of the 1960s—so too with the French feminists who could not be inventing "theory" if a space had not been created by the women's movement. In both cases, both groups posited a theory that excluded many of the people who made that space possible. Hence, one of the reasons for the surge of Afro-American women's writing during the 1970s and its emphasis on sexism in the black community is precisely that when the ideologues of the 1960s said black, they meant black male.

I and many of my sisters do not see the world as being so simple. And perhaps that is why we have not rushed to create abstract theories. For we know there are countless women of color, both in America and in the rest of the world, to whom our singular ideas would be applied. There is, therefore, a caution we feel about pronouncing black feminist theory that might be seen as a decisive statement about Third World women. This is not to say we are not theorizing. Certainly our literature is an indication of the ways in which our theorizing, of necessity, is based on our multiplicity of experiences.

There is at least one other lesson I learned from the black arts movement. One reason for its monolithic approach had to do with its desire to destroy the power that controlled black people, but it was a power that many of its ideologues wished to achieve. The nature of our context today is such that an approach which desires power single-mindedly must of necessity become like that which it wishes to destroy. Rather than wanting to change the whole model, many of us want to be all the center. It is this point of view that writers like June Jordan and Audre Lorde continually critique even as they call for empowerment, as they emphasize the fear of difference among us and our need for leaders rather than a reliance on ourselves.

For one must distinguish the desire for power from the need to become empowered—that is, seeing oneself as capable of and having the right to determine one's life. Such empowerment is partially derived from a knowledge of history. The black arts movement did result in the creation of Afro-American studies as a concept, thus giving it a place in the university where one might engage in the reclamation of Afro-American history and culture and pass it on to others. I am particularly concerned that institutions such as black studies and women's studies, fought for with such vigor and at some sacrifice, are not often seen as important by many of our black or women scholars precisely because the old hierarchy of traditional departments is seen as superior to these "marginal" groups. Yet, it is in this context that many others of us are discovering the extent of our complexity, the interrelationships of different areas of knowledge in relation to a distinctly Afro-American or female experience. Rather than having to view our world as subordinate to others, or rather than having to work as if we were hybrids, we can pursue ourselves as subjects.

My major objection to the race for theory, as some readers have probably guessed by now, really hinges on the question, "For whom are we doing what we are doing when we do literary criticism?" It is, I think, the central question today, especially for the few of us who have infiltrated the academy enough to be wooed by it. The answer to that question determines what orientation we take in our work, the language we use, the purposes for which it is intended.

I can only speak for myself. But what I write and how I write is done in order to save my own life. And I mean that literally. For me, literature is a way of knowing that I am not hallucinating, that whatever I feel/know is. It is an affirmation that sensuality is intelligence, that sensual language is language that makes sense. My response, then, is directed to those who write what I read and to those who read what I read—put concretely—to Toni Morrison and to people who read Toni Morrison (among whom I would count few academics). That number is increasing, as is the readership of Alice Walker and Paule Marshall. But in no way is the literature Morrison, Marshall, or Walker create supported by the academic world. And, given the political context of our society, I do not expect that to change soon. For there is no reason, given who controls these institutions, for them to be anything other than threatened by these writers.

My readings do presuppose a need, a desire among folk who, like me, also want to save their own lives. My concern, then, is a passionate one, for the literature of people who are not in power has always been in danger of extinction or of co-optation, not because we do not theorize but because what we can even imagine, far less who we can reach, is constantly limited by societal structures. For me, literary criticism is promotion as well as understanding, a response to the writer to whom there is often no response, to folk who need the writing as much as they need anything. I know, from literary history, that writing disappears unless there is a response to it. Because I write about writers who are now writing, I hope to help ensure that their tradition has continuity and survives.

So my "method," to use a new "lit. crit." word, is not fixed but relates to what I read and to the historical context of the writers I read and to the many critical activities in which I am engaged, which may or may not involve writing. It is a learning from the language of creative writers, which is one of surprise, so that I might discover what language I might use. For my language is very much based on what I read and how it affects me, that is, on the surprise that comes from reading something that compels you to read differently, as I believe literature does. I, therefore, have no set method, another prerequisite of the new theory, since for me every work suggests a new approach. As risky as that might seem, it is, I believe, what intelligence means—a tuned sensitivity to that which is alive and therefore cannot be known until it is known. Audre

Lorde puts it in a far more succinct and sensual way in her essay, "Poetry Is Not a Luxury."

> As they become known to and accepted by us, our feelings and the honest exploration of them become sanctuaries and spawning grounds for the most radical and daring of ideas. They become a safe-house for that difference so necessary to change and the conceptualization of any meaningful action. Right now, I could name at least ten ideas I would have found intolerable or incomprehensible and frightening, except as they came after dreams and poems. This is not idle fantasy, but a disciplined attention to the true meaning of "it feels right to me." We can train ourselves to respect our feelings and to transpose them into a language so they can be shared. And where that language does not yet exist, it is our poetry which helps to fashion it. Poetry is not only dream and vision; it is the skeleton architecture of our lives. It lays the foundations for a future of change, a bridge across our fears of what has never been before.[1]

Note

1. Audre Lorde, "Poetry Is Not a Luxury," in Audre Lorde, *Sister Outsider* (Trumansburg, N.Y.: Crossing Press, 1984), 37.

Karla Holloway

Karla Holloway received her Ph.D. from Michigan State University and is currently the William R. Kenan Professor of English at Duke University. Her publications include *Codes of Conduct: Race, Ethics, and the Color of Our Character* (1995) and *Passed On: African-American Mourning Stories* (2002).

Revision and (Re)membrance

A Theory of Literary Structures in Literature by African-American Women Writers

There were no memories among those pieces. Certainly no memories to be cherished.

—TONI MORRISON, *THE BLUEST EYE*

A stream of linguistic madness that merges the images of an internally fractured psyche and an externally flattened physical world is the opening and closing linguistic figuration in Toni Morrison's *The Bluest Eye*. We come to learn that the injured spirit belongs to Pecola and that the opening scene of the fictional Dick-and-Jane house that her metaphorically blued eyes see ("Here is the house. It is green and white. . . . It is very pretty. Here is the family. Mother, Father, Dick and Jane live in the green-and-white house."[7]) is the one-dimensional remnant of the illusory world that has claimed her.

This fragmented and flattened stream is just one of the shapes of language in Morrison's shifting novel. There is also the ironically poetic and visually vivid language that describes Claudia's struggle to rise above the depression in her physical world:

> She spent her days, her tendril, sap-green days, walking up and down, her head yielding to the bent of a drummer so distant only she could hear. . . . she flailed her arms like a bird in an eternal, grotesquely futile effort . . . intent on the blue void it could not reach—could not even see—but which filled the valleys of the mind. (158)

Colors and textures thicken this novel as if they are the only dimensions left of language and vision that are able to tell the story of Pecola's madness. Even though the sisters who befriend her are saved by "the greens and blues in [their]

From *Black American Literature Forum* 23 (Winter 1990); permission from Karla Holloway and the African American Review.

mother's voice [that] took all the grief out of the words" (24), Pecola is left with the biting shards of all the grief that surrounds her. "The damage done was total" (158), her one-time friend Claudia reflects. The only language which remains for her is the internalized monologue of a narrative stream whose shape, sound, and sense contain the fractured psyche of the tragically injured Pecola. It alone can testify that her madness was framed by the recurrence of a shifting textual language. Each change in the narrative reminds the reader of another of its forms. Eventually it is this characteristic of a shifting language which frames the recursive structures (signals of textual reflexiveness) of Morrison's first novel.

My purpose in this essay is to suggest ways in which the recursive structures of language in literature by contemporary African-American women writers are signaled by what is essentially a "multiplied" text. Recursive structures accomplish a blend between figurative processes that are reflective (like a mirror) and symbolic processes whose depth and resonance make them reflexive. This combination results in texts that are at once emblematic of the culture they describe as well as interpretive of this culture. Literature that strikes this reflective/reflexive posture is characteristically polyphonic. The textual characterizations and events, the settings and symbolic systems are multiple and layered rather than individual and one-dimensional. This literature displays the gathered effects of these literary structures to the extent that, when we can identify and recognize them, we are also able to specify their relationship to thematic and stylistic emphases of the traditions illustrated in these works. Because all of the structures share complexity—features of what I refer to as both the "multiplied text" and the "layered" text—I have chosen to use the term *plurisignation* as a means of illustrating the dimensions of vision and language in the contemporary literature of writers in this tradition.[1]

Plurisignant texts are notable by their translucence. One interesting consequence of this imagery is a certain "posturing" of the textual language. This posture places the narrative language at a formative threshold rather than on an achieved and rigid structure. This is not to suggest that thesis and content are constantly *in potentia* in these texts. It means instead that these works are often characterized by the presence of a translucent flux and identified by a shifting, sometimes nebulous text. The characteristic of words and places in these works is their representation of events and ideas that revise and multiply meanings to the point that their external ambivalence is but an outward sign of internal displacement. The result for these translucent works is textural dissonance.

Whether it is gender or culture or a complication of both that has directed the works of contemporary African-American women writers toward this exploration of the state of being of its voices, the various linguistic postures within these texts are clearly intertextual. Writing in *Figures in Black*, Henry Louis Gates suggests that "shared modes of figuration result only when writers read each other's texts and seize upon topoi and tropes to revise in their own texts . . . a process of grounding [that] has served to create formal lines of continuity between the texts that together comprise the shared text of blackness" (128–29). Considerations of gender weave an additional texture into this line of continuity.

The translucence I refer to begins to have an interesting quality when viewed not only as method in literature, but as an objective dimension of the literature. It is this kind of complexity that becomes a "formal line of continuity" and that identifies the discrete aspects in the texts of African-American women's writing. One might look, for example, at how black women in the literature of these authors visualize themselves. Instead of reflections that isolate and individuate, characters such as Gwendolyn Brooks's Maud Martha or Ntozake Shange's Sassafrass see themselves surrounded by a tradition of women like them.

Sassafrass's ancestral women come "from out of a closet" and beg her to "make . . . a song . . . so high all us spirits can hold it and be in your tune" (80–81). The "Lady" that Sassafrass conjures calls to "multitudes of brown-skinned dancing girls" (81) who become Sassafrass's spirit-informants, assuring her a place in their own line of continuity as they stabilize her spiritual relationship to them. Shange's achievement is a text that recalls ancestral voices to assist her own obviously contemporary story. For example, it is when Sassafrass's living begins to echo a blues song that the text dissolves into italics and the "Lady" comes from the closet. When this ancestral "Lady sigh[s] a familiar sigh" (180), Sassafrass herself enters the italicized narrative. This is a signal that there is no level of the story, no space in this narrative that is not here:

> The Lady turned to the doorway on her right and shouted, "Come on, y'all," and multitudes of brown-skinned dancing girls with ostrich-feather headpieces and tap shoes started doing the cake-walk all around Sassafrass, who was trying

to figure out the stitching pattern on their embroidered dresses. (81)

The message for Sassafrass is that the texture of their appearance (the "stitching pattern") is as important as their lineage. These ladies are there to instruct her and, even more importantly, to replace the abusive Mitch, who, Shange writes, had been "on her mind" (82). The mixture of images that Sassafrass learns to live with—the creation banner over the stove, the looms that revision her own growing-up in her mother's house, her writing and her recipes—are all fragments of the spiritual energy she will need in order to rescue her spirit from the disabling presence of Mitch.

The poignancy in Shange's writing extends from her successful mingling of languages. Poetry and music exist in the same spaces as dialogues and dreams. Women's sharing of their most intimate and creative language with each other is a significant feature of Shange's method. Part of this sharing is clearly evident in the recipes and letters from Sassafrass's, Cypress's, and Indigo's mother, but it is also an important dimension of the lesbian relationships in this novel. Some of the most generative and thickest language surrounds Shange's descriptions of the women's dance collective the Azure Bosom.

Dense in color and texture, and full and resonant in shapes and forms, this collective represents the deepest levels of the stylistic effort in *Sassafrass, Cypress & Indigo*. Here, the language is as full-bodied as the women's gender dance, "a dance of women discovering themselves in the universe" (141). In the house Cypress shares with the dancers from the Azure Bosom, she sees "herself everywhere . . . nothing different from her in essence: no thing not woman" (139). In this novel, Shange brings full circle the revelation of her dramatic choreopoem *for colored girls*. Here, the generational dimensions of womanself are explored as a variety of creative energies—Sassafrass's weaving and writing, Cypress's dance, and eventually Indigo's personification of biological creativity. She becomes a midwife—a creatrix. Because it is Indigo's vision that both opens and closes the story, she is Shange's final coalesence of the extended imaginative dimensions of the novel. Indigo represents the metaphorical bridge between African-American women and their African ancestry. She is an elemental link, embodying the qualities of air ("a moon in her mouth"), earth ("'earth blood, filled up with the Geechees long gone'"), and water ("'and the sea'" [1]). It is not until Sassafrass wears white and sees a vision of her "Mother" (Shange capitalizes this word, giving it a resonance and depth that extends beyond her immediate biological mother) that she finds the spirit she shares with her sister Indigo. By this time in the story, Indigo has come to embody the midwifery talents of her mentor Aunt Haydee. We are told that her place in the ancestral tradition Haydee represents is appropriate because, more than having "an interest in folklore," Indigo "was the folks" (224).

Maud Martha's vision of her place in the line of ancient folks that claim Sassafrass as one of them is vision as well as revision. Her recursive glance represents both a call from her history and a response from her own psyche:

A procession of pioneer women strode down her imagination; strong women, bold; praiseworthy, faithful, stout-minded; with a stout light beating in the eyes. Women who could stand low temperatures. Women who would toil eminently, to improve the lot of their men. Women who cooked. She thought of herself, dying for her man. It was a beautiful thought. (200–01)

That Maud Martha's imagination shifts in this novella just enough so that she does not become the sacrificial victim of a man who would define the parameters of her own dream for her is its thesis. Instead, Maud Martha learns to include her own self as something "decently constant" to depend upon—similar to the discovery of Toni Morrison's Sethe (in *Beloved*), who learns to accept that she is her own "best thing"—and learns as well that "learning was work." Significantly, Maud Martha does not revision the procession of women from her imagination. Instead, she learns to revisualize the nature of their work. In *Maud Martha*, translucence is related to the shifting presence of Maud and her dreams. For example, her husband tells her that the place he visualizes for her, their apartment, will be her "dream." But the reader is confronted with textual structures that insist on their own dreaminess: the silences that fracture each scene and the stifling spaces of Maud's life (both the apartment and her marriage) that define her liminality. Maud's thoughts mix themselves into these structures as if they are actually translucent. In an episode that describes Maud's sparing the life of a tiny mouse which "vanishes" after her act of liberation, Brooks writes, "Suddenly, she was conscious of a new cleanness in her. A wide air walked in her. . . . In the center of [her] simple restraint was—creation" (212–13).

Equally as significant a moment and also an illustration of the revision that occurs when "modes of figuration" are shared is the moment that follows the embrace between Ciel and Mattle in Gloria Naylor's *The Women of Brewster Place*. I find in Maud's sudden translucence (the wide air that "walked" in her) a luminous quality similar to Ciel's moan, a sound so "agonizingly slow, it broke its way through [her] parched lips in a spaghetti-thin column of air that could be faintly heard in the frozen room" (103).[2] Both moments mark occasions that initiate a cleansing of psychic despair. Maud realizes that she is good, and Luciela realizes her grief.

The Women of Brewster Place is a novel where time and place (space) immediately collide. The first section, "Dawn,"

is an introduction to the history of Brewster Place, which Naylor characterizes as a "*bastard child*" (1). The focus in the novel is on the women of this place, whose own histories are as bastardized as their contemporary locus. Mattle, Ciel, Etta Mae, "The Two," and Kiswana are all women separated from their familial sources and are left alone to become the communal "daughters" of the place. Such spiritual dislocation, complicated by the vapid air of Brewster Place, exacts its tragic due. In the last section of the novel, "Dusk," Brewster Place "wait[s] for death, which is a second behind the expiration of its spirit in the minds of its children. . . . the colored daughters of Brewster, spread over the canvas of time, still wake up with their dreams misted on the edge of a yawn" (192).

In this work, the metaphor of a place serves as an ancestral presence. Brewster Place exists both before the women who inherit it and afterwards. Its fundamental irony, and Naylor's bitter commentary on these spiritually dispossessing city spaces, is that Brewster Place is generatively inadequate and sterile. Over and over again African-American women's texts present characters poised between a spiritual place and a place that has been defined for them, assigned by some person, or extracted from some ritual they are unable to remember.

The quality of translucence that reveals such plurisignant texts is also one that complicates the identities of the tellers of the stories. The boundaries between narrative voices and dialogue often become obscure, merging one into the other.[3] Speech that is circumvented has come to be a discrete feature of the African-American women writers' canon. The result of this frustration, this struggle towards articulation, is that voice in these writer's works is manipulated—inverted from its usual dimensions and re-placed into non-traditional spheres (layers) of the text. In this formulation, speech is often liminal, translucent, and subject to disarray, dislocation (in the Freudian sense of *Verschetbung*), and dispersion. Only the thematic emphasis on the recovery of some dimension of voice restores the balance to the text between its voices and those collected into its rearticulated universe. Such empowerment at the metaphorical level—storms and hurricanes that have psychically disruptive potentials, trees that are serene and knowledgeable, rivers whose resident ladies (goddesses) hold the promise (or denial) of fertility—provides poetic activation of the textual voices in African-American women writers' texts.

II

Only the final section . . . raises the poetry to a sustained high level . . . recall[ing] the English metaphysicals . . . fus[ing] African and European elements as in the beat of Mr. Soyinka's early verse.

—WILLIAM RIGGAN, REVIEWING SOYINKA'S
MANDELA'S EARTH AND OTHER POEMS

Indeed, the basic difference between British and Igbo experiences and values are what make it necessary . . . to have to bend the English language in order to express Igbo experience and value in it.

—CHINWEIZU (EMPHASIS ADDED)[4]

Shift

I cite the Riggan review and the Chinweizu excerpt as a means of focusing on both the nature of textual revision and the substance of the interpretive discourse that often follows the work of writers whose cultural sources are non-Western. Central to my definition of metaphorical revision in the texts of African-American women writers is an acknowledgment of the cultural sources of their (re)membered theses. What becomes increasingly important to my consideration of the intertextual nature of the literature produced by black women writers is the premise that the plurisignant text has a multiple generation as well as a multiple presence. Both source and substance are traceable through the culturally specific figurations of language that are discrete figures in literature by black women authors. Shift happens when the textual language "bends" in an acknowledgment of "experience and value" that are not Western. A critical language that does not acknowledge the bend, or is itself inflexible and monolithic, artificially submerges the multiple voices within this literature. For this reason, critical strategies that address the issues within these texts must in one sense be mediative strategies between the traditional ideologies of the theoretical discourse and the ancestry of the text itself. Such mediation demands a shift in the scope (if not the tone) of critical terminology—a redirection that calls attention to different (and often contrary) ideologies. This is a task that demands a particular kind of assertiveness. This assertiveness directs my discussion on the nature of shift and revision.

My primary argument is this: When the interpretive spaces of the Afrocentric text are culturally specified, and when theory attends to the dimensions of gender that are discrete in the figurations of texts by black women writers, the tangential accomplishment of such specification and articulation is a presentation of the plurisignant text as the ideal center of the critical discourse among the cultural etymologies of words within the critical and textual traditions. Texts by black women writers are those which are most likely to force apart the enclosed spaces of critical inquiry. The ideologies especially challenged by the plurisignant text are those held by the "resident theoreticians"—those who have gerrymandered the districts of the interpretive community to the extent that all texts and theorists who do not succumb to the lexical tyranny of the English metaphysicals (and their descendants) are effectively redlined. Such a community has decided upon its membership by a tacit agreement on the formal methods of interpretation and has effectively enclosed the terms of inquiry and imprisoned methodology in the lexical tyranny of Western ideologies. However, by disabling the definitions—that is, by acknowledging a textual language that is translucent and in flux—both the text and (ideally) the inquiry surrounding the text are freed from the tyranny of the West. This act of liberation is directly related to the language within black women writers' texts because their plurisignant nature models the cultural complexity of the language that would engage a "liberated" interpretive community.

In a rather serious "play" with the issues of critical theorizing, Barbara Christian's essay "The Race for Theory" identifies black women as having the historical claim as the "race" (and gender) for theory because:

> people of color have always theorized . . . in forms quite different from the Western form of abstract logic . . . in the stories we create, in riddles and proverbs, in the play with language because dynamic rather than fixed ideas seem more to our liking. . . . And women . . . continuously speculated about the nature of life through pithy language that unmasked the power relations of their world. It is this language, and the grace and pleasure with which they played with it, that I find celebrated, refined, critiqued in the works of [black women writers].(68)[5]

Christian's familiar note that the form of black women's textual language is a hieroglyph ("familiar" because it is a figure Zora Neale Hurston used to describe "Negro" Speech) that is both "sensual and abstract . . . beautiful and communicative" (68) is an appropriate metaphor as well for the activities of criticism and interpretation of these texts.

However, instead of grace and dynamism, pleasure and pithy speculation, the more likely dimensions of literary assessment have been those that reflect the sort of cultural chauvinism evident in William Riggan's assessment of Wole Soyinka's 1988 book of poetry. Riggan, who is only able to critically appreciate Soyinka's verse when the author "reaches the level of the English metaphysicals" with poetry that reflects its European ancestry, would constrict the African and African-American writer's literary domain. Such ethnocentrism is in fact responsible for disabling the relationship between African and African-American texts and their literary traditions rather than encouraging their (mediative) dialogue.

The idea that the plurisignant text calls attention to the syncretic relationship between individual novels and the novels within the cultural as well as gender-specified genre suggests that the polyphonic nature of these texts is essential not only to their internal figurations, but is also definitive of the tradition that collectively identifies them. Not only do the texts of African-American women writers articulate the dimensions of cultural pluralism in their world, but the perceptual "outsidedness" of these authors (a factor of both gender and culture) propels a revision in the critical discourse about their literature. In such a discursive space, "shift" becomes a necessary mediation between the reader and the text and encourages a dialogue among critical postures within the interpretive community. Shift positions the alternative interpretations represented by the assertions of culture and gender within the textures of this literature. The critical result is a theoretical acknowledgment of the multiplied text.

In case a shifting text and a shiftiness in critical vocabulary seem too problematic for what is generally an urge towards firmness in literary theory, let me suggest a perspective of Paul Ricoeur's as a potentially stabilizing one. In "Hermeneutics: The Approaches to Symbol," Ricoeur notes that "it is only when . . . interpretation is seen to be contained in the other that the antithetic is no longer simply the clash of opposites but the passage of each into the other" (88). Ricoeur is certain of a textural point of intersection in symbols. The concrete moments of a dialectic represent a "peak of mediation." He notes:

In order to think in accord with symbols one must subject them to a dialectic; only then is it possible to . . . come back to living speech. In returning to the attitude of listening to language, *reflection passes into the fullness of speech . . . the fullness of language . . . that has been instructed by the whole process of meaning.* (88, emphasis added)

I suggest that it takes only a slight shift for an understanding of Ricoeur's comment regarding the "passage of each into the other" to extend to the "Others" who are the subjects and authors of African-American literature. The metaphorical figuration that results from this reformulated "other" (the symbols, the speech, the reflective language that Ricoeur includes in the processes that make meaning) is a symbolic reflection of my initial claim about the translucent nature of the plurisignant text. This refiguration brings me to a point where a reconsideration of gender and culture in what I have described as the "translucent" texts of African-American women writers is appropriate.

III

[T]he unconscious is the discourse of the Other. . . . The dimension of truth emerges only with the appearance of language.

— LACAN

(RE)MEMBRANCE

In a reflection on the use of folk material as "imagery and motif" as well as "a basic element of the inner forms" of African-American literature, Keith Byerman's conclusion is

that its use "implies a fundamentally conservative [i.e., preservationist], organic vision on the part of these writers" who recognize the "wholeness, creativity, endurance[,] and concreteness" in maintaining the perspectives of the past as "vital to their own sensibilities" (276). Byerman underscores an important relationship between folk material and the perspectives of the past it recovers in his concluding chapter of *Fingering the Jagged Grain.* However, the "wholeness" and "concreteness" that he suggests are features of this (re)membrance of the past are in fact antithetical to the issue he attempts to resolve in his study. Actually, the search for wholeness is representative of the critical strategies of Western cultures. It represents a sensibility that privileges the recovery of an individual (and independent) text over its fragmented textural dimensions. Byerman's discussion is an example of the negative dialectic that can disable the relationship between interpretive effort and the textual tradition. Although he clearly understands the thematic effort of these works as an attempt to diminish the importance of "individual identity [which] does not exist separate from the community" (277), it is because the "concrete" history which engages the community and its members is a disabling (and therefore translucent) history that literature by African-American women writers actually dissembles the "wholeness" of this revived folkloric text. This is, however, not an act of textual sabotage.

Such activity in African-American women writers' texts is paradoxically an effect of *(re)membrance*—a word which cannot, in this canon where the "shared" tradition belies the scattering effects of the diaspora as well as its contradictory "gathering," simply mean "wholeness." Such an image gives a critical edge to what Morrison's Sethe calls in *Beloved* "rememory." Sethe's vision of history has a translucence akin to that described at the opening of this essay. It is "a picture floating . . . a thought picture" that has as much a place in her vision of the past as it has in the actual past. Consequently, it represents a multiplied (and seemingly contradictory) form of memory because although it achieves its presence through its translucence, its form is a consequence of Sethe's visualization. It is this kind of implicit dualism that calls attention to the cultural traditions within this literature and that begs the questions of gender. For example, it is important to acknowledge the West African ideologies represented in the narrative traditions in African-American women's literature because such tracery would assure our exploring the vestiges of folktales in the African-American text in conjunction with the historically female voices of/in the tales. The tellers, the mode of telling, the complications and sometimes obfuscations of telling become critical not only to the "folkloric" tradition, but to the larger narrative traditions as well. The specificity of voice as well as its assignation are facets of the (re)membered texts by women of the African diaspora.

In "Reshuffling the Deck," Claudia Tate comments on the canon, noting that

> unlike the black aesthetics, black feminist criticism examines not only its discursive territory but its own methodologies as well, *realizing that they are not ideologically neutral.* . . . The criticism's placement in traditional, academic, humanistic discourse gives rise to this reflexive posture because critics involved in this enterprise realize that the very terms for engaging in this discourse, that is, formulating hypotheses and evolving praxes, inherently valorize cultural production that is white, patriarchal, and bourgeois-capitalistic. (120, emphases added)

Tate recognizes, in this essay that reviews contemporary works in Black feminist criticism, the "changing literal and figurative terms of the game," which is a tacit recognition of the quality of "shift" and the nature of (re)membrance. The figuration that is accomplished in these texts is one that reshapes the familiar structures of memory and that implicates a pre-text for African-American women's writing that would, if tapped into, address the significance of their race and culture and gender. The mythopoeic territory for these writers is a territory defined through the reconfiguration of memory. (Re)membrance does not imply the wholeness Byerman (for example) figures as a result of the folkloric traditions in Black literature. Instead, (re)membrance is activation in the face of stasis, a restoration of fluidity, translucence, and movement to the traditions of memory that become the subjects of these works. The substance of literary traditions, whether European or African or American or combinations thereof, is reconstituted in such a literary ethic.

In a recognition that the text of feminist literary studies is discrete, Lillian Robinson calls for the "next step in the theoretical process" which will be "for the female nontext to become the text" (32). Robinson identifies this nontext as the "creative incapacity" equated with silence and sees the restoration of voice as a discrete aspect of a feminist critical tradition. But it is exactly this kind of definition which, as it asserts the feminist text, simultaneously squeezes the black woman writer's literary tradition into a space too narrow to contain it. The (re)membered textural source of this gender-specified literary tradition includes a *cultural* source which is based in a collective orature. Robinson, who clearly understands that there is significant empowerment through language, curiously reaches for restoration of "a common literary heritage" within the restored "voice" of women's texts. However, such restoration may very well undermine the cultural specificity of women's language in the African-American text. The "common" heritage which Robinson concludes may be

the "real thing" for feminist criticism is one she artificially simplifies to a decision that "people have to live in a house, not in a metaphor" (34). It is precisely because of this kind of formulation that critical theories of African-American women's texts must clarify the distinctiveness of the traditions those texts embody and the specificity of the heritage that resonates in the texts, lest those traditions and that heritage be subsumed into a feminist-inspired "commonness."

Consider my final epigraph. How can the discourse of the Other possibly be perceived as a monologue? Truth, language, and alterity (otherness) find their definition within the "discursive territories" of a literary heritage that values and affirms pluralism. A consideration of the text, specifically its language, is exactly what forces critical inquiry back into a textual tradition and forward toward a theory that unequivocally addresses the source, meanings, and cultural complications represented within the textual language. Because the African-American woman's literary tradition is generated from a special relationship to words, the concerns of orature and the emergence of a textual language that acknowledges its oral generation must affect the work of the critics of this tradition.

The revised and (re)membered word is both an anomaly in and a concretizing of the traditions represented in literature by African-American women. Such seeming contradiction, rather than calling attention to a weakness, should draw attention to the need to identify, call, and specify the plurisignance within the texts of this tradition. This is a task of definition as much as it is an act of interpretation. Interestingly, the critical task participates in the "layering" that is intrinsic to the texts of African-American women writers. I find in what the editors of *Yale French Studies* identify as the need to read "collectively, [to speak] in a plural voice" the dimension of feminist criticism that is most like the texts of the African-American woman's tradition, and it is because of this similarity that I basically agree with Lacan's judgment that it is our own "unconscious" that is the actual Other. The presence of the differing self, the "Other" is established through a recursive project, one that repeats the text in order to produce the text. As Christopher Miller effectively argues in "Theories of Africans: The Question of Literary Anthropology":

> By defining the Other's difference, one is forced to take into account, or to ignore at one's peril, the shadow cast by the self. But without some attention to the African past, some effort to describe the Other, how can we accurately read the African present? There are in fact two ways to lose identity, be it one's own or someone else's . . . by segregation in the particular or by dilution in the "universal." (300)

Miller's citation of Césaire's comment on the loss of identity is a maxim critical to the textual and accompanying critical need for a reflective (re)membrance of the textual source which is, after all, the basis of its identity. Within such a perspective, the nature of a critical language is redefined and is subsequently shifted towards the full-bodied voices of the shared traditions reflected within the literature.

Notes

1. I use *plurisignation* in an effort to distinguish the idea of multiple meanings from a text that is (simply) ambiguous. Rather than meaning either one or the other of these terms, a plurisignant text signals the concurrent presence of multiple as well as ambiguous meanings.

2. Interestingly, "luminous" moments in this literature are often accompanied by a visual translucence that effectively includes the textual language as a factor in the shimmering quality of the metaphorical intent.

3. Zora Neale Hurston is the foremother in African-American literature of merged textual voices. *Their Eyes Were Watching God*, especially, uses this device in the blending of the poetic narrative voice and the poetic dialect of Janie's storytelling and reflective dialogues with her friend Pheoby. For further discussion of this dimension of narrative, see Holloway.

4. My preference here, and indeed the thoughtful advice of a reader of this essay, was to use citations that dealt more directly with the women writers under consideration. However, there is a compelling reason that the Riggan/Chinweizu epigraphs serve as appropriate choices for my discussion in this section. In focusing on Riggan's comment about Soyinka, I am able to draw attention to the paucity of critical response that African women writers have received outside of those theorists sympathetically interested in the traditions their gendered and encultured literature reflects. On the other hand, African male writers have managed to enter the wider critical arena (in other words, white males comment on their work). Unfortunately, this extended audience minimally (if at all) appreciates or understands the cultural traditions in the literature. The Riggan response is so striking in its ethnocentrism that it begs to be highlighted. (Carol Boyce Davies relates this issue of critical inattention to African women writers in the thoughtful discussion of her introduction.) As a consequence of Riggan's assessment, Chinweizu's comment on the cultural dimensions within a linguistic system, especially as he directly comments on the "British" experience which Riggan celebrates, is a particularly poignant example of my point concerning the cultural sources of (re)membered theses.

5. Christian's essay bewails the lack of clarity in the critical enterprise, arguing that it underscores a central inattentiveness to text. In addition she argues that this criticism is as "hegemonic as the world it attacks." Christian's comments have the effect of reducing "valuable" critical activity to a practical criticism (similar to her own enterprise) while undermining the theoretical because it "has silenced many of us to the extent that some of us feel we can

no longer discuss our own literature." Ironically, Christian's protest against writers whose criticism ignores the third world and continues to exert its control over the Western world implies the need for a textual exploration of the "center" of the literature of African and African-American women writers from the center that their texts identify.

Works Cited

Brooks, Gwendolyn. *Maud Martha*, 1953. *Blacks*, Chicago: David, 1957, 141–322.

Byerman, Keith. *Fingering the Jagged Grain*. Athens: U of Georgia P. 1985.

Christian, Barbara. "The Race for Theory." *Feminist-Studies* 14.1 (1988): 67–80.

Davies, Carol Boyce. *Ngambika: Studies of Women in African Literature*. Trenton: Africa World P. 1986.

Gates, Henry Louis, Jr. *Figures in Black: Words, Signs and the "Racial" Self*. New York: Oxford UP, 1987.

Holloway, Karla. *The Character of the Word: The Texts of Zora Neale Hurston*. New York: Greenwood, 1987.

Miller, Christopher. "Theories of Africans: The Question of Literary Anthropology." *"Race," Writing and Difference*. Ed. Henry Louis Gates, Jr. Chicago: U of Chicago P. 1985. 281–300.

Morrison, Toni. *The Bluest Eye*. 1970, New York: Pocket, 1972.

———. *Beloved*. New York: Knopf. 1987.

Naylor, Gloria. *The Women of Brewster Place*. New York: Viking, 1982.

Ricoeur, Paul. "Hermeneutics: The Approaches to Symbol." *Existential Phenomenology to Structuralism*, Ed. Vernon Gras. New York: Dell, 1973, 87–118.

Robinson, Lillian. "Canon Fathers and Myth Universe." *New Literary History* 19.1 (1987): 23–36.

Shange, Ntozake. *Sassafrass, Cypress & Indigo*. New York: St. Martin's, 1982.

Tate, Claudia. "Reshuffling the Deck: Or, (Re)Reading Race and Gender in Black Women's Writing." *Tulsa Studies in Women's Literature* 7.1 (1988): 119–31.

Audre Lorde

Audre Lorde was the author of numerous works of prose and poetry and held the Thomas Hunter Chair of Literature at Hunter College until her death in 1992. Her publications include *The Black Unicorn* (1978), *The Cancer Journals* (1980), *Zami: A New Spelling of My Name* (1982), *Sister Outsider: Essays & Speeches* (1984), and *A Burst of Light* (1989).

The Master's Tools Will Never Dismantle the Master's House*

I agreed to take part in a New York University Institute for the Humanities conference a year ago, with the understanding that I would be commenting upon papers dealing with the role of difference within the lives of american women: difference of race, sexuality, class, and age. The absence of these considerations weakens any feminist discussion of the personal and the political.

It is a particular academic arrogance to assume any discussion of feminist theory without examining our many differences, and without a significant input from poor women, Black and Third World women, and lesbians. And yet, I stand here as a Black lesbian feminist, having been invited to comment within the only panel at this conference where the input of Black feminists and lesbians is represented. What this says about the vision of this conference is sad, in a country where racism, sexism, and homophobia are inseparable. To read this program is to assume that lesbian and Black women have nothing to say about existentialism, the erotic, women's culture and silence, developing feminist theory, or heterosexuality and power. And what does it mean in personal and political terms when even the two Black women who did present here were literally found at the last hour? What does it mean when the tools of a racist patriarchy are used to examine the fruits of that same patriarchy? It means that only the most narrow perimeters of change are possible and allowable.

The absence of any consideration of lesbian consciousness or the consciousness of Third World women leaves a serious gap within this conference and within the papers presented here. For example, in a paper on material relationships between women, I was conscious of an either/or model of nurturing which totally dismissed my knowledge as a Black lesbian. In this paper there was no examination of mutuality between women, no systems of shared support, no interdependence as exists between lesbians and women-identified women. Yet it is only in the patriarchal model of nurturance that women "who attempt to emancipate themselves pay perhaps too high a price for the results," as this paper states.

For women, the need and desire to nurture each other is not pathological but redemptive, and it is within that knowledge that our real power is rediscovered. It is this real connection which is so feared by a patriarchal world. Only within a patriarchal structure is maternity the only social power open to women.

Interdependency between women is the way to a freedom which allows the *I* to *be*, not in order to be used, but in order to be creative. This is a difference between the passive *be* and the active *being*.

Advocating the mere tolerance of difference between women is the grossest reformism. It is a total denial of the creative function of difference in our lives. Difference must be not merely tolerated, but seen as a fund of necessary polarities between which our creativity can spark like a dialectic. Only then does the necessity for interdependency become unthreatening. Only within that interdependency of different strengths, acknowledged and equal, can the power to seek new ways of being in the world generate, as well as the courage and sustenance to act where there are no charters.

Within the interdependence of mutual (nondominant) differences lies that security which enables us to descend into the chaos of knowledge and return with true visions of our future, along with the concomitant power to effect those changes which can bring that future into being. Difference is that raw and powerful connection from which our personal power is forged.

As women, we have been taught either to ignore our differences, or to view them as causes for separation and suspicion

*Comments at "The Personal and the Political Panel," Second Sex Conference, New York, September 29, 1979.

rather than as forces for change. Without community there is no liberation, only the most vulnerable and temporary armistice between an individual and her oppression. But community must not mean a shedding of our differences, nor the pathetic pretense that these differences do not exist.

Those of us who stand outside the circle of this society's definition of acceptable women; those of us who have been forged in the crucibles of difference—those of us who are poor, who are lesbians, who are Black, who are older—know that *survival is not an academic skill.* It is learning how to stand alone, unpopular and sometimes reviled, and how to make common cause with those others identified as outside the structures in order to define and seek a world in which we can all flourish. It is learning how to take our differences and make them strengths. *For the master's tools will never dismantle the master's house.* They may allow us temporarily to beat him at his own game, but they will never enable us to bring about genuine change. And this fact is only threatening to those women who still define the master's house as their only source of support.

Poor women and women of Color know there is a difference between the daily manifestations of marital slavery and prostitution because it is our daughters who line 42nd Street. If white american feminist theory need not deal with the differences between us, and the resulting difference in our oppressions, then how do you deal with the fact that the women who clean your houses and tend your children while you attend conferences on feminist theory are, for the most part, poor women and women of Color? What is the theory behind racist feminism?

In a world of possibility for us all, our personal visions help lay the groundwork for political action. The failure of academic feminists to recognize difference as a crucial strength is a failure to reach beyond the first patriarchal lesson. In our world, divide and conquer must become define and empower.

Why weren't other women of Color found to participate in this conference? Why were two phone calls to me considered a consultation? Am I the only possible source of names of Black feminists? And although the Black panelist's paper ends on an important and powerful connection of love between women, what about interracial cooperation between feminists who don't love each other?

In academic feminist circles, the answer to these questions is often, "We did not know who to ask." But that is the same evasion of responsibility, the same cop-out, that keeps Black women's art out of women's exhibitions, Black women's work out of most feminist publications except for the occasional "Special Third World Women's Issue," and Black women's texts off your reading lists. But as Adrienne Rich pointed out in a recent talk, white feminists have educated themselves about such an enormous amount over the past ten years, how come you haven't also educated yourselves about Black women and the differences between us—white and Black—when it is key to our survival as a movement?

Women of today are still being called upon to stretch across the gap of male ignorance and to educate men as to our existence and our needs. This is an old and primary tool of all oppressors to keep the oppressed occupied with the master's concerns. Now we hear that it is the task of women of Color to educate white women—in the face of tremendous resistance—as to our existence, our differences, our relative roles in our joint survival. This is a diversion of energies and a tragic repetition of racist patriarchal thought.

Simone de Beauvoir once said: "It is in the knowledge of the genuine conditions of our lives that we must draw our strength to live and our reasons for acting."

Racism and homophobia are real conditions of all our lives in this place and time. *I urge each one of us here to reach down into that deep place of knowledge inside herself and touch that terror and loathing of any difference that lives there. See whose face it wears.* Then the personal as the political can begin to illuminate all our choices.

Deborah McDowell

Deborah McDowell received her Ph.D. at Purdue University and is currently the Alice Griffin Professor of English at the University of Virginia. Her publications include *'The Changing Same': Black Women's Literature, Criticism, and Theory* (1995) and *Leaving Pipe Shop: Memories of Kin* (1996).

New Directions for Black Feminist Criticism

"What is commonly called literary history," writes Louise Bernikow, "is actually a record of choices. Which writers have survived their times and which have not depends upon who noticed them and chose to record their notice."[1] Women writers have fallen victim to arbitrary selection. Their writings have been "patronized, slighted, and misunderstood by a cultural establishment operating according to male norms out of male perceptions."[2] Both literary history's "sins of omission" and literary criticism's inaccurate and partisan judgments of women writers have come under attack since the early 1970s by feminist critics.[3] To date, no one has formulated a precise or complete definition of feminist criticism, but since its inception, its theorists and practitioners have agreed that it is a "corrective, unmasking the omissions and distortions of the past—the errors of a literary critical tradition that arise from and reflect a culture creature, perpetuated, and dominated by men."[4]

These early theorists and practitioners of feminist literary criticism were largely white females who, wittingly or not, perpetrated against the Black woman writer the same exclusive practices they, so vehemently decried in white male scholars. Seeing the experiences of white women, particularly white middle-class women, as normative, white female scholars proceeded blindly to exclude the work of Black women writers from literary anthologies and critical studies. Among the most flagrant examples of this chauvinism is Patricia Meyer Spacks's *The Female Imagination*. In a weak defense of her book's exclusive focus on women in the Anglo-American literary tradition, Spacks quotes Phyllis Chesler (a white female psychologist): "I have no theory to offer of Third World female psychology in America. . . . As a white woman, I'm reluctant and unable to construct theories about experiences I haven't had."[5] But, as Alice Walker observes, "Spacks never lived in nineteenth-century Yorkshire, so why theorize about the Brontës?"[6]

Not only have Black women writers been "disenfranchised" from critical works by white women scholars on the "female tradition," but they have also been frequently excised from those on the Afro-American literary tradition by Black scholars, most of whom are males. For example, Robert Stepto's *From Behind the Veil: A Study of Afro-American Narrative* purports to be "a history . . . of the historical consciousness of an Afro-American art form—namely, the Afro-American written narrative."[7] Yet, Black women writers are conspicuously absent from the table of contents. Though Stepto does have a token two-page discussion of Zora Neale Hurston's *Their Eyes Were Watching God* in which he refers to it as a "seminal narrative in Afro-American letters,"[8] he did not feel that the novel merited its own chapter or the thorough analysis accorded the other works he discusses.

When Black women writers are neither ignored altogether nor merely given honorable mention, they are critically misunderstood and summarily dismissed. In *The Negro Novel in America*, for example, Robert Bone's reading of Jessie Fauset's novels is both partisan and superficial and might explain the reasons Fauset remains obscure. Bone argues that Fauset is the foremost member of the "Rear Guard" of writers "who lagged behind," clinging to established literary traditions. The "Rear Guard" drew their source material from the Negro middle class in their efforts "to orient Negro art toward white opinion," and "to apprise educated whites of the existence of respectable Negroes." Bone adds that Fauset's emphasis on the Black middle class results in novels that are "uniformly sophomoric, trivial and dull."[9]

While David Littlejohn praises Black fiction since 1940, he denigrates the work of Fauset and Nella Larsen. He maintains that "the newer writers are obviously writing as men, for men," and are avoiding the "very close and steamy" writing that is the result of "any subculture's taking itself too seriously, defining the world and its values exclusively in the

From *Black American Literature Forum* 14 (1980): 153–159.

terms of its own restrictive norms and concerns."[10] This "phallic criticism,"[11] to use Mary Ellman's term, is based on masculine-centered values and definitions. It has dominated the criticism of Black women writers and has done much to guarantee that most would be, in Alice Walker's words, "casually pilloried and consigned to a sneering oblivion."[12]

Suffice it to say that the critical community has not favored Black women writers. The recognition among Black female critics and writers that white women, white men, and Black men consider their experiences as normative and Black women's experiences as deviant has given rise to Black feminist criticism. Much as in white feminist criticism, the critical postulates of Black women's literature are only skeletally defined. Although there is no concrete definition of Black feminist criticism, a handful of Black female scholars have begun the necessary enterprise of resurrecting forgotten Black women writers and revising misinformed critical opinions of them. Justifiably enraged by the critical establishment's neglect and mishandling of Black women writers, these critics are calling for, in the words of Barbara Smith, "nonhostile and perceptive analysis of works written by persons outside the 'mainstream' of white/male cultural rule."[13]

Despite the urgency and timeliness of the enterprise, however, no substantial body of Black feminist criticism— either in theory or practice—exists, a fact which might be explained partially by our limited access to and control of the media.[14] Another explanation for the paucity of Black feminist criticism, notes Barbara Smith, is the lack of a "developed body of Black feminist political theory whose assumptions could be used in the study of Black women's art."

Despite the strained circumstances under which Black feminist critics labor, a few committed Black female scholars have broken necessary ground. For the remainder of this essay I would like to focus on selected writings of Black feminist critics, discussing their strengths and weaknesses and suggesting new directions toward which the criticism might move and pitfalls that it might avoid.

Unfortunately, Black feminist scholarship has been decidedly more practical than theoretical, and the theories developed thus far have often lacked sophistication and have been marred by slogans, rhetoric, and idealism. The articles that attempt to apply these theoretical tenets often lack precision and detail. These limitations are not without reason. As Dorin Schumacher observes, "the feminist critic has few philosophical shelters, pillars, or guideposts," and thus "feminist criticism is fraught with intellectual and professional risks, offering more opportunity for creativity, yet greater possibility of errors."[15]

The earliest theoretical statement on Black feminist criticism is Barbara Smith's "Toward a Black Feminist Criticism." Though its importance as a groundbreaking piece of

scholarship cannot be denied, it suffers from lack of precision and detail. In justifying the need for a Black feminist aesthetic, Smith argues that "a Black feminist approach to literature that embodies the realization that the politics of sex as well as the politics of race and class are crucially interlocking factors in the works of Black women writers is an absolute necessity." Until such an approach exists, she continues, "we will not even know what these writers mean."

Smith points out that "thematically, stylistically, aesthetically, and conceptually Black women writers manifest common approaches to the act of creating literature as a direct result of the specific political, social, and economic experience they have been obliged to share." She offers, as an example, the incorporation of rootworking, herbal medicine, conjure, and midwifery in the stories of Zora Neale Hurston, Margaret Walker, Toni Morrison, and Alice Walker. While these folk elements certainly do appear in the work of the writers, they also appear in the works of certain Black male writers, a fact that Smith omits. If Black women writers use these elements differently from Black male writers, such a distinction must be made before one can effectively articulate the basis of a Black feminist aesthetic.

Smith maintains further that Zora Neale Hurston, Margaret Walker, Toni Morrison, and Alice Walker use a "specifically black female language to express their own and their characters' thoughts," but she fails to describe or to provide examples of this unique language. Of course, we have come recently to acknowledge that "many of our habits of language usage are sex-derived, sex-associated, and/or sex-distinctive," that "the ways in which men and women internalize and manipulate language" are undeniably sex-related.[16] But this realization in itself simply paves the way for further investigation that can begin by exploring some critical questions. For example, is there a monolithic Black female language? Do Black female high school dropouts, welfare mothers, college graduates, and Ph.D.s share a common language? Are there regional variations in this common language? Further, some Black male critics have tried to describe the uniquely "Black linguistic elegance"[17] that characterizes Black poetry. Are there noticeable differences between the languages of Black females and Black males? These and other questions must be addressed with precision if current feminist terminology is to function beyond mere critical jargon.

Smith turns from her discussion of the commonalities among Black women writers to describe the nature of her critical enterprise. "Black feminist criticism would by definition be highly innovative," she maintains. "Applied to a particular work [it] can overturn previous assumptions about [the work] and expose for the first time its actual dimensions." Smith then proceeds to demonstrate this critical postulate by interpreting Toni Morrison's *Sula* as a lesbian novel, an interpretation she believes is maintained in "the emotions expressed, in the definition of female character and in the way that the politics of heterosexuality are portrayed." Smith vacillates between arguing forthrightly for the validity of her interpretation and recanting or overqualifying it in a way that undercuts her own credibility.

According to Smith, "if in a woman writer's work a sentence refuses to do what it is supposed to do, if there are strong images of women and if there is a refusal to be linear, the result is innately lesbian literature." She adds, "because of Morrison's consistently critical stance toward the heterosexual institutions of male-female relationships, marriage, and the family," *Sula* works as a lesbian novel. This definition of lesbianism is vague and imprecise; it subsumes far more Black women writers, particularly contemporary ones, than not into the canon of Lesbian writers. For example, Jessie Fauset, Nella Larsen, and Zora Neale Hurston all criticize major socializing institutions, as do Gwendolyn Brooks, Alice Walker, and Toni Cade Bambara. Further, if we apply Smith's definition of lesbianism, there are probably a few Black male writers who qualify as well. All of this is to say that Smith has simultaneously oversimplified and obscured the issue of lesbianism. Obviously aware of the delicacy of her position, she interjects that "the very meaning of lesbianism is being expanded in literature." Unfortunately, her qualification does not strengthen her argument. One of the major tasks ahead of Black feminist critics who write from a lesbian perspective, then, is to define lesbianism and lesbian literature precisely. Until they can offer a definition which is not vacuous, their attempts to distinguish Black lesbian writers from those who are not will be hindered.[18]

Even as I call for firmer definitions of lesbianism and lesbian literature, I question whether a lesbian aesthetic is not finally a reductive approach to the study of Black women's literature which possibly ignores other equally important aspects of the literature. For example, reading *Sula* solely from a lesbian perspective overlooks the novel's density and complexity, its skillful blend of folklore, omens, and dreams, its metaphorical and symbolic richness. Although I do not quarrel with Smith's appeal for fresher, more innovative approaches to Black women's literature, I suspect that "innovative" analysis is pressed to the service of an individual political persuasion. One's personal and political presuppositions enter into one's critical judgments. Nevertheless, we should heed Annette Kolodny's warning for feminist critics to

be wary of reading literature as though it were polemic . . . If when using literary materials to make what is essentially a political point, we find ourselves virtually rewriting a text, ignoring certain aspects of plot or characterization, or over-simplifying the action to fit our "political" thesis, then we are neither practicing an honest criticism nor saying anything useful about the

nature of art (or about the art of political persuasion, for that matter).[19]

Alerting feminist critics to the dangers of political ideology yoked with aesthetic judgment is not synonymous with denying that feminist criticism is a valid and necessary cultural and political enterprise. Indeed, it is both possible and useful to translate ideological positions into aesthetic ones, but if the criticism is to be responsible, the two must be balanced.

Because it is a cultural and political enterprise, feminist critics, in the main, believe that their criticism can effect social change. Smith certainly argues for socially relevant criticism in her conclusion that "Black feminist criticism would owe its existence to a Black feminist movement while at the same time contributing ideas that women in the movement could use." This is an exciting idea in itself, but we should ask: What ideas, specifically, would Black feminist criticism contribute to the movement? Further, even though the proposition of a fruitful relationship between political activism and the academy is an interesting (and necessary) one, I doubt its feasibility. I am not sure that either in theory or in practice Black feminist criticism will be able to alter significantly circumstances that have led to the oppression of Black women. Moreover, as Lillian Robinson pointedly remarks, there is no assurance that feminist aesthetics "will be productive of a vision of art or of social relations that is of the slightest use to the masses of women, or even one that acknowledges the existence and struggle of such women."[20] I agree with Robinson that "ideological criticism must take place in the context of a political movement that can put it to work. The revolution is simply not going to be made by literary journals."[21] I should say that I am not arguing a defeatist position with respect to the social and political uses to which feminist criticism can be put. Just as it is both possible and useful to translate ideological positions into aesthetic ones, it must likewise be possible and useful to translate aesthetic positions into the machinery for social change.

Despite the shortcomings of Smith's article, she raises critical issues on which Black feminist critics can build. There are many tasks ahead of these critics, not the least of which is to attempt to formulate some clear definitions of what Black feminist criticism is. I use the term here simply to refer to Black female critics who analyze the works of Black female writers from a feminist or political perspective. But the term can also apply to any criticism written by a Black woman regardless of her subject or perspective—a book written by a male from a feminist or political perspective, a book written by a Black woman or about Black women authors in general, or any writings by women.[22]

In addition to defining the methodology, Black feminist critics need to determine the extent to which their criticism intersects with that of white feminist critics. Barbara Smith and others have rightfully challenged white women scholars to become more accountable to Black and Third World women writers, but will that require white women to use a different set of critical tools when studying Black women writers? Are white women's theories predicated upon culturally specific values and assumptions? Andrea Benton Rushing has attempted to answer these questions in her series of articles on images of Black women in literature. She maintains, for example, that critical categories of women, based on analyses of white women characters, are Euro-American in derivation and hence inappropriate to a consideration of Black women characters.[23] Such distinctions are necessary and, if held uniformly, can materially alter the shape of Black feminist scholarship.

Regardless of which theoretical framework Black feminist critics choose, they must have an informed handle on Black literature and Black culture in general. Such a grounding can give this scholarship more texture and completeness and perhaps prevent some of the problems that have had a vitiating effect on the criticism.

This footing in Black history and culture serves as a basis for the study of the literature. Termed "contextual" by theoreticians, this approach is often frowned upon if not dismissed entirely by critics who insist exclusively upon textual and linguistic analysis. Its limitations notwithstanding, I firmly believe that the contextual approach to Black women's literature exposes the conditions under which literature is produced, published, and reviewed. This approach is not only useful but necessary to Black feminist critics.

To those working with Black women writers prior to 1940, the contextual approach is especially useful. In researching Jessie Fauset, Nella Larsen, and Zora Neale Hurston, for example, it is useful to determine what the prevalent attitudes about Black women were during the time that they wrote. There is much information in the Black "little" magazines published during the Harlem Renaissance. An examination of *The Messenger*, for instance, reveals that the dominant social attitudes about Black women were strikingly consistent with traditional middle-class expectations of women. *The Messenger* ran a monthly symposium for some time entitled "Negro Womanhood's Greatest Needs." While a few female contributors stressed the importance of women being equal to men socially, professionally, and economically, the majority emphasized that a woman's place was in the home. It was her duty "to cling to the home [since] great men and women evolve from the environment of the hearthstone."[24]

One of the most startling entries came from a woman who wrote:

The New Negro Woman, with her head erect and spirit undaunted, is resolutely marching forward, ever conscious of her historic and noble mission of doing her bit toward the liberation of her people in particular and the human race in general. Upon her shoulders rests the big task to create and keep alive, in the breast of black men, a holy and consuming passion to break with the slave traditions of the past; to spurn and overcome the fatal, insidious inferiority complex of the present, which . . . bobs up ever and anon, to arrest the progress of the New Negro Manhood Movement; and to fight with increasing vigor, with dauntless courage, unrelenting zeal and intelligent vision for the attainment of the stature of a full man, a free race and a new world.[25]

Not only does the contributor charge the Black woman with a formidable task, but she also sees her solely in relation to Black men.

This information enhances our understanding of what Fauset, Larsen, and Hurston confronted in attempting to offer alternative images of Black women. Moreover, it helps to clarify certain textual problems and ambiguities of their work. Though Fauset and Hurston, for example, explored feminist concerns, they leaned toward ambivalence. Fauset especially is alternately forthright and cagey, radical and traditional, on issues that confront women. Her first novel, *There Is Confusion* (1924), is flawed by an unanticipated and abrupt reversal in characterization that brings the central female character more in line with a feminine norm. Similarly, in her last novel, *Seraph on the Suwanee* (1948), Zora Neale Hurston depicts a female character who shows promise for growth and change, for a departure from the conventional expectations of womanhood, but who in the end apotheosizes marriage, motherhood, and domestic servitude.

These two examples alone clearly capture the tension between social pressure and artistic integrity which is felt, to some extent, by all women writers. As Tillie Olsen points out, the fear of reprisal from the publishing and critical arenas is a looming obstacle to the woman writer's coming into her own authentic voice. "Fear—the need to please, to be safe—in the literary realm too. Founded fear. Power is still in the hands of men. Power of validation, publication, approval, reputation . . ."[26]

While insisting on the validity, usefulness, and necessity of contextual approaches to Black women's literature, the Black feminist critic must not ignore the importance of rigorous textual analysis. I am aware of many feminist critics' stubborn resistance to the critical methodology handed down by white men. Although the resistance is certainly politically consistent and logical, I agree with Annette Kolodny that feminist criticism would be "short-sighted if it summarily rejected all the inherited tools of critical analysis simply because they are male and western." We should, rather, salvage what we find useful in past methodologies, reject what we do not, and, where necessary, move toward "inventing new methods of analysis."[27] Particularly useful is Lillian Robinson's suggestion that "a radical kind of textual criticism . . . could usefully study the way the texture of sentences, choice of metaphors, patterns of exposition and narrative relate to [feminist] ideology."[28]

This rigorous textual analysis involves, as Barbara Smith recommends, isolating as many thematic, stylistic, and linguistic commonalities among Black women writers as possible. Among contemporary Black female novelists, the thematic parallels are legion. In Alice Walker and Toni Morrison, for example, the theme of the thwarted female artist figures prominently.[29] Pauline Breedlove in Morrison's *The Bluest Eye*, for example, is obsessed with ordering things:

> Jars on shelves at canning, peach pits on the step, sticks, stones, leaves. . . . Whatever portable plurality she found, she organized into neat lines, according to their size, shape or gradations of color. . . . she missed without knowing what she missed— paints and crayons.[30]

Similarly, Eva Peace in *Sula* is forever ordering the pleats in her dress. And Sula's strange and destructive behavior is explained as "the consequence of an idle imagination."

> Had she paints, clay, or knew the discipline of the dance, or strings; had she anything to engage her tremendous curiosity and her gift for metaphor, she might have exchanged the restlessness and preoccupation with whim for an activity that provided her with all she yearned for. And like any artist with no form, she became dangerous.[31]

Likewise, Meridian's mother in Alice Walker's novel *Meridian* makes artificial flowers and prayer pillows too small for kneeling.

The use of "clothing as iconography"[32] is central to writings by Black women. For example, in one of Jessie Fauset's early short stories, "The Sleeper Wakes" (1920), Amy, the protagonist, is associated with pink clothing (suggesting innocence and immaturity) while she is blinded by fairy-tale notions of love and marriage. However, after she declares her independence from her racist and sexist husband, Amy no longer wears pink. The imagery of clothing is abundant in Zora Neale Hurston's *Their Eyes Were Watching God* (1937). Janie's apron, her silks and satins, her head scarves, and finally her overalls all symbolize various stages of her journey from captivity to liberation. Finally, in Alice Walker's *Meridian*, Meridian's railroad cap and dungarees are emblems of her rejection of conventional images and expectations of womanhood.

A final theme that recurs in the novels of Black women writers is the motif of the journey. Though one can also find this same motif in the works of Black male writers, they do not use it in the same way as do Black female writers.[33] For example, the journey of the Black male character in works by Black men takes him underground. It is a "descent into the underworld,"[34] and is primarily political and social in its implications. Ralph Ellison's *Invisible Man*, Imamu Amiri Baraka's *The System of Dante's Hell*, and Richard Wright's "The Man Who Lived Underground" exemplify this quest. The Black female's journey, on the other hand, though at times touching the political and social, is basically a personal and psychological journey. The female character in the works of Black women is in a state of becoming "part of an evolutionary spiral, moving from victimization to consciousness."[35] The heroines in Zora Neale Hurston's *Their Eyes Were Watching God*, in Alice Walker's *Meridian*, and in Toni Cade Bambara's *The Salt Eaters* are emblematic of this distinction.

Even though isolating such thematic and imagistic commonalities should continue to be one of the Black feminist critic's most urgent tasks, she should beware of generalizing on the basis of too few examples. If one argues authoritatively for the existence of a Black female "consciousness" or "vision" or "literary tradition," one must be sure that the parallels found recur with enough consistency to support these generalizations. Further, Black feminist critics should not become obsessed in searching for common themes and images in Black women's works. As I pointed out earlier, investigating the question of "female" language is critical and may well be among the most challenging jobs awaiting the Black feminist critic. The growing body of research on gender-specific uses of language might aid these critics. In fact, wherever possible, feminist critics should draw on the scholarship of feminists in other disciplines.

An equally challenging and necessary task ahead of the Black feminist critic is a thoroughgoing examination of the works of Black male writers. In her introduction to *Midnight Birds*, Mary Helen Washington argues for the importance of giving Black women writers their due first:

> Black women are searching for a specific language, specific symbols, specific images with which to record their lives, and, even though they can claim a rightful place in the Afro-American tradition and the feminist tradition of women writers, it is also clear that, for purposes of liberation, black women writers will first insist on their own name, their own space.[36]

I likewise believe that the immediate concern of Black feminist critics must be to develop a fuller understanding of Black women writers who have not received the critical attention Black male writers have. Yet, I cannot advocate indefinitely such a separatist position, for the countless thematic, stylistic, and imagistic parallels between Black male and female writers must be examined. Black feminist critics should explore these parallels in an effort to determine the ways in which these commonalities are manifested differently in Black women's writing and the ways in which they coincide with writings by Black men.

Of course, there are feminist critics who are already examining Black male writers, but much of the scholarship has been limited to discussions of the negative images of Black women found in the works of these authors.[37] Although this scholarship served an important function in pioneering Black feminist critics, it has virtually run its course. Feminist critics run the risk of plunging their work into cliché and triviality if they continue merely to focus on how Black men treat Black women in literature. Hortense Spillers offers a more sophisticated approach to this issue in her discussion of the power of language and myth in female relations in James Baldwin's *If Beale Street Could Talk.* One of Spillers's most cogent points is that "woman-freedom, or its negation, is tied to the assertions of myth, or ways of saying things."[38]

Black feminist criticism is a knotty issue, and while I have attempted to describe it, to call for clearer definitions of its methodology, to offer warnings of its limitations, I await the day when Black feminist criticism will expand to embrace other modes of critical inquiry. In other words, I am philosophically opposed to what Annis Pratt calls "methodolatry." Wole Soyinka has offered one of the most cogent defenses against critical absolutism. He explains:

> The danger which a literary ideology poses is the act of consecration—and of course excommunication. Thanks to the tendency of the modern consumer-mind to facilitate digestion by putting in strict categories what are essentially fluid operations of the creative mind upon social and natural phenomena, the formulation of a literary ideology tends to congeal sooner or later into instant capsules which, administered also to the writer, may end by asphyxiating the creative process.[39]

Whether Black feminist criticism will or should remain a separatist enterprise is a debatable point. Black feminist critics ought to move from this issue to consider the specific language of Black women's literature, to describe the ways Black women writers employ literary devices in a distinct way, and to compare the way Black women writers create their own mythic structures. If they focus on these and other pertinent issues, Black feminist critics will have laid the cornerstone for a sound, thorough articulation of the Black feminist aesthetic.

Notes

1. Louise Bernikow, *The World Split Open: Four Centuries of Women Poets in England and America, 1552–1950* (New York, 1974), 3.

2. William Morgan, "Feminism and Literary Study: A Reply to Annette Kolodny," *Critical Inquiry*, 2 (Summer 1976), B11.

3. The year 1970 was the beginning of the Modern Language Association's Commission on the Status of Women, which offered panels and workshops that were feminist in approach.

4. Statement by Barbara Desmarais quoted in Annis Pratt, "The New Feminist Criticisms: Exploring the History of the New Space," in *Beyond Intellectual Sexism: A New Woman, A New Reality*, ed. Joan I. Roberts (New York, 1976), 176.

5. Patricia Meyer Spacks, *The Female Imagination* (New York, 1976), 5. Ellen Moers, *Literary Women: The Great Writers* (Garden City, N.Y., 1977) is another example of what Alice Walker terms "white female chauvinism."

6. Alice Walker, "One Child of One's Own—An Essay on Creativity," *Ms.*, August 1979, 50.

7. Robert Stepto, *From Behind the Veil: A Study of Afro-American Narrative* (Urbana, Ill., 1979), x. Other sexist critical works include Donald B. Gibson, ed., *Five Black Writers* (New York, 1970), a collection of essays on Wright, Ellison, Baldwin, Hughes, and Leroi Jones, and Jean Wagner, *Black Poets of the United States: From Paul Lawrence Dunbar to Langston Hughes*, trans. Kenneth Douglas (Urbana, Ill., 1973).

8. Stepto, *From Behind the Veil*, 166.

9. Robert Bone, *The Negro Novel in America* (1958: reprint, New Haven, Conn., 1972), 97, 101.

10. David Littlejohn, *Black on White: A Critical Survey of Writing by American Negroes* (New York, 1966), 48–49.

11. Ellman's concept of "phallic criticism" is discussed in a chapter of the same name in her *Thinking About Women* (New York, 1968), 28–54.

12. Introduction to *Zora Neale Hurston: A Literary Biography* by Robert Hemenway (Urbana, Ill., 1976), xiv. Although Walker makes this observation specifically about Hurston, it is one that can apply to a number of Black women writers.

13. Barbara Smith, "Toward a Black Feminist Criticism," *Black American Literature Forum* 14 (1980): 411–12.

14. See Evelyn Hammonds, "Toward a Black Feminist Aesthetic," *Sojourner*, October 1980, 7, for a discussion of the limitations on Black feminist critics. She correctly points out that Black feminist critics "have no newspapers, no mass-marketed magazines or journals that are explicitly oriented toward the involvement of women of color in the feminist movement."

15. Dorin Schumacher, "Subjectives: A Theory of the Critical Process," in *Feminist Literary Criticism: Explorations in Theory*, ed. Josephine Donovan (Lexington, Kent, 1979), 34.

16. Annette Kolodny, "The Feminist as Literary Critic," Critical Response, *Critical Inquiry*, 2 (Summer 1976), 824–25. See also Cheris Kramer, Barrie Thorne, and Nancy Henley, "Perspectives on Language and Communication," *Signs*, 3 (Spring 1978), 638–51, and Nelly Farman, "The Study of Women and Language: Comment on Vol. 3, no. 3," *Signs*, 4 (Fall 1978), 152–85.

17. Stephen Henderson, *Understanding the New Black Poetry: Black Speech and Black Music as Poetic References* (New York, 1973), 31–46.

18. Some attempts have been made to define or at least discuss lesbianism. See Adrienne Rich's two essays, "It is the Lesbian in Us . . ." and "The Meaning of Our Love for Woman is What We Have," in *On Lies, Secrets and Silence* (New York, 1979), 199–202 and 223–30, respectively. See also Bertha Harris's "*What We Mean to Say*: Notes Toward Defining the Nature of Lesbian Literature," *Heresies*, 1 (Fall 1977), 5–8, and Blanche Cook's " 'Women Alone Stir My Imagination': Lesbianism and the Cultural Tradition," *Signs*, 4 (Summer 1979): 718–39. Also, at least one bibliography of Black lesbian writers has been compiled. See Ann Allen Shockley's "The Black Lesbian in American Literature: An Overview," *Conditions, Five*, 2 (Fall 1979):133–42.

19. Annette Kolodny, "Some Notes on Defining a 'Feminist Literary Criticism,' " *Critical Inquiry*, 2 (Fall 1975), 90.

20. Lillian S. Robinson, "Working Women Writing," *Sex, Class, and Culture* (Bloomington, Ind., 1978), 226.

21. Robinson, "The Critical Task," *Sex, Class, and Culture*, 52.

22. I am borrowing here from Kolodny, who makes similar statements in "Some Notes on Defining a 'Feminist Literary Criticism,' " 75.

23. Andrea Benton Rushing, "Images of Black Women in Afro-American Poetry," in *The Afro-American Woman: Struggles and Images*, ed. Sharon Hatley and Rosalyn Terborg-Penn (Port Washington, N.Y., 1978), 74–84. She argues that few of the stereotypic traits which Mary Ellman describes in *Thinking About Women* "seem appropriate to Afro-American images of black women." See also her "Images of Black Women in Modern African Poetry: An Overview," in *Sturdy Black Bridges: Visions of Black Women in Literature*, ed. Roseann P. Bell et al. (New York, 1979), 18–24. Rushing argues similarly that Mary Ann Ferguson's categories of women (the submissive wife, the mother angel or "mom," the woman on a pedestal, for example) cannot be applied to Black women characters, whose cultural imperatives are different from white women's.

24. *The Messenger*, 9 (April 1927), 109.

25. *The Messenger*, 5 (July 1923), 757.

26. Tillie Olsen, *Silences* (New York, 1978), 257.

27. Kolodny, "Some Notes on Defining a 'Feminist Literary Criticism,'" 89.

28. Lillian S. Robinson, "Dwelling in Decencies: Radical Criticism and Feminist Perspectives," in *Feminist Criticism*, ed. Cheryl Brown and Karen Olsen (Metuchen, N.J., 1978), 34.

29. For a discussion of Toni Morrison's frustrated female artists see Renita Weems, "Artists Without Art Form: A Look at One Black Woman's World of Unrevered Black Women," *Conditions: Five*, 2 (Fall 1979), 48–58. See also Alice Walker's classic essay, "In Search of Our Mothers' Gardens" for a discussion of Black women's creativity in general.

30. Toni Morrison, *The Bluest Eye* (New York, 1970), 88–89.

31. Toni Morrison, *Sula* (New York, 1980), 105.

32. Kolodny, "Some Notes on Defining a 'Feminist Literary Criticism,'" 86.

33. In an NEH Summer Seminar at Yale University in the summer of 1980, Carolyn Naylor of Santa Clara University suggested this to me.

34. For a discussion of this idea see Michael G. Cooke, "The Descent into the Underworld and Modern Black Fiction," *Iowa Review*, 5 (Fall 1974), 72–90.

35. Mary Helen Washington, *Midnight Birds: Stories of Contemporary Black Women Writers* (Garden City, N.Y., 1980), 43.

36. Ibid., xvii.

37. See Saundra Towns, "The Black Woman as Whore: Genesis of the Myth," *The Black Position* 3 (1974), 39–59, and Sylvia Keady, "Richard Wright's Women Characters and Inequality," *Black American Literature Forum* 10 (1976), 124–28, for example.

38. Hortense Spillers, "The Politics of Intimacy: A Discussion," in Bell et al., eds., *Sturdy Black Bridges*, 88.

39. Wole Soyinka, *Myth, Literature and the African World* (London, 1976), 61.

Carla Peterson

Carla Peterson received her Ph.D. from Yale University and is currently Professor and Director of the Africa and the Americas Committee at the University of Maryland. Her publications include *The Determined Reader: Gender and Culture in the Novel from Napoleon to Victoria* (1986) and *"Doers of the Word": African-American Women Speakers and Writers in the North (1830-1880)* (1995).

From Chapter 1: "Doers of the Word": Theorizing African-American Women Speakers and Writers in the Antebellum North

The Social Spheres of African-American Women

Within this general context of nineteenth-century African-American discursive practices, how can black women's culture and writing be specified? We need first of all to locate the particular position(s) of black women within Northern urban communities—to examine the different spaces they inhabited, to look at how they crossed social and geographic boundaries and negotiated "private" and "public" spheres. In so doing we must emphasize spatial plurality by remaining attentive to the ways in which the categories of race, gender, class, and culture complicated the politics of location of nineteenth-century black women. From such a perspective of heterogeneity, general paradigms break down; the private-public dichotomy must be adapted to specific historical circumstance. As we shall see, the discourse of these black women constitutes a particular form of hybridity in its disruption not only of the discourse of the dominant culture but also of that of the black male elite.

Historians of the dominant culture have typically located nineteenth-century women within the "private" sphere as opposed to the "public," which remained the province of men. More recently, however, scholars have insisted that this private-public dichotomy is too reductive and needs to be reconceptualized. They point out, first of all, that the private sphere is everywhere infiltrated by the public. Women's duties as laborers in the household, as procreators, and as socializers

of children are all carried out in the name of the public interest; they may more properly be termed "domestic" rather than "private." Moreover, in antebellum America the Southern slave household itself defied the ideology of separate spheres as it contained within it aspects of both productive and reproductive relations, regulating both the labor and sexual relations of master and slave classes.[38] Finally, black men in the North obviously could not participate in activities in the national public sphere to the same extent as men from the dominant culture given the limitations imposed on their civil and political rights. Such a constraint helped minimize although it did not eradicate the domestic-public dichotomy in Northern black communities.

Like white women, black women saw "domestic economy" as an empowering cultural model. Yet the domestic sphere of black society cannot be conceptualized in the same way as that of the dominant culture. Indeed, given the economic system that undergirded Northern black communities, as well as the demographic situation of black women—greater percentage than men, low fertility and birthrate—African-American familial life cannot be construed in the same terms as the white middle-class family.[39] We cannot make assumptions about the primacy of the nuclear family nor of women as wives and mothers; we need to think instead in terms of broader domestic networks, both kin and nonkin. In fact, almost all the women studied in this book followed the "anomalous" pattern of late marriage or early widowhood and consequently bore no, or few, children. They were thus freed from many of the domestic obligations that burdened most women, black and white. But, ever aware of the importance of preserving the integrity of black family life and its domestic networks, these black women sought to make of the family a site of cultural resistance. They constitute striking examples of how, to quote Mina Caulfield, "families, generally under the leadership of women, have fought back, defending subsistence production as it becomes more precarious, cementing family bonds and building new networks of mutual support as the old ones come under attack, consolidating and developing cultures of resistance—cultures which, like the role of women and family life itself, have been devalued under imperialist ideology."[40] Thus, Stewart, Prince, and Watkins Harper insisted that black women dedicate themselves to proper household maintenance, child rearing, gardening, diet, and hygiene. Still other women, like Sarah Mapps Douglass, spoke out on issues of women's physiology and anatomy, underscoring the need for black women to care for their bodies.[41]

Furthermore, the activities of black women, like those of black men, extended beyond the family into the ethnic community sphere. Black women joined in female benevolent associations that coexisted alongside similar men's organizations in order to take care of others in the community and, in particular, of each other. They involved themselves in what we could call the politics of domestic economy, which provided a solid base for cooperative community action. Stewart, Prince, Watkins Harper, and Jacobs, for example, devoted themselves to moral reform activities, creating "asylums" to shelter destitute young women, organizing mutual aid societies to succor the needy, or participating in the free produce and temperance movements. Stewart and Forten joined literary societies—the former Boston's Afric-American Female Intelligence Society in 1832, the latter a Philadelphia women's society in 1858—designed to enhance the intellectual and moral quality of black women's lives.[42] Black men, who were themselves deeply engaged in moral reform work, encouraged these benevolent activities, which they saw as necessary to the success of racial uplift. This community sphere thus functioned as an intermediate sphere situated somewhere between the domestic/private and the public. It can be viewed as "public" as it is located outside the "home" and remains preoccupied with the welfare of the general population, but it is also "domestic" in that it represents an extension of the values of "home" into the community; and it is "private" insofar as it is able to remain hidden, abstracted from the gaze of the dominant culture. For nineteenth-century African Americans, this sphere was vital to the preservation of both the bodily integrity and the psychic security of families and individuals.

Finally, many of these black women—Truth, Lee, Stewart, Prince, and Watkins Harper, for example—entered the national public sphere as workers, principally domestics or seamstresses. In this unprotected public sphere, black women suffered indignities and assaults not experienced by their white counterparts. In an autobiographical essay, Remond enumerated the many different places from which black women (and men) were likely to be expelled on account of racial prejudice: "They are excluded from public hotels, . . . omnibus[es], . . . steam-boats . . . places of amusements."[43] As public workers black women gained little prestige but did achieve economic independence as well as the geographic mobility and physical freedom that would enable them to take part in the public work of evangelism, abolitionism, temperance, and women's rights. In the postbellum period such activity was expanded to include increased participation in the temperance and women's rights movements as well as vocal support for the Fifteenth Amendment, collaboration with the educational institutions of the Freedmen's Bureau, and, in the case of Truth, lobbying for the granting of western territory to the freed people.

Importantly, however, significant limits *were* placed on black women's activities beyond the community level, in the ethnic public sphere of black national institutions dominated by men of the elite. It is true that several of the women studied here did form close personal friendships with men of this elite who, impressed by the women's extraordinary talent, disregarded the cultural constraints imposed on women's public activities to act as their mentors. Thus, David Walker became Stewart's role model; after his death she praised him as one who "has distinguished himself in these modern days by acting wholly in the defense of African rights and liberty";[44] as bishop of the AME Church, Richard Allen offered Jarena Lee an unofficial preaching role in Philadelphia's churches; Martin Delany was instrumental in helping Shadd Cary shape her ideas concerning political nationhood; Charles Lenox Remond encouraged his sister Sarah's activities as an antislavery lecturer; and, finally, William Watkins proposed a framework of Christian social justice that would later be that of his niece Watkins Harper as well. Nevertheless, these women were officially excluded from those black national institutions mentioned earlier through which men of the elite came together to promote public civic debate on practical issues of racial uplift as well as those more theoretical considerations of black nationality.[45] For example, in the first several years of its existence women were denied membership in the American Moral Reform Society; moreover, women were neither allowed to attain leadership positions in the AME Church nor permitted to voice their opinions at the annual national conventions; finally, considerable opposition was mounted within the black community against Shadd Cary's editorship of the *Provincial Freeman*. In thus restricting the role of black women in the articulation of racial uplift programs, the black male leadership strove, in what it believed were the best interests of the community, to contain heterogeneity, silence difference, and gender blackness as male.

Black Women and Liminality

How, then, could black women enter into the arena of public civic debate? I suggest that they did so by "achieving" an additional "oppression," by consciously adopting a self-marginalization that became superimposed upon the already ascribed oppressions of race and gender and that paradoxically allowed empowerment.[46] In so doing, these women entered into a state of liminality defined, following Victor Turner, as that moment and place in which an individual, separated from society, comes to be "betwixt and between the positions assigned and arrayed by law, custom, convention and ceremonial," and in which the creation of *communitas* becomes possible: "*Communitas* emerges where social structure is not. . . . [I]t transgresses or dissolves the norms that govern structured and institutionalized relationships and is accompanied by experiences of unprecedented potency."[47] From the perspective of the black women studied in this book, these liminal spaces came to function, however temporarily, as their "center," offering them greater possibilities of self-expression as well as the potential to effect social change. Yet even in their marginal positions these women were not purely "outside of" but remained "a part of"; as such they were never fully free from, but remained in tension with, the fixed social and economic male-dominated hierarchies that structured Northern urban life.

For the older generation of women, Truth and Lee, for example, the liminal space they chose to enter was the clearing, the site of religious evangelical activities that had been unleashed by the Second Great Awakening and drew the powerless—women, blacks, rural folk, and all those dislocated by the economic upheaval of the Jacksonian market revolution—to religion as a source of power. In such places social hierarchies of race, class, and gender are overturned and deconstructed as the congregants merge in varying degrees of religious ecstasy with the Godhead. For the somewhat younger women, Stewart, Watkins Harper, Remond, and Shadd Cary, their liminal place became that of the public platform from which they lectured to "promiscuous assemblies," audiences composed of both men and women. As oratory was deemed to be a specifically masculine genre and public speaking an activity proper only to men, these women were charged with unsexing themselves through an unseemly exposure of the female body. White women—Frances Wright, Angelina Grimké, Abby Kelley, Lucretia Mott, to name a few—were also engaged in public lecturing during this period and were equally vulnerable to public scorn and hostility.[48] But these women generally found themselves cushioned by their race, class affiliation, family ties, and secure economic status. In contrast, public speaking often led to greater social and economic uncertainty for black women. In making the decision to engage in such activities, they often left their employment as teachers, seamstresses, or domestics to live on their own, separated from family and community; public lecturing became their chief means of livelihood, frequently rendering them dependent on the generosity of their audiences and hosts. Finally, for almost all the women studied, marginality was engendered by the act of travel in which the mere fact of geographic displacement (as with Lee) or the journey away from "home" to another location (the frontier of Canada for Shadd Cary, the swamps of the South Carolina

Sea Islands for Forten) could open up new sites of empowerment or simply challenge the very notion of a stable home for African Americans.

It is important to note, however, that these women often entered the liminal space of *communitas* alone and could remain isolated within it despite the fact that their activities were designed to enhance community welfare. Indeed, these women did not always become part of the *communitas* but rather held an ambiguous insider/outsider status in relation to it. Moreover, if the absence of social structure made *communitas* possible for these women, it was its very existence that enabled black men to organize themselves in the ethnic public sphere. The elite's exclusion of black women from its national organizations, coupled with the women's lack of public power to create similar formal institutions, prevented black women leaders from joining together to form a national political community of their own in the antebellum period.

As Ann Boylan has noted, black women eagerly joined the broad racially mixed antislavery movement, participating "in many Female Anti-Slavery Societies, and in the three Anti-Slavery Conventions of American Women held between 1837 and 1839."[49] Furthermore, a number of the black women under study here were clearly cognizant of each other's cultural work, and their paths did sometimes cross. An 1854 article by Shadd Cary entitled "The Humbug of Reform" contains a reference to a speech given by Sojourner Truth.[50] Given Truth's widespread reputation, most of the other women probably also knew of her public activities; and Truth and Jacobs undoubtedly collaborated in their activities with the Freedmen's Bureau in Virginia during the Civil War. In addition, we know that Stewart and Prince both worshiped at the First African Baptist Church in Boston while Thomas Paul was still pastor there. Watkins Harper and Shadd Cary clearly knew of one another through the intermediary of William Still, met in the late 1850s and probably again in the 1890s at the foundation of the National Association of Colored Women. A mentor-protégé relationship brought Remond and Forten together from approximately 1854 to 1858. Finally, as a leading member of post-Reconstruction Washington D.C. black society, Forten, who by then had married the well-known Presbyterian minister Francis Grimké, was undoubtedly acquainted with Watkins Harper, Jacobs, and Shadd Cary. Watkins Harper mentions Forten in an essay written in the mid 1870s and corresponded with Francis Grimké during the 1890s; Grimké also wrote a moving tribute to Jacobs on the occasion of her death; finally, both Forten Grimké and Shadd Cary attended meetings of the Bethel Literary and Historical Association in the 1880s and 1890s.

As noted earlier, antebellum black women did come together in significant numbers to create their own local organizations—principally literary, antislavery, and mutual aid societies—designed to take care of family and community needs. It is impossible to underestimate the importance of such local associations in helping the development of black women's organizational skills, encouraging self and community empowerment, and validating practical work as an essential component of nation building. Yet in the final analysis the creation of a national network of black women leaders that would allow them as a group to enter into the arena of public civic debate and engage in sustained written production did not occur in the antebellum period. It was not until the Reconstruction period that black women joined the national organizations of black men and white women in significant numbers; and it was not until the early 1880s that they were able to create national organizations of their own that would come to function as their own "home places."

If such liminal spaces functioned as centers of empowerment, however, they also remained sites of oppression, separating the women from their "homes" and "native" communities, forcing an unfeminine exposure of the body, and thus further reminding them of their difference. Indeed, nineteenth-century black women were conceptualized by the dominant culture chiefly in bodily terms, in contrast to middle-class white women whose femininity, as defined by the cult of true womanhood, cohered around notions of the self-effacing body. According to this ideology, white women were to be hidden in the privacy of the domestic sphere, where they were encouraged to develop purity of mind and soul, impose complete emotional restraint on their physical movements through stringent rules of etiquette, and veil their already pale and delicate bodies in clothes that, following the sentimental ideal of transparency, would translate inner purity into outward form.[51] In contrast, the black woman's body was always envisioned as public and exposed. If in Europe this exposed body was caged and subjected to minute scientific inquiry, in the United States it was perceived, at least initially, as an uninhibited laboring body that was masculinized.[52] In descriptions in *Journey in the Seaboard Slave States*, for example, Frederick Law Olmsted emphasized the exposure of the female slave's body: "The dress of most of them was . . . reefed up . . . at the hips, so as to show their heavy legs, wrapped round with a piece of old blanket, in lieu of leggings or stockings. Most of them worked with bare arms, but wore strong shoes on the feet, and handkerchiefs on their heads." Olmsted further noted that no distinction appears to have been made between the "muscular" field work of male and female slaves: "The women . . . were engaged at exactly the same labor as the men; driving the carts, loading them with dirt, and dumping them upon the road; cutting down trees, and drawing wood by hand, to lay across the miry places; hoeing, and shoveling."[53]

Intimately linked in the white imagination to this masculine labor of slave women were those more feminine forms of work—the reproductive labor of childbirth, the obligation

to fulfill the sexual pleasure of slave masters, and the nurturing of the latter's children. In Fanny Kemble's *Journal*, descriptions of the bodily suffering of slave women repeatedly associate the vicissitudes of "hard field work" with those of childbearing, emphasizing in particular "the terrible hardships the women underwent in being thus driven to labor before they had recovered from childbearing"; and an 1861 report commissioned by the federal government and reprinted by Remond noted that "cases occurred where the negress was overtaken by the pains of labour, and gave birth to her child in the field." Much less sympathetic, but perhaps more typical, was Olmsted's conflation of labor and sexuality in his depiction of the sensuality of slave women engaged in field work: "Clumsy, awkward, gross, elephantine in all their movements; pouting, grinning, and leering at us; sly, sensual, and shameless, in all their expressions and demeanor; I never before had witnessed, I thought, anything more revolting."[54] Feminine attributes and functions of the black female body were thus commonly represented in degraded terms as abnormal excessive sexual activity; and, when superimposed on masculine ones, led to the creation of a complexly ambiguous portrait of the nineteenth-century black woman. As a result, the public exposure of black women cultural workers on the margins could only be perceived by the dominant culture, and by a segment of the black male elite as well, as a form of social disorder that confirmed notions of the black female body as unruly, grotesque, carnivalesque.[55] In her 1846 *Memoirs*, for example, Zilpha Elaw recounts a conversation with a minister's wife who "assuming the theologian, reprobated female preaching as . . . disorderly and improper."[56]

Such cultural constructions could quite possibly result in the transformation of the black female subject into an "abject creature" who internalizes the images of herself as dirty, disorderly, and grotesque.[57] Although the writings by, and about, the women studied in this book may at times suggest racial insecurity, they are much more frequently pervaded by portraits of a sick and debilitated body. Indeed, almost all these women were plagued throughout their lives by illnesses that often remained undiagnosed but whose symptoms were headaches, fevers, coughs, chills, cramps, or simply extreme fatigue. In such instances illness may quite possibly have occurred as a consequence of the bodily degradation to which these women were subjected or as a psychosomatic strategy for negotiating such degradation. In either case the black female body might well have functioned as what Elaine Scarry has called the "body in pain," whereby the powerless become voiceless bodies subject to pain and dominated by the bodiless voices of those in power. In her book Scarry enumerates different mechanisms through which the voiceless body of pain can be transformed into a bodiless voice of power: most generally, the human subject seeks to alleviate pain by giving it a place in the world through verbal articulation; in the Judeo-Christian tradition,

God authorizes man to divest himself of his body and seek power through the making of material artifacts, including language; in Christian interpretations of death, finally, the resurrection of the soul privileges the verbal category over the material by endowing man with an immortal voice.[58] Similarly, for Kristeva, abjection may be spiritualized by means of the Christian ritual of communion in which "all corporeality is elevated, spiritualized, and sublimated"; but, most importantly, it is "the Word . . . [that] purifies from the abject."[59]

How, then, did nineteenth-century black women social activists conciliate these differing interpretations of the black female body as empowered, on the one hand, and disordered on the other? The need to negotiate between these two extremes was particularly urgent for black female public speakers who offered themselves so vulnerably to the public gaze. In her *Memoirs*, for example, Zilpha Elaw recollected with pain how "the people were collecting from every quarter, to gaze at the unexampled prodigy of a coloured female preacher. . . . I observed, with very painful emotions, the crowd outside, pointing with their fingers at me, and saying, 'that's her,' 'that's her.'"[60] Audience response to Watkins Harper's public lecturing was even more telling, however, in its grotesque evocation of the black woman speaker as variably masculine and painted: "I don't know but that you would laugh if you were to hear some of the remarks which my lectures call forth," she wrote in a letter to William Still. "'She is a man,' again 'She is not colored, she is painted.'"[61] In this comment the black woman speaker is predictably masculinized, and she is also racialized as "painted." Yet the term "painted" also resexualizes her, and dangerously so, as an actress, and perhaps even a prostitute. In fact, these women lecturers needed in some sense to become actresses in order to negotiate their public exposure in front of "promiscuous assemblies"; and, as we shall see, their acting strategies ranged from deliberate attempts to call attention to the materiality of the black female body in both its productive and reproductive functions in order then to subvert the dominant culture's construction of it (Truth), to efforts to decorporealize the body from the outset and present the self as a disembodied voice (Watkins Harper).

I would argue that from their dislocated and liminal positions these black women ultimately turned to the *literary representation* of self-marginalization—to the writing of self, spirituality, and travel, the reprinting of public lectures, and the creation of fictional worlds—in an attempt to veil the body while continuing their racial uplift activities in the public sphere. In particular, they turned to writing in reaction to, and in tension with, their exclusion from black national institutions. Striving to achieve an empowering narrative authority, they hoped that their writing would both challenge the power of those institutions to which they had been barred access *and* compel these institutions to legitimate their social activism in the public sphere.

My study of African-American women in the nineteenth century is loosely organized around the liminal sites I identified earlier—religious evangelism, travel, public speaking—as well as the writing of fiction. The discussion of each woman begins with an attempt to narrativize and interpret those important social and biographical facts that might help us better to appreciate her cultural production. It then turns to an analysis of the cultural production itself, whether the speech in its printed form which, although never ascertainable, often sustains the fiction of the actual social exchange, or the written text. Taken together, my analyses suggest the possibility of tracing significant shifts in the use of literary discourses and generic conventions.

I argue that these black women appropriated many different cultural discourses ranging from a reliance on Africanisms to the adoption of standard literary conventions in order to become producers rather than mere consumers of literary expression. In her role as an itinerant lecturer, Truth was not only a Christian "doer of the word" but also a participant in the African belief in *Nommo*, or the Word as the productive life force that brings about generation and change. In addition, Truth employed Africanisms, folk proverbs and sayings, and African-American idioms in her lectures, creating what the dominant culture regarded as a quaint idiosyncratic speech; in fact, however, Truth's speech constitutes a serious political discourse through which she sought to define the specific positionality of nineteenth-century black women.[62] To prophesy the future of both black and white races in America and the role of black women in its making, Lee and Stewart grounded their sermons and spiritual writings in biblical discourse—particularly that of the Old Testament Prophets and the New Testament book of Revelation—producing powerful texts that their readers and audiences, however, often interpreted as mere emotional outbursts filled with indecipherable meanings. Watkins Harper, Forten, and Jacobs appropriated the sentimental discourse that had entered and permeated white women's culture by way of the eighteenth-century European cult of sensibility in order to invoke figures of sentimentality—the African-American slave (man, woman, child, or family), the drunkard husband or father, the seduced woman, the child dying of hunger—that would excite the readers' compassion and move them not to emotional consumption but to productive action. Given the particular social and cultural construction of black women's lives, such writing differed in significant ways from that of black men in its ability to imagine cultural possibilities specifically engendered by women's space and women's work. Finally, in the postbellum period black women sought to take advantage of the expansion and institutionalization of literary culture; and in becoming increasingly involved in the already existing national organizations of black men and white women while gradually creating institutions of their own, they hoped to appropriate new forms of social discourse that would help them further their cultural work.

As these black women narrated their thoughts and experiences, the location and perspective of the narrating *I* in relation to that which is narrated gained particular importance as evidenced by their careful manipulation of point of view, thus demanding from us a critical consideration of genre. Indeed, for these women the question of genre was not so much a choice of literary convention as an epistemological issue: how to represent the relationship of the self to the self and the Other. The only woman unable to author her own life story, Truth was obliged to confide its telling to white women abolitionists whose ethnobiographies construct her as irrecoverably Other. In asserting their desire and ability to narrate their own life stories themselves, Lee, Prince, Jacobs, and Forten wrote spiritual and secular autobiographies as well as journals in which the *I* seeks to narrate itself from its own constructed point of view. In composing travel accounts and ethnographies, Prince and Shadd Cary sought to deflect the public's gaze from themselves in order to represent the Other. Finally, in turning to more explicitly fictional modes and techniques in the 1850s, Wilson, Watkins Harper, and Jacobs created fictionalized versions of both self and Other from multiple perspectives, thereby striving to escape the scrutiny of the dominant culture and achieve perspectives of omniscience denied them in their actual historical moment and place.

Notes

Chapter 1

38. For more extensive discussions of these points, see Linda K. Kerber, "Separate Spheres, Female Worlds, Woman's Place: The Rhetoric of Women's History," *Journal of American History* 75 (1988): 9–39; Joan Kelly, "The Social Relation of the Sexes," in *Women, History, and Theory* (Chicago: University of Chicago Press, 1984), 1–18; Elizabeth Fox-Genovese, *Within the Plantation Household* (Chapel Hill: University of North Carolina Press, 1988), 37–99.

39. Curry, *The Free Black in Urban America*, 8–12.

40. Mina Davis Caulfield, "Imperialism, the Family, and Cultures of Resistance," *Socialist Revolution* 2 (1974): 74.

41. Dorothy Sterling, *We Are Your Sisters: Black Women in the Nineteenth Century* (New York: Norton, 1984), 129.

42. See also Dorothy B. Porter, "The Organized Educational Activities of Negro Literary Societies, 1828–1846," *Journal of Negro Education* 5 (October 1936): 556–66; and Sterling, *We Are Your Sisters*, chaps. 9–11.

43. Sarah P. Remond, "Sarah P. Remond," in *Our Exemplars, Poor and Rich; or Biographical Sketches of Men and Women*, ed. Matthew Davenport Hill (London: Cassell, Petter, and Galpin, 1861), 281.

44. M. Stewart, *Meditations*, 67.

45. For other discussions of the exclusion of black women from organizations of the male elite in the antebellum period, see Horton, "Freedom's Yoke," 51–76; and Winch, *Philadelphia's Black Elite*, 121.

46. See Michelle Zimbalist Rosaldo, "Woman, Culture, and Society: A Theoretical Overview," in *Woman, Culture, and Society*, ed. Michelle Zimbalist Rosaldo and Louise Lamphere (Stanford, Calif.: Stanford University Press, 1974), 28–30, for the use of the terms "ascribed" and "achieved" in anthropological discourse.

47. Victor Turner, *The Ritual Process: Structure and Antistructure* (Ithaca, N.Y.: Cornell University Press, 1977), 44–45, 126–28.

48. For a more extensive discussion of white women orators in the antebellum period, see Lillian O'Connor, *Pioneer Women Orators: Rhetoric in the Ante–Bellum Reform Movement* (New York: Columbia University Press, 1954).

49. Ann Boylan, "Benevolence and Antislavery Activity among African American Women in New York and Boston, 1820–1840," in *The Abolitionist Sisterhood: Antislavery and Women's Political Culture*, ed. John Van Horne and Jean Fagan Yellin (Ithaca, N.Y.: Cornell University Press, 1994), 120.

50. Mary Ann Shadd, "The Humbug of Reform," *Provincial Freeman*, May 27, 1854.

51. I paraphrase here the discussions of Barbara Welter, "The Cult of True Womanhood: 1820–1860," *American Quarterly* 18 (Spring 1966): 152; and Karen Halttunen, *Confidence Men and Painted Women* (New Haven, Conn.: Yale University Press, 1982), 71–91, 97.

52. For a discussion of European perceptions of the black female body, see Sander L. Gilman, "Black Bodies, White Bodies: Toward an Iconography of Female Sexuality in Late Nineteenth-Century Art, Medicine, and Literature," *Critical Inquiry* 12 (Autumn 1985): 204–42.

53. Frederick Law Olmsted, *A Journey in the Seaboard Slave States* (1856; New York: Negro Universities Press, 1968), 432, 386–87.

54. Frances Anne Kemble, *Journal of a Residence on a Georgian Plantation in 1838–1839*, ed. John A. Scott (Athens: University of Georgia Press, 1984), 293; *The Negroes and Anglo–Africans as Freedmen and Soldiers*, ed. Sarah Parker Remond (London: Victoria Press, 1864), 12; Olmsted, *Journey in the Seaboard Slave States*, 388.

55. For a discussion of the female grotesque, see Mary Russo, "Female Grotesques: Carnival and Theory," in *Feminist Studies/Critical Studies*, ed. Teresa de Lauretis (Bloomington: Indiana University Press, 1986), 213–29.

56. Zilpha Elaw, *Memoirs of the Life, Religious Experience, Ministerial Travels, and Labours of Mrs. Elaw*, in *Sisters of the Spirit*, ed. William L. Andrews (Bloomington: Indiana University Press, 1986), 147.

57. Julia Kristeva, *Powers of Horror: An Essay on Abjection*, trans. Leon S. Roudiez (New York: Columbia University Press, 1982), 10.

58. Elaine Scarry, *The Body in Pain: The Making and Unmaking of the World* (New York: Oxford University Press, 1985), 233–34, 219.

59. Kristeva, *Powers of Horror*, 120, 23.

60. Elaw, *Memoirs*, 91.

61. Quoted in William Still, *The Underground Railroad* (Philadelphia: Porter and Coates, 1872), 772. White women speakers such as Frances Wright were equally vulnerable to the charge of masculinization.

62. The issue of Africanisms in nineteenth–century African–American cultural life is extremely complex and, to a certain extent, must remain speculative. Historians of slavery have determined that kidnapped slaves came generally from West African and Central African tribes. Although the tribes undoubtedly had their own specific cultural forms, Sterling Stuckey has suggested that the experiences of the Middle Passage and of slavery must be seen as "incubators of slave unity across cultural lines, cruelly revealing irreducible links from one ethnic group to the other"; furthermore: "What we know of slave culture in the South, and of that of blacks in the North during and following slavery, indicates that black culture was national in scope, the principal forms of cultural expression being essentially the same. This is attributable mainly to the similarity of the African regions from which blacks were taken and enslaved in North America, and to the patterns of culture shared more generally in Central and West Africa" (Stuckey, *Slave Culture*, 3, 82).